D0623358

Annals of His Time

Series Chimalpahin

Susan Schroeder, Series Editor

Annals of His Time

Don Domingo de San Antón Muñón
Chimalpahin Quauhtlehuanitzin

Edited and translated by

James Lockhart, Susan Schroeder,
and Doris Namala

Stanford University Press
Stanford, California
2006

The present book belongs to an ongoing informal Series Chimalpahin organized by Susan Schroeder as general or series editor to publish the entire extant output of Chimalpahin in critical editions in English and the original language. Further volumes, whose venue, editorship, and even content are still not fully determined, are to be expected in due course. In the name of flexibility, the items in the series will not bear volume numbers. The two-volume *Codex Chimalpahin*, edited by Arthur Anderson and Schroeder, should be counted as part of this effort.

Stanford University Press
Stanford, California

Printed in the United States of America on acid-free, archival-quality paper

Library of Congress Cataloging-in-Publication Data

Chimalpahin Cuauhtlehuanitzin, Domingo Francisco de San Antón Muñón, 1579–1660.
Annals of his time : don Domingo de San Antón Muñón Chimalpahin Quauhtlehuanitzin / edited and translated by James Lockhart, Susan Schroeder, and Doris Namala.
p. cm.—(Series Chimalpahin)
Introduction in English; English and Nahuatl on opposite pages.
Includes bibliographical references and index.
ISBN 0-8047-5454-3 (cloth : alk. paper)
1. Chimalpahin Cuauhtlehuanitzin, Domingo Francisco de San Antón Muñón, 1579–1660. 2. Manuscripts, Nahuatl—Mexico—Mexico City. 3. Aztecs—History. 4. Aztecs-Politics and government. 5. Aztecs—Social life and customs. I. Lockhart, James. II. Schroeder, Susan. III. Namala, Doris. IV. Title. V. Series.

F1219.54.A98C45 2006
972'.018—dc22 2005028443

Original Printing 2006
Last figure below indicates year of this printing:
15 14 13 12 11 10 09 08 07 06

Contents

Some major blocks of text

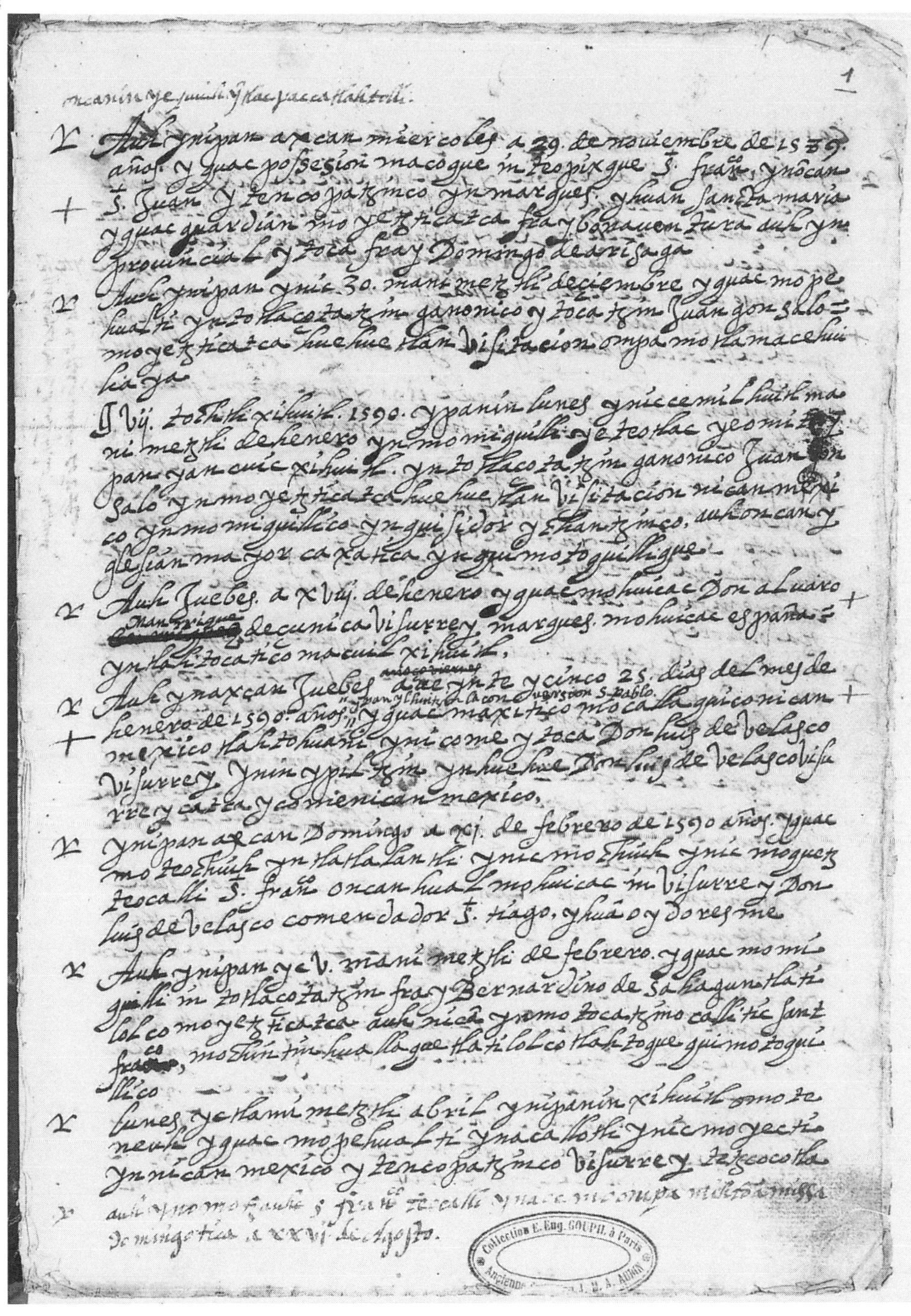

Figure 1. First page of the Paris manuscript. Fonds Mexicain 220, p. 1. Reproduced with the permission of the Bibliothèque Nationale de France.

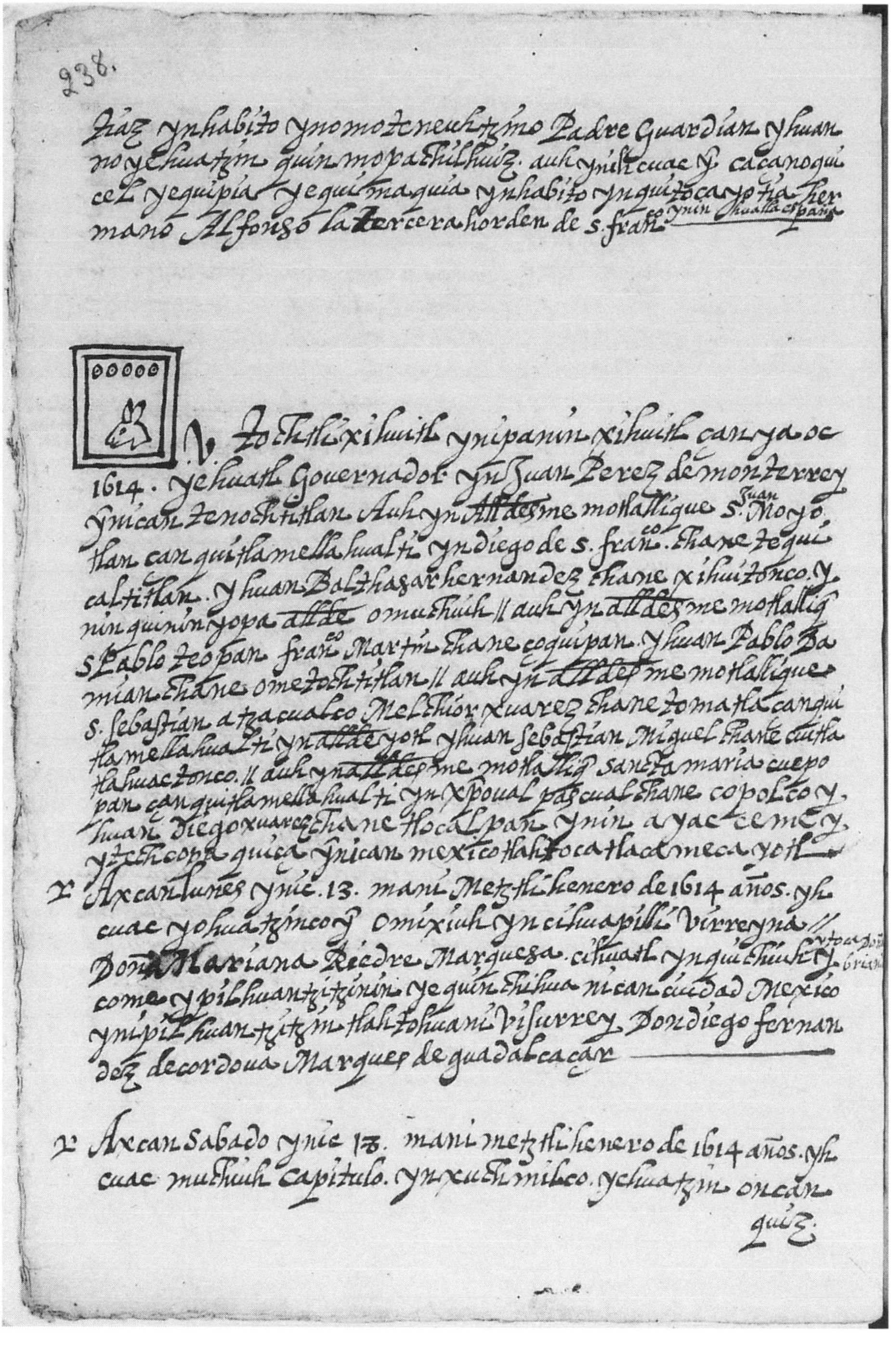

Figure 2. Annals entry for the beginning of the year 5 tochtli, 1614, with standard information about the election of the cabildo officials of Tenochtitlan. Fonds Mexicain 220, p. 238. Reproduced with the permission of the Bibliothèque Nationale de France.

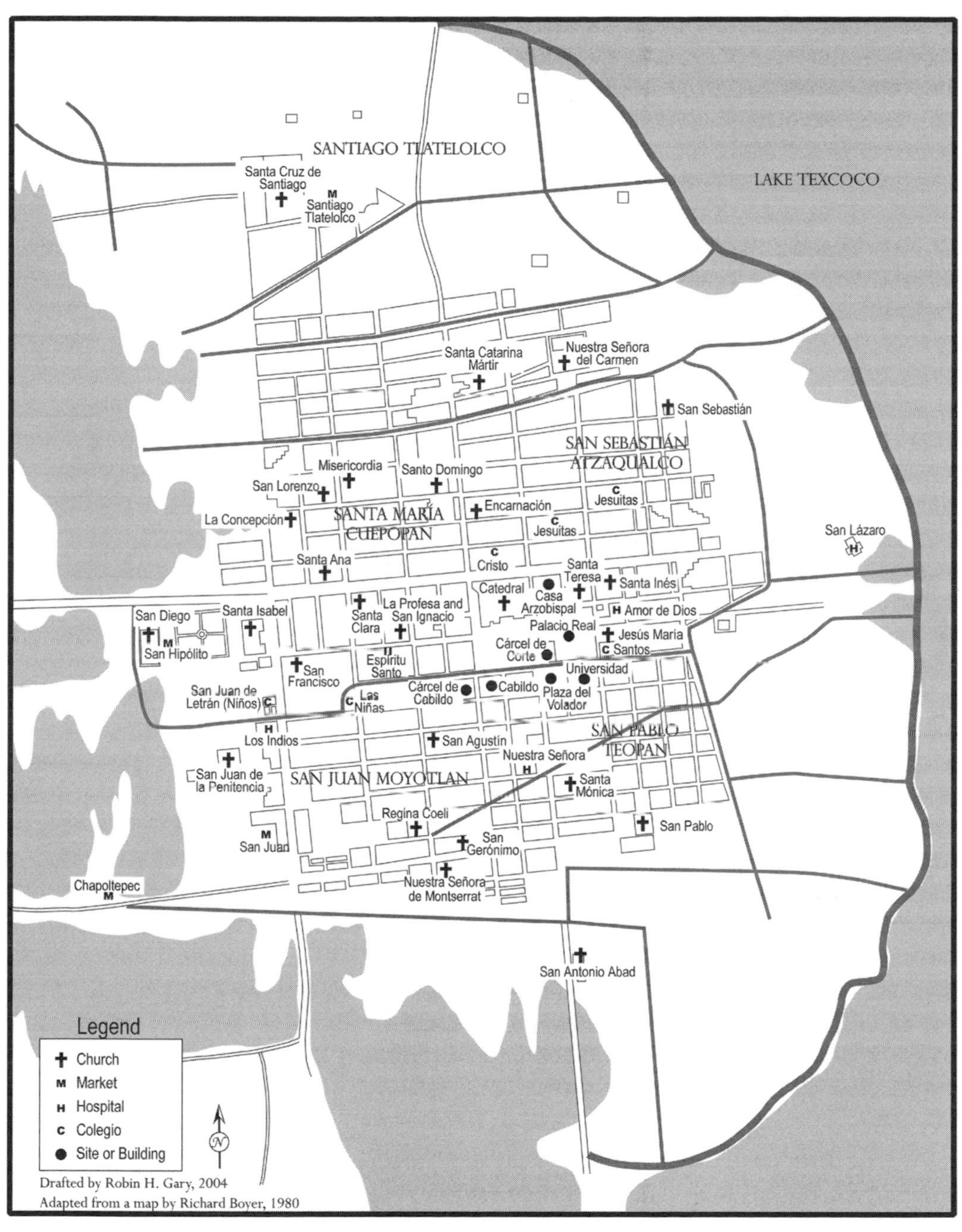

Map 1. Mexico City in Chimalpahin's time.

Annals of His Time

Introduction

yn ipampa yc nican nictlallia nicmachiyotia yn imiquilitzin ynin omoteneuhtzino huey teopixqui omoyetzticatca yniqu iuhqui yxiptlatzin omochiuhtzinoticatca nican Sancto Padre ynic huel omohuelitiltiaya yniqu icatzinco ypampatzinco miec Jubileos oquimotemaquillitia yn iuh otiquittaque auh monequi no quimatizque oncan in quittazque ytocatenehuallocatzin yn aquique çatepan ye nemiquihui yn amo quimottilique yn amo quimiximachilique ynin yc huey teopixqui ocatca ypampa yuh ninomati caocac yuhqui nican Mexico oc ce teopixqui yttoz yn oc ompa ye tonitztihui ypan cahuitl

The reason that I set down and record here the death of this said late great religious is that he became like the representative of the holy Father here because he was fully authorized to go along issuing many jubilees in his name and on his behalf, as we saw. And also those who will live later, who didn't see and know how great a religious he was, need to know of him and see his name mentioned, because I think that in future times another religious like him will not be seen again here in Mexico.

(From Chimalpahin's entry for September 7, 1614.)

Annals of His Time

The premier practitioner of the genre of Nahuatl annals in the form they took after the conquest was born in 1579 in Amaquemecan (Amecameca), baptized apparently as Domingo Francisco, then went very young to Mexico City, and eventually came to be known there as don Domingo de San Antón after the church where he worked, sometimes referring to himself in magnificent fashion as don Domingo de San Antón Muñón Chimalpahin Quauhtlehuanitzin. Scholars somehow settled on calling him Chimalpahin, one of two names of earlier lords of Amaquemecan that he appropriated to himself, and though that convention is not well founded, it is too late to protest, and we will call him Chimalpahin too.[1]

The item we publish here is devoted overwhelmingly (despite one abbreviated resumé of Mexica history from the beginning) to events occurring in the time after Chimalpahin was born, and indeed the momentum accumulates as he reaches the years of his early prime. After very brief annual entries for the 1570s and 80s, clearly set down after the fact, for the 1590s and early 1600s we find usually from two to four pages. For 1604 to 1608 we see an increase to five to nine pages a year, and then a further large and rapid increase in the first years of the second decade of the seventeenth century, when Chimalpahin was in his thirties, reaching a maximum of 41 pages for 1613 before the series as we know it halts in 1615. A reader cannot avoid the impression that the material certainly from about 1608 to the end, and possibly from considerably earlier, was first written primarily at the time of the events, and it deals for the most part with things the author saw or heard about as they happened. No wonder that from as early as the eighteenth century

1. We even retain the practice, originating with the author himself, of writing the name with an *h*, though by standard orthography it is not justified. The second element of the name appears to be a preterit agentive form of the verb *paina*, "to run, hasten," in which a glottal stop is not otherwise attested.

the work was being called the *Diario*, diary or journal. The word "Diario" by now has a tradition as strong as it is lasting, but there can be no doubt that it did not originate with Chimalpahin, and we consider it to be highly misleading.

For a century and more after his rediscovery in the late nineteenth century, translators and commentators gave their attention above all to his massive effort to tell the precontact history of central Mexico (principally Amaquemecan and Mexico Tenochtitlan),[2] but recently his extensive and equally impressive writing on postcontact times has also drawn attention,[3] and the present publication is part of that trend.

The texts published here belong in the clearest and fullest way to the tradition of Nahuatl annals, a genre concerned primarily with events of interest to the public, and indeed to the public of the author's own local sociopolitical entity. They are no diary; Chimalpahin's own activities are barely mentioned, his feelings fully and openly expressed only on rare occasions. And indeed it would have been against the annals tradition to give the work a title at all, or even perhaps to conceive it as a separate entity as opposed to other texts Chimalpahin wrote or compiled.[4] We publish this set of annals separately, respecting its character as an independent corpus and sequence in the original, but in a sense it belongs together with a large number of similar entries scattered through Chimalpahin's other manuscripts despite their often preponderantly precontact subject matter, and we hope that in due course all this material can be subjected to a common analysis.

---

2. The Paris annals that have come to be called the "Relaciones" constitute the bulk of Ch.'s writings about the precontact era. Dating to the time that the materials seem first to have become available in Paris, Rémi Siméon published the sixth and seventh Relaciones in French in 1889. The Germans followed after an interval, with several scholars translating and publishing different Relaciones; Ernst Mengin published the fifth Relación in German (1944, 1949, 1950), followed by a handsome series of volumes with facsimiles of all the Paris Relaciones. In 1958 Walter Lehmann and Gerdt Kutscher published more selections from the same sources. Günter Zimmermann, the most accomplished member of this school, published portions of the second, third, and eighth Relaciones in 1960, and in 1963–65 he brought out his invaluable transcription of both the corpus of Relaciones and Ch.'s contemporary annals (the so-called "Diario," the text edited here). A set of analytical notes to the edition conveyed many of Zimmermann's insights, but a planned full translation of the texts never came to pass. In the edition Zimmermann reorganized all of the Relaciones into chronological order by individual entry. On the one hand he for the first time brought out the scope of Ch.'s work and made research in it more feasible, while on the other hand he obscured the integrity of the individual texts and caused considerable confusion regarding the nature of annals and of Ch.'s oeuvre. A recent publication by Elke Ruhnau (Chimalpahin 2001A) with all of the Relaciones sums up the accomplishments of the German school.

In the time after World War II Mexican scholars also began publishing portions of the Relaciones in Spanish translation, often without transcriptions; most of this work is mentioned in Schroeder 1991, pp. 26–30. Far the best of these efforts, by Rafael Tena (Chimalpahin 1998), embraces the entire Relaciones, containing both a full transcription and an excellent translation.

3. As in Chimalpahin 2001 (the Tena edition) and Namala 2002.

4. See the passage on pp. 238–39, at n. 4, which could be construed as including Ch.'s contemporary annals within the same framework or as a later part of the same work as preconquest portions.

Although the original strong pictorial component of postconquest annals has virtually disappeared in Chimalpahin (only in some of the later years do we find even any pictorial representation of the Nahuatl year signs),[5] in every other way the work published here has the characteristics of a classic set of annals, in addition to some transformations and developments of those characteristics that are rarely seen elsewhere. In the annals tradition, the present work is organized into year units, giving both the Spanish calendar year and what is taken for its Nahuatl preconquest-style equivalent. Within each year every entry is separate from every other, connected only by a strictly chronological sequence of months and days.

The content is broadly speaking ultra-typical of Nahuatl annals both before and after the conquest: the celebration of the local sociopolitical entity by detailing its officers and public functions and in other ways; a record of the installation and removal of local high officials; reports of plagues, storms, and earthquakes, and of scandalous and other locally newsworthy events. Its main anomaly is its breadth. Almost any set of annals one can point to will concentrate overwhelmingly on and have as its focal point the author's home entity, where he invariably writes. The same principle obtains in Chimalpahin, but his migration gave him two homes. The primary focus in his contemporary annals is on the place of his residence as an adult, when he was doing the writing of the present text, on the indigenous Mexico Tenochtitlan and the Spanish Mexico City, including the amorphous single overall entity that they were becoming; the double nature of that entity explains much that seems quite unique in Chimalpahin's work here. But the reader will also find many traces of his roots in Amaquemecan and even specifically in Tzaqualtitlan Tenanco within it.

Chimalpahin's contemporary writings have many possible uses. It appears to us that they illuminate in the first instance the author's mentality and conceptual equipment, and to an extent Nahua mentality and concepts in his time more generally. They are surely the best developed of known annals material with a postconquest range, not forgetting the Tlaxcalan don Juan Buenaventura Zapata y Mendoza, whose writings can be considered at least in the same class.[6] Although the Nahua annalists may report facts mentioned nowhere else, especially on matters purely inside the indigenous context, the annals should not be taken for objective reporting, nor is their main value a contribution of facts. Chimalpahin, exceptional though he is in many ways, is the same as the others in this respect. The most obvious use of Chimalpahin's writing on his own time is in intellectual and cultural studies dealing with Nahua attitudes and concepts in the urban centers of central Mexico in the first half of the seventeenth century. The picture that emerges is one of persistence, if in a modified form, of Nahua concepts, structures, and values at the very core of Nahua-Spanish contact.

With his well developed writings, his repeated use of the same terms in many slightly varying contexts, Chimalpahin offers a rich opportunity for the study of Nahua categories of various kinds. Studies based primarily on his writings with precontact content, though ranging over the whole corpus, have already illuminated his sociopolitical

5. Although Ch. is a rather extreme example, the gradual diminishing of the pictorial element is a fact of the evolution of the genre; also, from early on there were annals without a pictorial element, such as the "Annals of Juan Bautista" (Reyes García 2001).

6. See Lockhart 1992, pp. 391–92.

categories.[7] In his contemporary writings Chimalpahin makes copious use of Nahua social categories.[8] He demonstrates how Nahuatl responded to the need to talk about indigenous people as a single ethnic group by expanding the semantic range of existing terms as well as mining the language's great potential for new formations. The most all-embracing of these terms, the related *macehualli* and *nican tlaca*, will be discussed in greater detail below under matters of translation (p. 17), in which they figure so strongly. Both used native vocabulary and built on while extending native meanings. They even both appeared at first above all in the first person plural, with the prefix *ti-*, "we," which had been used in preconquest times to indicate ethnic or gender solidarity. This form proved transitional, since as the new meanings became established the *ti-* was increasingly dropped, as we see happening in the very texts published here.

Despite these large ethnic terms, the use of already established references to smaller groups of indigenous continued to predominate. Chimalpahin's writings demonstrate that the *altepetl* and *tlaxilacalli* (i.e., the Nahua ethnic state and its constituent parts; see the discussion below, pp. 17–18) still functioned as the Nahuas' primary source of ethnic identity, since individuals and groups are identified by altepetl and tlaxilacalli names, and the terms *altepehuaque* and *tlaxilacaleque* ("people of the altepetl and tlaxilacalli") abound. At the same time, however, *altepehuaque* undergoes some semantic change, as its meaning extends to embrace the non-indigenous population too. *Chaneque* ("possessors of homes, residents, citizens") also becomes an ethnically open term, as it refers to people of any ethnicity who reside within the limits of an altepetl or tlaxilacalli. The term *tlacanechicoltin* ("people gathered from various places") in reference to the non-Nahua indigenous residents of Mexico Tenochtitlan is a Nahuatl construction but apparently not part of the basic traditional vocabulary and may have been influenced by Spanish designations of outsiders.

Regarding Chimalpahin's categories for non-indigenous people we find a very different scenario. Here well established Spanish loanwords prevail, suggesting that by Chimalpahin's time people of non- or partially indigenous descent had long been accepted as part of the Nahuas' daily lives. Much as with the relatively fewer occurrences of the archaic *nican tlaca* in reference to the indigenous, Chimalpahin rarely calls the Spaniards *cristianos*, "Christians," which tended to be the preferred term in the early postconquest years. Instead, the hybrid word *castilteca* and Spanish *españoles*, as well as forms with double plurals, one from each language, *españolestin* and *españolesme*, far outnumber the earlier term. A careful analysis of these contemporary annals even suggests that *castilteca* too was declining during the time of Chimalpahin's literary activity. Whereas *castilteca* and the double plurals of *españoles* dominate in the earlier entries, after 1613 they disappear entirely. During the same time period, between 1613 and 1615, simple *españoles* without the double plural appears 50 times. Thus we learn in Chimalpahin not only about Nahuatl social categorization but something about the chronology of its evolution.

In the context of all other ethnic groups, Chimalpahin uses Spanish loanwords from the beginning. Whether it be other Europeans, blacks, Japanese, or people of mixed descent, Chimalpahin calls these groups exactly as the Spaniards did. Even Nahuatl

7. Schroeder 1991, pp. 119–97; Lockhart 1992, pp. 14–44, passim.

8. For more on the categories and topics of Ch. as discussed in the following several paragraphs, see Namala 2002.

tliltique, literally "blacks," in reference to people of African descent represents a direct translation of Spanish *negros*. Perhaps the use of *criollo* is a bit of an exception, as Chimalpahin always pairs it with the Nahuatl circumscription *nican tepiltzin*, "a child of people here," implying his relative unfamiliarity with the word, and after all it was only at that time beginning to come into use in Spanish to refer to ethnic Spaniards, and that usually in the restricted realm of officeholding.

Chimalpahin's gender categories partake of some of the same trends observed with ethnic categories. As with the evolution of Nahuatl words that came to designate indigenous people as a group in the postconquest years, the basic Nahuatl gender terms *cihuatl*, "woman, female" and *oquichtli*, "man, male," also took on a distinct ethnic dimension by referring not merely to women and men but specifically to indigenous women and indigenous men. With men, the form using *ti-*, "we," also appears with ethnic meaning, extending its preconquest use to indicate the solidarity of males as a group.[9] Regarding Spanish women and men, Chimalpahin consistently uses Spanish loanwords, if not always in exactly the same way as in Spanish texts.[10] Chimalpahin's vocabulary demonstrates that Spanish gender terms were subjected to the same gendered rules as their Nahuatl counterparts, for the male and female terms were generally borrowed separately.

In his reporting in general, so close to traditional annals fare, Chimalpahin documents a thriving indigenous culture despite or perhaps because of the interconnectedness of the indigenous and Spanish worlds. For example, Chimalpahin's often repeated respect for the ruling authorities, indigenous and Spanish alike, speaks to the annalist's deeply felt responsibility to portray the greatness of his altepetl, and it is both Spanish and indigenous officials, both secular and ecclesiastic, who more than anyone else represent this greatness. Altepetl reportage and magnification is thus Chimalpahin's basic thrust, and a quite noncommittal but approving stance is his main mode, both of these things fully within the Nahua annals tradition. If we look at the text as a whole, we will soon grasp that demographic decline, economic woes, and other scourges of the indigenous population are not major themes, and not much space is devoted to them. When Chimalpahin does turn to such a topic, it is usually to speak of something that was of great public concern in Mexico City, often among high civil and ecclesiastical officials, as in his reporting of great loss of indigenous life in connection with the vast project of draining the Valley of Mexico, the *Desagüe*. Likewise, negative comments on officials are rare, and when we see them, the reason is often, apparently, that the majority consensus in Spanish officialdom, especially in the ecclesiastical sector, was also negative, as with the criticism of the Franciscan fray Gerónimo de Zárate, chaplain at the central Franciscan establishment for indigenous people, San José, or of Archbishop Guerra for his continued frivolities after a major earthquake had struck and devastated the city.[11] At times, it is true, we seem to detect a more personal note, as when Chimalpahin deplores the denuding of the slopes of Chapultepec, which he had thought so beautiful, as the result of a Spanish effort to locate some entirely illusory deposits of gold, with the wood of the formerly glorious

9. I.e., in precontact and even postcontact usage any group of men was called "we men" if a man was speaking; the same expression now took on an ethnic coloration as well. For a subtlety of this usage see pp. 182–83, n. 7.

10. See below, p. 20, for the meaning of *señora* in Nahuatl.

11. Pp. 194–201, 212–13, 250–51 (Zárate), pp. 188–93 (Guerra).

felled trees going for cooking.[12] Even here in a sense the greatness of the altepetl is at issue.

In Chimalpahin's portrayal of natural phenomena and in particular natural disasters his split personality in terms of upholding indigenous traditions versus embracing modernity sometimes comes to the fore. On the one hand, he fully accepts and eagerly passes on to his readers modern scientific explanations of, for example, a solar eclipse, clearly rejecting his ancestors' non-Christian religious interpretation of such an event. On the other hand, and again mirroring his own times, Chimalpahin is not immune to superstitious beliefs regarding this matter, either, and not merely indigenous beliefs, for the Spaniards had their own superstitions, not clearly distinguished from scientific findings, on such matters. Ultimately, church processions replace ancient Mexica rituals as a means of coping with natural disasters in the annalist's accounts. They also become symbols of unity, joining together the altepetl's Spanish and indigenous citizens in their plea to a common deity for help, as well as in the display of altepetl magnificence. Yet processions by cofradías and various other kinds of organizations are also a way in which a series of sociopolitical, corporate, and religious entities and subentities, Spanish and indigenous, expressed themselves within a framework of rivalry, and Chimalpahin reports the processions with a sharp sense of their significance within the politics of entities.

It becomes clear that Chimalpahin's notion of the altepetl was in the process of changing, as the Spanish city that was developing within its boundaries became more and more integrated with the indigenous entity and into Chimalpahin's writing. This tendency is seen in other annals too but is more pronounced in Chimalpahin's work, in part because of the nature of the capital city, in part because Chimalpahin was himself so embedded in the Spanish ecclesiastical world. While ethnicity remains an important factor in the definition and acceptance of localized identities, spectacles and scandals illustrate the ever-changing boundaries of rivalry and unity, as they cut across ethnic lines. For example, Chimalpahin's entries show that localized identities continue to reflect the original Nahua arrangement of Mexico Tenochtitlan's four separate and separately functioning parts, each of them displaying a strong sense of microethnic identity and pride; moreover, his often condescending remarks regarding Tlatelolco not only reinforce his Tenochca perspective, but also acknowledge the separate, if clearly inferior, status of that altepetl, even though from the Spanish point of view it was becoming just another part of the colonial City of Mexico. And Chimalpahin gives us examples of pride and separatist tendencies among Mexica entities far smaller than the four great districts.

In his few explicit statements about his motives for writing his contemporary annals, Chimalpahin tends to stress the need to convey to future generations how things in the altepetl were in his day. He wants future citizens to know and be amazed that the area around the church of San Antón, by their time well developed, had in his been almost a lake; he thinks they will need to know that there had been such a figure as a particular Jesuit savant whom Chimalpahin and many others admired.[13] If we look at his writing itself as mute evidence on this point, over and above the traditional annalist's stance we can detect a reporter's urge to portray unusual events vividly, as with the great earthquake or the arrival of the Japanese.[14] We also find him intent on explaining to indigenous

12. Pp. 300–03.

13. Pp. 258–59 (San Antón), 284–87 (Jesuit).

people and even to himself new Spanish or European lore that has just been relayed to him by some Spaniard, generally an ecclesiastic, as in his discussion of the mechanics of the solar eclipses just alluded to, or in his treatise on the order of San Antonio Abad.[15]

In the long run the serious reader of this large portion of Chimalpahin's work will learn how his qualities are reflected, if sometimes subtly, in virtually all parts of it. At first the reader may get an ultimately false impression of an endless series of short, trivial, uncommunicative entries. Until one acquires the background and then develops the sensitivities needed to appreciate such material fully, it can be helpful to concentrate on some of the more spectacular passages in the work, where Chimalpahin's qualities are more immediately evident. Some of the outstanding examples are the already mentioned earthquake account (pp. 186–93) and the descriptions of the Japanese (pp. 170–73, 272–77);[16] others include the funeral procession of Archbishop Guerra (pp. 200–11), the tales related to an alleged uprising by those of African descent (214–25), and two accounts about women who opposed the erection of crosses and were miraculously struck down (pp. 250–57). First reactions may vary to the description of the solar eclipse (176–85) and the accounts of water channeling projects (96–107, passim, and 292–95).

Processions and other public events in Mexico City play such a role in Chimalpahin that one gains a better sense of things if one knows the general layout of the Mexico City of his time, especially the location of churches and public buildings. With no attempt to be exhaustive, we have provided a map which we hope will be of use to the reader.

We have done our best in the English translation to give the reader most of the content and a good deal of the flavor of the Nahuatl original. Something that cannot easily be conveyed in a translation is the way that Chimalpahin used Spanish loanwords in his Nahuatl original; only a survey of the transcription of the original will give one a full sense of how Chimalpahin on the one hand was very conversant with a large amount of Spanish lore and concepts, and the corresponding Spanish loanwords had become a prominent feature of his vocabulary, no more problematic to him than vocabulary of native origin. But the reader of the transcription will also see many forms that from a Spanish point of view are misspelled; virtually all of these represent typical sound substitutions used by Nahuatl speakers in the long time before Nahuatl acquired the Spanish sounds that were lacking in its phonetic repertoire, using unvoiced stops instead of voiced stops for example. Presumably such substitutions were typical of Chimalpahin's pronunciation despite his in some ways great erudition in Spanish matters. We even find "fuente," the word for a fountain, with the intention *puente*, "bridge,"[17] because Nahuatl lacked [f] and used [p] as the closest equivalent, so that from the point of view of a Nahuatl speaker *f* and *p* were pronounced identically and could be interchanged. One wonders if this type of pronunciation was only for loanwords in Nahuatl, or if Chimalpahin carried it into Spanish conversation as well. A bit of writing in Spanish is to be found in our text, and it is perfectly spelled by the Spanish standards of the time, though its syntax and idiom subtly betray a non-native speaker.[18]

14. Pp. 186–93; 170–73, 272–77.

15. Pp. 176–85 (eclipse), 278–83, 290–93 (San Antonio Abad).

16. Related bits about the Japanese, rounding out the story, are on pp. 174–77, 236–37, 278–79, 282–83, 290–91, and 294–95.

17. Pp. 300–01 at n. 5.

18. As on pp. 232–33 at n. 1.

The Manuscript and its History

The primary original manuscript of the set of annals published here is housed in the Bibliothèque Nationale, Paris (BNP), as Fonds Mexicain 220, and is in remarkably good condition.[1] It is bound in velum with five leather ties through the spine, with two additional leather ties to close the volume. Written on the spine in brown stencil-like letters is "Diario d. D. Domingo d. S. Antón."[2] The paste-downs on the inside front of the binding are pages from *Vida del Venerable Padre* . . ., which is similar to the treatment of a copy of Chimalpahin's version of Francisco López de Gómara's *Conquista de México* (1552) made by Lorenzo Boturini Benaducci ca. 1740.[3] The annals text numbers 284 pages (the pagination was added later by another hand).

The beginning of the text as presented here is a separate manuscript fragment that is now located in Mexico City.[4] No doubt remains that Chimalpahin intended its contents to go with those of the main manuscript, not only because the years and months mesh perfectly, but because of specific indications made by the author in the originals. Lead-in words added at the lower right of the last page of the first section are identical with the first words of the main part. On that same last page Chimalpahin made a notation that an entry slightly out of chronological order should be inserted further on, and at the correct place on the first page of the main manuscript he indicated that the entry from above should be inserted.[5] The set as we know it, then, starts with the year 1577, 7 House, two years before Chimalpahin was born.[6] The fragment continues to 1589, 6 House, usually with an entry for each year. The annals for 1589 then merge into the main BNP text (beginning with the same year), which is characterized thereafter by many more details for each year.

Although the existence of a lead-in from the last page of the fragment to the first page of the main part would seem to indicate that at one time the two were joined together, such a conclusion cannot be drawn with certainty. It seems rather that when doing the present fragmentary first part, which is attached to another set of material, the idea of composing a major sequence concentrating upon his own lifetime may have gradually dawned upon Chimalpahin, and that having decided upon such a project he transferred to a new manuscript but did not carry out the laborious recopying required to start afresh from the beginning. It is also not clear that the section we are including as the first part was conceived of by Chimalpahin as a beginning of anything. Indeed, with the exception of the genealogical work on his home entity which he called a chronicle,[7] it is not clear that

1. See Schroeder 1991, pp. 27–29, for a more detailed treatment of the physical history of Ch.'s known manuscripts.

2. Schroeder visited the Bibliothèque Nationale in 1995 to examine both the manuscripts 74 and 220 of the Fonds Mexicain. She returned in 2001 to check the present transcription against the original. This description incorporates her observations on these occasions.

3. Browning Manuscript, CASE 5011, Newberry Library, Chicago.

4. For background on the manuscript see Reyes García 1971.

5. See pp. 32–33, nn. 4, 5, 6.

6. Ch. was born on Tuesday, May 26, 1579, the year 9 Reed in his scheme. The date of his death has not been verified.

7. Entitled by Ch. "La genealogia y declaracion de la DeScenden[cia] linage E generaçion y Origen de sus antepas[ados] del Señor Don domingo Hernandez Ayopochtzin. . ."

he considered any of his various collections of papers to be well defined separate units. He may have thought of them as portions of a single large work. Even in this first part he refers to a viceroy's not having any encomienda "either,"[8] i.e., either he had somewhere else written material for his contemporary annals sequence going back even farther in time than 1577, or he viewed similar statements he had already made in other connections as belonging to the same work in a larger sense.

Despite its relative cleanness, throughout the whole primary manuscript one will find marginal and superscript additions and words and passages crossed out. Part of Chimalpahin's normal procedure are dashes connecting the text with the right margin in the case of short lines, especially at the end of paragraphs. Each verso page has a lead-in word or words at the bottom anticipating the beginning of the following recto page. These words are not mentioned or reproduced here, except for the crucial one connecting the two parts of the manuscript. Perhaps only a total of five lead-ins from bottom verso to top recto are missing in the entire main manuscript. There are no recto to verso lead-ins.[9] The paper is European and linen-like in finish, with paper size, ink, and writing quite uniform (especially when one compares this set with Chimalpahin's other manuscripts); most entries are neat, unhurried, and well spaced. The last entry is on p. 282, dated October 14, 1615, and concludes a little over half way down the page.

How to answer the question of whether or not the present ending of our principal manuscript also represents the end of Chimalpahin's enterprise of keeping contemporary annals systematically is related in part to events that occurred after 1615. Pp. 283 and 284 of the manuscript contain a copy made by don Carlos de Sigüenza y Góngora (a Mexico City savant and bibliophile, 1645–1700) of what was apparently the first part of the diary of bachiller Gregorio Martín de Guijo of Mexico City, beginning in October 1623.[10] An entry for June 22, 1624, tells of the sudden death of Chimalpahin's patron, fray Agustín del Espíritu Santo, after which the church of San Antonio Abad was commandeered by a group of Augustinian friars who refused to leave but then were forcibly evicted, after which in turn city officials closed the church the next month. This move must have put Chimalpahin out of his primary job. Somehow he managed to add occasional bits of information to his other annals up to at least the year 1631.[11]

What became of Chimalpahin's manuscripts upon his death is not certainly known, but we have some reason to believe that they were acquired by don Hernando de Alva Ixtlilxochitl, affiliated with Tetzcoco and famous for his historical writings in Spanish.[12] Alva Ixtlilxochitl was a great collector of pictorial and alphabetic manuscripts, which he

---

8. In the entry for 1580, pp. 26–27 at n. 6.

9. Occasional small paper pasteovers are found covering the text or on the margins and may be considered irrelevant because they are mostly in French, clearly of a much later date, and never in Ch.'s handwriting.

10. For the remainder of the diary, see Guijo 1952.

11. For an item from 1629 see Chimalpahin 1963, p. 41; for one from 1631 see ibid., p. 49.

12. Although Alva Ixtlilxochitl held the position of judge-governor in both Tetzcoco and Tlalmanalco, and he was a prominent person, Ch. never mentions him, perhaps because Alva Ixtlilxochitl was much more Hispanized, of partly Spanish descent and writing almost exclusively in Spanish. Though he was the approximate contemporary of Ch. as to birthdate, he was in effect of a later cohort.

used to exalt his home region in his books. Since Sigüenza is known to have inherited much of Ixtlilxochitl's collection, it is natural to suspect that the writings of Chimalpahin were among it. What is certain is that the manuscripts of both Alva Ixtlilxochitl and Chimalpahin became part of Sigüenza's impressive collection of antiquities. Toward the bottom of the last page of our primary manuscript with Chimalpahin's writing on it, in a hand that closely resembles that of Sigüenza, is written: "Although the good don Domingo de San Antón Chimalpahin lived longer, I did not find any more personal papers on this matter other than those contained here, etc."[13]

The facts as known, then, are that it was not until some years after 1615, in 1624, that Chimalpahin's circumstances of employment changed in a way that might have affected his production of the contemporary annals, and that he made some additions to his writings even after that time. Yet Chimalpahin's manuscript ends on a half-filled page, something that otherwise does not occur in it, and there was some slacking off of the pace of writing already in 1614 compared to 1613. Among the mass of Chimalpahin's writing that was once in Sigüenza's possession he found nothing more apparently closely related to it. We can only suspect that Chimalpahin in fact halted the effort here, perhaps to concentrate more on preconquest material.

Upon his death Sigüenza willed his collection of books and manuscripts to the Jesuits' Colegio de San Pedro y San Pablo in Mexico City. Yet no copy of the will is extant, and we do not know for certain that all of Chimalpahin's works were delivered to the colegio as prescribed. Fray Agustín de Vetancurt, a close friend of Sigüenza writing at the end of the seventeenth century, credits Chimalpahin as one of his sources of information for his history of ancient Mexico in his "Catálogo de autores impressos, y de instrumentos manuscritos." It is not clear whether he knew Chimalpahin's writing while it was still in Sigüenza's hands or after transferral to the Jesuits.

The first published record of Chimalpahin's manuscripts comes from Lorenzo Boturini's catalog (1746). However, Chimalpahin's "Diario" is not mentioned by Boturini, and it was only in recent years that Schroeder discovered that it had been in the library of the Jesuits' secondary school for Nahua boys, the Colegio de San Gregorio in Mexico City. An inventory of the library's collection was made upon the expulsion of the Jesuits (1767), and the manuscript was listed among the Nahuatl-language materials in the collection.

The record of the subsequent whereabouts of the contemporary annals manuscript is sketchy, but most likely it became part of a large collection of manuscripts, rare books, and other antiquities that were acquired by Joseph Maria Alexis Aubin in the 1830s during a buying trip to Mexico, then being taken to Paris in 1840. E. Eugène Goupil purchased the same materials from Aubin in 1889, and his widow donated the entire collection of 384 manuscripts and other items to the Bibliothèque Nationale de France in 1898. It is likely that the contemporary annals were acquired separately from Chimalpahin's other Nahuatl annals at the BNP, for they have different catalog numbers, and the contemporary annals are paginated, whereas all of his other manuscripts are numbered by folio.

13. The comments by Sigüenza at the end of Ch.'s contemporary annals are not signed, but Schroeder has compared the writing with signed remarks by Sigüenza on a manuscript attributed to Alva Ixtlilxochitl, MS 374, vols. 1 and 2, in the Bible Society Library, Cambridge University.

Only eighteen folios of manuscript by Chimalpahin remain in Mexico. Referred to as the "Anales Tepanecas," this manuscript is housed in the Archivo Histórico of the Instituto Nacional de Antropología e Historia. It is the last two folios in this set that Chimalpahin designated as belonging with his larger contemporary annals manuscript.

Let us now try to see what the above rather technical considerations add up to. We have already expressed the suspicion that the project of an annals sequence covering Chimalpahin's own lifetime, with current entries added indefinitely into the future once he had reached the year in which he was writing, seems to have come to him bit by bit, and that the new cleaner manuscript now in Paris represents the point at which he undertook the enterprise definitively.

The manuscript, however, contains some apparently contradictory clues. The mere fact of additions, deletions, and changes points toward an original, that is, that Chimalpahin first wrote down his thoughts in exactly this form on this very paper. These features surely tell us that the author continued to revise the manuscript, but they do not necessarily prove that it was the first form the material took in the author's hands. Indeed, we find some cases in which whole phrases were left out inadvertently, then placed between the lines or in the margins, phrases without which the other material would make no sense.[14] We also find entries which appear to be current with the event narrated, and then in the body of the entry will appear some retrospective remark, such as that the image referred to is still there today, and this obviously posterior comment is part of the material written in the original lines, not an insert.[15] On reflection, however, one sees that these things do not necessarily prove that Chimalpahin had written an earlier version, merely that there was an earlier version of that particular entry on which he was basing himself, and he could equally well be copying from texts written by others, as we know he so frequently did. One must also consider the cost of paper to a person in Chimalpahin's circumstances, the effort of recopying, and the fact that he did not recopy and physically integrate the first part of the sequence, even though it was quite imperative to do so. On balance, we consider it probable that the version we now have represents in most cases Chimalpahin's only redaction of the material. On the basis of the facts mentioned above we can also speculate that the full-scale enterprise of contemporary annals, having gone on for several years, ended in 1615 as it appears to in the manuscript.

To such considerations one can add the evidence of Chimalpahin's orthography. The general impression given by the whole, in both its parts, is of a sameness of the hand and of the spelling, so that nothing would seem to say that it was not all written at the same time. Chimalpahin was trained in a mainly standard form of Nahuatl orthography of the late sixteenth and early seventeenth centuries, a style sometimes referred to as Franciscan, but in truth it was simply the general style in educated circles of that time before some innovations came in in the course of the early seventeenth century, often associated with the Jesuits, but actually somewhat broader than that. The most unusual feature of Chimalpahin's writing is the use of *uhc* for syllable-final [k^W]. The three main styles

14. As for example on pp. 212–13 at n. 4, or on pp. 262–63 at n. 4, or on pp. 280–81 at n. 3.

15. See the example on pp. 258–59, where a house presently being built in one part of the entry is later referred to as already finished. For examples of an even larger interval of time, see pp. 16–17, n. 3.

were *cuh*, as in most mundane Nahuatl writing, *cu* as in Molina, and *uc* as in Carochi. The word "lord" will often be seen in mundane writing as "tecuhtli"; in Molina it is "tecutli," in Carochi "teuctli." Chimalpahin is rare in writing "teuhctli," but this feature like much else in the manuscript never varies.

Other aspects do vary, and what is more, they evolve meaningfully across the manuscripts. In Chimalpahin's mature style, a syllable-final, word-internal glottal stop is often but not always represented in writing, taking the form of an *h*. With some common roots the *h* ultimately becomes almost invariable in the author's renderings. Such is not the case uniformly throughout our manuscripts, however. If we take the common word *iquac*, "at that time, when," which in pronunciation has a glottal stop at the end of the first syllable, one will find no instance of *h* ("ihquac") in the fragment in Mexico City. The same is true in a large initial part of the manuscript proper; the first instance of "ihquac" that we have seen comes on p. 121 of the manuscript, in an entry for September 1609. Then both versions occur, until with the entries for 1612 and after, the version with the *h* becomes predominant, in long stretches universal. Virtually the same story can be told for the word *tlatoani*, "ruler," first often "tlatohuani," then almost always "tlahtohuani"; the trend with related words is the same.

In the early part of the text Chimalpahin follows the convention of his time (and indeed it continued to be the main convention in Nahuatl writing for long afterward) in rendering [k^{W}a] as *qua*. Taking again the same word *iquac*, we find that it appears in the early fragment and in a large first part of the main manuscript in several variants, but always with *qua*. But in the 1612 entries, variants with *cua* become predominant, and after that *qua* is virtually absent. The same trend is seen with other words containing [k^{W}a].

Although its study is more subjective and we have not gone into it as thoroughly as the orthography, some traces of evolution can also be detected in Chimalpahin's mainly stable calligraphy. For example, at one point late in the game he seems to change the orientation and shape of the character representing the cedilla; he also begins to write more capital *E*'s.

All this evidence of orthographic and calligraphic evolution strengthens the notion that Chimalpahin was writing the manuscript bit by bit over an extended time, hence that what we have is truly his original version, with much of the part after perhaps 1605 or so written close to the time of the events as they occurred. The evidence also strengthens the connection between the two parts of the manuscript, showing a seamless continuity of trends from the fragment into the main part. In this context we can be even more assured that the change over the course of the text in Chimalpahin's ethnic terminology, alluded to in the first section above, represents an evolution in his usage over the years covered.

Some Aspects of the Edition

Conventions. The transcription in our edition adds nothing and attempts to retain all the letters, diacritic marks and abbreviations of the original as closely as they can be

1. We do not capitalize anything Ch. does not. An element of subjectivity enters in because only certain letters have an actual different form for capital and lower case; in others one must judge from variations in size alone. Perhaps we have put too many capital J's in the transcription because Ch.'s universal *j* is a large letter. Some other letters, notably *f*, present somewhat similar problems. We do sometimes include in brackets characters which are not clear in the manuscript.

reproduced in print.[1] As in comparable editions, however, the original spacing of letters is disregarded in favor of spacing by the norms of present-day grammarians; as in similar cases, the justification is not only the lack of entire consistency in the original but great difficulty in determining whether at a certain juncture it intends a space between letters or not, as one might indeed expect in a situation where the "space" as we know it did not exist.[2]

Many instances of syllable-final *n* and sometimes *m* are written in Chimalpahin, and in the work of other writers of his time, as a variously curved line over the preceding vowel. One can dispute whether this overbar is exactly the same in appearance as the diacritic that Chimalpahin puts where one would expect a Spanish tilde (~) (neither of them in practice is confined to a position directly over the letter affected). Following precedent in some printed books of that time and of this, we have reproduced both signs the same, as a tilde over a printed letter.

Reproduction of the original extends to punctuation and lack thereof. Some otherwise highly respectable editions of Nahuatl texts still follow the policy of repunctuating everything as though it were in modern English, Spanish, or German. One problem with such a procedure is that it commits the transcription once and for all to a particular interpretation of the sentence structure, precisely the part that we moderns are least likely to grasp. It also involves abandoning distinctions made in the original which not only can help in comprehending the meaning and organization of the text, but can place the text at a certain point in the tradition of Nahuatl orthography, often telling a great deal about its affiliations.

To indicate paragraph-like entities or the beginning of an entry, Chimalpahin like many others uses a sign in which two curved lines converge at a horizontal line forming the foot of the character; we have reproduced it as an underlined *v*. A separate entry usually begins at the left margin, ending wherever the words dictate, and we have followed the original exactly in this respect. To indicate divisions or new topics within such an entity, Chimalpahin sometimes uses a double or single diagonal (// or /). We have reproduced these signs just as in the original. It may be that the double diagonal indicates a more significant division than a single one, but we are not sure. At times one can detect hardly any justification for the presence of a given diagonal. Since these signs and the spacing of units are the best indication available of the author's sense of the organization of his material, we have reproduced them also in our translation in the corresponding places and have strictly followed the original's division into units or lack thereof.

At the level of words and sentences, Chimalpahin has signs that in appearance more or less approximate the period, comma, semicolon, and colon. They do not, however, behave like punctuation marks in European writing, either of that time or of ours. They come out of a tradition in which Nahua writers used one or all of these marks to indicate the end of a phonological/semantic phrase.[3] In Chimalpahin's writing, however, the origin of the practice can hardly be detected. In effect the marks come mainly at the end of

2. See Lockhart 1992, pp. 338–339; Lockhart 1993, pp. 26–27; and Lockhart 1995, pp. 134–35. To the justifications may be added that even experts, much less neophytes, are severely hampered in scanning the texts unless they are respaced. The deterrent effect of an unspaced printed text is much greater than that of a handwritten original.

3. Lockhart 1992, pp. 339–40; Lockhart 1993, pp. 25–26; Lockhart 1995, p. 134.

significant words, especially nouns, and particularly certain favorite nouns which usually bear such a mark. They also, as in Spanish writing, often accompany numbers, appearing even on both sides of the number. The period and comma are identical in their function and manner of distribution; the semicolon and colon are possibly different at times, but mainly they too follow the same lines. Chimalpahin thus had little motivation to distinguish period from comma or colon from semicolon. Rather than a clearly demarcated dot for a period versus a dot plus a curved line for a comma, he produced a continuum, some pure dots, some dots with the barest hint of a tail, some with a small tail, and some with a long one. The editors have not been entirely of one mind as to where along this line the point of demarcation should be. In the end, dots with only tiny additional marks were counted as periods, the rest as commas. Since there is no difference from Chimalpahin's point of view, the matter can rest there. Semicolons and colons presented the same problem, even less significant because they are far fewer in number.

It was Chimalpahin's general policy (not universally observed, however) to draw a dash from the last letter on a given line of text to the normal right margin. Since these lines have no syntactic or other grammatical or semantic function but are part of the physical allocation of the text on the original written page and would be out of place on a page with a different physical allocation of letters, they have been omitted in the transcription. A special case are some lines or dashes, occasionally ornamented, that Chimalpahin sometimes put at the end of a paragraph-like unit, occasionally without reaching the right-hand margin. We have reproduced some of these lines.

Translation philosophy. Our translation policy is a simple one, to try to give the closest equivalents available in idiomatic modern English, taking advantage of the progress in grammar and lexicon achieved over the last generation,[4] and also of experience with the wider variety of older Nahuatl texts circulating during the same time.[5] In choosing between an idiomatic English version that corresponds closely to the sense of the original and a more literal rendering which is less idiomatic and does not give the sense, we prefer the first alternative. We take advantage of the indications given in subordinating particles of various kinds to build longer English sentences than were often characteristic of older translations, believing that in the original too the syntax is often complex and long of breath. Yet while we generally tend toward a pragmatic rather than a literal translation, we are also trying to convey to a reader who does not know Nahuatl a number of important things in the original that do not correspond to anything in normal English discourse. Thus to the quite self-explanatory basic side of our translations the reader will find rather numerous exceptions, which do call for explanation. Explaining them will at the same time throw light on Chimalpahin's procedures and vocabulary.

---

4. As in Andrews 1975, Carochi 2001, Karttunen 1983, Launey 1979, and Lockhart 2001.

5. The translations here are comparable to those in Karttunen and Lockhart 1987 (the less literal of the two versions), Lockhart 1993, and Sousa, Poole and Lockhart 1998.

6. As in the entry for June 6, 1593, where an eagle was put on top of a church "as it appears today" (pp. 42–43); or the entry for July 23, 1594, in which the Discalced moved to a new site, and the remainder of the entry says that they were there thirteen years before moving again (pp. 50–51); or the entry for April 4, 1599, in which some images were set up "as they appear today" (pp. 66–67); or the entry for September 7, 1603, in which a church was inaugurated "where today mass is said" (pp. 76–77); or the entry for October

Axcan. A great many of Chimalpahin's entries begin with the word *axcan*, meaning in this context "today." It gradually becomes clear that many entries so beginning were not written on the actual day of the events narrated; surely not those in the early part of the work, occurring when Chimalpahin was still a child (though these entries may have been copied from others which in fact were written closer to the events). Not infrequently we see evidence that some or even the bulk of an entry was written years after the fact.[6] In view of its use in the original one might be justified in rendering this kind of *axcan* as "at this point," or leaving it out altogether, as Rafael Tena quite justifiably does at times in his 2001 Spanish edition of these texts. But since the word is an important item in the stylistics of Chimalpahin and of Nahuatl annals in general, and it is lacking in many entries, we have felt it best to give the reader the full information, putting "today" every time that this sort of *axcan* appears.

Macehualli and nican tlaca. An important item in Chimalpahin's vocabulary is *macehualli*. The word may originally have meant "human being"; by the sixteenth century it most often referred to social rank, to a commoner as opposed to a noble, although in the plural or collective it still could approach the sense "the people." By around 1600 this word, while often retaining its earlier senses, was becoming the primary term for indigenous people when their altepetl or other affiliations were not mentioned, often appearing in the first person plural.[7] Its field of reference in this sense was virtually the same as Spanish *indio*, "Indian," and in some cases it can be seen as an attempt to find an equivalent for the Spanish word. Its implications are not at all the same, however, so we have not felt it appropriate to translate *macehualli* as Indian. "Indigenous person or people" could have been justified in many cases, but the evolution and ramifications of the word are of such interest and complexity that we have retained "commoner," from which even a reader with no knowledge of Nahuatl can track the word through the text and see that it sometimes refers to indigenous people of low rank, and sometimes—generally or always in the plural—to the indigenous population in general (in one case it even refers to the indigenous population of an Asian region).[8]

Through much of the sixteenth century, before "macehualli" became dominant, the same sense had been expressed by the phrase *nican titlaca*, "we people here," which faded after 1600. Chimalpahin, however, still sometimes uses it as a stylistic alternative to "macehualli" or uses the two as a pair for effect. The expression is quite transparent, and we have retained the literal translation.

Altepetl. With the key term *altepetl* we have taken a somewhat different tack, retaining the Nahuatl term itself in the English translation, as has already been done in many publications in the field of Nahuatl studies and Mexican ethnohistory. It is becoming a part of the vocabulary of early Mexican history as important as the Spanish

---

18, 1603, in which the brothers of San Juan de Dios arrived, who "today are at the Hospital de los Desamparados" (pp. 76–77). Note that all these examples are from the earlier part of the text. In later years instances are fewer, as in the entry for November 17, 1610 (pp. 168–69), which speaks of some names being inscribed in a chapel "as they now appear." Other cases are more subtle or debatable.

7. See Lockhart 1992, pp. 115–16. The ethnic sense was present from an early time; see a fully developed instance, even in the first person plural, from the 1560s in the "Annals of Juan Bautista" (Reyes García 2001, pp. 152–53, paragraph 36).

8. See Namala 2002 for more detail.

"encomienda," and indeed, an altepetl was usually the basis of an encomienda.[9] The word, originally a doublet meaning "water(s) and mountain(s)," had come to be the primary term in Nahuatl for an independent state. In central Mexico it referred usually to a local ethnic state, of which there were many in the region before the Spanish conquest, and most of them survived into Chimalpahin's time, seen by the Spaniards as indigenous municipalities, but still called altepetl by the Nahuas when using their own language. The altepetl was the master institution of the Nahua world both before and after contact, and it is important that we gain a full understanding of the word's meaning and use in a variety of contexts. In Chimalpahin's usage here, it will be seen that he can mean any individual sociopolitical entity of the traditional type, including the indigenous corporation of Mexico Tenochtitlan as it existed under the Spaniards, but it seems at times to indicate the total complex formation of the capital city, including Spaniards and their corporation as well as the indigenous component.[10] When the word is used with a plural sense (not always easy to detect because Chimalpahin like most Nahuatl speakers did not make any external distinction between singular and plural), it usually refers to the various altepetl surrounding Tenochtitlan throughout the Valley of Mexico, or perhaps at times in an even wider area. The term will also be found occasionally as a description of entities in Europe, Asia, and South America, sometimes seeming to refer to vast realms and sometimes to individual cities; such instances are hard to assess because it is not always certain that Chimalpahin himself understood the nature of the foreign entity.

Tlaxilacalli. The constituent parts or districts of an altepetl were called primarily *tlaxilacalli*, and we have retained the Nahuatl word in the English as with the broader term and for the same reason, to allow readers of English only to follow the terminology of Nahuatl sociopolitical organization. It was once thought that entities at this level were uniformly called *calpolli*, but such turns out not to be the case, at least for the post-contact period. In other annals with a larger precontact content, Chimalpahin tends to call the entities calpolli as long as they are migrating and tlaxilacalli after they have settled permanently and taken on a landed dimension.[11] The word itself has not yet been securely analyzed, though it seems to have *calli*, "house," as the last element; there is a glottal stop before the *x*.

Mexico. In Chimalpahin "Mexico" still has the traditional Nahuatl meaning of the area inhabited by the Mexica in the narrower ethnic sense, limited to Tenochtitlan and Tlatelolco; sometimes the meaning seems to be Tenochtitlan only, and sometimes the whole mixed Spanish-indigenous capital of New Spain. Yet since the indigenous connotation still predominates, we have not felt it appropriate to translate "Mexico City" except in the relatively few instances where the Spanish loanword *ciudad* is used in addition. Let the reader understand, then, that "Mexico" in our translation refers approximately to the area now called Mexico City. The term was not yet and long afterward would not be used for New Spain as a whole or for the country we call Mexico today. At some point the word, in Spanish at least, seems to have come to refer to Mexico City and its environs, more or less the Valley of Mexico, but just when such usage became common is not yet

9. For more on the altepetl and tlaxilacalli see Lockhart 1992, pp. 14–58, and Schroeder 1991, pp. 119–53.

10. See Namala 2002.

11. Schroeder 1991, pp. 143–53.

well understood, and there is no hint of it in Chimalpahin. In Spanish, *mexicano* from an early time meant the Nahuatl language, and in Nahuatl *mexicatl*, "Mexica person," was sometimes used among the migrants in north Mexico to mean all Nahuatl speakers,[12] but again Chimalpahin has no reflection of such usage.

One will see reference in the translation to the four parts of Mexico Tenochtitlan, in the Nahuatl usually simply *nauhcan*, literally "in four places." Tenochtitlan was a complex altepetl consisting of four separate sub-altepetl, each large and complex in itself. The units are of the type that Chimalpahin calls *tlayacatl altepetl* in referring to his native Amaquemecan, but he never uses that word for the four parts of Tenochtitlan; indeed he gives them no specific appellation at all. The four parts rotated in all matters in a counter-clockwise direction starting with San Juan Moyotlan in the southwest, then going on to San Pablo Teopan in the southeast, San Sebastián Atzaqualco in the northeast, and finally Santa María Cuepopan in the northwest. In an ongoing rotation there was really no distinction of first and last, but in virtually any listing of Chimalpahin's the order will put San Juan first and go through the list to Santa María.[13] The municipal council building for all Tenochtitlan (the *tecpan* or palace, variously translated here) was also in San Juan Moyotlan. Tlatelolco, though a Mexica altepetl, was separate from Tenochtitlan and did not partake in the four-part order. The Spaniards may not always have been aware of the distinction.

Other altepetl. The names of Nahua altepetl are generally given in the translation in their standard Nahuatl form, though a few well known names retain their Spanish form so that the reader can be sure that that is the settlement that is in question: thus Tlaxcala, Tacuba, Tacubaya, rather than Tlaxcallan, Tlacopan, and Atlacuihuayan. Nevertheless, the well known Amecameca, since it was so important to Chimalpahin as his homeland and because he understood the entity in such a different way than the Spaniards, appears here as Amaquemecan.

Teopixqui. In postcontact times the Nahuatl word *teopixqui*, having originally referred to priests of the indigenous gods, was expanded by normal processes to mean Christian priests. But since mendicant friars were so predominant in the first decades after the conquest, the word normally meant friar or at least religious, a member of a religious order (such as a Jesuit), with the Spanish loanword *clérigo* being used for secular clerics. Nevertheless, in principle the word could refer to any Christian priest. Our usual translation is friar or religious, but occasionally, depending on the context, priest. At times it is not entirely clear whether Chimalpahin means religious, all clergy, or secular priests.

Celar/seral/selar. A puzzling word in Chimalpahin's vocabulary is "seral," "selar," or "celar," which refers to some institution or building on the central square of Mexico City in his time and must be a loan from Spanish. "Seral" occurs eight times in the present corpus, "celar" four times, and "selar" twice. It has been proposed[14] that "selar," which could conceivably be the basic form despite being the least used by Chimalpahin, is from Spanish *seglar*, "secular," and stands for the longer phrase *cabildo seglar*, "secular (municipal) council," as opposed to the *cabildo eclesiástico*, the ecclesiastical council,

12. As in Anderson, Berdan and Lockhart 1976, Doc. 23.

13. See for example the passage of 1600 in which for the first time four alcaldes were named (pp. 66–67).

14. Tena in Chimalpahin 2001, p. 420.

i.e., the cathedral chapter. This interpretation is tempting, but the situation is still puzzling. The written form "selar" (probably pronounced [sela:l] by Chimalpahin, so that "seral" would merely be a preferred hypercorrection representing the same pronunciation) is a plausible rendering of Spanish *seglar*, for the Nahuas would have had problems with the [gl] cluster and would have been likely to reduce it. One implausibility in this interpretation, however, is the relative rarity of the word *seglar* in Mexican Spanish sources of the sixteenth and early seventeenth century. It surely was not on the lips of the general populace on ordinary occasions and is hardly in the same class with other words that the Nahuas took as their own and changed in meaning, like their *tomin*, "money," originally derived from a Spanish coin of that name, or their *señora* (often pronounced [xino:la']), "Spanish woman."

Whatever the origin, the word in Chimalpahin does seem to refer to the building housing the Mexico City municipal council or cabildo on the southeast corner of the main square, and can be translated as municipal building or cabildo building. Chimalpahin's entries show unambiguously that his seral or selar was a notable edifice on the square, that it was distinct from the viceregal palace, that it had an arcade in front of it, and that it was the headquarters of the corregidor of Mexico City. These attributes are sufficient to indicate what the word means; moreover, if the seral is not the cabildo building, that important feature of the central square of Mexico City is left unaccountably unmentioned. The word sometimes seems to refer specifically to the jail associated with the building, and it occurred to us that the origin might be Spanish *cárcel*, but too much omission and metathesis must be postulated to make this derivation at all likely.[15]

The expression was by no means new with Chimalpahin. The Codex Osuna, prepared in Mexico City in 1565, has an instance in which the sense seems fully developed. A Spaniard who is pictured as involved in land allocation is labeled an "alcaldes çelar."[16] Although only one alcalde is shown, the accompanying text has the reliable plural "alcaldesme," so that this does not seem to be a hypercorrect plural actually meaning a singular. From the nature of the activities and the fact that the alcalde pictured is accompanied by a regidor, it is clear that they are from the Spanish cabildo of Mexico City. The exact meaning of "çelar" is left somewhat ambiguous; it could equally well mean "secular" (secular alcalde) or "municipal building" (alcalde from the municipal building) but since it does not agree in number with "alcaldes," it seems more likely that it is a substantive referring to the institution or the building. Freestanding loan adjectives hardly existed at this time and were very rare even in Chimalpahin's time.

The so-called Annals of Juan Bautista, done in Mexico City in the 1560s, contain the word three times, always in the form "celar." Luis Reyes in his recent excellent edition puts forth the interpretation that the meaning is "roof terrace," based on the phrase "celar

---

15. The *c* with which the word begins four times in Ch. might have more affinity with *cárcel*. In the early seventeenth century *s* and *c/z* seem to have been converging in Mexican Spanish as [s], whereas in earlier decades the Nahuas perceived them differently, keeping the Spanish *c/z* the same in their writing, where it represented [s], but often converting *s* to *x*, pronounced [sh]. That the word begins with *c* in both the "Juan Bautista" annals and the Codex Osuna (see the two notes immediately following) is ominous for the interpretation of the word as originating in *seglar*, implying, as we in fact have come to believe for now, that the form at its inception began with *c*.

tlapanco" found in the margin at one point. Reyes believes that the notation was made by a person learning to translate Spanish and that "celar" and "tlapanco," "roof terrace," are to be taken as equivalents. Possibly so, but it is our belief that the phrase just as likely says that the events referred to were viewed from the roof of the cabildo building. Two occurrences in the text proper are highly obscure and do not settle the meaning to our satisfaction.[17]

Tlatoani. A term almost as crucial for Nahua sociopolitical organization as "altepetl" is *tlatoani*, literally "speaker" and in practice the dynastic ruler of an altepetl.[18] The word underwent constant evolution in the postcontact period. Much change had already occurred before Chimalpahin's time, and it continued after that. We might well have kept the Nahuatl word in our English, but it is so frequent and would in many situations be so awkward that we have translated it instead. "Ruler" in our translation usually renders *tlatoani* in the sense of dynastic ruler of an altepetl. The plural, "rulers," most often represents the plural of the Nahuatl word, *tlatoque*, but the sense is often not of several dynastic rulers but of the members of an indigenous municipal council, usually that of Mexico Tenochtitlan. This different meaning of the plural was widespread in Nahuatl as early as the mid-sixteenth century. The word also appears in Chimalpahin (and other Nahuatl writings) applied to certain high Spanish officials, above all the viceroy and sometimes Audiencia judges as well. Here the term, although surely very meaningful, has something of the flavor of an additional courtesy title, and our most usual translation is "lord." Chimalpahin uses the Spanish loanword *obispo*, "bishop," but also, often in tandem with it, *teopixcatlatoani*, which we translate as "priestly ruler." At times other high ecclesiastical officials also receive the appellation. A related term in Chimalpahin's usage, seen less here than in other works of his but still present, is *quauhtlatoani*, literally "eagle speaker" or "eagle ruler," meaning ruler through war or more broadly through individual merit rather than dynastic claim. In view of the nature of the office, we translate it as "interim ruler."

Treatment of saints, names of feasts, etc. We go very far toward putting not only the names of churches but the corresponding names of saints and religious concepts or events in Spanish. Most would agree that it is better to call the main Franciscan establishment in Mexico City the church of San Francisco rather than of St. Francis. Once that step is taken, if we then give the saint the name of Francis (and the churches are named more frequently than the saints), the unity of the two is lost. Also, after enough exposure to these matters one tends to develop a sense that the Spanish terms have a different feeling and even to an extent a different meaning than their English equivalents. Thus with a very few exceptions for ad hoc reasons, the names of the churches and saints are in Spanish, as well as such things as Anunciación, Purificación, etc.

Other names. Nahuatl names are given in our standard orthography in the translation. Spanish names, whether of Nahuas or of Spaniards, are given using modern Spanish spelling conventions for clarity of identification. Given the vagaries of Chimalpahin's orthography of loanwords, full clarity has not always been established. When reconver-

16. *Códice Osuna*, f. 7v. Ch. himself has exactly the same phrase, "alcalde celar," in an entry for March 25, 1594 (pp. 50–51).

17. Reyes García 2001, pp. 150–51, 152–53, 240–41.

18. See Lockhart 1992, pp. 18, 31–35, and Schroeder 1991, pp. 162–93.

sion of Chimalpahin's letter substitutions leads to a well known Spanish name, we have proceeded with confidence and made no comment. With less well known names, we have carried out a certain amount of research in publications, both of that time and of ours, to identify officials, clerics, and other prominent persons, but we were not able in the present context to perform such research exhaustively. In some cases where we are not sure of the intended name we have simply inserted a note with the comment "Name not established." We have little doubt that quite a few persons named in the text will later be identified with greater precision.

Commentary on problems of translation. Our position on how to deal with translation uncertainties is an intermediate or provisional one. Many translators of this kind of material have provided virtually no notes or commentary other than alternate readings of words apparently incorrect in the original, if that. As translations have grown more sophisticated in recent years, more commentary is called for. Yet the field has not yet reached the stage of definitive editions, in which every single passage of dubious or contested meaning would be discussed in detail, all alternatives presented, and the thinking behind them elucidated. In the present state of things, such a procedure would lead to notes more copious than the texts, without corresponding profit. We have discussed in the notes only certain problems that have particularly occupied us and that have a relatively limited scope, for many larger puzzles are not yet ripe for discussion. One cannot complain unduly of Chimalpahin's difficulty despite the richness of his vocabulary and syntax, for his often repeated words and phrases give us many clues toward their decipherment, but the very nature of the annals genre, in which some unattested technical term may surface in a brief entry without much or any context and never be repeated again, can present problems which in the short run have no solution.

Reference numbers for the notes appear in both the transcription and the facing translation, even when the topic concerns only one of the two, to help the reader keep track of parallel words and passages on the two sides, for it is our experience that even the veteran reader of Nahuatl can use such help. Words or short passages which are repeated in the notes literally from Chimalpahin, or which are given as it is thought he intended them, are in roman and in quotes: "teuhctli," "tlahtohuani," etc. Nahuatl words cited in the abstract are in italics and in our standard orthography: *teuctli*, *tlatoani*, etc.

Acknowledgments

Intellectually, our greatest debt is to Rafael Tena. Our transcription and translation was complete in a first draft before we became aware of his Spanish edition of the same material published in 2001, but it has helped us very considerably nevertheless. Tena's translations are on a distinctly higher level than those of any earlier translator of Chimalpahin working in Spanish.[1] We have compared his translation quite systematically with our own. In many cases where there is a difference (aside from those which are the result of somewhat divergent philosophies of translation), by our understanding either interpretation could be justified; in other cases we believe we have hit on a more accurate solu-

1. It may be that consultation with Luis Reyes has had its effect here, but we have come to the conclusion that Tena is a translator of exceptional qualities in his own right.

2. Notably in the case of *señora*, which Tena does not recognize as meaning "Spanish woman of any rank."

tion.[2] But in yet other cases Tena had found a solution which we had not yet recognized, and in such cases after full consideration we have often followed him in that conclusion, with consequent gain to the translation.[3]

Our debt is nearly as large to Stafford Poole, C.M., whose deep knowledge of the Mexican church in the sixteenth and seventeenth centuries, and beyond that of church lore of all kinds, has been essential to our explorations and saved us from many an egregious error. We have consulted him again and again, often several times on the same matter, and we vastly appreciate his patience with us as well as his advice. In some cases we have specifically acknowledged him in notes, but his contribution goes well beyond that. On the other hand, to spare him we did not consult him on every last church-related point, so any mistakes remaining in such matters are our own responsibility. We also express our gratitude to Frances Berdan, whom we consulted on some points of indigenous-style dress.

No thanks are enough for Rebecca Horn, who from a gift copy and without our prior knowledge did a full proofreading after we had finished, finding a multitude of errors we had sought in vain.

We are exceedingly grateful to Madame Monique Cohen, Conservateur general of the Bibliothèque Nationale de France, Département des Manuscrits, Division Orientale, for granting Schroeder access to Chimalpahin's manuscripts in 1995 and again in 2001. We thank the Stone Center for Latin American Studies at Tulane University for subvention assistance.

3. Tena follows older policies of transcription, adding modern-style punctuation and capitalization and not reproducing abbreviations as in the original, in addition to which the division into words is occasionally erroneous, especially in mistaking a possessive prefix *in-* for the particle *in*. In fact, Zimmermann, as sophisticated as he was, preceded Tena in a good many of these errors and may have influenced him. Tena also, again like Zimmermann, does not rigorously respect Ch.'s original units in terms of paragraphs and sections.

Transcription and Translation

[*f. 17*] ¶ vii. calli xihuitl, 1577.[1] v̲ ypan in ỹ xihuitl oquimihcuilhui yamoxtzin libro in itoca d las moradas ỹ la madre Teresa de Jesus [. . .] car[. . .][2] yn ipan in yn ipan metztli Januarius. xxxi. mani necocollo. februarius. xxviii. mani necocollo, Março xxxi. mani ypan ceuh yn cocolliztli, auh yxquich yc micohuac ynic nohuian ypan nueua españa timicque yn timacehualtin yhuan tliltique auh çan quexquich yn españoles. micque yhuan ypan in ~~onez~~ huell onez yquac ynic cenca chicahuac opopocaya citlalli tlanextli ytech omoquetz. oc achi tlaca yn pehuaya, yhuan yquac mochiuh yn tlahuahuanaliztli yn iuh mochihuaya, ye huecauh yc quintlamahuiçoltique yn tlatoque[3] yhuan yquac yancuica maxitico. yn Padreme descalços St. franco teopixque çan moquixtitiquizque mohuica a la china,

¶ viii. tochtli xihuitl 1578. yquac ypan in tlayahualloloc yn ompa la compaña de Jesus yn teatinos.[4] ypampa ompa motlallito yn inecauhcatzin yn imomiyotzin Sanctome ompa hualla Roma oncan oneohuac yn igl̄a mayor. ynic tlayahualloloc,

¶ ix. acatl xihuitl. 1579. ypan in yquac momiquilli yn totlaçotatzin fray Alonso de molina St. franco teopixqui totemachticatzin catca. auh ye no ceppa yquac necocoloc (yeztli toyacacpa quiz) huel totocac yn cocoliztli miec tlacatl yn momiquilli, auh no yquac ypan pascua nauidad y hualmohuicaque monjastin yn ipilhuan Sancta clara yn axcan oncan moyetzticate petlacalco ompa huallehuaque ompa catca achtopa yn trinidad[5] glericostin yn quinpachohuaya achtopa.

¶ x. tecpatl xihuitl 1580. ypan in yquac quiz mohuicac quitlalcahui yn altepetl mexico, yn visurrey Don martin enrriquez ynic mohuicac peru yn tlahtocat matlactli omey xihuitl qualli ynic tlapachoco mexico. auh çanno yquac maxitico yn visorrey Don lurenço xuarez de mendoça conde de coruña ynin anotle ẽcomienda quipiaya[6] yn mocallaquico mexico ypan metztli yc 4. mani octubre martes ypan ylhuitzin St. franco, // Auh no yquac maxitico yn padreme Sant franco descalços yn moyetzticate uerta yhuan huitzillopochco, / yhuan quitohua oc ceppa ypan metztli yc ix. mani octubre Domingotica yn opeuh popocaya citlalli ca cenca nohuiyan yttoc cenca huey yn ipocyo mochiuh vmpa y motlalli yn tonatiuh ycallaquiyampa[7]

¶ xi. calli xihuitl 1581.
¶ xii. tochtli xi[*f. 17v*]huitl 1582. ypan in yn iquac ypan metztli ynic xxii. mani Julius.

---

1. This beginning portion now exists separately from the bulk of the manuscript. See introduction, p 10.

2. This sentence, in the transcription from "ypan" to "car[. . .]," was added above the line in Ch.'s hand but in a different ink.

3. It is not entirely clear whether the reference is, as so often, to the Mexica cabildo members, or to high Spanish authorities, or to indigenous rulers of olden times.

4. Although it was not proper usage, the Jesuits were often called Theatines. Even Mother Teresa is said to have confused the Theatines with the Jesuits. The Congregation of Regular Clerics was founded at Rome in 1524. Gian Pietro Caraffa (later Pope Paul IV), the first superior of the group, was bishop of Chieti (Theate in Latin), thus the name Theatines. The Theatines carried out conversion campaigns in Europe, Russia, and India,

[*f. 17*] ¶ 7 House year, 1577.[1] v In this year mother Teresa de Jesús [. . .] wrote her book named *De las moradas*.[2] In this year, in the month of January, 31 [days], there was sickness; during the 28 [days] of February there was sickness; in the 31 [days] of March the sickness abated. And during this time there were deaths all over New Spain; we commoners died, and the blacks, but only a few Spaniards died. And in this year there clearly appeared a comet with a very distinct tail; radiance arose from it, beginning while there was a bit of daylight. And at this time striping [for gladiatorial sacrifice] was performed as it was in ancient times; with it they honored the rulers.[3] And at this time for the first time there arrived the fathers who are Discalced friars of San Francisco; they just passed through on their way to China [the Philippines].

¶ 8 Rabbit year, 1578. In this year was when there was a procession to the [church of] the Company of Jesus, the Theatines,[4] going to place there the relics and bones of saints which had come from Rome; the procession set out from the cathedral.

¶ 9 Reed year, 1579. In this year our precious father fray Alonso de Molina, Franciscan friar, passed away; he was our preacher. And this was when there was a sickness again (blood came from our noses). The sickness really raged; many people died. And this was also when, at Christmas, the nuns who are children of Santa Clara came to where they now are, at Petlacalco; they came from where they were first, at Trinidad;[5] secular priests were in charge of them at first.

¶ 10 Flint year, 1580. In this year was when Viceroy don Martín Enríquez left, went from, and abandoned the altepetl of Mexico to go to Peru. He ruled 13 years and governed well in Mexico. At the same time Viceroy don Lorenzo Suárez de Mendoza, Count of Coruña, arrived; he had no encomienda either.[6] He entered Mexico on Tuesday the 4th of the month of October, the feast day of San Francisco. // And this was also when the Discalced Franciscan fathers arrived, who are at the orchard and in Huitzilopochco. / And they say that in this month, on the 9th of October, on Sunday, a comet began to appear again. It was seen everywhere, with a very large tail; it placed itself in the west.[7]

¶ 11 House year, 1581.
¶ 12 Rabbit year, [*f. 17v*] 1582. In this year, on the 22nd of the month of July, on the

---

but not the Americas until the twentieth century. The Society of Jesus was founded by Ignatius de Loyola in 1540 and also had schools and other establishments in Europe and Asia, but it was only the Jesuits who came to the Americas in the sixteenth century.

5. See Muriel 1991, 2: 139, "una de las más hermosas iglesias de la ciudad de México es sin duda la de la Santísima Trinidad anexa al Hospital de San Pedro."

6. The passage sounds like it refers to an encomienda in New Spain, but possibly it means being a comendador of a military order in Spain. The fact that it says "anotle encomienda," "no encomienda either," implies that this set (as Ch. viewed it, at least, for he may have imagined a unity across manuscripts) once contained earlier entries than those we now have. The sentence was added above the line.

7. This sentence, in the transcription from "ca cenca" to "ycallaquiyampa," was added in the margin below.

ypan ylhuitzin Sancta maria magdalena yquac acico yn aotli Sant Juan auh yn ipan metztli ynic xxxi. mani deciembre yn huetzico atl tianquizco acaxic, yquac mochalli yn acaxitl yn tianquizco mani chiquacenxiuhtica yecahuico

¶ xiii acatl xihuitl 1583. ypan in yquac moyecti motlacuicuilli yn acallotli yn nican mexico yn izqui acallotli nohuiampa huitza yn altepetl ypan tlaca // auh no yquac motlallique Beatati[1] yn oncan teopan Sancta monica ypilhuan oncan huitzillan, // no yquac hualmohuicac crucifixo yn ompa monextitzino totollapan +. Sant guilermo.[2] ça iuh huiptla de ramos Sant Pablo maxitico auh çatepan hualmohuicac. yn Sant. augustin. xolloco quimonamiquillito yn ixquichtin teopixque augustinos. fran^{cos}, Dominigos clerigos. teatinos. yhuan yquac yancuican motlayahualhuique yn Santo Domingo ypilhuan huel mahuiztic yn itlayhiyohuiliztzin tt^{o} Dios. ynic motecpanno yquac ypan metztli ynic xxix. Junius. ypan ylhuitzin S^{t}. Pedro yhuan S^{t}. Pablo apostoles. yn omomiquilli tlahtohuani Don lurenco [sic] xuarez de mẽ̃doça Cõde de coruña. visurrey qualli ynic tlapachoco mexico ompa motocac yn inacayo Sant. fran^{co}, yn tlahtocatico onxihuitl ypan chicuhcnauhtetl metztli[3] v cequintin quimachiyotia nimã yquac ỹ visurey m[o?u?]chiuhtzino - [?] Don P[^{o}?] moy[a] de contreras arçobpo. yn o iu[h] momiquill[i] dõ lure[nço] +[4]

¶ i. tecpatl xihuitl. 1584. ypan ĩ yn xihuitl oncan matlacpohualxihuitl ypan yepohualxihuitl quichiuhque ynic cate mexica tenochtitlan yquac ypan in omopehualti yn al~~lde~~. de corte Santiago de vera ynic mohuicac china quinmohuiquilli tlapitzq̃. nahuintin auh ça huallaque hualmocuepq̃. çan icel yn quihuicaque chirimias quipitza atlixocan ychan // auh no yquac omochiuhtzino bisitador general yn ipan nueua españa niman omochiuhtzino gouernador visurrey yn teoyotica tlahtohuani Don P^{o}. moya de contreras. arçobispo. mexico. yhuan ynquisidor mayor [*f. 18*] Mochiuhtica yn iquac omomiquilli tlahtohuani Don lurenço xuarez de mendoça visurrey ynic niman ipan ocallac gouernador visurrey omochiuhtzino yn arçobispo, Auh no yquac mito yn ixquichtin teopixque yn S fran^{co} .S. augustin, S^{t}: Domingo aocmo yehuantin motemachtilizque y nohuian altepetl ypan yehuantin calaquizque yn clerigos. yhuan yn altepetl ypan tlaca tlahtoque nohuian tlacuepaco tlananquillico yn inp̃apatzinco teopixque / auh no yquac omoyancuilli yn iglesia mayor teopancalli —

¶ 2. calli xihuitl. 1585. ypan in mochiuh ynic tlayahualloloc yn ipampa Sancto Concilio yn teoyotica necentlaliliztli Sancto Domingo hualpehualloto. oncan hualhuilohuac y Sant. augustin yhuan yn ixquichtin teopixque obisposme yn motlayahualhuique Don fray bartolome de ledesma obispo huaxacac S^{to}. Domingo teopixqui Don fray Domingo de alçura obispo xalixco teopixqui S^{to}. Domingo. Don fra gre^{o}. montãno obispo, campech teopixqui[5] S^{to}. Domingo. Don diego Romano obispo tlaxcallan teopixqui Sant P^{o}.

1. Pious women wearing a habit but lacking full and formal affiliation with an order.

2. The bringing of the crucifix of Totolapan to the capital in 1583 is referred to again on pp. 140–41.

3. The words "ypan cenpohualli onmatlactl ypan eylhuitl," "and 33 days," are marked out. But the same numbers appear again in this connection on pp. 140–41 at n. 3. The

feast day of Santa María Magdalena, was when the aqueduct reached San Juan. And on the 31st of the month of December water ran in the fountain in the marketplace; at that time the fountain that is in the marketplace was inaugurated. [The work on the aqueduct and fountain] took six years to finish.

¶ 13 Reed year, 1583. In this year was when all the canals here in Mexico were cleaned and cleared out; from everywhere the people of the [various] altepetl came. // And it was also when *beatas*,[1] children of Santa Mónica, were established at Huitzillan. // It was also when the crucifix was brought that appeared in San Guillermo Totolapan;[2] it arrived in San Pablo two days before Palm Sunday and later was brought to San Agustín Xoloco; all the Augustinian, Franciscan, and Dominican friars, the secular priests, and the Theatines went to meet it. And this is when the children of Santo Domingo went in procession for the first time; it was splendid how the passion of our lord God was arranged. This was when, on the 29th of the month of June, on the feast day of San Pablo and San Pedro Apóstoles, the ruler don Lorenzo Suárez de Mendoza, Count of Coruña, viceroy, passed away; he governed well in Mexico. His body was buried at San Francisco. He ruled for 2 years and 9 months.[3] v Some record that right then after don Lorenzo died, don Pedro Moya de Contreras, archbishop, became viceroy.[4]

¶ 1 Flint year, 1584. In this year the Mexica had spent 260 years in Tenochtitlan. This was when the alcalde de corte, Santiago de Vera, set out for China [the Philippines]. He took along four players of wind instruments, but they came back and returned; [in the end] they took only a player of the chirimía from Atlixxocan. // This was also when the spiritual ruler don Pedro Moya de Contreras, archbishop in Mexico, was made inspector general in New Spain, and then he was made governor, viceroy, and chief inquisitor; [*f. 18*] when the lord don Lorenzo Suárez de Mendoza, viceroy, passed away, the archbishop entered as appointed governor and viceroy. And this was also when it was said that all the friars, the Franciscans, Augustinians, and Dominicans, were no longer to preach in the altepetl everywhere; the secular priests were to enter. And the rulers of the people in the altepetl everywhere came to appeal and help on behalf of the friars. / This was also when the cathedral building was renovated. —

¶ 2 House year, 1585. In this year it happened that there was a procession because of the Holy Council, the spiritual assembly. It started from Santo Domingo and came to San Agustín, and all the priests who were bishops went in procession: don fray Bartolomé de Ledesma, bishop of Oaxaca, a Dominican friar; don fray Domingo de Arzola, bishop of Jalisco, a Dominican friar; don fray Gregorio Montaño, bishop of Campeche,[5] a Dominican friar; don Diego Romano, bishop of Tlaxcala, a priest of San Pedro, a secular

---

odd 33 days, more than any month, also occurs elsewhere in the corpus.

4. This sentence, in the transcription from "cequintin" to "lure[nço]," is in the right margin.

5. Torquemada 1975, 1: 649, has Montalvo as the bishop's name but speaks of Yucatan rather than Campeche.

clerico. Don fray Juan de medina obispo michhuacan[1] teopixqui Sant. augustin [Yquac yn oxitin coro yglesia] mayor [in ipan lunes a xv] dias de henero 1585 años oncan mochihuazquia cõcõcilio[2] ~~oc cequintin vevet[. . .] quimachiyotia ye quin inpan in~~ [i?]quac yn gou^{or}. visurrey mochiuhtzino arçobp̄o. mexico ~~auh amo nelli ca ye omito ye ompa tlacpac.~~[3]

v Ça huallatzauhctia yn arçobispo casolla quihuallaquitia yhuan ytopil ymitra auh çan moch capa yn quitlallitiaque obisposme / Don fray gomez de cordova obispo quauhtemalla[4] teopixqui Sant Jeronimo. auh ynin mochiuh ypan yc 20. Enero ypan ylhuitzin S^{t}. Sebastian

v Auh ynic tzonquiz ypan yn ilhuitzin S^{t}. lucas çanno iuh tlayahualloloc eylhuitl viernes. Sabado Domingo auh çanno ypan yn omito xihuitl 1585. años. no yquac maxitico visurrey Don aluaro Manrrique de çunica quinhualhuicac yn Padreme carmenitas (ypan metztli a 17. nouiembre)

¶ iii. tochtli xihuitl. 1586. yquac ypan in calacq̃ Sant Sebastian domĩgo possesion macoque teopixque carmenistas ypan 29. de enero. ynic mocallaquique. tlayahualloliztica. oncan oneohuac yn [*f. 18v*] Sancto Domingo yc quimocuillique ynic cemicac oncan moyetztiezque ynin teopixque yehuantin yn motenehua descarços ypilhuantzitzinhuan yn totlaçonan[5] Sancta maria del carme.

v Auh çanno yquac axcan miercoles[6] yn ipan Sant Bernabe ylhuitzin yc xi mani Junio. yquac ommopehualti yn teoyotica tlahtohuani arçobispo. ynic mohuicac castillan ye teotlac yn omopehualti Don Pedro moya de contreras. caxtolxihuitl once yn omotlahtocatillico mexico, yexihuitl ynquisidor moyetzticatca auh niman yc quimocuilli yn teoyotica ytlahtocayo arçobispo, matlacxihuitl yn arçobispo moyetzticatca auh ynin ynic mohuicac españa. yn igou^{or}.tzin conmotlallitehuac yn ipampatzinco tlapachoz Sta. ygl̄a mexico yehuatzin yn docto[7] don Sancho Sanchez de muñon maestreescuela[8] gou^{or}. y vi[cario general yn s^{ta}. ygl̄a catedral de mexico][9] yhuan mochi arçobispado yn icatzinco Don P^{o}. moya de contreras arçobispo mexico. del consejo del rey n̄r̄o Señor[10] —

¶ iiii. acatl xihuitl. 1587.

¶ v. tecpatl xihuitl 1588. ypan in cenca totocac cocoliztli yhuan yquac mixnamicque teopixque descalços yhuan S^{t} francisco yn iquac mochallaniaya yn itechpa comisario auh cenca achi huecahuac yn innetequipachol moteylhuiaya yn audiencia

v Auh çanno ypan yn xihuitl yn omoteneuh maxitico Juez visitador comisario quihualmihualli papa ynic quintlatetemollico S^{t}. fran^{co} teopixque auh yn maxitico ypan yc xix. mani octubre Juebestica

1. Torquemada, ibid., has "don fray Juan de Medina Rincón, obispo de Michuacan."

2. This sentence, the material from "Yquac" to "cõcõcilio" in the transcription, was added along the left margin. The portions in brackets are now worn away in the original and are taken from the Tena edition.

3. This sentence is on the right margin, in the transcription from "oc cequintin" to "tlacpac." As can be seen in the transcription, a substantial portion is marked out. The translation above represents only the unerased portions. The original statement would be: Other elders note that it was not until this year that the archbishop of Mexico was made governor and viceroy, but it is not true, for it was declared above.

priest; don fray Juan de Medina, bishop of Michoacan,[1] an Augustinian friar. The choir in the cathedral collapsed on Monday the 15th day of January of the year 1585; they were going to hold the council there.[2] At that time the archbishop was made governor and viceroy.[3]

v The archbishop came at the end, wearing a chasuble, with his staff and miter, and all the bishops came wearing capes. / Don fray Gómez de Córdoba, bishop of Guatemala,[4] a Hieronymite friar [was one of the bishops]. And this happened on the 20th of January, on the feast day of San Sebastián.
v And when [the council] ended it was on the feast day of San Lucas; processions were also held in the same fashion for three days, Friday, Saturday, and Sunday. In the same said year of 1585 was also when the viceroy don Alvaro Manrrique de Zúñiga arrived, on the 17th of November; he brought along the Carmelite fathers.

¶ 3 Rabbit year, 1586. In this year, Sunday the 29th of January, was when the Carmelite friars entered [the church of] San Sebastián and were given possession. They entered in procession, having set out from [*f. 18v*] Santo Domingo. They took [possession] so that these friars called Discalced, children of our precious mother[5] Santa María del Carmen, would be there forever.
v And likewise at this time, today Wednesday[6] the feast day of San Bernabé, the 11th of June, was when the spiritual ruler the archbishop don Pedro Moya de Contreras set out to go to Spain; it was afternoon when he departed. He ruled in Mexico for 16 years; for three years he was inquisitor and then he assumed his spiritual rulership as archbishop. He was archbishop for ten years, and when he went to Spain he left installed as his governor to govern the holy church in Mexico dr.[7] don Sancho Sánchez de Muñón, *maestrescuela*[8] [in the cathedral chapter], governor [and vicar general of the cathedral][9] and all the archbishopric in the name of don Pedro Moya de Contreras, archbishop of Mexico, of the council of the king our lord.[10] —

¶ 4 Reed year, 1587.

¶ 5 Flint year, 1588. In this year sickness raged greatly. And this was when the Discalced friars and the Franciscan friars disputed, when they argued about the commissary, and their worries lasted quite a while; they made complaint to the Audiencia.
v And in this same said year the commissary arrived as a judge inspector sent by the pope to investigate the Franciscan friars, and he arrived on Thursday the 19th of October.

---

4. Torquemada, ibid., has "don Gómez de Roxas, Obispo de Quauhtemallan."
5. Ch.'s intention was no doubt "totlaçonantzin."
6. The words "axcan miercoles" are written above the line.
7. For "doctor."
8. A cathedral dignitary nominally charged with teaching divinity.
9. Reconstructed from Galicia Chimalpopoca's copy in accordance with Reyes García 1971 and Chimalpahin 2001.
10. The last part of the paragraph was added and spills over into the margins.

¶ vi. calli xihuitl. 1589. ypan in xihuitl otlallolin ypan yc 10 mani abril ypan martes ynic oppa mochiuh yc 26. mani abril huel totocac niman oppa mochiuh tlallolinaliztli

Fue Gregorio Lopez a aquella soledad de Sancta fee a 22 de mayo de 1589 segundo dia de pascua de espiritu santo donde prosiguio sus exercicios de oracion. y contemplaciõ hasta el dia de su muerte.[1]

v̲ yn axcan ypan lunes yc .9. de Julio yquac omomiquilli yn ichpoch marques visurrey cuyohuacã yn mic[2] ytoca Doña fran^{ca} blanga ypan misa omito yn oncan Sant Joseph oncan motocac ỹ S fran^{co}

v̲ Auh yn iquac miercoles yn ipan yvisperastzin Sant Andres apostol Jueues a xxx de nouiembre[3] yquac omacoque yn Sant. fran^{co} teopixque possesion ynic huel imaxca yez teocalli S^{t}. Juan yhuan Sancta maria. yn oquimacac possesion al~~lde~~ de corte Seruandes. auh vel ipã ilhuitzin S. Andres oncan misa mito cuepopan.[4]

v̲ Sabado ypan yc .5. mani de agosto yn ipan ilhuitzin quiz sancta maria de la nieues motenehua cepayauhcihuapilli yquac motlallitzino in de nr̅a Señora de Monserate yn ipan tlaxillacalli S. Juan tequixquipan.[5]

v̲ Auh[6] yn ipan axcan miercoles a 29. de nouiembre de 1589. años. yquac possesion macoque in teopixque S^{t}. Fran^{co}, yn õcan S^{t}. Juan ytencopatzinco yn marques.[7] yhuan Sancta maria yquac guardian[8] moyetzticatca fray bonauentura auh yn prouincial ytoca fray Domingo de arisaga[9]

v̲ Auh yn ipan ynic .30. mani metztli deçiembre yquac mopehualti[10] yn totlaçotatzin ganonico ytocatzin Juan gonsalo moyetzticatca huehuetlan visitacion ompa motlamacehuiliaya

¶ vii. tochtli xihuitl. 1590. ypan in lunes ynic cemilhuitl mani metztli de henero yn momiquilli ye teotlac ye omito ypan yancuic xihuitl. yn totlaçotatzin ganonico Juan gonsalo yn moyetzticatca huehuetlan visitacion nican mexico yn momiquillico. ynqui-

---

1. For this material in Spanish about Gregorio López, no longer visible in the original, we rely on the version of Luis Reyes.

2. This clause, in the transcription "cuyohuacã yn mic," was added above the line.

3. This phrase, in the transcription "jueues a xxx de nouiembre," was added above the line.

4. The material in the transcription from "auh" to "cuepopan," corresponding to the second half of the sentence in the translation, is added above the line.

More importantly, in the left margin at this point are added the words "ynin tlatolli tlatzintla yetiuh," "this statement is to go below." They represent a rare notation by Ch. to himself for the rearrangement of the manuscript and definitively connect this fragment to the larger portion in Paris. See n. 6 just below.

5. At the bottom of the transcription are the words "Auh yn ipã" as a lead into the next page. The first page of the material from Paris in fact begins "Auh yn ipan," proving again that the sections belong together and are consecutive.

6. Here the main manuscript now in Paris begins with p. 1. In the upper margin, in Ch.'s hand but in fainter brown ink, is a notation "oncan in yequiuh ỹ tlacpac ca tlahtolli.," "there is where the statement above is to come to be," or less literally, "the above entry is to be put there," i.e., the entry for Thursday November 30 in the now separate fragment kept in Mexico, marked there for moving, is to be placed in chronological se-

¶ 6 House year, 1589. In this year, on Tuesday the 10th of April, there was an earthquake, and it happened again on the 26th of April; it was very strong; then there was an earthquake again.
Gregorio López went on the 22nd of May of 1589, the second day of Pentecost to that solitary place of Santa Fe, where he pursued his exercises of prayer and contemplation until the day of his death.[1]
v Today on Monday the 9th of July was when the daughter of the Marqués and viceroy named doña Francisca Blanca passed away; she died in Coyoacan.[2] A mass was said for her at San Josef, and she was buried at San Francisco.
v And on Wednesday the eve of San Andrés Apóstol, Thursday the 30th of November,[3] was when the Franciscan friars were given possession so that the churches of San Juan and Santa María would be fully their property. The one who gave them possession was the alcalde de corte Cervantes, and right on the feast day of San Andrés mass was said in [Santa María] Cuepopan.[4]
v On Saturday, the 5th of August, when the feast day of Santa María de las Nieves, called the snow lady, was celebrated, the [image of] Nuestra Señora de Montserrat was placed in the tlaxilacalli of San Juan Tequixquipan.[5]
v Today,[6] on Wednesday the 29th of November of the year 1589, was when the Franciscan friars were given possession of San Juan and Santa María at the order of the Marqués.[7] Fray Buenaventura was the father guardian[8] at that time, and the name of the provincial head was fray Domingo de Arisaga.[9]
v On the 30th of the month of December our precious father the canon whose name is Juan Gonzalo [began].[10] He had been at [the church of] Visitación in Huehuetlan, where he had been doing penance.

¶ 7 Rabbit year, 1590. On Monday, first day of the month of January of the new year, in the afternoon, the aforementioned canon, our precious father Juan Gonzalo, passed away; he had been at [the church of] Visitación in Huehuetlan. He came here to Mexico to die,

---

quence after the first entry on this page, for November 29. The meshing statements represent positive proof that the two parts belong together and are consecutive. An alternative interpretation might be that in both notations "tlahtolli" (literally "that which is said," hence "statement, words, language," and many related senses) refers to the entire first section of contemporary annals material and that the meaning is that that section is to be attached to the main part. But in view of the placing of the notations, especially the first one, and the situation with one entry being out of chronological sequence, we greatly prefer the first explanation. Either would tie the two parts together.

7. San Juan Moyotlan and Santa María Cuepopan were two of the four great constituent parts of the indigenous entity Mexico Tenochtitlan, the other two being San Pablo Teopan and San Sebastián Atzaqualco. The Franciscans received possession of both the churches in the areas and the whole ecclesiastical jurisdiction.

8. "Guardian" (*guardián*), in usage almost always "father guardian" (*padre guardián*), was the title of the prior of a Franciscan establishment. Here the main Franciscan church of Mexico City is surely meant.

9. Mendieta 1980, pp. 542–43, 770, lists a fray Domingo de Areizaga as the eighteenth provincial head.

10. What he began is not clear. With *-on, pehua* means to set out for somewhere, but *-on* is missing. The expected sense would be "arrived." See the entry just below.

sidor ychantzinco. auh oncan yglesian mayor caxatica yn quimotoquillique.

v Auh Juebes. a xviii. de henero yquac mohuicac Don aluaro Manrrique de çunica visurrey marques. mohuicac españa. yn tlahtocatico macuilxihuitl,

v Auh yn axcan Juebes a veynte y cinco 25. dias del mes de henero de 1590. años. ypan ylhuitzin la conuersion S. pablo. yquac maxitico mocallaquico nican mexico tlahtohuani ynic ome ytoca Don luis de velasco visurrey ynin ypiltzin yn huehue Don luis de velasco visurrey catca yc ome nican mexico,

v yn ipan axcan Domingo a xi. de febrero de 1590 años. yquac moteochiuh yn tlatlalantli. ynic mochiuh ynic moquetz teocalli S$^{t.}$ Fran^{co} oncan hualmohuicac in visurrey Don luis de velasco comendador S^{t}.tiago. yhuã oydoresme

v Auh yn ipan yc v. mani metztli de febrero. yquac momiquilli in totlaçotatzin fray Bernardino de sahagun tlatilolco moyetzticatca auh nicã yn motocatzino callitic sant fra^{co}, mochintin huallaque tlatilolco tlahtoque[1] quimotoquillico

v lunes yc tlami metztli abril yn ipan in xihuitl omoteneuh yquac mopehualti yn acallotli ynic moyecti yn nican mexico ytencopatzinco visurrey tetzcoco tla-

v auh yn omotzauhc s. Fran^{co} teocalli yn aocmo ompa mihtoa missa domingotica a xxvi de Agosto.[2]

[*p. 2*]copan mexico huel ce metztli moyecti yn izqui acallotli.

v yn ipan yc vii. de octubre yquac analloc cuitlaxcohuapan ytoca Don Antonio ypiltzin catca Don carlos quinto ytiachcauhtzin in Don Pelipe Rey españa yntlan nenca portugal tlaca auh y hualhuicoc nican mexico ypan lunes a xxix dias octobre ytech tlan yaoyotl quichihuaznequia nican otzaqualoc corte.

v Domingo a xiiii. de octubre yquac mocallaqui quimotlalilique Sacramẽto, in Sant. Josep. tlamayauhcampa yc cenpeuh in ye ompa missa quitta castilteca yhuan yc peuh ynic moxitini teocalli sant Fran^{co},

v yn ipan in xihuitl omoteneuh 1590 yquac momiquilli yn s^{to}. Padre[3] Sixto quinto sant. Fran^{co} teopixqui catca.

¶ viii. acatl xihuitl 1591. ypan in lunes yc 4. mani metztli de febrero yquac missa ypantzinco mito in santo Padre Sixto, quinto. S. Joseph yn missa ypã mito mochintin oncan mohuicatza in teopixque s^{to}. Domingo. s^{t}. augustin, teatinos. calmenitas. descarços. mercenadios. yhuan oncã mohuicatza visurrey

v martes a v. dias del mes de febrero yquac macoque possesion in Padreme descalços oncan in sanct ipolito. yquiyahuayoc ytecopatzinco visurrey ciudad tlaca quinmomaquillique a~~lld~~es. regidores. yn oncan moteocaltitzinoque auh ce tlacatl español pilli monetolti yn quiquetzaz teocalli ytoca Don matheo de moleon matlactli omome mill pesos. yn quihuenchiuh teocuitlatl ynic mochihuaz teocalli

v ypan yn Domingo yc tlami metztli março yquac quipehualtiq̃ yn españolesme netolleque ynic tlaxitinique mestiços chichimeca tliltique cequi castilteca yehuatl yn iglesia s^{t} Fran^{co} teocalli quixitinique

v yn ipan viernes. sancto a 12. de abril. yquac peuh tzintic in yancuic cofradia in suledad. Sant. Joseph. ynnenonotzaltica mochiuh yn teopixque prouincial fray Domingo yhuan

1. I.e., the members of the Tlatelolco cabildo.
2. This part was added later at the bottom of p. 1.

at the home of the Inquisitor, and they buried him at the cathedral in a separate tomb.
v Thursday the 18th of January was when don Alvaro Manrrique de Zúñiga, viceroy and Marqués, left and went to Spain; he ruled for five years.
v Today, Thursday the 25th day of the month of January of the year 1590 on the day of the conversion of San Pablo, was when the second ruler of the name of don Luis de Velasco, viceroy, arrived and entered here in Mexico; he is the child of don Luis de Velasco the elder who was viceroy, the second one here in Mexico.
v Today, Sunday the 11th of February of the year 1590, was when the groundbreaking was blessed for the building and erection of the church of San Francisco; the viceroy don Luis de Velasco, comendador of Santiago, and the judges of the Royal Audiencia came.
v On the 5th of the month of February was when our precious father fray Bernardino de Sahagún passed away. He had been at Tlatelolco, and he was buried here at San Francisco, inside the church. All the Tlatelolco rulers[1] came to bury him.
v Monday the last of the month of April in the said year was when cleaning of the canals here in Mexico began by order of the viceroy. In Tetzcoco, Tacuba, [*p. 2*] and Mexico, all the canals were cleaned for a whole month.
v And the church of San Francisco was closed, and mass was no longer said there, on Sunday the 26th of August.[2]
v On the 7th of October was when one called don Antonio, who was the child of don Carlos V and older brother of don Felipe, king of Spain, was arrested in Puebla. He had lived among the Portuguese. He was brought here to Mexico on Monday the 29th day of October; he was accused of wanting to make war, and he was shut up in the court jail.
v Sunday the 14th of October was when the Sacrament was installed and put inside [the church of] San Josef, on the right side. With that the Spaniards for the first time began to attend mass there, and with that the demolition of the church of San Francisco began.
v The said year of 1590 was when the Holy Father[3] Sixtus V passed away; he was a Franciscan friar.

¶ 8 Reed year, 1591. On Monday, the 4th of the month of February, was when a mass was said for the Holy Father Sixtus V; it was at San Josef that the mass for him was said. All the religious came: the Dominicans, the Augustinians, the Theatines, the Carmelites, the Discalced, the Mercedarians; and the viceroy came too.
v Tuesday, the 5th day of the month of February, was when the Discalced fathers were given possession [of land] close to San Hipólito. By the viceroy's order the municipal people, the alcaldes and regidores [of the Spanish cabildo], gave it to them, and they established a church there. A Spanish person, a nobleman, named don Mateo de Moleón, vowed to construct the church, making an offering of twelve thousand pesos in gold to build the church.
v Sunday, the last of the month of March, was when the Spaniards who had taken vows began having mestizos, Chichimecas, blacks, and some Spaniards carry out demolition work; they demolished the church of San Francisco.
v Good Friday, the 12th of April, was when the new cofradía of the Soledad was first founded at San Josef. It was done with the agreement of the following friars: the pro-

3. I.e., pope.

guardian fray Bonauentura yhuan tiuinidores[1] yehuãtin ynmacehual mochiuh in mexica huell ipan tlahtoque fray gr^{mo} yhuã [*p. 3*] fray Fran^{co} de ganboa // auh lunes a 29. de abril. yquac quitamachiuhque quitenexhuique yn teocalli s^{t} Francisco yn iuh yez yehuatl ynic ye moteca tepantli

v Domingo yc ix. mani metztli de Junio. de 1591 años. yquac papacohuac yn ipampatzinco arçobispo Don Pedro monya de cõtreras. quimomaquillique yn ompa españa huey tlahtocayotl yc quimohuecapanilhui in Rey. su mag^{d}. yn macoc conJejoyotl de indias Presidente y nican yc nohuian nueua españa ycemactzinco quimocahuilli yn nican mexico
v lunes a 17. de Junio. de 1591 a^{o}s. yquac onpeuhque tlaxcalteca yancuic mexico chiuhcnauhtlan yn namicoto oncan papaquiltiloque yollaliloque yn ica tlaqualtzintli y nohuian altepetl ypã tlahtoque[2] yhuan in mexico tlatilolco s^{t}. Fran^{co} teopixque quinmohuiquillique oncã teochihualloque nahuatiloque in chiuhcnauhtlan in visurrey. no oncan quinmonamiquillito yhuã no omentin yahque tlapitzque tlatzotzonque[3] mexica ce s^{t}. Pablo ychan ytoca augustin cano ynic ome ytoca Domingo sanchez. s^{t}. Juã ychan.

v Domingo a .7. de Julio yquac tlayahualoloc S^{to}. Domingo huilohuac yxquixtin[4] yn teopixque tlayahualloque ynic chicueteocaltin yhuan tlahtoque oydoresme ypampa ynic tlayahuallolocypãpa yn ipiltzin Rey ynic huel maxitiz castilla

v Domingo yc xxi. mani metztli Julio de 1591 a^{o}s. yãcuica motlayahualhui sacramento yn Sant. Antonio abbad. in xolloco auh ynic motlayahualhui yntlaytlaniliztica mochiuh yn capellan Joseph mendez yhuã yn Padron Diego de muñon quimotlatlauhtilique in maestre escuella[5] yhuã Provisor. arçobispo yxiptlatzin
v agosto ypan yn acico. agustin cano yn quincahuato tlaxcalteca yancuic mexico çan composteria[6] quincahuato oncã hualmocuepque yhuan cequintin quinhualhuicaque chichimeca teanaco tenechicoco yn nicã mexico [*p. 4*]

v yn ipan yvisperatzin ytlacatilitzin : tlaçopiltzintli Jesus. temaquixtiani ypan martes. a 24. de diçiembre de 1591 años. yquac quimanque Retabla. mage yn oncan pochteca[7] ymandas manca ye oncan quimanque quiquetzque yn ixiptlatzin Sancto fray Diego. Sanctiego yc mitohua amo corona quipiaya[8] çan quateçontzin motilon catca yhuã portero. yhuan cocirotia[9] yxquich quimochihuiliaya y netitlaniztequitl yn tlatequipanoliztli

¶ ix. tecpatl xihuitl. 1592. yn ipan in martes a 21. de henero. yquac tlayxmanaloc in Sanct ipolito tianquizco huel mocencauh yn inauhcampayxti ynic mexico yhuan tlatilolco mito acaxitl oncan momanaz yhuan moquahuaqui mohuexoaqui auh in ye teotlac niman yc tzatzihuac in tiyanquizco. Sant. lazaro mito aocac ompa tiamiquiz in Sant ipolito, yn moztla yxquich tlacatl nican tiamiquiz auh çan quezquilhuitl yn ontiamicoc niman oc

1. Members of a council authorized to resolve serious matters for the order.
2. Perhaps the cabildos, or perhaps more literally the governors and dynastic rulers.
3. Perhaps specifically fifers and drummers.
4. For "yxquichtin."
5. See p. 31, n. 8.

vincial head, fray Domingo, and the father guardian, fray Buenaventura, and the *definidores.*[1] It was done for the benefit of the Mexica; fray Gerónimo and [*p. 3*] fray Francisco de Gamboa urged it strongly. // And Monday, the 29th of April, was when they measured and spread lime, [marking out] how the church of San Francisco will be, so they can begin laying the walls now.

v Sunday the 9th of the month of June of the year 1591 was when there was rejoicing because there in Spain they granted the archbishop don Pedro Moya de Contreras the great rulership with which the king, His Majesty, exalted him; he was given the presidency of the Council of the Indies, by which [the king] left [matters] everywhere in New Spain, and here in Mexico, entirely in his hands.

v Monday the 17th of June of the year 1591 was when the Tlaxcalans left for New Mexico. At Chiucnauhtlan people went out to meet them and feted them and encouraged them by feeding them. The rulers of the altepetl[2] all around and the Franciscan friars of Mexico and Tlatelolco accompanied them; there they were blessed and bid farewell for Chiucnauhtlan. The viceroy also went there to meet them. And also two Mexica musicians[3] went; one is from San Pablo, named Agustín Cano; the second is named Domingo Sánchez, from San Juan.

v Sunday the 7th of July was when there was a procession going to Santo Domingo; all[4] the friars from eight churches went in procession, as well as the lords judges of the Royal Audiencia. The reason for the procession was so that the child of the king would be able to reach Castile [safely].

v On Sunday, the 21st of the month of July of the year 1591, the Sacrament was taken in procession for the first time at [the church of] San Antonio Abad in Xoloco, and the procession took place at the request of the chaplain Josef Méndez and the patron Diego de Muñón; they asked the maestrescuela[5] and the vicar general, the archbishop's deputy.

v In August there arrived Agustín Cano, who went to convey the Tlaxcalans to New Mexico; he only went with them as far as Compostela;[6] he and several Chichimecas who accompanied them came back from there to come here to Mexico to get and collect [more] people. [*p. 4*]

v The eve of the birth of the precious child Jesus the savior, Tuesday the 24th of December of the year 1591, was when they set up an altarpiece and image where the carrying platform of the merchants[7] had been; they set up and erected there the image of the saint fray Diego de San Diego, who it is said did not have the tonsure,[8] but was just a lay friar and doorkeeper and acted as cook;[9] he did all the errands and menial work.

¶ 9 Flint year, 1592. Tuesday the 21st of January was when things were dismantled at the San Hipólito market. Great preparations were made in the four parts of Mexico and in Tlatelolco. It was said that a water tank was to be set up there, and trees and willows were planted. And in the afternoon a proclamation was made in the marketplace of San Lázaro saying that no one was to engage in business any longer at San Hipólito, that the next

6. Compostela, now in southern Nayarit, was founded as the capital of New Galicia.

7. In view of the term *pochteca*, these were presumably indigenous merchants, but that is not fully established.

8. I.e., was not ordained.

9. The form "cocirotia" is apparently for "cocinerotia."

ceppa ompa momanato in tianquiztli yn õcan mocaltitzinohua Padreme descalços. yhuan yn tlatilolca moztlacahuica ompa tiamicozquia yn inchan tlatilolco auh yc moteylhuique audiencia yn mexica cihua amo huel neltic[1]

v Domingo a 23. de febrero. yquac yglesia mayor mocenquixtitzinoque in teopixque[2] yn izquican moyetzticate nican ynic mexico ypampa iuh mocac mito ohualla ypãnotzin ytamachiuhca yn imiccaquimiliuhcayotzin tt^{o}. Dios. yn motenehua savanas. ompa hualla in Roma

v Juebes a 5. de marça. yquac netlatiloc in tlequiquizcalco yn oncan mochihua tlequiquiztli altepehuaque cohuatequitque[3] yn motlatique achi quezquintin huel temamauhti ynic quixolocac[4] ynnacayo oncã quinhualhuicaque ospital real cequi patique yhuan cequintin momiquillique

v lunes yc 3. de febrero. de 1592 años. yquac motlallitzinoq̃ yn la compaña de Jesus. teatinos teopixque yn oncan corte quiahuac catca huell ipan in sant. blas. ylhuitzin catca yohualtica mocallaquico niman quimotlallilique sacramento yhuan quimopilhuique campana quinmotocayotillique de los prouesos. yn oncã mohuetzitico teopixque [*p. 5*] Auh yn iquac oquimomachiltique Sant. Fran^{co} teopixque niman mocentlalitzinoque yn Dominigos. augustinos clerigos. in oteylhuitzinoto yn audiencia yxpantzinco visurrey Don luis de velasco. yhuan quisidor sanctos garcia. yhuan no yquac nican moyetztica Don fray Domingo de salaçar china obispo, quinmolhuilli tleyn ticchihuazque ca omotzontec ompa yn españa camo nican omochiuh ca ompa ohualla yn huelitiliztli auh cenca yx[5] mixnamictzinoque nimã onmopehualtique yn castillan s^{t}. Fran^{co} teopixque moteylhuitzinoto aocmo huelitique

v axcan viernes a xvii. de febrero yquac nican quizque chachapoltin tlatilolcopa hualitztiaque ye tlapoyahua[6] can nohuiã cenmantiaque ynic yaque, // auh yn ipan lunes a 20 de abril de 1592. ye no ceppa huallaque otzillin nahui ora iuhqui hecatepoztli[7] hualmoquetztiaque ça cenmantiaque nohuian yahyaque s^{t}. miguel tlacopan atlacuihuayan cuyohuacã

v Domingo a 26. de abril yquac quimonpehualtique yn ocellome castillan quinhuicaque onteme tecpan comonidad.[8] manca auh no yquac mochiuh in tlahtocatilmatli tlauhtonatiuh yc ontetl. ocelonacazminque xiuhtilmatli yc tlapãtiuh chalchiuhtlatenyo[9] yhuan cactli iuh mito quimottiliz. in Principe Rey Don Phelipe, portadortin[10] yn quitzonque.

---

1. Much is left unsaid about the market moves and manipulations. See Gibson 1964, pp. 352–58, 395, for some information on the development of markets in Mexico City in the sixteenth to eighteenth centuries.

2. *Teopixqui* here probably means religious specifically, as so often in Ch.

3. Although Mexico Tenochtitlan was very much an altepetl, *altepehuaque* unqualified is most often used in Ch. to refer to the people of a whole larger area. The Spanish repartimiento system for procuring temporary labor was still viewed by the Nahuas as their traditional rotary labor, *coatequitl*, which at the base it was.

4. We have located no transitive verb *xoloca*. Possibly there is a relation to *xoloni*, for a wound or the like to get worse, or to intransitive *xoloca* and some associated verbs having to do with folding, bending, wrinkling.

5. In the Nahuatl, "yx" must be for "yc."

day everyone was to do business here [in San Lázaro]. But for only a few days was business done there; then the market was set up again where the Discalced fathers are housed. And the Tlatelolca had been deceived, for they were going to do business at their home of Tlatelolco, but the Mexica women brought complaint about it before the Audiencia, and it was not permitted to be carried out.[1]

v Sunday the 23rd of February was when the clerics[2] from all the places where they are here in Mexico assembled because, as was heard and was said, the cloth fit to our lord God, his shroud, called sheets, had arrived here; it came from Rome.

v Thursday the 5th of March was when people were burned at the armory, where firearms are made. Those who were burned were citizens of [surrounding] altepetl doing repartimiento labor,[3] quite a few of them; it was truly frightening how it [damaged? wrinkled?][4] their flesh. They brought them to the royal hospital; some got well, and some died.

v Monday the 3rd of February of the year 1592 was when the Theatine religious who were outside the court jail established themselves at [the church of] the Company of Jesus. It was right on the feast day of San Blas; they entered at night, then they installed the Sacrament and hung up the bell. They called the religious who settled there the professed. [*p. 5*] And when the Franciscan friars found out about it, they and the Dominicans, Augustinians, and secular priests assembled and went to complain to a convocation before the viceroy don Luis de Velasco and the inquisitor Santos García, and also don fray Domingo de Salazar, the bishop of the Philippines, was here at that time, and he said to them, "What are we to do? The judgment was made there in Spain and it was not done here, for the permission came from there." They had great arguments over it,[5] then Franciscan friars set out for Spain to make complaint; they could no longer [achieve anything].

v Today, Friday the 17th of February, was when grasshoppers came by here, coming from the direction of Tlatelolco. It was getting dark;[6] they spread out everywhere as they went. // And on Monday, the 20th of April of 1592, they came again, at four o'clock. They came raised up like a [tornado?],[7] they spread out and went everywhere: to San Miguel, Tacuba, Tacubaya, Coyoacan.

v Sunday the 26th of April was when they sent two jaguars off to Spain; they took two that had been at the community palace;[8] also at that time was made a rising sun ruler's cloak and second a turquoise cloak with a diagonal jaguar design and a greenstone border,[9] with sandals, it was said for the prince and king don Felipe to see. [The embroiderers][10]

6. Possibly the meaning is that the locusts covered the sky and made it dark. "Can" just after this is for "çan."

7. The term *ecatepoztli*, literally "wind-axe," refers to some portentous meteorological phenomenon. For an example see Lockhart 1993, p. 242. Reference to its rapid motion and appearing out of nowhere point to a tornado, but the meaning is not fully established.

8. The courthouse and cabildo headquarters in San Juan Moyotlan, apparently.

9. We have not accounted for "yc tlapãtiuh," which literally seems to say "goes broken with." Perhaps one of the motifs interrupted the other.

10. Given standard letter substitutions of the time, "portadortin" apparently contains *bordador*, a professional tailor specializing in embroidery. A more remote possibility would be *portador*, exactly the form given in the Nahuatl, which refers to the bearer of a message or present.

auh yn iten quichiuhque tlatenchiuhque tianquizpan tlaca yvan ce tlahpoyahuac quetzaltonatiuh yn ipan mantiuh ynĩ ye vecauh mexico tlahtoq̃. quimoq̃tiaya moch ya

v Yn ipan in ciudad mexico a 25. de mayo. yquac hualla acico yn itlahtollotzin arçobispo Don P^{o}. moya de cõtreras ynic omomiquilli yn ompa castilla auh yn iuh mocac tlahtolli yn ipan carta yn hualicuiliuhtia yn momiquilli ypã de febrero. auh yn ipã 29. de mayo. yquac peuh yn itepoz miccatepoztli ynic nohuian tzillin yn ipã yxquich teocalli mani mexico. yn ihtic altepetl caxtolomey tonatiuh in tzilinia campanas. // auh ypã caxtolilhuitl Junio de 1592 años. in missa ypantzinco mito yn iglesia mayor. motlalli monomento,[1] auh ynic chicueteocalli nican moyetzticate teopixque cecentetl missa mayor ypã quimitalhuique,
v martes yc tlami metztli de Junio de 1592. años. yquac peuh in Sant. Pablo, [*p. 6*] Teocalli ynic motlallan. motenexten yc quichiuhque possesion yn teopixque Sant. augustin Padreme yn onca moyetzticate yhuan gou^{or} Don Antonio valeriano al~~lde~~s. Fran^{co} de la cruz. yhuã hernando garcia Don Juan martin yhuã mochintin Sant Pablo tlaca pipiltin Regidores. ypampa ca oaxcatilloque omacoque yn teopixque ypampa mochi tlacatl tetl quicuic quinapallo in teopixque in contlalliq̃. tlatatacco tenexçoquititlan.

v Yn ipan xihuitl de 1592. yquac motlalli yn tlacallaquilli nanahui tomines oome tomin çan tlahuenchihualiztli mochiuh yn ihuicpatzinco Rey yn quimomaquiliaya in jordadosme cenhuetz ynic nohuian altepetl ypan ynic tlantica cemanahuatl ytlal tecpan in tecaquiltiloc ynic mochihuaz momanaz. oncan ticpehualtique in totequiuh al~~lde~~ fran^{co} de la cruz regidor mayor Thomas de Aquino merino pablo ximenez tequicaltitlan[2]

v Miercoles a xvi. de Setiembre yquac tapachiuhque nohuian cẽca tlaxicac in tlapanco yhuan mieccan xixitin papachiuh in calli netlapacholloc,

v Juebes a xii. de octubre yquac mopitz ye yohua in campana S^{t}. Joseph español in quichiuh yehuatl yn huey campana St Josepeh ypã motlatolti fray geronimo de çarate

¶ x. calli xihuitl. 1593. a^{o}s Domingo a 28. de març o yquac yohuatzinco tlahuizcalpan in St Joseph teopan yn ocenquixohuac yn onetecoc[3] yn ohualquiz totatzin fray Juan de S^{t}tiago niman ye yc tepehuia ymecauh yca in tehuitequi ynic hualtequixtia ythualco yhuan quauhtica tehuitec auh niman ic quicauh[4] yn itequiuh. yehuatl. yxquetzalloc in fray Pedro de req̃na quimonahuatilli. conmissario fray ber^{no} ynic yehuatl capellan mochiuh in S^{t}. Joseph. yhuan fr. Jer^{mo} de çarate conmisario çan ĩ quimoquixtili ytlaytlaniliztica teteuhctin[5] peticio quicalaquiq̃ —

1. A wooden ceremonial structure set up in the area in front of the main altar, a catafalque, sometimes fashioned in imitation of a church.

2. Ch. must have copied the last sentence directly from a source, perhaps not even the same one that supplied the material for the rest of the entry. *Merino* was a title given to various sub-cabildo offices.

3. The meaning of "yn cenquixohuac" by itself is "when everyone had assembled." "Yn onetecoc" apparently means the same. Although the most frequent meaning of reflexive

were the ones who sewed it, and marketplace people who make borders did its borders, and a dark sun of fine plumes was spread out on it. The rulers in Mexico wore this long ago. It all went [to Spain].

v In the city of Mexico on the 25th of May was when news came and arrived of the archbishop don Pedro Moya de Contreras, that he had died in Spain, and as the news was heard in the letter that came written, he passed away in February. The 29th of May was when the bells for him began, so that they were tolled in all the churches there are in Mexico. The bells tolled in the altepetl for eighteen days. // And on the 15th day of June of the year 1592, mass was said for him in the cathedral. The monument[1] was set up, and in eight churches here the priests in them said a high mass for him in each one.

v Tuesday the last of the month of June of the year 1592 was when [*p. 6*] groundbreaking and spreading lime for a church began at the church of San Pablo, with which the friars, the Augustinian fathers, who are there now took possession, and the governor [of Tenochtitlan] don Antonio Valeriano, the alcaldes Francisco de la Cruz, Hernando García, and don Juan Martín, and all the nobles and regidores of San Pablo, because the friars were given possession, all took and carried in their arms stones which the friars placed in the excavation among the cement.

v The year of 1592 was when a tribute of four reales for each person was established, [plus] two reales each which was just an offering made to the king, who gave it to the soldiers; it fell upon the altepetl everywhere as far as the end of the lands of the world. At the palace it was announced that it was to be raised and offered. At that point we, the alcalde Francisco de la Cruz, the regidor mayor Tomás de Aquino, and Pablo Jiménez, official at the tribute house, began our periods of office.[2]

v Wednesday the 16th of September was when we were flooded; the roofs leaked greatly everywhere, and in many places the houses collapsed and fell in, and people were caught underneath.

v Thursday the 12th of October, at night, was when the bell of San Josef was cast; it was a Spaniard who did it. It was the big bell of San Josef; fray Gerónimo de Zárate was in charge of it.

¶ 10 House year, 1593. Sunday the 28th of March was when, very early in the morning, at dawn, when everyone had assembled[3] at the church of San Josef, our father fray Juan de Santiago came out, whereupon he chased people away, he lashed them with his whip, so that he drove people out of the patio, and he beat people with a stick. Then because of that he relinquished his post.[4] Fray Pedro de Requena was put in [the post in his place]; the commissary fray Bernardino gave him the order for him to be made chaplain at San Josef, along with fray Gerónimo de Zárate. The commissary ejected him only at the request of the lords;[5] they put in a petition.

---

teca is to lie down, it also has to do with things spreading, etc., and here it seems to be synonymous with the *cenquiça* that immediately precedes it.

4. Was made to relinquish it, apparently. *Niman ic* generally means "thereupon," but here *niman*, "then," and *ic*, "for that reason," seem to be intended separately.

5. Apparently meaning the members of the indigenous cabildo of Mexico Tenochtitlan. This sentence is in the margin.

v Domingo a xi. de abril yquac quichallique yn incapilla netolleque españoles. in naza-Reno ypilhuan huell ipan motlalli in de ramos. ynic moteochiuh quauhxihuitl hitic quixohuac ynic tlayahualoloc / auh yn ipã visperas oncã machtilloque yn españolesme yehuatl motemachtili Reynoso. S. Fran^co —

v Domingo a xxv. de abril yquac moteochiuh in custodia yn imaxca tepetlatzinca natiuidas tlaca niman yhuan [*p. 7*] Yn icehualcaltzin yn palio yhuan teocuitlatlecaxitl sesario[1] / auh yn huehuetlan tlaca niman no yciuhca centetl quinextique quicouhque in costodia huel mahuiztic

v martes a xxvii. de abril yquac motatacac yn atlauhtli yn atoyac hicac yn iohui atl in quauhtla huallaticac mololhui ynic motatacac mexico. tlatilolco yhuã chinampaneca[2] yhuan tepaneca.[3] in quitatacaque atlauhtli atoyatl

v Yn ipan Domingo Spũ pasqua penthecostes ypã yc 6. mani metztli de Junio de 1593 años. ipã Spũ pasqua yquac quiquetzque in quauhtli yn icpac teocalli St Joseph tlapanixquac yn iuh neztica axcan yhuan yquac quimextequacuillotique[4] in teocalli in atenamitl yn tecpantoc tlapanixq̃c ytencopatzinco mochiuh in totatzin fray Jeronimo de sarate yquac yecauh in temimilchayahuac[5] ynic motlapacho in tlamayecampa

v Viernes yc 4. mani metztli de Junio yquac peuh moquetzaco in quiyahuitl aço he ome ora[6] yn moquetzaco auh yn hualathuic visita general ye cuel cenca çoquititlan mochiuh auh çan niman iciuh[7] hueyx macoc yn atl tlaapachiuh yn nicã mexico, yhuan ynic nohuian chinampa yn inauhcampaixti yhuan cẽca nohuian tlaxicac in techachan cenca netoliniloc // auh niman yc huahuac in toctzintli in nohuian chinampa

v Juebes yc xvii : mani metztli de Junio. yquac motlayahualhui in Sacramento auh amo huel mochiuh amo huel mohtlatoquilti çan callitic yn motlayahualhui yn iglesia mayor. ynic ahuel moquixti ypampa cenca quiyauh huel totocac in quiahuitl. yhuan cenca çoquititlan catca chiuh[8] auh yn ixquichtin maceuhque huel mocencauhque ynic mexico yhuã tlatilolco yhuã yn ixquichtin nepapan oficialesme mochĩtin cecentlamantli quichiuhque yn ineahuiltiliz yn ipãpa iuh mochiuh yc motlanahuatilli yn audiencia Real yhuã ciudad ~~alldes~~ hor^o. cerar corregidor mayor huey pena quitlalli yn aquin amo mahuiltiz. Justiciatica tlatzacuiltilozque / auh in yehuatzin fr Jeronimo de sarate temachtiani Sant. Joseph. no cenca huell ipan motlatolti yc motlatlaquauhnahuatilli in papaquiliztli

1. Here Ch. gives Nahuatl explanations before using the Spanish loanwords.

2. The Spanish word *chinampa* means an intensively cultivated strip or plot of earth, usually artificially built up, sitting in the midst of water in marshes, shallow lakes, and the like. The Nahuatl word was *chinamitl*, to which the locative *-pan* was so often added, giving *chinampan*, that that was the form (minus a weak final *n*) that the Spaniards borrowed and that has become known in English. A large area south and east of Mexico Tenochtitlan was dominated by chinampas, and its inhabitants were known as *chinampaneca*, chinampa people or inhabitants.

3. An ethnic group spreading across several altepetl on the western side of the valley.

4. In the form "quimextequacuillotique," *tequacuilli* is a statue or idol, followed by an assimilated form of the nominal suffix *-yo*, giving a collective sense; *-tia*, of which we have here the preterit plural, means to provide to someone or something what the nom-

v Sunday, the 11th of April, was when they inaugurated the chapel of the Spaniards who had taken vows as children of the Nazarene; it was established right on Palm [Sunday]. The way it was blessed was that leaves of trees were brought from inside and taken in procession. / And during vespers the Spaniards heard a sermon; the Franciscan Reinoso preached.

v Sunday, the 25th of April, was when a monstrance belonging to the Tepetlatzinca, the people of Nativitas, was blessed, as well as [*p. 7*] a structure to give it shade, a canopy, and a golden fire-bowl, a censer.[1] / And then the people of Huehuetlan also quickly produced one; they bought a very splendid monstrance.

v Tuesday, the 27th of April, was when the ravine was excavated at the river, [where] the channel of water [canal] comes from the forest; [people] were collected for digging in Mexico and Tlatelolco; also people of the chinampa territories[2] and Tepaneca[3] excavated the ravine and river.

v Sunday the holiday of the Holy Spirit, Pentecost, on the 6th of the month of June of the year 1593, was when they erected the eagle on top of the church of San Josef, on the front side of the roof, as it appears today, and it was when they put [cloud images?][4] on the parapet of the church, lined up in a row at the front of the roof. It was done by order of our father fray Gerónimo de Zárate. At this time the [row of columns?][5] with which the right-hand side was covered was finished.

v Friday the 4th of the month of June was when rain began to fall; it lasted perhaps two hours,[6] and at dawn on the morning of the general inspection it had already become very muddy. And then very quickly[7] the water grew and rose so that it was flooded here in Mexico, and in the chinampas in all four parts, and it leaked very much everywhere in people's houses; there was great misery. // And after that the young maize plants dried up in the chinampas everywhere.

v Thursday the 17th of the month of June was when the Sacrament went in procession, but it could not be done, it could not make progress on the road; it went in procession only inside the cathedral, since it couldn't be taken out because it rained very much; the rain really pelted down, and it became[8] very muddy. All the dancers prepared themselves well, in Mexico as well as Tlatelolco, and all the different tradespeople performed their acts of entertainment as separate groups; the reason it was done that way is that the Royal Audiencia along with the alcaldes ordinarios of the [Spanish] city and the corregidor mayor at the municipal building ordered it and set a big fine for whoever should not take part in the celebration; they would be punished by the officers of the law. / And fray Geró-

---

inal core of the construction designates. The puzzling part of the word is "-mex-," an element apparently modifying *tequacuilli*, which we are unable to identify. Perhaps it is for *-mix-* from *mixtli*, "cloud." Conceivably the *x* is weakened from *tz* and the intention is *-metz-* from *metztli*, "moon." The most frequent decoration of the edge of the roof of sixteenth-century Mexican churches was a row of merlons or *almenas*, and that is probably what is meant.

5. *Temimilchayahuac* could refer to the columns arrayed around an internal patio, including those integrated into balustrades.

6. We take "ome ora" to be durative. It may be, however, that the time by the clock is meant. For a clear case of durative use of *hora* see pp. 304–05, entry for Sept. 9, 1615.

7. For "iciuhca."

8. For "mochiuh," apparently, although it seems that "catca" would suffice.

mochihuaz yhuã quihto in corregi^{or}, mayor yn aquique huel mahuiztic quichihuazq̃. motlaxtlahuizque macozq̃ tomines. — [*p. 8*]

v auh yn ipan Domingo a a[1] 20 de Junio yquac yequene motlayahualhui motlatoquilti yn Sacramento ynin çan huel oc mixcahui yn iglesia mayor tlayahualoloc auh yxquich mochiuh in papaquiliztli macehualiztli xochillacatzoque miec tlamantli mochiuh ynic motimalloque in mexica yhuã tlatilolca yhuã amo çan quexquich yn andas tlayahuallo yhuã yn vanderas. auh in Sant Josep caltitlan yn oncan motenamiquiliani teopixque oncã quinmomanillique in Sant Fran^{co}. yhuan S^{t}. Diego huel paño yn quinmoquentillique ynneololoeltzin auh actihuetz in tlapechtli poztec yn quahuitl auh oncan ytlacauhque in Sanctome ymatzin[2] poztec in S^{t}. Fran^{co}. yhuã yn St Diego no ytlacauh

v Domingo a 27. de Junio yquac motlayahualhui in Sacramento in S^{t}. Fran^{co}. yhuan S^{t}. Augustin S^{to}. Domingo yhua tlatilolco yn tlayahualoloc auh yn ixquich mochiuh S^{t}. Fran^{co}. yn ixquichtin nepapan oficialesme mochintin cecentetl tlapechtli quitlallique oncan quichiuhque yn intlachihual yhuan oncan papacque mitotique in quauhtlapechco pochteca tepozpitzque teopã tlaca quauhxinque yhuã Jordadosme. acalchimaltica quinnamicque yn acalloco yn iquiahuac. castaneda huel huey papaquiliztli mochiuh aic iuhqui mochihuani yn omochiuh auh yehuatzin missa oquimitalhuico in tlahtohuani quisidor[3]

v Yn ipan axcan Domingo yc xviii. mani metztli de Julio de 1593. años. yquac hualmohuicaque mocallaquico in Sant Juan de la penitencia yn cihuapipiltin monjastin Sancta clara ypilhuantzitzin çan oc macuiltin yn hualmohuicaque ye teotlac in mocallaquico otzillin nahui ora yxquichtin quinmocahuillico in teopixque St Fran^{co}. guardian diunidores comissario prouincial quinmoyomahuilico ynic quinmotlalilico yhuan corregidor mayor yhuan miequintin castilteca. yn quihualmohuiquillique çan ica Coche yn huallaque ompa hualquizque yn S^{t}.ta clara
v Yn ipan axcan viernes. yn ipan ylhuitzin tt^{o} Dios. motenehua [*p. 9*] Trasfiguracion yc 6. mani metztli agosto. yquac quimotlallilico in Sacramento yn oncan St Juan baptista de la penitencia yc cenca quimocnelili yn ialtepetzin tt^{o}. Dios. yc quimomahuiçotili quimotenyotilli yn moyotecayotl.[4] // auh no mohuicatza yn tlahtoque yn visurrey yhuan oydores. quimoyomahuillico ynic quimotlalilico Sacramento mochi hualla yn ãdas yn nohuian Jujetos. yhuan in teopixque necoc motecpãtzinoque ynic hualmohuicaque
v Yn ipan axcan Domingo a v. de Septiembre yquac macehualloc yn oncan quanpatlanilizquauhtitlan yc motlanahuatilli visurrey michcuicatl[5] yn meuh yxquichtin huallaque in chinampaneca xochmilca nauhteuhctin[6] yxquich hualla yn intlahuiz yn ipan macehuaco yhuan yn mexico. tlatilolco oficialesme yhuan tlacopaneca yn macehuaco cenca tlamahuiçoque in tlahtoque yhuã obispome
v Yn ipan axcan Domingo a tres dias del mes de octubre de 1593. años in yehuatzin teo-

1. The word "a" is inadvertently repeated in the original.
2. Or hands, or arm or arms.
3. Here as often happened, the *in* is left off *inquisidor*, having been taken to be the Nahuatl article/subordinator of that shape.
4. San Juan Moyotlan, one of the four main parts of Tenochtitlan, first in order and seat of the municipal government.

nimo de Zárate, preacher at San Josef, also did a great deal to see to it; he strongly ordered that the celebration be carried out. The corregidor mayor said that those who did it really splendidly would be paid, they would be given money. [*p. 8*]

v And Sunday, the[1] 20th of June, was when the Sacrament finally went in procession and went on its way [outdoors]; this was still confined to going in procession in the cathedral area. All the celebration and dancing was performed, they strung flowers together, and many different things were done, of which the Mexica and the Tlatelolca were proud; and a great many carrying platforms and banners went in procession. And at San Josef, next to the church, where the friars usually meet people, they set up San Francisco and San Diego, they clothed them well in woolens as their raiment, but the platform collapsed; the wood broke, and the saints were damaged. San Francisco's hand[2] broke off, and San Diego was also damaged.

v Sunday, the 27th of June, was when the Sacrament went in procession at San Francisco, San Agustín, and Santo Domingo, and there was a procession in Tlatelolco. And everything was done at San Francisco. All the different tradespeople set up a platform each. There they carried out their activities, and the merchants, blacksmiths, church attendants [musicians], and carpenters celebrated and danced on the wooden platforms. And the soldiers [mock warriors] met them in war boats in the canal outside the place of Castañeda. A very great celebration took place; never had anything happened like what happened. And the lord inquisitor[3] came to say mass.

v Today, Sunday, the 18th of the month of July of the year 1593, was when the lady nuns, children of Santa Clara, came and entered San Juan de la Penitencia; for now only five came; they entered in the afternoon at four o'clock. The Franciscan friars, the father guardian, the definidores, the commissary, and the provincial head all came in person to deliver them and set them up, and the corregidor mayor and many Spaniards accompanied them. They came by carriage, leaving from Santa Clara.

v Today, Friday, the feast day of our lord God called [*p. 9*] Transfiguration, on the 6th of the month of August, was when the Sacrament was brought to be placed in San Juan Bautista de la Penitencia, whereby our lord God greatly favored his altepetl and gave honor and fame to the entity of Moyotlan.[4] // And also the lords viceroy and Audiencia judges came in person to place the Sacrament; all the carrying platforms [with saints] came from the subject settlements all around, and the friars came in rows on both sides.

v Today, Sunday the 5th of September, was when there was dancing next to the pole for head-flying [the *volador*]. The viceroy ordered it; it was a fish song that was sung.[5] The chinampa people, the Xochimilca, the people of the four lords[6] all came, bringing all their insignia with which they danced. Also the tradespeople of Mexico and Tlatelolco and the people of Tacuba came to dance. The lords and the bishops greatly marveled at it all.

v Today, Sunday, the 3rd day of the month of October of the year 1593, the ruler in di-

5. There might have been one song or many of them; the *michcuicatl*, fish song, is a genre seen in the Cantares Mexicanos. Ch. himself refers to michcuicatl again in Chimalpahin 1963–65, 2: 41.

6. A group of altepetl south of Mexico City. See Gibson 1964, p. 443, under Mexicalzingo.

yotica tlahtohuani ynquisidor Sanctos garcia quimocuilli in teoyotica ytlahtocayotzin ynic obispo. mochiuhtzino oncan teochihualloc in Sant. Josep yn St. Franco yehuatl quimoteochihuilli in visitador. Don diego Roma [cu]itlaxcohuapan obispo. auh quauhtlapechtli moman in Sant Joseph temimiltitlan tlamellauhyan tlayxpan yxquichtin mohuicatza in teopixque yn izquican moyetzticate teopixque yhuan tlahtoque visurrey. yhuan oydores. yhuan ciudad tlaca al~~lde~~s. horos yxpantzinco mochiuh in comissario. yhuan prouincial. // auh in imoztlayoc lunes yn ipan ylhuitzin catca Sant Franco. a 4. de octubre yquac nez yn quauhtli quichiuhque tlacuilloque tenochtli quichiuhque ycpac ycaca quauhtli auh in totatzin S Franco ypã mehuiltitica yuhq̃ ma ycauallo ypã moyetztica ythualco cruz ytzintla yn yn quiquetzq̃ cenca mahuiçolloc yhuã ypan mehuiltitica yn Sant. Franco huell ipã tlato fr. Jermo. de çarate temachtiani[1] —

v̲ Yn ipan axcan a .5. de octobre de 1593. años. ypan martes yn onicallac yteopanchantzinco notlaçottatzin Señor Sant. Antonio Abbad. ỹ nican xolloco nehuatl Domingo de St. Anton muñon chimalpahin ompa nochan tzaqualtitlã tenanco Amaquemecan chalco, [*p. 10*]

¶ xi. tochtli xihuitl 1594. años. yn ipan a 3. de henero lunes yquac momiquilli yn tlacatl in tlacopan tlahtohuani catca ytoca Don Juan cortes ypiltzin catca yn tlacatl Don Antonio cortes totoquihuaztli. Domingo yohuan yn momiquilli yn otlathuic lunes ye monoltitoc yquac quimotoquillique chiuhcnauhxihuitl yn ontlahtocat yn oquipacho altepetl tlacopan // auh nahui metztli yn ayac tlahtohuani catca // auh niman yc hualla yn tlaxcallan Juez ytoca Don leonardo xicotencatl quimixquechilli yn visurrey ynic yehuatl quipachoto altepetl tlacopan.

v̲ Yn ipan abril de 1594 años. yn o iuh onquiz ynezcalilitzin tto. Dios. in pasqua Resurretion yquac miquanitzinoque yn teopixque yn iztac abito quimaquitzinohua ypilhuãtzitzinhuan yn totlaçonantzin Sancta maria de las mercedes Redemptio de captiuos yn teopixque quinmotocayotilia mercenadios. ompa motlallitzinoto yn ipan tlaxillacalli tomatla yquiahauc in tzauhqui[2] español ytoca lucas de tueñas. auh yexihuitl yhuan yey metztli yn moyetzticatca Sant ipolito ypan tlaxillacalli teocaltitlan

v̲ Juebes. a 24. de febrero yn ipan ylhuitzin Sant. mathias apostol yc omilhuitl neçahuallo quaresma yquac vey. tlayahualoliztli mochiuh ompa hualpeohuac in Sant. Jeronimo oncan hualhuilohuac in de monserate tequixquipan ynic tlayahualloloc oncan quimotlallilico yn ilhuicac cihuapilli de nuestra señora de monserate. quimonapalhuitica yn itlaçoconetzin huellacencahualoc yn otlica quauhtlapechtli motlatlalli yn otlica ochpanco tolquatectli[3] vanderas. auh in yomatzinco visurrey yhuã tlahtoque oydores yn oncan mohuicatza ynic quimotlallilico cihuapilli Dios. ynantzin motlayahualhuiq̃ —

v̲ Nican peuh tzintic ynic ye piello yn ilhuitzin Sancto Thomas de aquino, Sancto Domingo teopixqui yc tzatzihuac yn nohuian caltzallan ynic tecaquitilloc ynic yxquich

---

1. This episode and its meaning are briefly discussed in Lockhart 1992, p. 236.
2. Literally weaver in the Nahuatl; the meaning of *obrajero* is not merely one who weaves but one who runs if not owns a textile shop.

vine matters, the inquisitor Santos García, took up his divine rulership, being made bishop. He was consecrated at San Josef, [which is] at San Francisco; it was the inspector don Diego Romano, bishop of Puebla, who consecrated him. A wooden platform was set up at San Josef, next to the stone pillars, right in front. All the religious from all the places where they are came, and it was done in the presence of the lords viceroy and Audiencia judges, and the members of the [Spanish] cabildo, the alcaldes ordinarios, and the [Franciscan] commissary and the provincial head. // The following day, Monday, on the feast day of San Francisco, the 4th of October, was when the eagle which the painters made was revealed. They made a prickly pear cactus on top of which stood an eagle, and our father San Francisco was sitting on it, as if he were on his horse. They set it up at the foot of the cross in the patio. It was greatly marveled at, and San Francisco sits on it. Fray Gerónimo de Zárate, preacher, really favored [the project].[1]

v Today, Tuesday, the 5th of October of the year of 1593, I, Domingo de San Antón Muñón Chimalpahin, from Tzaqualtitlan Tenanco, Amaquemecan, Chalco, entered the church of my precious father the lord San Antonio Abad here in Xoloco. [*p. 10*]

¶ 11 Rabbit year, 1594. Monday the 3rd of January was when the lord ruler of Tacuba, whose name was don Juan Cortés, passed away. He was the child of the lord don Antonio Cortés Totoquihuaztli. It was Sunday night when he passed away; at dawn Monday he was already lying [dead]. That was when they buried him. He was ruler and governed the altepetl of Tacuba for nine years. // And for four months no one was ruler. // Then a judge named don Leonardo Xicotencatl came from Tlaxcala; the viceroy appointed him, so that he went to govern the altepetl of Tacuba.

v April of the year 1594, after the resuscitation of our lord God, the holiday of the Resurrection [Easter] had passed, was when the friars who wear white habits, the children of our precious mother Santa María de las Mercedes y de la Redención de Cautivos, the friars they call Mercedarians, moved. They went to establish themselves in the tlaxilacalli of Tomatlan at the entryway of the house of Lucas de Dueñas, a Spaniard who was an *obrajero*.[2] For three years and three months they had been at San Hipólito in the tlaxilacalli of Teocaltitlan.

v Thursday the 24th of February, the feast day of the apostle San Matías, the second day of fasting at Lent, was when a great procession took place. People began at San Gerónimo and came to [the church of] Montserrat in Tequixquipan in procession; they came there to set up [the image of] our Lady of Montserrat, who carries her precious child in her arms. Things were well prepared along the way; wooden platforms were set up in different places along the way on the main road, and banners.[3] And the viceroy and lords judges of the Audiencia came in person to establish the Lady, mother of God; they went in procession. —

v Here began and was founded the observation of the feast day of Santo Tomás de Aquino, a Dominican friar. It was proclaimed in the streets everywhere to inform people how until

3. Ch. seems to mean that the *tolquatectli* are the same thing as the banners. By its parts the construction looks like it would mean a reed or rush with the top part cut off. We have not found the word *quatectli* as such, but from Molina's verb "quatecuia. nino." it appears to refer to a cloth head covering.

cahuitl ayc opieloya yniquilhuitzin. quiçaya. cecexiuhtica Sancto — [*p. 11*] Auh yn axcan yc peva in cecexiuhtica ylhuitzin quiztiaz huey pielloz quihualmihualli ytlanahuatiltzin in Sancto Padre in moyetztica Roma ypan a vii. de marco de 1594. años ypan lunes motlali yn ilhuitzin Sancto. yn ipan in omoteneuh xivitl —

v Yn ipan axcan viernes. yc xi. mani metztli de março de 1594. años. yquac possesion quimocuilli macoc yn arcediano Don Juan de ceruantes. ynic yxiptlatzin mochiuh yn arçobispo Bonilla, oncan yn iglesia mayor macoc ytencopatzinco mochiuh. yn arcobispo.[1] Bunilla ynin visitador. mochihuato yn Perũ, auh castillan quimocuillito ynic arçobispo, mochiuh auh ompa yn quihualmacac yn ihuelitiliz ynic ypampa gouernador mochiuh yn arcediano ỹ nican ciudad mexico yn oquic yxquichcauh visita quichihuato perũ, auh huel tlacencahualloc yn iglesia mayor huel huey papaquiliztli mochiuh yn iquac macoc teoyotica tlatocayotl cenyohual in papacohuac quahoocotl in tlatlac yn icpac teocalli yhuã mahuiltique yn españolesme, yhuan yn cavildo. / yn dean / arcediano, prouisor. canonigos.tin yn ixquichtin clerigos.

v Yn ipan axcan sabado a xix. de março yn ipan ylhuitzĩ Sant. Joseph yquac mochalli momamal in vandera chichiltic tamasco yn itech icuiliuhtoc ytech micuillo tlachinolli teoatl[2] quitentocatoc yhua yn tlahtoque yn otlahtocatico mexico mochi tenochtli ymac ycuiliuhtihui tlatoq̃ yhua quauhtli tlahtocayotl conaquitica auh ypan metztica in totlaçotatzin. S. Fran^{co}, iuhqui ma cauallo pohui ycruz ymaquicac yhuan in yamatzin[3] quimoçohuilitica. auh tlapanixquac y mopillo. yn oncã S Josepeh cenca quimahuiço. in tlahtohuani visurrey yhuã tlahtoq̃, oydoresme —

v Yn ipan axcan Domingo. a xx. de março de 1594. años. yquac yancuic monasterio de monjas motlalli in teatinos caltitlan motocayoti ytocayocan de nr̃a Señora Encarnacion yquac motlallitzinoque in cihuapipiltin ompa hualmoquixtique in de la comcepcion ynic õpa mohuetziltito [*p. 12*] Yancuic monasterio. ynin ypilhuantzitzinhuan yn totlaçonantzin de la conception

v Yn ipan axcan Juebes. a xxiiii. de março de 1594. años. yquac molnamic yn imiquillitzin tlahtohuani visurrey yn huehue Don luis de velasco catca yn itatzin catca totlahtocauh visurrey yn axcan moyetztica yn quenin mochiuh yn iquac momiquilli yn ipan xihuitl mill y quinientos y sesenta y quatro años. in ye axcã cenpohualli onmatlactli xihuitl. ypan yey metztli yn omolnamiquico munomẽto motlalli in callitic S^{t}. Domingo yn õcan missa ypãtzinco mitto. yxquichtin oncan cenquizque in teopixque in missa ypã quimitalhuique yhuan tlayahualloloc yn ithualco teopã gonatica[4] quimonapalhuique yn iyomiyo oydoresme in quinapalloque, auh yn õtzonquiz missa oc cecni quimotoquilliq̃ yn iyomiyotzin. yhuan quinmotlaqualtilli yn ixquixtin[5] teopixq̃. —

v Yn ipan viernes a xxv. de março de 1594 años. yn ipan yhuilhuitzin[6] anuciacion Sancta maria yquac hualmohuicaque in monjastin yn oncan Sant. Juan bap^{ta}. de la penitẽcia, yn ipilhuan Sancta clara chicueyntin in ye no hualmohuicaque yc matlactin omomen mochiuhque yn achto nahuintin huallaque auh çan quihualhuillanque yca coche yntlan hual-

1. For "arçobispo." The version given here of the appointments differs somewhat from that on pp. 152–53.

2. Or one could take it that the pictographic symbol *atl tlachinolli* (water and scorched fields), which was a traditional metaphor for battle or war, was literally reproduced along the edges.

now the saint's feast day had never been observed and held each year; [*p. 11*] but now it would start going along being held every year, observed in grand style. The Holy Father who is in Rome sent his order that the feast day of the saint was set on the 7th of March of the year 1594, on a Monday of the said year.

v Today, Friday, the 11th of the month of March of the year of 1594, was when the archdeacon don Juan de Cervantes was given and took possession [of his office] by which he became the deputy of Archbishop Bonilla. [Possession] was given to him at the cathedral; it was done by order of Archbishop[1] Bonilla, who went to Peru appointed as inspector [general]. He went to Spain to get the appointment as archbishop, and from there he gave him power that on his behalf the archdeacon was made governor [of the archdiocese] here in the city of Mexico until he had gone to perform his inspection in Peru. Things were well prepared at the cathedral, and a very great celebration was held when he was given the divine rulership; all night people celebrated, torches were burned on top of the church, and the Spaniards, and the cathedral chapter, the dean, the archdeacon, the vicar general, the canons, and all the secular priests made merry.

v Today, Saturday the 19th of March, the feast day of San Josef, was when the banner of crimson damask was initiated and inaugurated, on which is painted, along the edges of which were painted [scenes of] war,[2] and the rulers who governed in Mexico all go painted on the branches of a cactus, and [they put in?] an eagle [representing] the rulership, and on it is our precious father San Francisco, as though it were considered a horse; he has a cross in his hand and he displays a paper.[3] It was hung above the portal at San Josef; the lord viceroy and the lords judges of the Audiencia greatly marveled at it.

v Today, Sunday the 20th of March of the year 1594, was when a convent of nuns was newly established next to the house of the Theatines. It was called and is at the place called Nuestra Señora de la Encarnación. When the ladies established themselves, they departed from [the convent of] Concepción, so that they settled [*p. 12*] at the new convent; they were children of our precious mother of Concepción.

v Today, Thursday the 24th of March of the year 1594, was when the death of the lord viceroy, the late don Luis de Velasco the elder, who was father of our ruler the present viceroy, was remembered. How it happened when he died in the year of 1564, thirty years and three months ago now, was remembered. The catafalque was set up inside the church of Santo Domingo, where mass was said for him. All the religious assembled there and said a mass for him, and there was a procession in the church patio. In a cradle[4] they carried his bones; it was the Audiencia judges who carried them. When mass was finished, they buried his bones in another place, and he [the present viceroy?] fed all[5] the friars.

v Friday, the 25th of March of the year 1594, on the feast day[6] of the Annunciation of St. Mary, was when nuns, children of Santa Clara, came to San Juan Bautista de la Penitencia. There were eight more who came, with which the first four who came became twelve. They brought them by carriage; their relatives rode along next to them, and the

---

3. That is, a paper with a legend written on it, what the Spaniards called a *letrero*.
4. The letters "gona" seem to correspond to Spanish *cuna*.
5. For "ixquichtin."
6. For "ylhuitzin" or possibly "yn ilhuitzin."

yetiaque yn inhuanyolque quĩhualmohuiquilli al~~lde~~ celar[1] gonsalo gomez de ceruantes yhuã alguacil mayor. Balthasar mexia yhuã castilteca mahuiztique auh in teopixq̃. oncan quinmochielico. S. Ju^{o} auh yn tlahtoque mexico al~~ldes~~ Regidores[2] yhuan yn ixquichtin macehualtin toquichtin cihua quinnamiquito ohtlica yhuan cequintin huell ompa Sancta clara quimanillito. auh yn oacico Sant. Juan caltenco xochitica namicoque yhuã quinxochitzetzelloque huel quinmahuiztilique yn cihuapipiltin auh oncan hualmohuicaq̃ yn tlahtoque oydores yhuan visurrey oncan machtilloque yn ipã missa

v Yn iquac o iuh onquiz yn inezcaliliztzin tt^{o}. Dios. yn ipan .x. abril 1594 a^{o}s. yn oquiz pasqua çan yquezquilhuiyoc. nimã Yc omopehualti yn teoyotica tlahtohuani obispo. Don Fran^{co} Sanctos garcia ompa mohuicac in tonallan[3] ompa motlalli [*p. 13*] Yn itequitzin ynic teoyotica motlahtocatillito tonallan confirmacion quimotemaquilitia ynic mohuicac in oncan tlatilolco, auh yn ixiptlatzin. mochiuh in quimopatilli inquisidor. mochiuh ytoca Don Bartholome lubo querrero

v Yn Padreme mercenadios yn iquac mohuicaque motlallitzinoto yn iquiahuac luis de tuẽnas. tzauhqui. ypan tlaxillacalli tomatlan. çan ic onquiz in pasqua Resurretion ypã abril de 1594 años. yexihuitl yhuan nahui metztli yn oncã catca ypan tlaxillacalli St ipolito teocaltitlan. novian nenq̃. acan tlaqualitaq̃. auh çan matlactetl once metztli yn ompa catca tomatla yc niman hualmiquanique in toçanitlan yquiahuac yn diego mexia cerda ypan metztli de febrero de 1595. años. ychan volundate. yc ce onca motlaliq̃.

v Yn ipan axcan sabado a xxiii. de Julio de 1594. a^{o}s. yn mahuiztililoni Padreme yn huey tlamacehualiztli quimopielia descalsos yquac hualmiquanitzinoque yn oncan yancuic yncaltzin oquimoquechillique Sant ipolito quiyahuac yn ihuicpa tlaxillacalli huehuecalco // auh yn ompa moyetzticatca a la huerta sant cosme sant damian matlacxihuitl omey yhua chicontetl metztli yn oncan yc hualmiquanitzinoque yancuic teopan S^{t}. Diego. huehuecalco.

v Yn ipan axcan ylhuitzin Sanctiago apostol ypan xxv. de Julio. de 1594 a^{o}s. nican motenehua yn ipan axcan xihuitl ticate yhuan huehue xihuitl xi. tochtli. yquac cenca huey. netoliniliztli topã mochiuh cenca tlatonalhuac huellayhiyohui in tonacayotl huahuac teteyn yhuã cequi cehuechililoc ayaxcan yn quiyahuico amo cenca totocac çan tlaçoquiyauh tlacuilolquiyauh auh cenca mayanaloc ynic mexico yhuan ỹ nohuian huelaçotic in tlaolli in ce tomĩ ça aquiton catca aoc huel centlaxcalchiquihuitl. ça iuhqui. ce cacahuatl momatia ce tomin // Auh yn iquac cenca oncatca yn michin yn xoxohuiltin ça xicaltica quintamachihuaya yn mediotica auh yn cetica tlaolquahuacalli ynic quitamachihuaya yhuã oncatca nez yn izcahuitli[4] —

v Auh yn ipan yquac ylhuitzin S^{t}. bartholomen a 24. de agosto 94. a^{o}s. in yehuantin atlacuihuayan tlaca ynic motlayecoltiaya yztac octli[5] yquac quiquixtique mãdamento [*p.*

1. Gonzalo Gómez de Cervantes had held many positions as judge and administrator, including that of governor of Tlaxcala. It is possible that some higher post, based in the municipal building, is meant here, yet the same phrase apparently meaning one of the alcaldes on the Spanish cabildo appears much earlier in the Codex Osuna (see introduction, p. 21). See introduction to Gómez de Cervantes 1944.

2. The members of the indigenous cabildo.

alcalde [of the municipal cabildo],[1] Gonzalo Gómez de Cervantes, and the alguacil mayor Baltasar Mejía, and highly esteemed Spaniards came accompanying them. The friars came to await them at San Juan, and the rulers of Mexico, the alcaldes and regidores,[2] and all the commoners [indigenous people], men and women, went to meet them along the way, and some went all the way to Santa Clara to get them. And when they got just outside San Juan, they were met with flowers and had flowers sprinkled over them; they greatly honored the ladies. The lords Audiencia judges and the viceroy came; there they heard a sermon during mass.

v After the great festivity of the Resurrection of our lord God had passed and the festivity been held on the 10th of April of the year of 1594, only a few days after that the ruler in divine matters, the bishop don Francisco Santos García, departed. He went to Tonallan,[3] where his office was established, [*p. 13*] so that he went to be ruler in divine matters in Tonallan. He went along administering [the sacrament of] confirmation to people as he went to Tlatelolco. The person appointed his deputy, who replaced him and became inquisitor, was don Bartolomé Lobo Guerrero.

v The Mercedarian fathers went to establish themselves next to the house of Luis de Dueñas, obrajero, in the tlaxilacalli of Tomatlan, just after the festivity of Resurrection had passed, in April of the year 1594. For three years and four months they were in the tlaxilacalli of San Hipólito Teocaltitlan. They lived everywhere and were satisfied nowhere. For only eleven months were they in Tomatla, then they moved to Toçanitlan, next to the house of Diego Mejía Cerda, in the month of February of the year 1595, at the house of [the Voluntad?], where they settled once and for all.

v Today, Saturday the 23rd of July of the year of 1594, was when the revered fathers who observe the great penitence, the Discalced, moved to their new house that they built outside of San Hipólito in the direction of the tlaxilacalli of Huehuecalco. // They were at the garden of San Cosme and San Damián for thirteen years and seven months, from where they moved to the new church of San Diego in Huehuecalco.

v Today, on the feast day of the apostle Santiago, on the 25th of July of the year 1594, here it is mentioned that in the year we are in now, the year 11 Rabbit in the old style, was when very great misery came upon us. It got very dry. The maize really suffered; it got all dry and cracked up, and some froze. It hardly rained; it did not rain hard, but only drizzled and sprinkled. There was a great famine, so that in Mexico and everywhere maize became very expensive. One real could buy only a little bit, no longer even one full basket of bread; a real was considered no more than a cacao bean. // And when there were lots of fish, catfish, they would measure out just a gourd vessel full for half a real, and for one real they would measure out a maize container full, and there were small lake worms that appeared.[4]

v On the feast day of San Bartolomé, the 24th of August of the year 94, the people of Tacubaya, who make their living with white pulque,[5] got an order [*p. 14*] from the vice-

3. Means Jalisco. See entry for May 20, 1596, pp. 56–57.

4. Perhaps the meaning is that the worms, in Mexican Spanish *izcahuite*, were sold and eaten, or possibly the worms got mixed in with the fish.

5. It is not clear to us if this means simply pulque in general, or if white pulque is a special kind. Molina gives white wine for *iztac octli*.

14] Quinmomaquilli visurrey Don luis de velasco. ynic huel quinamacazque nican mexico ayac quincuiliz. yhuan amo ac quimilpiz. quinmottilique mandamiento gou^{or} mexico Don Antonio valeriano al~~ld~~esme

v̲ Yn ipan axcan sabado a xxvii de agosto. de 1594. años. yn huehuetlan visitacion yquac mocalaquique in Sancto Domĩgo teopixque ynic ompa motlalitzinoto ytencopatzinco Sancto Padre yhuan yn Rey. amo çan nican macoque castilla hualla tlanahuatilli yquac quimocahuillique Sant. Fran^{co} teopixque yn ompa missa conmitalhuiaya / auh yn S^{t}. Domĩgo teopixque quin yehuãtzitzin otlatocayotique ynic axcan motenehua de la piedad ypãtzinco mochiuh ỹ Don luis de velasco visurrey.

v̲ Yn ipan ciudad mexico a xi. de Setiembre de 1594 años. in yehuatzin mahuiztililoni huey teopixqui yhuã huey tlamatini Don Sancho Sanchez de muñon maestrescuela moyetzticatca yn nican mexico. ytlanequiliztzintica mochiuh ynic ompa moyetztiez ypan tlaxillacalli tepetlatzinco natiuidas. achtopa quimonemililito in teocalli auh ye iuh tihuallaci ylhuitzĩ in cihuapilli auh yn ipan Domingo matlaquilhuitl once mani metztli de Setiembre in maestrescuela mohuicac in tepetlatzinco yehuatzin missa quimitalhui auh yn fray Jeronimo de çarate motemachtilli yhuã quimitalhui ynic ompa moyetztiez tlahtohuani maestrescuela çan ye ypan in yn omoteneuh xihuitl de 1594. años.[1]

¶ xii. acatl xihuitl : 1595 años. ypan in. sabado. a xxviii. de henero yquac Capitulo mochihuato yn xochimilco ompa mocentlallitzinoque yn teopixque yehuatl quimochihuilli in comissario yancuic fray P^{o}. de pilla[2] ye iuh nepa ome metztli macoc ynic conmissario mochiuhtzino // auh yn prouincial motlalli ytoca fray esteuã de alçua[3] auh no yquac mocallaquique teopixque yn iztacalco S^{t}. Mathias. yn motlallitzinoto ytoca fray Fran^{co} Reynoso. achto huel mohuetziltito yancuican tlalmacehuato yn ompa. auh ỹ fr. P^{o}. de Requena movicac quauhtitlan capillero catca nican S. Joseph. auh yn fr. Jer^{mo}. de çarate ya chollolan auh yehuatzin hualmohuicac nicã S. Josep. ỹ fr. Fran^{co} de ganboa. yhuan fr. gaspar hortis. de aRi[4] — [*p. 15*]

Miercoles a vii. de Junio. de 1595 a^{o}s. yquac tianquizco Sant ipolito. yc tzatzihuato yn ipampa totollin tictequitizque ynic mexico yn timacoque totequiuh chicome mill. y quatro cientos y tantos. gallinas.[5] yn icohualloca ytech oquiz yn ome to^{s}. nanahui tomines cecentomin me^{o}. yhuan ynic nohuiã altepetl ypã cenhuetz ynic titequimacoque ytencopa yn visurrey auh yn izquicã titetlamamaca // Sanct ipolito. / desmanparado. // ospital real. / huitzillan / contaduria / de las. vobas.[6] chiquaceccan yn titequimacoque.

v̲ Yn ipan axcan Domingo yc ix. mani metztli de Julio de 1595. años. yn tlaçocihuapilli de moserate. in moyetztica ypan tlaxillacalli tequixquipan yquac hualmiquani yn iteocaltzin yn ochpantenco huey otli ypan yn tlamellahua Sanct Pablo ohtli, yn iuh neztica

---

1. A cathedral dignitary surely would not abandon his post for a tlaxilacalli church. Presumably the maestrescuela was to be there for a short visit or to associate himself with the church in an honorary fashion.

2. Mendieta 1980, pp. 545, 784, notes a "fray Pedro de Pila, comisario general," the seventeenth to hold the office. He was apparently raised in New Spain and had been provincial head in Michoacan.

3. Mendieta 1980, pp. 543, 770, lists fray Esteban de Alzúa as 23rd provincial head.

4. The name, added above the line, seems incomplete. Tena in Chimalpahin 2001, p. 59, supplies Aréizaga.

roy don Luis de Velasco that they would be able to sell [their pulque] here in Mexico City. No one was to take it from them or arrest them. They showed the order to the governor of Mexico City, don Antonio Valeriano, and the alcaldes.
v Today, Saturday the 27th of August of the year 1594, was when the Dominican friars entered [the church of] Visitación in Huehuetlan, so that they went to establish themselves there by order of the Holy Father and the king. The order was given to them not just here, but it came from Spain. At this time the Franciscan friars, who had said mass there, left. / The Dominican friars gave it a new name, so that today it is called "de la Piedad." It was done in the time of the viceroy don Luis de Velasco.
v In the city of Mexico, on the 11th of September of the year 1594, it happened by the wish of the very reverend great priest and savant don Sancho Sánchez de Muñón, who was maestrescuela [at the cathedral] here in Mexico, that he was to be in the tlaxilacalli of Tepetlatzinco Nativitas. First he went to reconnoiter the church, and then as we were coming to the feast day of the Lady, on Sunday the 11th day of the month of September, the maestrescuela [definitively] went to Tepetlatzinco. He said mass, and fray Gerónimo de Zárate preached and said that the lord maestrescuela was going to stay there, in the same said year of 1594.[1]

¶ 12 Reed year, 1595. Saturday, the 28th of January, was when a general meeting [of the Franciscans of the province] was held in Xochimilco; the friars assembled there. The new commissary, fray Pedro de Pila,[2] called the meeting; it was over two months before that he was given the appointment as commissary. // And the provincial head who was put in is named fray Esteban de Alzúa.[3] And this is also when the friars entered San Matías Iztaccalco; the one who went to establish himself there was named fray Francisco Reinoso; first he went to get really settled and to acquire land there. And fray Pedro de Requena went to Quauhtitlan; he had been the chaplain here at San Josef. Fray Gerónimo de Zárate went to Cholula, and fray Francisco de Gamboa came here to San Josef, along with fray Gaspar Ortiz de Arri . . . .[4] [*p. 15*]
Wednesday the 7th of June of the year 1595 was when a proclamation was made at the San Hipólito market about how we are to pay tribute in chickens in Mexico; we were assigned a tribute of 7,400-odd chickens.[5] The money to pay for them came from the four reales plus two reales each [that we pay], a real and a half each, and this tribute that we were assigned by order of the viceroy fell upon all the altepetl around. And we deliver it in the following places: // San Hipólito, / Los Desamparados, // Hospital Real, / Huitzillan, / Contaduría, / Hospital de las Bubas;[6] we were assigned [to pay] tribute in six places.
v Today, Sunday the 9th of the month of July of the year 1595, was when the church of the precious lady of Montserrat, which is in the tlaxilacalli of Tequixquipan, was moved here onto the highway, at the edge of it, the big road going straight to San Pablo, as it

5. By the general context it is highly probable that chickens were involved, but on purely linguistic grounds there is uncertainty, since *totolin* in Nahuatl and *gallina* in Spanish were both used for the hen of both the chicken and the turkey.

6. Muriel 1990, 1: 161, cites a letter from Bishop Zumárraga in 1540 mentioning an "hospital de los enfermos de bubas." (We take *bubas* to mean syphilis.) From its first location it took over the buildings of the first Colegio de Niñas Indias. Called the Hospital del Amor de Dios, it was located at the corner of Moneda and Academia.

axcan —

v Lunes a xxiii. de octubre yquac tlecoc mopilloto yn campana yn icpac campanario. yn S^{t}. Joseph. pilcac ye teotlac in quitlecahuique quimoteochihuillique in teopixque ynin yehuatzin quimochihuilli yn ganboa yhuã fr gaspar —

v Yn ipan axcan martes. a xxiiii. de octubre de 1595. a^{o}s. yquac mohuicac in tlahtohuani visurrey Don luis de velasco, yey hora tzilini yc moquixti yn quimotlalcahuilli altepetl mexico. ynic mohuicac peru[1] yn otlahtocatico macuilxihuitl ypan matlactetl metztli // auh ypan peuh in Sant. Fran^{co} . teocalli auh o panhuetz yn mohuicac auh ça ixquich in capilla in teocalcalcuitlapilli[2] yn ayamo tlami yn quimocahuilitia

v Yn ipan axcan Juebes. yc omilhuitl mani metztli de Nouiembre de 1595. a^{o}s. huel iquac yn miccaylhuitl oncan maxitico yn tepeyacac yn visurrey. Don gaspar de çuniga y Azeuedo Conde de monterrey. ompa quimopapaquiltilique yn castilteca yhuã ompa macehuato yn mexica yhuan chinampaneca // auh qui Domingo mocallaquico, [*p. 16*] Yn ihtic altepetl mexico tenochtitlan ypan a v. de nouiembre de 1595 a^{o}s. ỹ maxitico in yancuic tlahtohuani Dõ gaspar de çuniga. visurrey. ye teotlac ỹ maxitico. auh ỹ mocallaquito audi^{a}. ye tlapoyahua otzillin or̅o̅n̅

v Auh ypan in deziembre de 1595. a^{o}s. yn momanaco Cocoliztli çahuatl Salanbio ynic micohuac huel totocac yn cocoliztli ynic nepallehuiloc yztac octli heheloquiltic tletlematzin miya yn ipã yztac octli.[3] yc patihuaya auh huel cenca micohuac yn cecemilhuitl huel miec in motocaya auh yn ipan 1596. a^{o}s. amo quiz. amo caxahuac yn cocoliztli çan ye yhui totocac huel ixpoliohuac in telpochtli yn ichpochtli in tlapallihui yn huehuentzin ylamatzin piltzintli conetzintli, auh nohuian calpã. ỹ mexico moteyolcuitiliaya. y teopixq̃. yhuã tlaqualtzĩtli quitemacaya. in castilteca. yvã teyzminaya —

v axcan jueves inic .30. yc tlami metztli noviembre de 1595. años ypan ilhuitzin S. Andres yni quimocuili yauitotzin S. Anton yn padre fr. Aug^{tin} del Sp̅i̅u̅ S.^{to} teotlac yehuatzin quimomaquilico yauito ỹ Doctor hernando ortiz de hinoxosa canonigo yhuan Prouisor omoyetzticatca ỹ nican arçobispado mexico.

v Yn iquac Domingo. yn itlamian metztli deziembre de 1595. a^{o}s. yquac tlayahualoloc Sant Sebastian hualpehualoto ompa huilohuac in Sant. lazaro. acalcaltitlan huel mahuiztic yn mochiuh yxquich tlacatl ompa huia yn timacehualtin yhuan castilteca ompa motemachtilli yn totatzin fray helias de S^{t}. Juan bap^{ta}. calme totatzin ynin mochiuh ynic tlayahualoloc ypampa cocoliztli ynic moyolcehuitzinoz tt^{o}. Dios. yhuã yehuatzin yn tlaçocihuapilli Sancta maria

¶ xiii. tecpatl xihuitl 159.6. a^{o}s. yn ipan lunes yc .2. mani metztli abril. yquac yecauh in campanario S. Josep. ycpac quiquetzque in cruz tepoztli yhuan tlatenexaltilliçotl[4]

---

1. Or: and went to Peru.

2. Probably for "teocalcuitlapilli," though if *calcuitlapilli* is taken as a unit meaning "the back of a building," and *teocal-*, "church," is taken as bound to that unit, the construction is possible. The reference is no doubt to the apse.

3. *Eloquiltic* seems to be an adjectival form based on *elotl* (*elote* in Spanish), a green ear of corn on the plant, and *quilitl*, any of a variety of green plants of the type used for salads. *Tlemaitl* is a sort of ladle to carry fire in and probably could refer to a ladle or

presently appears. —

v Monday the 23rd of October was when the bell that hangs on top of the belltower at San Josef was raised up and hung; it was already afternoon when they raised it up. The friars blessed it; Gamboa did it, along with fray Gaspar. —

v Today, Tuesday the 24th of October of the year 1595, was when the lord viceroy don Luis de Velasco went away. It was three o'clock when he came out and left the altepetl of Mexico to go to Peru;[1] he ruled for five years and ten months. // In his time the church of San Francisco was begun, and it was completed when he left; he left only the chapel at the back of the church[2] unfinished.

v Today, Thursday, the 2nd day of the month of November of the year 1595, right on the Day of the Dead, the viceroy don Gaspar de Zúñiga y Acevedo, Count of Monterrey, arrived in Tepeyacac. There the Spaniards greatly feted him, and the Mexica and people of the chinampas went there to dance. // And then on Sunday he came to enter [*p. 16*] inside the altepetl of Mexico Tenochtitlan; it was on the 5th of November of the year 1595 that the new ruler don Gaspar de Zúñiga, viceroy, arrived; it was in the afternoon that he arrived, and when he entered the Audiencia [building] it was getting dark, and the bell was ringing for prayer.

v It was in December of the year 1595 that an epidemic of measles broke out, from which people died; the epidemic really raged. People were helped with white pulque; *eloquiltic tletlematzin* was drunk in white pulque,[3] with which it was cured. There were a very great many deaths; every day very many were buried. And it did not end in the year of 1596, the epidemic did not subside, but raged vigorously. Absolutely everyone perished: youths and maidens, grown men, old men and old women, and little children. And in the houses all around Mexico the religious heard confession, and the Spaniards gave people food and bled them.

v Today, Thursday the 30th, at the end of the month of November of the year 1595, on the feast day of San Andrés, Father fray Agustín del Espíritu Santo took the habit. In the afternoon Dr. Hernando Ortiz de Hinojosa, who was canon and vicar general here in the archbishopric of Mexico, came to give it to him.

v Sunday the end of the month of December of the year 1595 was when there was a procession; people started from San Sebastián and went to San Lázaro Acalcaltitlan. It was done in a very marvelous way: everybody went, we commoners and the Spaniards. Father fray Elías de San Juan Bautista, a Carmelite father, preached. The reason this was done and there was a procession was because of the epidemic, so that our lord God and the precious lady Saint Mary would be appeased.

¶ 13 Flint year, 1596. Monday, the 2nd of the month of April, was when the belltower at San Josef was finished. On top they placed an iron cross and a green coating,[4] as it

---

spoon more generally. The words refer to specific herbs used for a variety of purposes. See Sahagún 1979, Book 10, f. 105v, and Book 11, ff. 100, 136, 140, or Sahagún 1950–1982, Book 10: 151, and Book 11: 136, 143, and Cruz 1996, 1: 82–83, 98; 2: f. 58v, for *eloquilitl* and *eloquiltic*. For *tletlematzin*, see Sahagún 1979, Book 10, ff. 100, 109v, or Sahagún 1950–1982, Book 10: 142, 157, and Hernández 2000, p. 181. There is the question again of whether *iztac octli* could be white wine.

4. Whitewash or stucco? The word is based on *tenexaltia*, "to wash with lime."

xoxoctic yn iuh neztica axcan ynin yehuatzin quimochihuilli in fray fran^co^ ganboa guardian S^t^. Josepeh

v Yn ipan metztli febrero yhuan março abril yhuã xihuitl. yquac macuilcan onpeuhque in Joldadosme a la china, / gallifornia, / yancuic huehue mexico = la uaaña / a la florida yhuicpa Sant Juan de lua yc macuilcan yn yaoquiçato castilteca.

v Yn ipan ciudad mexico tenochtitlan nueua españa [*p. 17*] Ynic nohuian axcan ypan miercoles sancto.[1] yc matlaquilhuitl mani metztli de abril de 1596. años. yn itic altepetl. S. Fran^co^ S. Joseph. capilla yn quimoyacanilia[2] yxquich monesterio. ynic mexico, oncan omochiuh omotlalli centlamantli Sancta cofradia yancuic tlayahualloliztli ypilhuantzitzin in Sancto fray diego. ompa hualla in Roma quinhualmomaquilli yn Sancto Padre huel iquac quizque in miercoles Sancto yey hora[3] quizque huell oncan in Sant Josep. motecpanque yn quimoquixtilique yehuatl yn xochitepanco yc quimotlatlauhtili ytlaçotatzin dios. yhuan ynic quimonahuatili ytlaçonantzin Sancta maria motocayotia despedimiento de nuestra Señora. auh nextic yn invandera yhuan nextic yn escapulario cõtlalique ymelpan

v axcan a xiiii. de mayo 96. años. yquac momiquili Sancho Lopez secretario motocac Sant Fran^co^,

v Yn ipan lunes. a xx. de mayo de 1596. anos. ynic omochiuh tlayahualloliztli yn ipãpa ynetlecahuiliztzin tt^o^. Dios. amo oncã huillohuatza in Sant. Fran^co^. ye ompa huillohuac trinidad.[4] yhuã yn Sant. augustĩ // auh ynic omilhuitl martes. de la cassa prouesa teatinos corte quiyahuac catca yn huillohuaya auh ynic iuh mochiuh chalanaliztli ynnepantlatzinco catca in teopixque clerigos. Dominigos. Franciscos. yhuan descomunion catca yehuatl iuh quichiuh yn Don Juan de ceruantes yquac gouernador mochiuhticatca ypampa yn arçobispo

v Auh yn ipan lunes. omoteneuh a xx de mayo 96. a^o^s. yquac hualmohuicac maxitico yn obispo. xalixco Don Francisco Sanctos garcia[5] ye tlapoyahua maxitico nican mexico //. auh yn momiquilli ypan Juebes. a xxvii. de Junio 96. a^o^s. // auh yn ompa motlahtocatillito xalixco çan õxihuitl ypan nahui metztli auh ỹ motocac ynacayotzin yglesia mayor. oncã yn miquiltiticac Sancto crucifixo, [*p. 18*]

v Yn ipan axcan Sabado a xx de Julio. de 1596 años. yquac motlayahualhui Sacramento yn monjas Regina celi. yc mochalli momamal in yancuic teopancalli matlaquilhuitl yn tlanepantla[6] moyetzticatca Sacramento auh yzquilhuitl momoztlaye missa mitohuaya // auh yn oyecahuico teocalli matlacxihuitl omey yn omochihuaco yc omomamal

v el sancto hermitano. gregorio lopez. murio sabado à mediodia: que se contaron veỹte de Julio de este año de 1596. dia en que la sagrada Religion de los Padres carmelitas celebra la fiesta del Sancto Helias Primer Padre y fundador de la vida solitaria. la qual greg^o^. lopez. tan perfectamente auia seguido. viuio cinquenta y quatro años. y los treynta y tres dellos en soledad depositose el cuerpo en la yglesia de Sancta fee. junto al Altar mayor; al

1. Wednesday before Easter, not Ash Wednesday.
2. Literally "which leads"; it is not entirely clear to us whether Ch. is saying that San Francisco was the first established, was the leading monastery, or the first to have a cofradía of San Diego.

now appears. Fray Francisco de Gamboa, father guardian at San Josef, did this.

v In the months of February, March, and April of this year soldiers set out for five places: China [the Philippines], / California, / New Old Mexico, = Havana, and / Florida, in the direction of San Juan de Ulúa, the fifth place where the Spaniards went off to war.
v In the city of Mexico Tenochtitlan and [first?] in all New Spain, [*p. 17*] today Holy Wednesday,[1] on the 10th day of the month of April of the year 1596, in the altepetl, at San Francisco, at the chapel of San Josef, first of all the monasteries in Mexico City,[2] a holy cofradía was made and established, [with] a new procession of the children of the holy fray Diego. [The permission] came from Rome, the Holy Father bestowed it upon them. They came out right on Holy Wednesday, they came out for three hours.[3] Right at San Josef those who came out lined up. [On their carrying platform was a scene about how] in the flower garden [Jesus] prayed to his precious father God and said goodbye to his precious mother St. Mary, called Farewell to Our Lady. And their banner is gray, and gray is the scapular they placed on their chests.
v Today, the 14th of May of the year 96, was when Sancho López, the secretary, died. He was buried at San Francisco.
v On Monday, the 20th of May of the year 1596, when the procession on account of the ascension of our lord God was held, they did not come to San Francisco; they went to the [church of] the Trinidad[4] and to San Agustín. // And on the second day, Tuesday, it was to the Casa Profesa of the Theatines, outside the court jail, that they went. Because it was done this way, there was friction among the friars and secular priests, the Dominicans and the Franciscans, and there were excommunications. The one who did [the excommunication] was don Juan de Cervantes, at that time appointed governor on behalf of the archbishop.
v The said Monday, 20th of May of the year 96, was when the bishop of Jalisco, don Francisco Santos García, came and arrived here.[5] It was dark when he arrived here in Mexico. // And he died on Thursday the 27th of June of the year 96. // He ruled in Jalisco for only two years and four months. His body was buried in the cathedral, where the holy crucifix stands. [*p. 18*]
v Today, Saturday the 20th of July of the year 1596, was when the Sacrament went in procession to the nunnery of Regina Coeli, with which the new church building was inaugurated. For ten days the Sacrament was [publicly displayed],[6] and during that time mass was said daily. // It took thirteen years to finish and build the church until it was inaugurated.
v The holy hermit Gregorio López died Saturday at noon, on the calendar the 20th of July of this year of 1596, the day when the holy order of the Carmelite fathers celebrates the feast day of Saint Elías, first father and founder of the solitary life, which Gregorio López had followed so perfectly. He lived for 54 years, 33 of them in solitude. His body was

3. *Hora* without *tzilini*, "to ring," sometimes refers to duration rather than clock time in Ch., but possibly the meaning is "at three o'clock." See also the case on p. 42 at n. 6.
4. Stafford Poole brings to our attention that the ascension of Christ was traditionally celebrated on a Thursday, the fortieth day after Easter.
5. See also the entry for April 10, 1594, pp. 50–51.
6. Literally in the middle, presumably out in the open in the main part of the church.

lado del Euãgelio.[1]

v̲ Domingo a xxix. de Seti^{e}. 96 a^{o}s. yquac peuh ynic tlayahualoloc yn iglesia mayor. yhuan in nohuian teopan yhuan mõjas. ynpampa tlatlatlauhtiloc yn omictiloque x̄p̄ianosme yn atl itic luderanos yn temictique yhuan ingleses. tlaca in temictiq̃ auh ypampa y nohuiã ynpampa tlatlatlauhtiloc, // no yhquac nican ypan in oyecauh yn teocalli S. Pablo yn çan omotlapacho yn iglesia

auto. grande de mexico.

v̲ Yn ipan axcan Domingo yc chicueylhuitl mani metztli de diçiembre de 1596. años. yn ipan ylhuitzin de la concepcion de nuestra Señora, yquac quintlatique Judiosme tlateotocanime macuiltin, señorasme nahuintin castilteca yc ix. tlacatl. auh ỹ tlachichihualtin collotin matlactin. ix caxtilteca. yc 10tli señora yc õce quauhtanatli tẽtia oncan ce yyomiyo yc centecpãtli tlatlaq̃.

v̲ Auh colotin tlachichihualtin matlactin chiuhcnahui castilteca ce señora. yc matlactli yc once quauhtanaco tentia yyomiyo. yc centecpantli tlatlaque[2] //. Auh yn mochintin teyttitiloque yetecpantli onchiuhcnahui tlacatl

v̲ Auh yn tetlatzontequilianime in Justicia quimochihuillique ynquisidores. omentin yn tlahtoque ce tlacatl ytoca el Doctor Don Bartholome Robo guerrero ynquisidor mayor. ynic ome ytoca Don Alonso de peralta ynquisidor menor. // auh yn quinteyttitique oncan in selar callixquac huey quauhtlapechtli oncan moman yhuan yn oncan motlallique tlahtoq̃. visurrey. oydoresme. auh yn oncã motemachtilli a la china arçobispo. ytoca Don fray ignacio de millas.[3] // auh ye teotlac yn tlatilloto tlateotocanime Sant ipolito, auh yn nohuian altepetl ypan tlahtoque pipiltin yhuan al~~de~~sme mayortin corregidorti thenienteti yhuan castilteca yxquichtin cẽquiçaco yn tlachiaco tlamahuiçoco, yhuã yn ixquichtin teopixque yn nohuian moyetzticate yxquichtin mohuicatza // auh yn iquac ye quinhuica ynic miquizque yn ixquichtin

Auh y mochintin teyttitiloq̃ ynic mocenpohua. in teyttitiloq̃. 69. tlacatl. selar ỹ teyttitiloq̃. auh ye teotlac ỹ tlatiloto S.t ipolito.[4] [*p. 19*]

Teopixque yn nican moyetzticate mexico. ynic chicuetetl monasterios. huel quimololhuitiaque ynic quintlalnamictique yn tlaneltoquiliztica quinyolcuitique. auh yn ipã mochiuh yn ixiptlatzin. arçob̄p̄o. Don Juan seruãtes. auh ỹ prouisor ytoca Doctor. ortiz

—

v̲ Martes. a xxiiii. de [d]iciembre de 1596. años. yquac theniente mochiuh yn tlacatl Don Juan m̄īn quipallehui yn Don Antonio valeriano gou^{or} ypampa ohuehuetix. ochicavac yhuan aocmo tlacaqui[5] ypampa quipallehui yn ica gouernacio mexico ytencopatzinco mochiuh yn visurrey huell iquac yn visita general quichihuaco yn nican tecpan oncan yn quimacac varra yn quinahuati auh aculman catca yn iquac onxihuitl ypan macuiltetl metztli yn Jueztito acolman yn Don Juan m̄īn yn ompa tlahtocatito.

¶ 1. calli xihuitl, 1597. años. yn iquac Sant Sebastian ylhuitzin catca yn ipã lunes. a xx

1. Despite being in Spanish, this paragraph added in the margin is in Ch.'s hand. The Spanish seems perfect, although one might have expected "el" before "sabado."

2. Apparently inadvertent repetition.

3. Name unconfirmed.

buried in the church of Santa Fe, next to the main altar, on the Gospel side.[6]
v Sunday, the 29th of September of the year 96, was when processions began at the cathedral and the churches everywhere, and at the nunneries. There were prayers for the Christians who were killed across the sea. Lutherans and English people were the killers, and for that reason there were prayers everywhere for [those killed]. // Also at this time the church of San Pablo was finished; the church was just roofed over.

Great auto da fe in Mexico City.

v Today, Sunday the 8th day of the month of December of the year 1596, on the day of the Conception of Our Lady, was when they burned five Jews who were idolaters, and four Spanish women, making nine people, and ten effigies, nine Spaniards and the tenth a Spanish woman, and the bones of an eleventh that were in a wooden basket, making twenty that burned.
v There were ten effigies, nine Spaniards and one Spanish woman, making ten, and the bones of an eleventh that were in a wooden basket, making twenty that burned.[2] // And in all 69 people were displayed to the public.
v Those who passed sentence, who did justice, were the two lords inquisitors, one named dr. don Bartolomé Lobo Guerrero, inquisitor major, and the second named don Alonso de Peralta, inquisitor minor. // And [for] those whom they showed to the public, at the portal of the municipal building a large wooden platform was set up, and there the lords viceroy and Audiencia judges sat, and there the archbishop of the Philippines, named don fray Ignacio de Millas,[3] preached. // It was already afternoon when the idolaters were taken to be burned at San Hipólito. And from the altepetl all around the rulers and nobles, and alcaldes mayores, corregidores, tenientes, and Spaniards all came to assemble, look, and behold, and all the friars from everywhere came. // And when they took them to die, all the [*p. 19*] friars who are here in Mexico City in the eight monasteries went surrounding them completely, reminding them of the faith and hearing their confessions. This happened in the time of the deputy of the archbishop, don Juan de Cervantes, and the vicar general named dr. Ortiz.
As to all those who were shown to the public, those who were shown add up to 69 people; it was at the municipal building that they were displayed, and in the afternoon they were taken to be burned at San Hipólito.[4]
v Tuesday, the 24th of December of the year 1596, was when the lord don Juan Martín was made deputy. He aided don Antonio Valeriano, governor, because he had grown old and aged and no longer could hear.[5] For that reason he helped him with the governance of Mexico. It was done by order of the viceroy, right during the general inspection that he came to make here at the municipal building [of the indigenous municipality]. There he gave him the staff of office and notified him. At the time he had been in Acolman; it was two years and five months since don Juan Martín had gone to serve as judge in Acolman and rule there.

¶ 1 House year, 1597. When it was the feast day of San Sebastián, on Monday the 20th

4. This sentence is in the margin on p. 18 of the original.
5. *Tlacaqui* is literally to hear, but the meaning is probably could no longer understand, had become senile.

de henero de 1597. años. in yehuatzin totlaçotatzin fray Alonso vrbano guardian S. Franco onpohualli pesos. quinmotlaocolili in cocoxque yc mocouh tlaolli tlaxcalli marquexodi xochiqualli, xocotl,[1] quinmamacaya in cocoxque yn ipan cecentlaxillacalli ynic St. Juan yhuan Sancta maria quiyomahuiaya yn Regidoresme Doctorme yxquetzalloque ynpan yn quimitaya cocoxque yn tleyn intech monequi yn boticapatli yn intech monequia ynic patiloya auh cẽca huel totocac yn cocoliztli huel micohuac yxquichtin momiquillique yn piltzintli in ye qualtzin yn moquequetza yn mohuillana yn telpochtli yn ichpochtli yn tlapallihui yn iyolloco toquichtin yhuan cihua yhuan yn huehuetque yn illamatque huel ixpoliohuac ynic micohuac yhuan castilteca

v Yn ipan axcan Juebes. yc 13. mani metztli de março de 1597. años. yquac Sanct ipolito tzatzihuato auh ynic tzatzihuato, ypampa ynic tiquinnemitizque quaquehueque[2] molati yhuan temamani[3] yhuã carnerostin yhuan quanacame totolme yhuã necapatiloz nechichihualoz espada daga mopiaz. auh moch licencia motquitinemiz. ynic chicahuaz ayac çan nen y iuh nemiz ynic ayac. yca mocayahuaz yhuan yn cohuatequitl yn ipã Semana Sancta yhuan pasqua Resuretion ayamo mochihuaz oc moca[*p. 20*]huaz quin iquac yn oquiz pasqua mochihuaz. cohuatequitl

v Yn ipan axcan Domingo a xx de março[4] de 1597. años. ye iuh caxtolilhuitl mozcallitzino yn temaquixtiani xp̄o yquac yn ixiptlatzin Sant. Jacinto. quimolhuichihuillilique yancuicã motlayahualhui oncã quimanillico ỹn iglesia mayor. ompa quimohuiquillique yn Sancto Domĩgo. ypãpa Sancto Domingo teopixqui huey Sancto yhuã mietlamantli[5] yn quimomaquilli tto. Dios. huelitiliztli ynic quimochihuilia tlamahuiçolli yn quenamicatzintli Sant Diego. çan no iuhqui yehuatzin

v Juebes. a xiiii. de agosto. de 1597. aos. yquac hualmohuicac yn tlaçocihuapilli Sancta maria de los Remedios. yn moyetztica totoltepec yxquich tlacatl ompa yaque yn toquichtin yn cihua yn castilteca yn señoratin, tlacxipanhuique moch camdelas quitquique ynic quihualmotlahuililitiaque cequintin huel acique yn õpa totoltepec auh cequintin ça otliça quimonamiquilique yglesia mayor yn quimoquechilito auh matlaquilhuitl yn nican moyetzticatca mexico

v Yn ipan axcan viernes yc 10. mani metztli de octubre de 1597. años. yquac mocallaquique in teopixq̃. yn Sancta maria asumption la Redonda ynic mocallaquique ytencopatzinco So. padre yhuan yehuatzĩ Rey. ynic cemicac ompa moyetztiezque // auh yn iquac Domingo ypã castilli[6] onnahui mani octubre yquac tlayahualoliztica mohuicac yn tlaçocihuapilli Sancta maria mopitzinohuaya Sant Joseph. auh yquac prouincial yn fray Juan Lazcano, auh yn guardian yãcuican mohuetziltito yn mocallaqui ytoca fray diego Redon yhuã oc cequintin teopixque

v Auh yn inpan mochiuh pipiltin[7] Don miguel garcia yxtlahuel, diego Sanchez. al~~lde~~.[8] andres garcia [*p. 21*] Cohuacuech Regidortin niculas. hernandez mathias hernandez.

---

1. In view of the most usual meaning of *tlaxcalli*, the bread may well have been tortillas. The difference in meaning between *xochiqualli* and *xocotl* here is not clear to us; both are used for fruit.

2. For "quaquahueque." The word often refers specifically to oxen, and in view of the context that may be the meaning here as well.

3. Presumably primarily horses.

of January of the year 1597, our precious father fray Alonso Urbano, father guardian of San Francisco, favored the sick with forty pesos, with which was bought shelled maize, bread, caramels, and fruit.[1] They distributed it to the sick in each tlaxilacalli of San Juan and Santa María. The regidores and doctors who were appointed to look after the sick, [to get them] what they needed [in the way of] medicine from the pharmacy for their cure, took care of it personally. The epidemic raged very terribly, there was a great deal of death. Infants who can already raise themselves up quite well and crawl, youths and maidens, grown men, mature men and women, and old men and women, all died. There was total destruction by death. Also Spaniards [died].

v Today, Thursday the 13th of the month of March of the year 1597, was when an announcement was made at San Hipólito, and what was proclaimed was about how we are to maintain cattle,[2] mules and mounts,[3] and muttons, and chickens, and there will be wearing of Spanish capes and dressing [in Spanish style], and having swords and daggers, but [whoever does it] will go about carrying a license to confirm it all; no one is to go about that way just on his own, so that no one will be deceived. And rotary draft labor will no longer be done during Holy Week and the festival of the Resurrection. [*p. 20*] It will be left off for a while, and when the festival has come to an end, draft labor will be done.

v Today, Sunday the 20th of [April?][4] of the year 1597, two weeks after the resurrection of Christ the Redeemer, was when they held a feast day for the image of San Jacinto and it went in procession for the first time. They came to the cathedral to get it and took it to Santo Domingo, because [San Jacinto] was a Dominican friar and a great saint, and our lord God gave him many kinds[5] of powers to perform miracles. He was just like San Diego.

v Thursday, the 14th of August of the year 1597, was when the precious lady, Santa María de los Remedios, who is in Totoltepec, came here. Everyone went [to see her], indigenous men and women, Spaniards and Spanish women. They went on foot, all carrying candles to light her way here. Some got all the way to Totoltepec, and some just met her on the way to the cathedral where they went to lodge her. She was here in Mexico City for ten days.

v Today, Friday the 10th of the month of October of the year 1597, was when the [Franciscan] friars entered [the church and jurisdiction of] Santa María de la Asunción la Redonda. They entered by order of the Holy Father and the king, so that they will be there always. // And Sunday the 19th[6] of October was when the precious lady Santa María who was kept at San Josef was taken there in procession. At this time fray Juan Lazcano was provincial head, and the father guardian who was newly seated, the one who entered, along with some other friars, was named fray Diego Rendón.

v It happened during the period of office of the members of the [indigenous] cabildo[7] don Miguel García Ixtlahuel, Diego Sánchez, the alcalde[8] Andrés García Coacuech, [*p. 21*] and the regidores Nicolás Hernández and Matías Hernández.

---

4. March in the text. If March 13 was Thursday, the 20th cannot have been Sunday.
5. For "miectlamantli."
6. For "castolli."
7. Literally nobles.
8. It is not clear just whom the word alcalde applies to; perhaps all those named were alcaldes except for the last two.

v Domingo a vii. de diziembre de 1597. años. yc ontetl Dominica aduien[t]o in yehuatzin fray Juan de castillo yc motemachtilli quimotecaquitilli ynic momiquillique teopixque yn ompa a la china chiquacemintin Sant. Franco ypilhuantzitzin descalços teopixque ynic momiquillique Cruztitech quinmamaçohualtique ytech quitetzotzonque yn inmatzin auh yn huel momiquillique yn ipan altepetl ytocayocan xabon yhuan oc cequintin xp̄ianosme ompa tlaca yn xabon yni mochtintzitzin momiquillique quinmocepanmictillique ytencopa mochiuh yn ompa huey tlahtohuani xabon

¶ 2. tochtli xihuitl, 1598. años. miercoles. a 4. de febrero yquac mocuic nextli auh yn ihuiptlayoc viernes ypan .vi. de febrero, yn ompa St. ma. la Redonda ompa peuh ynic tlayahuallolotiuh viernestica yehuatzin quimopehualtilli in fray lope yzquierdo. yhuan fray diego Redon guardian auh yn ichicueylhuiyoc viernes ypan a xiii. de febrero, yn çan ye ypan xihuitl omoteneuh de 1598. años. yquac tlayahualoloc in Sant. Franco. ythualco cenca yc moquallanalti in Ganboa yhuã fray Juan ynic achtopa ompa peuh St. ma. auh yc cemicac peuh mochipa iuh mochiuhtiaz yn cecexiuhtica yn ipã quaresma yn viernestica tlayahualolotiaz.
v Miercoles a 4. de março de 1598. aos. yquac momiquilli yn tlahtohuani prouisor. Doctor ortiz de hinojosa ye tlapep̄etzintli catca ynic obispo moyetztiezquia quauhtemallan yntlacamo momiquiliani auh cenca huecauh yn tlahtocat in prouisortic.
v Yn ipan viernes Sancto, ypan xx. de março de 1598 años. yn Sant. Pablo. tlaca yquac quimonextilique yn tto. Dios. yn motenehua de n̄ra Señora de la Soledad. yquac conpehualtique ynic yancuican tlayahualloque ypan 3. hora teotlac ytencopatzinco y maestro doctor don Juan de seruantes arcediano Mexico yhuan gouor. ycatzinco yn teoyotica tlahtohuani don Alonso fernandez de bonilla arçobispo mexico. no yhuan ynin tlayahualloliztli ynic huel mo[*p. 22*]chiuh no yehuatzin yhuelitilizticatzinco yn tlahtohuani don gaspar de çuniga y azeuedo conde de monterrey visurey. ytlaytlaniliztica mochiuh yn hernando de S. m̄n chane S. Pablo. yhuã o cequintin[1] tlaca. auh yn ihuelitzin conde xuchmilco yn quicuito yhquac vmpa moyetzticatca. yehica ypampa in yehuantin S. Juan tlaca moyoteca quinhualixnamique contradicion quinhualchihuiliaya yn S. Pablo tlaca yhuan S. Sebastian tlaca auh yn axcan çan centlachicahuililoque. y S. Sebastian tlaca ynic huellayahualotiazq̃ cecexiuhtica ynin ca achtopa yehuantin ye quiçaya

ypan fr. franco de ganboa capillero S. Josep S. Franco.[2]
v Yn ipan Junio. de 1598. años. ytlamian yn metztli yquac quimocahuilli yn itequitzin guardian fray alonso vrbano. callitic guardian moyetzticatca auh yn conmopatilli ytoca fray Juan de Salas. auh yn fray alonso vrbano mohuicac huertas Sant Cosme,

v Yn ipan Julio yhuan xihuitl 98. aos. yquac hualla acico. amatl in yancuic mexico ynic omaxitique teopixque Sant Franco fray Alonso martinez conmissario mochiuhtia, auh yhuan ce quihuicaque Donado amaquemecan ychan ytoca franco faustino quetzalmaçatzin auh ynic hualla tlahtolli ypampa ynic huel omaxitito yn ihtic altepetl auh yn iquac ohacico tlahtolli nican mexico cenca papacohuac yhuan tlayahualloloc yn iglesia mayor,

1. For "oc cequintin."

v Sunday, the 7th of December of the year 1597, the second Sunday of Advent, fray Juan del Castillo preached about and announced to the people that friars in China [the Orient] had died, six Franciscan friars, Discalced. The way they died was that they spread their arms out on crosses and nailed their hands to them. They really died in the altepetl called Japan, and other Christians, people from there in Japan, all died. They killed them all together; it was done at the order of the great ruler in Japan.

¶ 2 Rabbit year, 1598. Wednesday, the 4th of February, was when ashes were taken, and two days later, on Friday the 6th of February, they began holding a Friday procession at Santa María la Redonda; fray Lope Izquierdo began it, along with fray Diego Rendón, the father guardian. And a week later, Friday the 13th of February, in the same said year of 1598, was when there was a procession in the patio of San Francisco. Gamboa and fray Juan [del Castillo] got very angry that it began first at Santa María, but it began being done on a permanent basis that way; there is to go along being a procession on the Friday of Lent every year.

v Wednesday the 4th of March of the year 1598 was when the lord vicar general dr. Ortiz de Hinojosa passed away; he was already chosen and was going to be bishop in Guatemala if he hadn't died. He ruled as vicar general for a very long time.

v On Good Friday, the 20th of March of the year 1598, was when the San Pablo people produced [the image of] our lord God called Nuestra Señora de la Soledad. At that time they first began to go in procession at 3 o'clock in the afternoon, by order of the master of theology dr. don Juan Cervantes, archdeacon [at the cathedral of] Mexico and governor through the ruler in divine things don Alonso Fernández de Bonilla, archbishop in Mexico. For this procession to be permitted it also *[p. 22]* had the authorization of the lord don Gaspar de Zúñiga y Acevedo, Count of Monterrey, viceroy. It was done at the petition of Hernando de San Martín, citizen of San Pablo, and some other[1] people. They went to get permission from the Count at Xochimilco, where he was at the time, because the people of San Juan, the Moyoteca, contested and contradicted the San Pablo people and the San Sebastián people. But now the San Sebastián people have been entirely confirmed in being able to go in procession every year, for they were the ones who came out first.

Fray Francisco de Gamboa was chaplain at San Josef, at San Francisco, at this time.[2]

v In June of the year of 1598, at the end of the month, was when the father guardian fray Alonso Urbano relinquished his office; he had been guardian inside the [Franciscan] establishment. One named fray Juan de Salas replaced him, and fray Alonso Urbano went to the gardens of San Cosme.

v In July of the year of 98 was when a letter came and arrived from New Mexico about how the Franciscan friars, with fray Alonso Martínez appointed as commissary, reached there, and they took along a lay brother from Amaquemecan named Francisco Faustino Quetzalmaçatzin. And when news came and arrived that they were able to reach and enter the altepetl [New Mexico], there was great rejoicing here in Mexico, and a procession was held at the cathedral.

---

2. In the margin on p. 21 of the original.

v Sabado. a x. de octubre de 1598. a^{o}s. yquac yc tzatzihuac tianquizco yn ipampa çoquicamdelero angelesme. yhuã yn tlapopochhuilloni temetzhuilli yn aço Sancto anoço Sancta yhuan yn ihetl ytech quitlalia mochi tecahualtilloc yc motlanahuatilli yn quimopiallia Sancto Oficio inquisidor, descumonion yc huetz cahualtilloque yn çoquichiuhque

v Yn ipan axcan Domingo yc vi. mani metztli de diziembre de 1598. años. yquac ye teotlac maxitico yn imomiyotzin descalço P^{e}.me. yn momiquillique xabon, yn ipan tlalli a la china ye teotlac yn maxitico teopixque quinhualmonapalhuique caxatica huallonotia auh yn ixquichtin teopixque nican moyetzticate mexico yxquichtin quimonamiquillito, yn omaxitico S^{t}. Diego. niman huehuetz tlequiquiztli. auh ynic moquillique[1] yn iuh mochiuh ompa. nauhtetl yn tilmatli. ytech tlacuilloli mopipillo, teopan S^{t}. Joseph. yxquich tlacatl quittac quimahuiço yn españoles yn timacehualtin auh ytech man[2] yn micuillo caltech yn oncan Sant Joseph, ytencopatzinco mochiuh [*p. 23*] Yn ganboa. yhuan fray Juan yquac motlapialiaya yn nican mexico / auh yn ipantzinco mochiuh callitic guardian fray Juan de Salas. auh in prouincial fray Juan de lazcano commissario general fray P^{o} de pilla fiscal francisco Sandoual Sindico. yhuan gou^{or} Don Antonio Valeriano Don Juan m̄n al~~lde~~s. me Don antonio de mendoça gabriel xuarez. auh o iuh momiquilli yn antonio ximenez

¶ iii. acatl xihuitl 1599. años. yn ipan axcan a x. de febre^{o} yquac acico tlahtolli yn ompa castilla yn ipampa omomiq̃lli cemanahuac tlahtohuani Don Philipe Segundo Rey n̄ro Señor. yn iquac machiztico nican mexico ye iuh nauhtetl metztli momiquilli yn ipan metztli yc xviii. mani octubre yn ipan xihuitl de 1598 años. yn momiquilli ompa españa // auh yn iquac oquimomachilti in ye momiquiliz. niman quimixquechilli quimonahuatilli yn itlaçopiltzin[3] çanno ytocatzin Don felipe. quimomaquilli yn itlahtocayo yn icoronatzin ynic yehuatl quipachoz cemanahuac altepetl. auh yn omotlahtocatilli Rey. onpohualxihuitl omey.____ yn oquimopachilhui altepetl cemanahuac auh yn o iuh acico tlahtolli niman yc peuh in nohuian tzilli[4] campana yn miccatepoztli yhuan nahuatilloque yn españoles.me mochintin moçauhque luto quitlallique

v Domingo a xiiii. de março de 1599. años. yqu etetl Semana quaresma. yquac mochihuazquia Joramento ynic tlatennamicozquia yn ipampa omotlahtocatlallitzino yn tlahtovani Don Philipe tercero telpochtli Rey españa yhuã nican nueua españa auh ayamo huel mochiuh çan iuh xitinohuac // auh yn mochihuato ypan viernes. a xix. de março de 1599 años. yquac ylhuitzin quiz. yn S^{t}. Joseph.

v Domingo a xxviii. de março de 1599 a^{o}s. yquac yvisperatzĩ yvigiliatzin mitto, yn huey tlahtohuani Rey Don felipe huehue yglesia mayor yn mochiuh munomento. motlalli [*p. 24*] Yquac oncan mochallanique yn teopixque yn clergios. Dominigos. Franciscos. ynic quizque tecpan Palacio yn quinequi Dominicos. yhuan Franciscos. çan inhuehuemamania yn manalozquia ynic tecpanalloque ceceyaca cecetlamantin teopixque ye nepa tlayacac quinmanaya yn teopixque S^{t}. Domingo yhuan S^{t}. Fran^{co} auh yn ome perochias belacruz. yhuan S^{t}. ta catharina martyr. ye huehuechiuhtiazqui[5] ça tlatzacuitiazquia tlayacac quin-

---

1. For "momiquilique."

2. A very speculative interpretation, requiring that the intention was "ytech moman" (and even transitive *mana* does not seem quite the right verb). The phrase "ytech man" should mean "it was taken from, based upon," etc.

v Saturday, the 10th of October of 1598, was when a proclamation was issued in the marketplace about the clay candleholders in the shape of angels and the leaded censers in the form of a male or female saint and the tobacco that they put in them. It was all forbidden. The inquisitor of the Holy Office ordered that it be observed on pain of excommunication. The potters were forbidden [to make them].

v Today, Sunday, the 6th of the month of December of the year 1598, in the afternoon, was when the bones of the Discalced fathers who died in Japan in the land of China arrived. It was afternoon when the friars arrived; they came carrying them enclosed in chests. All the religious who are here in Mexico went to meet them; when they reached San Diego, the guns were discharged. How they died[1] and what happened there was painted on four cloths which were hung at the church of San Josef; everyone saw and admired them, the Spaniards and we commoners. And what was painted [was put?][2] on the wall at San Josef. It was done at the order of [*p. 23*] Gamboa, and fray Juan was in charge at that time here in Mexico. / And it was done in the time of the internal guardian fray Juan de Salas, the provincial head fray Juan de Lezcano, the commissary general fray Pedro de Pila, the fiscal and syndic Francisco Sandoval, and [in the indigenous municipal government] the governor don Antonio Valeriano [with the aid of] don Juan Martín, and the alcaldes don Antonio de Mendoza and Gabriel Juárez; Antonio Jiménez had died.

¶ 3 Reed year, 1599. Today, the 10th of February, was when word arrived from Spain about how the universal ruler don Felipe the Second, the king our lord, had passed away. When it became known here in Mexico, it had been four months since he had died; it was on the 18th of the month of October in the year of 1598 that he died there in Spain. // When he knew that he was about to die, he appointed and notified his legitimate child,[3] likewise named don Felipe, and gave him his rulership and crown so that he would govern the universal altepetl. And the king ruled for forty-three years that he governed the universal altepetl. And when the news had come, pealing[4] of the bells began everywhere, and the Spaniards were all notified to fast and wear mourning clothes.

v Sunday, the 14th of March of the year 1599, the third week of Lent, was when the oath was going to be taken in which [the cross] was to be kissed because the ruler don Felipe the Third, the younger, was installed as king in Spain and here in New Spain, but it could not be done yet, but was canceled. // And it was done on Friday the 19th of March of 1599, when the feast day of San Josef was celebrated.

v Sunday the 28th of March of the year 1599 was when the evening rites and vigil of the great ruler and king don Felipe the elder were said; it was done at the cathedral, and the catafalque was set up. [*p. 24*] At that time the priests—the secular priests, Dominicans, and Franciscans—argued. On leaving the palace the Dominicans and Franciscans wanted things to be arranged in the old way as to how they were lined up: there at the head of the separate groups of friars and priests they used to put the Dominican and Franciscan friars in front, and the two parishes Vera Cruz and Santa Catarina Mártir were going to [do it in the ancient fashion];[5] they were just going to come last. In front they put the said Do-

3. Literally precious child.
4. For "tzilini" or possibly "tzilin."
5. The verb seems to lack an object prefix, and the sense is far from certain.

mãca yn omoteneuhque teopixque Dominigos Fran^{cos}. auh yehuatl yc mochallanique yc çan ixneliuhque yn ontlamãtin teopixque auh yn oc cequintin yn izqui tlamãtin nepapã teopixq̃. mexico moyetzticatca atle yc tlachallanique çan qualli moquixtique ynic motecpantiaque yehuantzitzin motlayacatilitiaque yn Padreme descalços S^{t}. Fran^{co} ypilhuãtzitzin tlayacac mantiaque ynic callacohuac yglesia mayor. yn ipan in mochiuh ye omito Domingo ye teotlac yc quixonhuac yn palacio, auh ymoztlayoc ypã lunes yn mochiuh yn horra ymissatzin auh nohuian huallaque yn altepetl ypan moyetzticate teopixque yn ipan motlatlatlauhtillico yn huey tlahtohuani Rey.

v̲ Domingo de ramos. a 4. de abril de 1599. años. yquac mochalli in letablo Sant. augustin ynic moman cenca mahuiztic magen[1] yn iuh neztimani axcan moch tlacamani[2] yn Sanctosme yhuan in Corona pilar

v̲ Yn ipan axcan Juebes yc ix. mani metztli de Setiembre de 1599. años. yquac hualla in Don Jeronimo Lopez ynic gou^{or}. Juez mochihuaco nican mexico. xaltocan ychan tlatilolco, tlapiaya, auh yn Don Juan. m̄īn̄, nican tlapiaya, auh compatlaco niman yc ya tlatilolco ompa tlahtocatito gou^{or} Jueztito ompa,

¶ iiii. tecpatl xihuitl, 1600. años. yn ipan in xihuitl de mill y seyscientos yn ipan yancuic metztli de henero yquac ontzintic yn alcaldesme nahuintin motlallique cecen ixquetzalloque yn inauhcampayxti

oc cequintin quimachiyotia ypan in ỹ hualla don Geronimo lopez gou^{or}. mexico ypan metztli octubre de 1600 a^{o}s. amo nelli ỹ ca ye tlapic neltitica ynic hualla mexico[3] [*p. 25*]

v̲ Sant. Juan motlalli al~~lde~~. Juan bonifacion —

v̲ Sant. Pablo. motlalli al~~lde~~ hernando garcia —

v̲ Sant. Sebastian motlalli al~~lde~~ Don Antonio de mẽdoça

v̲ Sancta maria motlalli al~~lde~~ Diego Sanchez —[4]

v̲ martes a xv. de febrero de 1600 a^{o}s. yn Don Juan gano de moteuhcçoma[5] español, quinexti yn moteuhcçomatzĩ catca ypan quixeuh in Don hernando de aluarado teçoçomoctzin.[6] quinapalloque, yca andas. yhuan balio yc quicaltitiaque yxpan[7] macehuallotia. ynic hualla tecpan quiyahuac yxpan^{co} necico in Visurrey _____ yhuan mahuiltique castilteca

v̲ Domingo yc centetl Domingo quaresma ypan. cẽpohualilhuitl mani metztli de febrero yhuã xihuitl de 1600. años. in yehuatzin temachtiani fr. Juan de torquemada quimochihuilli quimoteyttitilli neyxcuitilli tomachiyouh yn timacehualtin yn tonemiliz yuh tlamito quaresma in vi tetl Domingo auh yn izquitetl viernes ynic tlayahualoloc cecentlamãtli neztia yn itlayhiyohuiliztzin totemaquixticatzin x̄p̄o. // axcan y[pan] viernes ye yohua ynic 25. mani metztli de hebrero de 1600. a^{o}s. ypan ylhuitzin S. Mathias Apostol omomiquilli yn tlayectenehualli tettatzin fr. Sebastian de Aparicio. teopixqui S Fran^{co} quateçontzin cuitlaxcoapan S. Fran^{co}. momiquilli. ynin chane españa yn oncan

1. It may be that in Nahuatl *imagen*, "image," could refer to a whole ensemble. The pair *retablo imagen* occurs more than once in Nahuatl documents.

2. From one or two instances in mundane documents it begins to appear that the meaning of *tlacamani* is in the round, but certainty has not been achieved. Note that Luis Reyes translates the similar "tlacaycatiuh" in the so-called "Anales de Juan Bautista" with a reference to sculpture (Reyes García 2001, pp. 230–31).

minican and Franciscan friars. And what they argued about was that the two groups of friars were just mixed in together. All the other different groups of friars who were here in Mexico City argued about nothing, but came out well as to how they went lined up; the Discalced fathers, children of San Francisco, led the way, they went in front entering the cathedral. This happened, as was said, on Sunday; in the afternoon was the departure from the palace, and the next day, Monday, his [the king's] honors and mass were held, and the friars who are in the various altepetl everywhere came; they came to pray for the great ruler the king.

v Palm Sunday, the 4th of April of the year 1599, was when the altarpiece at San Agustín was inaugurated; very splendid images[1] were set up, as they appear today, with the saints all like people,[2] and the columns or pillars.

v Today, Thursday the 9th of the month of September of the year 1599, was when don Gerónimo López came; he came appointed as governor and judge here in Mexico. He is from Xaltocan, and had been in charge in Tlatelolco. Don Juan Martín was in charge here, and [don Gerónimo] came to replace him, whereupon he went to Tlatelolco to rule and serve as governor and judge there.

4 Flint year, 1600. In the year of 1600, in the new month of January, was when it began that four alcaldes were put in office. One was chosen for each of the four parts [of Mexico Tenochtitlan]:

Others record that don Gerónimo López, governor in Mexico, came in the month of October of the year 1600. It is not true; it is made up. It is true that he came to Mexico [in September of 1599].[3] [*p. 25*]

v In San Juan Juan Bonifacio was installed as alcalde. —

v In San Pablo Hernando García was installed as alcalde. —

v In San Sebastián don Antonio de Mendoza was installed as alcalde.

v In Santa María Diego Sánchez was installed as alcalde.[4] —

v On Tuesday, the 15th of February of the year 1600, don Juan Cano de Moctezuma,[5] a Spaniard, produced [a representation of] the late Moteucçoma. Don Hernando de Alvarado Tezozomoctzin[6] impersonated Moteucçoma. They carried him on a platform and went sheltering him with a canopy. In his presence[7] people went dancing as he came in front of the palace. They came to appear before the viceroy _____, and the Spaniards celebrated.

v Sunday, the first Sunday in Lent, on the 20th day of the month of February in the year 1600, the preacher fray Juan de Torquemada held and showed [a play or spectacle] as a model for the lives of us commoners. Lent lasted for six Sundays, and each Friday in procession one of the passions of Christ our redeemer went along being shown. // Today, on Friday evening, the 25th of the month of February of the year 1600, on the feast day of San Matías the apostle, the lauded father fray Sebastián de Aparicio, a Franciscan lay friar, passed away. He died at San Francisco in Puebla. He was from Spain, and was born

3. Added in the lower left margin.
4. The four great parts are in their normal order.
5. Although Ch. writes the name in his usual fashion within the Nahuatl tradition, in Spanish don Juan used the form Moctezuma.
6. The famous interpreter and historian in Nahuatl and Spanish.
7. Apparently meaning going along before him.

huel motlacatilli ypan altepemaytl[1] ytocayocan Gudiña. yn ipan tlahtocayotl Galicia. yn ipan yeyantli de viedma. yntlahuillanalpan yntech pohui yn tlahtoq̃ condes de Monterrey. yn ittatzin ytoca catca Juan de Aparicio. auh yn inantzin ytoca Teresa del Prado tlalchiuhq̃.

—

v̲ Miercoles. a iii. de mayo. de 1600. a^{o}s. huel ipan yn Sancta velacruz ylhuitzin yquac acico yn itlahtollo. arçobispo. Don alonso fernandez bonilla ynic ompa. omomiquilli perũ, auh niman yc peuh in nohuian tzillin campana yn miccatepoztli achi quezquilhuitl in tlatzillin auh çatepã missa ypan mito yn iglesia mayor.

v̲ axcan yc 15. mani metztli Setiembre de 1600 a^{o}s. yquac nican mexico maxitico Eȳtin. S. Benito. teopixq̃. fr. bernardino. Prior yhuan fr. Juan de la vitoria yhuã fr. domingo monserate motlalitzinoco[2]

v̲ Yn ipan axcan Domingo yc caxtolli omome mani metztli de Setiembre de 1600 años. yquac motlallique mõjastĩ in de las vobas hospital quiahuac ompa hualquizque yn concepcion oncan quinhualhuicaque yn iglesia mayor. auh yn ocenquizque tlahtoq̃.[3] yhuã yxquichtin castilteca niman ye ic netecpano. tlayahualoliztica quinmocahuilliton yn oncan yancuic monasterio Sancta ynes. ynĩ monjastin ypilhuantzitzinhuan totlaçonantzin con[*p. 26*]ception yn onca mohuetziltito auh ynin monasterio yehuatl ytlaquetzal ychan catca in diego cauallero,

v̲ Domingo a xii. de nouiembre de 1600. a^{o}s. yquac ylhuitzin quiz in San. Diego. huel mahuiztic ynic tlachichihualloc auh quimotlalilique tlayxpã[4] yn inemiliztzin yn otlica yxtlahuacã ylhuicac tlaxcaltzintli quinhualmomaquilli yn tt^{o}. Dios. angelesme quihualcuiq̃. oncã quimoqualtique yn ixtlahuacan // auh ynin tlaxcalli yquac moteochiuh. yn iuh yehuatzin S^{t}. nicolas de tolentino moteochiuhtiuh ytlaxcaltzin cexiuhtica çan no iuh mochihuaz yn ipan ylhuitzin S^{t}. Diego

v̲ Yn ipan axcan lunes. yc ii. once[5] mani metztli deziembre. de 1600. a^{o}s. yquac momiquilli yn tlacatl yn Don Juã m̅ī̅n̅. gou^{or}. Juez. tlatilolco moyetzticatca, ce xihuitl. yhuã nahui metztli, yn motlahtocatilli. tlatilolco. auh ymomextin. yn inamictzin. yn ompa momiquillique ymomextin. ompa toctitoc yn innacayo. auh chicoccã yn oquipacho altepetl, calli ymanyan, tlatilolco, xochmilco / cuitlahuac, acolman mexico, yc chicoccã in tlatilolco. oppa omilochti yc oppa yn yn axcan ompa omomiquilli

v̲ Yn ipan omoteneuh. lunes in metztli yhuã xihuitl yquac ce piltzintli quimozcalili in S^{t}. Diego. huey tlamahuiçolli yn mochiuh. yn iquac omomiquilli niman quihualhuicac yn inantzin in teopan yxpã quimotequilli in S^{t}. Diego. cenca choquiztica quimotlatlauhtilli yn itlacotzin[6] dios. S^{t}. Diego. auh yn oquimohuelcaquiti yn tlatlatlauhtilli. niman mozcalli yn piltzintli yn omozcalli nimã yc peuh ye ic tlatzitzillicac yxquichtin quimottilique yn teopixque. yhuan castilteca,

v̲ Auh yn ipan .xiiii. deziembre de 1600 a^{o}s. Juebes. oc ceppa ce quimozcalili piltzintli. in S^{t}. Di^{o}. cenca no mahuiçoloc. yn piltontli yn mozcalli,

v̲ Auh çanno ypan in deziembre de 1600 a^{o}s. [*p. 27*] Ye iuh tihuallaci, ytlacati-

---

1. Literally, altepetl branch.
2. This portion is in the left margin.
3. Ch. often means the members of the indigenous cabildo of Mexico Tenochtitlan by this word, but perhaps Spanish dignitaries are intended as well or instead.

right in the village[1] named Gudiña in the kingdom of Galicia, in the area of Biedma, which belonged to and was a dependency of the rulers who were Counts of Monterrey. The name of his father was Juan de Aparicio, and his mother was named Teresa del Prado; they were workers on the land.

v Wednesday, the 3rd of May of the year 1600, right on the feast day of the Santa Vera Cruz, was when news arrived about the archbishop don Alonso Fernández de Bonilla, that he had died in Peru. Thereupon the bells began to peal everywhere. The pealing went on for quite a few days, and afterward a mass was said on his behalf in the cathedral.

v Today, the 15th of the month of September of the year 1600, was when three Benedictine friars arrived here in Mexico; fray Bernardino, the prior, and fray Juan de la Victoria and fray Domingo de Montserrat came to establish themselves.[2]

v Today, Sunday the 17th of the month of September of the year 1600, was when nuns established themselves outside the Hospital de las Bubas. They came from [the nunnery of] la Concepción and were brought to the cathedral. And the rulers[3] and all the Spaniards gathered together, whereupon the order was arranged by which they were going to take them in procession to the new nunnery of Santa Inés. These nuns who went to settle there were children of our precious mother of Concepción. [*p. 26*] And this convent was erected by and had been the home of Diego Caballero.

v Sunday, the 12th of November of the year 1600, was when the feast day of San Diego was celebrated. It was really marvelous how everything was adorned. In front[4] they put his life. Traveling through the desert, our lord God gave them bread from heaven; angels brought it, and they ate it in the desert. // And this bread was blessed at that time; it will be done on the feast day of San Diego the same way as the bread of San Nicolás de Tolentino goes along being blessed each year.

v Today, Monday the 11th[5] of the month of December of the year 1600, was when the lord don Juan Martín, who was governor and judge at Tlatelolco, passed away. He ruled at Tlatelolco for a year and four months. And the bodies of both of them, him and his spouse, who both died there, lie buried there. There were seven places where he governed an altepetl, in Calimaya, Tlatelolco, Xochimilco, / Cuitlahuac, Acolman, and Mexico. The seventh place was Tlatelolco; he returned a second time. This was the second time, when he died there now.

v The said Monday, [the same] month and year, was when San Diego revived a small child; it was a great miracle that was performed. When [the child] passed away, its mother brought it to the church and laid it before San Diego. With heavy weeping she prayed to the beloved[6] of God, San Diego. And when he had approved her prayer, the child came back to life. After it had revived, the bells began to peal everywhere because of it. All the friars and Spaniards saw [the miracle].

v And on the 14th of December of the year 1600, a Thursday, San Diego brought a child back to life again. The child who was revived was greatly marveled over as well.

v Likewise in December of the year 1600, [*p. 27*] as we arrived at the birth of our lord

4. Of the procession? Of San Diego's carrying platform? Stafford Poole informs us that this feast was normally held on November 13th.

5. Ch. would hardly use the Spanish word *once* here. Most likely "once" means "plus one" even though the implied word "ten" is not present. The "ii" itself means eleven.

6. For "itlaçotzin."

lizpantzinco tt^{o}. Dios. yquac momiquilli yn tlahtohuani maestrescuela Don Sancho Sanchez de muñon huey teopixqui latinmatini catca clerigo.

¶ v. calli xihuitl. 1601. años. yquac ypan in motlallique alcaldesme nican mexico. macuiltin omochiuhque —
v̲ Martin xuarez. cozcaquauh fiscaltia[1] S^{t}. Juan ychan
v̲ Miguel Sanchez. hueton Regidortia S^{t}. Juan ychan —
v̲ Don Bartholome fran^{co} xochiquen yc oppa alldetic. S^{t}. Pablo ychan :

v̲ Don miguel Sanchez yc vi. pa alldetic. atzaqualco ychã
v̲ Gabriel xuarez yc oppa alldetic. S^{t}. ta maria ychan
v̲ ypan in yn xihuitl omoteneuh ypan otlamico yn itlacatilizxiuhtzin temaquixtiani. ohacic nauhtzonxihuitl yc onpehua yn axcan yancuic xihuitl Seisciẽtos. y vno. años.
v̲ yn ipan lunes. yc viii. mani metztli de henero yquac momiquilli oydor. balderama ycxipoçahuac quitequillique yn Doctoresme. ynic patiz auh aocmo huel patic yc momiquilli S^{t}. Domingo motocac
v̲ yn ipan axcã Sabado a iii. de febrero. de 1601. in yehuatzin cenca mahuiztililoni huey Sancto Sant. blas. obispo. martyr yquac tzintic peuh yn ilhuitzin quiztiaz cecexiuhtica pialoz ayac tlatequipanoz. auh pregones yc mochiuh auh tlayayahualoloc[2] prossesion mochiuh ompa hualpeohuac yn iglesia mayor. ynic oncan hualhuilohuac Sancta vera cruz. ypampa ca ompa mopia yn ixiptlatzin auh yxquichtin tlayahualloque yn tlahtoque oydores. alldes de corte hordinario, yhuan Regidores. ciudad. celar. auh yn omoteneuh tlayahualloliztli ynic mochiuh çan nican[3] ytlanahuatiltica yn prouisor. ypampa yquac mãca cocoliztli tozcamiahualiztli,[4] mochi tlacatl yuh mochiuh [*p. 28*]
v̲ Yn ipan cemilhuitl Domingo yc xi. mani metztli de febrero de 1601. a^{o}s. yn itlaçopilhuantzitzin Sancta clara cihuateopixque yquac mohuetzitique yn ayoticpac yancuic monasterio, yn ichan cihuapilli Doña Catharina de peralta ycnocihuatl yc tlahuenchiuh yn ical ypampa amo pilhua yehica ynic teopantli mochiuh yn icaltzin chiquacemintin yn hualmohuicaque monjastin ce ytocatzin Doña ana Sotelu de moteuhcçoma yn fundadoras. mochihuaco auh yeppa cequintin oncan cate motenehua Beatasme auh cenca mahuiztic ynic tlayahualoloc ynic quinmocahuilico nohuian huallaq̃ yn teopixq̃. yn izquican moyetzticate / auh yc motocayoti yn teopan La visitacion descalças.
v̲ Yn axcan ypan cemilhuitl Domingo. yc nahuitl[5] mani metztli de março de 1601. a^{o}s. yquac momamal ynĩteocaltzin Sant Fran^{co}. teopixque in yancuic teocalli yece oc miec yn itlacapa ynic mocencahuaz çan oc cenca yehuatl yn omochalli in letablo huel mahuiztic tlacenpanahuia ynic mahuiztic in tablero,[6] yn pilar corona yn cassamiento tabernacolo yn Sanctome hitic mani yn incaltzĩ yn corona centecpantli oncastolli once. auh ça iuh nahuilhuitl mocuiz nextli[7] yn teocalchalliloc in teocalmamalihuac — auh nohuian hualmohuicq̃. in teopixque yhuan yn tlahtoque visurrey. Oydoresme —
v̲ yehuatzin yn visurrey. Don Gaspar de çuñiga // alldes. de corte

1. The word "fiscaltia" is preceded by a smear or blot which appears to contain a letter or letters. Their appearance seems to exclude the otherwise tempting "ofiscaltia."
2. For "tlayahualoc," unless the rare reduplication of *ya* is intentional.
3. I.e., not by an order from Spain.
4. We have not been able to identify the disease in question.

God, was when the lord maestrescuela don Sancho Sánchez de Muñón, a great priest and knower of Latin, who was a secular priest, passed away.

¶ 5 House year, 1601. In this [year] when alcaldes were installed here in Mexico, five were appointed:
v Martín Juárez Cozcaquauh, who had been serving as fiscal,[1] from San Juan;
v Miguel Sánchez Huenton, who had been serving as regidor, from San Juan;
v Don Bartolomé Francisco Xochiquen, who became alcalde for the second time, from San Pablo;
v Don Miguel Sánchez, who became alcalde for the sixth time, from Atzaqualco;
v Gabriel Juárez, who became alcalde for the second time, from Santa María.
v In the said year the birth year of the Savior came to an end; 1600 years were completed, with which the present new year of 1601 begins.
v Monday, the 8th of the month of January, was when the Audiencia judge Valderrama passed away. He had a swollen foot that the doctors cut off for healing, but he was no longer able to heal, so that he died. He was buried at Santo Domingo.
v Today, Saturday the 3rd of February of 1601, was when it was instituted and begun that when the feast day of the very reverend great saint San Blas, bishop and martyr, will go along being celebrated and observed each year, no one is to work. Proclamations were made about it, and there was a procession,[2] beginning at the cathedral and coming to Santa Vera Cruz, because his image is kept there. And the lords civil and criminal judges of the Audiencia, and the alcaldes ordinarios and regidores of the [Spanish] city all went in procession. It was done just here[3] by order of the vicar general, because at that time there was an epidemic of throat [inflammation?];[4] it happened that way [with] everyone. [*p. 28*]
v A Sunday, the 11th of the month of February of the year 1601, was when the nuns who are the precious children of Santa Clara settled at a new convent in Ayoticpac, the home of the lady doña Catarina de Peralta, a widow. She made an offering of her house because she was childless, wherefore her house became a church. Six nuns came; the one named doña Ana Sotelo de Moctezuma came as one of the founders. Previously there were some of those called *beatas* there. And the procession with which they brought them was very splendid; the friars came from everywhere, from all the different places where they are. / And the church was named La Visitación [of the] Discalced nuns.
v Today, a Sunday, the 4th[5] day of the month of March of the year 1601, was when the church of the Franciscan friars, the new church, was inaugurated, although there was still much along the side of it to be finished; only the altarpiece especially was inaugurated, very magnificent; exceedingly splendid were the [woodwork],[6] the pillars or columns, and the casing of the tabernacle, with thirty-six saints inside their housings, [on] their columns. Four days before ashes were to be taken[7] the inauguration of the church occurred. From everywhere came the friars and the lords viceroy and Audiencia judges.
v The viceroy was don Gaspar de Zúñiga. // Criminal judges of the Audiencia:

5. For "nahuilhuitl."
6. A *tablero* could be a finished plank or several, a counter with an edging, a board for playing chess and other such games, etc. Just after this, "corona" is Ch.'s rendering of Spanish *columna* (then often written "coluna"), with common letter substitutions.
7. Four days before Ash Wednesday.

v Maldonado presidente —
v Don Fran^co dello —
v Don Juan funsega —
v Sanctiago de rriego. —
v el Doctor villagran[1] —
v el lliceciado Don P^o. de otalora
v Don marcos guerrero —
v el lliceciado. ayala —
v el lliceciado Diego nuñez morquecho —

v Auh yn mexico tlahtoque Don Antonio Valeriano. huehue Don Jeronimo lopez gou^or. mexico, Don Juan bap^ta. tlahtohuani gou^or tlatilolco, al~~ld~~esme mexico mīn xuarez [*p. 29*] Miguel Sanchez. Don Bartholomẽ. Don miguel Sanchez. Gabriel xuarez. yhuã fiscal. Joseph xuarez. antonio Raphael sindico escriuano yglesia. fran^co Sanchez corregidor. mexico.[2]

v Auh yn teopixcatlahtoque yn inpantzinco omochiuh omomamal teocalli. fray P^o. de pila. conmissario. fr Bonauentura de paredes prouincial. fray P^o. de la cruz. guardian. fray fran^co de ganboa guardian S^t. Joseph. fr. Juan de torquemada temachtiani, yhuan fr. fran^co hormendia presidente.[3] yehuantin in yn imixpan^co, mochiuh. ynic mochalli teocalli yn oyecahuico teocalli. matlacxihuitl omome // auh ye iuh nauhpohualxihuitl ypã onxihuitl yhuan õtetl metztli onoque yn españolesme. ynic acico mexico. nican ynic tlalmacehuaco

v Ynquisicion Sancto oficion yn omochiuh yn quimochihuillique yehuantin ynquisidores. ypan castolli onnahui quaresma neçahuallo yn auto omochiuh[4] —

v Sabado. yc xxiiii. mani metztli. de março de 1601. años. yn icruztzin. temaquixtiani ompa hualla Sancto Domingo, oncan quimoquechillico yn quauhtlapechticpac yn oncan teyttitiloque. yn tlateotocani yn atlaneltocani yxquichtin ompa cenquizque in teopixque ynic chicuetetl hordenes. hualmotecpãtzinotiaque ynic quimanilito Sancta cruz. teopixque quihualmonapalhuitiaque yhuã sesario. yc quihualmopopochhuilitiaque yn cruz.

v Auh yn ipan axcan Domingo. ypan ylhuitzin yn tlaçocihuapilli ynic quimotlapalhuico. Angel S^t. gabriel. yn motenehua anunciacion yc xxv. mani metztli de março de 1601 a^os. yquac omochiuh ỹ sancta yglesia yJusticiatzĩ y motenehua auto. Sancto oficion ynquisicion, oncan yn tecpan quiahuac portales. motlalli quauhtlapechtli yn õcan motlallitzinoque tlahtoque ynquisidores. yhuã visurrey yhuã oc cequintin tlahtoque yhuan teopixque auh yxquichtin tlamahuiçoco. yn altepetl ypan tlaca [*p. 30*] Yhuan yn españolesme yn nohuian cate cenquiçaco yn estacia. tlaca.[5]

v Auh yn teyttitiloque, castolloce çan collotin. tlachichihualtin, moch amaquahuitzeque tlatleycuilolli, yn quihualmaquitiaque. moch tlahtolli yn imelpan. huallicuiliuhtia, yehuan yn omicque yhuan cequintin ocholloque auh yn imomiyo. caxatica quinhualnapalloque, no tlatleycuillolli caxa yhuã miquiztzontecontlacuillolo, moch tlatilloque yquac quitlatique yn iyomiyo Antonio machado, sastre. yhuan ynmaestro catca yn Judiosme. yn iyomiyo ompa quiquixtito yn Sant. augustin teopan auh yn huel tlaca. tlatlaque yeyntin.

1. Maldonado is apparently licenciado Antonio Maldonado, Santiago del Riego don Domingo de Santiago del Riego, Doctor Villagrán Doctor Francisco Alonso de Villagrán, licenciado Ayala licenciado Andrés de Ayala. See Schäfer 1934; Martínez 1948; Monroy Castillo 1987–88.

2. Of the indigenous corporation? Or of the entire district?

v Maldonado, the president [of the Audiencia]. —
v Don Francisco Tello. —
v Don Juan Fonseca. —
v Santiago del Riego. —
v Doctor Villagrán.[1] —
v Licenciado don Pedro de Otalora.
v Don Marcos Guerrero. —
v Licenciado Ayala. —
v Licenciado Diego Núñez Morquecho. —

v And the [indigenous] rulers in Mexico: don Antonio Valeriano the elder, don Gerónimo López, governor in Mexico; don Juan Bautista, lord governor in Tlatelolco; alcaldes in Mexico, Martín Juárez, [*p. 29*] Miguel Sánchez, don Bartolomé, don Miguel Sánchez, Gabriel Juárez, and the fiscal Josef Juárez, the syndic and notary of the church Antonio Rafael, and Francisco Sánchez, corregidor in Mexico.[2]

v And the authorities among the friars in whose time it happened that the church was inaugurated were: fray Pedro de Pila, commissary; fray Buenaventura de Paredes, provincial head of the order; fray Pedro de la Cruz, father guardian of the monastery; fray Francisco de Gamboa, father guardian at San Josef; fray Juan de Torquemada, preacher; and fray Francisco Ormendia, president;[3] it was in their presence that it happened that the church was inaugurated. The church was finished in thirteen years. // And it had been 82 years and two months that the Spaniards were present, since they arrived in Mexico coming to acquire the land.

v What happened [at?] the Holy Office of the Inquisition, that the inquisitors did, on the nineteenth day of Lent, [when] there was fasting, was that an auto da fe was held.[4]

v Saturday, the 24th of the month of March of the year 1601, the cross of the Savior was brought from Santo Domingo and set up on top of a wooden platform where the idolaters and unbelievers were displayed. All the religious of eight orders gathered there, coming lined up to go get the holy cross. Friars came carrying it, with a censer with which they wafted incense smoke on the cross.

v And today, Sunday, on the feast day of the precious Lady, when the angel San Gabriel came to greet her, called the Annunciation, the 25th of the month of March of the year 1601, was when the justice of the holy church, called an auto da fe, [of] the Holy Office of the Inquisition, was held; outside the palace, at the arcades, a wooden platform was set up, where the lords inquisitors and the viceroy and other lords and friars took their seats. And all the people from the altepetl [the ones in the whole surrounding area] came to watch, [*p. 30*] and also the Spaniards who are everywhere around, the people of the estancias,[5] assembled.

v Of those who were displayed sixteen were only effigies; they all had peaked paper [caps], and wore things branded on them; they all came with legends written on their chests [of what they had done wrong]. [The effigies were of] those who had died, and of some who had fled. And they came carrying their bones in chests; the chests were also branded and bore death's heads painted on them. All [the effigies and bones] were burned. At that time they burned the bones of Antonio Machado, a tailor, who was also teacher of

3. At present the name is unconfirmed, nor is it yet known what he was president of.

4. This whole entry is more than usually obscure and uncertain. Perhaps it is incomplete. Perhaps it is intended as a title for what follows.

5. Probably meaning estancias in the sense of the rural Spanish properties, but possibly also relating to "estancia" as an outlying indigenous settlement.

nahuintin yezquia çan mocauh yn ce tlacatl huehuenton quihto ca oc onca yn tleyn quimocuitiz. yc oc ceppa quicuepque ynquisiciõ

v Yhuan yquac oncan teyttitiloc yn isabel machada Judia ychpochtli ychpoch catca yn omoteneuh antonio machado sastre Judio. yhuan oncan teyttitiloq̃. ce clerico. ytoca plata, yhuã ce monja. yhuan ce beata,
v Yn ipan axcan miercoles. yc matlaquilhuitl once mani metztli. abril de 1601. a^{os}. yquac quimotlaxillique yn huey cruz. cenca huiac catca yn icaca Sant. Fran^{co}. ythualco yn quimoquechilitiuh. totlaçotatzin fray Pedro de gante quateçontzin maestro, yhuan yn matlactin omomentin teopixque yn achto yancuican. maxitico nican mexico, auh yn tlaquetztli ypan xihuitl. de mill 531. años. auh yn huehue xiuhxiuhtlapohualli[1] matlactlomey acatl, ye iuh matlacxihuitl omey acico yn españolesme yn iquac moquetz auh yn oycaca in cruz. yepohualxihuitl ypan chiuhcnauhxihuitl, ypan hetetl metztli, ypan matlaquilhuitl once mani metztli, abril, auh yn ohuetzico yn omotlaz. ye iuh nauhpohualxihuitl ypan onxihuitl yhuan yey metztli ypan matlaquilhuitl once cahuitl yn acico. españoles. / miyequintin in tlahtoque yn ipan omicque virreyesme. Oydoresme. yn otlahtocatico. mexico yhuan in mexica tlahtoque pipiltin yhuan ob̄p̄ome, [*p. 31*] Yhuan tlahtocateopixque yn omonemiltico nican mexico tenochtitlan
v viernes a iiii. de mayo de 1601 años. yquac momiquilli oydor. ytoca Don fran^{co} tello, S^{t}. augustin yn motocac ynacayotzin
v Domingo. a vi. de mayo de 1601 a^{os}. yquac nez yn ixiptlatzin tlaçocihuapilli S^{t}ta maria yehuatl ynic momiquillitzino motenehua tranleo.[2] tepetlacalco monoltitoc. viernes yn quimoteochihuillique auh yn ipan Domingo. omoteneuh yxquich tlacatl quimotennamiquilli yn icxitzin yhuan ymatzin tlahtoq̃ al~~ld~~es. regidores. yhuã yn ixquichtin timacehualtin[3] / auh ynin tlaçocihuapilli yehuatzin quimonextili yn totatzin fray fran^{co} de ganboa

¶ vi. tochtli xihuitl 1602. años. ypan in yn xihuitl Juebes. a xxv. de abril. yquac momamal yn ospital del esp̄ū Sancto p̃ethecostes tlayahualoloc. yglesia mayor. hualpeohuac, oncan quimotlallilico Sacramento oncã huitza visurrey. yhuan yxquichtin tlahtoque oydores. yc mochalli. yc momamal in teocalli
v yn ipan axcan Domingo yc xiii. mani metztli de octubre de 1602. a^{os}. yquac maxitico arçobispo. Don fray garcia de S^{t}.ta maria de m̃edoça y Çuñiga[4] Sant. Jeronimo teopixq̃. ye teotlac yn mocallaquico mexico.
v axcan miercoles. yc xi. mani metztli ____ de mill. 602. años. in tlahtohuani visurrey Don gaspar yquac tlatilolco mohuicaya[5] ypampa cohuatequitl quimonemilili ynic polihuizquia ypampa cenca yc motolinia yn mexica tlatilolca achi huecauh ynic mochiuh tlahtolli pregones: yc mochiuh caquitilloque in castilteca auh amo huel mochiuh amo

1. The letters "xiuh" have been inadvertently repeated.
2. The word *tránsito* can refer to the death of holy persons (*Diccionario de Autoridades*). Several times Ch. uses Nuestra Señora del Tránsito. As Stafford Poole tells us, Latin *translatio* had the same sense, and Ch. may have been affected by that form.
3. This passage could be interpreted as that the members of the indigenous cabildo and the indigenous populace in general participated, or that the first part refers to the cabildo

the Jews. They went to take his bones from the church of San Agustín. And three real people were burned. It was going to be four, but one elderly man was left out. He said he still had something to confess, for which reason they took him back to the Inquisition [building].

v And at that time Isabel Machado was displayed, a Jewish woman, young and unmarried, who was the daughter of the said Antonio Machado, the Jewish tailor. And a secular priest named Plata, a nun, and a beata were displayed.

v Today, Wednesday, the 11th day of the month of April of the year 1601, was when they took down the big cross, very high, that stood in the churchyard of San Francisco, that was raised by our precious father fray Pedro de Gante, the lay friar and teacher, along with the twelve friars who first arrived here in Mexico. It was raised in the year of 1531, 13 Reed in the old year[1] count; it was thirteen years after the Spaniards arrived when it was put up. And the cross had stood for 69 years and three months on the 11th day of April, and when it fell and was taken down, it had been a time of 82 years, three months, and 11 days since the Spaniards arrived. / Many lords died in its time [while it was standing], viceroys and Audiencia judges who came to rule in Mexico City, and Mexica rulers and nobles, and bishops, [*p. 31*] and friars in authority who lived here in Mexico Tenochtitlan.

v Friday, the 4th of May of the year 1601, was when the Audiencia judge named don Francisco Tello passed away; his body was buried at San Agustín.

v Sunday, the 6th of May of the year 1601, was when the image of the precious lady Santa María was shown to the public. That is the one of how she died, called del Tránsito;[2] she is lying in a tomb. They blessed her on Friday, and on the said Sunday everyone kissed her hands and feet: the rulers, alcaldes, regidores, and all of us commoners.[3] / And our father fray Francisco de Gamboa produced [was responsible for showing] this precious lady.

¶ 6 Rabbit year, 1602. In this year, Thursday the 25th of April, at Pentecost, was when the hospital of Espíritu Santo was inaugurated. There was a procession beginning at the cathedral. They came to establish the Sacrament there; the viceroy and all the lord Audiencia judges came there because the church was inaugurated.

v Today, Sunday the 13th of the month of October of the year 1602, was when the archbishop don fray García de Santa María de Mendoza y Zúñiga,[4] a Hieronymite friar, arrived; it was afternoon when he entered Mexico.

v Today, Wednesday the 11th of the month of ____ of the year 1602, was when the lord viceroy, don Gaspar, went[5] to Tlatelolco on account of considering how draft rotary labor was to be abolished, because the Mexica Tlatelolca are greatly afflicted by it. Discussion lasted rather long, proclamations were made about it, the Spaniards were informed, but it

---

of the Spanish municipality and the rest to the entire indigenous population. Ch.'s use of the word *tlatoque* makes the first more likely.

4. Monroy Castillo 1987–88, 1: 95, gives the name as don García de Mendoza y Santa María.

5. The use of the imperfect instead of the usual preterit leaves the impression that perhaps Ch. means that the viceroy was going to go but didn't, or was in the process.

huel poliuh

v ypan in metztli de Septiembre. de 1602. a^{o}s. yquac hualla acico yn itenyotzin yn imahuiçotzin Sant Raymundo ynic otlateochihualtic[1] ytetzinco pohui in Sancto Domingo predicador. [*p. 32*]

¶ vii. acatl xihuitl. 1603. años. yn ipan in xihuitl. yn ipan axcan Domingo. yc xx. mani abril yquac auto. mochiuh yn Sant. Joseph. centecpantli teyttitiloque Judiosme yn tlateotocanime

v Yn ipan axcan Domingo yc xvii. mani metztli agosto de 1603. años. yn Sancto yancuic Sant Raymundo. Sancto Domingo teopixqui yquac tlayahualloliztica quimoquechillito yn icapillatzinco yn ompa S^{to}. Domingo. tlapechtli motlatlalli ynic tlayahualoloc yglesia mayor. hualpeohuac ynic quimocallaquillito teopan huel quicencauhque yn ixquichtin teopixque yhuan tlahtoque oydores. al~~ld~~es de cortesme

v axcan miercoles yc 2. mani metztli. de Septi^{e}. de 1603. años. yn Sancto Domingo teopixque yquac motlallique yn quapatlanallizquauhtitlan. calnacazco ychan catca Don fran^{co} tello al~~ld~~e de corte Sant luis. yc tlatocayotiq̃. yn Sancto Domingo teopixque yhuan yncolegio[2] quichiuhque

v Domingo yc .7. mani metztli de Septi^{e}. de 1603 a^{o}s. yquac teocalchallique teocalmamalque yn La compañia de Jesus. in teatinos. teopixque. huel mahuiztic. in teocalli quimochihuillique. yn axcan. oncan missa mitohua La compañia de Jesus.

v Axcan Domingo. yc .v. mani metztli. de octubre de 1603 años. yquac mohuicac yn tlahtohuani visurrey. Don Gaspar de çuniga açeuedo conde tetzcoco. motlallito oncã quimochiyelli yn yancuic tlahtohuani visurrey Don Juan de mendoça y luna marques. oncan motatzinoq̃. yn tetzcoco.

v Domingo yc xix. de octubre de 1603 a^{o}s. yn tlaçocihuapilli, yn monextitzino[3] atiçapan yquac quimocahuillito, yn ompa a la huerta Sant cosme. Sant. Damian cemicac ompa moyetztiez tlayahualoliztica yn quimocahuillito, guardian fray fran^{co} de ganboa. yxquich tlacatl ompa mohuicaya. [*p. 33*]

v Yn ipan axcan Sabado. yc xviii. mani metztli de octobre de 1603. años. yquac mito capitulo. yn ompa xochimilco yn guardian. fray fran^{co}, ganboa. mohuicac tlatilolco. auh yn guardian mochiuh ytoca fray Juan de castaneda

v auh çanno ypan in yn omoteneuh metztli ynic 18. mani de octubre de 1603. a^{o}s. yquac ohuallaque oacico yn ihtic altepetl mexico in yehuantin teopixque quateçontzitzin, yn ipilhuan Beato Juan de Dios. yn quimocuitlahuia hospitales. yn axcan oncan cate hospital yn desmaparados.

v Domingo. a xxvi. de octubre de 1603. años. yn tlahtohuani visurrey. Don Juan de mendoça y luna marques de montesclaros. ytech pohui comendador Sanctiago, yquac maxitico mocallaquico yn ihtic altepetl mexico ciudad tenochtitlan ye macuilli hora yn maxitico, quihualmohuiquilli[5] ycihuauh[4] ytoca Doña Anna Mexia Manrrique, virreyna.

v Auh yn tlahtohuani Don gaspar de çuñiga y Azeuedo conde de monterrey. conpatlato yn

1. The meaning is that he was beatified, yet here and below he is also called a saint.
2. *Colegio*, a place of both residence and instruction.
3. It could be either that the Virgin appeared or that her image was produced, shown.

could not be done, it could not be abolished.

v The month of September of the year 1602 was when the news of the fame and honor of San Raimundo came and arrived, that he became a blessed one;[1] he is a Dominican, a preacher. [*p. 32*]

¶ 7 Reed year, 1603. In this year, today, Sunday the 20th of April, was when an auto da fe was held at San Josef; twenty Jews who were idolaters were displayed.

v Today, Sunday the 17th of the month of August of the year 1603, was when they went in procession to set up the new saint San Raimundo, a Dominican friar, in his chapel at [the church of] Santo Domingo. Platforms were set up. The procession began at the cathedral, and they went to put him in the church [of Santo Domingo]. All the priests and religious, and the lords civil and criminal judges of the Audiencia took him there.

v Today, Wednesday the 2nd of the month of September of the year 1603, was when the Dominican friars established themselves near to the head-flying pole, at the corner, in what used to be the home of don Francisco Tello, criminal judge of the Audiencia. The Dominican friars named it San Luis and made it their college.[2]

v Sunday the 7th of the month of September of the year 1603 was when the Company of Jesus, the Theatine religious, inaugurated a church. The church they built was very splendid, where today mass is said at the church of the Company.

v Today, Sunday the 5th of the month of October of 1603, was when the lord viceroy don Gaspar de Zúñiga y Acevedo, the Count, went to stay in Tetzcoco; there he awaited the new lord viceroy, the Marqués don Juan de Mendoza y Luna. They saw each other in Tetzcoco.

v Sunday the 19th of October of the year 1603 was when they went to deliver the precious lady [the Virgin] who appeared[3] at Atiçapan to the orchard of San Cosme and San Damián; she is to be there always. The father guardian [of San Josef], fray Francisco de Gamboa, went in procession to deliver her; everyone went there. [*p. 33*]

v Today, Saturday the 18th of the month of October of the year 1603, was when a chapter meeting [of the Franciscan province] in Xochimilco was announced. The father guardian fray Francisco de Gamboa went to Tlatelolco, and one named fray Juan de Castañeda became guardian [at San Josef].

v Likewise in the said month, on the 18th of October of the year 1603, was when the lay brothers, children of the blessed Juan de Dios, who take care of hospitals, and today are at the Hospital de los Desamparados, came to and arrived in the altepetl of Mexico.

v Sunday, the 26th of October of the year 1603, was when the lord viceroy don Juan de Mendoza y Luna, Marqués of Montesclaros, who possesses the position of being a comendador of the order of Santiago, reached and entered the altepetl of Mexico, the city of Tenochtitlan. It was at five o'clock that he arrived. His wife,[4] named doña Ana Mejía Manrrique, the virreine, accompanied him.[5]

v And the lord don Gaspar de Zúñiga y Acevedo, Count of Monterrey, went to Peru to

---

4. Ch. mainly uses *-namic*, "one's spouse," for wife, but occasionally also *-cihuauh*, "one's woman, wife," an anticipation of later usage. For such usage see Pizzigoni 2002.

5. The meaning could equally well be that he brought her.

ompa Peru. yn Don luis de velasco visurrey. catca yn ompa Peru, ompa tlahtocatia auh yn o iuh conpatlato. aoctle ytequiuh mochiuh auh yc niman hualpeuh hualmocuep. yn ça niman ipan in xihuitl omoteneuh hualla yn nicã ypã nueua españa. atlacuihuayan motlallico oncã mocehuico auh çatepann onya ompa motlallito yn imacehualpan toltitlan,

¶ viii. tecpatl xihuitl 1604. años. ypan in yn xihuitl oncan ohuacico yn matlacpohualxihuitl ypan nauhpohualxihuitl quichiuhque ynic cate in ye yxquichcauh yc acico mexica yn tenochtitlan,

v Yn ipan axcan martes. ypan ymilhuitzin Reyesme yc. 6. mani metztli de henero yquac quimacehuitique[1] yn tlahtohuani. visurrey Don Juan de mendoça y luna nohuian huallaque yn altepetl ypan tlaca yn macehuaco mitotico, [*p. 34*]

v Domingo, yc xxi. mani metztli de março de 1604 años. yn iquac hin huey papaquiliztli. mochiuh in palacion tlapãco, amatlecomitl motecpan yn atenantitech. yn oncan tlatlac sepo camdela. moch tlapallo[2] yn amatl yn ihtic tlatlac camdela huell onquiztoca in tlapanco, atenãtitech, yhuan vandera motetecac, auh yn celar yn huey tlapanco quahuitl motlatlalli yn oncan tlatlac, tletlalliloc. auh nohuian tletlallique yn incaltenpan castilteca auh nohuian huitza yn altepetl ypã tlaca. auh in castilteca mahuiltique motlatlalloque in yohualtica

v In ipan axcan Juebes. ypan ylhuitzin S^{t}. maria mg^{na}. ypan metztli Julio. xxii. dias. de 1604. años. yquac momiquilli yn totlaçotatzin fray fran^{co} de ganboa guardian moyetzticatca tlatilolco, auh nican momiquillico S^{t}. Fran^{co}, yn quimotoquillique vmpa S^{t}. Joseph. altar mayor. yxpan // Auh ynic quimotoquillique. huel mocencauh. yn inauhcampayxti teteuhctin yhuan macehualtin, auh yn tlatilolco. gou^{or}. al~~ld~~esme Regidores. yhuan yxquichtin tlatilolca huel quihualcencauhque yn quimotoquillico // auh yxiptlatzin mochiuh yn fray Juan de torquemada guardian mochiuhtzino tlatilolco,

v Yn ipan axcan viernes. yc xxvii. mani metztli de agosto. de 1604. a^{o}s ça iuh moztla. ylhuitzin. S^{t}. augustin. auh huel iquac peuh in tlapaquiyahuitl. ynic momanaco huell ipan yn ivisperatzin S^{t}. augustin. chicueylhuitl yn quiyauhtimanca. cemilhuitl cecẽyohual, huel tetlaocoltin yn topan mochiuh yhuan nohuiã tlatlaxicac yn tochachan in timacehualtin. yhuan castilteca yhuan in teopan nohuian. atl nenez. mollon yn atl in S^{t}. Fran^{co} in S^{t}. augustin. in S^{t}. Domingo. in La compañia teatinos. auh ynic cecemilhuitl yhuan yn cecenyohual quiyauh ca nohuian ynic moch ipan nueua españa. yquac nohuian mollon motlatlapo yn aoztotl,[3] ynic cenca miec oncan oquiz atl, yhuan yn intech tetepe nohuiampa hualtemoc yn atl, auh ynic nohuian ypan nueua españa. mieccan yn atocohuac yhuan netlapacholloc xixitin yn calli yhuan yquac cequi [*p. 35*] hualmomimillo yn ceppayahuitl huallixxitin yn iztac tepetl,[4] // auh oc cenca nican mexico yn ipan ohualtemoc yn tepetitech atl ynic cenca ypan otemico yc polihuizquia yn altepetl, auh ynic nohuiampa hualtemoya yn huallamiequiliaya yn atl. huel huey ynic macoc, auh mieccan papachiuh xixitin yn calli. yhuan ahapachiuh acallac yn calli yc mocalcauhque. in chaneque. yhuã yn otli nohuian popoliuh. yhuan yn chinamitl. huel nohuian poliuh. auh yn atlixocan tla-

---

1. One would have expected "quimacehuilique."
2. It is not clear whether the color was from the paper or from the flame inside.

replace don Luis de Velasco, who was viceroy in Peru and ruled there. And when [don Gaspar] had replaced [don Luis], he was left without office, and thereupon he started back and returned; he came here to New Spain right away, in the same year, and came to settle and rest in Tacubaya. Afterward he went and settled among his vassals [at his encomienda] in Toltitlan.

¶ 8 Flint year, 1604. In this year it reached 280 years since the Mexica arrived in Tenochtitlan.

v Today, Tuesday, the feast day of the Magi, the 6th of the month of January, was when they danced for[1] the lord viceroy don Juan de Mendoza y Luna; the people from the various altepetl all around came to dance. [*p. 34*]

v Sunday, the 21st of the month of March of the year 1604, was when a great celebration was held on the roof of the palace. Paper fire pots [luminarios] were lined up on the parapet, in which tallow candles burned; the paper inside which the candles burned was all colored,[2] the parapet of the roof was entirely full, and banners were unfurled, and on the main roof of the municipal building logs were placed that burned there, that were set on fire. And the Spaniards everywhere set fires beside their houses. And the people of the altepetl [of the countryside] came from everywhere. And the Spaniards played, they ran here and there in the night.

v Today, Thursday, the feast day of Santa María Magdalena, the 22nd day of the month of July of 1604, was when our precious father fray Francisco de Gamboa, who was father guardian at Tlatelolco, passed away. He came here to [the church of] San Francisco to die; they buried him at San Josef facing the main altar. // And when they buried him, everyone was there, the lords and commoners of all four parts [of Mexico Tenochtitlan], and the governor, alcaldes, regidores of Tlatelolco, and all the Tlatelolca, they all came to bury him. // And fray Juan de Torquemada became his replacement; he was made father guardian at Tlatelolco.

v Today, Friday, the 27th of the month of August of the year 1604, the day before the feast day of San Agustín, was exactly when a fine, lasting rain set in, right on the eve of San Agustín. It kept raining for a week, night and day; what happened to us was really pitiful. And it leaked in our homes everywhere, those of us commoners and those of the Spaniards, and in the churches everywhere water appeared and sprang up, at San Francisco, San Agustín, Santo Domingo, the Company of Jesus [belonging to] the Theatines. And since it rained every day and night, everywhere in all New Spain at this time [wells][3] sprang up and opened, so that very much water came out of them, and water descended from the mountains everywhere, and in many places all over New Spain things were carried away by the water and people were buried; the houses fell in, and at this time [*p. 35*] some of the snow came rolling down on Iztactepetl,[4] its surface came falling in [there was an avalanche]. // And the water from the mountains descended especially to Mexico here, so that it greatly filled up, and the altepetl was about to perish because of it. And since everywhere the water descended and increased, it rose very greatly, and in many places the houses collapsed and crumbled, and they were flooded and sank under the water,

3. *Aoztotl* is literally water caves or cavities.
4. Iztactepetl, literally white mountain, is the same as today's Iztaccihuatl.

mellahua otli. huey atezcatl huey atl mochiuh auh yn inchan españoles. nohuian mollon. yn atl. yc cenca omomauhtique miequimtin yc mocalcauhque yc quitlalcahuique yn altepetl mexico. yc nohuiampa altepetl ypan yahque ompa motlallito, auh yn ixquich otli. yn huehuey otli. mochi apachiuh, cocoton. in tepeyacac yn cohuatlayauhcan. in St. miguel. otli. yn tlacopan azcapotzalco huel nohuian apachiuh,[1] // auh yn izquican huehuey teocalli omoteneuh mexico. ca yzquican tlaxicac yhuan ynic yzquican yhtic atl mollon. ynic cẽca tetentimoman y nohuian teopan monasterios. yc nimã cacocque quitlaltenque yn capilla yhuã ytlacapan teocalli St. augustĩ yhuã cacocque yn altar mayor. yhuan in Retablo.[2] // auh no iuh quichiuhque yn St Domingo yn tlalpantli çan ixquich quitlaltenque yn capilla mayor yhuan yn itlacapan yn ipãpa no oncan yhtic mollonia atl / auh çan no iuh mochiuh yn La compañia de Jesus. auh ynic cenca omomauhti omotequipacho yn yn tlahtohuani visurrey Don Juan de mendoça y luna marques de montesclaros. auh yc 3. ye ylhuitl mani metztli Septie. yn achi oquiz yn tlapaquiyahuitl. ynic cecemilhuitl yhuã cecenyohuatl[3] quiyauh, auh yc niman oncan peuh in ye quiztiuh yn ça ye tlapixalquiyauhtimani // auh yc 10. mani metztli Septie. ynic mocenpohua ynic peuh cecemilhuitl cecenyohual manca quiyahuitl yn tlapaquiyahuitl ynic quiçaco ynic tlamico caxtolylhuitica yn quiçaco yn ipan in omoteneuh metztli Septie ynic ompa peuhtica ypan metztli agosto.

v Lunes. a xi. de octubre de 1604. años. yquac peuh in St. Franco yn expa tlayahualloloya cemilhuitl, yohuatzinco. nepantla tonatiuh. ye teotlac. quimoquixtiliaya in Sacramẽto [*p. 36*] Auh yn izquican teopan monasterios. yn teopixque oncan moyetzinoticate. yhuan monjas. nohuian tlayahualoloc. yn ipampa ynic otapachiuhque yn nican mexico tenochtitlan. yn huey atl. huel macoc moteponaço. auh yn ixquich acallotli, huel teten yn atl huel pepexon titillin. yn nohuian auh huel mauhtiloc mitohuaya tley ye topan mochihua mexico,

v Yn ipan axcan viernes a 15. de octubre de 1604 años. yquac tlayahualoloc tlamacehualoc yn nican mexico huel ihui Juebes Sancto. mochihuani ynic tlayahualoloc / yn ipãpa atl, yn oapachiuh mexicayotl / auh yn tlayahualoque yxquichtin. españolesme. Vela cruz perochia. cenquixohuac ompa cenquizque. yn izquitetl cofradias. / auh in timacehualtin. St. Franco. St. Joseph. cenquizque[4] niman ye yc oneohua in quixohuato oncan ayoticpac yquiyahuac yn augustin guerrero. yn monepanoto. macehualtin yn españoles. me ynic oncã oncetiac tlayahualoliztli, niman ye huillohua yn quixohuato conception monjas. niman Sto. Domingo. nimã Encarnacio. Sancta catharina de Sena. tecpan quiyahuac yglesia mayor. auh yn tlayahualo andas. St. maria tlatquitl. crucifixo. palio. yc quimocaltilitiaque in tto Dios. ytloctzinco mantiaq̃ ychtecq̃ crucifixos. niman yhuan guion[5] vandera tepiton nimã yhuã cruz manca[6] niman yhuã vandera yey huehuey. tliltic tlayacanque // tlatilolca.

---

1. Tacuba and Azcapotzalco have the air of being an afterthought; perhaps the statement that it was flooded everywhere applies only to them. Indeed, in this whole section some of the names could refer to the roads blocked and others to the places where they were cut.

2. In the Nahuatl an original *l*, making "letablo," has been changed into *R*.

3. For "cecenyohual."

4. Here "cenquizque," "assembled," is in third person, not agreeing with the first person "timacehualtin," "we commoners," showing that the first person form was becoming

for which reason the inhabitants left their houses. And the roads everywhere disappeared, and also the chinampas absolutely everywhere. The road going straight to Atlixxocan became a great lake or ocean, and water sprang up in the homes of the Spaniards everywhere, by which they were greatly frightened; many for that reason left their houses, abandoned the altepetl of Mexico, and went to the altepetl in the country all around to stay. And the roads, the highways, were all flooded. The roads [going to] Tepeyacac, Coatlayauhcan, and San Miguel and to Tacuba and Azcapotzalco were cut. It was flooded everywhere.[1] // And in each of the said big churches in Mexico it leaked, and inside each of them water sprang up, so that the churches and monasteries all around got very full, so that then they raised [the floor level] and filled [the space] with earth in the [main] chapel and on the sides of the church of San Agustín, and they raised the main altar and the altarpiece.[2] // And they did the same with the floor in Santo Domingo—they only filled with earth the main chapel and the sides—because water was springing up in the inside there too. / And the same was done at the Jesuit church. The lord viceroy, don Juan de Mendoza y Luna, Marqués of Montesclaros, was very alarmed and concerned by it. And on the 3rd day of the month of September, the strong rain, with it raining all day and all night,[3] stopped somewhat, and thereupon it began coming to an end and just drizzling. // And on the 10th of the month of September it totaled fifteen days [two weeks] from the time the strong rain began falling day and night until it ended and finished; it ended in the said month of September, having begun in the month of August.

v Monday the 11th of October of the year 1604 was when holding processions three times a day at San Francisco began; early in the morning, at midday, and in the afternoon they would bring the Sacrament out. [*p. 36*] And there were processions in all the churches and monasteries, wherever there were priests and nuns, because of how we were flooded here in Mexico Tenochtitlan; the lake really rose and swelled, and all the canals were entirely full of water, it rose and filled things up everywhere. There was great fear; it was said, What is happening to us in Mexico?

v Today, Friday, the 15th of October of the year 1604, was when there was a procession and penitence here in Mexico, just as is customarily done on Holy Thursday. / The reason for the procession was the water, that everything pertaining to Mexico was flooded. / And all the Spaniards went in procession; they assembled at the parish of Vera Cruz; all the cofradías assembled there. And we commoners assembled[4] at San Josef, at San Francisco. Thereupon everyone set out and departed; at Ayoticpac, outside the house of Agustín Guerrero, the commoners and Spaniards joined, so that there the procession became one. Then everyone went to the nunnery of Concepción, then to Santo Domingo, then to Encarnación, then to Santa Catarina de Sena, and outside the palace at the cathedral. A carrying platform belonging to Santa María [district] went in procession, [with] a crucifix. They went along sheltering our lord God with a canopy. Next to him went the crucified thieves, then also a *guión*,[5] a small banner, then also crosses with cloth decorations,[6]

---

a frozen expression, no longer always thought of as first person plural in the usual sense of including the speaker. Just below appears "macehualtin" in the third person with the same meaning.

5. A standard on a crosspiece, an ensign.

6. "Cruz manca" includes Spanish *manga*, "sleeve." The reference is to a cloth ornamentation hanging down from the horizontal part of the cross.

ça tlatzauhctiaque. yei yn invandera oncan quiquixtique. huehuey. cruz. soledad. guion cruz. yhuã cruz manca, // auh in Vela cruz. Sancto. ligno cruz andasco. micatiltitiuh. palio. yc quimocaltilitihui yhuã totlaçonãtzin nuestra señora del rosario. huey andasco miquiltitiuh teopixque quimonapalhuique. yhuan miyequintin teopixque motlayahualhuique. auh yn tlayahuallo. yn mohuitec. yn tlamaceuhque aço quen exiquipilli in ye mochi mocenpohua macehualtin yhuan españoles.me. auh oc cenca miec yn mohuitec españoles. yn amo macehualtin. auh yc no ceppa [*p. 37*] Necuepaloc. callacohuato. yn ompa hualquiz. tlayahualoliztli.//.

v Auh çan ya yehuatl. ypan in in metztli omoteneuh octubre. yn opeuhque mexica tenochca. ytencopatzinco yn visurrey Don Juan de mendoça y luna ynic otequitque. ynic quichiuhque. quipahpatique. quiyancuillique. yn tetenamitl y nohuian oytlacauhca. yn ococoyonca. ynic cen iquac tlachiuhtli yn ipan tlahtohuani. huehue Don luis de velasco. visurrey. yn ipan 12. tecpatl xihuitl 1556. años. yquac tlahtocatia yn omoteneuh visurrey. nican tenochtitlan. yn iquac yc no apachiohuaca. mexica onpohualxiuhtica. onchiuhcnahuitica. yn axcan yn o no nicuel iuh mochihuaco. ynic ye no otlaapachihuico. yn ye no yehuatl ypampa yn omopahpati. o nohuian mochi motzatzauhc. yn atetenamitl yn ocuicuitlacoyonca. ompa hualpeuhtica in moyectili ynic mopahpati. yn coyonacazco nimã ye Sant. Sebastian. niman Sant. Pablo. niman ye mixiuhcã. nimã ye acachinanco. auh huel ixquichcauh yc nemohuac yn ipan ce metztli octubre. ynic mochichiuh. auh huel inoma yn tlahtohuani visurrey. Don Juan de mendoça y luna. yn ipan ontlahtohuaya. yn quimonmottiliaya tequitque ynic mopahpati. tetenamitl. acaltica. yn quimohuiquilitinenca. ynic no yhuan quimonemililiaya yn quenin huel quimanahuiz. altepetl. mexico tenochtitlan. ynic cenca ye apachihui. ynic nohuiampa ypan ye huitz atl. quauhcopa[1] hualtemo cenca quimotequipachilhui yn tlahtohuani visurrey. yn altepetl. mexico. ynic atica ye polihuiz-[*p. 38*]Nequi. auh yn ontlah.[2] yn oconchiuhque. yn oconpahpatique. mexica. yn ixquich omoteneuh tetenamitl. yc ye no cuel centlamantli motlalli yn intequiuh tenochca.

v Auh çan ye no ypan in yn omoteneuh metztli octubre de mill 604 años. otequimacoque. in nauhcame chalca. ytencopatzinco yn tlacatl. visurrey yn opeuh ye quauhtemohuillo. yn izquican chalco yehuatl tequiuhtiloque. in chalca. in quamimilli in motenehua morrillos.[3] cenca yc motolinique ompa. canato. ompa quiquixtito. yn ixilla.[4] yztac tepetl. yhuan popocatepetl. ytech yn quitequito. amaquemeque. yhuan caxitico. atenco. yn oncan ayotzinco. yn çan inneyxcahuil mochiuh yn amaquemeque.[5] yn nican hualla mexico. quãmimilli. morrillos yxquich .vi. mill. —

v Sabado a xxvii. de nouiembre. de mill 604 años. yquac motamachiuh yn atl. yn nican ahuatzalpan[6] motenehua. mecatica mopouh quiyomahuico, nahuatlahtoque Juan grande. fran^{co} de leyba. yhuan mexico tenochtitlan. gou^{or}. Don Jeronimo lopez. mestiço. yhuan al~~ld~~esme. yhuan tlatilolco. gou^{or}. Don Juan bap^{ta}. yhuan al~~ld~~esme. yhuan chinampaneca. culhuaque. xochmilca. cuitlahuaca. mizquica.[7] ynic motamachiuh. ypampa atenamitl.

1. The expression *quauhcopa* possibly refers to a particular direction in this context.
2. The intention of "ontlah" seems to be "ontlan."
3. A type of rough wooden beam for rafters or pilings.
4. Usually in the belly or womb, in compounds *-xillan* can mean side, flank.

and then also three large black banners went ahead. // The Tlatelolca just came last. They brought out three of their large banners, a cross of Soledad, a [processional?] cross, and a decorated cross. // And the true cross, a cross with a relic of the true cross, went standing on a carrying platform, [they] went sheltering it under a canopy. And our precious mother Nuestra Señora del Rosario went standing on a large carrying platform; priests carried it, and many priests went in procession. During the procession the penitents scourged themselves. Perhaps there were some twenty-four thousand [participants] counting everybody, commoners and Spaniards. But many more Spaniards scourged themselves than commoners. Thereupon they returned once again [*p. 37*] and went in where the procession had started.

v It was in the same said month of October that the Mexica Tenochca began, at the order of the viceroy don Juan de Mendoza y Luna, to perform work duty, so that they built, fixed, and renewed the walls [of the dikes] which had been damaged and were full of holes everywhere. They had first been built during the time of the lord viceroy don Luis de Velasco the elder in 12 Flint year, the year of 1556. At that time the said viceroy was ruling here in Tenochtitlan, when because the Mexica were flooded then too, 49 years before now, since the same thing happened again, that everything was flooded, therefore because of that also the dikes that had holes in their sides were fixed and all closed up everywhere. The cleaning up and fixing began at Coyonacazco, then San Sebastián, then San Pablo, then at Mixiuhcan, then at Acachinanco. They were busy at it the whole month of October until it was fixed. And it was the lord viceroy don Juan de Mendoza y Luna in person who saw to it and supervised the workers so that the walls would be repaired; he went about accompanying them in a boat. He was also pondering how he could protect the altepetl of Mexico Tenochtitlan, since it was already very much flooded and the water came into it from everywhere, descending from the forests.[1] It greatly worried the lord viceroy how the altepetl of Mexico was about to perish from water. [*p. 38*] When the Mexica had finished[2] building and repairing all the said walls, thereupon the Tenochca were assigned a different task.

v And in the same said month of October of the year of 1604, the people of the four parts of Chalco were given tasks by order of the lord viceroy. Bringing down logs [from the forest] began everywhere in Chalco. The Chalca were assigned the round wooden beams called *morillos*,[3] because of which they suffered greatly. They went to get them and take them out from the slopes[4] of Iztactepetl and Popocatepetl, and the Amaquemeque[5] went there to cut them, and they brought them to the shore at Ayotzinco. Of the wooden columns or morillos that were brought here to Mexico, a total of 6,000 were the exclusive responsibility of the Amaquemeque.

v Saturday, the 27th of November of the year 1604, was when the water was measured here at what is called the drained area.[6] It was counted by [measuring] ropes. It was done personally[7] by the interpreters Juan Grande and Francisco de Leiva, the governor in Mexico Tenochtitlan don Gerónimo López, mestizo, and the alcaldes [in Mexico], and the

---

5. People of Amaquemecan.

6. Possibly the intention is Ahuatzalpan as the proper name of an area of settlement. Or the meaning may simply be dry land.

7. Possibly the reference to doing it personally applies only to the interpreters and officials.

motecac

v Auh niman axcan ypan lunes. yc xxix. de nouiẽbre de 1604. años. netequimacoc. in mexico. in tlatilolco. yhuan yn nohuian SoJetos.[1] huel mocencauh yc niman quipehualtique in mexica. in ye quiteca yancuic tetenamitl. yn tlalmantli nohuian [*p. 39*] Motatacac. yn nican tlaxillacalpan. Sant. Juan yn calçolli. moxixitinin. yhuan yn ixquich huexotl mochi motlaz. ynic tlaquauhtzotzonaloc. oncan peuh yn xolloco. S^t^. Antonio Abbad. oztocaltitlan in ye mochihua in ye moteca yancuic tetenamitl yc çan ompa ontlantica yn xoconochnopalyacac yn amanalcopa y oquitzacuillique yn atl. ypampa yn cenca hualpexonticallaquia yn ihtic ciudad[2] ynic ye tlaapachohua ca mochi tepeatl yn oncan hualmomana ahuatzalpan. auh ynic tetequimacoc, yn ipan yzqui altepetl omoteneuh. yn chinãpanecatl. ca huel ixquich nican quichihuaco. yn itequiuh. ynic cenchinampanecatl. // Auh yn oyecauh yn omotecac yancuic atenamitl. auh ye no cuelle yn otlih. in tlamellahua. atlixocan. yn nican ypan tlaxillacalli. tepetitlan. mohuecapano. moquauhtzotzon. yhuan moteman monauhcampahui tehuãme in xochmilca. auh yn tlatilolca. atle oncã quichiuhque. ypampa yn inchan no ochichiuhque. yn tlamellahua tepeyacac. quitequipanoque yhuan yn ixquich altepehua y nepa chaneque // — auh yn nican tenochtitlan. ynic tlamico atenamitl yhuan yn otlih. tlamellahua atlixocã ye ytlamiã in metztli de diciembre. yn ipan xihuitl. omoteneuh. // auh no niman iquac motzaquato. yn mexicatzinco huey acallotlih. ynic aocmo oncan hualcallaquiz. chicahuac atl. mexicopa in ye nepa huitz huallauh quizqui yn 8: tecpatl xihuitl.

¶ ix. calli xihuitl 1605: años. ypan in in yancuic xihuitl. yhuan in yancuic metztli. henero. yquac Opeuh in ye tequitihua. in ye ochichihualo. yn ompa hecatepec. Sant. x̄p̄oual. huel on[*p. 40*]can yn itocayocan acalhuacan ytencopatzinco yn tlahtohuani. visurrey. Don Juan de mendoça y luna mochi tlacatl. oncan tequitico yn anahuacatl. in techyahuallotoc. çan inneyxcahuil mochiuh yn altepehuaque amo tehuanme. in mexica auh inic ompa tequitihuac hecatepec. acalhuacan macuiltetl metztli ypan tlamico. in metztli Mayo. // auh yn o iuh ontlanque yn intequiuh ompa hecatepec yn altepehuaque. auh niman no cuelle onahuatilloque ynic ohuacalloyectico ohuacalotlaçoquiquixtico nohuian. yn ipan izqui acallotli. mexico. yhuan oochichihuaco. ootlatlaltemaco. ocacocuico yn izqui huehuey otlih. mexico. ynic oncan cenca omotolinico oapizmiquico. tlaqualtica in macehualtin. altepehuaque. yn ipan in xihuitl. omoteneuh. de 1605. años.
v Auh no yquac yn ipan in xihuitl. omoteneuh yn ipan metztli agosto yn momiquilli tlacatl huehue Don Antonio Valeriano azcapotzalco ychantzinco. ynin gouernador catca ỹ nican mexico tenochtitlan. ynin ymontzin catca in tlacatl Don diego de aluarado huanitzin. auh cenca huecauh yn quimopiallico. altepetl. tenochtitlan auh ynic momiquillico. ye iuh nepa. matlacxihuitl. quimocahuilica ymac yn Don Juan m̄ī̄n. yn igouernaciotequitzin catca. huehue Don Antonio Valeriano. ca mocehuiticatca[3] ynic onmomiquillico.
v Auh yn axcan ypan yc 21. mani metztli [*p. 41*] Setiembre de 1605. años. ypan ylhuitzin Sant. Matheo. Apostol. yquac omachiztico. ohualla tlahtolli yn ompa españa.

1. Both altepetl had constituent parts located at some distance; here Ch. uses the Spanish term *sujeto*.

2. Here Ch. apparently uses *ciudad* for the whole entity, not just the municipal council

governor in Tlatelolco, don Juan Bautista, and the alcaldes [in Tlatelolco], and the people of the chinampa area, the people of Colhuacan, Xochimilco, Cuitlahuac, and Mizquic, did it personally. The reason it was measured was because dikes were built.

v Then today, Monday the 29th of November of the year 1604, tasks were assigned; it was fully arranged in Mexico and Tlatelolco and all the subject settlements everywhere,[1] whereupon the Mexica began to build new walls [dikes]. Everywhere the leveled ground [*p. 39*] was dug up. Here in the [various] tlaxilacalli of San Juan, the old houses were demolished, and all the willows were felled so that trunks were pounded in [i.e., in pile driving]. Making and laying the new walls began at Xoloco, at San Antonio Abad [in?] Oztocaltitlan; closing off the water went as far as Xoconochnopalyacac, toward Amanalco, because water came entering inside the city[2] and greatly filling it up, flooding everything, for all the water from the mountains spread where [normally] it is dry. And as to the tasks assigned to each of the said altepetl of the chinampa people, they came here to do all their tasks as chinampa people. // And when the new dikes were built and finished, in addition the road going straight to Atlixxocan here in the tlaxilacalli of Tepetitlan was raised; there was pile driving for it and stones were placed. It was done by the four parts [of Tenochtitlan] along with the Xochimilca. The Tlatelolca did nothing because they also worked fixing roads in their home area. And [the one] going straight to Tepeyacac was worked on by all the inhabitants of the altepetl out there. // — The dikes here in Tenochtitlan and the road going straight to Atlixxocan were finished at the end of the month of December in the said year. // This is also when the big canal was closed at Mexicatzinco so the strong waters coming from beyond would no longer enter Mexico. End of 8 Flint year.

¶ 9 House year, 1605. In this new year and new month of January was when tribute work began, fixing roads at San Cristóbal Ecatepec at the exact place [*p. 40*] called Acalhuacan, by order of the lord viceroy don Juan de Mendoza y Luna. All the people of Anahuac [the lake region] who surround us came to work there; it was done exclusively by the people of the altepetl [of the hinterland], not together with the Mexica. Work went on at Acalhuacan in Ecatepec for five months and finished in the month of May. // And when the people of the country altepetl had finished with their work at Ecatepec, then they were again given orders to come clean the canals, to remove the rubbish everywhere in all the canals in Mexico and to repair roads, to level land for roads and raise all the highways in Mexico, so that they suffered greatly in it; the commoners of the hinterland altepetl were starving for lack of food in the said year of 1605.

v And it was also in the said year, in the month of August, that the lord don Antonio Valeriano the elder passed away. He was from Azcapotzalco and was governor here in Mexico Tenochtitlan—he was the son-in-law of the lord don Diego de Alvarado Huanitzin—and he was in charge of the altepetl of Tenochtitlan for a very long time. When he died, it had been ten years since don Antonio Valeriano the elder had left his duties as governor in the hands of don Juan Martín, for he was in retirement[3] when he passed away.

v Today, the 21st of the month [*p. 41*] of September of the year 1605, on the feast day of San Mateo Apóstol, was when it became known and news came from Spain that the

or the Spanish part of the settlement.

3. Literally resting.

ynic omotlacatilli. yehuatzin Principe. yn itlaçopiltzin tohueytlahtocauh Don felibpe tercero. Rey. de españa. yn o iuh machiztico. niman yquac nohuian tlatzitzilicac yn izquican teopan mexico. ypan matlactlomome tzillini. nepantla tonatiuh / auh yn ipan in cemilhuitl. ynic onyohuaco. yn ipan oraçion mochiuh. in ye tlapoyahua[1] yn oncan palacio tlapanticpac. yn ichan visurrey yhuan yn ibentanas nohuian quitlatlatique. sepo candelas. aço huel ontzontli yn amatlecomitl quitecaque yn quitetecpanque. atenantitech. yn tecpan tlapanticpac. yhuan y nohuian oncan omoteneuh bentanas. yn oncan tlatlatlaya sepo candelas. auh no yhuan yn oncan celar tlapanticpac cenca miec yn tlatlapanalquahuitl. piuas[2] yhuan tlatlatlac. çanno yhui yn oncan tecpan quiyahuac amo çan quexquich yn quahuitl yhuan yn piuas. quitlatlatique. auh niman ye no yehuatl. in couetes. amo çan quexquich in quitlatlazque. oncã palacio. yn tecpan yhuan yn mochintin castilteca. yn inchachan. yn incahcalticpac. yhuan yn incacaltenpa amo çan quexquichi yn quitlatique. quahuitl. ỹ nican mexico. yhuann oc ceppa nohuian tlatzitzilicac yn izquican teopan. auh ynic nohuian mexico. iuh mochihu in. ca yc tlanahuatiloc. yc pena motlalli. yn ihtic ciudad mexico. tenochtitlan. // Auh yn ipan ye chiuhcnahui tzilli. in ye yohuac yquac peuhque yn españolesme [*p. 42*] Yn tlahtoque cauallerostin. cauallotlatlalochtiq̃ yn tecpan quiyahuac mochi cenca tlaçotli yn innechichihual. contlallique. çanno yhui quincencauhque. quinchichiuhque. yn incaulloshuan[3] no yhui yn intlilticahuan. yn intlacahuan huel quĩcencauhque. yn innechichihualtica. yn oncan quintocatinemia intecuiyohuan. auh yehuatl achtopa conpehualti n cauallotlatlalochtin ỹ visurrey. yhuan oc ce cauallero. ytloc ycatia quimonpehualtilique.[4] yn oc cequintin tlahtoque oome mantihui. yn tlatlatlalochtique. auh yuh oquihtoque. in huehuetque españolesme. ayc iuhqui omottac. ce visurrey. yn nican mexico. yn maca ce iuhqui. oquichiuh. in ye nepa achtopa. otlahtocatico. visurreyesme. nican mexico: yn iuh yehuatzin oquimochihuili. Don Juan de mendoça y luna. marques de montesclaros. yhuan oc cequi miectlamantli. in mochiuh yquac ypan ylhuitzin catca S^t^. Matheo. ynic papacohuac yn ipampatzinco. ynic omotlacatilli. Principe. auh yn iuh hualicuiliuhtia. tlahtolli. yn españa. ypan yc viii. mani metztli. abril. yn ça ye ypan in xihuitl de 1605 años. ypan Viernes Sancto. in motlacatilli yehuatzin Principe. Don felipe Domingo Victor de austria. yn itlaçopiltzin tohueytlahtocatzin Rey. Don felipe tercero. yn axcan moyetztica españa. auh yn ipampa. ynic ontetl ypan quimotocayotilique. yn tlahtocapiltzintli Principe. ynic ytocatzin. mochiuh Domingo [*p. 43*] Ca yehica. ypampa yn oncan moquatequitzino. yn iquac piltzintli moyetzticatca. yn itlaçotzin tt^o^. Dios. yn tlacemicnopilhuiani. Sancto Domingo de guzman. yn ihtic nequatequilizacaxitl. yn villa. yn oncã quimoquatequillique. auh çan no oncan yn oquimoquatequilique. yn tlahtocapiltzintli Principe. ynic oncan oquimocuilli yn itocatzin Sancto Domingo. Ca iuh omachiztico. yn nican mexico.

v Auh ynic oppa axcan yc 4. mani metztli de octubre. de 1605. años. ypan ylhuitzin Sant. Fran^co^ ye no ceppa omochiuh papaquiliztli miec tlamãtli. yn ipan moquixtique. yn ipan mixeuhque. ynic mahuiltique. españolesme. ynic tlaquetzque ynic tetlahuehuetzqui-

---

1. Alternatively, On this day, when night fell, at the time when prayers were said and it was getting dark . . .

2. In "piuas" for *vigas*, *p* for initial *v* [b] is a normal substitution. With *u* ([w] or [b/v]) for *g*, it sometimes happened that the letter for any voiced medial consonant was exchanged with any other.

3. For "incaualloshuan."

prince, the heir of our great ruler don Felipe III, king of Spain, was born. As soon as it was known, bells were rung everywhere in all the churches in Mexico, at twelve o'clock, at noon. / And all day until night fell there was prayer on his behalf.[1] When it was dark, on the roof of the palace, the residence of the viceroy, and in its windows everywhere they lit tallow candles, they laid out perhaps 800 paper firepots [luminarios] which they lined up on the parapet of the roof of the palace, and everywhere in the said windows where tallow candles were burning. And also on the roof of the municipal building, very much kindling and beams[2] were burned, and likewise outside the palace they burned a great deal of wood and beams. And then they also shot off a great many rockets at the palace, and all the Spaniards at their various homes, on top of their houses, and at the entrance to their houses, burned a great deal of wood here in Mexico. And the bells were rung in all the churches and everywhere in Mexico once again; the reason it was done was that it was so ordered, and a fine was set up in the city of Mexico Tenochtitlan [if the bells were not rung]. // And at nine o'clock at night, the Spanish lords, the gentlemen, began to [*p. 42*] make their horses run outside the palace. The attire they wore was all very splendid; in the same fashion they prepared and adorned their horses,[3] and in the same fashion they fully prepared as to their outfits their black slaves who went following their lords there. The viceroy was the one who first began the horse running, and another gentleman rode beside him. They started[4] the other lords, who went along in pairs making their horses run. And the older Spaniards said that such a thing had never been seen, that any viceroy here in Mexico should have done such a thing, back from when the first viceroys came to rule here in Mexico, such as don Juan de Mendoza y Luna, Marqués of Montesclaros, did. And many more things were done on the feast day of San Mateo to celebrate because the prince was born. And as the news came written from Spain, it was on the 8th of the month of April in the same year of 1605, on Good Friday, that the prince, don Felipe Domingo Víctor de Austria, the heir of our great ruler the king don Felipe III, who rules now in Spain, was born. And the reason why they gave the royal child, the prince, his second name, so that his name became Domingo, [*p. 43*] was that where the beloved of our lord God, the greatly deserving saint Domingo de Guzmán, was baptized when he was an infant in the baptismal font of the town where they baptized him, was the same place where they baptized the royal child, the prince, so that from there he took the name of Santo Domingo, as became known here in Mexico.

v Today, the 4th of the month of October of the year 1605, on the feast day of San Francisco, a celebration was held again, for a second time; the Spaniards appeared in many guises and representing many things for amusement, to tell tales and make people laugh. They all went everywhere in the streets, following the various roads in Mexico. They

4. Possibly challenged or attacked? It is not clear to us yet whether the participants are racing, displaying their horses' paces, or performing mock jousting (*juego de cañas*). In Carochi 2001, p. 273, reflexive *tlatlaloa*, in the first person plural with long vowel reduplication, is explained by examples of those who ride at jousts or run in pairs, making swirls or circles around something.

tique. mochintin. nohuian nenque. yn caltzallan. cohotocaque. yn mexico. xayacatl. conaquitinemia. yhuann amatl. amatlacuiloltepitoton. quitemacatinemia yn oncan ipan icuiliuhtoc. in tleyn nepapan tehuetzquititlahtolli yn oquicuiloque. yn çan quiyoyocoxque yn çan quipipicque. in çan quiyoyollohuique tlatlaquetzalli tlahtolli. auh yhuan ye no ceppa. cauallotlatlalochtique. yn españolesme. in tlahtoque. ypan chiquacẽ tzillini. in ye teotlac. ye no ceppa yhu in mochiuh yn iuh achtopa mochiuh ye no ceppa yehuatzin achtopa mocauallotlatlalochtili. yn tlahtohuani visurrey. quimonmopehualtilili[1] yn tlahtoq̃ ynic cauallotlatlalochtique.

v Yn ipan axcan yc viii. mani metztli octubre de 1605. años. yquac maxitico. nican mexico in yehuatzitzĩ [*p. 44*] Padreme Sant. Augustin. descalços. yn quintocayotia. Regoredos.[2] matlactlomome. ompa hualmohuicaq̃. in españa. auh çan onmoquixtitiquizque. in mexico. mohuicaque a la china. ynic ompa motemachtilizq̃

v Auh no yquac. yn ipan in xihuitl. omoteneuh de 1605. años. cenca omochiuhque. yn mimichtin. in xoxohuiltin. yn amillome.[3] yhuan no cenca miectin yn omochiuhque tocame. yn caltitech. yn nican mexico.

v Yn ipan axcan yc 8. mani metztli. de diciembre de 1605. años. yquac omachiztico. omicohuac yn a la china. ye iuh nepa ce xihuitl. yn ipan ylhuitzin catca Sant. Fran^{co}. yn omochiuh yaoyotl. amo cẽca miectin yn micque españolesme. auh ye oc cẽca tlapanahuia miectin. in micque in mictilloque yn ompa tlaca. macehualtin in motenehua Sangreyes.[4]

—

¶ x. tochtli xihuitl. 1606. años. ypan in in yancuic xihuitl. yhuan ypan in yancuic metztli henero. yn ohuacico. yn ohualla ycedulatzin. yn itlanahuatiltzin. yn tohueytlahtocatzin Rey Don felipe tercero. yn ipampa yn quin nepa omochiuh congrecacion[5] y nohuian ypan altepetl. ceceyaca cece yn itlahuillanalpan yn itlatititzalpan[6] motenehua. ysojetos. in campa. inyeyan. ymonoyan in macehualtzitzintin. yn quaxochtli. quitztoca. in quaxochpiaya. yquaniloque. mochintin tlaliloto. ytzontecompa.[7] yn altepetl. yn inpopohuian. auh yc cenca innetoliniliz. mochiuh. yn macehualtzitzinti. auh iuh quimocaquilti. yn tohueytlahtocauh. Rey. ye õxiuhtica. nepa nohuian omochiuh yn congrecacion. ynic axcan ohualmotlatitlani ohualmotlanahuatilli yn tohueytlahtocatzin. y iuh quihualmitalhui. [*p. 45*] Yc nitlanahuatia. yntla quinequizque mochintin. macehualtin. yn ohualliquaniloque. yn imaltepeuh ypan yn inpopohuian yntla oc ceppa mocuepazque. ma mocuepacan. ca yyollocacopatiz. yntla quinequizque mocuepazque yn campa inyeyan ymonoyan catca.— auh aocmo huel iuh mochiuh. aocac omocuep yn macehualli. ça iuh omocauhque yn oncan oyquaniloque. auh ça cana yn omocuepque. yn campa inyeyampa. macehualtin

v Yn axcan Domingo. yc 26. mani metztli de febrero de 1606 años. yquac otlatiloc. ce tlacatl. molato. çan tlapic teopixqui clerigo omochiuhca. amo tlateochihualli catca ymac obispo. huecauh yn missa oquitohuaya oteyolcuitiaya. otetlaceliltiaya. otequatequiaya otenamictiaya yn ompa campa oquiztinenca ypan altepetl. yn ompa canin motlapialia.

---

1. The same question arises here as in the immediately preceding note. But the phrase just before the word tends to point in the direction of simply going first.

2. Retired, of strict observance.

3. In Mexican Spanish, *juiles* and *amilotes*.

4. Ethnic Chinese.

went about wearing masks and giving people little pieces of paper with writing, on which were written whatever various joking words they had written, that they had just composed, made up, and improvised. And also the Spanish lords made horses run again, at six o'clock in the afternoon. It was done again as it was done the first time; again the lord viceroy ran a horse first, he started[1] the lords running horses.

v Today the 8th of the month of October of the year 1605 was when [*p. 44*] the discalced fathers of San Agustín, called Recoletos,[2] arrived here in Mexico; twelve came from Spain. They just quickly passed through Mexico; they went to China [the Philippines] to preach there.

v Also in this said year of 1605 there were many fish, trout-like fish [*xoxohuiltin*] and white fish [*amilome*],[3] and there were also many spiders around the houses here in Mexico.

v Today, the 8th of the month of December of the year 1605, was when it became known that there were deaths in China [the Philippines] a year ago or more, on the feast day of San Francisco, when there was fighting. Not very many Spaniards died, but there were a great many more of the people there, the indigenous inhabitants called Sangleyes,[4] who died and were killed. —

¶ 10 Rabbit year, 1606. In the new year and new month of January, the cedula and order of our great ruler the king don Felipe III came and arrived here, concerning the *congregaciones*[5] that were carried out a little while back in the [various] altepetl all around. In each one, each of its dependencies,[6] called sujetos, where the poor commoners were and dwelt, looking to and guarding their boundaries, were all moved and taken to be settled in the headtown[7] of the altepetl to which they belonged; through this the commoners suffered great afflictions. But our great ruler the king heard about it two years after the congregaciones were carried out everywhere, so that now our great ruler has sent a message here and given orders, saying, [*p. 45*] "I order that if all the commoners who were moved in the altepetl to which they belong want to go back again [to where they came from], let them go back; it is to be by their own free will if they want to return to where they used to be and live." — But it could no longer be done, none of the commoners went back, but stayed where they were moved to; only in rare cases did the commoners return to where they had been.

v Today, Sunday the 26th of the month of February of the year 1606, was when a mulatto was burned. He had falsely made himself a secular priest; he was not ordained by a bishop. For a long time he had been saying mass, hearing confessions, administering communion, baptizing and marrying people in the various altepetl he had gone passing

5. Systematic resettlements of indigenous people organized by the Spaniards, usually to concentrate them more.

6. The Nahuatl terminology for dependencies speaks of entities dragged or pulled along with the overall entity.

7. The term used is a literal Nahuatl translation of Spanish *cabecera*.

clerigostin yn motenehua beneficiados.[1] yn iquac yntlan callaquia yn oquic yn aço oc cana ommohuicaya ytech mocauhtihuia. ynic oc yehuatl inyeyampa mocahuaya. teoyotica. quinpalehuiaya. quichihuaya yehuatl. in ixquich omoteneuh teotequitl. missa. quitohuaya. çan tlapic yc tetlateotoquiltiaya. yn cacocuia tlaxcalli. yn amo tlateochihualli. yn amo nelli huel yehuatzĩ ynacayotzin tt^{o}. Dios. y motenehua Sacramento. auh maçonellihui yn quitohuaya, yn ixquich teotlatolli[2] camo pouhqui. yn oquic amo ytlateochihual obispo. auh machiztito. yn ompa ynquisicio. yn amo tlateochihualli. anoc. yn ompa Sancto oficio. ypan. auh yn oyttoc yn ca nelli iuhqui. yc tlatiloc. auh ye quin iquac opehu in. yn ipan in xihuitl. yn oc ompa titztihui yn aquin. iuhqui quichihuaz. yn çan tlapic missa quihtoz. niman. tlatiloz. yn ompa Sancto oficio. La ynquisicio. ca iuh hualmotlanahuatilia. in yehuatzin in tocenquizcahueyteopixcatzin. Sancto Padre. in Ro[*p. 46*]ma. moyetztica. yehuantin quinhualmonahuatilia ynquisidoresme. ynic yehuantin. quimochihuilizque Justicia. nican mexico. ca yntequitzin in ynin omochiuh ypan quaresma.

v Yn ipan axcan quaresma yc 16. mani metztli. Março de 1606. años. no yquac momiquilli in Don Bartholome fran^{co}. xochiquentzin al~~lde~~ catca. nican mexico ynin ipiltzin yn Don Pablo xochiquentzin catca

v Auh no ypan yn axcan. omoteneuh quaresma. yn ipan Juebes Sancto. yquac yancuican. achto. oquizque. yn ipilhuantzitzin Sancta Catharina Martyr. huel qualli. ynic quiz tlayahualoliztli. yehuatl in motenehua La Sangre de christo.

v Yn ipan axcan yc 5. mani metztli abril. de 1606. a^{o}s. yquac omotlapoto yn atenamitl. mexicatzinco. ynic tzauhcticatca ynic oncan hualquiçaz atl. çan oc cecni n mocuitlacoyonito. atenamitl. ypampa acallac in teocalli. cuitlahuac. yhuan mizquic. yhuan no ypampa yn ompa ynic oyaque ocholloque yc omocalcauhque. çan mochipa quiztimani yahtimani miyequintin macehualtin. yn ompa chaneque omoteneuh ye quicahua yn imaltepeuh. ye hui ypan oc cequi atl tepetl. yehica ypampa yn incal yn inchachan oc ohuacallac. yhuan miec yn opapachiuh yn oxixitin. auh y manel oc cequi calli. yn oc huel mamani yece ca ça tlatlacacitimani yn atl. ynic mocalcauhque macehualtin.

v Yn ipan axcan yc 2. mani metztli Mayo. de 1606 años. yquac omomiquilli in Don diego Romano. obispo cat[ca] tlaxcallan.

v Yn axcan. yc 2. mani metztli Junio de 1606. años yquac. Perù.[3] ohualla tlahtolli omachiztico ỹ nican [*p. 47*] Mexico. Omomiquilli. yn ompa Perù. in yehuatzin tlacatl. yn tlahtohuani Don Gaspar. de çuñiga. y Azeuedo. Conde de monterrey. visurrey. catca yn ompa Perù. iuh machiztico. yc x. mani metztli. de febrero. viernestica in momiquilli. aminaliztli.[4] yn quimohuiquilli. ynic momiquilli. auh iuh mitohuaya yntla huel oc mocueptzinohuani. yn ompa españa. ca ycamalerotzin mochiuhtzinozquia. yn tohueycihuatlahtocauh. Reyna. Doña margarida austria. yn inamictzin yn axcan moyetztica tohueytlahtocauh Don felipe Tercero.

v Yn ipan axcan Domingo. yc 23. mani metztli Julio. de 1606. años. yquac yn ompa tzaqualtitlan tenanco. amaquemecan momiquilli. in quimohuiquilli tt^{o}. Dios. yehuatzin.

---

1. Curates.

2. *Teotlatolli* often means sermon, but here it seems to refer to the words uttered during the sacraments.

3. "Peru" in many instances has a very small mark above the *u*, somewhere between a dot and a small vertical mark. It is not like any of Ch.'s other diacritics. Thus it is probably not an overbar to indicate a nasal, though many Nahuas wrote "pelon," etc.

through, where secular priests called *beneficiados*[1] were in charge, when he entered where they were; as long as they were gone somewhere it would be left to him, while he was left in their place, to help them with divine matters, doing all the said churchly tasks. He would say mass and falsely sanctify the bread he lifted up, which was not blessed, not really the body of our lord God, called the Sacrament. Although he said all the divine words,[2] it did not count, as long as he was not ordained by a bishop. It became known at the Inquisition that he was not ordained; he was arrested [and held] in the [building of] the Holy Office. When it was seen that it was truly that way [as reported], he was burned for it. From that point it began, in this year and for the future, that whoever should do likewise, say mass falsely, will immediately be burned at the Holy Office of the Inquisition; so orders come from our supremely great priest the Holy Father who is in Rome; [*p. 46*] he orders the inquisitors here to do justice here in Mexico, for that is their duty. This happened during Lent.

v Today, during Lent, the 16th of the month of March of the year 1606, was also when don Bartolomé Francisco Xochiquentzin passed away. He was alcalde here in Mexico and was the child of don Pablo Xochiquentzin.

v Also in the just now mentioned Lent, on Maundy Thursday, was when for the first time the children of Santa Catarina Mártir came out; the procession turned out very well. It is the one called the Blood of Christ.

v Today, the 5th of the month of April of the year 1606, was when the dike at Mexicatzinco was opened, that had been closed, so that water will come out there. For now, only one place in the dike was opened, because the churches in Cuitlahuac and Mizquic were submerged, and also because of those there who left their houses and went and fled; many commoners are always leaving and going. The said residents there have already left their altepetl and gone to other altepetl because their houses and homes were still submerged, and many collapsed and crumbled, and although there are other houses spread about, yet they are half filled with water, so that the commoners left them.

v Today, the 2nd of the month of May of the year 1606, was when don Diego Romano, who was bishop of Tlaxcala, passed away.

v Today, the 2nd of the month of June of the year 1606, was when news came from Peru[3] and it was known here [*p. 47*] in Mexico that the lord ruler don Gaspar de Zúñiga y Acevedo, Count of Monterrey, who was viceroy in Peru, passed away there. It became known that it was on the 10th of the month of February, a Friday, that he passed away; [dysentery][4] carried him off, so that he died. And it was said that if he had been able to return to Spain, he would have become the chamberlain of our great lady ruler, the queen, doña Margarita de Austria, spouse of our present great ruler, don Felipe III.

v Today, Sunday the 23rd of the month of July of the year 1606, was when my late precious father, Juan Agustín Ixpintzin, a lord, who was the son of the lady doña Luisa

---

Perhaps it is intended as the grave accent sometimes used at this time to show stress, and we have so reproduced it.

In other cases, the mark above the *u* is identical to Ch.'s overbar or tilde, and we have reproduced it as a tilde.

4. Molina defines *amina* as being ill because of the water not agreeing with one after having eaten green foods.

notlaçotatzin. moyetzticatca. Juan augustin yxpintzin teuhctli. yn itelpochtzin catca cihuapilli. Doña luisa. xochiquetzaltzin.[1] auh ynic omonemiltico tlalticpac yn ixquichcauh onpohualxihuitl. oncaxtolli. yn ipan in metztli omoteneuh. yquac momanaco. matlaltotonqui.[2] iuh quihtoque. yn tlamatinime yehuatl techhuicac[4] yni ipan in xihuitl omoteneuh yn quitocayotia planeta Marte. huey citlalli.[3] huel ihiyo.[5] yn cocoliztica.

v Yn ipan axcan lunes. yc 2. mani metztli octubre de 1606. años. yey tzillini ye yeotlac. yquac momiquilli. in teoyotica. tlahtohuani Don fray Garcia de Stta maria de mendoça y çuñiga. arçobispo. omoyetzticatca ỹ nican ypan huey altepetl ciudad mexico. tenochtitlan. ynin Sant. Jeronimo teopixqui. auh yn o iuh momiquilli. quin imoztlayoc ypã martes. ye teotlac. yvisperatzin ypan Sant. Franco tlayahualoliztica. yn quihualmoquixtilique y[*p. 48*]chantzinco. oncan quimotoquilico. yn inacayotzin yn iglesia mayor. altar mayor. yn motoquiltitoc auh ynic teoyotica omotlahtocatillico. mexico. çan huel nauhxihuitl.

v Yn ipan axcan miercoles. yc 4. mani metztli. octubre de 1606. años. ypã Sant. Franco. ylhuitzin ye teotlac yn maxitico. yn mocallaquico. nican mexico in yehuatzin visitador. general. ytoca el llicеciado. Diego lantẽras y velasquez.[6] yn ompa ohualmohuicac españa. oquihualmihualli. in tohueytlahtocauh Rey. ynic yehuatzin motlachiyeltiz. nican ypan nueua españa

v Auh yn axcan ynpan yc 24. mani metztli octubre de 1606. años. yquac ompa yn tzaqualtitlan tenanco amaquemecan. omomiquilli. omopolihuilti. yn tlacatl cihuapilli nocitzin Doña Martha de St.tiago. amaxochtzin tenanco tepopolla cihuapilli oncan. ychantzinco ynin ynamictzin. catca yn pilli Don Domingo Hernãdez. ayopochtzin. tzaqualtitlan tenanco amaquemecan ychantzinco. auh ynic omonemiltico cihuapilli tlalticpac. yepohualxihuitl. onmatlactli ypãn onxihuitl. ynin ychpochtzin catca. yn tlacatl. Don Juan Hehuacayotzin. pilli. oncan ychantzinco catca yn tecpan yn itocayocan tlayllotlacan tecalco. ytech pohui yn altepetl. tenanco texocpalco tepopolla. chalco.

v Auh yn ipan axcan yc 6. mani metztli de diciẽbre. de 1606. años. yquac ye no occan quitlapoto. quicoyonito. yn mexicatzinco atenamitl. yn oncan hualquiça atl. yn oncan yancuic buentes. quichiuhque. yhuan yancuic puertas. oncan quitlatlallique. ynic tzauhctiez. yn iquac quenmanian yntla oc ceppa. apachiohuaz. mexico. yc motzaquatiuh [*p. 49*] Yn atl. auh yn ipan quitlapoto. atenamitl mexicatzinco ypampa yn cenca ye apachihuia. yn izqui altepetl chinãpan catqui. in culhuacan. xochmilco. cuitlahuac. mizquic

v Auh çan no ypan in yn izquilhuitia. omoteneuh metztli octubre.[7] yquac ohualla. tlahtolli in La china. omachiztico. ye oquitlanque. in españolesme. yn altepetl. yn oncan ytocayocan Maluco. ye ytechtzinco. ponhui. in yehuatzin. tohueytlahtocauh Rey Don Felipe. Tercero. yn ompa españa. moyetztica. yhuan yuh machiztico. yn oncan tlahtocatia. Maluco. yn Rey. mochiuhticatca. cacique in christianosme. yhuan no yquac yn ipan in xihuitl omoteneuh yquac ompa momiquilli yn La china. yn oncã manilla. yn gouer-

---

1. The name Juan Agustín Ixpintzin is without don and consists of two first names plus a possibly made up or little used indigenous name; it comes very low on the naming scale for the early seventeenth century. Perhaps Juan Agustín was illegitimate; his father is not mentioned.

2. *Totonqui* means hot; *matlal-* refers to a dark color most often indicated as green. The word is thought to refer to typhus; see Cook 1998, p. 138. We thank Linda Newson for giving us the information and the reference.

Xochiquetzaltzin, passed away and our lord God took him.[1] He lived on earth for 55 years. The said month was when *matlaltotonqui*[2] broke out. The wise men said that what they call the planet Mars, a great star,[3] governed us[4] in the aforementioned year; it is really its emanation[5] with the epidemic.

v Today, Monday the 2nd of the month of October of the year 1606, at three o'clock in the afternoon, was when the ruler in divine things, don fray García de Santa María de Mendoza y Zúñiga, who was archbishop here in the great altepetl and city of Mexico Tenochtitlan, passed away; he was a Hieronymite friar. After he died, right on the next day, Tuesday, in the afternoon on the eve of [the feast day] of San Francisco, they brought him in procession [*p. 48*] out of his home [the archiepiscopal palace] and came to bury his body in the cathedral; it is at the main altar that he lies buried. He ruled in Mexico in divine matters for only four full years.

v It was today, Wednesday the 4th of the month of October of the year 1606, on the feast day of San Francisco, in the afternoon, that the inspector general, whose name is licenciado Diego Landeras y Velásquez,[6] arrived and entered in Mexico here. He came from Spain; our great ruler the king sent him here to look at things here in New Spain.

v Today, the 24th of the month of October of the year 1606, was when the noble lady my grandmother, doña Marta de Santiago Amaxochtzin, a noblewoman of Tenanco Tepopolla, who was from there, passed away and perished in Tzaqualtitlan Tenanco, [a division of] Amaquemecan. She was the spouse of the nobleman don Domingo Hernández Ayopochtzin from Tzaqualtitlan Tenanco [in] Amaquemecan. The lady lived on earth for 72 years. She was the daughter of the lord don Juan Ehuacayotzin, a nobleman, whose home was at the palace at the place called Tlailotlacan Teccalco belonging to the altepetl Tenanco Texocpalco Tepopolla, [a part of] Chalco.

v Today, the 6th of the month of December of the year 1606, was when they went to a second place to open and make holes in the dike at Mexicatzinco for the water to come out, where they built new bridges and placed new gates so the dike can be closed; if there is a flood in Mexico again sometime, the water will be closed off with them. [*p. 49*] And the reason they went to open the dike at Mexicatzinco was that all the altepetl in the chinampa country—Colhuacan, Xochimilco, Cuitlahuac, and Mizquic—were flooded.

v And on the same day in the said month of October[7] was when news came from China [the Philippines] and it became known that the Spaniards had gained the altepetl called Malucca, which already belongs to our great ruler the king don Felipe III, who is in Spain, and it became known that the Christians captured the one who had ruled in Malucca and had been made king there. And also at that time in the said year was when the governor of the Philippines, who governed all the Christians who dwell there, passed

3. It may be that *huei citlalin*, literally "great star," actually means planet. In Molina the expression is glossed as Venus specifically.

4. Or accompanied us?

5. Literally "its breath."

6. Given as licenciado Diego Landeras de Velasco in Torquemada 1975, 1: 737, and other sources.

7. Sic, meaning December?

nador. momiquilli. ompa yntepachocauh catca yn ixquichtin christianosme. yn ompa onoque. quizqui. yn x. tochtli xihuitl.

¶ xi. acatl xihuitl. 1607. años. ypan in xihuitl. ypã metztli. Março. yquac ocehuico yn cocoliztli matlaltotonqui yn manca. cenca chicahuac yc micohuac in nican mexico. ce xihuitl. yn manca

v Auh ye ytlamian ynin omoteneuh metztli Março. ca nohuian huaquico yn atl. yn ipan ayxtlahuatl. yn oncan huehuey yc momanca atl. auh çan huel ome metztli yn ontlaahuacca. yn huel onpoliuhca atl. ynic cennohuian chinampa. yn çan iyocan: nican mexico. yn ipan metztli. abril. tlaahuaqui. yhuan yn ipan metztli. Mayo. tlaahuaqui huel popoliuhca. yn atl chinampa. yhuan yn ayxtlahuacan. huel teteyn tzatzayan yn tlalli. auh çan niman aocmo tlaahuecatlan mochiuh. yn ipan huehuey acallotli. ỹ nicã mexico. ca huel popolihuico. yn huaquico. yn omoteneuh tlacpac atl. yn ça huel achiton ica. yc apachihuizquia. altepetl mexico. tenochtitlan. yn ipan huehue xivitl viii tecpatl. de 1604. años. yn iquac ypã yehuatl moyãcuilli mochi nohuian yn itlacauhtoca. yn ça cuicuitla[*p. 50*]Coyontoca. yn atenamitl. auh yn manca atl. nican mexico. yn amo huel huaquia. onxihuitl. ypan tlacoxiuhtica. ynic huaquico yn ipan in xihuitl omoteneuh

v Auh yn axcan ypan metztli Junio. ye no nicuel momanaco. in quiyahuitl. // auh yn ipan Sant. Juã bap^ta^. ylhuitzin quiz. yquac cenca yequene chicahuac. yc cen peuh yn momanaco. quiyahuitl. yn cecemilhuitl. yhuan ceceyohuatl.[1] ye quiyahui ynic nohuian ypan nueua españa. ynic ye no nicuel opeyonico otemico atl. nican mexico. ynic cennohuian ahuatzalpan huehuey ayxtlahuacã omochiuh yhuan yn mochi chinamitl huel popoliuh yn apachiuh. yhuãn iquac. yn ompa azcapotzalco. cuitlaxitin ce atlauhtli. yn oncan ytocayocan quauhyahualolco. yn oncan hualcuitlaquiçaya atl. tepeatl. cenca hualtillahuatihuia. yn hualtemoya. quauhtla. ynic oncan ypã hualhuia ypã hualxelihuia. yn altepetl. azcapotzalco. yc ye polihuizquia. yquac ompa catca. yn tlahtohuani. Don luis de velasco. ayatle ytequiuh. çan ompa mocehuitzinoticatca.

v Yn axcan ypan yc 20. mani metztli. Junio. yquac ohualla tlahtolli. yn ompa españa. omachiztico. ynic ye no nicuel. quihualmomaquilia. yn tohueytlahtocauh Rey. yn itlahtocayo. yehuatzin tlacatl Don luis de velasco. ynic visurrey ye no nicuel mochiuhtzinoz. ỹ nican. ypan nueua españa. auh ompa ypan acico yn itlahtocayo. yn imacehualpan.[2] azcapotzalco. yn quihualmotitlanilili ytlahtocayo yehuatzin. yn tohueitlahtocauh[3] Don felipe tercero. yn ompa moyetztica castilla. —

auh ynic ompa cuitlaxitin. atlauhtli. [*p. 51*] Yn azcapotzalco. yn oncan quauhyahualolco. yehuantin quitzaquato yn mexica. yhuan tepaneca. oc yehuatzin. ytencopatzinco. mochiuh ynic ompa atzaqualloto. yn tlahtohuani visurrey Don Juan de mendoça y luna. huel inomatzinco. ompa mohuicaya. yn quimottillito. yhuan no yehuatzin. ompa ypan motlahtolti. yn atzaqualiztli. yn tlahtohuani Don luis de velasco. yn oquic ayemo hualmohuetzitia nican mexico. ypan ytlahtocayo.

v Auh yn axcan ypan yc 29. mani metztli Junio. ypan ylhuitzin. Sant. Pedro yhuan Sant. Pablo. apostolosme. yquac moquixti. ypan ce tzillini yn quitlalcahui. huey altepetl

1. For "cece(n)yohual."

2. The younger don Luis de Velasco held encomiendas in both Azcapotzalco and nearby Toltitlan (see an entry of October 26, 1603, pp. 78–79 [top]). See Gerhard 1972, p. 248.

away in Manila. End of 10 Rabbit year.

¶ 11 Reed year, 1607. In this year, in the month of March, was when the epidemic of the fever matlaltotonqui, which had greatly raged, and from which there were many deaths here in Mexico, subsided. It had gone on for a year.

v At the end of this said month of March, the water dried up everywhere in the expanses of water where the great waters had spread out. For fully two months it was dry and the water was entirely gone all over the chinampa district; here in Mexico in particular, it was dry in the month of April, and it was dry in the month of May. The water was entirely missing in the chinampas, and on the lakes the land [the lake floor] was full of cracks and crevices. And there was no deep water left at all in the big canals here in Mexico, for the water mentioned above had entirely disappeared and dried up, when only a very little while before the altepetl of Mexico Tenochtitlan was about to be covered over by water, in the old-style year of 8 Flint, the year of 1604, in which all the dikes everywhere that had gone bad, that had holes in their sides, [*p. 50*] were renovated, when the waters spread out here in Mexico and it did not not dry out for two years and a half, until it dried out in the said year.

v Now in the month of June the rains broke out again. // When the feast day of San Juan Bautista was celebrated was when finally and at last the rains began to come on very strongly, raining all day and all night[1] all over New Spain, so that again the water spilled over and filled up Mexico here, so that the dry land everywhere became large lakes, and all the chinampas entirely disappeared and were flooded. And it was when the sides of a ravine in Azcapotzalco at the place called Quauhyahualco collapsed, where the water from the mountains was coming out the sides; the water came very heavily, descending from the forests, so that it came down upon and spread over the altepetl of Azcapotzalco, causing it almost to be destroyed. At that time the ruler don Luis de Velasco was there, not yet in office; he was just in retirement there.

v Today, the 20th of the month of June, was when news came from Spain and it became known that our great ruler the king is again giving the rulership to the lord don Luis de Velasco, so that he will be made viceroy again here in New Spain. And [news] of his rulership reached him [when he was] among his vassals in Azcapotzalco;[2] our great[3] ruler don Felipe III who is in Spain sent him the rulership. —

And when the sides of the ravine collapsed [*p. 51*] in Azcapotzalco, at Quauhyahualco, the Mexica and Tepaneca went to close it. Going to close off the water there was still done by order of the lord viceroy don Juan de Mendoza y Luna, who went there in person to inspect it, and also the ruler don Luis de Velasco looked after closing off the water previous to coming here to Mexico to settle down in his rulership.

v Today, the 29th of the month of June, the feast day of San Pedro and San Pablo, apostles, at one o'clock, was when the lord viceroy don Juan de Mendoza y Luna, Marqués of

3. The *i* in this word is not written clearly and might be imagined not to be there except that it is needed.

ciudad. mexico tenochtitlan in yehuatzin tlahtohuani visurrey. Don Juan de mẽdoça. y luna marques de montesclaros. ompa mohuicac Perù. auh yn omoyetztiaco[1] ynic omotlahtocatilico nican mexico. ynic ye nohuian ypã nueua españa, yexihuitl ypan chicuetetl. metztli.

v Auh niman hualmoman yn metztli Julio. yn ipan in mani quiyahuitl.

v Yn ipan axcan Domingo. yc 15. mani metztli Julio. de 1607 a^os. yquac ypan macuilli tzillini ye teotlac. yn maxitico. yn mocallaquico. yhtic altepetl mexico tenochtitlan. yc mohuetzitico. ynic ye no nicuel oncan no ceppa conmanilli yn itlahtocayo. tlahtohuani Don luis de velasco. yc oppa visurrey. omochiuhtzino. ỹ nican mexico. ompa hualmehuiti yn azcapotzalco. ynic motlallitzinoco yn itlahtocaycpalpan. auh ynic çan catca ỹ mocehuitzino yn atle ytequiuh catca yexihuitl ypã chiquacentetl. metztli. ynic ompa hualmohuicac [*p. 52*] Perũ. ompa visurrey. moyetzticatca. yehuatzin ompa quihualmopatillito. yn conde Don Gaspar de çuñiga y azeuedo.

v Yn inpan[2] axcan yc 26. mani metztli. Julio de 1607. años. ypan ylhuitzin Sancta Ana. ye teotlac yquac ompa omicohuac. in hueyapan yn ipan acallotli.[3] ynic ompa huillohua tetzcoco: noço nican yc hualhuillohua mexico. auh yeh nican. mexico. hualhuia yn acalli. yehuatl yn quitocayotia. navio. yn hueyapan pollaquico. auh yhtic hualyetihuia miec tlatquitl. yn cacahuatl. xiquipiltica hualloonotihuia. caxtolli tlacatl onnahui : yn ihtic hualyetihuia acalli. yn españolesme. yhuan çan quezquintin yn macehualtin. yn mochintin. yhtic hualyetihuia acalli hueyatl. ynepantla. yn pollaquico. yn oncan momiquillique. yn espanolesme. ce Sant. augustin teopixqui. telpochtli. ayemo missa quichihuaya. yhuan yn oc ce español ytoca Diego de paz. procurador.[4] audiencia real catca. yn oncan mochtin. momiquillique matlanhuique. auh ça nahui tlacatl yn momaquixtique yn ca atitlan yahque. tlamanellotiaque. ynic ompa atenquiçato chimalhuacan atenco. auh in yehuantin oc cequintin. yn atitlan momiquillique. çatepan ye yquezquilhuitiyoc. in necico: matlactlomome tlacatl. yn ompan quinquixtique. yn quimanque. chimalhuacan atenco yn mimiccatzitzinti. ompa tocoque. auh çan chiquacentetl metztli. yn onmonec acalli yn nabio. ynic achto nezca. necoccampa. yc tepanahuilloya. ỹ nican onehuaya mexico. tlaca. yc onpanahuilloya ynic ompa huia in tetzcoco. auh yn ompa tetzcoco. ompa [*p. 53*] Yc hualtepanahuiloya. yn ompa huallehuaya tetzcoco tlaca. yc huel hualpanahuiloya ynic nican hualhuia mexico. ynic yehuatl yca. amo huecauh panolloya. yn acalli. auh ynic tlamictico ynic pollaquico hueyapan. çan ic cotonico. ypampa ỹ tepanahuiaya. amo huecauh yn onmonec yn nabio. yninn iaxca catca. yn Don Juan de aluarado. gouernador tetzcoco.

v Auh ynic tlamico. metztli omoteneuh Julio. cenca chicahuac yn manca quiyahuitl.

v Auh yc niman hualmoman in metztli agosto. çan no yhui yn ipan cenca chicahuac yn mani quiyahuitl. ynic mottac. cenca ye tleco. ye temi ye peyoni ye moteponaçohua. yn atl. ynic nohuian cenmexico. tenochtitlan. ye apachihui yn altepetl. ynic ye no ceppa oquitzatzaquato. yn õpa mexicatzinco atenamitl. yn tlatlapouhticatca yn quitlapoca yexcan yn oncan hualquiçaya atl. nican mexicopa hualhuia. yc quicaxahuaya. ynic cennohuian chinampa ye polihuizquia yn izquicã ypan altepetl. omoteneuh. yn culhuacan. yn xoch-

---

1. For "omoyetztieco."

2. For "ipan."

3. *Acalotli* normally is a canal used for boats, but since it means "boat road," it might have the sense of a commonly used route or channel across the lake.

Montesclaros, left and abandoned the great altepetl and city of Mexico Tenochtitlan and went to Peru. He had been[1] ruler here in Mexico and all New Spain for three years and eight months.

v Then came the month of July, in which there was rain.
v Today, Sunday, the 15th of the month of July of the year 1607, at 5 o'clock in the afternoon, was when the ruler don Luis de Velasco arrived in and entered the altepetl of Mexico Tenochtitlan, coming to establish himself to take his rulership again, having been made viceroy for the second time here in Mexico; he came from Azcapotzalco to take his seat on his throne as ruler. He was in retirement and without office for three years and six months since he came from [*p. 52*] Peru, where he was viceroy; the Count don Gaspar de Zúñiga y Acevedo went there to replace him.

v Today, on[2] the 26th of the month of July of the year 1607, the feast day of Santa Ana, in the afternoon, was when people died on the great lake, [on the boat route?][3] that goes to Tetzcoco or comes here to Mexico. The boat, the kind they call a ship, was coming here to Mexico when it sank on the lake. Inside it came many goods; cacao beans came in bags. Nineteen Spaniards were riding in the boat, but only a few commoners; all who were riding inside the boat sank in the middle of the lake. Among the Spaniards who died there was an Augustinian friar, a youth who did not yet say mass [was not fully ordained], and another Spaniard named Diego de Paz, who was *procurador*[4] in the Royal Audiencia. All of them died there; they went into the water. There were only four people who escaped, who went into the water and went along swimming, so that they came out at the shore at Chimalhuacan Atenco. Of the others who died in the water, several days later twelve people showed up; they brought them out and took them at Chimalhuacan Atenco, and the dead were buried there. The boat or ship had been used for only six months since it first was built. It took people across in both directions. People of Mexico leaving from here were taken over by it to go as far as Tetzcoco. And at Tetzcoco [*p. 53*] people coming from Tetzcoco were brought by it in this direction, brought the whole way until they came to Mexico, so that with the boat, people were taken across in a short time. But when it caused the deaths and sank in the lake, the [service] of taking people across was discontinued. The ship was not used for long; it belonged to don Juan de Alvarado, governor in Tetzcoco.

v As the said month of July came to an end, there were very strong rains.
v Then came the month of August, in which likewise there were very strong rains, so that one saw that the waters greatly rose, filled everything up, spilled over, and swelled so that the whole altepetl of Mexico Tenochtitlan was flooded everywhere, so that again they went to close the dike at Mexicatzinco, which was open in various places; they had opened it in three places, from where water was coming out and coming toward Mexico here. The reason they made [the water] diminish was that [everything] was about to be

4. A *procurador* was commonly a barrister practicing before a court, usually without a law degree from a university, but the word was also used for special representatives or lobbyists for certain entities, and also for certain kinds of prosecuting attorneys.

milco. yn cuitlahuac. yn mizquic. yn cẽca ye polihuia. yn ica atl. ynic tzauhcticatca. ynic ye onxihuitl ypã tlacoxihuitl: huetzico ĩ ye quipolozquia. in ye capachozquia nican mexico. ynic yehuatl. ypampa quitzatzacca. Auh yhuan ye no oquitlatlapoca. auh ypan in yn omoteneuh metztli agosto. yhuan yn ompa omoteneuh mexicatzinco. mochi quitzatzaquato. yn atenamitl.

v Auh yn nican mexico. yn izquitetl. huehuey teopãcalli yhtic yn Sancto Domingo cenca mollonia. meyaya. cenca tentimoma yn ihtic atl. aocac [*p. 54*] huel oncallaquia. yhuan aocmo huel missa oncã mochihuaya. ypampa huel yuh mitoz ca ça tlacacitimania yn atl. ytlacapã[1] ỹ teocalli. yc quimoquixtilique. in sanctissimo sacramento. auh ça oncan claustro. yn mochihuaya missa. auh no yhuan. yn ompa teopan la compañia de Jesus yn tictocayotia teatinos. yn ihtic çan no iuh mochiuh. cenca no meyaya mollonia. no cenca tẽtimoma yn atl : aocmo no huel callacohuaya yn itic teopancalli. yhuan aocmo no huel oncan missa mochihuaya. no yc quimoquixtilique yn sanctissimo sacramẽto. yc motzacca yn teopancalli.

v Auh yn Sant. Fran.^co teopancalli. yn ihtic amo cenca miec ynic molon ynic mex atl. çan quexquich yca.

v Auh yn iglesia. mayor. teopancalli yhtic çan qualcan catca. ye quin ye pehuaznequia yn moloniznequia atl.

v Auh yn Sant. Augustin. yn ihtic teopancalli atle molon yn atl. çan qualcan catca. ypampa cenca quihuecapanoque. ynic quitlaltenque. in ye nepa. onxihuitl. ypan tlacoxihuitl. yn iquac no tlaapachiuhca mexico. // auh çan yehuantin yn huehuey teopancalli ỹ nican omoteneuhque. auh amo nican yhuan motenehua yn oc cequi. teopancalli yhuan yn monasterios. yn oncan moyetzticate monjastin. amo yhuan nican motenehua ypampa. ca nohuian mollon yn atl. yn inchachantzinco yn inmonasterios. yn iuh mochi tlacatl. quittac: yhuan quimati.

v Auh ynic nauhcampa quiztica. ynic nauhcampa xeliuhtica. yn mexicayotl tenochcayotl. yn Sant. Juan Moyotlan. yn Sant. Pablo. teopan. yn Sant. Sebastian atzaqualco. yn Sancta Maria. cuepopan. ynic nohuiã omoteneuh ynic cen ixquich mexico tenochtitlan [*p. 55*] Ca nohuian tlaapachiuh. auh ça yxquich yyolloco yn altepetl : ça tepitzin ica. yn tlalli mocauh yn amo apachiuh. yn iuh omoteneuh. ca ixquich tlacatl oquittac yhuan quimati yn mexico tlaca.

v Auh yn ixquichtin. mexica tenochca. yn onoque yn huel chinampa chaneque. ca ça nohuian acaltica yn callaquia ynchachan. ypampa yn ixquich yc huecapan. tlalticpactli yn omoteneuh yyolloco altepetl mexico huel quitencuitima[2] quixacitimomanaco yn ixquich omoteneuh. yc huecapan tlalticpactli yn atl. yc macoc. ynic moteponaço. auh ynic nohuian auh ynic caltzallan yn altepeyotl. mexico. ytloc ynahuac yn otlih: cocoton yn tlani. yn campa tlatlacomoliuhtica. yn amo huecapanixtoc. tlalpantli. çan tel yevatl yn apachiuh: yhuan yn nohuian ypan xolal. cacalac yn atl. auh yn campa huecapanixtoc tlalpantli. ça yyoca mocacauh. y nohuian. auh no yhuan ypampa. yn atl. yc nequapanchichihualoc nohuian ça yehuatl. ypan huilohuaya. yn quapantli. yhuan nohuiã yn caltechtli motzintlaltenãyoti. pitzatzitzinica. otlih. ypan pohuia ypan huilohuaya.[3] yhuan cenca

1. This expression, occurring more than once, may be the equivalent of "in the nave."
2. The meaning of the verb *tencui* (literally "to take the edge of") is not clear, but it seems to be being used as an approximate equivalent of *ixaci*, "to reach all of."

lost all over the chinampa district, in all the said altepetl—Colhuacan, Xochimilco, Cuitlahuac, Mizquic—which were greatly destroyed through the water having been closed off. Two and a half years before [the waters] were about to destroy and flood Mexico here, because of which they had closed [the dike at Mexicatzinco]. But they had already opened it in various places, and in the said month of August and at the said Mexicatzinco they went to close all the dikes.

v Here in Mexico inside each of the great churches, [starting with] Santo Domingo, much water sprang and gushed forth; the inside got very full of water. No longer could anyone [*p. 54*] go in, and mass could no longer be held there, because it can really be said that the church was half filled with water along the sides,[1] so that they removed the most Holy Sacrament, and mass was held only in the cloister. And also in the church of the Jesuits, whom we call Theatines, the same thing happened inside; the water also greatly gushed forth and sprang up, and the inside got very full. It was no longer possible to go inside the church, and mass could no longer be held there either, for which reason they also removed the most Holy Sacrament and closed the church.

v Inside the church of San Francisco not very much water sprang and gushed forth, just a bit.

v The cathedral was usable inside; the water was just barely beginning to spring forth.

v Inside the church of San Agustín no water sprang forth; it was in good shape, because they had greatly raised [the floor] by filling it in two and a half years before, when Mexico had also been flooded. // It is only the great churches that are mentioned here; the other churches are not mentioned here as well, and the convents where there are nuns are not mentioned here either, because the water sprang up everywhere in the buildings of their nunneries, as everyone saw and knows.

v In the four parts into which the entity of Mexico Tenochtitlan is divided, San Juan Moyotlan, San Pablo Teopan, San Sebastián Atzaqualco, and Santa María Cuepopan, everywhere in the said parts, in absolutely all of Mexico Tenochtitlan [*p. 55*] it was flooded everywhere. Only in the central part of the altepetl was a little land left that was not flooded. As mentioned, all the people in Mexico saw and know about it.

v All the Mexica Tenochca who lived on chinampas and really had their homes there entered their homes everywhere in boats, because the ground was so deep beneath the surface of the water. The said central part of the altepetl of Mexico was entirely affected,[2] as much as was mentioned, so that the ground was deep under the water, which rose and swelled. Everywhere in the streets near the central part of Mexico, the roads were interrupted in the low part, where there are big holes and the level ground was not elevated; that part was flooded, and the water entered the house lots everywhere. The only places left were wherever the ground had been raised. Also because of the water, wooden bridges were fixed up [improvised]; everywhere people went only on the bridges and on the sidewalks everywhere, which were provided with walls of earth as a foundation; they served as narrow roads and people walked on them.[3] Very many of the houses of Span-

3. The preceding several sentences are among the most difficult for us today in the whole larger text, and the translation involves more than the usual amount of speculation.

miec yn apachiuh yn acallac yn incal españolesme. yc mocalcauhque. yhuan cequi miec yn actihuetz yn papachiuh. yncal çan tel yehuatl. yn xancalli. tzitzinciyahuac. ynic huallactihuetz. auh no yhui oc cenca miec yn incal macehualtin. yn actihuetz. yn papachiuh yc quicauhque. auh yn ipampa yn atl. cenca quinmauhtiaya. quintequipachohuaya yn quittaya. yn ixquichtin españolesme. yc ye macomanazquia. ye mochtin. cholozquia. ye quicnocavazquia. yn altepetl mexico. tenochtitlan. auh yc niman in yehuatzin tlahtohuani visurrey Don luis de velasco. Pena quinmotlalili yn ix[*p. 56*]Quichtin. españolesme. ynic ayac. quiçaz. quitlalcahuiz. yn altepetl mexico. ypampa. ỹ cenca mochintin. ye mocomoniznequia. cenca ye momocihuiaya. ye mamanaya. yn ipampa atl. ynic cenca omacoc. omoteponaço. omopepeyontimoma nohuian. yn ipampa yc ye conmatizquia nohuiampa yn altepetl. ypampa ca cenca teyçahui ỹ manca quiyahuitl. yn ipan iquac yn omoteneuh xihuitl yn amo mochiuh mochiuh[1] in ye onxihuitl ypã tlacoxihuitl. ynic apachiohuac ynic quiyauh yn ipantzinco. yehuatzin mochiuh tlahtohuani visurrey. Don Juan de mendoça y luna. marques de montesclaros. auh yn axcan ypan in xihuitl yn titlahtohua. de 1607. años. yn ipan huehue xihuitl xi. acatl. ynic oppa ohuapachiohuaco. ye quin ipan in ohuapachihuico. yn tianquiztli. Sanct ipolito. aocmo oncan otiamicoya. yhuan yn Sant. Juan tianquiztli. no apachiuh centlacoltica. auh yn oc centlacolli. amo apachiuh ca quexquichton yn mocauh yehuatl. ypan tiamicoya. ça mocenmatia. oncan yn tiamicoya. yn ipampa moch apachiuh yn tianquiztli Sancto polito.

v Auh yn Santiago. tlatilolco. no yhuan nohuian apachiuh. yn altepetl. auh ça yxquich yn ompa tianquiztli yn amo apachiuh. ynic yehica ompa quihuicazquia. ompa quimanazquia. yn tianquiztli Sanct ipolito. yhuan yn tianquiztli. Sant Juan. yc moteylhuiaya yn tlatilolca. auh yece amo huel mochiuh. yc mixnamicque.[2] yn tenochtitlan tlaca.

v Auh in yehuatzitzin yn ixquichtintzitzin teopixque. fraylestin. yhuan no yehuantzitzin yn ixquichtintzitzin. cihuateopixque. in monjastin. yn mexico. monoltitoque. mochtintzitzin. [*p. 57*] Motequipachotzinoque. yn ipampa teopan yhuann ica yn incaltzin. in monasterios. ynic cenca ye nohuian. ye apachihuia. yhtic molon yn atl. auh yc yehuatl. nohuian. ypampa tlatlatlauhtiloc. yn quiyahuitl. manca. huel izquican yn teopan tlayahualoloya. yexpa in momoztlaye. yohuatzin^{co} niman ye nepantlah tonatiuh. niman ye teotlac çan callitic. yn ipampa yc cehuiz. mocahuaz yn quiyahuitl. quimocehuiliz. yn tt^{o} Dios. auh ynic tlamico metztli. agosto. cenca chicahuac yn manca quiyahuitl. ynic cenca tlaapacho mexico

v Auh niman ic hualmoman yn metztli Septiembre yn ipan in manin quiyahuitl. auh yn ipan in omoteneuh metztli. ypã niman quipehualtique yn ihtic Sancto Domingo teopancalli. in ye anoquillo. cenca ça tetlaocoltican. ça atezcapan catca. auh mochi quiyahuac quihuallazque. quiquixtique quinoquique. yn atl. tlapixque yn anoquique. oncan auh yn iquac. yn tlaanoquiloc callitic. niman in tlalpantli y nohuian callitic cacocque. quihuecapanoque.

v Auh çan no iuh quichiuhque. yn ompa la compañia de Jesus. yn teatinos. yhuan no quiyahuac quihualazque. quiquixtique quinoquique yn atl. in callitic catca. no yhuan yn tlalpantli. cacocque quihuecapanoque.

v Auh yn ipan axcan ynic 3. mani metztli. omoteneuh. Setiembre. de 1607. años. yquac nohuian opeuh yn izquican teopan mexico. ye tlatzillinilo. iuhqui descumunio. yc mo-

1. The word "mochiuh" is inadvertently repeated in the original.

iards were flooded and submerged, so that they abandoned their houses, and in places many of their houses fell in and collapsed. Especially adobe houses got soaked at the base, so that they fell in. Likewise even more of the houses of the commoners fell in and collapsed, so that they left them. The problems with the water greatly scared and concerned all the Spaniards who saw them, so that they were on the point of getting disturbed, all fleeing, and leaving the altepetl of Mexico Tenochtitlan orphaned. Thereupon the lord viceroy don Luis de Velasco set a fine for all [*p. 56*] the Spaniards so that no one would leave and abandon the altepetl of Mexico, because they were all about to get very agitated; they were disturbed and worked up about the water, how it greatly rose, swelled, and spilled over everywhere. For this reason they were about to go to the altepetl [in the countryside] all around, because the rains there were at that time, in the said year, were very frightening, the like of which had not happened[1] two and a half years before, when there was flooding because of the rain that happened in the time of the lord viceroy don Juan de Mendoza y Luna, Marqués of Montesclaros. Now in the year we are talking about of 1607, in the old-style year of 11 Reed, there was flooding for a second time; in this year [for the first time ?] the San Hipólito market was flooded; commerce no longer went on there. And half of the San Juan market was also flooded, but the other half was not flooded, a little bit of it was left, and buying and selling was done there, everyone thought that business was done there because the entire San Hipólito market was flooded.

v̲ And in Santiago Tlatelolco the altepetl was flooded everywhere too, and only the market there was not flooded, for which reason they were going to move the markets of San Hipólito and San Juan there and set them up, about which the Tlatelolca brought suit, but it could not be done; the Tenochtitlan people had differences among themselves about it.[2]

v̲ And all the religious, the friars, and also all the female religious, the nuns, who lived in Mexico were all [*p. 57*] worried about the churches and the monasteries, their houses, how they were greatly flooded everywhere and water sprang up inside. And because of that everywhere there was praying because of the rain. At every church there were processions, three times a day, early in the morning, then at noon, and then in the afternoon, just inside the buildings, so that the rain would subside and cease, that our lord God would bring it to a halt. When the month of August came to an end, the rains were very strong, so that there was great flooding in Mexico.

v̲ Then came the month of September, in which there were rains. In the said month they began pumping out water from inside the church of Santo Domingo, which was a very sad sight; it was just a pond. They diverted all the water back outside, removed and pumped it. It was house servants who did the bailing out there. When the inside of the building had been bailed out, they raised and heightened the floor and the whole inside of the building.

v̲ They did the same thing at the church of the Jesuits, the Theatines, and they also diverted back outside, removed and pumped out the water that had been inside the building, and also raised and heightened the floor.

v̲ Today on the 3rd of the said month of September of the year 1607 was when ringing began at all the churches in Mexico; the ringing was like when excommunication is

---

2. Or opposed it?

tlalia. ynic tlatziliniloya. cenca tetlaocolti. yhuan temauhti. teyçahui. auh ca ye ypampa yn tlatzilinia. in cenca chicahuac manca quiyahuitl. yc quiyauhtlaçalloya. yn iquac mocaquia tepoztli. ynic nohuian mexico. tlaocoltlatzilliniloya [*p. 58*] Ca yc cenca tlaocoyaloya: netequipacholloya. in mexico. auh çan iquac yn. yn iuh mochihuaya. in mixtica. tlayohuatimomanaya. in ye quiyahuiznequi. niman ic pehuaya. yn tlatzilliniloya. noyan.[1] teopan oncan quipehualtiaya. yn iglesia mayor. ca ytla[2] nel yohualtica yn çaço quēma ca tlatziliniloya yzquicã ynic quiyauhtlaçalloya auh yn iuh mochiuh yn tlatzilliniloc mexico. mochi yn ipan metztli omoteneuh Setiembre.

v Auh yn axcan sabado. yc 15. mani metztli yn omoteneuh Setiembre de 1607. años. yquac peuh yn ompa amaquemecan chalco. yn aotli. ye motataca. ytēcopatzinco. yn tlahtohuani Don luis de velasco visurrey. ynic mochiuh. ynic ompa tequitihuac quinauhcanhuique yn chalca. ce español. ypan icaca ytoca. Ylescas. yn quimotequiuhti aotlih. yehuatl quinemili. quimachiyoti. yn iyohui yezquia atl. ynic ompa ytztiazquia nepa chimalhuacampa. ynic tlanahuati. ye motataca. aotlih. yn iuh quitohuaya yn iuh momatia. huel ompa quitlaçazquia. ompa quitztiltitiazquia chimalhuacampa. yn nicã mexicopa hualtemo ome ceppayahuatl. yn itech yztac tepetl huiz.[3] amaquemecan hualquiça oncan ayapãco. hualmonamiqui. ynic ça cettitihuiz. tepopolla hualquiça. yhuan ce popocatepetl ytech hualtemo yn atl quitocayotia tetzauhatl ypampa y mochipa tetzahuatiuh[4] yc quiça. ynin çan xopantla ỹ hualmoyacatia. oncan hualtenepanohua y calla amaq̃mecan. ynic moch oncan hualquiça omoteneuh tepopolla. yhuan ce tlalmanalco hualtemo yn atl mochi oncan hualcallaqui. yn chalco atenco ynic cenca oncan hualtlatemiltiaya hualtlatlapihuiliaya. ynic nohuian chinampa ynic cenca ye tlaapachohuaya. auh yehuatl ypampa yn. ynic ompa cohuitiaya. atl chimalhuacampa quintzacuilizquia[5] yn izqui omoteneuh atl. nahuittiazquia. [*p. 59*] Yn ompa yc cohuitiaya amaquemecan. aocmo oncã hualcallaquizquia. yn chalco. atenco. ye mochi ompa quitlaçazquia. yn ompa omoteneuh chimalhuacan. auh mochintin. ompa atatacato. yn ixquichtin yn nauhcanme chalca macehualtin.

v Auh çã no yquac ye no nicuel oquauhtemohuique quauhtla. yn omoteneuhque nauhcanme chalca. yehuatl quitemohuique yn quamimilli yn motenehua morrillos. çan oquixquich caxtolpolhualli. yn intequiuh mochiuh yn quitemohuique amaquemeque. yn hualla nican mexico.

v Auh yn ipan axcan yc 21. mani metztli Setiembre de 1607. años. yquac ypan ylhuitzin quiz. Sant. Matheo apostol. yquac mochi tlacatl. oquittac. ce citlalli popocaya : ohualnez ylhuicatitech. ye nipa hualitztia mictlampa y norte. yhuicpa yn azcapotzalcopa. auh can[6] ihuian huallotlatocatia ynic nican motlallico. tonatiuh ynepillohuayan. yn iquac callaquia tonatiuh. yn onpoliuh. niman hualnecia yn popocaya citlalli. hualmoquetzaya ycuitlapil. yn itlanex. cenca huiac. çan iuhquin ayauhpoctli. yn hualmoquetzaya. ynic hualnecia. ypocyo. mochipa yuh hualnecia. yn maca çan hualmapillohuaya. ye nican tocpacpa. yn quihualquetzaya ycuitlapil. tonatiuh yquiçayampa onitzticaya.

v Auh çã no ypan in yn ipan ilhuitzin quiz. Sant. Matheo. oncan ye no nicuel ceppa missa mito. yn ihtic teopancalli Sancto Domingo. ye otlayecchichihualoc. ye qualcan yn

1. For "nohuiyan."
2. For "yntla."
3. For "huitz."

promulgated, very mournful, frightening, and startling. The reason for the ringing was that the rains were very heavy; there was such a cloudburst when the bells were heard that the bells were tolled in sorrow all over Mexico, [*p. 58*] for there was great sorrow and concern in Mexico over it. At this same time it would happen that darkness would come because of clouds when it was about to rain, and thereupon the bells would begin to be rung in the churches everywhere.[1] They began it at the cathedral; if[2] it was truly night, or whenever it was, there would be ringing everywhere because of the cloudbursts, and ringing went on that way in Mexico all during the said month of September.

v Today, Saturday, the 15th of the said month of September of the year 1607, was when digging of a water channel began at Amaquemecan Chalco by order of the lord don Luis de Velasco, viceroy. As to how it was done and the duties were carried out, the Chalca did it by their four divisions. A Spaniard named Illescas was in charge of it; he assigned duties for the channel, he thought out and designed the path that the water would take, so that it would head off to the side, toward Chimalhuacan. In ordering the channel to be excavated he said and thought that he could direct and go along aiming toward Chimalhuacan two streams of snow water that come down toward Mexico here, coming[3] from Iztactepetl to Amaquemecan, that meet and unite at Ayapanco, coming to Tepopolla, and a stream of water that comes down from Popocatepetl that they call the thick water, because it always runs thick[4] as it comes by—it only comes rushing out in the spring—and comes to join [the others] at the settlement at Amaquemecan, so that it all comes by the said Tepopolla, and a stream that comes down from Tlalmanalco; all of it comes into Chalco Atenco, so that there it would come filling up its channel and increasing so that it would cause great floods all over the chinampa region. It was because of this that they were channeling the water toward Chimalhuacan. They were going to close off [for someone?][5] all the said waters going in four separate streams [*p. 59*] and divert them through Amaquemecan; they would no longer enter Chalco Atenco but all be directed to the said Chimalhuacan. And all the commoners of all four parts of Chalco went to do the water excavation.

v At the same time the people of the said four parts of Chalco again brought wood down from the forest. They brought down round logs called morillos; for the time being the quota of the Amaquemeque was set at only three hundred, which they brought down and which were brought here to Mexico.

v Today, the 21st of the month of September of the year 1607, was when the feast day of San Mateo Apóstol was celebrated and when everyone saw a comet that appeared in the sky; it headed this way from off to the north, from toward Azcapotzalco. It came along slowly,[6] settling as the sun was getting low; when the sun went down and disappeared, the comet became visible. The light of its tail took shape, very long, its smoke appearing like vapor as it shaped up. It always appeared that way, not just pointing toward us, but putting its tail here over our heads, looking toward the east.

v Also in this [month], when the feast day of San Mateo was celebrated, mass was said again inside the church of Santo Domingo. Things had been fixed up, and the inside was

---

4. Presumably with ice or mud. It is possible, however, that the word has to do with the root *tetzauh-*, referring to something extraordinary, frightening.

5. The reason for the applicative in "quintzacuilizquia" is not clear.

6. For "çan."

ihtic. yn ipampa yc tlatlacauhca. atl yn manca yhtic. // Auh yn la compañia de Jesus. ye quin çatepan Domingo. yn motlapo teopancalli. ypan ylhuitzin catca. yn ichpochtli Sancta Vrsula. ca ça tzauhcticatca. ynic ye no yehuantzitzin teopixque. omotlayecchichihuillique. yn tlalpãtli [*p. 60*] Oquimacocuillique. ynic no cenca tentimanca atl teopan. // Yhuan yn ypan in omoteneuh metztli miyequintin atlan micque yn matlanhuique macehualtin. yhuan yn ipan in omoteneuh metztli Setiembre. ynic tlamico. huel hualnecia ynic popocaya citlalli.

v Auh niman ic hualmoma yn metztli. octubre. mochi yn ipan in popocaya citlalli. yhuan yn ipan in metztli ça quezquilhuitl. yn onquiyauh. ye ytlacoyoc ynepantla. yn oquiçaco quiyahuitl. // auh çan no yquac yn ipan in omoteneuh metztli octubre de 1607. años. yquac ohualla tlahtolli yn ompa españa. omachiztico. nican mexico. ye ce xihuitl çanno yehuatl. ypan yn omoteneuh metztli octubre de 1606 años. yn ipan omomiquilli in yehuatzin tlahtocapilli Don diego luis de moteuhcçoma yhuitltemoctzin. yn ipiltzin tlacatl Don Pedro de moteuhcçoma tlacahuepantzin. ye omito yuh machiztico ye ce xihuitl yn omomiquilli. ynin Don diego luis de moteuhcçoma yhuitltemoctzin ye yxhuiuhtzin yn tlacatl catca huey tlahtohuani emperador. Moteuhcçomatzin xocoyotl. auh in yehuatzin Don diego luis de moteuhcçoma yhuitltemoctzin. yn ompa españa oquincauhtia ynamic huel española yn cihuapilli ytoca Doña fran[ca] de la cueba yhuan ypilhuantzitzin chiquacemĩ mestiçoti. yehica ye omito yn innantzin ca huel española. nahui oquichtli. ome cihuatl.

v ynic ce ytoca Doña Maria miyahuaxochtzĩ

v ynic ome ytoca Don P[o] desifun de la cueba de moteuhcçoma

auh yn oc cequintin amo huel momati yn intoca. yn ipilhuantzitzin Don diego luis de moteuhcçoma yhuitl. temoctzin. [*p. 61*]

Auh niman hualmoman in metztli Nouiembre de 1607. años, yn iquac ypan in ça yquezquilhuiyoc yn onpolihuico. yn popocaya citlalli. tonatiuh ycallaquiyampa temoc. ynic poliuh.

v Auh yn axcan yc 5. mani metztli nouiembre de 1607. años. yquac ye no nicuel oquinmonahuatili. yn visurrey ỹ nauhcame chalca. ynic ompa quauhtequizque. quauhquixtizque. yn quauhtla quauhtemohuizq̃. yehuatl quinmotequitilli yn quamimilli yn motenehua morrillos. auh ynic nenque yn quauhtecque. chalca. mochi yn ipan metztli nouiembre.[1]

v Auh ye ytlamian ynin omoteneuh metztli. nouiẽbre. de 1607. años. yn iquac ompa amaquemecan yn español. ylescas. oquicauh yn aohuitataquiliztli yn quichihuaya. quiquetzaya. ynic nepa quitlaçazquia. ynic nepa quitztiltitiazquia chimalhuacampa. atl. ome metztli ypan tlaco ynic ne[2] cohuitiaya. auh ye ytechpa onacia yn xocoyoltepec motenehua. yn oc achi nican hual. yn tlalli aocmo huel mohuecatlanohuaya ye tepatlapan[3] yn tlani. yn oncan quiquetzaya aotlih. yn oncã yazquia atl. auh ynic quiyeyecoca atl yn español. çan onmotzotzonaya[4] nepa calyacac.[5] auh y nepa milpan. aocmo huel onyauh çan hualmocuepaya. yn atl. auh ynic aocmo huel mohuecatlanohuaya aotlih. yehuatl ypampa ynic amo huel quichiuh ynic nepa quitlaçazquia atl. çan concauh. quimauhca-

---

1. Or: The Chalca woodcutters were involved in it during the whole month of November.

2. Apparently "ne" is for *nen*, which is included in many expressions of trying unsuccessfully to do something.

good for walking on; the reason why it had become unusable was that water was inside. // The Jesuit church was opened later, on Sunday the feast day of the virgin Santa Ursula; it had been closed while those religious too fixed things up and raised the floor, [*p. 60*] because that church too was very full of water. // And in the said month many commoners died in the water and drowned. And at the end of the said month of September the comet was still fully visible.

v Then came the month of October, during all of which the comet was there. During this month it rained for only a few days; in the middle of the month the rain stopped. // In this same month of October of the year 1607 was when word came from Spain and it became known here in Mexico that a year before, likewise in the said month of October, of the year 1606, there had passed away the royal nobleman don Diego Luis de Moteucçoma Ihuitltemoctzin, child of the lord don Pedro de Moteucçoma Tlacahuepantzin. As was said, it became known that he had died a year before. This don Diego Luis de Moteucçoma Ihuitltemoctzin was the grandchild of the late lord high ruler and emperor Moteucçoma the younger. Don Diego Luis de Moteucçoma Ihuitltemoctzin left behind in Spain a spouse, a noblewoman who was fully Spanish named doña Francisca de la Cueva, and six children who were mestizos, because, as was said, their mother was fully Spanish. Four of them are male, two female.

v The first is named doña María Miyahuaxochtzin.
v The second is named don Pedro [Tecifón?] de la Cueva de Moteucçoma.
The names of the other children of don Diego Luis de Moteucçoma Ihuitltemoctzin cannot be established. [*p. 61*]
Then came the month of November of the year 1607. A few days into this month the comet disappeared; it went down and disappeared toward the west.

v Today, the 5th of the month of November of the year 1607, was when the viceroy again ordered the people of the four parts of Chalco to cut trees in the forest and remove them; he gave them the duty of bringing down the round logs called morillos. The Chalca were involved in cutting trees during the whole month of November.[1]

v At the end of the said month of November of 1607 was when the Spaniard Illescas stopped the excavation of a water channel in Amaquemecan that he was making and constructing to divert and aim the water to one side, toward Chimalhuacan. For two months and a half he tried[2] to make the channel for the water. He got to what is called Xocoyoltepec, a bit this side of it, and the earth could be dug no deeper, there was rocky earth[3] underneath where he was making the channel that the water would go through. When the Spaniard tried the water [i.e., tried running it through the channel], it just was blocked at[4] the houses[5] and fields to one side; the water could go no farther and would just run back. That the water channel could not be deepened more was why he could not divert

3. For "tepetlapan."
4. Or hit up against.
5. Since *tlayacac* can mean a populated district, perhaps *calyacac* can have much the same sense. See also pp. 216–17 at n. 3.

yttac. ynic amo huel ompa yauh atl. auh niman oc cecni otlayeyecoco yn ocohuitiaya. oncan yn omoteneuh ayapanco yn imonepanohuayan atl. oncan quipehualti yn tlatacaya.[1] ompa quicaya[2] y motenehua amanalco. tepopolla nepa ynahuac. yn quihuicazquia atl [*p. 62*] auh amo no huel quichiuh. çan concauh no yn oncan.

v̲ Auh yn axcan ytlamian ynic 30. mani metztli nouiembre de 1607. años. ypan ylhuitzin Sant. Andres. apostol. yquac oquipehualtito. yn aotlih ye motataca in ye motlapohua in ye motlacohuiltequi. tepetl. yn motenehua citlaltepetl. yn õcann opeuh huehuetocan. ynic motatacac motlapo. ynic ompa quiçatiuh atl. yn nicã otlaapacho mexico. auh in yomatzinco. ompa mohuicaya yn tlahtohuani visurrey. Don luis de velasco. yxpantzinco. yn quipehualtito. in ye motataca. aotlih. yn ompa huehuetocan yn citlaltepec. çan tequitl. hualmocueptzinoto. auh yehuantin. altepehuaque yn techyahuallotoq̃ yn ompa tequitito. yn quichiuhto tequitl. auh yn amaquemeque amo tehuanme. yn iuh nimã ye onneciz.

v̲ Auh yn mexica no yquac quipehualtique in ye quipatlahua. tetenamitl. yn oncan hospital caltitlan. Sant. Lazaro. ytencopatzinco. mochiuh. yn tlahtohuani visurrey. yc quinmonahuatillica yn mexica. ypan calquetzazque yn iquac tla oquipatlauhque tetenamitl.

v̲ Auh yc niman hualmoma yn metztli de diciembre. de 1607. a^{o}s. yn ipan in. in yehuantin amaquemeque. yquac quitlamico. ynic quauhquixtique. ynic quauhtemohuique. quauhtla yn chalca. yn intequiuh mochiuh yn quitemohuique. ỹ nonqua çan inneyxcahuitl.[3] mochiuh amaquemeque. vii mill. yn quamimilli morrillos yn quitecque. ypan in xihuitl. [*p. 63*] Omoteneuh de 1607. años. cenca yc motolinique yn cecencalli. ỹ namiqueque. yn intequiuh mochiuh. matlatlactetl. omehey. ypan mochi tlacatl cepan ya. ayac mocauh. auh yn quaxochpã tlaca. yn atlauhteca. yn ça ye yhuan ompa pouhque amaquemecan. yn intequiuh mochiuh morillos. yn quauhtla quiquixtique. nahui 4. mill. auh ynic mochi. mocenpohua. yn amaquemecan tequitl mochiuh. in ye mochi matlactloce mill in morillos. yn nican hualla mexico. // auh in ye mochi. ynic mocemacicapohua ynic mocentlalia. yn ixquich yntequiuh mochiuh morillos. yn ipan ic nauhcan xeliuhtica. ynic nauhcan quiztica. chalcayotl. yn tlalmanalco. yn amaquemecan. yn tenanco. yn chimalhuacan.[4] yhuan yn ixquich ica. ynic nohuian yn intlatititzalpan. yn intlahuillanalpan. yn izquican omoteneuh altepetl chalco. ynic omocentlalli mochi. yn izquican yntequiuh mochiuh morillos. ochenta mill. yn monauhcanhui yn nican mexico hualla: // auh ypan pasqua nauidad. ytlaçotlacatilizpantzinco yn tt^{o} Dios. yn peuhque chalca. in ye quihualcahua morillos mexico. —

quizqui yn ii.[5] acatl xihuitl. de 1607. años. —

¶ xii. tecpatl xihuitl. 1608. ypan in in yancuic xihuitl. ypan ypan[6] yancuic metztli henero. yquac macoque in al~~lde~~yotl. yn Don diego luis de moteuhcçoma. atzaqualco chane. ynin ypiltzin. yn tlacatl. yn ompa omomiquillito. españa. Don diego luis de moteuhcçoma. yhuitltemoctzin. ynic ome motlalli al~~lde~~. quiniyopa yehuatl yn Don Antonio valeriano. telpochtli. Sant. Juan [*p. 64*] Moyotlan chane ynin yxhuiuhtzin yn huehue

1. For "tlatatacaya."

2. "Quicaya" may be for "quiçaya," as assumed in the translation, but there are other possibilities, such as that a syllable is missing as in "tlatacaya" and that the intention is another transitive verb with Illescas as subject.

3. For "inneyxcahuil."

the water to one side but abandoned it and was afraid of it, since the water could not go in that direction. Then he tried to make a channel for the water elsewhere; he began digging[1] at the said Ayapanco where the streams join, where the water goes by[2] the place called Amanalco [in] Tepopolla; he was going to conduct the water to one side close to there, [*p. 62*] but he couldn't do that either, but abandoned it there also.

v Today, the 30th, the last of the month of November of the year 1607, on the feast day of San Andrés Apóstol, was when they went to begin excavating a water channel to open up and cut through the mountain called Citlaltepetl; excavation and opening up began at Huehuetocan, so that the water that flooded Mexico here would go out that way. The lord viceroy don Luis de Velasco went there personally. In his presence they began to excavate the water channel at Huehuetocan and Citlaltepec; he hardly got there before he returned. The citizens of the various altepetl that surround us went there to work, to do labor duty, but the Amaquemeque did not go along, as will soon be seen.

v At the same time the Mexica began to widen the dikes close to the hospital of San Lázaro. It was done by order of the lord viceroy, who had instructed the Mexica to erect houses on the dikes when they had widened them.

v Then came the month of December of the year 1607. This month was when the Amaquemeque finished getting out trees, when the Chalca brought down trees from the forest. The separate and exclusive[3] quota assigned to the Amaquemeque was to bring down 7,000 round logs, morillos, that they cut in the said year [*p. 63*] of 1607. They were greatly afflicted by it; the married [men] of each household were assigned thirteen each. Everyone went together, no one stayed behind. The people of the border, the inhabitants of Atlauhtlan, who were also counted with Amaquemecan, were assigned 4,000 morillos to get out of the forest, so that the total duty of Amaquemecan was 11,000 morillos, which were brought here to Mexico. // The sum and grand total of the quota of morillos for the greater entity of Chalco, consisting of and divided into four parts, Tlalmanalco, Amaquemecan, Tenanco, and Chimalhuacan,[4] and all of the dependencies everywhere of the said altepetl of Chalco, with the total of the quotas of all the entities, was 80,000 morillos that were delivered by the four parts and brought here to Mexico. // On the Christmas holiday, the precious birth of our lord God, the Chalca began to come to deliver the morillos to Mexico. —

End of 11[5] Reed year, the year 1607. —

¶ 12 Flint year, 1608. In the new year, in[6] the new month of January was when positions as alcalde were given to don Diego Luis de Moteucçoma, citizen of Atzaqualco, child of the lord don Diego Luis de Moteucçoma Ihuitltemoctzin, who died in Spain, and second don Antonio Valeriano the younger, citizen of San Juan Moyotlan, who was made alcalde for the first time; [*p. 64*] he is the grandchild of don Antonio Valeriano the elder. And

4. The four are in their usual order.

5. Here "ii" means not Roman number 2, but 11, as frequently happens with writers of the time. See also pp. 68–69 at n. 5.

6. Here "ypan" is inadvertently repeated.

Don Antonio valeriano. yhuan yn ipan in xihuitl yancuic. yhuan ypan yancuic metztli henero. yxquich ypan oquauh[1] yn chalca. in nican mexico. quicallaquico yehuatl. y morillos.

v Auh yhuã ypan in yn omoteneuh metztli. henero yquac oquicauh yn aotlih quittatacaya español ylescas. yn oncan amanalco. yc occan tlatatacaya. atle huel quichiuh.

v Yhuan yn ipan in omoteneuh metztli henero mochipa. omoyeyeco[2] yn quiyahuitl. ynic mochi nohuian ypan nueua españa.

v Auh niman hualmoman yn metztli de febrero yquac ypan in. onecico nican mexico. huey apan yn motenehua atotoltin[3] yn ayc onecia nican

v Yn ipann axcan yc 4. mani metztli de febrero. de 1608. años. yquac oquincauhque. yn Sant. Ṡebastian. teopixque. y moteneuhtzinohua calmenistas. descarços. yn mexica atzaqualca. yn intechtzinco pohuia. yehuantzitzin. quinmopachilhuiaya yn omoteneuhtzinoque teopixque inn omoteneuhque mexica atzaqualca. auh çan yehuantzitzin yyollocacopatic. yn omoteneuhtzinoque. teopixque calmenitas. ynic quinmocahuillique. macehualtin. auh yn ixquichcauh oquinmopachilhuique atzaqualca cenpohualxihuitl ypan yexihuitl. ynic çan quimonmocahuillico yn ipan in omoteneuh xihuitl. auh yn mexica atzaqualca. atzaqualca.[4] [*p. 65*] Camo caxcancauhque. oquixquich yntlapal quichiuhque. ynic amo quicahualiztlamatia. yn atzaqualca. yn inteopancal ca huey Pleito. yc quichiuhque. yehica ypampa. yn huehue teopancalli omoteneuh Sant. Sebastian. ca huel imaxca yntlatqui. yhuan yntlal. yn ipan icac teopantli. yntlaquetzal yn huehuetque. yn incolhuan yntahuã catca. yn mexica macehualtin atzaqualca mochi ymaxca catca auh yece çan niman aocmo huelitique. ynic macozque. ynic moteylhuiaya. auh oc Justiciatica nahuatilloque. yn atzaqualca yn oquic mottaz monemilliz. yn quenĩ mochihuaz. yn Pleyto. achi quexquichcauh yn oquiuhcauhticatca

v Auh yn iquac yn omoteneuh ynic quinmocahuillique teopixque calmenitas. yn atzaqualca. auh in yehuantzitzin. Sant. augustin. teopixque. no niman iquac quinmanillique yn omoteneuhque atzaqualca. ytencopatzinco mochiuh yn tlahtohuani visurrey. Don luis de velasco. ynic yehuantzitzin. quinmopachilhuia ynic axcan. teoyotica quinmopallehuilia. çan oc yehuatzin. quinmoyollaliliaya yn Padre fray Juan de missango. çan oc mopatlatinemia. yn teopixque. yn quinmomachtiliaya. atzaqualca. yn oquic ayemo motlalliaya yn vicario. achi ye quexquichcauhtica yn motlallico yn vicario. oc mochix ye quin ipan quiz ynic mochihuaco capitulo. Sant. augostin. yehuatl achto. yn vicario. mochiuh. yn atzaqualca. yn Padre fray augostĩ [*p. 66*] de Sant. Pablo. yece çan oc oncan moyetzticatca yn Sant. augustin.[5]

v Auh yn ipan ĩ omoteneuh metztli de febrero. de 1608. años. yquac no cenca miecpa. yn moyeyeco[6] quiyahuitl. achi quezquipan yn quiyauh.

v Auh çan ye no ypan in. yn omoteneuh metztli de febrero. yn peuh. ynic nohuian nican yhtic ciudad mexico tenochtitlan. ynic quitlaltenque. ynic quihuecapanoque. yhuan quitemanque. yn huehuey otlih. çan yehuantin. quichiuhque yn mexica.

v Auh ye ytlamian in. yn omoteneuh metztli de febrero de 1608. años. yquac mochintin.

---

1. It appears that "oquauh" is for "oquauhtemohuique."

2. Tentatively, fitfully? Such a meaning of *yeyecoa* has not yet been located in dictionaries.

3. See Sahagún 1950–1982, Bk 11, pp. 27, 29–30.

during the whole new month of the new year the Chalca [brought down][1] trees; they came to deliver the morillos here in Mexico.

v In the said month of January was also when the Spaniard Illescas abandoned the water channel he was excavating at Amanalco, the second place where he excavated. He was unable to do anything.

v And in the said month of January the rain was always [by fits and starts?][2] everywhere in all New Spain.

v Then came the month of February; in this month what they call pelicans,[3] that had never appeared here, came and appeared here in Mexico on the big lake.

v Today, the 4th of the month of February of the year 1608, was when the friars at San Sebastián called Discalced Carmelites left the Mexica Atzaqualca, who had belonged to them; the said friars had governed the said Mexica Atzaqualca, and it was voluntarily that the said Carmelite friars left the commoners. They governed the Mexica Atzaqualca for twenty-three years until they left them in the said year. But the Mexica Atzaqualca[4] [*p. 65*] did not give them up quickly; they made every effort, for the Atzaqualca did not want to be deprived of their church building. They carried on a great lawsuit over it, because the old church building called San Sebastián is fully their property, and the church stands on their land, built by those of old, who were their fathers and grandfathers. It was all the property of the Mexica Atzaqualca commoners, but they were absolutely unable to have it given to them, so that they initiated a suit; the Atzaqualca were ordered by the court that while it was being looked into and considered how the suit was to be conducted, for a while things would stay as they were.

v When as mentioned the Carmelite friars left the Atzaqualca, the Augustinian friars right then took over the said Atzaqualca—it was done by order of the lord viceroy don Luis de Velasco—so that now they govern them and help them in holy matters. At first Father fray Juan de Mijango consoled them. Provisionally the friars just went along taking turns teaching the Atzaqualca until a vicar should be installed; it was quite a while until a vicar was installed. They waited to select him until a general chapter meeting of the Augustinians was held. The first vicar appointed for the Atzaqualca was Father fray Agustín [*p. 66*] de San Pablo, but for the time being he resided at the Augustinian church.[5]

v The said month of February of the year 1608 was when again [it rained intermittently?];[6] it rained quite a few times.

v In the same said month of February they began everywhere here in the city of Mexico Tenochtitlan to fill in the land to raise the highways and to pave them with stones; only the Mexica did it.

v At the end of this said month of February of the year 1608 was when all the people of

4. Here "atzaqualca" is inadvertently repeated.

5. For further background on the incident see Gibson 1964, p. 373; Mendieta 1980, p. 435; and Torquemada 1975, 3: 228–29.

6. See n. 2 just above about the same word.

onotzalloque nohuian. yn anahuaca. yn techyahuallotoque. ytencopatzinco. yn visurrey. ynic oncan huallaque mochintin macehualtin. yn tlacpac omotocateneuh. yn itocayocan huehuetocan citlaltepec oncan otequitico. ynic omoquetz. yn aotlih. ynic omotatacac ynic omotlapo. omotlacohuiltec. omocoyoni yn tepetl. yhuan miccaomitl. ompa quiquixtique. ceme yehuatl. ymomiyo yniquin quẽma. yn onemico. nican ypan tlalli. yn quintocayotitihui. yn quinteneuhtihui huehuetque tocihuan tocolhuan. quinameti. tlacahueyaq̃. catca. auh ynin ca ceme yehuantin ymomiyo yn ompa quiquixtique. atatacoyan. oncan quihualhuicaque yn Sant Pablo. quimottili. yn visurrey. // auh yhuan cenca miec tlacatl. macehualli oncan omomiquillico. yhuan cequintin. omococo[1] oncan yn omoteneuhque altepetl ypan tlaca. yn otequitico. ypan in ontetl metztli henero. yhuan febrero. yhuann ipan yn oc cequi metztli. // auh çan inceltin. yn amaquemeque [*p. 67*] Yn amo ompa tehuanme. otequitito. çan yehuatl yntequiuh mochiuh yn tlacpac omoteneuh morillos. quauhtlan quiquixtique.

v Yn axcan Domingo. yc 2. mani metztli. Março de 1608. a^{os}. yquac momiquilli yn tlacatl Don Juã de aluarado. Gouernador catca tetzcoco.

v Auh çan ye no yehuatl ipan in yn Domingo omoteneuh. no yquac momiquilli. yn cihuapilli. Doña maria. ceron. yn ichpochtzin. Don martin ceron tlahtohuani xochmilco. mexico. yn momiquillico. ynĩ cihuapilli. yehuatl yn chalco tlalmanalco. cihuamontli. catca. yn inantzin. Don Alonso de la cerda. piltzintli. ynin ytlaçopiltzin yehuatl quicauhtiuh. yn Don hernando de la cerda telpochtli tlahtocapilli tlalmanalco. catca.

v Yn axcann ipan yc 2. mani Mayo. de 1608. años. yquac onmopehualti. omoquixti. nican mexico in yehuatzin teoyotica. tlahtohuani. Don Alonso. de muta. obispo. xalixco. Guadraxara. omoyetzticatca. auh çan onmoquexquichcahuitytiquiz yn nicã mexico. auh yn axcan omoteneuh quin ic yancuicã ompa mohuica. ye mocallaquia. yn cuitlaxcohuapa. obispo. ompa mochiuhtzinohua ynic õpa mochipa. moyetztiez. ompa oquimiquanilli yn tohuey. tlatocauh Rey. auh çan nican omoquixtitiquiz. mexico. amo ma omohuecahualtitiquiz. ynin yehuatzin obispo. huel nican mexico. tlacat. nican tepiltzin. criyoyo mitohua yntech quiça yn pipiltin conquistadoresme

v Yn axcan ypan yc 29. mani metztli Mayo. de 1608. años. yquac ohualla tlahtolli. yn ompa españa omachiztico. omomiquilli çan oquixixilque. yn Don fran^{co} [*p. 68*] de velasco coregidor catca yn Madrid ynin ypiltzin yn tlahtohuani Don luis de velasco. visurrey yn axcan. yc oppa motlahtocatillia nican mexico moyetztica. auh yninn omotocateneuh ypiltzin yn omictiloc ompa españa. nican mexico. tlacat. nican ya.[2] nican tepiltzin. criyoyo mitohua.

v Auh yhuan çan moch cen ohualla yn españa yn itlahtollo Don fran^{co} de velasco. yn intlahtocatequiuh. omentin. tlamatinime.[3] ce Doctor. yhuan ce lliceciado. yn oquinhualmotequimaquilli tohueytlahtocauh Rey. ynic ce ytoca El lliceciado. chapez. fiscal. mochiuh. yn ompa audiencia Guadraxara. yn xalixco. ynin españa. chane. auh nican mexico. ye ochanchihuaya. ynic nican ytequiuh o ypan acico.

v Auh inic omentin nican ohualtequimacoque yehuatl. yn Doctor. Grauajar. oydor.

1. Or were hurt.

2. Although *nican ya* literally means "left here," it seems from the context that perhaps the intention was something different; *nican yol* would be another way of saying "was born here."

the lake region everywhere who surround us were called by order of the viceroy so that all the commoners came to the above named place called Huehuetocan at Citlaltepec. They came there to work so that a water channel was constructed, so that there was excavation so that the mountain was opened up, cut into, and a hole made in it. And they removed bones of the dead from there; some of their bones were like those who lived formerly here on earth, whom the ancients, our grandmothers and grandfathers, named and called giants; they were tall people. And they removed some of their bones from the place of water excavation and brought them to San Pablo; the viceroy saw them. // And very many commoners died there, and some of the said people from the various altepetl [fell sick].[1] They came to work there in two months, January and February, and in some other months. // Only the Amaquemeque [*p. 67*] did not go along with the others to work; their only duty was that they removed the above mentioned beams from the forest.

v Today, Sunday the 2nd of the month of March of the year 1608, was when the lord don Juan de Alvarado, who was governor of Tetzcoco, passed away.
v The same said Sunday was also when the lady doña María Cerón, daughter of don Martín Cerón, ruler in Xochimilco, passed away. She came to Mexico to die. This lady was daughter-in-law [of the ruler?] in Chalco Tlalmanalco, mother of the small child don Alonso de la Cerda; he was the legitimate child [heir] whom the late don Hernando de la Cerda the younger, nobleman of the royal dynasty of Tlalmanalco, left behind.
v Today, the 2nd of May of the year 1608, was when the ruler in holy matters don Alonso de Mota, bishop of Jalisco, set out from and left Mexico here. He had been in Guadalajara, and he passed through Mexico here spending only a short time. The one just mentioned is going for the first time to and entering Puebla as bishop, appointed there so that he will always be there; our great ruler the king transfered him there, and he only passed quickly through Mexico here, not spending a long time at all. This bishop was born right here in Mexico, the child of people here, called a criollo; he comes from the noble conquerors.
v Today, the 29th of the month of May of the year 1608, was when word came from Spain and it became known that don Francisco de Velasco, who was corregidor in Madrid, passed away; they just stabbed him. [*p. 68*] He was the child of the ruler don Luis de Velasco, viceroy, who is now ruling for a second time and is here in Mexico. This just named child of his who was killed in Spain was born here in Mexico and left,[2] a child of people here, called criollo.
v And also together with the news about don Francisco de Velasco there came from Spain [news of] the rulerly [governmental] offices of two learned men,[3] one a doctor and one a licenciado, to whom our great ruler the king gave offices. The first is named licenciado Chaves, who was made *fiscal* of the Audiencia of Guadalajara in Jalisco; he is from Spain, but he made his home here in Mexico, so that [news of] his office reached him here.
v The second of those given office here is doctor Carvajal, who was made a judge in the

3. Apparently Ch.'s translation of Spanish *letrado*, a person who holds a university degree, especially in law.

mochiuh yn ompa audiencia. quauhtemallan. ynin totepantlahtocauh[1] catca. ỹ nican mexico audiencia real. ynin huel nican tlacat. huel nican tepiltzin. mexico. ye quin icel. yancuican criyoyo. oydor. omochiuh. ye quin oncan yc pehua yn. yn oydortizque criyoyosme çan niman ipan in yn omoteneuh xihuitl ya quauhtemallan yn omoteneuh oydor.

v Auh no yhuan çan moch cen ohualla yn intlahtocatequiuh. omomentin[2] omoteneuhque tlamatinime. no yquac ohualla. in tehuantin. timacehualtin. yn topallehuilloca. techhualmotitlanililia yn tohueytlahtocauh Rey. Don felipe tercero. yprouisiontzin quihualmotitlani. yn itechcopa yn mimiccatzitzinti. yn intestamentos. quichiuhtihui. ynic ayac quitlacoz. [*p. 69*] Yn tley. yntlanequiliz quitotihui, yhuan quenin tetlamamacatiazque. hualtlalililo. machiyotl. octacatl yn ipan huilohuaz. ytech manaz. yn tlatquixexeloliztli. yn iuh maxiltiz. moneltiliz. yn tley. yntlanequiliz. mimicque. ynic aocmo çan quinamoyazque. teopixque. yn iuh quimochihuilia. ynic çan teopan mochi quimocallaquilia. yn tleyn in tlatqui. quicauhtihui mimiccatzitzinti. auh ynic yehuatzin hualmotlanahuatilia. tohueytlahtocatzin. Rey. yn timacehualtin yn cocoxqui. yc quichihuaz. ỹ testamento. çan iyollo tlama yez. quiyomahuiz. yn quihtoz. huel ytlanequiliztica quitlaliz. yn itlahtol. ynic quixexelotiaz. yn iaxca. ytlatqui. yn momiquiz. nanahuatiqui. quichihuaz huel quihtotiaz. yn tleyn. ytlanequiliz. yez. ynic mocacauhtiaz. ynic niman yehuatl mochihuaz moneltiliz maxiltiz. yn intlahtol. yc mocacauhtihui mimicque. oc cẽca yehuantin. yntla oncate yn huel teoyotica. oquinchiuhque. ynpilhuan. huel innahuatil. yn quintlamamacatiazque. yn iquac yntzonquiçalizpan. yn tetahuan[3] anoço tepilhuan necoc[4] yuh ca tlahtocatenahuatilli. auh ynic huel mochihuaz. ynic nohuian. altepetl ypan. ceceyaca cece escriuanostin. yxquetzalozque. çan quixcahuizque yn quichihuazque testamentos. yn iuh ytech neztica prouission real.

v Yn axcan ypan yc 12. mani metztli. de Junio. yquac omomiquilli. yn Don Jeronimo lupez. Juez Gouernador. catca. nican mexico tenochtitlan. ynin mestiço. xaltocan. ychan. auh inic ojuezgouernadortico. tenochtitlan. matlacxihuitl. ypan chicuetetl metztli. ypan cenpohualli once tonatiuh.

v Yn axcan ypan yc. 16. mani metztli de Junio. de 1608. años. yquac maxitico. mocallaquico nican mexico. in yehuatzin. teoyotica. tlahtohuani. Don fr. Juã [*p. 70*] de valle. obispo. teopixqui Sant. Benito. españa. ohualmohuicac. çan nican mexico. moquixtitiquiz. ompa mohuicac ompa ytequipantzinco. yn Guadraxara. yn xalixco.

v Yn axcan ypan yc 21. mani metztli. de Junio. de 1608 años. yquac. ohualcallac. yn Don Juan bap^{ta} Juez gou^{or} mochihuaco. nican mexico. tenochtitlan. ynin tlatilolco huallehuac. ompa Juez gou^{or} catca. ynin malinalco ychan auh ynic hualla tenochtitlan. yehuatzin quihualmocallaquilli. yn tlahtohuani. visurrey. Don luis de velasco. auh yn tlatilolco. ypan oncallac. conpatlato. yehuatl yn Don Melchior de Sotu. Juez gouernador. mochiuh. yn tlatilolco. ynin huell oncan. chane. yece ompa huallehuac yn cuitlahuac. ompa Juez. gouernador catca.

v Yn ipan axcan yc 18. mani metztli. de Julio. de 1608. años. yquac macoque possecion. yn Sant. Augustin teopixque. axcatilloque. yn calli yhuan tlalli. oncã yn itocayocan ahuatonco. yn çan ye ypan tlalli atzaqualco. yn oncan omohuetziltique. yn omoteneuh-

1. In the sense of advocate, lawyer, apparently; perhaps he held the position called Defender of the Indians.

2. For "omentin."

3. The Nahuas did not normally use the plural of the word "father" to mean "parents of

Audiencia of Guatemala; he had been our intercessor[1] here in the Royal Audiencia in Mexico. He was born right here, the child of people right here in Mexico; he alone has become the first criollo Audiencia judge. It only began with this that criollos should become Audiencia judges. Right away in this said year the said judge went to Guatemala.

v And also at the same time as [news of] the governmental positions of the two[2] said learned men, there came [news that] our great ruler the king don Felipe III is sending us commoners something to help us. He is sending his provision about the testaments that the dead make, so that no one will go against [*p. 69*] whatever will they express and how they distribute things to people when they die. A sample or model has been set up for them by which people are to go and from which the division of property is to be taken, and how whatever is the will of the dead is to be fulfilled and realized, so that the friars will no longer steal it, as they do, so that whatever property the dead leave, they just deliver it all to the church. And our great ruler the king sends orders [concerning] us commoners that the way a sick person is to make a testament is just as he/she sees fit, and he/she is to speak in person; entirely voluntarily he/she is to issue his/her statement about how he/she is dividing his/her property. The person giving orders on dying [the testator] is to do it, is to go along really saying what his will will be as to how [the property] is to be left to various people, so that the statements [that the dead leave behind] will be immediately executed, carried out, and fulfilled, especially of those who have truly legitimate children that they engendered; they are to distribute to them all that is bequeathed them at the death of either the parents[3] or children.[4] Thus is the royal order. And so that it can be done, in each of the altepetl all around a notary is to be put in office who will do nothing but make testaments, as appears in the royal provision.

v Today the 12th of the month of June was when don Gerónimo López, who was judge-governor here in Mexico Tenochtitlan, passed away. He was a mestizo from Xaltocan, and he came here to serve as judge-governor in Tenochtitlan for 10 years, 8 months, and 21 days.

v Today, the 16th of the month of June of the year 1608, was when the ruler in holy matters the bishop don fray Juan [*p. 70*] del Valle, a Benedictine friar, arrived and entered into Mexico here. He came from Spain; he just passed through Mexico here quickly and went to his place of office in Guadalajara, in Jalisco.

v Today, the 21st of the month of June of the year 1608, was when don Juan Bautista entered here into Mexico Tenochtitlan as appointed judge-governor; he came from Tlatelolco, where he had been judge-governor, and his home was Malinalco. As to how he was brought to Tenochtitlan, the lord viceroy don Luis de Velasco brought him in. And don Melchor de Soto went to enter Tlatelolco and take his place, appointed judge-governor in Tlatelolco. His home was right there, but he came from Cuitlahuac, where he had been judge-governor.

v Today, the 18th of the month of July of the year 1608, was when the Augustinian friars were given possession and made owners of the house and land at the place called Ahuatonco, on Atzaqualco land, where the said Augustinian friars established themselves,

---

both genders" as the Spaniards did, but that appears to be Ch.'s meaning here, where he is explaining a text in Spanish.

4. The interpretation of the word *necoc* (on both sides) in this context as either one or the other is speculative.

tzinoque. Sant. Augustin teopixque. ynic oncan moquetz yn iteopancaltzin Señor. Sant. Sebastian oncan ye no yncenteopan mochihuaco yn mexica atzaqualca yquac quixitinique. yn incapilla. yn inteopan catca atzaqualca. yn ompa ycaca ynhuehuechan yn axcan ompa moyetzticate. teopixque calmenitas. descarsos. yn ipilhuantzitzin totlaçonantzin Sancta maria del calme. ye omito tlacpac yn achto yehuãtzitzin. cenpohualxihuitl ypan exihuitl. yn quinmopachilhuique. yn tenochca atzaqualca.

v Yn ipan axcan. yc 18. mani metztli Setiembre de 1608 años. yquac otlamico. omotlapoto. yn aotlih. yn motatacac. ynic motlacohuiltec tepetl. yn ompa citlaltepec. ynic nepa tullampa contlazque cõtlachiyeltique. ynic conyacatique. ynic nepa onquiça. yauh yn atl. yn tlamauhtiaya. [*p. 71*] Yn tlaapachohuaya. nican mexico. auh quiyomahuito. yn tlahtohuani visurrey. Don luis de velasco. yxpantzinco. yn motlapoto. yhuan no yehuatzin oncan yxpantzinco mochiuh yquac oncan maxitico. in yehuatzin cenca mahuiztililoni teoyotica tlahtohuani. arçobispo. Don fray Garcia guerra. teopixqui Sancto Domingo ye quin ic ompa mohuicatz. yn españa. ynic oncã citlaltepec. quimonamiquilli visurrey.[1] yniquinehuantzin. ymixpantzinco, motlapo. aotlih. yn oncan yauh atl. yehuatzin. quimoteochihuilli. yn arçobispo. yn oncan omoteneuh onquiça atl. auh çan ic oncan hualmehuititzino çan ic oncan hualmoquixtitiquiz. yn arçobispo. ynic quihualmoteochihuilitiquiz. yn aotlih citlaltepec. auh yn ixquichcauhtica. yc nemohuac ynic aotatacoc. ynic motlacohuiltec tepetl. ynic motlapoco. ynic tlamico yyohui atl. chiuhcnauhtetl. metztica. ypan caxtollonahuilhuitl. auh ye o mito. tlacpac. mochintin. oncan tequitico. yn altepehuaque. yn techyahuallotoque. yn ipan ixquichcauh nemohuac. auh amo tehuanme. ompa otequitito. yn mexica. çã nican mexico ochichiuhque

v Auh yn ipan axcan lunes. yc 29. mani metztli de Setiembre. de 1608. años. yquac ypan Sant. Miguel ylhuitzin. maxitico. mocallaquico. nican yhtic yn altepetl ciudad mexico tenochtitlan in yehuatzin omoteneuhtzino. yn cenca mahuiztililoni. teoyotica tlahtohuani. Don fray Garcia Guerra. arçobispo mexico. ye omito teopixqui. Sancto. Domingo. yn axcã moyetztica teoyotica motlahtocatilia. techmopa[*p. 72*]chilhuia. tenochtitlan. yc chiquacen arçobispo ỹ nicã mexico. auh ynic hualmohuicac ynic maxitico. mexico. oc confirmacio quihualmotemaquilitiquiz yn quauhtitlan. yhuan tepotzotlan. auh çã huel onxihuitl yn ayac arçobispo. catca nican mexico.

v Yn ipan axcan yc 15. mani metztli de octubre de 1608. años. yquac nican mexico. omaxitico. omocallaquico. in yehuatzin cenca mahuiztililoni teoyotica tlahtohuani Don fray Balthasar. Acobarrobias.[2] obispo huaxacac. teopixqui Sant. Augustin. ye quin ic opa hualmohuicac. yn huaxacac çan onxihuitl yn ompa motlapiallito. auh ynic nican mexico. omoquixtitiquiz. oc nauhtetl. metztli ypan tlaco nican omoyetzticatca. auh ye quin ipan. de 1609. años. ye ytlamian metztli Março quaresma yn onmopehualti ompa mohuicac yn michhuacan ompa comiquanilli yn tohueytlahtocauh Rey. ynic ompa ye no yehuatzĩ motlapachilhuiz. yc mopatlac yn huaxacac.

— Yhuan nican motlalia. motenehua. yn ipan yn itlamian in yn omoteneuh xii. tecpatl xihuitl. de 1608. años. in ye quexquichcauh yn ompa ytzinecan yn oquimochihuilli. yn oquimoyocolli. cemanahuatl yn tt° Dios. ynic oquimotlalili yn ilhuicatl yn tlalticpactli. yhuan yn ixquich tlamantli. yn ipan onoc. yhuann oc cequi tlahtolli nicã motecpana. in

1. Or the viceroy met him.

so that there was built the church of the lord San Sebastián, and it also became the general church for the Mexica Atzaqualca when they demolished what had been the Atzaqualca's chapel and church, where their old home stood, where now the Discalced Carmelite friars reside, children of our precious mother Santa María del Carmen. It was said above that first they were in charge of the Tenochca Atzaqualca for 23 years.

v Today, the 18th of the month of September of the year 1608, was when the opening of the water channel was finished, which was being excavated to cut through the mountain at Citlaltepec, whereby they diverted and aimed the water which was frightening everyone [*p. 71*] and flooding things here in Mexico to one side, toward Tula; they guided it so that it goes out to one side. The lord viceroy don Luis de Velasco went in person, and [the channel] was opened in his presence, and it was also done in the presence of the very reverend ruler in holy matters the archbishop don fray García Guerra, a Dominican friar, who arrived there at that time; he had just come from Spain, so that he met the viceroy at Citlaltepec,[1] so that the water channel by which the water goes was opened before the two of them together. The archbishop blessed the said place where the water comes out; thereupon he set out in this direction; the archbishop just passed by on his way here, he blessed the Citlaltepec channel in passing. And the time people were involved in excavating the channel and cutting through the middle of the mountain until the passage for the water was finished and opened was nine months and nineteen days. It was said above that the people of all the altepetl surrounding us came there to work during the time it was going on. The Mexica did not go there to work with the others but repaired roads here in Mexico.

v Today Monday the 29th of the month of September of the year 1608, the feast day of San Miguel, was when the very reverend ruler in holy matters don fray García Guerra, archbishop in Mexico, who as already said is a Dominican friar, arrived and entered here in the altepetl and city of Mexico Tenochtitlan; he is the one who now resides, rules in holy matters, and governs us [*p. 72*] in Tenochtitlan, the sixth archbishop here in Mexico. And before coming to and arriving in Mexico, he performed confirmations in Quauhtitlan and Tepotzotlan passing through on the way here. For fully two years no one had been archbishop here in Mexico.

v Today, the 15th of the month of October of the year 1608, was when the very reverend ruler in holy matters don fray Baltasar Covarrubias,[2] bishop in Oaxaca, Augustinian friar, arrived and entered Mexico here. It was the second time he came from Oaxaca; he was in charge there for only two years. When he passed through Mexico here, he stayed here for four and a half months. Not until the year of 1609, at the end of March, in Lent, did he set out and go to Michoacan, where our great ruler the king transferred him so that there too he would govern; it was exchanged for Oaxaca.

— Here at the end of the said 12 Flint year, the year 1608, is set down and mentioned how long it has been since the beginning of the universe, since our lord God made and created it, since he established heaven and earth and all the different things on it; and some other paragraphs are arranged here about what happened long ago, as will soon appear in

2. Given as Covarrubias in Torquemada 1975, 3: 384–85.

tleyn ye huecauh omochiuh yn iuh nimã ye onneciz. nican tecpantoc.

v Yn iquac yn itzinpeuhyoc. yn ochihualoc yn yocoyalloc cemanahuatl. ye caxtoltzonxihuitl ypan caxtolpohualxihuitl. ypan yepohualli ypã ce xihuitl. ynic axcan ypan in yn itlamian yxiuhtzĩ tt^{o} Dios. de 1608 años. [*p. 73*] Auh ye matlactzonxihuitl ypan chicuepohualxihuitl ypan macuilxihuitl. yn oapachiohuac nohuian cemanahuac. yn motenehua Diluuio. yc mochiuh yn ipãtzinco yehuatzin Noe. ca ye yzquixihuitl ynic axcan ypan ĩ yn itlamian yxiuhtzin. tt^{o}. Dios. de 1608. años.

v Auh yn omotlalli. altepetl Roma. ye macuiltzonxihuitl. ypan caxtolpohualxihuitl. ypan yepohualxihuitl. ypan ce xihuitl. ynic axcan ypan in yn itlamian yxiuhtzin tt^{o}. Dios. de 1608. años.

v Auh yn omotlacatillitzino. tt^{o}. Dios. ye nauhtzonxihuitl. ypã chicuexihuitl ynic axcan mocenpohua ynic tlami yxiuhtzin de 1608 años.

v Auh ya yetzonxihuitl ypan caxtolpohualxihuitl. ypan yepohuallocaxtolli. ypan ce xihuitl axcan yn omomiquillitzino. Jesu christo. y nelli ytlaçopiltzin. Dios. ynic cruztitech. quimotlalilitzinoque. Judiosme. ynic otechmomaquixtillico. tlalticpac titlaca. ca ye yzqui xihuitl oquichiuh ynic axcan ypan in yn itlamian yxiuhtzin de 1608. años.

v Auh ya yetzonxihuitl. ypan caxtolpolhualxihuitl. ypan onpohuallocaxtolli ypan nauhxihuitl. axcan ynic oncan achtopa yn acaltica atenquiçaco. aztlan teoculhuacan yn huehuetque chichimeca mexica çã hualpepetlauhtiaque. yn campa huallaque ynic oncan atenquiçaco motlallico aztlan teoculhuacan ca ye yzquixihuitl oquichiuh ynic axcan ypan yn itlamian yxiuhtzin tt^{o}. Dios. de 1608. años.

v Auh ya yetzonxihuitl ypan caxtolpohualxihuitl. ypan cenpohuallocaxtolli ypan yexihuitl. axcan yn otlalpoliuh Jerusalem. ynic motzoncuic yn imiquiliztzin. yn Dios. ytlaçopiltzin Jesu christo. yni[*p. 74*]c ompa tlalpoloto. vespassiano. ca ye yzquixihuitl. oquichiuh ynic axcan ypan in yn itlamian yxiuhtzin tt^{o}. Dios. de 1608. años.

v Auh ya yetzonxihuitl ypan caxtolpohualxivitl ypan cenpohuallonnahui xihuitl axcan yn opeuhq̃ huehuetque chichimeca yn ompa ye huitze aztlan teoculhuacã yn oncan ye hualquiztimani chicomoztoc quinehuayan ynic ye moxexellohua ynic yetlatlamãcahuitze. ynic nican omotecaco. omocecenmanaco. yn ipan tlalli motenehua nueua españa. o iuh ye ce xihuitl mocuecuep ynin tlahtol yn iquac opeuhque ye hualquiztimani. yn achtopa çan oc centetl catca yn intlahtol. auh cenpohuallocaxtolli xihuitl. yn çan oc ompa cepan onoca cepan catca yn aztlan. auh çan oncan quiçaco ỹ chicomoztoc. ca ye yzquixihuitl oquichiuh ynic axcan ypan in. yn itlamian yxiuhtzin tt^{o}. Dios. de 1608. años.[1]

v Auh ye ontzonxihuitl ypan chiconpohualxihuitl. axcan. yn motlallico. yn huallaque nican culhuacan yn huehuetque chichimeca. yn culhuaque ye ynpan acico ye chanonoque yn xochmilca. yhuan yn atlacuihuayan calque yc cate yn axcan oncan onoque. ca ye yxquich ye yzquixihuitl oquichiuh ynic axcan ypan in yn itlamian yxiuhtzin tt^{o}. Dios. de 1608. años. anoço de 1609 años.

v Auh ye centzonxihuitl ypan caxtolpohualxihuitl. ypan chiuhcnauhpohualxihuitl. ypan matlactlomome xihuitl.[2] axcan yn achto yc peuh tlahtocayotl. ỹ nican culhuacan yehuatl achto. quihualpehualti yn tlahtocatlaliloc. [*p. 75*] Yn itoca yn tepiltzin[3] huehue nauhyotzin tlahtohuani culhuacan ynic yehuatl ytlacamecayotitech otemoco oquiçaco yn

1. It is not clear how this entry can be reconciled with the one three further down.

2. This number of years would be given in a more standard fashion as *ontzonxihuitl ipan nauhpohualxihuitl ipan matlactlomome xihuitl* or *matlacxihuitl omome*.

what is arranged here.
v When the universe was made and created at the very beginning, it was 6,361 years before now at the end of the year of our lord God 1608. [*p. 73*] It is 4,165 years since there was flooding everywhere in the universe, called the deluge, which happened in the time of Noah; that is how long it has been until now at the end of this year of our lord God 1608.

v From the establishment of the altepetl of Rome it has been 2,361 years until now at the end of the year of our lord God 1608.

v Our lord God was born 1,608 years ago, which is the total until now at the end of his year of 1608.
v It was 1,576 years before now that Jesus Christ, truly the precious child of God, died, when the Jews put him on the cross so that he redeemed us people of earth; that is how many years it has been until now in this year at the end of the year [of our lord God] 1608.
v It was 1,559 years ago when the ancient Chichimeca Mexica first landed in boats at Aztlan Teocolhuacan. They just came naked from where they had been when they landed and established themselves at Aztlan Teocolhuacan. That is how many years it has been until now at the end of the year of our lord God 1608.

v It has now been 1,538 years since Jerusalem was destroyed, by which the death of Jesus Christ, the precious child of God, was avenged, when [*p. 74*] Vespasian went there to lay waste to the land. That is how many years it has been until now at the end of this year of our lord God 1608.
v It has now been 1,524 years since the ancient Chichimeca who had come to Aztlan Teocolhuacan gradually began to come in this direction, to Chicomoztoc Quinehuayan, coming divided into three separate groups, to spread out and disperse here in the land called New Spain. After a year their languages changed; when they began to come in this direction bit by bit, at first they still had a single language. For 35 years they dwelt and were together at Aztlan, and from there they came to Chicomoztoc. That is how many years it has been until now at the end of this year of our lord God 1608.[1]

v It has now been 940 years since the ancient Chichimeca who were Colhuaque came and settled here in Colhuacan; they found the Xochimilca already there living in their homes, and the people of Tacubaya were already where they now dwell. That is the total of how many years it has been until now at the end of this year of our lord God 1608 or 1609.

v It has now been 892 years[2] since the rulership was first begun here in Colhuacan; the person who first began it and was made ruler [*p. 75*] was named Tepiltzin[3] Nauhyotzin the elder, ruler in Colhuacan, so that from his line have come and descended all the rulers in Colhuacan. The second was named Acamapichtli, who first came to rule here in Te-

3. It is equally likely that *tepiltzin* is to be interpreted as something on the order of a title, person of high birth.

izquintin culhuacan tlahtoque. yhuan ynic ome ytoca acamapichtli yn otlahtocatico achto nican tenochtitlan. ynic no yehuatl ytlacamecayotitech otemoco oquiçaco yn izquintin mexico tenochtitlan tlahtoque ca ye yzquixihuitl oquichiuh ynic peuh tlahtocayotl ynic axcan ypan in yn itlamian yxiuhtzin tt^o^. Dios. de 1608. años.

v̲ Auh ye centzonxihuitl. ypan chiconpohualxivitl ypan macuilxihuitl axcan yn ompa huallehuaq̃. aztlan teoculhuacan yn mexica huehuetque aztlã tlaca chichimeca. auh ynic ompa cenca huecahuaq̃. ynic õpa catca aztlan teoculhuacan, ontzonxihuitl ypan matlacpohualxihuitl ypan matlactli onnahui xihuitl. yn iuh neztica yntlapohual[1] huehuetque. ynic niman ompa ohualolinque ohuallehuaque ynic nican ye hualnenemi. ca ye yzquixihuitl. oquichiuh ynic axcan ypan in yn itlamian yxiuhtzin tt^o^ Dios. de 1608. años.

v̲ ye iuh nepa õtzonxivitl ipã matlacpoalli xivitl ypã yepoalli onnahui xivitl motlacatilitzino ỹ tt^o^. Dios.[2]

v̲ Auh ye centzonxihuitl ypan chiconpohualxihuitl ypan ce xihuitl. axcan yn huehuetque mexica azteca chichimeca. ynic ompa hualolinque hualquizque aztlan teoculhuacan ynic ohualnenenque. nohuian otlihpa. ohualnentiaque. ynic niman oncan acico. yn canĩ quahuitl cenca tomahuac yn ahuehuetl yn inpan poztec[3] oncan oc nauhxiuhtique yn mexica. catca. ynic oncan motlallico. ytzintlan mocehuiaya yn ahuehuetl. ynin quahuitl. omoteneuh ỹpan poztec mexica. çan no yehuantin yntlaaquil. mochiuh yn az[*p. 76*]teca. yn iuh quitotihui huehuetque. ye iuh matlactlomome xihuitl. oncan cate. yn aztlan teoculhuacan. yn ipan xii. calli xihuitl .61. años. yn caquique quahuitl. yn ahuehuetl. auh yn ixiuhtzin tt^o^. Dios ye iuh ye nepa yepohualli ypan ce xihuitl motlacatillitzino ynic caquique quahuitl. yn çatepan ynpan poztec. yn ipan v. tecpatl. 1068. a^o^s. ynic huallaque huehuetque. yn inpan poztec otlihpan yn itzintlan mocehuiaya mexica. auh ynic cenca huecauhtica ycaca yn ahuehuetl ynic tlaaquilli. yhuan ynic poztequico ỹpan mexica yn ixquichcauhtica ontzonxiuhtica ypan matlacpohualxiuhtica ypan chicuexiuhtica ca ye yzquixihuitl oquichiuh ynic axcan ypan in yn itlamian yxiuhtzin tt^o^. Dios. de 1608. años —

v̲ Auh yhuan ye centzonxihuitl ypan chiquacenpohualxihuitl ypan matlactlonnahui xihuitl. yn ipan xii. acatl xihuitl. 1075 años. yn oncan quiçaco chicomoztoc quinehuayan yn mexica azteca chichimeca huehuetque oncan chicoxiuhtique ynic mitohua motenehua chicomoztoca auh ypan in yn omoteneuh xii. acatl. yn hualolinque. ynic hualnenenque ynic ye huitze hualacxipetlatiaque nohuian quauhtla. çacatla. tepetla. atlauhtla cuillotla.[4] nequametla. tzihuactla[5] teocotla[6] xihuallacatla.[7] y hualnentiaque ymehuatilma hualyetia yn chichimeca. o iuh ye nepa hualquizque matlactlomome xihuitl yn ompa aztlan. yn ipan in omoteneuh xii. acatl. ynic niman hualnenenque oncan huallehuaque yn omoteneuh chicomoztoc quinehuayan [*p. 77*] Ca ye yzqui xihuitl. oquichiuh. ynic axcan ypan in yn itlamian yxiuhtzin tt^o^. Dios. de 1608 años.[8]

v̲ Auh yhuan ye centzonxihuitl. ypan onpohualli onchiuhcnahui xihuitl. yn ipan vi. tecpatl xihuitl 1160. años. axcan yn ompa hualolinque huallehuaque chicomoztoc quinehua-

1. In effect, calendar.
2. This entry is in the margin.
3. This expression could equally well mean that the tree literally fell on top of them or that it split during their stay.
4. Brewer and Brewer 1971, p. 122, has *cuilōtl*, stick; Molina has *cuilotic*, someone slim.
5. See Sahagún 1979, Book 11, f. 201, or Sahagún 1950–1982, Book 11, p. 218.

nochtitlan, so that from his line too have come and descended all the rulers in Mexico Tenochtitlan. That is how many years it has been until now at the end of this year of our lord God 1608 since the rulership began.

v It has now been 545 years since the Mexica, the ancient Aztlan people and Chichimeca, left Aztlan Teocolhuacan, where they spent a very long time; they were at Aztlan Teocolhuacan 1,014 years, as appears in the count[1] of the ancients, until they set out and came in this direction, wandering toward here. That is how many years it has been now at the end of this year of our lord God 1608.

v It had been 1,064 years since the birth of our lord God.[2]

v It has now been 541 years since the ancient Mexica Azteca Chichimeca set out from and left Aztlan Teocolhuacan in this direction, wandering toward here, coming wandering on the roads everywhere, until they came to a place where a very thick tree, a cypress, broke while they were there;[3] first the Mexica were there for four years, establishing themselves and resting at the base of the cypress. This said tree that broke over the Mexica had also been planted by the Azteca; [*p. 76*] the elders say that when they had been at Aztlan Teocolhuacan for twelve years in 12 House year, the year 61 [in the Christian calendar], they planted the cypress tree, and in the years of our lord God he had been born 61 years before when they planted the tree that afterward split on them in the year of 5 Flint, 1068, when the ancient Mexica came along the way and it split on them while they were there resting at its base. The cypress stood for a very long time from when it was planted until it split when the Mexica were there: 1,008 years. That is how many years it has been now at the end of this year of our lord God 1608.

v And also, 534 years ago, in the year 12 Reed, 1075, the ancient Mexica Azteca Chichimeca left Chicomoztoc Quinehuayan; they spent seven years there, so that they are called and named Chicomoztoca. In the said 12 Reed they set out in this direction, wandering toward here, coming barefoot everywhere, through woods, grass, mountains, ravines, thickets,[4] palms, maguey patches,[5] bushy places,[6] [marshy places?];[7] the Chichimeca came wearing leather cloaks. In the said 12 Reed it had been 12 years since they left Aztlan in this direction, so that they walked along in this direction coming from the said Chicomoztoc Quinehuayan. [*p. 77*] That is how many years it has been until now at the end of this year of our lord God 1608.[8]

v And also, 449 years ago, in the year 6 Flint, 1160, now the ancient Chichimeca who were Totolimpaneca Amaquemeque got on their way and left Chicomoztoc Quinehuayan

6. *Teocotl*, literally "rock pine," is a kind of bushy plant producing an incense.

7. In "xihuallacatla," *aca-* is reed, *-tla* place of abundance; the first part could contain *xiuh-*, something green or related to leaves, but that leaves an impossible *-al* or *-all*; everything before *acatla* is probably a single element.

8. The years and intervals given in different entries in this section by no means always seem congruent with one another. We leave a thorough investigation and rationalization of this aspect to future research or other scholars.

yan. yn chichimeca huehuetq̃. totolimpaneca Amaquemeque. yn ompa yntlahtocauh quihualhuicaque ytoca hecatzin teuhctli chichimecateuhctli. tlaquitzcaliuhqui[1] auh ynic cenca huecahuaque ynic ompa catca yn aztlan teoculhuacan. yn chichimeca totolimpaneca ontzonxihuitl ypan caxtolpohualxihuitl. ypã yepohualxiuhtique. ynic nimann ompa hualolimque huallequaque ynic ohualnenenque. ca ye yzquixihuitl oquichiuh ynic axcan ypan in yn itlamian yxiuhtzin tt°. Dios. de 1608. años.

v̲ Auh yhuan ye centzonxihuitl ypan onpohualxivitl ypan ce xihuitl. yn ipan i. tecpatl. de 1168. años. yn copehualti teyacanalizyotl. yn quauhtlequetzqui oc ompa y cohuatepec yn ihuicpa tullam. ca ye yzqui xihuitl oquichiuh ynic axcan ypan in yn itlamian yxiuhtzin tt°. Dios. de 1608. años.

v̲ Auh yhuan ye centzonxihuitl. ypan nauhxihuitl yn ipan xii. calli xihuitl 1205. años. yn quicauh teyacanalizyotl. yn quauhtlequetzqui. yn teyacan cẽpohualxihuitl ypan caxtollomey. xihuitl. // auh ça niman iquac yn ipan omoteneuh xihuitl. motlalli yn acacitli yn teyacanaz. ca ye yzquixihuitl oquichiuh. ynic axcan ypan in yn itlamian yxiuhtzin tt°. Dios. de 1608. años. [*p. 78*]

v̲ Auh yhuan ye caxtolpohualxihuitl ypan nauhpohualxihuitl ypan matlactlomome xihuitl. yn ipan xiii. acatl xihuitl. 1219. años. yn quicauh teyacanalizyotl. yn acacitli. yn teyacan caxtolxihuitl auh ça niman iquac yn ipan omoteneuh xihuitl. motlalli yn citlalitzin yn teyacanaz. ca ye yzquixihuitl oquichiuh ynic axcan ypan in yn itlamian yxiuhtzin tt°. Dios. de 1608 años.

v̲ Auh yhuan ye caxtolpolhualxihuitl. ypan yepohuallocaxtolli ypan onxihuitl yn ipan 2. tochtli xihuitl. 1234. yn quicauh teyacanalizyotl. yn citlallitzin yn teyacan caxtollonce xihuitl. // auh çan niman iquac yn ipan omoteneuh xihuitl motlalli tzĩpan ỹ teyacanaz. Ca ye yzquixihuitl oquichiuh ynic axcan ypan in yn itlamian yxiuhtzin tt°. Dios. de 1608 años.

v̲ Auh yhuan ye caxtolpolhualxihuitl ypan yepohuallocaxtolli ypan ce xihuitl. yn ipan. 3. acatl xihuitl 1235 años. yn quicauh teyacanalizyotl. yn tzinpan yn teyacan onxihuitl. // auh ça niman iquac yn ipan omoteneuh xihuitl. motlalli yn tlaçotzin yn teyacanaz. ca ye yzquixihuitl oquichiuh ynic axcan ypan in yn itlamian yxiuhtzin tt°. Dios. de 1608. años

v̲ Auh yhuan ye caxtolpolhualxihuitl ypan yepohuallomatlactli ypan ce xihuitl yn ipan vii. acatl xihuitl. 1239. años. yn quicauh teyacanalizyotl yn tlaçotzin. yn teyacan macuilxihuitl. // auh ça niman iquac yn ipan omoteneuh xihuitl motlalli yn tozcuecuextli yn teyacanaz. ca ye yzqui xihuitl. oquichiuh ynic axcan ypan in. yn itlamian yxiuhtzin tt°. Dios. de 1608. años. yn tozcuecuextli. oncan ypan molpilli oncan quilpillique [*p. 79*] Yn ixiuh[2] yn tecpayocan ynic quinhualyacã mexica.

v̲ Auh yhuan ye caxtolpohualxihuitl ypan yepohuallonchiuhcnahui xihuitl. yn ipan. ix. calli xihuitl 1241. años. yn acico oncan chalco atenco yn huehuetque chichimeca totolimpaneca yn amaquemeque yehuatl tlahtohuani hualmochiuhtia yn huehueteuhctli yn chichimecateuhctli. yhuan acico quĩhualhuicac yeyntin ypilhuan ynic ce ytoca tliltecatzin. ynic ome ytoca xochitzin. yniquey. ytoca. atonaltzin. auh ynic acico ynic ompa huallehuaque yn chicomoztoc quinehuayan ynic tlayahualloque ye nauhpohualxiuhtica ypan onxiuhtica. ynic motlallico oncan chalco atenco auh ca omomiquillitacico. yn ipan omoteneuh xihuitl ix. calli. yn tlatohuani huehueteuhctli yn chichimecateuhctli. yn tlah-

1. The word seems to contain *tlactli*, torso; *itzcalli*, side; and *iuhqui*, being a certain way.

in this direction, accompanying their ruler named Eecatzin teuctli, the Chichimecateuctli, [with a twisted body?].[1] To show how very long the Chichimeca Totolimpaneca had stayed while they were at Aztlan Teocolhuacan, they spent 1,160 years until then they got under way and set out to come walking in this direction. That is how many years it has been until now at the end of this year of our lord God 1608.

v And also, 441 years ago, in the year 1 Flint, 1168, Quauhtlequetzqui began the leadership; it was still at Coatepec, toward Tula. That is how many years it has been until now at the end of this year of our lord God 1608.

v And also, 404 years ago, in the year 12 House, 1205, Quauhtlequetzqui left the leadership, having been leader for 38 years. // And right then in the said year Acacitli was installed to be leader. That is how many years it has been until now at the end of this year of our lord God 1608. [*p. 78*]

v And also, 392 years ago, in the year 13 Reed, 1219, Acacitli left the leadership, having been leader for 15 years. And right then in the said year Citlalintzin was installed to be leader. That is how many years it has been until now at the end of this year of our lord God 1608.

v And also, 377 years ago, in the year 2 Rabbit, 1234, Citlalintzin left the leadership, having been leader for 16 years. // And right then in the said year Tzimpan was installed to be leader. That is how many years it has been until now at the end of this year of our lord God 1608.

v And also, 376 years ago, in the year 3 Reed, 1235, Tzimpan left the leadership, having been leader for two years. // And right then in the said year Tlaçotzin was installed to be leader. That is how many years it has been until now at the end of this year of our lord God 1608.
v And also, 371 years ago, in the year 7 Reed, 1239, Tlaçotzin left the leadership, having been leader for five years. // And right then in the said year Tozcuecuextli was installed to be leader. That is how many years it has been now at the end of this year of our lord God 1608. In the time of Tozcuecuextli the years were bound there;[2] they bound [*p. 79*] the years at Tecpanyocan when he came leading the Mexica.

v And also, 369 years ago, in the year 9 House, 1241, the ancient Chichimeca Totolimpaneca, the Amaquemeque, arrived at Chalco Atenco. Huehueteuctli, the Chichimecateuctli, came as their ruler; with him arrived and he brought along three children of his, the first named Tliltecatzin, the second named Xochitzin, and the third named Atonaltzin. And when they arrived, it had been 82 years that they had been wandering around since leaving Chicomoztoc Quinehuayan until they settled at Chalco Atenco. And the ruler Huehueteuctli, the Chichimecateuctli, died on arriving in the said year of 9 House, having ruled for 68 years during which he came governing the Amaquemeque. And right then in

2. I.e., the end of a 52-year cycle and the beginning of another was celebrated.

tocat. yepohualxihuitl ypan chicuexihuitl. yn quinhualpachotia amaquemeque. auh çan niman iquac yn ipan xihuitl omoteneuh motlahtocatlalli yn ipiltzin. ynitoca atonaltzin. chichimecateuhctli. mochiuh yn oncan chalco atenco. ca ye yzquixihuitl oquichiuh ynic axcan ypan in yn itlamian yxiuhtzin tt^{o}. Dios. de 1608. años.

v Auh yhuan ye caxtolpolhualxihuitl ypan onpohualli ypan onxihuitl yn ipan xi. calli xihuitl. 1269. años. yn acito yn ompa ycpac tepetl amaqueme ynic õpa monamiquito. y nahuintin tlahtoque chichimeca. achtopa yehuantin ompa acito. yn totolimpaneca. yn tliltecatzin chichimecayaotequihua. yhuan yni teyccauhtzin Atonaltzin chichimecateuhctli. amaq̃mecan tlahtoque. auh niman ynpa onacito oc no omentin tenanco tlahtoque ynic ce yehuatl yn itoca quahuitzatl teuchtli. tlayllotlac teuhctli. ynic ome ytoca huehue ytzquauhtzin atlauh[*p. 80*]tecatl teuhctli.[1] auh yn atonaltzin chichimeca teuhctli. yn ihuan quahuitzatl teuhctli tlayllotlacteuhctli momiminque oncan yn icpac tepetl amaqueme yni ipampa quitohuaya yn atonaltzin ayac cacizquia[2] ynic chichimecatl. ynic hehey. quimotlaxillique yni inmiuh ayac huel mominque. auh yn çatepan yn omottaque yn omonenehuillique yn çan neneuhque ynic chichimeca. niman quimotlapanique yn tepetl amaqueme ynic niman oncan quitlallique yn ome altepetl. yni cecca ytztlacoçauhcan totolimpa amaquemecan. ynic occan tzaqualtitlan tenanco chiconcohuac amaquemecan. yhuan yquac quitlallique yn ixquich ynquaxoch ynic niman motlallique. ca ye yzqui xihuitl. oquichiuh ynic axcan ypan in yn itlamian yxiuhtzin tt^{o}. Dios. de 1608. años

v Auh yhuan ye caxtolpohualxihuitl ypan cenpohuallomatlactli ypan ome xihuitl. yn ipan vii. tochtli xihuitl. de 1278. años. yn miquico. tozcuecuextli yn teyacan onpohualxihuitl. // auh çan niman iquac yn ipan omoteneuh xihuitl quitlahtocatlallique in mexica yn huehue huitzillihuitl yntlahtocauh mochiuh. ynin ye oncan yn chapoltepec quitlallique. ca ye yzqui xihuitl oquichiuh ynic axcan ypan in yn itlamian yxiuhtzin tt^{o}. Dios. de 1608. años.

Vehuehuitzillihuitl yn inãtzin ytoca catca tlaquilxochitzin[3]

v Auh yhuan ye caxtolpohualxihuitl ypan matlacxihuitl. yn ipan 2. acatl xihuitl 1299. años ypan toxiuh molpilli. yquac oncan cacique. yn acoculco. chapoltepec yn huehue huitzillihuitl. tlahtohuani catca yntlan y mexica. chichimeca ynic oncan quinyaoyahualloque chapoltepec ynic nahualpoliuhq̃. nauhcampa[4] huicalloque ỹ mexica. mochoquilitiaque. auh yn huehue huitzillihuitl. ompa huicoc ompa quimictito. yn culhuacan. ytencopa mochiuh yn tlahtohuani coxcoxtli. auh yn tlahtocat. — [*p. 81*] huehue huitzillihuitl. cenpohualxihuitl ypan ome xihuitl. // auh yc niman oncan onehuaque. yn acoculco yn chapoltepec in mexica. çan ya yehuatl ypan yn omoteneuh 2. acatl. 1299. años. yn iquac oncan callaquico. ypan altepetl. culhuacan yn mexica azteca. yquac oncan tlahtocati. yn tlacatl coxcoxtli. auh ye iuh nepa matlacpohualxihuitl ypan cenpohualloncaxtolli ypan yc oce. ynic ompa huallolimque. ynic ompa hualquizque. yancuic mexico aztlan. yn mexica. ynic nohuian hualquizq̃. hualnenenque otlihpa. ynic oncan tetlan motlallico culhuacan. mexica. // auh no yhuan ye iuh nepa matlacpohualxihuitl ypan cenpohualxihuitl. ypan macuilxihuitl. yn ipan vii. acatl xihuitl de 1073 años ynic ompa hualolimque ynic ompa hualquizque yn çan oncan chicomoztoc quinehuayan. in mexica azteca. ynic nohuian otlihpa hualnentiaque. ynic oncan tepan callaquico culhuacan yn ipan omoteneuh xihuitl. ome acatl auh nauhpa yn otlihpa. yn inpan toxiuh molpilli mexica.

1. Lord of Atlauhtlan.
2. Literally catch him.

the said year his child named Atonaltzin was installed as ruler and became Chichimecateuctli at Chalco Atenco. That is how many years it has been until now at the end of this year of our lord God 1608.

v And also, 342 years ago, in the year 11 House, 1269, they arrived on top of the mountain Amaqueme, so that the four Chichimeca rulers met there. First arrived the Totolimpaneca [rulers], Tliltecatzin the Chichimecayaotequihua and his younger sibling Atonaltzin, the Chichimecateuctli, rulers in Amaquemecan. And then when they were there two more arrived, rulers in Tenanco, the first named Quahuitzatl teuctli, the Tlailotlac teuctli, and the second named Itzquauhtzin the elder, the Atlauhtecatl [*p. 80*] teuctli.[1] And Atonaltzin the Chichimecateuctli and Quahuitzatl teuctli the Tlailotlac teuctli shot arrows at each other on top of the Amaqueme mountain, because Atonaltzin said that no one could equal him[2] as a Chichimeca, so that they each shot three arrows, but they couldn't hit anyone. Afterward they looked at each other and came to agreement that they were equal as Chichimeca. Then they divided the mountain Amaqueme between them, so that they established two altepetl there, the first Itztlacoçauhcan Totolimpan Amaquemecan, and the second Tzaqualtitlan Tenanco Chiconcoac Amaquemecan, and at that time they established all their boundaries, whereupon they settled down. That is how many years it has been until now at the end of the year of our lord God 1608.

v And also, it was 332 years ago, in the year 7 Rabbit, 1278, that Tozcuecuextli, who was leader for 40 years, died. // And right then in the said year the Mexica installed as ruler Huitzilihuitl the elder, who became their ruler; they installed him at Chapoltepec. That is how many years it has been until now at the end of the year of our lord God 1608.

Huitzilihuitl the elder's mother was named Tlaquilxochitzin.[3]

v And also, 310 years ago, in the year 2 Reed, 1299, in which our years were bound, was when at Acocolco Chapoltepec they captured Huitzilihuitl the elder, who was ruler among the Mexica Chichimeca, when they were being surrounded at Chapoltepec, so that the Mexica were treacherously defeated and were taken off in all four directions;[4] they went weeping. And Huitzilihuitl the elder was taken to Colhuacan, where they killed him; it was done by order of the ruler Coxcoxtli. — [*p. 81*] Huitzilihuitl the elder was ruler for 22 years. // Thereupon the Mexica left Acocolco Chapoltepec; it was in the same said year of 2 Reed, 1299, when the Mexica Azteca entered the altepetl of Colhuacan. At that time the lord Coxcoxtli was ruler there. And it had been 236 years since the Mexica set out and left New Mexico, Aztlan, toward here and came in this direction walking everywhere on the roads, until the Mexica settled among others at Colhuacan. // And it had also been 225 years, in the year 7 Reed, 1073, since the Mexica Azteca set out and left Chicomoztoc Quinehuayan toward here, so that they came walking along the roads everywhere until they entered among others at Colhuacan in the said year of 2 Reed. And while the Mexica were on the way, our years were bound four times while they came

3. In the margin.
4. This expression might refer instead to all four parts of the entity.

ynic hualnentiaque. ynic cenca huecauhtica. ynic oncan acico culhuacan.

v Auh yhuan ye centzonxihuitl ypan matlacpohualxihuitl. ypan cenpohuallomatlactli xihuitl. oncan cate culhuacan yn culhuaque. ynic oncan ynpã callaquico. mexica. auh yhuan ye iuh nepa centzõxihuitl. ypan chiuhcnauhpohualxihuitl. ypan yexihuitl. yn oncan tlahtocayotl culhuacan ynic oncan callaquico mexica yc _____[1] tlahtohuani oncan yn coxcoxtli.

v Auh yhuan ye iuh nepa matlacpohualxihuitl ypan yepohualxihuitl poliuhque yn tullam tlaca ynic momoyahuaque quicauhque yn imaltepeuh [*p. 82*] yehuatl quichichiuh yn diablo. yn yaotl[2] yn tezcatlipoca. ynic poliuh altepetl. tullam. ye yxquichcauh opoliuh. ynic oncan motlallica culhuacan mexica.

v Auh yhuan yn iuh oncan motlallico culhuacan mexica. yn ipan omoteneuh 2. acatl xihuitl. yquac oncan quinpehuato yn xochmilca. çan mochĩtin quinnacaztlazque. yn inmalhua mexica.

v Auh yn o iuh quimictique huehue huitzillihuitl yn culhuaque. auh ça niman iquac yn ipan omoteneuh xihuitl yn 2. acatl 1299. años. motlalli yn tenoch. yn teyacanaz. ye omoteneuh ome acatl. ynic quilpillique. yn ixiuh yn culhuacan. ompa yn quitlallique. ca ye yzqui xihuitl oquichiuh ynic axcan ypan in itlamian yxiuhtzin tt^{o}. Dios. de 1608. años. yc macuilpa oncan ypan toxiuh molpilli. in mexica yn cuhhuacan[3] in ye yxquich ica yc ompa huitze aztlan.

v Auh yhuan ye caxtolpohualxihuitl ypan ome xihuitl. yn ipan x. acatl xihuitl 1307 años. yn omomiquillico tlacatl coxcoxtli tlatohuani catca culhuacan. yn tlahtocat. cenpohualxihuitl ypan chicoxihuitl. auh yn quauhtlahtoloc yn ayac tlahtocat culhuacan caxtolli once xihuitl. yn o y mic[4] coxcoxtli ca ye yzqui xihuitl oquichiuh ynic axcan ypan in yn itlamian yxiuhtzin tt^{o}. Dios. de 1608 años.

v Auh yhuan ye matlacpohualxihuitl ypan nauhpohualxihuitl ypan chiquacenxihuitl [*p. 83*] Yn ipan. xiii. acatl xihuitl. 1323. años. ypan in tlamico. ynic quauhtlahtolloc yn culhuacan caxtolxihuitl once yn ayac tlahtocat. // auh yn tiçaapan culhuacan ynic ompa onoca yn mexica. cenpohualxiuhtique onmacuilli. // auh ypan in yn omoteneuh yn xiii. acatl xihuitl in yancuica ye yc quipehualtia in yaoyotl in culhuaque. ynic quinhualtocaque. yn mexica oncan motlallico. y nexticpac. cexiuhtique oncan yn xihuitl. ce tecpatl. 1324. años. nimã oncan hualpeuhque ynic acico tenochtitlan ca ye yzqui xihuitl oquichiuh ynic axcan ypan in. yn itlamian. yxiuhtzin tt^{o}· Dios. de 1608. años.

v Auh yhuan ye matlacpohualxihuitl ypã nauhpohualxihui[5] ypan macuilxihuitl yn ipan omoteneuh ce tecpatl xihuitl 1324. a^{o}s. yn motlahtocatlalli yn tlahtohuani huehue acamapichtli tlahtohuani culhuacan. // auh no yquac yn ipan in xihuitl omoteneuh yquac peuh yn xochiyaoyotl yn ompa chalco. yehuantin quichiuhque yn chalca yn tlacochcalca ca ye yzqui xihuitl. oquichiuh ynic axcan ypan in yn itlamian yn ixiuhtzin tt^{o}. Dios. de 1608. años.

v Auh yhuan ye matlacpohualxihuitl ypan nauhpohualxihuitl. ypan nauhxihuitl. yn ipan 2. calli xihuitl 1325. años. yn omotlallico. nican atl ihtic tenochtitlan. yn mexica. matlactli omomentin yn acico. ye omito ynic ce yehuatl hualquauhtlahtotia hualteyacan yn

1. Gap left in original to be filled in later.

2. Yaotl, meaning literally "enemy," was a proper name in general and was one of the names of Tezcatlipoca because of his warlike attributes. See Durán 1994, p. 53, n. 4, and Sahagún 1979, Book 3, f. 8v, or Sahagún 1950–1982, Book 3, p. 12.

walking, it was such a very long time until they arrived in Colhuacan.

v And also, the Colhuaque had been in Colhuacan for 630 years when the Mexica entered among them. And there had been a rulership in Colhuacan for 583 years when the Mexica entered there; Coxcoxtli was the _____th[1] ruler there.

v And also, it had been 260 years since the people of Tula disappeared, when they dispersed and abandoned their altepetl; [*p. 82*] it was the devil Yaotl[2] Tezcatlipoca who caused the altepetl of Tula to perish; it had perished that long ago when the Mexica settled in Colhuacan.

v And also, when the Mexica had come to settle in Colhuacan, in the said year 2 Reed, at that time they went to conquer the Xochimilca; the Mexica cut off the ears of all their captives.

v After the Colhuaque had killed Huitzilihuitl the elder, right then in the said year 2 Reed, 1299, Tenoch was installed to be leader. In the said year 2 Reed, when they bound their years at Colhuacan, they installed him there. That is how many years it has been until now at the end of the year of our lord God 1608. This was the fifth time our years were bound in the time of the Mexica, at Colhuacan,[3] in the whole time since they came from Aztlan.

v And also, it was 302 years ago, in the year 10 Reed, 1307, that the lord Coxcoxtli, who was ruler in Colhuacan, passed away, having ruled for 27 years. There was interim rule and no one was ruler in Colhuacan for 16 years after Coxcoxtli died.[4] That is how many years it has been until now at the end of the year of our lord God 1608.

v And also, 286 years ago, [*p. 83*] in the year 13 Reed, 1323, the 16 years of interim rule in Colhuacan, when no one was ruler, came to an end. // The Mexica spent 25 years living at Tiçaapan in Colhuacan. // And in the said 13 Reed year was when the Colhuaque began war anew and chased out the Mexica in this direction. They came to settle in Nexticpac; they spent a year there, the year 1 Flint, 1324. Then they set out from there in this direction until they arrived in Tenochtitlan. That is how many years it has been until now at the end of this year of our lord God 1608.

v And also, 285[5] years ago, in the said year 1 Flint, 1324, the ruler Acamapichtli the elder was installed as ruler in Colhuacan. // And in the said year was also when flower war began in Chalco; the Chalca and Tlacochcalca did it. That is how many years it has been until now at the end of the year of our lord God 1608.

v And also, it was 284 years ago, in the year 2 House, 1325, that the Mexica came to settle here within the waters, in Tenochtitlan. There were twelve who arrived, as has been said: first, the one who came as interim ruler and leader was named Tenoch; the second

3. For "culhuacan."
4. Intention possibly "o yuh mic."
5. For "nauhpohualxihuitl."

itoca tenoch ynic ome ytoca quauhtli yolqui. ynin no hualte[*p. 84*]Yacan. yniquey ytoca tzonpantzin. ynic nahui ytoca Ahuexotl. ynic macuilli ytoca yzhuac tlaxquitl. ynic chiquacen ytoca Ocomecatzin. ynic chicome ytoca chicopachmani. ynic chicuey ytoca Ahatzin. ynic chiuhnahui ytoca tençacatetl. ynic matlactli ytoca Acacitli. ynic matlactloce ytoca copil teomama. ynic matlactlomome ytoca xiuhcaque teomama. yehuantin in yn huehueyntin[1] yn acico. tenochtitlan. tehuanme acico yn oc omentin yn itoca xocoyotl. yhuan tzintlatlauhqui. yc mactlactlonnahui yn acico chimeca[2] mexica. ca ye yzqui xihuitl oquichiuh ynic axca ypan in yn itlamian yxiuhtzin. tt^o. Dios. 1608. años. // auh ye iuh nepa caxtolpohualxihuitl ypan cenpohuallomatlacli ypan ce xihuitl cate yn azcapotzalca ynic acico mexica yn tenochtitlan. ynic mocentlallico.

v Auh yhuan ye matlacpohualxihuitl ypan yepohualxihuitl ypan matlactlomey xihuitl yn ipan xiii. tecpatl xihuitl. 1336. a^os. yn momiquillico. yn huehue acamapichtli tlahtohuani culhuacan yn tlahtocat. matlactlomey xivitl. ca ye yzqui xihuitl oquichiuh ynic axcan ypan in yn itlamian yxiuhtzin tt^o. Dios. de 1608. años.

v Auh yhuan ye matlacpohualxihuitl ypan yepohualxihuitl ypan matlactlomome xihuitl yn ipan i ce calli xihuitl. 1337. años yn moxeloque mexica. matlactlomome tlacatl yn omotlallito xaltilolco yn axcan ye tiquitohua tlatilolco. yn ompa yahque mexica. chichimeca. ynic ce [*p. 85*] Ytoca cuitlachquauhtli teomama. ynic ome ytoca xochilleletzin.[3] yniquey. ytoca cemacachiquihuitl. ynic nahui ytoca xomimitl. ynic macuilli ytoca callaomitl. ynic chiquacen ytoca Ocellopane. ynic chicome. ytoca atlanquahuitl. ynic chicuey ytoca yztac michĩ ynic chiuhcnahui. ytoca cocihuatli. ynic matlactli ytoca poyahuitl. teomama ynic matlactloce ytoca xiuhcoyollatzin ynic matlactlomome ytoca maltecatzĩ ca ye yzqui xihuitl oquichiuh ynic axcan ypan in yn itlamian yxiuhtzin tt^o. Dios. de 1608. años.

v Auh yhuan ye matlacpohualxihuitl. ypan onpohualxihuitl. ypan chiquacenxihuitl. yn ipa i. ce acatl xihuitl. 1363. años. yn omomiquillico yn tenochtzin. yn teyacan yn quauhtlahto. tenochtitlan. cenpohualxihuitl ypan caxtolli onnahui xihuitl. auh ynic mocenpohua yn ixquichcauh oquauhtlahto tenochtzin ynic ompa. quitlallique tiçaapan culhuacan. yepohualxihuitl ypan nauhxihuitl ynic onmomiquillico. yn o iuh momiquilli oc yexihuitl yn ayac oquauhtlahto çan ocactimãca yn tenochtitlan. auh ynic momiquillico ca ye yzqui xihuitl oquichiuh. ynic axcã ypan in yn itlamian yxiuhtzin. tt^o. Dios. de 1608. años.

v Auh yhuan ye matlacpohualxihuitl ypan onpohualxihuitl ypan ome xihuitl. yn ipan v. acatl xihuitl 1367. años. yn motlahtocatlalli. yn tlacatl. Acama[*p. 86*]pichtli. achto. tlahtoani tenochtitlan. ca ye yzqui xihuitl. oquichiuh. ynic axcan ypan in yn itlamian yxiuhtzin tt^o. Dios. de 1608. años.

v Auh yhuan ye matlacpohualxihuitl ypan cenpohualxihuitl ypan ome xihuitl yn ipan xii. acatl xihuitl 1387 años. yn omomiquilli ỹ tlacatl. acamapichtli. tlahtohuani catca achto tenochtitlan. yn tlahtocat cenpohualli ypan ce xihuitl. ca ye yzqui xihuitl oquichiuh ynic axcan ypan in yn itlamian yxiuhtzin tt^o. Dios. de 1608. años.

v Auh yhuan ye matlacpohualxihuitl ypan caxtolomey xihuitl yn ipan iii. acatl xihuitl. 1391 años yn omotlahtocatlalli yn tlacatl. ynic ome huitzillihuitl. tlahtohuani tenoch-

1. Literally the great ones. The word, however, sometimes simply means adults, and the names of the two who follow, Xocoyotl (youngest) and Tzintlatlauhqui (Red-bottom), strengthen the suspicion that such is the meaning. Normally in such accounts, however, each individual represents a constituent unit.

was named Quauhtliyolqui, who also came as leader; [*p. 84*] the third was named Tzompantzin; the fourth was named Ahuexotl; the fifth was named Izhuac Tlaxquitl; the sixth was named Ocomecatzin; the seventh was named Chicopachmani; the eighth was named Aatzin; the ninth was named Tençacatetl; the tenth was named Acacitli; the eleventh was named Copil, bearer of the god; the twelfth was named Xiuhcaque, bearer of the god. They were the principal ones[1] who arrived in Tenochtitlan; along with them arrived two others, named Xocoyotl and Tzintlatlauhqui, making fourteen Chichimeca[2] Mexica who arrived. That is how many years it has been until now at the end of this year of our lord God 1608. // And the Azcapotzalca had been there 331 years when the Mexica arrived and all came to settle in Tenochtitlan.

v And also, 273 years ago, in the year 13 Flint, 1336, Acamapichtli the elder, ruler of Colhuacan, passed away, having ruled for 13 years. That is how many years it has been until now at the end of this year of our lord God 1608.

v And also, 272 years ago, in the year 1 House, 1337, the Mexica divided. Twelve people went to settle in Xaltelolco, that we now call Tlatelolco, where some Mexica Chichimeca went: the first [*p. 85*] was named Cuitlachquauhtli, bearer of the god; the second was named Xochilleletzin;[3] the third was named Cemacachiquihuitl; the fourth was named Xomimitl; the fifth was named Callaomitl; the sixth was named Ocelopane; the seventh was named Atlanquahuitl; the eighth was named Iztacmichin; the ninth was named Cocihuatli; the tenth was named Poyahuitl, bearer of the god; the eleventh was named Xiuhcoyolatzin; the twelfth was named Maltecatzin. That is how many years it has been until now at the end of this year of our lord God 1608.

v And also, 246 years ago, in the year 1 Reed, 1363, Tenochtzin, who had been leader and interim ruler in Tenochtitlan for 39 years, passed away; the total of how long Tenochtzin was interim ruler from when they installed him at Tiçaapan in Colhuacan until he died was 64 years. After he had died, for three years there was no interim ruler; [the rulership] was vacant in Tenochtitlan. From his death, that is how many years it has been until now at the end of this year of our lord God 1608.

v And also, 242 years ago, in the year 5 Reed, 1367, the lord Acamapichtli [*p. 86*] was installed as the first ruler in Tenochtitlan. That is how many years it has been until now at the end of this year of our lord God 1608.

v And also, 222 years ago, in the year 12 Reed, 1387, the lord Acamapichtli, who was the first ruler in Tenochtitlan, passed away, having ruled for 21 years. That is how many years it has been until now at the end of this year of our lord God 1608.

v And also, 218 years ago, in the year 3 Reed, 1391, the lord Huitzilihuitl the second was installed as ruler in Tenochtitlan.[4] That is how many years it has been until now at the

---

2. For "chichimeca."
3. The name as given in the original is likely an error.
4. See p. 128, n. 1.

titlan.[1] ca ye yzqui xivitl oquichiuh ynic axcan ypan in yn itlamian yxiuhtzin tt°. Dios. de 1608. años

v Auh yhuan ye matlacpohualxihuitl ypan chiconxihuitl. yn ipan 1 ce tochtli xihuitl. 1402. a°s. yn otlacat. Neçahualcoyotzin tlahtohuani tetzcoco. ca ye yzqui xihuitl oquichiuh ynic axcan ypan in yn itlamian yxiuhtzin tt°. Dios. de 1608. a°s.

v Auh yhuan ye chiuhcnauhpohualxihuitl ypan matlactlonnahui xihuitl. yn ipan i. acatl xihuitl. 1315.[2] años. yn omomiquilli yn tlacatl ynic ome huitzillihuitl. tlahtohuani catca tenochtitlan yn tlahtocat. cenpohualli ypan macuilli xihuitl. // Auh ça niman iquac yn ipan omoteneuh xihuitl motlahtocatlalli yn tlacatl chimalpopoca tlahtohuani tenochtitlan. ca ye yzqui xihuitl oquichiuh ynic axcan ypan in yn itlamian yxiuhtzin tt°. Dios. de 1608. años. [*p. 87*]

v Auh yhuan ye chiuhcnauhpohualxihuitl ypan yexihuitl. yn ipan xii. tochtli xihuitl 1426. años. yn omomiquilli tlacatl chimalpopoca. tlahtohuani catca tenochtitlan. yn tlahtocat. matlactlomome xihuitl. çan quimictico yn tepaneca. ca ye yzqui xihuitl oquichiuh ynic axcan ypan in yn itlamian yxiuhtzin tt°. Dios. de 1608. años.

v Auh yhuan ye chiuhcnauhpohualxihuitl ypan õxihuitl. yn ipan xiii. acatl xihuitl 1427. a°s. yn omotlahtocatlalli yn tlacatl yn itzcohuatzin tlahtohuani tenochtitlan. ca ye yzqui xihuitl oquichiuh ynic axcan ypan in yn itlamian yxiuhtzin tt°. Dios. de 1608 años.

v Auh yhuan ye chiuhcnauhpohualli ypan ce xihuitl yn ipan i. tecpatl xihuitl 1428 años. yn opoliuh altepetl. azcapotzalco. ynic pehualoc ypan mochiuh yehuatl yn tlacatl Maxtlatzin yquac oncan tlahtocatia yn azcapotzalco. ca ye yzqui xihuitl oquichiuh ynic axcan ynpan in yn itlamian yxiuhtzin tt°. Dios. 1608.

v Auh yhuan ye chicuepohualxihuitl ypan caxtollomey xihuitl. yn ipan iiii. acatl xihuitl. 1431. años. yn omotlahtocatlalli yn tlacatl neçahualcoyotzin. tlahtohuani aculhuacan tetzcoco. ca ye yzqui xihuitl oquichiuh ynic axcan ypan in yn itlamian yxiuhtzin tt°. Dios. de 1608 años.

v Auh yhuan ye chicuepohualxihuitl ypan chiuhcnauhxihuitl yn ipan xiii. tecpatl xihuitl 1440 años. yn omomiquilli tlacatl ytzcohuatzin tlahtohuani catca tenochtitlan. yn tlahtocat matlactlonnahui xihuitl Auh çan niman iquac yn ipan omoteneuh xihuitl yn motlahtocatlalli yn tlacatl huehue Moteuhcçoma ylhuicamina chalchiuhtlatonac tlahtohuani. te[*p. 88*]nochtitlan. ca ye yzqui xihuitl oquichiuh ynic axcan ypan in yn itlamian yxiuhtzin tt°. Dios. de 1608. años —

v Auh yhuan ye chiconpohualxihuitl ypan caxtolli xihuitl. yn ipan i. tochtli xihuitl 1454. años yn iquac necetochhuiloc[3] mayanaloc. ynic nohuian ypan nueua españa. ca ye yzqui xihuitl oquichiuh ynic axcã ypan in yn itlamian yxiuhtzin tt°. Dios. de 1608 a°s.

Auh yhuan ye chiconpohualxihuitl ypan macuilxihuitl yn ipan xi. tecpatl xihuitl. 1464 años. yn otlacat neçahualpilli tlahtohuani tetzcoco ypiltzin. y neçahualcuyotzin. yquac cenca otonalhuacohuac motzitzineuh hehecatica yn quahuitl. ynic nohuian ca ye yzqui xihuitl oquichiuh ynic axcan ypan in yn itlamian yxiuhtzin tt°. Dios. de 1608. años.

v Auh yhuan ye chiconpohualxihuitl ypan nauhxihuitl yn ipan xii. calli xihuitl 1465.

1. The reference seems to be to the second Huitzilihuitl compared to Huitzilihuitl the elder in the entry for 1278. However, the new Huitzilihuitl was also second ruler of Tenochtitlan, and one might take it that Ch. had reversed the order of the words. Yet the fact that Ch. uses the same order two entries further below tends to indicate that he means the second Huitzilihuitl even if he was also the second ruler.

end of this year of our lord God 1608.[1]

v And also, it was 207 years ago, in the year 1 Rabbit, 1402, that Neçahualcoyotzin, ruler in Tetzcoco, was born. That is how many years it has been until now at the end of this year of our lord God 1608.
v And also, it was 194 years ago, in the year 1 Reed, 1315,[2] that the lord Huitzilihuitl the second, who was ruler in Tenochtitlan, passed away, having ruled for 25 years. // And right then in the said year the lord Chimalpopoca was installed as ruler in Tenochtitlan. That is how many years it has been until now at the end of this year of our lord God 1608. [*p. 87*]

v And also, it was 183 years ago, in the year 12 Rabbit, 1426, that the lord Chimalpopoca, who was ruler in Tenochtitlan, passed away, having ruled for twelve years; the Tepaneca came and killed him. That is how many years it has been until now at the end of this year of our lord God 1608.
v And also, it was 182 years ago, in the year 13 Reed, 1427, that the lord Itzcoatzin was installed as ruler in Tenochtitlan. That is how many years it has been until now at the end of this year of our lord God 1608.
v And also, it was 181 years ago, in the year 1 Flint, 1428, that the altepetl of Azcapotzalco was defeated, conquered. It happened in the time of the lord Maxtlatzin, who was ruling in Azcapotzalco. That is how many years it has been until now at the end of this year of our lord God 1608.
v And also, it was 178 years ago, in the year 4 Reed, 1431, that the lord Neçahualcoyotzin was installed as ruler in Acolhuacan Tetzcoco. That is how many years it has been until now at the end of this year of our lord God 1608.

v And also, it was 169 years ago, in the year 13 Flint, 1440, that the lord Itzcoatl, who was ruler in Tenochtitlan, passed away, having ruled for 14 years. And right then in the said year the lord Moteucçoma the elder, Ilhuicamina Chalchiuhtlatonac, was installed as ruler in [*p. 88*] Tenochtitlan. That is how many years it has been until now at the end of this year of our lord God 1608.

v And also, it was 155 years ago, in the year 1 Rabbit, 1454, that there was hunger and a great famine[3] all over New Spain. That is how many years it has been until now at the end of this year of our lord God 1608.
And also, it was 145 years ago, in the year 11 Flint, 1464, that Neçahualpilli, ruler in Tetzcoco, child of Neçahualcoyotzin, was born. At that time there was a great drought, and the trees everywhere were uprooted by the wind. That is how many years it has been until now at the end of this year of our lord God 1608.
v And also, it was 144 years ago, in the year 12 House, 1465, that the people of the four

2. Presumably for 1415.
3. From the very fact of this famous famine having occurred in 1 Rabbit, the expression *necetochhuilo*, impersonal of *mocetochhuia*, for people to experience things or have them happen to them 1-Rabbit style, came to mean for a famine to occur. The word occurs in other annals in this meaning with no reference to the specific year of 1 Rabbit.

años. yn opehualoc chalcatl. nauhcanme. yn ipan yehuatl huehue Moteuhcçoma ylhuicamina. ca ye yzqui xihuitl oquichiuh ynic axcan ypan in yn itlamian yxiuhtzin tt^{o}. Dios. de 1608. años.

v Auh yhuan ye chiconpohualxihuitl ypan ce xihuitl yn ipan 2. tecpatl xihuitl 1468. años. yn omomiquilli yn tlacatl huehue Moteuhcçoma ylhuicamina chalchiuhtlatonac tlahtohuani catca tenochtitlan yn tlahtocat. cenpohuallonchiuhcnahui xihuitl. ca ye yzqui xihuitl oquichiuh ynic axcan ypan in yn itlamian yxiuhtzin tt^{o}. Dios. de 1608. años.

v Auh yhuan quin huel axcan ye chiconpohualxihuitl yn ipan 3. calli xihuitl 1469 años. yn omotlahtocatlalli yn tlacatl Axayacatzin. tlahtohuani [*p. 89*] Tenochtitlan. ca ye yzqui xihuitl. oquichiuh ynic axcan ypan in yn itlamian yxiuhtzin tt^{o}. Dios. de 1608. años.

v Auh yhuan ye chiquacenpohualxihuitl ypan caxtollomome xihuitl yn ipan vi. tecpatl xihuitl. 1472. a^{o}s. yn omomiquilli yn tlacatl. y neçahualcoyotzin tlahtohuani tetzcoco. yn tlahtocat. onpohualxihuitl ypã onxihuitl. auh yn çan pilli catca cenpohuallonchiuhcnahui xihuitl yn oqu ic ayemo tlahtocatlalliloya auh ynic mocenponhua yn ixquichcauh nen tlalticpac ynic tlacat. yepohualxiuhtica ypan matlacxiuhtica oncetica. ynic onmomiquillico. // Auh çan niman iquac yn ipan omoteneuh xihuitl. motlahtocatlalli yn ipiltzin ytoca neçahualpilli tlahtohuani. tetzcoco. ynic motlahtocatlallico. ye chiuhcnauhxiuhtia. ca ye yzqui xihuitl oquichiuh. ynic axcan ypan in yn itlamian yxiuhtzin tt^{o}. Dios. de 1608. años.

v Auh yhuan ye chiquacenpohualxihuitl ypan caxtollonce xihuitl. yn ipan. vii. calli xihuitl 1473. años. yn opoliuh yn opehualloque tlatilolca yehuatl quinpeuh yn axayacatzin. ca ye yzqui xihuitl oquichiuh ynic axcan ypan in ytlamian yxiuhtzin tt^{o}. Dios. de 1608. años.

v Auh yhuan ye chiquacenpohualxihuitl ypan chicuexihuitl yn ipan 2. calli xihuitl. 1481. años yn omomiquilli. yn tlacatl Axayacatzin tlahtohuani tenochtitlan. yn tlahtocat. matlactlomey xihuitl. // auh çan niman iquac yn ipan omoteneuh xihuitl. motlahtocatlalli tlacatl tiçocicatzin tlahtohuani tenochtitlan. yehuatl cenca ypan otlahto. yn ical huitzillopochtli. ynic panhuetziz. ca ye yzqui xihuitl oquichiuh ynic axcan ypan in yn itlamian yxiuhtzin tt^{o}. Dios. de 1608. años. [*p. 90*]

v Auh yhuan ye chiquacenpohualxihuitl ypan yexihuitl. yn ipan vii. tochtli xihuitl 1486. años. yn omomiquilli tlacatl tiçocicatzin tlahtohuani tenochtitlan yn tlahtocat. chiquacenxihuitl. // auh çan niman iquac yn ipan omoteneuh xihuitl motlahtocatlalli yn tlacatl. ahuitzotzin tlahtohuani tenochtitlan. ca ye yzqui xihuitl oquichiuh ynic axcan ypan in yn itlamian yxiuhtzin tt^{o}. Dios. de 1608. a^{o}s.

v Auh yhuan ye chiquacenpohualxihuitl ypan ce xihuitl. yn ipan viii. acatl xihuitl 1487. a^{o}s. yn omomamal ycal diablo huitzillopochtli. ypan yn tlacatl ahuitzotzin. ca ye yzqui xihuitl oquichiuh ynic axcan ypan in yxiuhtzin tt^{o}. Dios. de 1608. años

v Auh yhuan ye macuilpohualxihuitl ypan matlacxihuitl yn ipan vii. acatl xihuitl 1499. años yn oquiz. acuecuexatl.[1] yn tlaapachoco tenochtitlan. ynin huel neltiliztli. ypan in tlacatl ahuitzotzin. yquac ypampa yn acuecuexatl mictilloque omentin tlahtoque. ynic ce yehuatl yn itoca tepiltzotzomatzin tlahtohuani catca cuyohuacan. ynic ome yehuatl. yn itoca huitzillatzin tlahtohuani catca huitzillopochco. ca ye yzqui xihuitl oquichiuh ynic axcan ypan in yn itlamian yxiuhtzin tt^{o}. Dios. de 1608 años.

---

1. A particular stream coming from the direction of Coyoacan used for providing fresh

parts of Chalco were conquered, in the time of Moteucçoma Ilhuicamina, the elder. That is how many years it has been until now at the end of this year of our lord God 1608.

v And also, it was 141 years ago, in the year 2 Flint, 1468, that the lord Moteucçoma Ilhuicamina Chalchiuhtlatonac, the elder, who was ruler in Tenochtitlan, passed away, having ruled for 29 years. That is how many years it has been until now at the end of this year of our lord God 1608.

v And also, after that it was 140 years ago to this very day, in the year 3 House, 1469, that the lord Axayacatzin was installed as ruler in [*p. 89*] Tenochtitlan. That is how many years it has been until now at the end of this year of our lord God 1608.

v And also, it was 137 years ago, in the year 6 Flint, 1472, that the lord Neçahualcoyotzin, ruler in Tetzcoco, passed away, having ruled for 42 years. He was just a nobleman for 29 years before he was made ruler, and the whole time he lived on earth from when he was born until when he died totals 71 years. // And right then in the said year his child named Neçahualpilli was installed as ruler in Tetzcoco; he was nine years old when he was made ruler. That is how many years it has been until now at the end of this year of our lord God 1608.

v And also, it was 136 years ago, in the year 7 House, 1473, that the Tlatelolca were defeated and conquered; Axayacatzin conquered them. That is how many years it has been until now at the end of the year of our lord God 1608.

v And also, it was 128 years ago, in the year 2 House, 1481, that the lord Axayacatzin, ruler in Tenochtitlan, passed away, having ruled for 13 years. // And right then in the said year the lord Tiçocicatzin was installed as ruler in Tenochtitlan. He greatly furthered the completion of the house [temple] of Huitzilopochtli. That is how many years it has been until now at the end of this year of our lord God 1608. [*p. 90*]

v And also, it was 123 years ago, in the year 7 Rabbit, 1486, that the lord Tiçocicatzin, ruler in Tenochtitlan, passed away, having ruled for six years. // And right then in the said year the lord Ahuitzotzin was installed as ruler in Tenochtitlan. That is how many years it has been until now at the end of this year of our lord God 1608.

v And also, it was 121 years ago, in the year 8 Reed, 1487, that the temple of the devil Huitzilopochtli was inaugurated, in the time of the lord Ahuitzotzin. That is how many years it has been until now at the end of this year of our lord God 1608.

v And also, it was 110 years ago, in the year 7 Reed, 1499, that the Acuecuexatl[1] came out [of its banks] and flooded Tenochtitlan; this is well authenticated, in the time of the lord Ahuitzotzin. At that time two rulers were killed because of the Acuecuexatl, the first named Tepiltzotzomatzin, who was ruler in Coyoacan, and the second named Huitzilatzin, who was ruler in Huitzilopochco. That is how many years it has been until now at the end of this year of our lord God 1608.

---

water to Tenochtitlan.

v Auh yhuan ye macuilpohualxihuitl ypan chiconxihuitl. yn ipan x. tochtli xihuitl 1502. años. yn omomiquilli tlacatl ahuitzotzin. tlahtohuani catca tenochtitlan. yn tlahtocat. caxtollomey xihuitl. // auh çan niman iquac yn ipan omoteneuh xihuitl motlahtocatlalli yn tlacatl Moteuhcçoma xocoyotl tlahtohuani tenochtitlan ca ye yzqui xihuitl oquichiuh ynic axcan ypan in [*p. 91*] Yn itlamian yxiuhtzin tt^{o}. Dios. de 1608. años —

v Auh yhuan ye nauhpohualxihuitl onmatlactli ypan onxihuitl yn ipan x. acatl xihuitl 1515 años. yn opoliuh ynic çan ya yn tlacatl neçahualpilli tlahtohuani catca aculhuacan tetzcoco. yn tlahtocat. onpohualxihuitl onchiquacen. auh ynic mocenpohua yn ixquichcauh nen tlalticpac. ynic tlacat. ye onpohualxiuhtica onmatlactica ypan nauhxiuhtica. ynic çan polihuico. ynic çan ya ca ye yzqui xihuitl quichiuh ynic axcan ypan in yn itlamian yxiuhtzin tt^{o}. Dios. de 1608. años.

v Auh yhuan ye nauhpohualxihuitl ypan matlactloce xihuitl yn ipan xi. tecpatl xihuitl 1516. años y motlahtocatlalli tlacatl cacamatzin tlahtohuani aculhuacan tetzcoco. ypiltzin y neçahualpiltzintli. ca ye yzqui xihuitl oquichiuh ynic axcan ypan in yn itlamian yxiuhtzin tt^{o}. Dios. de 1608. a^{o}s.

v Auh ye nauhpohualxihuitl ypan matlacxihuitl yn ipan 1. acatl xihuitl 1519. años. yn oacico españoles. yn omotlallico. nican ypan totlal yn motenehua nueua españa. ca ye yzqui xihuitl oquichiuh ynic axcan ypan in yn itlamian yxiuhtzin tt^{o}. Dios. de 1608. años. ye iuh nepa chiuhcnauhpohualxihuitl ypan caxtolxihuitl cate yn mexica. tenochtitlan. yniquinpan acico. españolesme.

v Auh yhuan ye nauhpohualxihuitl ypan chiuhcnauhxihuitl yn ipan 2. tecpatl xihuitl 1520. años. yn omomiquilli. tlacatl Moteuhcçoma. xocoyotl. tlahtohuani catca tenochtitlan. yn tlahtocat. caxtollonnahui xihuitl // auh çan niman ipan iquac yn ipan omoteneuh xihuitl [*p. 92*] Motlahtocatlalli yn tlacatl cuetlahuatzin[1] tlahtovani tenochtitlan. yquac ompa temi tlaxcallan yn españolesme auh çã nauhpohualilhuitl. yn ontlahtocat tenochtitlan. auh çan ye ypan yn omoteneuh xihuitl yn momiquilli. totomonaliztli.[2] yn quihuicac ca ye yzqui xihuitl oquichiuh ynic axcan ypan in yn itlamiã yxiuhtzin tt^{o}. Dios. de 1608. años.

v Auh yhuan ye nauhpohualxihuitl. ypan chicuexihuitl yn ipan 3. calli xihuitl 1521. años. yn motlahtocatlalli yn tlacatl quauhtimoctzin tlahtohuani tenochtitlan. yn iquac yn çan ye oc tlaxcallan temi yn españolesme. // Auh çan ye ypan in yn omoteneuh xihuitl. in ya yn poliuh mexicayotl. ynic quitlanque españolesme yn altepetl tenochtitlan auh çan niman iquac cacique yn españolesme. yn quauhtimoctzin tlahtohuani tenochtitlan. ca ye yzqui xihuitl oquichiuh ynic axcan ypan in yn itlamian yxiuhtzin tt^{o}. Dios. de 1608. años.

v Auh yhuan ye nauhpohualxihuitl ypan macuilxihuitl yn ipan vi. tecpatl xihuitl 1524. años. yn omaxitico. Padreme Sant. Fran^{co}. matlactin omomentin teopixque. // Auh no yquac ypan in yn omoteneuh xihuitl oncan matlacpohualxiuhtico yn mexica. ynic cate tenochtitlan. // Auh no yquac yn ipan xihuitl omoteneuh. yquac oncan cuyohuacan huicalloque oncan ylpitoya. tepoçotoya. in mexico. tlahtoque. yn quauhtimoctzĩ yhuan motelchiuhtzin. yhuan tlacotzin cihuacohuatl yhuan oquiztzin. yhuan huanitzin. oncan quinxotlatique ypampa yn coztic teocuitlatl yn quipolloque españolesme yn oncan tol-

1. The third letter in this word is a bit unclear, but it does seem to be *e* rather than the expected *i*; moreover, the form with *e* is repeated more clearly below, on p. 146.

v And also, it was 107 years ago, in the year 10 Rabbit, 1502, that the lord Ahuitzotzin, who was ruler in Tenochtitlan, passed away, having ruled for 18 years.// And right then in the said year the lord Moteucçoma the younger was installed as ruler of Tenochtitlan. That is how many years it has been until now at [*p. 91*] the end of this year of our lord God 1608.
v And also, it was 92 years ago, in the year 10 Reed, 1515, that the lord Neçahualpilli, ruler in Acolhuacan Tetzcoco, perished and went away [died], having ruled for 46 years; and all the time he lived on earth from when he was born until he perished and went away totals 54 years. That is how many years it has been until now at the end of this year of our lord God 1608.

v And also, it was 91 years ago, in the year 11 Flint, 1516, that the lord Cacamatzin, child of Neçahualpiltzintli, was installed as ruler in Acolhuacan Tetzcoco. That is how many years it has been until now at the end of this year of our lord God 1608.

v It was 90 years ago, in the year 1 Reed, 1519, that the Spaniards arrived and came to settle here in our land called New Spain. That is how many years it has been until now at the end of this year of our lord God 1608. The Mexica had been in Tenochtitlan for 195 years when the Spaniards found them here.

v And also, it was 89 years ago, in the year 2 Flint, 1520, that the lord Moteucçoma the younger, who was ruler in Tenochtitlan, passed away, having ruled for 19 years. // And right then in the said year [*p. 92*] the lord Cuitlahuatzin[1] was installed as ruler of Tenochtitlan; at that time the Spaniards were in Tlaxcala. For only 80 days he was ruler in Tenochtitlan; it was in the same said year that he passed away; pustules[2] were what carried him off. That is how many years it has been until now at the end of this year of our lord God 1608.

v And also, it was 88 years ago, in the year 3 House, 1521, that the lord Quauhtemoctzin was installed as ruler in Tenochtitlan, likewise still while the Spaniards were in Tlaxcala. // It was in this same said year that Mexica sovereignty perished when the Spaniards won the altepetl of Tenochtitlan, and right at that moment the Spaniards captured Quauhtemoctzin, ruler in Tenochtitlan. That is how many years it has been until now at the end of this year of our lord God 1608.

v And also, it was 85 years ago, in the year 6 Flint, 1524, that the Franciscan fathers, twelve friars, arrived. // And also at that time, in the said year, the Mexica attained their two hundredth year of having been in Tenochtitlan. // And it was also at that time, in the said year, that the rulers in Mexico, Quauhtemoctzin, Motelchiuhtzin, Tlacotzin the Cihuacoatl, Oquiztzin, and Huanitzin, were taken to Coyoacan, where they lay imprisoned in irons. There they burned their feet over the gold that the Spaniards lost at the Tolteca canal when they fled and they [the Mexica] chased them out of Tenochtitlan at night, so

2. The most common term for smallpox was *huei çahuatl*, "great rash," but *totomonaliztli*, pustules or blisters, was also used; it appears in the Florentine Codex, Book 12 (Lockhart 1993, 180–83). There can be little doubt that smallpox is meant here.

tecaacalloco. ynic cholloq̃ ynic quintocaque tenochtitlan yohualtica ynic yaca tlaxcallan ompa mopatito. // auh no yquac ypan yn omoteneuh xihuitl. ompa huillohuac. yn hueymollan [*p. 93*] Acallan. yquac poliuhque pehualloto. yquac yectlalliloto. yn hueymollan tlaca. auh yn omotocateneuhque yn izquintin mexico tlahtoque. yn ilpitoya cuyohuacan. oncan quimonehualtique yn ipan xihuitl omoteneuh. ynic ompa quinhuicac hueymollan acallan yn Don fernando cortes. marques del valle. auh çan nima ypan yn xihuitl omoteneuh ompa quiquatequique yn tlahtohuani Don fernando quauhtimoctzin. yn hueymollan. ca ye yzqui xihuitl. oquichiuh ynic axcan ypan in yn itlamian yxiuhtzin tt^{o}. Dios. de 1608. años.

v Auh yhuan ye nauhpohualxihuitl. ypan nauhxivitl yn ipan 7. calli xihuitl. 1525. años. yn omomiquillico. yn tlacatl Don hernando quauhtimoctzin. çan quĩpilloque ytech pochotl ynehuan yn Don P^{o} tetlepanquetzatzin tlahtohuani tlacupa. çan tẽtlapictli yn quitzauhctiaque. yehuatl quintlatzontequilli. yn marques. Don fernando cortes. ompa yn hueymollan quinpilloque. auh yn itech catca. tlahtocayotl quauhtimoctzin yn tenochtitlan. çan macuilxihuitl. yhuan ompa momiquillito. yn hueymollan yn Don carlos. oquiztzin. tlahtohuani catca azcapotzalco mexicapa. auh ynĩ tlahtohuani oquiztzin çan cocolmic yn õpa ondora auh yn Don Juan velasquez. yn tlacotzin cihuacohuatl. ompa quitlahtocatlallica. yn marques. yn hueymollan ye ytech hualyetihuia yn tlahtocayotl. tenochtitlan ye hualmocuepaya yn tlacotzin auh ye oncan nochiztlan quatzontlan yn onmomiquilico. ca ye yzqui xihuitl oquichiuh ynic axcan ypan in yn itlamian yxiuhtzin tt^{o}. Dios. de 1608. años. // auh çan niman iquac yn ipan omoteneuh xihuitl 7. calli xihuitl. 1525. años. yn oquauhtlahto Don Andres de tabian motelchiuhtzin yn tenochtitlan. [*p. 94*]

v Auh yhuan ye nauhpohualxihuitl ypan exihuitl yn ipan 8. tochtli xihuitl. 1526. años. yn omotlahtocatlalli yn Don Juan de guzman ytztlollinqui tlahtovani cuyohuacan. yquac axihuaco. ya yexiuhtica ynic huillohuaya. hueymollan. ca ye yzqui xihuitl oquichiuh ynic axcan ypan in ytlamian yxiuhtzin tt^{o}. Dios. de 1608. años.

v Auh yhuan ye nauhpohualxihuitl ypan ome xihuitl yn ipan 9. acatl xihuitl. 1527. años. yn opeuh nequatequiliztli. yn nican mexico Sant. Fran^{co}. ca ye yzqui xihuitl oquichiuh ynic axcan ypan in yn itlamiã yxiuhtzin tt^{o}. Dios. de 1608. años.

v Auh yhuan ye nauhpohualxihuitl yn ipan xi. calli xihuitl 1529. años. yn opeuh nenamictiliztli nican mexico. ynic axcan ypan in yn itlamian yxiuhtzin tt^{o}. Dios. de 1608. años.

v Auh yhuan ya yepohualxihuitl. ye oncaxtolli ypã nauhxihuitl yn ipan xii. tochtli xihuitl. 1530. años. yn opoliuhque yn opehualloto teoculhuacan tlaca. yquac ypan in ompa ya yn Don Andres de tabian motelchiuhtzin. auh ye yc hualmocuepaya. oncan momiquillico yn aztatlan. oncan ce chichimecatl quimin. yn oquauhtlahto motelchiuhtzin. tenochtitlan. macuilxihuitl. ca ye yzqui xihuitl oquichiuh ynic axcan ypan in yn itlamian yxiuhtzin tt^{o}. Dios. de 1608. años.

v Auh yhuan ya yepohualxihuitl ypan caxtollomome. xihuitl. yn ipan i. tecpatl xihuitl 1532. años. yn omotlalli yn oquauhtlahto. yn Don Pablo. xochiquentzin. yquac axihuaco mexico ya yexiuhtica. ynic ompa huillouaya teoculhuacan ca ye yzqui xihuitl o.quichiuh ynic axcan ypan in. yn itlamian [*p. 95*] Yxiuhtzin tt^{o}. Dios. de 1608. años. ynin huel neltiliztli.[1]

that they went to Tlaxcala to recuperate. // And also at that time, in the said year, a group went to Hueimollan [*p. 93*] Acallan [Honduras]; at that time the people of Hueimollan were defeated and conquered and set aright [i.e., reorganized Spanish fashion]. All the Mexica rulers whose names were mentioned before who were under arrest in Coyoacan were caused to depart in the said year when don Hernando Cortés, Marqués del Valle, took them to Hueimollan Acallan. Right then in the said year the ruler don Hernando Quauhtemoctzin was baptized in Hueimollan. That is how many years it has been until now at the end of this year of our lord God 1608.

v And also, it was 84 years ago, in the year 7 House, 1525, that the lord don Hernando Quauhtemoctzin passed away; they hanged him from a silk-cotton tree along with don Pedro Tetlepanquetzatzin, ruler in Tacuba. They paid the penalty because of false testimony; the Marqués don Hernando Cortés sentenced them, and they hanged them in Hueimollan. Quauhtemoctzin had the rulership in Tenochtitlan for only five years. Don Carlos Oquiztzin, who was ruler in Azcapotzalco Mexicapan, also passed away in Hueimollan, but this ruler Oquiztzin died of natural causes in Honduras. In Hueimollan the Marqués installed don Juan Velásquez Tlacotzin, the Cihuacoatl, as ruler; the rulership in Tenochtitlan was in the hands of Tlacotzin as he was returning, but in Nochiztlan Quatzontlan he passed away. That is how many years it has been until now at the end of this year of our lord God 1608. // And it was right then in the said year of 7 House, 1525, that don Andrés de Tapia Motelchiuhtzin became interim ruler of Tenochtitlan. [*p. 94*]

v And also, it was 83 years ago, in the year 8 Rabbit, 1526, that don Juan de Guzmán Itztlolinqui was installed as ruler in Coyoacan. At that time [Cortés and party] arrived here after having gone to Hueimollan for three years. That is how many years it has been until now at the end of the year of our lord God 1608.

v And also, it was 82 years ago, in the year 9 Reed, 1527, that baptism began here in Mexico, at San Francisco. That is how many years it has been until now at the end of this year of our lord God 1608.

v And also, it was 80 years ago, in the year 11 House, 1529, that marriage began here in Mexico until now at the end of this year of our lord God 1608.

v And also, it was 79 years ago, in the year 12 Rabbit, 1530, that the Teocolhuacan people were defeated and they went to conquer them. At that time, in this year, don Andrés de Tapia Motelchiuhtzin went there. He was already coming back from there when he passed away in Aztatlan; a Chichimeca shot him with an arrow there. Motelchiuhtzin was interim ruler in Tenochtitlan for five years. That is how many years it has been until now at the end of this year of our lord God 1608.

v And also, it was 77 years ago, in the year 1 Flint, 1532, that don Pablo Xochiquentzin was installed as interim ruler; at that time those who had gone to Teocolhuacan arrived in Mexico after three years. That is how many years it has been until now at the end of [*p. 95*] this year of our lord God 1608. This is really true.[1]

1. Or is well verified.

v Auh yhuan ya yepohualxihuitl ypan caxtolxihuitl. yn ipan iii. tochtli xihuitl 1534. años. yn oacico yancuican nican mexico. yn tlahtohuani Don Antonio de mendoça visurrey. ca ye yzqui xihuitl oquichiuh ynic axcan ypan in yn itlamian yxiuhtzin tto. Dios. de 1608. años.

v Auh yhuan ya yepohualxihuitl ypan matlactlomey xihuitl. yn ipan .v. tecpatl xihuitl 1536. años. yn omomiquilli Don Pablo xochiquentzin yn oquauhtlahto tenochtitlan macuilxihuitl ca ye yzqui xihuitl oquichiuh ynic axcan ypan ĩ yn itlamian yxiuhtzin tto. Dios. de 1608. años.

v Auh yhuan ya yepohualxihuitl ypan matlactloce xihuitl yn ipan vii. tochtli xihuitl. 1539.[1] años. yn omotlahtocatlalli yn omogouernadortlalli yancuican yn huel achto yn tlacatl Don diego de aluarado. huanitzin. tlahtohuani tenochtitlan. ompa canato. yn ecatepec ompa tlahtohuani catca achtopa. çan ce xihuitl yn ayac tlahtocat. ynic niman motlalli. ca ye yzqui xihuitl oquichiuh ynic axcan ypan in yn itlamian yxiuhtzin tto. Dios. de 1608. años.

v Auh yhuan ya yepohualxihuitl. ypan chicuexihuitl yn ipan 10. calli xihuitl 1541. años. yn omomiquilli tlacatl Don diego de aluarado huanitzin. tlahtohuani gouernador catca tenochtitlan. yn tlahtocat çan nauhxihuitl. // auh çan niman iquac yn ipan omoteneuh xihuitl. motlahtocatlalli mogouernadortlalli yn tlacatl. Don diego d St franco tehuetzquititzin. tlahto[*p. 96*]huani tenochtitlan. no yquac huillohuac yn xochipillan yquac poliuhque yn xochipilteca ompa motlahtocapacato[2] yn Don diego tehuetzquititzĩ ca ye yzqui xihuitl oquichiuh ynic axcan ypan ĩ yn itlamian yxiuhtzin tto. Dios. de 1608. años.

v Auh yhuan ya yepohualxihuitl ypan nauhxihuitl yn ipan i. calli xihuitl 1545. años. yn toyacacpa eztli quiz. ypan yquac moman in tiyanquiztli Sant ipolito. ca ye yzqui xihuitl. oquichiuh ynic axcan ypan in yn itlamian yxiuhtzin tto. Dios. de 1608. aos.

v Auh yhuan ya yepohualxihuitl ypan ce xihuitl yn ipan 4. tecpatl xihuitl 1548. años. yn omomiquilli Don fray Juan de çumaraga. obispo. catca mexico in teoyotica tlahtocat. tenochtitlan huel ixquichcauh cenpohualxihuitl ypan ce xihuitl. ca ye yzqui xihuitl oquichiuh ynic axcan ypan in yn itlamian yxiuhtzin tto. Dios. de 1608. años.

v Auh yhuan ye onpohualxihuitl ypan caxtollomey. xihuitl yn ipan vii. acatl xihuitl 1551 años. yn ohualla yn oacico mexico. yn huehue Don luis de velasco. visurrey ca ye yzqui xihuitl. oquichiuh ynic axcan ypan in yn itlamian yxiuhtzin tto. Dios. de 1608. años.

v Auh yhuan ye onpohualxihuitl. ypan caxtolxihuitl. yn ipan 10. tochtli xihuitl 1554. años. yn omomiquilli tlacatl. Don diego de st. franco. tehuetzquititzin. tlahtohuani tenochtitlan. yn tlahtocat. matlactlonnahui xihuitl. // auh no yquac hualmohuicac. yn ipann omoteneuh xihuitl. yquac maxitico yn mexico. ỹ Don fray Alonso de muntufar. arçobispo. mexico. ca ye yzqui xihuitl oquichiuh ynic axcan ypan in yn itlamian yxiuhtzin tto. Dios. de 1608. años. — [*p. 97*]

v Auh yhuan ye onpohualxihuitl ypan matlactlomome xihuitl. yn ipan xiii. calli xihuitl. 1557. años yn omotlahtocatlalli tlacatl Don xp̃oual de guzmã cecetzin. gouernador tenochtitlan. ynin ipiltzin yn Don diego huanitzin. auh yn oquic ayemo motlahtoca-

1. By the indigenous year cycle, the Christian calendar year should be 1538.

2. The construction "motlahtocapacato" contains the past of the outward moving purposive motion form and the reflexive prefix, and incorporates *tlatoani*, "ruler." What remains is *paca*, "to wash." The literal meaning would be "he went to wash himself as a

v And also, it was 75 years ago, in the year 3 Rabbit, 1534, that the lord don Antonio de Mendoza, the viceroy, arrived here in Mexico for the first time. That is how many years it has been until now at the end of this year of our lord God 1608.

v And also, it was 73 years ago, in the year 5 Flint, 1536, that don Pablo Xochiquentzin, who was interim ruler in Tenochtitlan for five years, passed away. That is how many years it has been until now at the end of this year of our lord God 1608.

v And also, it was 71 years ago, in the year 7 Rabbit, 1539,[1] that the lord don Diego de Alvarado Huanitzin was installed as ruler in Tenochtitlan and its very first governor. They went to get him from Ecatepec, where he was ruler first. For only a year there was no ruler; then he was put in office. That is how many years it has been until now at the end of this year of our lord God 1608.

v And also, it was 68 years ago, in the year 10 House, 1541, that the lord don Diego de Alvarado Huanitzin, who was ruler and governor in Tenochtitlan, passed away, having ruled only four years. // And right then in the said year the lord don Diego de San Francisco Tehuetzquititzin was installed as ruler and governor [*p. 96*] in Tenochtitlan. Also at that time a party went to Xochipillan; the Xochipilteca were defeated then. Don Diego Tehuetzquititzin went there to do his first notable deed as ruler.[2] That is how many years it has been until now at the end of this year of our lord God 1608.

v And also, it was 64 years ago, in the year 1 House, 1545, that blood came out of people's noses. In this year the San Hipólito market was set up. That is how many years it has been until now at the end of this year of our lord God 1608.

v And also, it was 61 years ago, in the year 4 Flint, 1548, that don fray Juan de Zumárraga, who was bishop in Mexico, passed away, having ruled in Tenochtitlan in spiritual matters for a full 21 years. That is how many years it has been until now at the end of this year of our lord God 1608.

v And also, it was 58 years ago, in the year 7 Reed, 1551, that don Luis de Velasco the elder, the viceroy, came to and arrived in Mexico. That is how many years it has been until now at the end of this year of our lord God 1608.

v And also, it was 55 years ago, in the year 10 Rabbit, 1554, that the lord don Diego de San Francisco Tehuetzquititzin, ruler in Tenochtitlan, passed away, having ruled for 14 years. // And also at that time, in the said year, don fray Alonso de Montúfar, archbishop in Mexico, came to and arrived in Mexico. That is how many years it has been until now at the end of this year of our Lord 1608. — [*p. 97*]

v And also, it was 52 years ago, in the year 13 House, 1557, that the lord don Cristóbal de Guzmán Cecetzin was installed to rule as governor in Tenochtitlan; he was the child of don Diego Huanitzin. Before he was installed to rule,[3] the [rulership] was vacant for only

---

ruler," but the reference is to a ruler accrediting himself through an initial act, often originally winning a battle or taking captives, but also any other ostentatious deed. See another example and its explanation in Reyes García 2001, pp. 154–55, n. 48.

3. See p. 138, n. 1.

tlalliaya.[1] çan onxihuitl. yn cactimanca tenochtitlan. ca ye yzqui xihuitl oquichiuh ynic axcan ypan in. yn itlamian yxiuhtzin. tt^o^. Dios. de 1608. años.
v Auh yhuan ye onpohualxihuitl ypan matlacxivitl. yn ipan 2. acatl xihuitl 1559. años. yn omoquetz quauhteocalli munomento. yn oncan Sant. Joseph. yniqu ipampa tlatlatlauhtiloc. in huey tlahtohuani Don carlos .v. emperador. ca ye yzqui xihuitl oquichiuh ynic axcan ypan in yn itlamian yxiuhtzin tt^o^. Dios. de 1608. años.
v Auh yhuan ye onpohualxihuitl ypan chiconxihuitl yn ipan v. tochtli xihuitl. 1562. años. yn omomiquilli tlacatl. Don xp̃oual de guzman cecetzin. tlahtohuani tenochtitlan. yn ipiltzin Don diego huanitzin. yn tlahtocat. chiquacenxihuitl. ca ye yzqui xihuitl. oquichiuh ynic axcan ynpan in yn itlamian yxiuhtzin tt^o^. Dios. de 1608. años.
v Auh yhuan ye onpohualxihuitl. ypan chiquacenxihuitl. yn ipan vi. acatl xihuitl 1563. años. yn omotlahtocatlalli tlacatl. Don luis. de S^t^a maria nacacipactzin.[2] gouernador tenochtitlan. ca ye yzqui xivitl oquichiuh ynic axcan ypan in yn itlamian yxiuhtzin tt^o^. Dios. de 1608. años.
v Auh yhuan ye onpohualxihuitl ypan macuilxivitl. yn ipan vii. tecpatl xihuitl. 1564. años. yn omomiquilli tlacatl. huehue Don luis. de velasco. visurrey. yquac tzin[*p. 98*]tic. yn tlacallaquilli nican mexico. ca ye yzqui xihuitl oquichiuh. ynic axcan ypan in yn itlamian. yxiuhtzĩ tt^o^. Dios. de 1608. años. yn tlahtocat. mexico 14. xihuitl
v Auh yhuan ye onpohualxihuitl ypan nauhxihuitl yn ipan viii. calli xihuitl. 1565. años. yn omomiquilli tlacatl Don luis de s^t^ta maria nacacipactzin tlahtohuani tenochtitlan. yn tlahtocat. yexihuitl. auh yehuatl in o ytech tlamico. ynic mexica tlahtocatepilhuan yn tenochca tlahtocatepilhuan yn aocmo yehuãtin. tlahtocati tenochtitlan. yc cen iquac cotonico. yn intlahtocatepacholiz. ca ye yzqui xihuitl oquichiuh ynic axcan ypan in yn itlamian yxiuhtzin tt^o^. Dios de 1608. años.
v Auh yhuan ye onpohualxihuitl ypan ye xihuitl yn ipan ix. tochtli xihuitl 1566. años. yn oquechcotonalloque. omentin tlahtoque[3] Alonso davilla. yhuan yteyccauh Gil goçales aluarado. yaoyotl yntech tlah[4] quichihuazquia. yuh mito macocuizquia. yn ipampa quitzauhtiaque. // auh çan no yquac yn ipan omoteneuh xihuitl. hualla yn tlacatl Don Gaston de peralta. visurrey. comendador s.tiago. ca ye yzqui xihuitl oquichiuh ynic axcan ypan in yn itlamian yxiuhtzin tt^o^. Dios. de 1608. años.
v Auh yhuan ye onpohualxihuitl. ypan ce xihuitl yni ipan xi. tecpatl xihuitl. 1568. años. yn ohualla mexico. yn Don fran^co^ ximenez. juez gouernador. mochihuaco. ỹ nican tenochtitlan. tecamachalco ychan yehuatl yc cen copehualtico. yn altepetl ypan ye hualhui yn juezgouernadores. in ye huallapachohua tenochtitlan. // auh çan no yquac yn ipan omoteneuh xihuitl. yn oyah castilla yn tlacatl Don Gaston de peralta visurrey. çan exiuhtico ỹ nican mexico tlahtocatico. // Auh çan no yquac [*p. 99*] Yn ipan omoteneuh xihuitl. yn ohualla yn acico mexico. yn tlacatl. Don Martin emrriquez. visurrey. ynin atle encomienda[5] quipiaya. ça ye yzqui xihuitl. oquichiuh ynic axcan ypan in yn itlamian yxiuhtzin tt^o^. Dios. de 1608. a^o^s.

1. The use, two times, of the verb *tlahtocatlallia* could be taken to mean that don Cristóbal was specifically installed in the office of tlatoani as well as governor, or it could be taken, as often with Ch., to mean that the governorship is in some sense equated with the rulership. Just below, in the entry for 1562, don Cristóbal is referred to unequivocally as tlatoani. Much the same situation with *tlatocatlalia* and the governorship occurs again in the 1563 and 1565 entries with don Luis de Santa María.

two years in Tenochtitlan. That is how many years it has been until now at the end of this year of our lord God 1608.

v And also, it was 50 years ago, in the year 2 Reed, 1559, that a wooden church, a monument [catafalque], was erected in [the church of] San Josef, because prayers were offered for the great ruler don Carlos V, the emperor. That is how many years it has been until now at the end of this year of our lord God 1608.

v And also, it was 47 years ago, in the year 5 Rabbit, 1562, that the lord don Cristóbal de Guzmán Cecetzin, ruler in Tenochtitlan, child of don Diego Huanitzin, passed away, having ruled for six years. That is how many years it has been until now at the end of this year of our lord God 1608.

v And also, it was 46 years ago, in the year 6 Reed, 1563, that the lord don Luis de Santa María Nacacipactzin[2] was installed to rule as governor in Tenochtitlan. That is how many years it has been until now at the end of this year of our lord God 1608.

v And also, it was 45 years ago, in the year 7 Flint, 1564, that the lord don Luis de Velasco the elder, the viceroy, passed away. At that time the payment of tribute was introduced [*p. 98*] here in Mexico. That is how many years it has been until now at the end of this year of our lord God 1608. He [Velasco] ruled in Mexico for 14 years.

v And also, it was 44 years ago, in the year 8 House, 1565, that the lord don Luis de Santa María Nacacipactzin, ruler in Tenochtitlan, passed away, having ruled for three years, and with him it came to an end that descendants of the Mexica and Tenochca rulers should rule in Tenochtitlan any more; at that time their governing as rulers was cut off forever. That is how many years it has been until now at the end of this year of our lord God 1608.

v And also, it was 43 years ago, in the year 9 Rabbit, 1566, that the two lords[3] Alonso de Avila and his younger sibling Gil González de Alvarado were decapitated. They were accused[4] of being about to make war. It was said that they were going to rebel, for which they paid the penalty. // And likewise at that time, in the said year, the lord don Gastón de Peralta, viceroy, comendador of Santiago, came. That is how many years it has been until now at the end of this year of our lord God 1608.

v And also, it was 41 years ago, in the year 11 Flint, 1568, that don Francisco Jiménez, from Tecamachalco, came to Mexico appointed as judge-governor here in Tenochtitlan. He first began it that judge-governors from various other altepetl have come to govern in Tenochtitlan. // And likewise at that time, in the said year, the lord don Gastón de Peralta, viceroy, went to Spain; he ruled here in Mexico for only three years. // And likewise at that time, [*p. 99*] in the said year, the lord don Martín Enríquez, viceroy, came to and arrived in Mexico; he had no encomienda.[5] That is how many years it has been until now at the end of this year of our lord God 1608.

---

2. The usual form is Nanacacipactzin, "mushroom alligator," and in that form it is generally taken to be derisive; Cipactzin by itself was one of the classic preconquest calendrical names.

3. Literally, rulers.

4. For "tlan."

5. See pp. 26–27 at n. 6.

v Auh yhuan ye cenpohualxihuitl ypan caxtollomome xihuitl. yn ipan 2. tecpatl xihuitl. 1572. años. yn omomiquilli Don fray Alonso de muntufar. arçobispo. mexico. yn teoyotica motlahtocatilli caxtollonnahui xihuitl. // Auh çan no yquac yn ipan omoteneuh xihuitl. yn quiz. mohuicac yn ichan tecamachalco. yn Don fran^{co} ximenez. Juez gouernador. catca tenochtitlan. yn tlahtocat. macuilxihuitl. ca ye yzqui xihuitl oquichiuh ynic axcan ypan in yn itlamian yxiuhtzin tt^{o}. Dios. de 1608. años.

v Auh yhuan ye cenpohualxihuitl ypan caxtollonce xihuitl. yn ipan 3. calli xihuitl. 1573. años. yn ohualla mexico. tenochtitlan yn tlacatl huehue Don Antonio. valleriano. tlamatini momachtiani Juez gouernador. mochihuaco tenochtitlan azcapotzalco. ychan. ynin ymontzin yn Don diego huanitzin. ca ye yzqui xihuitl oquichiuh ynic axcan ypan in yn itlamian yxiuhtzin tt^{o}. Dios. de 1608. años.

v Auh yhuan ye cenpohualxihuitl ypan caxtolxihuitl yn ipan iiii. tochtli xihuitl. 1574. años. yn omacoc teoyotica ytlahtocayo. Don Pedro moya de contreras. ynic arçobispo. omochiuhtzino mexico. ca ye yzqui xihuitl oquichiuh ynic axcan ypan in yn itlamian yxiuhtzin tt^{o}. Dios. de 1608. años.

v Auh yhuan ye cenpohualxihuitl ypan chiuhcnauhxihuitl. yn ipan x. tecpatl. xihuitl. 1580. años. yn o[*p. 100*]mohuicac perũ. yn tlacatl. Don Martin emrriquez. visurrey yn tlahtocat tenochtitlan. matlactlomey xihuitl. // auh çan no yquac yn ipan omoteneuh xihuitl. yn omaxitico mexico. yn tlacatl Don lurenço xuarez de mendoça conde de coruña visurrey ynin anotle encomienda[1] quipiaya ca ye yzqui xihuitl. oquichiuh ynic axcan ypan in yn itlamian yxiuhtzin tt^{o}. Dios. de 1608. años.

v Auh yhuan ye cenpohualxihuitl. ypan chiquacẽ xihuitl. yn ipan xiii. acatl xihuitl. 1583. años. yn ohualmohuicac nican mexico. yn crucifixos. yn õpa monextitzino Sant. guilermo. totollapan[2] Sant. Pablo maxitico. / auh çan no ypann iquac yn omoteneuh xihuitl. yn omomiquilli tlacatl Don lurenço xuarez de mendoça conde de coruña visurrey. yn tlahtocat. tenochtitlan onxihuitl ypan chicuetetl metztli. ypan cenpohuallonmatlactli ypan eylhuitl.[3] ca ye yzqui xihuitl oquichiuh ynic axcan ypan in yn itlamian yxiuhtzin tt^{o}. Dios. de 1608. a^{o}s.

v Auh yhuan ye cenpohualxihuitl ypan macuilxihuitl. yn ipan i. tecpatl xihuitl. 1584. años. yn omochiuhtzino bisitador general yn ipan nueua españa. niman gouernador visurrey. omochiuhtzino. yn teoyotica tlahtohuani Don Pedro moya de contreras. arçobispo. mexico. yn ipampa ynic omomiquilli visurrey. ca ye yzqui xihuitl oquichiuh ynic axcan ypan in yn itlamian yxiuhtzin tt^{o}. Dios. de 1608 años.

v Auh yhuan ye cenpohualxihuitl. ypan nauhxihuitl. yn ipan 2. calli xihuitl. 1585. años. yn omochiuh Sancto concilio. yn teoytica necentlaliliztli yn nican mexico. ynic tlayahualoloc. // auh no yquac. yn ipan omoteneuh xihuitl yn ohualla [*p. 101*] Yn omaxitico. mexico. yn tlacatl Don Aluaro Manrrique. de çuniga. marques. de Villa Manrrique. visurrey. ca ye yzqui xihuitl oquichiuh ynic axcan ypan in yn itlamian yxiuhtzin tt^{o}. Dios. de 1608. a^{o}s.

v Auh yhuan ye cenpohualxihuitl ypan ye xivitl. yn ipan 3. tochtli xihuitl. 1586. años. yn omopehualti mohuicac castilla. in teyotica tlahtohuani Don pedro moya de contreras. arçobispo. mexico. matlacxihuitl yn arcobispo. moyetzticat[4] mexico tenochtitlan. auh yhuan ynic visitador. yhuan ynic gouernador. mochiuhtzinco mexico yexihuitl. ca ye yz

---

1. See p. 139 at n. 5 and the further reference there.
2. The same topic is mentioned on pp. 28–29 at n. 2.

v And also, it was 37 years ago, in the year 2 Flint, 1572, that don fray Alonso de Montúfar, archbishop in Mexico, passed away, having ruled in spiritual matters for 19 years. // And likewise it was at that time, in the said year, that don Francisco Jiménez, who was judge-governor in Tenochtitlan, left and went to his home of Tecamachalco, having ruled for five years. That is how many years it has been until now at the end of this year of our lord God 1608.

v And also, it was 36 years ago, in the year 3 House, 1573, that the lord don Antonio Valeriano the elder, a sage and scholar, came to Mexico Tenochtitlan appointed judge-governor in Tenochtitlan; he was from Azcapotzalco and was the son-in-law of don Diego Huanitzin. That is how many years it has been until now at the end of this year of our lord God 1608.

v And also, it was 35 years ago, in the year 4 Rabbit, 1574, that don Pedro Moya de Contreras was given his spiritual rulership as appointed archbishop in Mexico. That is how many years it has been until now at the end of this year of our lord God 1608.

v And also, it was 29 years ago, in the year 10 Flint, 1580, that the lord don Martín Enríquez, viceroy, [*p. 100*] went to Peru, having ruled in Tenochtitlan for 13 years. // And it was likewise at that time, in the said year, that the lord don Lorenzo Suárez de Mendoza, Count of Coruña, viceroy, arrived in Mexico; he had no encomienda either.[1] That is how many years it has been until now at the end of this year of our lord God 1608.

v And also, it was 26 years ago, in the year 13 Reed, 1583, that the crucifix which appeared in San Guillermo Totolapan[2] was brought here to Mexico and arrived in San Pablo. / And it was likewise at this time, in the said year, that don Lorenzo Suárez de Mendoza, Count of Coruña, viceroy, passed away, having ruled in Tenochtitlan 2 years, 8 months, and 33 days.[3] That is how many years it has been until now at the end of this year of our lord God 1608.

v And also, it was 25 years ago, in the year 1 Flint, 1584, that the spiritual ruler don Pedro Moya de Contreras, archbishop in Mexico, was appointed visitor general in New Spain and then governor and viceroy, because of how the viceroy died. That is how many years it has been until now at the end of this year of our lord God 1608.

v And also, it was 24 years ago, in the year 2 House, 1585, that a holy council, a spiritual assembly, was held here in Mexico, because of which there were processions. // And it was also at that time, in the said year, that the lord don Alvaro Manrrique de Zúñiga, Marqués of Villamanrrique, viceroy, came to [*p. 101*] and arrived in Mexico. That is how many years it has been until now at the end of this year of our lord God 1608.

v And also, it was 23 years ago, in the year 3 Rabbit, 1586, that the ruler in spiritual matters, don Pedro Moya de Contreras, archbishop in Mexico, departed and went to Spain; he was archbishop[4] in Mexico Tenochtitlan for ten years, and also made inspector and governor in Mexico for three years. That is how many years it has been until now at the

3. The number "33" would appear to be in error, but see also pp. 28–29 at n. 3.
4. For "arçobispo. moyetzticatca."

qui xihuitl oquichiuh ynic axcan ypan in yn itlamian yxiuhtzin tt^{o}. Dios. de 1608. años.
v Auh ye caxtollonnahui xihuitl yn ipan vii. tochtli xihuitl. 1590. años. yn omohuicac españa. yn tlacatl Don Aluaro. Manrrique. de çuniga. marques de villa mãrrique visurrey. yn tlahtocat. tenochtitlan. macuilxihuitl. // auh çan niman iquac yn ipan omoteneuh xihuitl yn ohualmohuicac yn omaxitico mexico. ynic ome ytoca Don luis de velasco visurrey.
v Auh yhuan ye caxtolxihuitl. yn ipan .xi. tochtli xihuitl 1594. años. yn omacoc possion[1] quimocuilli yn arcediano. Don Juan de ceruantes. ynic yxiptlatzin ygou^{or}tzin. mochiuh el licenciado Don Alonso fernandez. de Bonilla arçobispo. mexico. yn oquic. visitador. mochiuhtzinoto perũ. ompa yn quihualmacac yn ihuelitiliz. ynic ygou^{or} mochiuh Don Juan de ceruãtes. ca ye yzqui xihuitl. oquichiuh ynic axcan ypan in yn itlamian yxiuhtzin tt^{o}. Dios. de 1608. años.
v Auh yhuan ye matlacxihuitl ypan nauhxihuitl yn ipan xii. acatl xihuitl 1595. años. yn omohuicac [*p. 102*] Perũ. yn tlatl[2] ynic ome ytoca Don luis de velasco. visurrey. yn tlahtocat. tenochtitlan macuilxihuitl ypan matlactetl metztli // auh çan niman iquac yn ipan omoteneuh xihuitl. yn ohualmohuicac yn omaxitico mexico yn tlacatl Don Gaspar de çuniga. y Azeuedo conde de Monterrey visurrey. ca ye yzqui xihuitl oquichiuh ynic axcan ypan in yn itlamian yxiuhtzin tt^{o}. Dios. de 1608. años.
v Auh yhuan ye matlacxihuitl ypann exihuitl yn ipan xiii. tecpatl xihuitl. 1596. años. yn theniente mochiuh yn tlacatl Don Juan mīn mestiço. quipallehui yn huehue Don Antonio Valeriano gouernador. tenochtitlan. ca ye yzqui xihuitl oquichiuh ynic axcan ypan in yn itlamian yxiuhtzin tt^{o}. Dios. de 1608. años.
v Auh yhuan ye matlacxihuitl yn ipan iii. acatl xixihuitl.[3] 1599. años. yn ohualla yn omotlallico mexico Don Jeronimo Lupez mestiço Juez gou^{or} mochihuaco yn mexico tenochtitlan. ynin xaltocan ychan auh yquac huel quicauh yn itequiuh ynic Juez gou^{or} catca huehue Don Antonio valeriano. yn tlahtocat tenochtitlan cenpohualli onchicome xihuitl. // auh yn theniente catca Don Juan mīn mestiço yn tenochtitlan. ynic quipallehui Don Antonio. valeriano. onxihuitl ypan chicuetetl metztli. ynic niman õpa yah tlatilolco Juez gouernadortito ompa ca ye yzqui xihuitl oquichiuh ynic axcan ypan in yn itlamian yxiuhtzin tt^{o}. Dios. de 1608. años.
v Auh yhuan ye chiuhcnauhxihuitl yn ipan iiii. tecpatl xihuitl 1600. años. yn ohualla tlahtolli [*p. 103*] Perũ. yuh machiztico. nican mexico. ompa omomiquilli yn teoyotica tlahtohuani el licenciado. Don Alonso. fernandez. de Bonilla. arçobispo. mexico. auh yn itech catca mexico arçobispoyotl. chiquacenxihuitl. ypan chiquacentetl metztli. auh yxquichcauh ypampa gouernador mochiuhticatca ỹ nican mexico. yn Don Juan de ceruantes. arcediano. ca ye yzqui xihuitl oquichiuh ynic axcan ypan in yn itlamian yxiuhtzin tt^{o}. Dios. de 1608. años.
v Auh yhuan ye chiconxihuitl yn ipan vi. tochtli xivitl 1602. años. yn omaxitico mexico. yn teoyotica tlahtohuani Don fray Garcia de s^{t}. ta maria de mendoça y çuniga. arçobispo. mexico. ca ye yzqui xihuitl oquichiuh ynic axcan ypan in yn itlamian yxiuhtzin tt^{o}. Dios. de 1608. años.
v Auh yhuan ye chiquacenxihuitl yn ipan vii. acatl xihuitl 1603. años. yn omohuicac Perũ yn tlacatl Don Gaspar de çuniga y Azeuedo. conde de monterrey. visurrey yn

1. For "possession."
2. For "tlacatl."

end of this year of our lord God 1608.

v And also, it was 19 years ago, in the year 7 Rabbit, 1590, that the lord don Alvaro Manrrique de Zúñiga, Marqués of Villamanrrique, viceroy, went to Spain, having ruled in Tenochtitlan for five years. // And it was right then in the said year that the viceroy don Luis de Velasco, the second of his name, came to and arrived in Mexico.

v And also, it was 15 years ago, in the year 11 Rabbit, 1594, that the archdeacon don Juan de Cervantes was given and took possession[1] of his office as appointed deputy and governor for licenciado don Alonso Fernández de Bonilla, archbishop in Mexico, as long as he has gone to Peru appointed inspector there; from there he gave him his authority so that don Juan de Cervantes was made governor for him. That is how many years it has been until now at the end of this year of our lord God 1608.

v And also, it was 14 years ago, in the year 12 Reed, 1595, that the lord[2] don Luis de Velasco, viceroy, the second of his name, went [*p. 102*] to Peru, having ruled in Tenochtitlan 5 years and 10 months. // And it was right then in the said year that the lord don Gaspar de Zúñiga y Acevedo, Count of Monterrey, viceroy, came to and arrived in Mexico. That is how many years it has been until now at the end of this year of our lord God 1608.

v And also, it was 13 years ago, in the year 13 Flint, 1596, that the lord don Juan Martín, mestizo, was appointed deputy and aided don Antonio Valeriano the elder, governor of Tenochtitlan. That is how many years it has been until now at the end of this year of our lord God 1608.

v And also, it was 10 years ago, in the year[3] 3 Reed, 1599, that don Gerónimo López, mestizo, came to Mexico and was installed as the judge-governor appointed in Mexico Tenochtitlan; he was from Xaltocan. And at this time don Antonio Valeriano the elder really left his office as judge-governor, having ruled in Tenochtitlan for 27 years. // And don Juan Martín, mestizo, who had been deputy in Tenochtitlan, aiding don Antonio Valeriano for 2 years and 8 months, then went to Tlatelolco to be judge-governor there. That is how many years it has been until now at the end of this year of our lord God 1608.

v And also, it was 9 years ago, in the year 4 Flint, 1600, that news came [*p. 103*] from Peru and it became known here in Mexico that the spiritual ruler licenciado don Alonso Fernández de Bonilla, archbishop in Mexico, had passed away there. He held the archbishopric for 6 years and 6 months, and for the whole time don Juan de Cervantes was appointed governor on his behalf here in Mexico. That is how many years it has been until now at the end of this year of our lord God 1608.

v And also, it was 7 years ago, in the year 6 Rabbit, 1602, that the spiritual ruler don fray García de Santa María de Mendoza y Zúñiga, archbishop in Mexico, arrived in Mexico. That is how many years it has been until now at the end of this year of our lord God 1608.

v And also, it was 6 years ago, in the year 7 Reed, 1603, that the lord don Gaspar de Zúñiga y Acevedo, Count of Monterrey, viceroy, went to Peru, having ruled in Tenoch-

---

3. In "xixihuitl." *xi* is inadvertently repeated.

tlahtocatico tenochtitlan. chiconxihuitl ypan matlactetl once metztli. // auh çã niman iquac yn ipan omoteneuh xihuitl. yn ohualla yn omaxitico mexico. yn tlacatl Don Juan de mendoça. y luna marques de mõtesclaros. visurrey. ca ye yzqui xihuitl oquichiuh ynic axcan ypan in yn itlamian yxiuhtzin tt^{o}. Dios. de 1608. años.

v Auh yhuan ya ye xihuitl yn ipan x. tochtli xihuitl 1606. años. yn omomiquilli. teoyotica tlahtohuani Don fray Garcia de s^{t}ta maria de mendoça y çuniga. arçobispo. mexico. yn teoyotica omotlahtocatilli tenochtitlan nauhxihuitl. ca ye yzqui xihuitl oquichiuh ynic axcan ypan in yn itlamian yxiuhtzin tt^{o}. Dios. de 1608. años. [*p. 104*]

v Auh yhuan ye ce xihuitl yn ipan xi. acatl xihuitl 1607. años. yn omohuicac Perù. yn tlacatl. Don Juan de mendoça y luna. marques de montesclaros. visurrey. yn otlahtocatico. tenochtitlan. yexihuitl. ypan chicuetetl metztli. // auh çan niman iquac yn ipan omoteneuh xihuitl. yn oquimanilli ytlahtocatequitzin yn tlacatl. Don luis de velasco. yc oppa visurrey. omochiuhtzino. ỹ nican tenochtitlan. ca ye ce xihuitl oquichiuh ynic axcan ypan in yn itlamian yxiuhtzin tt^{o}. Dios. de 1608. años.

v Auh ye omoteneuh tlacpac yn ipan in xihuitl xii. tepatl[1] xihuitl. 1608. años. yn omomiquilli Don Jeronimo lupez. Juez gouernador. tenochtitlan. yn otlahtocatico tenochtitlan. matlacxihuitl ypã chicuetetl metztli. ypan cenpohuallonce tonatiuh // auh çan niman ipan in yn omoteneuh xihuitl yn ohualcallac ỹ nican mexico. in tlacatl Don Juan bap^{ta} Juez gouernador. mochiuh yn tenochtitlan. malinalco. ychan yn axcan moyetztica. tlahtocati. ynin yc cenpohuallonmatlactli ypan ome i ye yntepachocahuan mexica tenochca. in ye yc ompa hualquizque in ye yc ompa huallolinque. yn inchan yn ompa huehue mexico aztlan quinehuayan chicomoztoc yn axcan quitocayotia yancuic mexico. auh ynic huel mellahuac momatiz. in ye yzquintin intepachocahuan mochihua mexica tenochca nican teneuhtoc yn intoca. nican motecpana ceceyaca.

v Ynic ce ytoca Moteuhcçoma. ynin oc ompa. yntlahtocauh catca in yancuic mexico. aztlan yn mexica.

v Ynic ome ytoca chalchiuhtlatonac ynin yevatl quinhualquixti. ompa quinhualpachotia [*p. 105*] Ynic ompa hualquizque huallolinque yancuic mexico aztlan quinehuayan chicomoztoc yn mexica. tenochca.

v Yniquey ytoca quauhtlequetzqui teomama —

v Ynic nahui ytoca acacitli.

v Ynic macuilli ytoca citlallitzin

v Ynic chiquacen ytoca tzinpan

v Ynic chicome ytoca tlaçotzin.

v Ynic chicuey ytoca tozcuecuextli.

v Ynic chiuhcnahui ytoca huehue huitzillihuitl tlahtohuani

v Ynic matlactli ytoca tenochtzin quimaxitico yehuatl quinhualpachotia quinhualyacan yn mexica. ynic acico tenochtitlan.

v Ynic matlactlonce ytoca acamapichtli tlahtohuani achto yn tenochtitlan

v Ynic matlactlomome ytoca huitzillihuitl. yc ome tlahtohuani

v Ynic matlactlomey ytoca chimalpopoca tlahtohuani

v Ynic matlactlonnahui ytoca ytzcohuatl tlahtohuani

v Ynic caxtolli ytoca huehue Moteuhcçoma ylhuicamina chalchiuhtlahtonac tlahtovani

1. For "tecpatl."

titlan 7 years and 11 months. // And it was right then in the said year that the lord don Juan de Mendoza y Luna, Marqués of Montesclaros, viceroy, came to and arrived in Mexico. That is how many years it has been until now at the end of this year of our lord God 1608.

v And also, it was 3 years ago, in the year 10 Rabbit, 1606, that the spiritual ruler don fray García de Santa María de Mendoza y Zúñiga, archbishop in Mexico, passed away, having ruled in spiritual matters in Tenochtitlan for four years. That is how many years it has been until now at the end of this year of our lord God 1608. [*p. 104*]

v And also, it was one year ago, in the year 11 Reed, 1607, that the lord don Juan de Mendoza y Luna, Marqués of Montesclaros, viceroy, went to Peru, having ruled in Tenochtitlan 3 years and 8 months. // And it was right then in the said year that the lord don Luis de Velasco took his office as ruler, appointed viceroy for the second time here in Tenochtitlan. He has put in one year until now at the end of the year of our lord God 1608.

v It was mentioned above that it was in the year 12 Flint,[1] 1608, that don Gerónimo López, judge-governor in Tenochtitlan, passed away, having come to rule in Tenochtitlan for 10 years, 8 months, and 21 days. // And it was right then in the said year that the lord don Juan Bautista entered Mexico here, appointed judge-governor in Tenochtitlan; he is from Malinalco, and he is ruling at present. He is the 32nd of those who have been governors of the Mexica Tenochca since they left and set out in this direction from their home there in Old Mexico Aztlan Quinehuayan Chicomoztoc, which today they call New Mexico. And so that it will be known correctly who all those who governed the Mexica Tenochca were, their names are mentioned here; here each one is listed.

v The first was named Moteucçoma; he was their ruler while the Mexica were still in New Mexico, Aztlan.

v The second was named Chalchiuhtlatonac; he brought them out and came governing them [*p. 105*] as the Mexica Tenochca left and set out in this direction from New Mexico, Aztlan Quinehuayan Chicomoztoc.

v The third was named Quauhtlequetzqui, god-bearer.

v The fourth was named Acacitli.

v The fifth was named Citlalintzin.

v The sixth was named Tzimpan.

v The seventh was named Tlaçotzin.

v The eighth was named Tozcuecuextli.

v The ninth was named Huitzilihuitl the elder, ruler.

v The tenth was named Tenochtzin; he brought them here, he came governing the Mexica and led them until they arrived in Tenochtitlan.

v The 11th was named Acamapichtli, the first ruler in Tenochtitlan.

v The 12th was named Huitzilihuitl, the second ruler.

v The 13th was named Chimalpopoca, ruler.

v The 14th was named Itzcoatl, ruler.

v The 15th was named the elder Moteucçoma Ilhuicamina Chalchiuhtlatonac, ruler.

v Ynic caxtollonce ytoca axayacatzin tlahtohuani
v Ynic caxtollonmome ytoca tiçocic. tlahtohuani.
v Ynic caxtollomey. ytoca Ahuitzotl tlahtohuani [*p. 106*]
v Ynic caxtollonnahui ytoca Moteuhcçoma xocoyotl huey tlahtohuani
v Ynic cenpohualli ytoca cuetlahuatzin
v Ynic cenpohuallonce ytoca quauhtimoctzin
v Ynic cenpohuallomome ytoca Don Andres. motelchiuhtzin
v Ynic cenpohuallomey ytoca Don Pablo xochiquẽtzin.
v Ynic cenpohuallonnahui ytoca Don diego de aluarado huanitzin.
v Ynic cenpohuallonmacuilli ytoca Don diego de Sant. Fran^{co}. tehuetzquititzin
v Ynic cenpohuallonchiquacen ytoca Don xp̄oual de guzman cecetzin.
v Ynic cenpohuallonchicome ytoca Don luis de s^{t}.ta maria nacacipactzin
v Ynic cenpohuallonchicuey ytoca Don fran^{co} ximenez. çan Juez
v Ynic cenpohuallonchiuhcnahui ytoca huehue Don Antonio valeriano.
v Ynic cenpohuallonmatlactli ytoca Don Juan m̄īn̄. theniente
v Ynic cenpohuallomatlactli once ytoca Don Jeronimo Lupez.
v Ynic cenpohuallonmatlactli ypan ome ytoca Don Juan bap^{ta}. ynin axcan moyetztica. de 1609. años.

v Auh çan o moch mocentlallique. nican yn oquauhtlahtoque. yhuan yn tlahtoque. yhuan in Juezgouernadoresme. omochiuhque nicã tenochtitlan mexico. [*p. 107*]

v Yhuan nican motenehua yn Gouernadoresme yhuan yn visurreyesme in ye otlapachoque yn ipan in nueua españa. in ye ixquichcauh yc oquitlanque. yhuan ynic yehuatl axcan ypan xihuitl de 1609.[1]

Auh ye omitoq̃ ye omoteneuhq̃ yn ipan tlacpac çã mocenmatoque yn tlahtoque Reyesme mexico. auh ça yuh neci. amo huel ticnonquatlalizque. amo huel ticnonquaquixtizque. ynic mocemitoz. ynic mochihuaz imemoriayo yn ipan in. yn Gouernadoresme. yhuan visurreyesme. in ye otlapachoque. yn ipan in nueua españa in ye ixquichcauh ypan yehuantin christianosme[2] ymaxcapan.

v Yehuatl achto catca yn Don fernando Cortes. Marques del valle gouernador. Justicia mayor y Capitan General. yn tlapacho huel ixquichcauh ynic quitlanico tlalli yn ipan xihuitl de 1519. yxquichcauh yc acic ynic omilhuitl mani metztli Julio. yn ipan. xihuitl de 1526. yn tlapacho chiquacenxihuitl ypan chicuetetl metztli.

v Auh yehuatl. yc ome Gouernador mochiuh in yehuatl el liceciado luis. Ponce ompa yntechcopa quiça ytlacamecayohuan yn tlahtoque Duques. yn ipan altepetl motenehua de arcos. mochiuh Juez de residencia. ỹ quiceli yn onmotlalli ypan ytepacholiz. yn Gouernacio. yc omilhuitl mani metztli Julio. yn ipan xihuitl de 1526. auh amo huel quitzonquixti yn itetlatetemoliliz. yn Residencia yehica. niman õmomiquillico. çan quexquichcauhtica

v Auh ynic momiquilli yn liceciado luis. Ponce. nimãn omotlalli yn ipan tepacholiztli. yn Gouernacio. yn iteniente. Marcos. de Aguilar. ompa ychan yn ipan altepetl de Exija. [*p. 108*]

v Auh yn onmomiquillico Marcos. de Aguilar. çan ome metztica auh ypatca yxiptla

1. An attempt may have been made to change this 9 into an 8.

2. With the third person demonstrative *yehuantin*, it appears that "Christians" here means the Spaniards, as it often did in colloquial Nahuatl. This whole sentence seems to

v The 16th was named Axayacatzin, ruler.
v The 17th was named Tiçocic, ruler.
v The 18th was named Ahuitzotl, ruler. [*p. 106*]
v The 19th was named Moteucçoma the younger, the great ruler.
v The 20th was named Cuitlahuatzin.
v The 21st was named Quauhtemoctzin.
v The 22nd was named don Andrés Motelchiuhtzin.
v The 23rd was named don Pablo Xochiquentzin.
v The 24th was named don Diego de Alvarado Huanitzin.
v The 25th was named don Diego de San Francisco Tehuetzquititzin.
v The 26th was named don Cristóbal de Guzmán Cecetzin.
v The 27th was named don Luis de Santa María Nacacipactzin.
v The 28th was named don Francisco Jiménez, only a judge.
v The 29th was named don Antonio Valeriano the elder.
v The 30th was named don Juan Martín, deputy.
v The 31st was named don Gerónimo López.
v The 32nd was named don Juan Bautista; he is now in office in the year 1609.

v Here all those who were interim rulers, rulers, and were appointed as judge-governors here in Tenochtitlan Mexico have been brought together. [*p. 107*]
v And here are mentioned the governors and viceroys who have governed in New Spain ever since they won it until the present year of 1609.[1]

The rulers and kings of Mexico were already spoken of and mentioned, and they are placed together above. It seems that we might likewise put in some separate place a total list and memorandum in this [text] of the governors and viceroys who have governed in New Spain ever since it has belonged to the Christians.[2]

v The first was don Hernando Cortés, Marqués del Valle, governor, high justice, and captain general, who governed the whole time from when he came to win the land in the year of 1519 until the 2nd day of July in the year of 1526, having governed for 6 years and 8 months.
v The second governor named was licenciado Luis Ponce, who came from the lineage of the lords dukes in the altepetl called Arcos. He was made judge of the residencia and received and was placed in charge of the government on the 2nd day of the month of July in the year of 1526, but he could not complete his investigation, the residencia, because he died right away, within a short time.

v When licenciado Luis Ponce passed away, his deputy Marcos de Aguilar was placed in charge of governing. He was from the altepetl of Ecija. [*p. 108*]

v When Marcos de Aguilar passed away in only two months, the treasurer Alonso de

make sense only if the words "amo huel" are construed as creating questions, reproduced indirectly in the translation here.

mochiuh yn ica yxquich yhuelitiliz oc ye ytech motlalli yn tesorero Alonso de estrada. ompa ychan yn ipan altepetl de ciudad Real. yn otlapacho yxquich yca ynic hualla yn españa yn achto yc motlallico audiencia. yexihuitl yn ey tlacatl tlapacho.

v Auh yn oacico yn huell achto. Audiencia mexico yehuatl ypan xihuitl de 1528. auh yn oydoresme huallaque oncan yntequiuh mochiuh yehuatl yn liceciado Alonso de la Parada. yhuan yehuatl yn liceciado franco Maldonado. yhuan yehuatl. yn liceciado Juan ortiz de Matienço. yhuan yehuatl yn liceciado Delgadillo. yhuan yquac macoc ynic Presidẽte mochiuh oncan audiencia yn Nuño de guzman Gouernador ompa yn Panuco.

v Auh ynin achto. Audiencia. omito. yn otlapacho. yn ogouernadortic. yexihuitl yxquich yca ynic acico yehuatl ypan xihuitl de 1530. auh yuh ytlahuelitaltzin. yuh quimonequilti yn tohueytlahtocauh quinmoquixtili mochintin yn catca. oydoresme. auh niman oquinhualmotitlani. yn inyeyampa oc centlamantin. ma iuh momati. yehuatl yn liceciado vasco. de Quiroga. yhuã yehuatl yn liceciado Alonso Maldonado. yhuan yehuatl yn liceciado franc.o Zaynos. fiscal del consejo. Supremo. yhuan yehuatl yn liceciado Juan de salmeron. yhuan Presidente. mochiuh yn oncan audiencia yn ipan tepacholiztli yn gouernacio. ynic nohuian ypan in nueua españa in yehuatzin Don Sebastian Ramirez. de fuenleal obispo yn ompa Sancto Domingo. ayhtic. yhuan yn Don fernando cortes Marques del valle. oc ceppa macoc [*p. 109*] Yancuican yehuatl yn itequiuh mochiuh yn tepacholiztli yn Gouernacio yn yaopan yc omachiyotiloc ynic capitan geral. mochiuh yn tlapacho audiencia macuilxihuitl.

v Auh yehuatl achtopa omachiyotiloc ynic visurrey. yhuan capitan General yn ipan in nueua españa. omochiuh yn Don Antonio de mendoça huel inehuan tlacati yn Marques de Mondejar. omacoc yuh yehuatl ypan xihuitl de 1534 yn otlapacho. yca yxquichcauh yehuatl ypan xihuitl acico. de 1550. niman mohuicac ompa motlapachilhuito yn ipan prouincias Pirù.

v Auh yehuatl yc ome visurrey mochihuaco yn huehue Don luis de velasco. cauallero. ompa yntechcopa quiça. ytlacamecayohuan yn pipiltin in yaoyotl yntequiuh[1] yn ompa chaneque. yn condestable de castilla.[2] yn otlapacho niman iquac yxquich yca yn ipan xihuitl de 1550. auh yxquich yca acico. yehuatl ypan xihuitl de 1564 momiquilli mexico. ompa toctitoc yn inacayo. Sancto Domingo. yn tlahtocat matlactlonnahui xivitl

v Auh yehuatl yquey visurrey. mochihuaco yn Don Gaston de Peralta Marques de falces. yn otlapacho. niman iquac yxquich yca. yn ipan xihuitl de 1566. auh yxquich yc acico ipã metztli marçо yehuatl ypan xihuitl de 1568. ynic mohuicac españa yn tlahtocatico ce xihuitl ypan macuiltetl metztli.

v Auh yehuatl yc nahui visurrey mochihuaco. yn Don Martin Enrriquez de Almansa. huel inehuan tlacati yn yn Marques de Alcañizes. yn otlapacho yca yxquichcauh ynic peuh achtopa metztli Nouiembre [*p. 110*] Yn ipan xihuitl de 1568. auh yxquich yc huallantica[3] yehuatl. ypan xihuitl de 1580. ynic mohuicac vmpa visurrey mochiuhtzinoto yn Pirù. yn tlahtocatico nican matlactlomey xihuitl.

v Auh yehuatl yc macuilli visurrey y mochiuhtzinoco yn Don lurenço xuarez de mendoça Conde de coruña yn otlapacho yca yxquichcauh yn ipan xihuitl de 1580. auh yxquich yc

1. This phrase apparently attempts to define the Spanish word *caballero*, "gentleman or knight," which precedes it.

2. Ch. apparently takes this expression for a place name or political unit.

Estrada, from the altepetl of Ciudad Real, became his substitute and replacement with his full authority, given to him before [his death]; he governed until the first Audiencia that was established came from Spain. The three [Ponce, Aguilar, and Estrada] governed for three years.
v The very first Audiencia of Mexico arrived in the year 1528, and the judges appointed to office in it were licenciado Alonso de Parada, licenciado Francisco Maldonado, licenciado Juan Ortiz de Matienzo, and licenciado Delgadillo, and at that time Nuño de Guzmán, governor of Pánuco, was appointed president of the Audiencia.

v This first Audiencia here mentioned governed for three years, until the year of 1530 came, and according as our great ruler saw best and wished, he removed all those who were judges, and then he sent here in their place another group; may it be known that they were licenciado Vasco de Quiroga, licenciado Alonso Maldonado, licenciado Francisco Ceynos, prosecuting attorney of the supreme council, and licenciado Juan de Salmerón, and appointed as president of the Audiencia in governing all of New Spain, don Sebastián Ramírez de Fuenleal, bishop in Santo Domingo out in the ocean. And don Hernando Cortés, Marqués del Valle, was again given [*p. 109*] the assignment of governing in war and designated captain general. The Audiencia governed for five years.

v The first to be designated viceroy and captain general in New Spain was don Antonio de Mendoza, a full brother of the Marqués of Mondéjar. He was given the post in the year of 1534 and governed until the year of 1550 came; then he went to govern in the provinces of Peru.

v The second who came appointed as viceroy was don Luis de Velasco the elder, a gentleman coming from the nobles who shared his lineage and whose task was warfare,[1] citizens of the high constable of Castile,[2] who then governed from the year of 1550 until the year of 1564 came. He passed away in Mexico; his body lies buried in [the church of] Santo Domingo. He ruled for 14 years.
v The third who came appointed as viceroy was don Gastón de Peralta, Marqués of Falces, who then governed from the year of 1566 until the month of March in the year of 1568, when he went to Spain. He ruled for a year and five months.

v The fourth who came appointed as viceroy was don Martín Enríquez de Almanza, full brother of the Marqués of Alcañices, who governed from the first beginning of the month of November [*p. 110*] in the year of 1568 until[3] the year of 1580, when he went to Peru, appointed as viceroy. He ruled here for 13 years.

v The fifth who came appointed as viceroy was don Lorenzo Suárez de Mendoza, Count of Coruña, who governed the whole time from the year of 1580 until the 29th of the month

3. The form "huallantica" could represent either standard *hual-an-ti-ca*, "is stretching in this direction," an expression used in speaking of spatial and temporal distances, or *hual-[t]lan-ti-ca*, "is coming to an end." In either case the meaning would be much the same.

huallantica. ypan yc 29 mani metztli Junio. yn ipan xihuitl de 1583. yn momiquillico. auh çatepan huicoc yn inacayo españa yn tlahtocatico nican onxihuitl ypan chicuetetl metztli ypan cenpohuallonmatlactli ypan eylhuitl[1]

v Auh ynic momiquilli yn conde de coruña. niman otlapacho. ogouernadortic yn teoyotica tlahtohuani Don P° Moya de contreras. Arçobispo mexico. ca ynic otetlatetemolli ynic visitador mochiuh yhuan ynic otlapacho yn ogourernadortic yn itequitzin catca yn conmanilli yehuatl ypan xihuitl de 1584 auh yxquich yca huallantica. yehuatl ypan xihuitl de 1586. ynic mohuicac españa.

v Auh yehuatl yc chiquacenvisurrey y mochiuhtzinoco yn Don Aluaro Manrrique de çuniga Marques. de villa Manrrique. yn otlapacho. yca yxquichcauh yn ipan xihuitl de 1585. auh yxquich yc huallantica yehuatl ypan xihuitl de 1590. ynic mohuicac ompa españa. yn tlahtocatico nican macuilxihuitl.

v Auh yehuatl yc chicome visurrey. mochiuhtzinoco yn tlacatl Don luis de velasco cauallero. yn ica ytlaquentzin yn ihabitotzin Sanctiago. ypiltzin [*p. 111*] Ynic ome visurrey. catca yn ipan in nueua españa yn otlapacho. yca yxquichcauh yn ipan xihuitl de 1590. auh yxquich yc huallantica yehuatl ypan xihuitl de 1595. ynic mohuicac ompa visurrey mochiuhtzinoto. yn Perũ. ỹ tlahtocatico macuilxihuitl ypã matlactetl metztli.

v Auh yehuatl yc chicuey visurrey. mochiuhtzinoco yn tlacatl Don Gaspar de çuniga y Azeuedo conde de Monterrey. yn otlapacho. yca yxquichcauh yn ipan xihuitl de 1595. auh yxquich yc huallantica. yehuatl ypan xihuitl de 1603. ynic mohuicac ompa visurrey mochiuhtzinoto. ompa motlapachilhuito yn ipan prouincias. Pirũ. yn tlahtocatico nicã mexico chicuexihuitl ypan matlactetl once metztli.

v Auh yehuatl yc chiuhcnahui visurrey mochiuhtzinoco yn tlacatl Don Juan de mendoça y luna marques de Montesclaros. yn mocallaquico mexico. ypan yehuatl xihuitl de 1603. yc 26. mani metztli octubre. yn otlapacho yca yxquichcauh auh yxquich yc huallantica yn ipan yehuatl xihuitl de 1607. ynic mohuicac vmpa visurrey mochiuhtzinoto. yn Perũ. yn otlahtocatico nican mexico. yexihuitl ypã chicuetetl metztli.

v Auh yn axcan motlapachilhuitica yc oppa motlahtocatillia yn ipan in nueua españa yn tlacatl Don luis de velasco. yn mocallaquico mexico. ypan yehuatl xihuitl de 1607. yc 15. mani metztli. Julio. ompa hualmehuiti yn azcapotzalco ompa mocehuitzinoticatca ynic ompa hual[*p. 112*]Mohuicac Pirũ huel qualli ynic quimonamiquillique. ynic oppa omohuetztico ytlahtocaycpalpan mexico. ma quimonequiltitzino yn tt°. Dios. ma quimotlamelahualtilli yhuan ma quimochicahuilli miec xihuitl. yn ipan ycenquizcatlayecoltilocatzin. yhuan yn ipan yn ipacholloca ynin tlahtocaaltepetl. yn iuh mochintin in altepehuaque quellehuia.[2] — \\\ —

Yhuan nican tenehualo. yn Arçobisposme in ye otlapachoco. yn ipan in nueua españa. in ye yxquichcauh yc oquitlanico yhuan ynic yehuatl axcan ypã xihuitl de 1608

v Yehuatl achto obispo mochihuaco. yn Don fray Juã de çumaraga. Sant. Fran^co^ teopixqui yn otlapacho yca yxquichcauh yn ipan xihuitl de 1528. auh yxquich yc huallantica. yehuatl ypan xihuitl de 1548. yn momiquillico. yn teoyotica motlahtocatilli mexico. cenpohualxihuitl ypan ce xihuitl.

v Auh yehuatl yc ome arçobispo. omochihuaco. yn Don fray Alonso de montufar. teopixqui Sancto Domingo. yn otlapacho yca yxquichcauh yn ipan xihuitl de 1554. o iuh ye

---

1. The same apparently erroneous number was given in the same context above (pp. 140–41 at n. 3).

of June in the year of 1583, when he passed away; later his body was taken to Spain. He ruled here for 2 years, 8 months, and 33 days.[1]

v When the Count of Coruña died, the spiritual ruler don Pedro Moya de Contreras, archbishop in Mexico, governed. His tasks were investigating as appointed inspector and governing. He took up [the governorship] in the year of 1584 until the year of 1586, when he went to Spain.

v The sixth who came appointed as viceroy was don Alvaro Manrrique de Zúñiga, Marqués of Villamanrrique, who governed the whole time from the year of 1585 to the year of 1590, when he went to Spain, having ruled here for five years.

v The seventh who came appointed as viceroy was the lord don Luis de Velasco, a knight of the habit of Santiago, the child of [*p. 111*] the second viceroy who was in New Spain, who governed the whole time from the year of 1590 until the year of 1595, when he went to Peru appointed as viceroy there, having ruled 5 years and 10 months.

v The eighth who came appointed as viceroy was the lord don Gaspar de Zúñiga y Acevedo, Count of Monterrey, who governed the whole time from the year of 1595 until the year of 1603, when he went to the provinces of Peru appointed as viceroy to govern there, having ruled here in Mexico for 8 years and 11 months.

v The ninth who came appointed as viceroy was the lord don Juan de Mendoza y Luna, Marqués of Montesclaros, who entered Mexico in the year of 1603, on the 26th of the month of October, and governed the whole time until the year of 1607, when he went to Peru appointed as viceroy, having ruled here in Mexico for 3 years and 8 months.

v Today the lord don Luis de Velasco is governing, ruling for the second time in New Spain. He entered Mexico in the year of 1607, on the 15th of the month of July; he came from Azcapotzalco, where he was living in retirement after [*p. 112*] coming back from Peru. They gave him a very good reception when he came to occupy his seat as ruler in Mexico for the second time. May our lord God see fit to send him in the right direction and give him health for many years in his entire service and in the governance of this royal altepetl, as all its citizens desire.[2]

And here are mentioned the archbishops who have come to govern here in New Spain ever since they [the Spaniards] won it until now in the year of 1608.
v The first who came appointed as bishop was don fray Juan de Zumárraga, a Franciscan friar, who governed beginning in the year 1528 until in the year of 1548, when he passed away, having ruled in spiritual matters in Mexico for 21 years.
v The second who came appointed as archbishop was don fray Alonso de Montúfar, a Dominican friar, who governed beginning in the year of 1554—it had been seven years

---

2. A close translation into Nahuatl of common Spanish formulas.

nepa chiconxihuitl momiquilli yn Don fray Juan de çumarraga. auh yxquich yc huallantica yehuatl. ypan xihuitl de 1572. yn momiquillico Don fray Alonso de mantufar. yn teoyotica motlahtocatilli mexico caxtollonnahui xihuitl

v Auh yehuatl yqu ey arcobispo.[1] omochiuhtzinoco. yn Don Pedro Moya de contreras. clerigo ynquisidor [*p. 113*] Achtopa catca mexico. yn otlapacho yca yxquichcauh yn ipan xihuitl. de 1574. o iuh ye nepa ye xihuitl momiquilli yn Don fray Alonso de montufar. auh yxquich yc huallantica yehuatl ypan xihuitl de 1586. ynic mohuicac españa Don P.º Moya de contreras. yn teoyotica motlahtocatilli mexico ynic arçobispo. moyetzticatca matlacxihuitl.[2] — Auh ynic mohuicac españa ompa mochiuhtzinoto presidente del Real consejo de indias. yn ompa moyetzticatca yca yxquichcauh yn ipan mohuicac xihuitl. auh yxquich yc huallantica yehuatl ypan xihuitl de 1592. ynic momiquilli ompa españa yn ompa moyetzticatca chiquacenxihuitl.

v Auh yehuatl yc nahui arçobispo. mochiuhtzino yn licẽciado Don Alonso fernandez de Bonilla. clerigo. ynin achto fiscal moyetzticatca yn ipan Sancto officio. ynquisicion niman inquisidor mochiuh y nican mexico. auh niman ompa onixquetzalloca ynic ompa obispo mochiuhtzinozquia yn yancuic yn motenehua nueuo Reyno de Galicia. auh çatepan. mohuicac visitador. mochiuhtzinoto. yn ipan tlahtocaaltepetl Pirù. auh ompa ypan moyetzticatca yn itequitzin. ynic visita quimochihuillia. ynic niman oquimixquechillique ynic arçobispo. omochiuhtzino mexico. auh yxquichcapa ompa yn quihualmomaquilli yn ihuelitiliz. ynic ypampa gouernador mochiuh Don Juan de ceruantes. arcediano. nican mexico. yn oquic ompa quimotlamiltilia ytequitzin. auh viernes yc xi mani metztli Março de 1594. yquac possecion macoc. yn Don Juan de ceruãtes. arcediano. ynic yxiptlatzin mochiuh yn arçobispo Bonilla. yn otlapacho yca yxquichcauh yn i[*p. 114*]Pann omoteneuh xihuitl de 1594. O iuh ye nepa yexihuitl ompa españa momiquilli yn Don Pedro Moya de contreras auh yxquich yc huallantica yehuatl ypan xihuitl de 1600. ynic momiquillico[3] yn teoyotica tlahtocayotl. ytechtzinco catca chiquacenxihuitl yxquichcauh ypampa gouernadortic yn mexico yn Don Juan de ceruantes arcediano.

v Auh yehuatl yc macuilli arçobispo. omochiuhtzinoco. yn Don Fray Garcia de Sancta Maria de mendoça y çuniga. teopixqui. Sant. Jeronimo. yn otlapacho yca yxquichcauh yn ipan xihuitl de 1602. o iuh ye nepa onxihuitl momiquilli. yn licenciado. Don Alonso fernãdez de Bonilla. auh yxquich yc huallantica. yehuatl ypã xihuitl de 1606. yn momiquillico Don fray Garcia de S.ᵗta maria de mendoça y çuniga. yn teoyotica motlahtocatilli mexico. nauhxihuitl.

v Auh yn axcan motlapachilhuitica. yn teoyotica motlatocatilia yn ipan in nueua españa. yn cenca mahuiztililoni Don Fray Garcia Guerra arçobispo. Sancto Domingo. teopixqui. yn mocallaquico mexico. ypan yehuatl in xihuitl de 1608. yc 29. mani metztli de Setiembre. huel qualli ynic quimonamiquillique. ma quimonequiltitzino. in ttº. Dios. ma quimochicahuillitzino miec xihuitl yn ipan ycenquizcatlayecoltilocatzin yhuan yn ipã yn ipacholloca ynin Sancta yglesia mexico tenochtitlan yn iuh mochintin ipan in altepehuaque quellehuia

— \\\ —

Yhuan Nican tenehuallo in yehuantzitzin cenca mahuiztililoni inquisidoresme. in ye omo-

1. For "arçobispo."
2. Perhaps the discrepancy is because he was also interim viceroy for a time.

since don fray Juan de Zumárraga had passed away—until in the year of 1572, when don fray Alonso de Montúfar passed away, having ruled in spiritual matters in Mexico for 19 years.

v The third who came appointed as archbishop[1] was don Pedro Moya de Contreras, a secular priest; first he was inquisitor [*p. 113*] in Mexico. He governed beginning in the year of 1574—it had been three years since don fray Alonso de Montúfar had died—until in the year of 1586, when don Pedro Moya de Contreras went to Spain, having ruled spiritually in Mexico as archbishop for ten years.[2] — And when he went to Spain he was made president of the Royal Council of the Indies; he was there beginning in the year when he went until in the year of 1592, when he died in Spain, having been there six years.

v The fourth who came appointed as archbishop was licenciado don Alonso Fernández de Bonilla, a secular priest; first he was prosecuting attorney in the Holy Office of the Inquisition, and then he was appointed inquisitor here in Mexico. Then he was chosen and was going to be made bishop in the new [region] called the New Kingdom of Galicia, but later he went appointed as inspector to the royal altepetl of Peru, and he was there at his task of carrying out the inspection when they named him to be made archbishop of Mexico. And from there he sent his power of attorney so that don Juan de Cervantes, archdeacon here in Mexico, was made governor on his behalf until he should finish his assignment there. Friday, the 11th of the month of March of 1594, was when don Juan de Cervantes, archdeacon, was given possession [of the office] and made the deputy of archbishop Bonilla; he governed from then [*p. 114*] in the said year of 1594—it had been three years since don Pedro Moya de Contreras had died in Spain—until in the year of 1600, when he[3] passed away. He held the spiritual rulership for six years, during which time don Juan de Cervantes, archdeacon, governed in Mexico on his behalf.

v The fifth who came appointed as archbishop was don fray García de Santa María de Mendoza y Zúñiga, a Hieronymite friar, who governed beginning in the year 1602—licenciado don Alonso Fernández de Bonilla had passed away two years before—until in the year of 1606, when don fray García de Santa María de Mendoza y Zúñiga passed away, having ruled in spiritual matters in Mexico for four years.

v Today the very reverend don fray García Guerra, archbishop, Dominican friar, is governing and ruling in spiritual matters in New Spain. He entered Mexico in the year of 1608, on the 29th of the month of September; they gave him a very good reception. May our lord God see fit to give him health for many years in his entire service and in the governance of this Holy Church in Mexico Tenochtitlan, as all the citizens there desire.

— \\\ —

And here are mentioned the very reverend inquisitors who have come to preside in Mexico

---

3. Meaning Bonilla; an earlier entry says he died in 1600, and it is seen below that Cervantes became bishop of Oaxaca in 1609. The version given here of the appointments differs somewhat from that on pp. 48–49.

yetztieco mex^{co} yn ipan in tetlatzontequililiztlahtocaycpalli. yn motenehua Sancto Officio. yn ipan ĩ [*p. 115*] Nueua españa. ynic ompa hualpeuhtica ypan xihuitl de 1571. ynic yehuatl huallantica axcan ypã xihuitl de 1608. ca yz tecpantoque —
v Yehuatzin achtopa inquisidor mochiuhtzinoco. yn Don Pedro Moya de contreras. auh çatepan Mochiuhtzino Arçobispo yn Mexico. yhuan Gouernador. yn ipan in Nueua españa. yhuan çatepan mochiuhtzino presidente del real consejo de indias. —
v Auh yehuatl yc ome inquisidor. mochiuhtzino yn licenciado Don Alonso Fernandez de Bonilla. ca onixquetzalloca ompa obispo mochiuhtzinozquia. in yancuic yn motenehua del nueuo Reyno de Galicia xalixco yhuan çatepan mohuicac ynic visitador. mochiuhtzinoto. yn ipan tlahtocaaltepetl Pirũ. auh ompa ypan moyetzticatca yn itequitzin ynic visita quimochihuilia ynic niman nican oquihualmixquechillique ynic arçobispo omochiuhtzino mexico. amo huel hualmohuicac. ompa momiquilli yn ipan altepetl ciudad de lima. çan ye oc ompa ypan moyetzticatca yn itequitzin ynic visita quimochihuilliaya. —
v Auh yehuatl yquey inquisidor mochiuhtzino yn licẽciado Granero de Aualos. auh çatepan mochiuhtzinoto obispo. yn ipan altepetl y motenehua charcas. yn õpa ypan Pirũ ompa momiquillito. —
v Auh yehuatl yc nahui inquisidor mochiuhtzino. yn licenciado Fran^{co} Sanctos Garcia. auh çatepan ompa mochiuhtzinoto obispo. yn yancuic y motenehua del nueuo Reyno de Galicia guadraxara xalixco. —
v Auh yehuatl yc macuilli inquisidor. mochiuhtzino. [*p. 116*] Yn Doctor Don Bartolomẽ lobo Guerrero. auh axcã arçobispo. mochiuhtzinotica in yancuic y motenehua del nueuo Reyno de Granada —
v Auh yn axcan cahuitl ypan moyetzticate yn ipan in cenquizca qualli Sancto tetlatzontequililiztlatocaycpalli. yn cenca mahuiztililoni Señores licenciados. Don Alonso de Peralta. yhuan Gutierre Bernardo de Quiros. Otzonquiçaco. yn matlactlomome xii. tecpatl xihuitl de 1608. años. —

¶ xiii. calli xihuitl. 1609. yn ipan in xihuitl omoteneuh yehuatl Gouernador yn tlacatl Don Juan bap^{ta}. malinalco ychan auh al~~ld~~es. çan ya yehuatl yn telpochtli Don Antonio valleriano. yn ixhuiuhtzin huehue Don Antonio valleriano catca azcapotzalco ychantzinco // yhuan Don miguel huetzin acatla chane al~~ld~~esme Sant. Juan moyotlan tenochtitlan yhuan Don melchior. S. Pablo chane.
v Auh yn axcan ypehuayan yn omoteneuh yancuic xihuitl. yhuan ypehuayan yancuic metztli henero. ypan omacocuizquia. yaoyotl oquichihuazquia. nicã mexico. yn tliltique. ynpan quichihuazquia yn intecuiyohuan yn españolestin. oquinmictizquia. auh amo quimonequiltitzino yn tt^{o} Dios. amo quinmomacahuilli yn españolestin. mictilozque. ca nimã machiztic niman ohuanoque yn tliltique. auh yuh mito. yntla huel quichihuani yaoyotl. yntla huelitini ca yehuantin. otlahtocatizquia. yn iuh machiztic yn ipan in yancuic tlalli nueua españa motenehua ye oquitlallica yntlahtocauh ce tliltic yn tlahtohuani yn Rey mochiuhca ytoca Don _____ Auh no ce tliltic cihuatl cihuatlahtohuani Reyna [*p. 117*] Omochiuhca. ytoca _____ yhuan yn oc cequintin tliltique. ye oquimomamacaca. yn ixquich nican altepetl yn oncan otlahtocatizquia. ynic cequintin Duquesme yhuan cequintin. marquesesme. yhuan cequintin condesme omochiuhca. yn iuh momatca oc yehuantin. otechmomacehualtizquia ỹ nican titlaca timacehualtin otiquintlayecoltizquia.
v Auh yn axcan ypan in yc i. mani metztli Março de 1609. años. yquac opeuh cenca chi-

on the royal seat of justice called the Holy Office here in [*p. 115*] New Spain, beginning in the year of 1571 until the present year of 1608; here they are listed. —

v The one who first came appointed as inquisitor was don Pedro Moya de Contreras; later he was made archbishop in Mexico and governor in New Spain, and later he was made president of the Royal Council of the Indies. —

v The second who was appointed as inquisitor was licenciado don Alonso Fernández de Bonilla; he was chosen to be made bishop in the new [region] called the New Kingdom of Galicia, Jalisco, and later he went appointed as inspector to the royal altepetl of Peru. He was there at his task, carrying out the inspection, when they named him to be made archbishop here in Mexico. He could not come; he died in the altepetl and city of Lima, still at his assignment, carrying out the inspection. —

v The third who was appointed inquisitor was licenciado Granero de Avalos. Later he was appointed bishop in the altepetl called Charcas, in Peru; he went there and died. —

v The fourth who was appointed inquisitor was licenciado Francisco Santos García. Later he went appointed as bishop to the new [region] called the New Kingdom of Galicia, to Guadalajara, in Jalisco. —

v The fifth who was appointed inquisitor was [*p. 116*] dr. don Bartolomé Lobo Guerrero. Now he has been made archbishop in the new [region] called the New Kingdom of Granada. —

v At present the very reverend lords licenciados don Alonso de Peralta and Gutierre Bernardo de Quiroz occupy the consummately good and holy royal seat of justice. The year 12 Flint, 1608, has come to an end. —

¶ 13 House year, 1609. In the said year the governor was the lord don Juan Bautista, from Malinalco, and the alcaldes were the same don Antonio Valeriano the younger, grandchild of the late don Antonio Valeriano the elder, from Azcapotzalco, and don Miguel Sánchez Huentzin, citizen of Acatlan, alcaldes for San Juan Moyotlan in Tenochtitlan, and don Melchor, citizen of San Pablo.

v Now at the beginning of the said new year and the beginning of the new month of January, the blacks were going to rebel and make war here in Mexico; they were going to make it on their lords the Spaniards, they were going to kill them, but our lord God did not want it so, he did not permit the Spaniards to be killed, for it became known right away, and the blacks were immediately arrested. It was said that if they had been able to make war, if they could have, they would have ruled, as it became known, in the new land called New Spain. They had already established a black as their ruler; the ruler and king who had been created was named don _____. And also a black woman had been chosen woman ruler and queen, named _____. [*p. 117*] And they had distributed all the various altepetl here to other blacks who would rule there; some had been made dukes, some marqueses, some counts. They thought they would make us local people, us commoners, their vassals; we were going to serve them.

v Today the 1st of the month of March of the year 1609 was when the rash called small-

cahuac momanaco yn çahuatl. yn motenehua viruelas. cenca miequintin yc momiquillique yn pipiltzitzinti. yn inpilhuã timacehualtin.[1] yhuan çan no yhui yn inpilhuan españolestin. yhuan yn inpilhuan tliltique. çan mochtin neliuhtiaque yn momiquilique. yhuan cequintin ye huehueỹtin tlaca. ynic momiquillique çahuatl ypan cehuico yn Mayo. ome metztli ypan tlaco yn manca.

v̲ Auh yn axcan yc 7. mani metztli Março. de 1609 años. yquac peuh yn ipan izqui acallotli nican mexico. yn omoyecti o nohuian moçoquiquixti. ytencopatzinco. yn tlahtohuani visurrey Don luis de velasco. auh yehuantin. oquichihuaco. yn tequitl. ynic nohuian cenchinampanecatl yhuan yehuantin chalca yn tequitico. mexico

v̲ Auh yn axcan quaresma ye ytlamian metztli Março de 1609. años. yquac nican mexico. onmopehualti. ynic ompa mohuicac michhuacan in yehuatzin cenca mahuiztililoni teoyotica tlahtohuani Don fray Balthasar. Acobarrobias teopixqui Sant. Augustin. huaxacac obispo. ocatca. auh yn michhuacan vmpa comiquanilli yn tohueytlahtocauh Rey. ynic ye no ye ompa yehuatzin motlapachilhuiz michhuacan yc mopatlac yn huaxacac ynin obispo nican otlacat mexico. nican tepiltzin. [*p. 118*]

v̲ Auh axcan sabado quaresma yc 4. mani metztli abril de 1609 años. yquac nican mexico onmopehualtique chicomentin Sant. Fran^co^ Padreme. mohuicaque yãcuic mexico. yehuatzin yn Padre fray fran^co^ de la peyna commissario mochiuhtia.

v̲ Auh axcan sabado ypan ylhuitzin Sant. Marcos. yc 25. Mani metztli abril de 1609 años. yquac nican mexico. omoquixti omohuicac cuitlaxcohuapan yn Don Juan de ceruantes arcediano mexico. yc mohuicac ynic ompa macoz teoyotica ytlahtocayo. ynic obispo muchiuh huaxacac

v̲ Auh axcan Domingo yc 26. mani metztli abril de 1609. años. yquac nican mexico. omaxitico. omocallaquico. in yehuatzin cenca mahuiztililoni teoyotica tlahtohuani Don diego Pasquez de mergado. obispo. yocadan clerigo. mohuica vmpa ỹ la china yn ipã altepetl Manilla ynic ye no ye ompa arçobispo mochiuhtzino.

v̲ Auh çan ic onquiz yn pasqua rresurecion çan ye ypan ye ytlamian yn metztli abril ni cuell omentin Sant. Fran^co^ Padreme mohuicaque in yancuic mexico. quinmohuiquillique 20. Juldadosme. yquac mochi ya yn ixquich ompa monequiz yn cartillas. quimomachtizque ompa tlaca yhuan ya cornedas. chirimias çacapoch yhuan ce organo yhuan campanas. yhuan yztac amatl clauos. yhuan oc cequi tlamantli yn ompa monequiz. moch ya yhuã quezquintin quinhuicaque officialesme yn tolteca yn quinmachtizque ompa tlaca yn ica yzqui tlamantli tequitl.

v̲ Axcan sabado yc 2. mani metztli Mayo de 1609 años. yquac pregon mochiuh ỹ nican mexico ye tzatzihuac ynic omotlalli yancuic oc ce visitador [*p. 119*] Ytoca Don Juã Billela[2] vmpa huallehuac yn Guadraxara yn xalixco. ompa presidente catca. yquac quicauh yn itequiuh yn oc ce catca visitador. yn itoca licenciado. Diego lanteras y velasquez.[3]

v̲ axcan Domingo yc 3. mani metztli Mayo de 1609. años. yquac teochihualoc ompa macoc yn ipan altepetl de los Angeles cuitlaxcohuapan yn teoyotica ytlahtocayo. yn Don Juan de ceruantes. obispo huaxacac. mochiuhtzino. yn o iuh macoc teoyotica ytlahtocayo.

---

1. As in some other places in the text, though *timacehualtin* is in itself first person plural, it is otherwise treated here as a third person, crossreferring with the third person noun *impilhuan*, "their children."

pox broke out very strongly. Very many children of us commoners[1] died of it, and likewise children of Spaniards and children of blacks; all died mixed together [without distinction], as well as some adults who died of smallpox. It abated in May, having gone on for two and a half months.

v̲ Today on the 7th of the month of March of the year 1609 was when cleaning out all the canals here in Mexico and removing the mud everywhere began at the order of the lord viceroy don Luis de Velasco. The different people from all over the chinampa region came to perform the tribute work, and the Chalca came here to Mexico to work.
v̲ Now during Lent, at the end of the month of March of the year 1609, was when the very reverend spiritual ruler don fray Baltasar Covarrubias, an Augustinian friar, who had been bishop of Oaxaca, set out from Mexico here and went to Michoacan. Our great ruler the king transferred him to Michoacan so that he would govern in the same way there; Oaxaca was replaced by Michoacan. This bishop was born here in Mexico, the child of people here. [*p. 118*]
v̲ Today, Saturday, during Lent, the 4th of the month of April of the year 1609, was when seven Franciscan fathers set out from Mexico here and went to New Mexico; Father fray Francisco de la Peina went appointed as commissary.
v̲ Today, Saturday, the feast day of San Marcos, the 25th of the month of April of the year 1609, was when don Juan de Cervantes, archdeacon of Mexico, left Mexico here and went to Puebla; he went there in order to be given his spiritual rulership, by which he was appointed bishop of Oaxaca.
v̲ Today, Sunday the 26th of the month of April of the year 1609, was when the very reverend spiritual ruler don Diego Vásquez de Mercado, bishop of Yucatan, a secular priest, arrived and entered Mexico here; he is going to China [the Philippines], to the altepetl of Manila, since he is likewise being made archbishop there.
v̲ Hardly had the Easter holiday passed, at the end of the month of April, when already two Franciscan fathers went to New Mexico; at that time they took along twenty soldiers, and everything that would be needed there went along: primers to teach the people there, and cornets, chirimías, trombones, and an organ, and bells, European paper, nails, and other things that would be needed there all went along, and they took some artisans, craftsmen, to teach the people there in all the different kinds of work.

v̲ Today, Saturday, the 2nd of the month of May of the year 1609, was when a proclamation was made here in Mexico; it was proclaimed that a new and different inspector general was put in office, [*p. 119*] named don Juan Villela,[2] who came from Guadalajara in Jalisco, where he was president [of the Audiencia]. At that time another inspector general that there had been, named licenciado Diego Landeras y Velásquez,[3] left his post.

v̲ Today, Sunday, the 3rd of the month of May of the year 1609, was when in the altepetl of Los Angeles, Puebla, the spiritual rulership of don Juan de Cervantes, appointed bishop of Oaxaca, was consecrated and given to him. After he had been given his spiritual

2. Name unconfirmed.
3. See pp. 92–93, n. 6.

yc niman oncan mohuicac ynic mohuetzitito. huaxacac ynin obispo. nican tlacat mexico nican tepiltzin[1] yntech quiça yn conquistadoresme
v Axcan martes yc 19. mani metztli Mayo de 1609. años. yquac nican mexico. ompeuh ynic ya españa Don Juan Gano de moteuhcçoma quinhuicac ynamic yhuan ypilhuan.

v Axcan Viernes yc 22. mani metztli Mayo de 1609. años. yquac nican mexico. onmopehualti ynic mohuicac españa. in yehuatzin visitador licenciado Diego lanteras y velasquez. yn visita nican quimochihuilico onxihuitl ypan tlaco xihuitl.
v Auh axcan ytlamian metztli Junio de 1609. anos. yquac otlamico yn izqui acallotli ypan mexico. omoyecti omoçoquiquixti. yn ipampa atl. yn moyecti ynic nemohuac nauhtetl metztli.
v Axcan juebes. yc 9. mani metztli Julio de 1609. años. yquac cathetratico omochiuhtzino yn escuelas real mexico in yehuatzin Padre maestro. fray diego de contreras. prior Sant. Augustin mexico. [*p. 120*]
v Axcan Viernes. yc 17. mani metztli Julio. de 1609. años. yquac omomiquilli yn itlaçotzin tt.º Dios. ỹ Padre Pedro Sanchez. teopixqui de la compañia de Jesus. nican mexico y momiquilli cenca ye omohuehuetillitia
v Axcan Sabado yc 18. mani metztli Julio de 1609. aºs. yquac oya onpeuh yancuic mexico. ce maestro tepozpitzqui. timacehualtin ytoca. ______ quimihualli visurrey ynic quinmachtiz ompa tlaca yancuic mexico 8.tin yn Juldadostin quinhuicac. españolesme

v Auh axcan Sabado yc i. mani metztli agosto. de 1609. años. ypan Sant. Pedro de ad vincula[2] ylhuitzin. yn otzonquiçaco. ypleyto in yehuatzin Padre frey Augustin del Spũ Sancto. yn itechcopa ynic motlacenmachiltiz yca ytlaquentzin yn ihabitotzin totlaçotatzin Señor Sant. Anton Abbad. oquimotlachicahuililique. oquimomelauhcatyttilique yn yehuantzitzin cuitlaxcohuapan obispo. Don Alonso de la muta y escobar yhuã provisor melchior marques. yehuantzitzin. oquixitinique. yn pleyto. nican mexico arçobispado. yn ixquich yc oquixnamicque yn itoliniloca omochiuh yn omoteneuhtzino Padre frey. Augustin del Spũ Sancto. ye mellahuac yn axcan ye yteopixcatzin. yntotlaçotatzin. Sant. Anton Abbad.
v Auh axcan viernes. yc .7. mani metztli agosto de 1609. años. yquac omotlapoto mexicatzinco [*p. 121*] Yn atl. yn oncan tzauhcticatca cecni yca tlatzacuilotl puente mitohua.

v Axcan lunes yc 31. de agosto de 1609. años. yquac Oquaquamiminalloc opahpacohuac nican mexico tenochtitlan vncan seral quiyahuac. ypampatzinco yc quiz yn ilhuitzin Sant ipolito Martyr Patron ỹ nican ciudad. mexico. yeylhuitl motlalli ynic tlamiminalloc yhuan cauallotlatlallochtique yn oncan curral. yn españolesme tlahtoque[3] yhuan acatica mominque auh yn intlatqui yn innechichihual contlallique ynic mocencauhque cenca mochi tlaçotli. cenca miyec ypatiuh yn intech contlallique mochintin tlahtoque

v Auh axcan miercoles yc 2. mani Metztli Setiembre. yc ya yeylhuitl pahpacohua Quaquamiminallo yn oncan Omoteneuh Seral quiyahuac yn ihquac ohualla curreo ypan macuilli tzillini ye teotlac yn ocaxitico yn oquihualhuicac tlahtolli españa. yn oqui-

1. The sense of *tepiltzin*, as often, may be child of prominent people.
2. Stafford Poole advises us that this is the feast commonly known in English as

rulership, he went to settle down in Oaxaca. This bishop was born here in Mexico, a child of people[1] here; he comes from the conquerors.

v Today, Tuesday, the 19th of the month of May of the year 1609, was when don Juan Cano de Moctezuma set out from Mexico here to go to Spain; he took his spouse and children.

v Today, Friday, the 22nd of the month of May of the year 1609, was when the inspector general licenciado Diego Landeras y Velásquez set out from Mexico here to go to Spain; he carried out the inspection here for two and a half years.

v Now at the end of the month of June of the year 1609 was when cleaning and clearing mud out of all the canals in Mexico came to an end; the activity on account of cleaning the water lasted for four months.

v Today, Thursday, the 9th of the month of July of the year 1609, was when Father fray Diego de Contreras, master [in theology] and prior of San Agustín in Mexico, was given a chair at the royal school in Mexico. [*p. 120*]

v Today, Friday, the 17th of the month of July of the year 1609, was when the beloved of our lord God Father Pedro Sánchez, religious of the Company of Jesus, passed away. It was here in Mexico that he died; he was very old at death.

v Today, Saturday, the 18th of the month of July of the year 1609, was when a master blacksmith, one of us commoners, named ____, set out and left for New Mexico. The viceroy sent him to teach the people there in New Mexico; he accompanied eight Spanish soldiers.

v It was today, Saturday, the 1st of the month of August of the year 1609, on the feast day of San Pedro ad Vincula[2] that the lawsuit of Father frey Agustín del Espíritu Santo in his persistent campaign about his habit of our dear father lord San Antón Abad came to a conclusion. The bishop of Puebla, don Alonso de la Mota y Escobar, and the executive officer of the bishopric, Melchor Márquez, confirmed him and decided his cause was just; they dismissed the suit here in the archbishopric of Mexico with which they so greatly opposed the said Father frey Agustín del Espíritu Santo, causing his suffering. Now he is rightly a religious of our precious father San Antón Abad.

v Today, Friday, the 7th of the month of August of the year 1609, was when a group went to Mexicatzinco [*p. 121*] to open up the water that was blocked there in one place with a closing device called a bridge.

v Today, Monday, the 31st of August of the year 1609, was when there was bullfighting and celebration here in Mexico Tenochtitlan, outside the municipal building, because of the celebration of the feast day of San Hipólito Mártir, patron here in the city of Mexico. Three days were set aside during which there was [bull]fighting, and the Spanish rulers[3] ran horses at the corral and jousted with reed darts. The gear and attire which they wore and prepared themselves with was all very fine; what all the rulers wore was very expensive.

v And today, Wednesday, the 2nd of the month of September, the third day of bullfighting and celebration outside the said municipal building, was when a courier came, at 5 o'clock in the afternoon, bringing news from Spain; he came to announce it at the waiting room

---

Saint Peter in Chains.

3. Here apparently meaning little more than prominent people or *caballeros*.

machiztico oncan ytlatlachiantzinco yn visurrey Don luis de velasco. yn ipantzinco acico yn castilla hualla tlahtolli ynic oquimomachiztillico. yn quenin yehuatzin tohueytlahtocauh Rey Don felipe tercero yn ompa moyetztica españa. ye oquimomaquilli ye ytech oquimopohuilli yn tlahtocayotl yn Marquesyotl yn ipan altepetl de Salinas. yn Don luis de velasco vmpa marques. omochiuhtzino

v Auh niman axcan Juebes ye yohua yc 3. mani Metztli yn omoteneuh Setiembre de 1609 años. ya yehuatzin ycatzinco ypampatzinco yn tlahtohuani visurrey Don luis de velasco marques de salinas yn opahpacohuac. mexico. yn oncan tecpan qui[*p. 122*]Yahuac Palacio bentana hualmoquetzino yn omoteneuhtzino visurrey yn quimopahpaquiltillique oncan hualmotztilitoya ynic oncan tlatzĩtla yxquichcapa ceceyaca oome mãtihui yn ixquichtin. caualleros españolesme in ye mochintin onpohuallonchicuey in ye no ni cuel mocencauhque yn intlaçotlatquitica vncan conmotlapalhuiaya yxpantzinco onmopachohuaya yn tlahtohuani moch tlacauallohuia candelas achas yn inmac tlatlatlatiuh ynin mochiuh ypan chicome tzillini ye yohuac yn pahpacohuac yhuan yn oncã tecpan tlapantenco y nohuian cenca miec yn õcan tlatlac sepocandelas. ynic mochiuh yn motenehua luminarios. yhuan no cenca miec yn oncan quitlatlazque couetes. yuan ynic nohuian oncan tecpan quiyahuac nohuian quauhtlaliloc tlatlac oncan yn quahuitl yhuan ynic nohuian yhtic ciudad yn incalticpac castilteca nohuian quitlatique quahuitl. yhuan nohuian tlatzitzillitzalloc yn izquican teopan mexico yn monasterios.[1]

v Axcan Sabado. yc 3. mani metztli de octubre de 1609. años. ypã yvisperatzin S. Fran^{co} yn omomiquilli y notlaçoycniuhtzin Padre helias donado pouhqui ytlatecpanalpantzinco yn señor Sanct Fran^{co} toctoc oncan yn Sant. Josep mexico. ynin xochmilco ychantzinco cenca huecauh yn omotlamacehuili yca habito. nehuatl. Domingo de S. Anton Muñon y nicniuhtzin onicatca

v Auh axcan Domingo yc ____ tia metztli Nouiembre de 1609. años. yquac yah yn Don Juan baptista Juez gouernador catca mexico. tenochtitlan ychan Malinalco [*p. 123*]

v Axcan lunes yc 30. mani Metztli Nouiembre de 1609. años. ypan ylhuitzin S. Andres Apostol. yhquac nican Mexico iglesia mayor. oteochihualloc omacoc teoyotica ytlahtocayo in yehuatzin inquisidor mayor. omoyetzticatca Don Alonso de Peralta ynic Arçobispo. mochiuhtzino yn ipan altepetl de las charcas yn ompa ypan tlalli perũ. auh yehuantzitzin quimoteochihuillique quimomaquillique yn teoyotica ytlahtocayo. yn omentzitzin teoyotica tlahtoque ynic ce yehuatzin yn Don fray Garcia guerra arcobispo[2] Mexico. ynic ome yehuatzin yn Don diego Pasquez de Mercado arçobispo de manilla de la china yhquac nican moyetzticatca. Auh yc niman yehuatzin inquisidor mayor. omochiuhtzino yn Don Gutierre Bernardo de Quiros. yc chicome yn ynquisidores mayores ye mochiuhtzinoa yn nican ypan huey altepetl ciudad mexico tenochtitlan. Otzonquiçaco yn Matlactlomey calli xihuitl. de 1609. años.

— \\\ —

¶ i. Tochtli xihuitl. 1610. yn ipan in yancuic xihuitl yehuatl Presidente mochiuhtica yn fran^{co} Sanches español ỹ nican mexico tenochtitlan yn ipampa gouernacio.[3] auh çan ya yehuatl allde yn telpochtli Don Antonio valleriano ihuan don miguel sanchez huetzin yhuan yn oc cequintin nauhcãpa alldesme.[4] // yhuan axcã miercoles yc 6. tia henero ypã

1. Or at all the monastery churches in Mexico?

2. For "arçobispo."

3. A sort of quasi-governorship of Mexico Tenochtitlan held by a Spaniard. See also

of viceroy don Luis de Velasco, where the news that came from Spain reached him; he came to announce that our great ruler the king, don Felipe III who resides in Spain, had given and assigned to don Luis de Velasco the rulership and Marquesado in the altepetl of Salinas, that he had been made Marqués there.

v And then today, Thursday, at night on the 3rd of the said month of September of 1609, there was celebrating in Mexico in honor of the lord viceroy don Luis de Velasco, Marqués of Salinas, outside the palace. [*p. 122*] The said viceroy came and stood at the palace window; while they feted him he looked on at each of all the Spanish cavaliers below going in pairs, 48 in all, again outfitted in their precious gear; there they greeted the ruler and bowed down before him, and everything was on horseback, with burning candles and tapers in their hands. This celebration took place at 7 o'clock in the evening. And on the palace roof everywhere very many tallow candles burned, making what are called luminarios, and they also set off many rockets there, and everywhere outside the palace logs were placed and wood burned there, and everywhere in the city the Spaniards burned logs on the roofs of their houses, and the bells were rung everywhere, in all the churches and monasteries of Mexico.[1]

v Today, Saturday, the 3rd of the month of October of the year 1609, on the eve [of the feast day of] San Francisco, my dear friend Father Elías, a lay brother belonging to the order of the lord San Francisco, passed away. He lies buried at San Josef in Mexico. He was from Xochimilco. He had served in the habit for a very long time. I, Domingo de San Antón Muñón, was his friend.

v Today, Sunday, the __th of the month of November of the year 1609, was when don Juan Bautista from Malinalco, who was judge-governor in Mexico, left. [*p. 123*]

v Today, Monday the 30th of the month of November of the year 1609, on the feast day of San Andrés Apóstol, was when the former chief inquisitor, don Alonso de Peralta, was consecrated and given his spiritual rulership here in the cathedral of Mexico as archbishop appointed in the altepetl of Charcas in the land of Peru. Those who consecrated him and gave him his spiritual rulership were the two spiritual rulers don fray García Guerra, archbishop[2] in Mexico, being first, and second don Diego Vásquez de Mercado, archbishop in Manila in China, who was here at the time. And thereupon don Gutierre Bernardo de Quiroz was made chief inquisitor. He was the seventh chief inquisitor appointed here in the great altepetl and city of Mexico Tenochtitlan. The year 13 House, 1609, has come to an end.

— \\\ —

¶ 1 Rabbit Year, 1610. In this new year Francisco Sánchez, Spaniard, was made president here in Mexico Tenochtitlan concerning the governorship.[3] And the same don Antonio Valeriano the younger was alcalde, along with don Miguel Sánchez Huentzin and the other alcaldes from the four parts.[4] // And today, Wednesday, the 6th of January, on the feast

---

the reference to Francisco Sánchez, corregidor of Mexico, in the entry for March 4, 1601 (pp. 72–73 at n. 2).

4. I.e., no new alcaldes had been appointed yet.

ylhuitzin de los Reyes yeyn tlahtoq̃ yquac omomiquili ỹ Don P^{o} çuga allde te corde y presidente de audiencia real de mexico

v Auh axcan ypan metztli febrero de 1610 años yquac omachiztico ohualla tlahtolli yn ompa a la china vmpa omomiquilli yn itlaçotzin tt^{o}. Dios. Don fr. Pedro de agurdo obispo de Sepon[1] ynin Sant. Augustin teopixqui in yehuatzin in nican mexico motlacatilli nican te[*p. 124*]Piltzin. quin iceltzin criyoyo momati yn obispo omochiuhtzino quin yehuatzin quimonpehualtilli ỹ nican tepilhuan in ye tleco in ye tlahtocati —

Yhuan yquac vmpa hualhuia yn la china yn Don Rodrigo ______ ymachtzin yn tlacatl Don luis de velasco visurrey. yn axcan motlahtocatilia auh çan huey apan polihuico. yn iuh machiztico

v Auh axcan Domingo yc 28. mani metztli huel itlamian febrero de 1610 años. yquac ypan matlactli tzillini tlaca ỹ nican mexico omoquixti ynic onmopehualti ynic ompa mohuicac. a la china in teyotica tlahtohuani Don diego Pasquez de mergado arçobispo de manilla. ynin clerigo. quinmohuiquilli matlactlomomentin Sant Augustin teopixque yn ompa motemachtilizque a la china // no yquac vmpa ya ỹ mariscal la china

v Auh yn ipan omoteneuh Domingo yn itlamian metztli febrero yquac nezque yn alldesme nauhcampa mexico tenochtitlan ye o iuh yalhua sabadotica tlalliloque yn San Juan moyotlan çan ya yehuatl yn telpochtli Don Antonio valleriano. yhuan Don diego _____ yn alcaldesme. auh yn Sant. Pablo yehuantin motlallique yn Don miguel Sanchez. yhuan Don Bernabe _____ Auh yn Sant Sebastian motlallique yehuantin yn tlacatl Don diego luis de moteuhcçoma yhuan melchior _____ auh yn Sancta Maria motlallique yehuantin yn Matia _____ yhuan Sebastian _____ quin oncan inn onpeuh yn escan omoteneuh Sant. Pablo. San Sebastian Sancta maria yn oome motlallique alldesme. ytencopatzinco [*p. 125*] Yn tlahtohuani visurrey. ypampa yn tequitl mopapatlazque yn quichiazq̃ yn tleyn tequitl[2]

v axcan sabado yc 28 Março de 1610 a^{o}s. yquac oteochihualoq̃. fr. augustin del sp̄ū Santo yca Euangelio yhuã Don diego Sutelo yca misa. —

v Auh axcan Sabado Sancto yc 10. mani metztli abril de 1610 años. yquac nican mexico moquixti ynic onmopehualti ynic ompa mohuicac Pirũ. yn teoyotica tlahtohuani Don Alonso de Peralta arçobispo de las charcas yn ompa ypan tlalli Perũ

v Auh no yquac ypan yn omoteneuh metztli abril. oc ceppa ompa otequitihuato yn huehuetocan citlaltepec ompa otequitito y nohuiampa tlaca altepehuaque yn tlaxcalteca yhuan chololteca. // yhuan mexicatzinco ohtli yn atenamitl mochiuhtoc mohuecapano motlalten motlachcuitlaz. oncan tequitico yn quauhnahuaca ynic centonayan tlaca yhuã chalca amaquemeque / ce metztli ynic nenque ye ytlacoyoc Metztli Mayo. yn quitlamico ohtli mexicatzinco

v Auh axcan miercoles yc 30 mani metztli Junio de 1610 a^{o}s. yquac ocallac yn Don Juan Perez de monterrey. mestiço gouernador mexico tenochtitlan nican mexico chane yquac quicauh ynic Presidente mochiuhticatca fran^{co} Sanchez. español. // no yquac hualla españa yn iBeatificacioyotzĩ ỹ Sant. ignacio de loyola fundador de la compañia de Jesus.

v Auh axcan Sabado ome tzillini ye teotlac yc 24. mani metztli Julio de 1610 años. yquac

1. The word appears to have been written both Sebon and Sepon, in what sequence is not clear.

day of the Kings, the three rulers, was when don Pedro de [Zúñiga?], alcalde de corte and president of the Royal Audiencia of Mexico, passed away.

v Now, in the month of February of the year 1610, was when it became known here and word came from China that the beloved of our lord God, don fray Pedro de Agurto, bishop of Japan,[1] who was an Augustinian friar, passed away there. He was born here in Mexico, a child of people here. [*p. 124*] He is thought to have been the only criollo made a bishop yet; he started it that children of people here are ascending and ruling.

And at this time don Rodrigo [de Vivero], nephew of the lord don Luis de Velasco, viceroy, who governs now, was coming from China [the Philippines], but he perished on the ocean, as became known.

v Today, Sunday the 28th of the month, at the very end of February of the year 1610, was when, at 10 o'clock in the morning, the spiritual ruler don Diego Vásquez de Mercado, archbishop of Manila, set out and departed to go to China. He is a secular priest and took with him twelve Augustinian friars who are to preach in China. // Also at that time the marshal went to China.

v The said Sunday, at the end of the month of February, was when the alcaldes from the four parts of Mexico Tenochtitlan were made public; they had already been placed in office the day before, Saturday: for San Juan Moyotlan the same don Antonio Valeriano the younger, and don Diego______ as alcaldes; and for San Pablo don Miguel Sánchez and Don Bernabé_______ were installed; and for San Sebastián the lord don Diego Luis de Moteucçoma and Melchor_____ were installed; and for Santa María Matías____ and Sebastián ____ were installed. Only then did it begin that in the three said parts of San Pablo, San Sebastián, and Santa María two alcaldes each were installed, at the order of the lord viceroy, [*p. 125*] to take turns with the duties and wait to see what duty there will be.[2]

v Today, Saturday the 28th of March of the year 1610, was when frey Agustín del Espíritu Santo was ordained deacon, and don Diego Sotelo was ordained priest. —

v Today, Saturday of Holy Week, the 10th of the month of April of the year 1610, was when the spiritual ruler don Alonso de Peralta, archbishop of Charcas in the land of Peru, set out and left Mexico here to go to Peru.

v Also, in the said month of April people went again to perform duty at Huehuetocan, at Citlaltepec. The people from altepetl everywhere went to work there, including the Tlaxcalans and the Cholulans. // And the Mexicatzinco road that has been made into a dike was raised; soil and sod were thrown on it. The people of Cuernavaca and all the people of the hot lands came to work there, and the Amaquemeque of Chalco spent a month at it. / It was already halfway through the month of May when they finished the Mexicatzinco road.

v Today, Wednesday the 30th of the month of June of the year 1610, was when don Juan Pérez de Monterrey, mestizo, from Mexico here, entered [office] as governor in Mexico Tenochtitlan; at that time Francisco Sánchez, Spaniard, left [the office] he had been appointed to as president. // At the same time [news] came from Spain of the beatification of San Ignacio de Loyola, founder of the Company of Jesus.

v Today, Saturday, at 2 o'clock in the afternoon, on the 24th of the month of July in the

2. In this important passage as elsewhere, the order of the four parts is the invariable one.

ypan yPesperastzin Sanctiago Apostol. yc teopancalmamalihuac yquac yecauh yn iteopancaltzin tlatilolco vmpa yn macoto yancuic teopan yn ipan omoteneuh Pesperaspan yn icomiendatzin Santiago yn telpochtli Don fernãdo altamirano. yn inconeuh yn inpiltzin Don Juan al[*p. 126*]tamirano. yhuan Doña Maria de dircios.[1] yn ichpochtzĩ tlahtohuani Don luis de velasco marques de Salinas visurrey. yn axcan moyetztica motlahtocatilia ca yxhuiuhtzin yn omoteneuh telpochtli Don fernãdo altamirano. caPitan de la guardia. ynin yn omoteneuh encomienda ca yehuatzin quihualmomaquilli yn tohueytlahtocauh yn ompa moyetztica españa Don felipe tercero. // auh no yquac moman in yancuic retablo. auh ye quin imoztlayoc Domingotica y huel ipan ilhuitzin Sanctiago. ynic 15. Julio. yn pahpacohuac yn ilhuitl mochiuh tlatilolco ynic motlapo teopancalli yehuatzin ymactzinco yecauh yn Padre fray Juan torquemada. yn tlamico

v Auh axcan Sabado yc 31. mani metztli huell itlamian Julio de 1610 años. yquac teopancalmamalihuac yn motenehua la cassa Professa yquac motlapo ynin yancuic teopancalli yn oncan yc occã moyetzticate la compañia de Jesus. teopixque yquac quimotlallilique yc mocallaqui yn Sacramẽto. oncan quimanillico yn iglesia mayor. huey tlayahualolliztica huey ylhuichihualiztica yhuan huel ipan motlalli yn omoteneuh Sabado yn ilhuitzin yancuican yc mochiuh ytlacemicnopilhuiani Sant Ignacio de loyola fundador de la compañia de Jesus. viscaya ychantzinco ynin huel yehuatzin achtopa intatzin huel yehuatzin yancuican ytlapehualtiltzitzinhuan ytlanextiltzitzinhuan yn la compañia de Jesus teopixque yn omoteneuhtzinoa teatinos. yn ipan in omoteneuh Sabado. yquac oceliloc ỹ nican mexico yni iyectenehualocatzin Sant Ignacio. y motenehua yBeatificacioyotzin. yn oquimomacahuili [*p. 127*]Sancto Padre Paulo quinto. yn axcan moyetztica Roma. auh ynic mochiuh ylhuitl yn tlayahualoliztli ye omito yglesia mayor yn quimanillico ỹ Sancramento. ynic quimohuiquillique otlipan oncã quimoquixtilico yn seral quiyahuac yxpan purtales. oncan ce mochiuh coloquio. niman quimoquixtilico Sant. Augustin teopancalli yxpan oncan puertatitlan yc ome coloquio omochiuh niman yc nepa calnacazco õnecolloloc niman hospital del es͞pũ Sancto quimoquixtilito yc nahui[2] coloquio oncã mochiuh. auh in yehuatzin tlacemicnopilhuiani huey tetatzin Patriarcha Sant. Ignacio yn ĩtatzin clerigos. teopixque la compañia de Jesus. ayemo motlayahualhui yn ipan in mochiuh[3] tlayahualoliztli ca çan oncan yn hospital del es͞pũ Sancto teopanquiyahuac yn conmonamiquillico Sacramento. yn Sant. Ignacio. oncan quihualmoquixtilique yn ichantzinco la cassa proffessa antastica yn ipilhuãtzitzinhuan quimonapalhuique auh yn oconmonamiquillico Sacramento niman yc quimoyacanilli ynic quimocallaquillito ychantzinco yn oncan yancuic teopan la cassa proffessa motenehua ynic ynehuantzin oncan quimopielizque yancuic teopan calli ynic axcan ye mitohua Sant. Ignacio ỹ teopan. auh ynin ylhuitl mochiuh oc cenca yehuantin quichiuhque yn vizcaya tlaca españolesme ypampa ca ynSanctotzin yn omoteneuhtzino. macuilpohualli yn moJuldados. chichiuhque yn arcabuz. quitlaztiaque yn quimoyacanillique sacramento yn ipan tlayahualoliztli mo[*p. 128*]chiuh yehuatl yncapitan mochiuhtia yn Don P^o^ odallola oydor. auh yn ipan missa yehuatzin motemachtili in cenca mahuiztililoni teoyotica tlahtohuani Don fray Garcia guerra arçobispo mexico. yn ihquac mochihuin ylhuitzin yancuican Sant Ignacio de loyola ye quin o yuh nepa onpohualloncaxtolli xihuitl momiquillitzino yn ompa Roma ytzon-

---

1. This surname, which appears several times in Ch. in different forms, is given as Ircio in Sarabia Viejo 1978.

year 1610, on the eve of [the feast day of] Santiago Apóstol, was when a church building was inaugurated in his name, when his church was finished in Tlatelolco. Don Hernando Altamirano the younger went to the new church on the said eve to be given his encomienda [in the order of] Santiago; he is the child of don Juan Altamirano [*p. 126*] and doña María de Ircio,[1] daughter of the lord don Luis de Velasco, Marqués of Salinas, viceroy, who is now in residence and governs, for the said don Hernando Altamirano the younger, captain of the guard, is his grandchild. Our great ruler who resides in Spain, don Felipe III, sent orders giving him the said encomienda. // At the same time a new altarpiece was set up, but not until the next day, on Sunday, right on the feast day of Santiago, the 15th of July, was there rejoicing and the feast day was celebrated in Tlatelolco, and the church was opened. It was finished and completed under the direction of Father fray Juan de Torquemada.

v Today, Saturday the 31st of the month, right at the end of July of the year 1610, was when the church called the Casa Profesa was inaugurated, and this new church was opened as a second place where the religious of the Company of Jesus reside. At this time they installed and brought in the Sacrament; they came to get it from the cathedral with a great procession and great celebration. It was installed right on the said Saturday, when for the first time the feast day of the all-deserving San Ignacio de Loyola, founder of the Company of Jesus, from Biscay, was celebrated. He was the very first father of the religious of the Company of Jesus, called Theatines, and they were first started and manifested by him. It was on the said Saturday that the blessing of San Ignacio, called his beatification, which the Holy Father Paul V, now residing in Rome, bestowed upon him, was received here in Mexico. [*p. 127*] As to how the feast day and procession were held, it was already said that they came to the cathedral to get the Sacrament and took it along the streets. They brought it by outside the municipal building, facing the arcades; there a speech was held. Then they brought it in front of the Augustinian church, next to the door, and a second speech was held. Then they turned around the corner on the far side and took it by the Hospital of Espíritu Santo, where a fourth[2] speech was held. The all-deserving great father and patriarch San Ignacio, the father of the priests and religious of the Company of Jesus, did not yet go in the said[3] procession. San Ignacio only came to meet the Sacrament outside the church at the Hospital of Espíritu Santo; his children [the Jesuits] brought him out of his home, the Casa Profesa, bearing him on a carrying platform. When he had come to meet the Sacrament, he led it, taking it into his home, the new church called the Casa Profesa, so that they will keep both of them at the new church, the church now being called San Ignacio. This feast day that was held was celebrated especially by the Spaniards who are Basques, because the said [San Ignacio] is their saint. A hundred men gotten up as soldiers, who went shooting off harquebuses, went ahead of the Sacrament. When the procession was held, [*p. 128*] don Pedro Otalora, judge of the Audiencia, went as their captain. And at the mass the very reverend spiritual ruler don fray García Guerra, archbishop in Mexico, preached. When the feast day of San Ignacio de Loyola was celebrated for the first time, it had been 55 years since he passed away in

2. Either "third" is meant, or even more likely, mention of a third site and occasion was inadvertently omitted.

3. It appears that "omoteneuh" was intended here.

teconpa yn cemanahuatl auh oc cenca huel momahuiçohua ynic oquiz ylhuichihuililocatzin mexico yn omoteneuhtzino Sant. Ignacio. yn ayemo ycenyo yn ilhuichihuililocatzin omochiuh ye niman hueylhuitl yn omochiuh ynic ycatzinco opahpacohuac ynic cenca miequintin çatepan oquinextique yn tlahueliloque oquimomahuizpolhuique yntlacuiloltica yn aquique conçaçalohuaya puertatitech yn oncan yglesia mayor yohualtica. auh quenmache oc tlapanahuia hueylhuitl mochihuatiuh yniquin quenman quimonequiltitzinotiuh tt^o. Dios ynic mochipauhtzinoz ynic quimocencahuilizque ynic Sancto cemahuiço macoz. ynic tlamiz. yn icanonizatoyotzin motenehua yehica ypampa yn axcan yntla çan oc in yectenehuallocatzin yBeatificacioyotzin general yniquilhuitzin omochiuh auh ye niman huey yn ilhuichihuililocatzin omochiuh mexico yn ayac oc ce Sancto yuh ycatzinco omochiuh ceppa nican Mexico.

v̲ Axcan miercoles. yc .8.tia Metztli Setiembre de 1610. años. yquac nican mexico ohualla tlahtolli yn ompa españa yuh omachiztico yn ompa Rey catca francia yn itoca [*p. 129*] Dõ henrriq̃. quarto. Oquimictique. auh yn quimicti çan ce ymacehual ybaxe ycalliticnencauh amo pilli amo cauallero çan cuitlapilli atlapalli. yn iuh machiztico çan otlica caltzallan yn quiquechcoton yhtic coche yetihuia yn tlahtohuani Rey. ynehuan yetihuia ce obispo Nuncio mitohua auh ynic quiquechcoton çan carta conmacaya yn oncann icocheco ynic no yehuatl hualtlachiaya hualmoquechanaya yn tlahtohuani yn oncan conquechcoton amo huel momati yn tle yca auh ynic otlica nenca Rey. yn ihtic ciudad quiytztinenca yn otli yn aço qualli ynic oncan pahpacohuaz. yn ipampa ynamic Reyna. ynic corona macoz. ynic cihuatlahtohuani francia.

v̲ Auh axcan sabado yc 18.tia metztli Setiembre de 1610 años. yquac oteochihualloc yca missa in yehuatzin notlaçotatzin fray Augustin del sp̄ū Sancto ytechtzinco pohui totlaçotatzin. Sant Antonio Abbad. çan ce ynehuan yquac o no teochihualoc yca Epistula yn fray Thomas de libera Santo Domingo teopixqui Amaquemecan chalco ychan ypiltzin Marcos de libera. yxhuimontzin yn tlacatl Don Juan de sandoual tequanxayacatzin teohuateuhctli tlahtohuani catca tlayllotlacã Amaquemecan chalco. auh ynin yn omoteneuhtzinoque omentintzitzin teopixque yehuatzin oquinmoteochihuilli yn cenca mahuiztililoni teoyotica tlahtohuani Don fray Garcia guerra arçobispo mexico. oncan yn Sancto Domingo moteteochihuilli Mexico. [*p. 130*]

v̲ Axcan lunes. yc 20.tia metztli Setiembre de 1610. años. yquac omomiquilli yn tlacatl Don Miguel Sanchez huetzin. acatla pilli ça ycel ocatca yniquitechpa oquizticatca yn itlacamecayo yn tlacatl catca yn huehue tlacayeleltzin cihuacohuatl condeStable mexico tenochtitlan. auh yn omoteneuh miccatzintli yehuatl o ytech tlamico yn acatla pilotl quicentlamitiuh

v̲ Axcan Dõmingo yc 10 metztli octubre de 1610 años. yquac omonamicti yn tlacatl Don Antonio valleriano telpochtli oquimonamicti yn cihuapilli Doña Barbara çan ihuayolcatzin. yn in omoteneuhque yccatotonhuan yn tlacatl Don diego de aluarado huanitzin tlahtohuani catca tenochtitlan

v̲ Axcan Domingo ye yohuac matlactli tzillini yc 31.tia metztli octubre de 1610 años. yquac omomiquilli yn Don Juan altamirano comendador Sanctiago ymõtzin catca yn tlacatl Don luis de velasco. Marques de Salinas. visurrey mexico yn axcan moyetztica motlahtocatilia auh ye quin lunes y motocac ye teotlac chiquacen tzilini yn quiquixtique ychan huel mahuiztic yuhquin Juebes Sancto ynic quihuicaque ynacayo ynic quitocato

Rome, capital of the world. And there was especially great wonderment about how the feast day of the said San Ignacio was celebrated before his feast day had been entirely established, that already a great feast day and celebration was held for him, as many scoundrels afterward manifested and made insults about him in writing, sticking them on the doors of the cathedral at night. How much greater even will be the celebration of the feast day when someday our lord God deigns that [San Ignacio] be purified and prepared so that he will be made a saint in full honor, so that what is called his canonization will be completed, because now it is still only because of his blessing, his general beatification, that his feast day was held, and then already his day was celebrated more greatly than was ever done for any other saint here in Mexico.

v Today, Wednesday the 8th of the month of September of the year 1610, was when news came from Spain to Mexico here and it became known that the late king in France, named [*p. 129*] don Enrique IV, was killed. The person who killed him was just one of his vassals, his page, a servant living in his house, not a noble, not a gentleman, just a commoner. As became known, when the ruler, the king, was riding in his coach together with a bishop called the nuncio [papal ambassador], just on the road, on the street, he cut off his head. As to how he cut off his head, he was just giving him a letter in his coach, so that the ruler looked this way and stretched out his neck, where he cut off his head, with what cannot be established. As to why the king was going along the streets inside the city, he was going inspecting the streets to see if they were good for celebrations there on account of his spouse the queen, when she was to be given the crown as queen in France.

v Today, Saturday, the 18th of the month of September of the year 1610, was when my precious father fray Agustín del Espíritu Santo was ordained as [a priest with permission to hold] mass. He belongs to [the order of] our precious father San Antonio Abad. At that time just one other person was ordained together with him, as subdeacon, fray Tomás de Ribera, a Dominican friar from Amaquemecan Chalco, child of Marcos de Ribera, grandson-in-law of the lord don Juan de Sandoval Tequanxayacatzin, Teohuateuctli, who was ruler in Tlailotlacan Amaquemecan Chalco. The very reverend spiritual ruler don fray García Guerra, archbishop in Mexico, ordained the two said religious; he performed the ordainment at Santo Domingo in Mexico. [*p. 130*]

v Today, Monday the 20th of the month of September of the year 1610, was when the lord don Miguel Sánchez Huentzin, a noble of Acatlan, passed away. He was the only one left, so that with him ended the line of the late lord Tlacaelleltzin the elder, the cihuacoatl, high constable in Mexico Tenochtitlan. With the said dead person the nobility of Acatlan came to an end, he terminated it once and for all.

v Today, Sunday the 10th of the month of October of the year 1610, was when the lord don Antonio Valeriano the younger got married; he married the noblewoman doña Bárbara, his relative. The aforementioned are the great-grandchildren of the lord don Diego de Alvarado Huanitzin, who was ruler in Tenochtitlan.

v Today, Sunday, at ten o'clock at night, on the 31st of the month of October of the year 1610, was when don Juan Altamirano, comendador of Santiago, passed away. He was the son-in-law of the lord don Luis de Velasco, Marqués of Salinas, viceroy in Mexico, who is now in residence and rules. On the following Monday he was buried. At 6 o'clock in the afternoon they brought him out of his home. The way they took his body and went to

Sant Fran.co yehuantzitzin quinapaloque yn izquican teopixque yn prouincialesme yhuã prioresme. yhuan oncan mohuicac ye quiyacatitia ỹ teoyotica tlahtohuani Don fr Garcia guerra arçobispo yhuan mochtin yn canonigosme yn cabildotlaca.[1] Auh yn tlahtohuani Don luis de velasco visurrey. [*p. 131*] ça motlatoquillitia ytloctzinco yyopochcopatzinco ycatia yn ixhuiuhtzin Don fernando altamirano capitã de la guardia çanno comendador S.tiago ypiltzin y moteneuh miccatzintli.

v Axcan can[2] Domingo yc 14.tia metztli Nuuiembre de 1610. años. yquac yancuic missa oquimochihuilli y notlaçotatzin fray Augustin del Spũ Sancto. yteopixcatzin yn totlaçotatzin Señor S. Antonio Abbad. nican yteopanchantzinco ciudad mexico. auh yehuantzitzin Padrinos. mochiuhtzinoque yn cenca mahuiztililonime Padres Juan de touar. redor colegio S. grego yhuã yehuatzin Sancti esteuan auh yn omotemachtili yehuatzin yn Padre Gaspar meneses. ymeyxtintzitzin la compañia de Jesus teopixque

v Axcan miercoles. yc 17.tia metztli Nouiembre de 1610 años. yquac omotlalli retablo yn oncan yglesia mayor. teopan yn oncan ycapillatzinco Señor Sant grego Thamaturgo obispo confesor Padron totepantlatocatzĩ mexico ytechpa ynic oapachihuia altepetl mexico tenochtitlan ynic amo huel opoliuh.[3] auh ynic quimotlalilique omoteneuhtzino Sancto yn oncan ycapillatzin huey tlayahualoliztica oncan quimanillico yn Sant. Augustin. yn ciudad tlaca. mochintin yn tlahtoque visurrey. oydores. ynic mochintin omicuiloque[4] oncan ycapillatzin Sancto yn iuh neztica axcan [*p. 132*]

v axcan lunes yc 15.[5] mani metztli Nouiembre de 1610 años. yquac nican mexico callaquico yn Don Rodrigo de vivero vmpa hualla Jabun a la china ynahuac. auh ynic yahca vmpa a la china yn oncan ytocayocan manilla oncan gouortito yn omoteneuh Don Rodrigo. ynin ymachtzin yn tlahtohuani Don luis de velasco visurrey. auh atlan poliuhca ye yc hualhuia nican mexico. mochi polihuico yn itlatqui auh ompa quinhuicac yn ayehecatl yn Jabun ompa atenquiçato ynic ypan callaquito yn huey tlatohuani emperador yn oncã tlahtocati Jabun oncan monotzque oncan quimocniuhti yn Don Rodrigo. yhuan oncan quihuallaneuhti quexquich ytlatqui y quihualcuic nican mexico Don Rodrigo. yhuan quezquintin oquinhualhuicac yn ompa tlaca Jabun. auh yn iuh machoca nican mexico ca atlan hueyapan omomiquillico ỹ Don Rodrigo ynic ompa huallehuaca manilla auh ya ce xiuhtica ynic axcan onecico ynic ocallaquico mexico. auh ynic callaquico çacan[6] oqu icel ỹ nican mexico. çan oc otlipan quinhualcauhtiquiz yhuiantzin yatihuitze ỹ nican huitze Jabun tlaca yn ompa quinhuallehuiti Jabun. yn o yuh atenquiçaco oncan al puerto acapolco çan niman quihualyacatitiquiz yn Don Rodrigo.

v Axcan Domingo yc 12 tia metztli de diciembre de 1610. años. yquac ye teotlac chiquacen tzilini yn ocallaquico monjastin. yn oncan monasterio Sancta Monica. nahuintin yhuã omentin noficias. ye chiquacemin yn onca callaquico cochetica. [*p. 133*] Y huallaque. vmpa hualquizque. yn huey Monasterio. concepcio. Ayoticpac. oncan fundadoras mochihuaco. yn monasterio. S.ta Monica. auh yehuatl oncan inPatron yhquac. mochiuh. yn Doctor Don fernando de villegas. quinpachoz. yn monjastin. oncan callaquizque. ca yuh yehuatzin quimomamaltilli in teoyotica tlahtovani Don fray Garcia Guerra arçobispo. Mexico. yehuatzin. quimomaquilli. yn Patronasco.

---

1. It seems that the members of the cathedral chapter are meant.
2. The *can* of "Axcan" is inadvertently repeated.
3. Or was not able to be destroyed.

bury him at San Francisco was truly impressive, like on Maundy Thursday. The religious who were provincial heads and priors of the different orders carried him; the spiritual ruler don fray García Guerra, archbishop, went ahead of him, along with all the canons and members of the cabildo.[1] And the lord don Luis de Velasco, viceroy, [*p. 131*] just followed behind. At his left side went his grandchild don Hernando Altamirano, captain of the guard, also a comendador of Santiago, child of the said deceased.

v Today,[2] Sunday the 14th of the month of November of the year 1610, was when my precious father fray Agustín del Espíritu Santo, religious of our precious father the lord San Antonio Abad, said mass for the first time here at his [San Antonio's] church in the city of Mexico. The very reverend fathers Juan de Tovar, rector of the Colegio of San Gregorio, and ______ San Esteban became sponsors, and Father Gaspar de Meneses preached; all three are religious of the Company of Jesus.

v Today, Wednesday the 17th of the month of November of the year 1610, was when an altarpiece was set up in the cathedral, in the chapel of the lord San Gregorio Taumaturgo, bishop, confessor, patron, and our intercessor in Mexico, concerning how when there was flooding here in the altepetl of Mexico Tenochtitlan, it was not entirely destroyed,[3] so that they established his chapel there for the said saint with a great procession. The members of the Spanish cabildo and all the high lords, viceroy and Audiencia judges, came to San Agustín to get him, so that all their names were inscribed[4] in the chapel of the saint as they now appear. [*p. 132*]

v Today, Monday the 15th[5] of the month of November of the year 1610, was when don Rodrigo de Vivero entered Mexico here. He came from Japan, close to China [the Philippines]. The reason the said don Rodrigo had gone to China, to the place called Manila, was to be governor there; he was the nephew of the lord don Luis de Velasco, viceroy. And he came to grief on the sea; as he was coming here to Mexico, all his possessions were lost, and the storms carried them to Japan, where he landed, so that he found there and entered the presence of the great ruler, the emperor, who rules in Japan. There they talked; [the emperor] made friends with don Rodrigo and lent him all the goods he brought here to Mexico, and don Rodrigo brought a few of the people from there in Japan. It had been thought here in Mexico that don Rodrigo had died on the water, the ocean, when he left Manila coming in this direction, but after a year he now appeared and entered Mexico. When he entered here in Mexico, it was just[6] by himself; he left behind on the road the Japanese who were coming here and leaving Japan to come at their leisure after they had landed at the port of Acapulco; don Rodrigo hurried ahead of them.

v Today, Sunday the 12th of the month of December of the year 1610, was when, at 6 o'clock in the afternoon, nuns entered the convent of Santa Mónica. There were four of them along with two novices, so that six entered. They came in a carriage; [*p. 133*] they left from the great convent of Concepción in Ayoticpac, coming as founders of the convent of Santa Mónica, and doctor don Fernando de Villegas became their patron at that time; he is to govern the nuns who enter there, for the spiritual ruler don fray García Guerra, archbishop in Mexico, gave him that responsibility, gave him the position of patron.

---

4. Or a painting of them was put there.

5. Monday the 15th is compatible with Wednesday the 17th even though the usual order is reversed.

6. For "ca çan."

v Axcan Juebes. teotlac. yc 16. mani metztli de diciembre de 1610. años. yhquac ye chiquacentzillini. nican yhtic ciudad Mexico. ahcico. yc callaquico. aço huel caxtollonnahui tlacatl. yn Jabon china tlaca. ce pilli ynteuhcyo yn quinhualhuicac. enbaxador. ynteuhctitlan yn huey tlahtohuani emperador jabon. tlamatca yeliztli paz. quichihuaco. yn inhuicpa christianosme. ynic ayc moyaochihuazque. çan mochipa tlamatcayezque. motlaçotlazque ynic huel callaquizque. españoles. mercaderes. pochteca. yn õpa Jabon. ayac huel quintzacuiliz. yn ompa tlaca. auh çanno yhui yehuantin Jabon tlaca. huel hualcallaquizque. ỹ nican Mexico. motlayecoltiquihui. nican quinamacaquihui. yn tleyn intlatqui ompa mochihua. ayac aquin huel nican. quintzacuilliz. ca yuh quinmonahuatilli yn quimottillico tlahtohuani visurrey Don luis de velasco. marques de Salinas. auh yehuatl nican quinhualhuicac. çan ce hueyatenquiçaco. yn Don Rodrigo. de viuero. vmpa Governadortito. yn ipan ciudad Manilla china. ynin ymachtzin. yn tlahtohuani Don luis de velasco Marques. visurrey Mexico. yniquimachtzin. ytechpa [*p. 134*] Yn inamictzin. catca. auh ynin omoteneuh Don Rodrigo de viuero. ca poliuhca huey apan. ynic hualhuia nican mexico. yuh machiztico yn axcan ye ce xihuitl. ypan de 1609. años. ynic ye chialloya. auh ayac quiçaco. çatepã yuh mihto. aço polihuico. yn acalli. aço tlapanico cana huey apan. anoçe o ypan pollaquico. yn ica tlatquitl. yn iuh mochihuani quenmanian. huel yuh nemachoc. yn Mexico. ca opolihuico. opollaquico yn acalli. yn ihtic hualyetihuia Don Rodrigo. auh ãca ce ye.[1] ayehecatl ỹpã moquetz. in huey apan. yn ica yehecatica atocotiaq̃. auh yn intlatqui. quihualcuia. moch atitlã quitlazq̃.[2] ça yuhq̃. ynic ompa quinhuicac vmpa atenquiçato. yn ipan huey tlahtocaaltepetl Jabon. ynic ompa çan tlamatca yocoxca. quihualnamicque yn Jabon tlaca. mottaque ynehuã yn tlahtohuani Emperador. Jabon. yuh machiztico. ytecpanchan ypalacio. yn mochantito cenca quitlaçotlac. quitlaqualtiaya. yhuan vmpa ypal motlatlanehui yn Don Rodrigo. yn Emperador. Jabon. cenca miyec mill yn itlatqui. vmpa quihualtlaneuhti. y nican quihualhuicac mexico Don Rodrigo. auh no yehuatl ypampa ynic quĩhualhuicac Jabon tlaca quicuico. yn izqui mil pesos. ytlaneuh Don Rodrigo. auh in yehuantin in omoteneuhque jabon tlaca. ynic nican huallaque. ca ya cequintin christianosme. auh cequintin oc tlateotocanime. ayemo moquatequiaya. yhuan çan ye mochiuh hualmochichiuhtiaque. yn iuh vmpa mochichihua. yn iuhqui çan inxicolhuipil quimaquia ypan mocuitlalpia yn intlacotian yn inpitzahuayan oncan quitecatihui ce gadana tepoztli yuhqui yn imespada ypã ponhui. yhuan çan iuhqui tlamantillahuia.[3] auh yn incac. yamanqui tlayamanilli cuetlaxtli [*p. 135*] Yn Motenehua gamoça. yuhquin ma çã xocpalvandes.[4] ypan pohui. yc caquia. ymicxic. yuhquin aquen momamamati. amo yocoxcatlaca. amo mocnomatcatlaca. çan iuhquin quaquauhti. yc nemi. auh huel moyequixquapetzohua. ynic moyequixquaytzxima huel yn quayollonepantla. conaxitia. ynic mixquapetzxima. auh çan in canahuacan. onpeuhtica. ynic ye moch incuexcochtlanpa. tlayahuallotoc. yn intzoncal. huey acatzoneque. ynquechpan ahci. ynic mohueyacatzontia. quiyacatequi.[5] yuhquin ma ychpopochtin. yc neci. yn ipampa yc motzonquentia. auh yn achi hueyac yntzon yn cuexcochtlan. yuhquin ma ynpiyoch.[6] quicetilia. ynic quillacatzcocolilpia.[7] auh yniquin quayollonepantli caxitia. ynic moyecytzquaxipetzxima. huel yuh ypan neci corona. quiteca. yn imicpac. yehica yn incanahuacan yhuan yncuexcochtlan. hueyac. yn intzon tlayahual-

1. The division of the words and their analysis at this point is uncertain.
2. To stay afloat, presumably.
3. Headgear for women, a light scarf over head and shoulders.
4. The form "vandes" equals *guantes*.

v Today, Thursday in the afternoon, the 16th of the month of December of the year 1610, at 6 o'clock, was when perhaps as many as nineteen people from Japan, in China, arrived and entered here in the city of Mexico. A noble, their lord, the ambassador, from the court of the great ruler the emperor in Japan, who brought them, came to make peace with the Christians so that they would never make war but always be at peace and esteem each other, so that Spanish merchants will be able to enter Japan and none of the people there will be able to impede them. And likewise the people of Japan will be able to come enter Mexico here to do business, to come here to sell their goods that are made there, and no one here will be able to impede them, for thus the lord Viceroy don Luis de Velasco, Marqués of Salinas, whom they came to see, informed them. Don Rodrigo de Vivero brought them here; they had all landed together; he had gone to be governor in the city of Manila in China, and was the nephew of the ruler don Luis de Velasco, Marqués, viceroy in Mexico; he was his nephew through [*p. 134*] his spouse. This said don Rodrigo de Vivero had gotten lost on the ocean as he was coming here to Mexico, as became known today. A year ago, in the year 1609, when he was already expected, no one came. Later it was said that perhaps the ship was lost, or broke up somewhere on the ocean, or sank in it with the goods as happens sometimes. It was really thought that the ship in which don Rodrigo was coming was lost and sank. It turns out[1] that a sea storm arose over them in the ocean, and they went along driven by the winds of the storm, and they threw all their goods they were bringing in the water,[2] and in that condition the storm carried them to where they landed in the great royal altepetl of Japan, where the people of Japan met them in peace; the ruler, the emperor in Japan [and don Rodrigo] met together. It became known that he went to reside at his palace; he made much of him, fed him, and there don Rodrigo borrowed from the emperor in Japan; he came having borrowed very many thousand [pesos] belonging to him that don Rodrigo brought here to Mexico. And also because of that don Rodrigo came bringing people of Japan to come get the so and so many thousand pesos that he borrowed. And some of the said people of Japan who came here were already Christians and some still idolaters who were not yet baptized. And they came gotten up as they are gotten up there; they wear something like an ornamented jacket, doublet, or long blouse, which they tie at their middle, their waist; there they place a catana [Asian cutlass] of metal, which counts as their sword, and they wear something like a mantilla.[3] And their footwear is soft, softened leather [*p. 135*] called chamois, counting just like foot-gloves[4] that they put on their feet. They seem bold, not gentle and meek people, going about like eagles. And their foreheads are very bare because they closely shave their foreheads, making the shaving of their foreheads reach to the middle of their heads. Their hair just begins at their temples, all going around toward the nape of their necks. They are long-haired; their hair reaches to their necks from their letting it grow long. They [cut only the tips?];[5] they look like girls because of the way they wear their hair. Their hair is rather long at the neck; they put together something like a *piochtli*,[6] which they tie in twisted, intertwined fashion,[7] reaching to the middle of the head with close shaving. It really looks like a tonsure that they display on their heads,

---

5. The verb *yacatequi* seems to contain *yacatl*, "nose, tip, point, front part," and *tequi*, "to cut." The word as such has so far not been located in works of reference or other texts.

6. Hair left on the nape of the neck of Nahua boys when they got a haircut.

7. Braid it? Make a bun?

lotoc[1] yhuan amo tentzoneque. yhuan çan iuhquin cihua xayaqueque. yhuan çan iztalecpopol. ynic chipahuaque. yn inxayac. çan iztalectic. moch iuhque yn Jabon tlaca. yuhqui yn nacayo. yhuan amo cenca quauhtique. yn iuh mochi tlacatl. oquimittac. auh ynic nican mexico. callaquico. cenca quimahuiztilique. yn yehuatl vmpa pille. yn inpillo hualmochiuhtia Jabon tlaca. chapoltepec quinamictito. yn icochetzin visurrey. yn huel ye in yaxcatzin. ynic moquixtia ohtlipan. yehuatl yn quimotitlanilili. yn ihtic hualmotlallique. ynehuan ce teopixqui descalso. yn ompa quihualhuicaque Jabon. quinhualnahuatlahtalhuitia. yhuã ce oydor. yn quinnamiquito. chapoltepec. ynic õcã [*p. 136*] yc quiçaco. huallaque. jabonti. auh ynic oncan huallehuaque chapoltepec. yn omoteneuh coche. yhtic hualyetiaque. ymeyxtin. yn pilli Jabon yhuan teopixqui descalso. yhuan oydor. ynic callaquico yhtic ciudad. mexico. S. Augustin. teopancaltitlan. motlallico. auh ye quin imoztlayoc. yn quimottilique tlahtohuani visurrey. auh ynic nican mexico catca ynic motlallico. Rey[2] yn quintlaqualtiaya.

¶ 2. Acatl xihuitl 1611. años. axcan yehuatl ipan ĩ yn ome acatl xihuitl. yn iuh quihtotihui. quiteneuhtihui. huehuetque tachcocolhuan. toxiuh molpillia yn õpohuallonmatlacxiuhtica ypan onxiuhtica. yuh mochiuhtiuh. yn molpillitiuh yn inxiuh huehuetque. yn maca çan temallacatl. ynic yatiuh. ynic mocuecueptiuh ynic momallacachotiuh. // auh yn ipan in yancuic xihuitl. yhuan yancuic metztli henero. yn ipan. omotlallique. al~~lde~~sme. Mexico. S. Juan Moyotlan tlaca Joseph xuarez tlecuiltzin. S. Anton acatla chane. yhuan Sebastian _____ atiçapan chane. auh fiscal. S. Fran^{co}. mochiuh. yn Don Antonio valeriano. telpochtli tequicaltitlã chane auh yn S. Pablo. tlaca al~~lde~~sme. mochiuhque. hernando teuhcxochitzin. tlachcuititlan chane. yhuan. _____[3]
v Axcan Miercoles. yc. 12. mani Metztli henero de 1611. [*p. 137*] Años yhquac yc onyohuac. ye matlactlonce tzillini. çan iciuhca yxtomamiquiliztica.[5] momiquilli. amo cocoliztli. ynic momiquilli. Señora[4] leonor Marin. Patrona yn teopan. S. Anton. ycnocihuatzĩtli yn illamatlacatl. ynamictzin catca yn señor. Diego de Muñon. Patrones. ocatca. yn iteopanchantzinco Señor. S. Anton Abbad. Mexico xolloco. ythatzitzinhuã moyetzticatca. yn cenca mahuiztililoni. Padre fray Augustin del Spīu Sancto. yteopixcatzin. yhuan fundador. yn iteopixcatlatecpanpantzinco.[6] yn ireligiontzin. Señor. S. Anton. yn axcan oncan ye no yehuatzin Patron mochiuhtzinotica. quimopiallia. yn iteopancaltzin Sancto. S. Antontzin. oncan quinmochillitica. yniqu in españa hualmohuicazque. yn teoyotica ynhermanotzitzinhuan teopixque. yn motenehua canonigos. reclares.[7] yhuã yc monotza comendadores. de S. Anton —
v Axcan Juebes. yc. 20 mani metztli henero de 1611 años. yhquac ypan ylhuitzin catca. S. Sebastian. yn mocallaqui sacramento. y yancuic teopan S. Sebastian. atzaqualco.

1. This whole passage about hairstyling broaches a topic very rare in older Nahuatl texts; the translation is likely to contain a substantial amount of error.

2. *Rey* for *virrey* or *visorrey* may have been a simple slip on Ch.'s part. It is not, however, unheard of in older Nahuatl texts in general.

3. The alcaldes for San Sebastián Atzaqualco and Santa María Cuepopan are not mentioned, though an empty space was left for them.

4. Note how exactly Ch. reflects Spanish usage here. He calls Leonor Marín señora because she was not entitled to the "doña" used so liberally with the wives of viceroys and

because long hair goes around from their temples to the nape of their neck.[1] And they do not have beards, and they have faces like women, and they are whitish and light, with whitish or yellowish faces. All the people of Japan are like that, that is how their corporal aspect is, and they are not very tall, as everyone saw them. When they entered Mexico here, the nobleman from there who came appointed as the leader of the Japan people was greatly honored. The carriage of the viceroy, his very own property, went to Chapoltepec to meet him as he was passing by on the road. He sent to him, sitting in the coach together, a Discalced friar whom they brought from Japan, who came to interpret for them, and a judge of the Audiencia who went to Chapoltepec to meet him, when the Japanese came by [*p. 136*] on the way here. And when they came from Chapoltepec, inside the said carriage rode all three of them, the nobleman from Japan, the Discalced friar, and the judge. When they entered the city of Mexico, they came to establish themselves next to the Augustinian church, and not until the next day did they see the lord viceroy; and while they stayed here in Mexico, it was the [vice]roy[2] who fed them.

¶ 2 Reed year, 1611. Now in this 2 Reed year, as the ancients our forebears said and mentioned, our years are tied, as was done every 52 years that the years of the ancients went along being tied, as though it were a wheel in its manner of going returning upon itself and revolving. // And in this new year and in the new month of January alcaldes were installed in Mexico: for the San Juan Moyotlan people, Josef Juárez Tlecuiltzin, citizen of San Antón Acatlan, and Sebastián _____, citizen of Atiçapan; don Antonio Valeriano the younger, citizen of Tequicaltitlan, became fiscal at San Francisco, and the alcaldes appointed for the San Pablo people were Hernando Teucxochitzin, citizen of Tlachcuititlan, and _____.[3]

v Today, Wednesday, the 12th of the month of January of the year 1611, [*p. 137*] was when at 11 o'clock at night señora[4] Leonor Marín passed away quickly and [unaccountably],[5] not of illness. She was patron of the church of San Antón, a widow and old woman, who was the spouse of señor Diego de Muñon; they were patrons of the churchly home of lord San Antón Abad in Mexico Xoloco and parents of the very reverend father fray Agustín del Espíritu Santo, religious and founder in the religious order[6] of lord San Antón, who now likewise becomes patron there and is in charge of the church building of the saint San Antón; there he is awaiting the time when his spiritual brothers will come from Spain, the religious who are called regular[7] canons and comendadores of San Antón.

v Today, Thursday, the 20th of the month of January of the year 1611, was when, on the feast day of San Sebastián, the Sacrament was brought into the new church of San

---

encomenderos. We can conclude that the Muñón family was of relatively modest social origins.

5. The sense of this word is deduced mainly from the context. In the form *ixtoma-miquiliztica*, *-miquiliztica* is "by death," and *ixtoma-* defines the type of death. The root resembles *ixtomahua*, which often has the sense of haphazardly, without apparent purpose or reason. See the same word in a similar context, pp. 214–25 at n. 2 (Apr 16, 1612).

6. For "iteopixcatlatecpantzinco."

7. Presumably for Spanish *reglares*.

yhquac yecauh and TT4tin padreme. yhuan atzaqualca. yn oncan quiquetzque ahuatonco. yexiuhtica. yn oyecahuico. teocalli. ynic quichiuhque atzaqualca. ya yehuantin ypan motlahtoltique. yn S. Augustin Padreme. canel yehuantin ye quinmopachilhuia. yn atzaqualca. in ye yxquich ica. ye quincauhque. yn achtopa yn tahuan yn intepachocahuan catca. calmenitas. descalços. Padreme. yn oquicuique. yn oquimotechtique. yn inhuehueteocal[1] [*p. 138*] catca atzaqualca. yn axcan yhtic cate. quipia yn calmenitas. ca yehuatl huel ymaxca. achtopa ỹ macehualtin[2] atzaqualca. çan oquincuillique. ynic oncan in hualmiquani. ahuatonco. yn iteocaltzin Señor S. Sebastian. oncan ye no ye quiquetzaco. yn atzaqualca. yhuan oncan omochiuh yn inmonasterio.tzin Padreme S. Augustin. ynic cemihcac oncan moyetztiezque. quinmopachilhuiz. que yn atzaqualca. yn axcan omoteneuh oncan omocallaqui Sacramento. cenca huey tlamahuiztililiztica. yhuan tlayahualoliztica. oncan quimanillico. yn huey teopan. colegio. de la compañia de Jesus. teatinos.

v̲ Axcan Domingo. ypan ome tzillini. ynic 23. mani metztli. henero de 1611. años. yhquac teopan. S. Fran^{co}. omoquatequique. omentin. yn ohuallaque Jabon tlaca. huel tlamahuiztililiztica. yn quatequilloque. moch oncan nezque. mochintĩ ymixpan mochiuh. yn ixquichtin nepapan teopixque mexico. onoque. ynic ce moquatequi. yehuatl yn pilli teuhctli Jabon. ytoca mochiuh yn onca ypan baptismo Don Alonso. teoyotica. ythatzin mochiuh yn Don hernando de altamirano. capitan de la guarda. yn ihquac auh ynic ome moquatequi Jabon tlacatl. ytoca mochiuh. lurenço. teoyotica ytatzin mochiuh. yn Don Pedro altamirano. yn moquatequique yn. huel ypan ylhuitzin catca. S. Ilefonso. arcobispo[3] de Toledo. // auh ye no nicuel. ynic omilhuitl. yn ipan lunes. ye no ceppa ce tlacatl. moquatequi. yn Jabon tlacatl. ytoca mochiuh pelipe. teoyotica ythatzin mochiuh yn Don gonçalo de monrroy.

v̲ Axcan sabado. yc .29. mani metztli henero de 1611. años. [*p. 139*] Yhquac capitulo. mochiuh nican mexico. S. Fran^{co}. yehuatl prouincial mochiuh. yn Padre fr. hernando[4] duran. cuitlaxcohuapan. ychan. criyoyo. quin huel yuhti axcan criyoyo. nican otlacat. ypan nueua españa. prouincial omochiuhca yn ompa yc ye yzqui xihuitl. ahcico. achto. matlactlomome. Padreme S. Fran^{co}. nican nueua españa. ca çan oc moch huitze castilla. yn omochiuhtinenca prouinciales. yn ipan izquitetl capitulo. onhualmochiuhtia. auh ca quin axcan ypan in yn omoteneuh capitulo. onpeuh ontzintic. ynic huel prouinciales. mochihuazque. criyoyos. ỹ nican tepilhuan nueua españa S. Fran^{co} teopixq̃. auh yn ipan capitulo. omoteneuh yn axcã. omochiuh. yhquac nican capilla S. Joseph. S. Fran^{co}. capillero. omochiuh yn fr. Jeronomio de çarate. capellan motenehua.

v̲ Axcan lunes. yc .7. mani metztli Março de 1611 años. yhquac nican mexico. quiz. onpeuh. yn sebastian vizcayno. vezino. mexico. general mochiuhtia. yn a la china acalli yc yah vmpa a la china.[5] yhquac niman quinhuicac. yn Jabon tlaca. ytloc quiquetztia.[6] yn pilli Jabon in ye ytoca Don Alonso. ye moespañolchichiuhtia. ynic mocuep ychan. nican quitlaçaco yn itech ompa hualyetiaca. ynechichiuh çan icel. yn motlapatillico nican mexico. yhuan çan ome metztico. ynic nican mexico catca. yn mocuepque ynchan cax-

1. The word could also be interpreted as "patrimonial church," inherited over generations and belonging to them by right.
2. Here meaning people, population of Atzaqualco.
3. For "arçobispo."
4. First "diego" was written, then crossed out.

Sebastián in Atzaqualco; at that time the new church building of the fathers of San Agustín was finished, and the Atzaqualca erected it at Ahuatonco. It took three years for the church to be finished and the Atzaqualca to make it. The Augustinian fathers saw to it because they have been governing the Atzaqualca ever since their first fathers and governors, who were the Discalced Carmelite fathers, left them. They took and appropriated to themselves the Atzaqualca's old church,[1] [*p. 138*] in which the Carmelites now reside and are in charge, for it was first truly the property of the commoners[2] of Atzaqualco. They just took it from them, so that the church of lord San Sebastián was moved to Ahuatonco; there the Atzaqualca likewise came to erect it, and there was built the monastery of the Augustinian fathers, so that they will forever reside there and govern the Atzaqualca. The Sacrament was brought in there, as was just mentioned, with great splendor; they came in procession to the great church and college of the Company of Jesus, the Theatines, to get it.

v Today, Sunday, at 2 o'clock on the 23rd of the month of January of the year 1611, was when at the church of San Francisco were baptized two of the Japan people who came. They were baptized with true splendor. It was done in the presence of all the different ecclesiastics who dwell in Mexico, who all appeared there. The first baptized was a noble and lord of Japan whose name upon baptism became don Alonso; don Hernando Altamirano, then captain of the guard, became his godfather. Lorenzo became the name of the second Japanese person baptized; don Pedro Altamirano became his godfather. It was right on the feast day of San Ildefonso, archbishop[3] of Toledo, that they were baptized. // And right away on the next day, on Monday, again a Japanese person was baptized; Felipe became his name; don Gonzalo de Monrroy became his godfather.

v Today, Saturday, the 29th of the month of January of the year 1611, [*p. 139*] was when a chapter meeting was held at San Francisco here in Mexico; father fray Hernando[4] Durán, from Puebla, criollo, became provincial head; this was the very first time that a criollo born here in New Spain had become provincial there in all the years since the first twelve Franciscan fathers arrived here in New Spain; all the provincials who had gone along being chosen in all the chapter meetings that were held over that time came from Spain, and not until this said meeting did it begin that criollos, children of people here in New Spain, Franciscan friars, can be made provincials. And it was in the meeting mentioned just now that fray Gerónimo de Zárate was made person in charge of the chapel of San Josef in San Francisco; he is called chaplain.

v Today, Monday, the 7th of the month of March of the year 1611, was when Sebastián Vizcaíno, citizen of Mexico, set out and left Mexico here, appointed general of the China boats going to China[5] [the Philippines]. At that time he then took the Japanese; he placed next to himself[6] the Japanese nobleman whose name was now don Alonso and who now went dressed as a Spaniard, to return to his home; here he threw away his outfit that he wore coming here. He was the only one to change [his clothing] here in Mexico.

5. Ch. generally writes just "china" for China (mainly meaning the Philippines), but here he participates in the common Nahuatl usage in which the word was construed to be "alachina."

6. Made second in command?

tollomome nican mocauhque. yeyntin mexico.

v Axcan martes. yc .10. mani metztli Mayo. de 1611. años tlahca. ypan matlactli tzillini. yhquac nican ciudad Mexico. moquixti. quitlalcahui yn altepetl. yn tlahtohuani Don luis de velasco. Marques. de Salinas. visurrey. oppa omochiuhtzino. nican mexico. nueua españa.[1] mohuica castilla. quihualmonochilli. yn tohueytlahtocauh Rey Don felipe tercero ynic ompa. presidente del consejo. de indias. mochiuhtzinoto. [*p. 140*] Auh ynic nican yc oppa motlahtocatillico. Mexico. yexivitl ypan matlactetl Metztli ypan cenpohuallonchiquacen tonatiuh. auh ynic nican moquixti mexico. tecpan palacio. ynic onmopehualti tlahtohuani Don luis de velasco. ynehuantzin. mantiaque. yn teoyotica tlahtohuani Don fr. Garcia Guerra arçobispo. Mexico. quimocahuillito. ohtlipan. vmpa quimoquechillito. S.ta Ana. tlatilolco. oncan monahuatitzinoque. ynic niman nepa omohuicac tlahtohuani Don luis de velasco. tepeyacacpa. auh yc hualmocueptzino. yn arçobispo. auh ynic nican moquixtique palacio. tlahtohuani Don luis de velasco. yn inehuantzin arçobispo. ynic netloc mantiaque. ye tlaopochcopa ycatia. yn arçobispo. ypan cecentetl. yncauallotzin. ye tlamayecamcopa yhcatia yn tlahtohuani Don luis de velasco. yn ixquich ica vmpa yc mocauhtzinoto. S.ta Ana. ynic oncan mochintin. quimocahuillito.[2] tlahtoque. auh yeyntin ỹ nican quincauhtia. ychpochhuan tlahtohuani Don luis de velasco. Marques de Salinas. ynic ce ycnocihuatl ytoca Doña Maria de dircio. ynamic catca Don Juan Altamirano. comẽdador S.tiago. ynic ome ychpoch ytoca Doña Beatriz de la encarnacio. Abbadessa del monasterio de regina celi. yniquey Itoca Doña Isabel de Jesus. monja. yhuan yn oncan moteneuh Regina celi. yhuan yhueltiuh nican quicauhtia yn itoca Doña Ana de castilla ycnocihuatl ynamic catca Diego de ybarra. comendador. S.tiago. yhuã moch nican quincauhtia. yn ixquichtin yhuanyolque yn imachhuan yxhuihuan. auh ça ymachcihuamo.[3] yn quimahtiuh vmpa españa. ypan aciz. yn itoca Doña Mariana de ybarra. ynamic catca yn ipiltzin Don Fran^{co} de velasco. yn ompa momiquilli españa. ỹ no vmpa quincauhtia ypilhuan. yn huel yehuantin yezque erederos. nema[*p. 141*]Queque. yezque. yn marquesado de Salinas. yntla momiquiliz. incoltzin. Don luis de velasco. yn mohuica axcan españa —

v Axcan viernes. yc .6. mani Metztli Mayo. de 1611 años yhquac momiquilli. yn itztapallapan cihuapilli. Doña Balbara. ychpochtzin. catca yn tlahtohuani Don Alonso Axayaca yxhuetzcatocatzin.

v Axcan lunes. yc .5. mani metztli Junio. de 1611. años. yn ohualtlathui. otlallolin yohualtica. yohualnepantla. yohualli xellihui yn ipehuayan lunes. yhquac yn cenca chicahuac tlallolin. çan tel niman onquiztiquiz. atle quitlaco. atle quimayauh tepãtli. ynic huallathuic lunestica. ye omochiuh yn tlallolinaliztli yohualtica —

v Axcan viernes teotlac. yey tzillini. ynic 10. mani metztli Junio. de 1611. años. ye no yhquac. oypantic. yxtlapachiuhca yn tonatiuh. yn iuh quihtotihui huehuetque. tonatiuh quallo. ca in yehuatl Metztli. yxpan momanca. in tonatiuh. huel poliuhca yn itlanex. tonatiuh. huel quitzacuillica. yn itlanextiliz. yhuan techtlayohuilica. huel iuhcan. mochiuhtihuetzca. yn ihquac chicuey tzillini ye yohua. ynic huel tlayohuatihuetzca niman moch neztihuetzca. yn cicitlaltin ylhuicatitech auh tel amo huecauh. ynic huel ontlayo-

1. Possibly this phrase could be taken as an early example of equation of Mexico and New Spain, but the interpretation in the main text is more likely.

2. Alternatively, to which all the lords conducted him.

They had been here in Mexico just two months when seventeen of them returned home; three stayed here in Mexico.

v Today, Tuesday, the 10th of the month of May of the year 1611, at 10 o'clock in the daytime, was when the ruler don Luis de Velasco, Marqués of Salinas, who was appointed viceroy twice here in Mexico in New Spain[1] departed from the city of Mexico here and left the altepetl. He is going to Spain; our great ruler the king don Felipe III summoned him, because he has been appointed president of the Council of the Indies there. [*p. 140*] The second time, he came here to Mexico to rule for 3 years, 10 months, and 26 days. And as the ruler don Luis de Velasco left the palace here in Mexico and departed, he and the spiritual ruler don fray García Guerra, archbishop in Mexico, went together; he left him along the way; he got him as far as Santa Ana in Tlatelolco; there they took their departure from each other, so that then the ruler don Luis de Velasco went beyond toward Tepeyacac, and thereupon the archbishop returned. And when the ruler don Luis de Velasco and the archbishop left the palace here together, going along next to each other, each of them on one of his horses, the archbishop went on the left; the ruler don Luis de Velasco went on the right, until they stopped at Santa Ana and there all the lords left him.[2] And the ruler don Luis de Velasco, Marqués of Salinas, left behind here three daughters of his: the first a widow, named doña María de Ircio, who was the spouse of don Juan Altamirano, comendador of Santiago; the second daughter of his, named doña Beatriz de la Encarnación, abbess of the convent of Regina Coeli; the third named doña Isabel de Jesús, also a nun in the said Regina Coeli; and he left here his older sister named doña Ana de Castilla, widow, who was the spouse of Diego de Ibarra, comendador of Santiago; and he left behind here all his nephews, nieces, and grandchildren who were his relatives; when he arrives in Spain he will find only his daughter-in-law[3] named doña Mariana de Ibarra, who was the spouse of his child don Francisco de Velasco who died in Spain, who also left behind there his children, the very ones who will be heirs of [*p. 141*] the marquesado of Salinas when their grandfather don Luis de Velasco, who is now going to Spain, dies.

v Today, Friday, the 6th of the month of May of the year 1611, was when the noblewoman of Iztapalapa doña Bárbara passed away; she was the daughter of the ruler don Alonso Axayaca Ixhuetzcatocatzin.

v Today, Monday, the 5th of the month of June of the year 1611, the night before, at midnight at the beginning of Monday, there was an earthquake; at that time there was a very strong earthquake, but it ended right away, damaging nothing and throwing no walls down; at dawn on Monday the earthquake at night was already over.

v Today, Friday, at 3 o'clock in the afternoon on the 10th of the month of June of the year 1611, was when the covering of the face of the sun happened, or as the ancients said, the sun is eaten, for the moon placed itself before the sun and the light of the sun entirely disappeared; it entirely blocked its shining and put us in the dark. It quickly became as when it is 8 o'clock at night, so that it quickly became full night, and then all the stars quickly appeared in the sky; but it wasn't full night for long, just a very short time, then

3. Since according to Ch. doña Mariana de Ibarra was married to the viceroy's son, she was certainly his daughter-in-law. But *-machcihuamon* would be one's niece-in-law. If she was a relative of Diego de Ibarra, his brother-in-law, she could perhaps be called niece-in-law by virtue of that connection. Diego's name is given as Antón on pp. 210–11.

huaca. çan huel achitonca. niman. oc ceppa. hualnez. yn tonatiuh. auh ye omihto. ynin mochiuh yehuatl yn quiteneuhtihui tachcocolhuan catca. tonatiuh quallo. ynic motlapololtiaya. canel amo huel oquimattiaque. yn quenin hui. yn quenin mochihua. ynic yzqui tlanepanoltitimani. yn ilhuicame ynic otlatoca. ynic momamallacachotihui. ynic mopapanahuitihui. ynic cecenteotlatoca. ynic yzqui tlanepanoltitimani. ylhuicame. — [*p. 142*]

v Auh nican ca centlamantli tlahtolmachiyotl. ytech tlaquixtilli yn iamoxtzin. yn iSermonariotzin. oquimotlallilitia. yn cenca mahuiztililoni Padre fray Juan bap^ta^. teopixqui. S. Fran^co^. moyetzticatca. ỹ nahuatlahtolpan. oquimotlallitia. yn oncan yhuan ytechpa motlahtoltitiuh yn tonatiuh. yn quenin polihui. yn iuh mihtohua quallo. auh macihui yn itechpa motlahtoltitiuh tonatiuh ynic tonahuatlahtolpan quimocuepillitiuh. yn itlahtolmachiyo yn iuh mochihua quenin quallo tonatiuh. ca amo no huel yxcoyantzinco. yneyxcahuiltlamachiliztzin. ynic tonahuatlahtolpan[1] oquimocuepilitia. oquimotlallilitia ca çano ytech quimoquixtili. ytech quimanilli yn intlahtol. yn ilhuicatlamatinime. in Philosophosme yn Astrologosme. yn oquihtotiaque. yn quenin mochiuhtiuh. yn iuh polihui. yn iuh quallotiuh tonatiuh yn ihquac ypanti. yn iuh tlayohuatimomana. yn quexquich yc hueliti polihui tonatiuh. yn iuh nican tecpantoc. tlahtolmachiyotl. yn çan huel yuh oquinamiquico. yn çan huel yuh oquinenehuillico. oquimopotico yn iuh axcan ypan viernes. otiquittaque omochiuh. ye onpehua yn tlahtolmachiyotl —

v Yz catqui tlahtolli in quenin yxpoyahuac in tonatiuh yhuan yn Metztli. yn tonatiuh. in Metztli. amo ça cen ilhuicatl ytech yn cate: onoque. ca cecentlanepanolli.[2] ytech onoque. yn ilhuicatl. ca yn tonatiuh. yc nauhtlanepanolli ylhuicatl. yn itech ca. auh in cecentlanepanolli ylhuicame. cecentlamantli. yc momallacachohua. auh yn ihquac. ypanti. yn Metztli yxpan momana. in tonatiuh. / huel yxquich ca yn quexquichcapa yc motzticate. / ca yc quitzacuillia. yn itlanextiliz. yhuan techtlayohuillia. in tehuantin. ynic amo huel tiquittazque yn itlanex. in tonatiuh / yn iuh axcan ypan viernes [*p. 143*] Otiquittaque. Oticmahuiçoque. O topan mochiuh // in tonatiuh auh yc ixcuichehua. yxpoyahua. yxmatlallehua. in tonatiuh. maçonellihui in ayc quicahua. yn itlanexyo. canel tlanexmeyalotl. Auh yehica yn oc cenca huey. in tonatiuh. yn ahmo mach iuhqui yn Metztli. amo huel mochihuaz. in Metztli. quicẽtzacuiliz. yn itlanextiliz. in tonatiuh. çan cequi. çan achiton. ahnoço cecni. yn oncan huel yxpan momana, auh yn oc ceccan. yn amo huel yxpan. cacitimomana. amo huel yxcuichehuaz. in tonatiuh. IZ. catqui. machiyotl. in cehualcalli. in huel tiquixnamictia in tonatiuh. ca quitzacuillia. yn itlanex. ynic amo topan tonaz. yece yn oc cequintin. yn amo quixnamictia. yn incehualcal. ca quittazque. yn itlanextiliz. in tonatiuh. yn inpan momanaz. ca çan ye no yuhqui. mochihua. in tonatiuh. ixcuichehualiz. ca oncan ixcuichehua. yxmatlallehua. yn huel yxpan momana. in metztli. auh yn oncan. amo yxpan momana. amo yxcuichehua. amo yxpoyahua. amo yxmatlallehua. auh ma huel yuh mochi tlacatl quimati. ca niman. amo huelitiz. in huecauhtica. yxpoyahuatiez. yxcuichehuatiez. yxmatlallehuatiez. in tonatiuh. ca çan iciuhca. onquiztiquiça: ca in quenin. nepantla tonatiuh. in tlamelauhca onmottitia. in cehualcalli. ca tettzacuillia.[3] ynic amo topan tonaz. yece niman in ye ommopillotiuh. in ye onmotzcallotiuh. tonatiuh. techtlanextilia. yn oncã amo techtlanextiliaya. ca çanno yuhqui. yn ihquac metztli. quitzacuillia. yn tonatiuh. amo huel mochihuaz. in huecauhtica. quixtzacuiliz. yehica. ca

1. These are rare references to Nahuatl using the term *nahuatlatolli*.

2. Placed one above the other, as in *calnepanolli*, a two-story house.

the sun appeared again. As was already said, when this happened our forefathers called it the sun being eaten, in which they were confused, for they did not know how the heavens go, how they are made, so that each one lies across the other as they go along revolving and crossing one another, how each one goes along, how each of the heavens crosses the others. [*p. 142*]

v Here is a separate instructive statement taken from the book and sermon collection which the very reverend father fray Juan Bautista, a late Franciscan friar, composed, that he did in the Nahuatl language, where among other things he talks about how the sun disappears, or as they say is eaten. Though he speaks of the sun to translate his statement into our Nahuatl language as to how it happens that the sun is eaten, it was also not entirely on his own and by his exclusive knowledge that he translated it and composed it in our Nahuatl language,[1] for he also took it from the statements of those who know the heavens, the philosophers and astrologers who had said how it happens, how the sun disappears and is eaten: when it happens, how it gets dark, for how long the sun can disappear. What happened and what we saw today, Friday, exactly matched and equaled the statement as it is arranged here. Now the exemplary statement begins:

v Here is an account of how the sun and the moon became dark. The sun and the moon are not in a single heaven, but are in separate heavens joined together.[2] The sun is in the fourth of the joined heavens. Each of the joined heavens rotates separately. When it happens that the moon places itself in front of the sun, / for fully as long as they are facing each other, / thereby [the moon] blocks [the sun's] shining and puts us in the dark, so that we cannot see the sunlight, / as we saw and beheld and happened to us on Friday. [*p. 143*] // And thereby the surface of the sun turns black, dark, or dark blue, although it never relinquishes its shining, for it is a source of light. And since the sun is much bigger than the moon, it cannot happen that the moon should entirely block the shining of the sun, but it can place itself directly in front of only some, or a little, or a particular part, but in the other part, which it cannot place itself completely in front of, the surface of the sun cannot blacken. Here is an example. A shady shelter that we cause to face the sun directly blocks its rays so that it does not shine on us, but the others who do not have shelters directly facing it will see the sunshine, it will present itself to them. The same thing happens with the blackening of the sun, for its surface blackens and turns dark blue where the moon directly faces it, and where it does not face it, its surface does not blacken, darken, and turn dark blue. And let everyone realize that the surface of the sun can by no means stay black, dark, dark blue for a long time, for it quickly passes. As at noon when the sun is shown straight on, a shady shelter protects us[3] so that it doesn't shine on us, but then when the sun inclines and goes off to one side, it shines on us where it didn't shine on us before; just so, when the moon blocks the sun, it cannot happen that it should block off its surface for long, because it [the sun] goes rotating [*p.*

3. For "tetzacuillia" or "techtzacuillia."

moma[*p. 144*]lacachotiuh. yhuan quitlalcahuitiuh. yn Metztli.[1] ynin tlahtolli. ye omihto. ytech tlaquixtili. yn ilhuicatlamachiliz. amoxtli. ca yehuantin. yntlatlalil. ỹtlanemilil. yn huey tlamatinime. in Philosophosme. in Astrologosme. in quinemillique. yhuan quihcuillotiaque. yn izquitlamantli. tlalticpacayotl. yhuan yn izquitlamantli. yn tiquitta. yn ticmahuiçohua. yn inyeliz. auh yn tachcocolhuan. yn huehuetque. yn oc tlateotocanime yn motenehua Gentilesme catca atle huel quimattiaque. yn itechpa in. yc ypampa yn omotlapololtitiaque.

v Auh yn axcan omoteneuh ypan cemilhuitl. viernes. ynic omixtlapachoca yca metztli tonatiuh. ynic mihtohua. oqualoc tonatiuh. ca yn ihquac. ayemo tihuallaci yn ipan in viernes. ca achtopa quihtoque. tenemachtique. in yehuantin tlamatinime yn españolesme. yn huel quimati. yn ilhuicatitech tlamatini. yn motenehua Astrologos. quihtoque. ca yn ipan viernes. tacizq̃. ynic .10. maniz metztli Junio. mixtlapachoz. yn tonatiuh tlayohuaz. matlactlonce tzilini pehuaz. tlacoçahuiaz. ynic tlayohuatiaz. auh ypan ome tzilini. tlamitiuh ynic oc ceppa tlanecitiuh. in ye teotlac. auh yn ixquich ica. tlayohuaz. amo qualli cahuitl yez. yn ixquich ica qualoz tonatiuh. cocolizyo yez. macayac. conacopayttaz. ma huel nepiallo. yhuicpa. ma necaltzaquallo. amoyac huel nenemiz. yn otlipan. ypampa. yn ihquac amo qualli yn ehecatl. quiztoz. yhuan no yxquich ica. ayac tlaquaz. ayac atliz. anoço cochiz. yn ixquich ica oc ceppa tlanecitiuh. ynic necitiuh tonatiuh. auh yevatl ypampa yn axcan omoteneuh ypan cemilhuitl [*p. 145*] Viernes mochi tlacatl mocaltzauhc. yn çan huell imman ihq̃c otlateneuhque. tlamatinime pehuaz. ynic tlacoçahuiaz. ynic tlayxcuichehuaz. ynic yxpoyahuaz tonatiuh. mochintin mocaltzacque. yn espanoles. yhuan yn timacehualti. çan niman aocac ohtli quitocaticatca. yn ihtic ciudad. Mexico. ça huel cacacticaca yn ohtli. yhuã cenca miyequintin Señorati. momauhtiaya. oc yohuatzinco. moyolcuitique yhuan tlacellique. mocencauhque teoyotica. auh ye oc cõpanahui. yn cahuitl yn imman ypan tlateneuhque. tlamatinime, ye quin ipan yn omochihuaco. ome tzillini ypan tlaco hora. yn opeuh huel yequene tlacoçahuia. yn çan ihuiãtzin. ye tlayohuatiuh aocmo chicahuac tonaya. yhuan mixtli. çan ipan oquiquiztinenca. tonatiuh. // auh yn ipãpa in. yn oc conpanahui yn ipan tlateneuhque tlamatinime. pehuazquia. matlactlõce tzillini ynic tlayohuatiazquia. yxquich ica tlamitiuh ypan ome tzillini ynic oc ceppa necitiuh tonatiuh. yniquipampa oc conpanahui. yuh mochi tlacatl momatca. ca aocmo mochihuaz yn iuh oquihtoca tlamatinime. yn iuh ypan mochihuaz tonatiuh. yc oquimiztlacamatque. oquihtoque cequintin españolesme. ca çan iztlacati yn tlein. quimomachiztia aço çan otlahuanque aço çan imihuincacopa. in tleyn oquihtoque tlamatinime in Astrologos. yn tlein mochihuazquia axcan yn imma. ypan otlateneuhque ca amo mochihua. ynic ye mochi tlacatl. hualquiz. yn ĩchachan ynic mocaltzacca. yn momalhuiyaya. españolesme. yhuan cequintin timacehualtin. ye nohuiã nenemohua. yn ohtlipan yc mexico. auh yehica. ypampa. ca ye oquipanahui yn oncã ypan hora quiteneuhque. omochihuazquia. ynic otlayohuazquia. mochi tla[*p. 146*]catl. conacopayttaya. yn tonatiuh. aquen ca. aquen mochihua huel macitica. yhuan tlanextia. yece aocmo chicahuac topan moquetzaya. yn itotonillo. aocmo tetlatiaya huel ce tzillininn opeuh. yn ça yuhqui. cocoxticatca. tonatiuh. anca ce yc[2] opeuh. yn ye tlayohuaz. auh ynic huellotiquittaque. mochi tlacatl nican nueua españa titlaca. ynic yxquich ihuelitzin. tt^{o}. Dios. yn çan iceltzin huel moch quimochihuillia. ytlamahuiçoltzin in tleyn quimonequiltitzinoa. quimochihuiliz. quimoteyttitiliz.

1. It is true that this passage could be interpreted as meaning that the moon leaves the sun behind, but since it was the sun that was moving and was the subject in the first part

144] and leaves the moon behind.[1] This statement, which as was already said was taken from a book about knowledge of the heavens, was composed and thought out by the great scholars, the philosophers and astrologers, who considered and wrote about all earthly matters and the nature of everything that we see and behold. And our forefathers, the ancients who were still idolaters, called pagans, were not able to find out anything about this because they lived in confusion.

v Today, on the said day of Friday, when the face of the sun had been covered by the moon, so that it is said that the sun is eaten, before Friday came, those Spanish sages who know all about it, who are scholars of the heavens, called astrologers, first said and warned people that when Friday the 10th of the month of June should come, the surface of the sun would be covered and it would get dark. At 11 o'clock the light would begin to fade, and it would get darker and darker. At 2 o'clock it would end and it would get light again in the afternoon. And it would be a bad time as long as it was dark; as long as the eclipse lasted it would be unhealthy. No one should look upward, everyone should guard well against it. They should all stay in their houses; nor would anyone be permitted to go about on the roads because at that time a bad air would be passing by, and also during that time no one should eat, drink, or sleep until it should get light again, until the sun should appear. Because of that on the said day of [*p. 145*] Friday all the people shut themselves up in their houses. At exactly the time when the wise men had predicted that the light would begin to fade and the surface of the sun would get black and dark, all the Spaniards and we commoners closed themselves in their houses. No one at all was walking the streets in the city of Mexico; the streets were entirely abandoned. And a great many Spanish women were afraid; while it was still very early in the morning they made confession and took communion, they prepared themselves spiritually. But it went past the time the wise men had predicted. It didn't happen until half past 2 o'clock that the light finally began to fade and it very slowly got dark; the sun was no longer shining strongly, and some clouds went along passing by the sun. // Because of this, that it went beyond the 11 o'clock when the scholars had predicted that it would begin to get dark until it would end at 2 o'clock and the sun would appear again, since it went beyond that, everyone thought that what the scholars had said would happen to the sun wasn't going to happen; they wrongly considered them liars. Some Spaniards said they are just lying about what they announce, maybe they just got drunk, maybe what the scholars and astrologers said is just drunken talk; what was going to happen, that they predicted for now, is not happening. So everyone, the Spaniards and some of us commoners, came back out of their houses where they had shut themselves in and sought protection, and everyone went walking on the streets everywhere around Mexico. And since it was already past the time they predicted for it to happen that it would become dark, everyone [*p. 146*] looked upward at the sun; there was nothing wrong with it, nothing the matter with it, it was entirely whole and was shining, although its heat no longer beat strongly down upon us, it no longer burned. Right at 1 o'clock the sun seemed to begin to weaken, so that it began[2] to get dark. And so that all of us people here in New Spain could see how only our omnipotent lord God can perform all his miracles, for he does what he wants to do, and

of the sentence, the interpretation in the main text seems more likely.

2. The thrust of "ce yc" is not clear. Perhaps "once and for all, finally, really?"

nican tlalticpac. ca quimochihuilia. yn quenin huel quimonextiliz. ca yn ihquac. yc ye pehua. ye tlacoçahuia. in ye mixtlapachoz. yca metztli tonatiuh. yn motenehua ye qualoz. yn ilhuicatl ca nohuiampa mixtli yc tzauhctimanca. acan huel hualnecia. auh çan iyocan. çan ixquich yn oncan yetiuh tonatiuh. çan mixcanactli. yn oncan huel yxpan yxco. quiquiçaya. auh in yequene yhquac yn ye ynma. in ye tlayohuaz. in ye ome tzillini ypan tlaco hora. yc niman opeuh. in ye miquania mixtli, in ye quitlalcahuia tonatiuh. ynic mochi tlacatl huel quittaz. yn quenin ipan yc mochihuaz tonatiuh. achi hueca yc quitlalcahui. tlanahuac çan huel hualmoyecyahualiuhcatecato ỹ mixtli. ynic quitlacahuilli tlanaliuhtiquiz. yn ilhuicatitech. ynic huel cempani. iyoca. hualtlalli[1] tonatiuh. auh yn o yuh in yoca hualmotlalli tonatiuh. ylhuicatitech. niman yc peuh yn huel ye tlacoçahuia. çan ihuiantzin. ye tlayohuatiuh ynic ye poliuhtiuh tonatiuh. ynic huel ixpan [*p. 147*] Ye yatiuh. ynic huel ixpan ye onmomana metztli, huel cacitimoman. ynic yahualtic tonatiuh. ynic quixtzacuilli. y çan ihuiantzin huel onpolihuico. tonatiuh auh ça huel pizcantzin.[2] ca yuhquin ce citlaltepitzĩ aquitzin. ytonameyo. hualnezca. yn ça ytloc ynahuac ytenco. hualquizticatca. yn ixcuichehuaca. yn ixpoyahualiz. yn ixmatlallehuaca. ynic oyxtlillehuatihuetzca[3] tonatiuh. ye omihto. huel iuhcan mochiuhtihuetzca yn ihquac chicuey tzillini. ye yohua. ynic huel. ontlayohuatihuetzca. ynic niman moch hualneztihuetzca cicitlaltin. yn ilhuicatitech. auh yn ixquich ica. ynic topan otlayohuaca. ynic otechtlayohuillica tonatiuh. in tehuantin nican titltlaca[4] timacehualtin. yn amo ticmati. yn quenin mochihua yn ilhuicame.[5] ynic ohtlatoca ynic momallacachohua ynic ypantic. axcan. omonepanixnamiquico. yn tonatiuh yhuan metztli, ynic cecenteylhuicatitech yn quexquich ca. yc motzticate. cecenteylhuicapan yn maca çan ohtlipan omocepanhuecapanetlocohuiyxnamiquico. ynic ytech yetihui. ynic momallacachotihui. yn ilhuicame. omonepanyxnamiquico. canel noço nauhteylhuicapan[6] in yatiuh tonatiuh. auh yn metztli. ca ye yc itech in yatiuh ynic centeylhuicapa. yn huel ye ytech yn quiyahuallohua tlalli. yn huell achto ytech. ynic onpeuhtoque ylhuicame. oncan yxquichcapa oconixcemacicatzacuillica yn huel ixquich ica. ynic yahualiuhtiuh. yn itlanextiliztica tonatiuh. ynic topã otlayohuaca. yn intzintla tinemi yc cenca mochi [*p. 148*] tlacatl. omomauhti. omiçahui. yn toquichtin.[7] yhuan oc cenca yehuantin. yn Señorati. yhuan ỹ nican titlaca timacehualtin cihuatzitzinti mochintin. mocaltenq̃. mocaltzacque. yn inchachan. ỹtlan oquintlallique Yn inpipilhuan. oncan tlatzatzatzi. yn mochoquilia yn ixquich ica tlayohuaca. quihtohuaya. tley ye topan mochihua. tley ye topan quimonequiltia in tt°. Dios. ototlahueliltic. ca ypampa totlatlacol. huel ixquich ica mocahuaco. yn chocaya ynic quiz. ynic polihuico tlayohualotl. yhuan cequintin tehteopã moteopancaltemato. yn toquichtin yhuan cihua vmpa moteochiuhticatca. ca no yehuantzitzin. yn teopixque. yc motemachtillique. yn iuh mochihuaz yn iuh axcan omochiuh quimitalhuique yn teopixque. ayac momauhtiz. miçahuiz. ynic qualoz tonatiuh. ca çan achitonca. yn tlayohuaz. teopan ximocenquixtiqui.

---

1. The form is in error, possibly for "hualmotlalli" as just below.

2. For "pitzcantzin."

3. *Huetzi* as a *-ti-* auxiliary denotes quickness of the action of the main verb, yet that meaning seems to go against what was said earlier.

4. For "titlaca."

5. In the complexity of his thoughts and his absorption in the topic Ch. seems to have gradually lost track of the grammatical structure here. He seems to have been going to say that we commoners, who do not know about these things, became greatly frightened, but his explanation of the things themselves became longer and longer, including whole inde-

show people here on earth, as he can manifest, for when the light began to fade and the surface of the sun to be covered by the moon, which is called being eaten, the sky was closed everywhere by clouds, [the sun] could appear nowhere; it went [was visible] only where thin clouds would pass back and forth in front of it. But then when it was finally time for it to get dark, at half past 2 o'clock, the clouds began to move off and leave the sun so that everyone could see what would happen to the sun; the clouds left it rather far to the side, they disposed themselves in a full circle, so that they left a space and the sky cleared, so that the sun positioned[1] itself [in the space] far above and entirely alone. And when the sun had taken a position by itself in the sky, the light really began to fail, it gradually got darker as the sun continued to disappear, as the moon [*p. 147*] went and placed itself right in front of it and placed itself entirely in the circle of the sun so that it blocked off its surface and the sun gradually disappeared entirely, and its light appeared very small,[2] like a tiny star, that came from the sides and edges of its blackness, darkness, dark blueness, when the surface of the sun had quickly[3] become black. As was said, it quickly became like 8 o'clock at night, so that it suddenly grew dark and all the stars suddenly appeared in the sky. The whole time that we had been in the dark, that the sun had been dark to us, we local people,[4] we commoners, who do not know how it happens,[5] how the heavens move along their routes and rotate, so that it happened now that the sun and the moon met each other and faced each other each from its separate heaven, at the distance they are from each other. It is not that they met together and joined together on a [single] route high above, on which the heavens go and rotate, meeting each other [colliding], for the sun goes in the four[th][6] heaven, and the moon goes in the first heaven that rotates all around the earth, the very first one with which the heavens begin, from there it completely blocked off the surface of the sun as it goes rotating with its light, so that dark fell upon us who live here below them, whereby everyone was greatly [*p. 148*] frightened and taken aback, the men[7] and especially the Spanish women and the local, commoner women, they all went into their houses, shut themselves up in their homes, and placed their children next to them, where there was a general shouting and crying as long as it was dark, saying, "What is happening to us now? What does our lord God want for us? Woe is us, it is because of our sins." The weeping didn't stop until the actual moment when the darkness ended and left. And some indigenous men and women went into the various churches and prayed there, for the ecclesiastics too preached about how what had now happened was to happen. The priests said, "No one is to be frightened or shocked that there is a solar eclipse, for it will be dark for only a little while; come

---

pendent sentences, until he returns to the expected result at the very bottom of his p. 147.

6. Ordinarily *ic* or *inic* would have been required before "nauhteylhuicapan" to make it ordinal.

7. *Toquichtin*, *oquichtli* in the first person plural, usually means indigenous men specifically in Ch. Here it is followed by and apparently paired with *señoratin*, which means Spanish women unambiguously. We are left wondering if here for once *toquichtin* refers to Spanish men, or to all men. The immediately following phrase seems to include wording for women of both ethnicities. Just below, however, *toquichtin* is paired with *cihua* alone, apparently returning to its sense of indigenous men.

nican timechyolchicahuazque.[1] ypampa ynic cequintin teopan mocaltemato, auh ye no ceppa peuh in ye neztiuh. in ye mixtlapotiuh. yniquixpan ye quiztiuh. ye quicauhtiuh. yn oquixtzacuillica. ye miquanitiuh yn Metztli, ynic yequene no ceppa huel tlanecico. topan. yn mochihu in huel ypan yey tzillini. ye teotlac. yn iuh mochi tlacatl. ypan omochiuh oquittac. auh yn ixquich ica in ynic tlayohuatihuetzca. huel yxquich ica. ça huel momatticatca[2] yn tonatiuh. çan huel tlanaliuhtoca, yn ixquich ica omoteneuh yc quiyahualiuhcatlalcahuica. mixtli çan huel oncan. ahciticatca. yn oncã ypan yc peuh ahcitoya. mixtli,[3] [*p. 149*] ynic otlayohuaca. ynic oqualoc tonatiuh çan niman aoctle ypan hualla. aoctle ypan oquiz. auh yn ihquac ye no ceppa no cuel ohualnez. yn huel ohualtehuilacachiuhcanez. mochi tonatiuh, in huel ye tlanextia, yc niman yxco hualmocençouh yn mixtli, yc nohuianpa yn ilhuicatl yc hualmixtzauhctimomah, yn omoteneuh mixtli, aocmo cenca cana hualnez. yn ixquich ica onaquito, tonatiuh. yn icacallaquiyampa. ynic onyohuato. yhuan oquihtoq̃. yn tlamatinime in Astrologos.me. oquinezcayoti ynic no yhuan ypampa yn iuh omochihuin. ce ciudad. huey altepetl polihuiz. yn campa mochihuatiuh. amo huel momati. yn tleyn ic polihuiz. yhuan ce huey tlacatl tlahtocapilli. motenehua Principe. momiquiliz. yn campa tlalli ypam momiquiliz. yhuann aqui. amo no huel momati yn campa mochihuatiuh ye quin ihquac necitiuh yn campa ye omochiuh. yece ye onez. ytech yn tonatiuh. ynic omixtlapachoca ca oquinezcayoti, yn iuh mochihuaz. O yhuin mochihuĩ ynic mihtohua oqualoc tonatiuh. yn ipan in omoteneuh cemilhuitl viernes, nican o mochi motecpan yn itlahtollo. yn iuh omochiuh. ynic nican quittazque. yhuan quimatizque. yn ixquichtin in quin ye tlacatizque in quin çatepan yc nemiquihui nican tlalticpac, yn aquique, amo ycah yuhqui quittazque. auh quemaca yn iquin canin quemma. cequintin. yn aquique. yuh quittatihui yece oc huecauh. oc miyec xihuitl quiçaz. yn ihquac oc ceppa yn iquin no cuel ynpantitiuh in çã ye iuh [*p. 150*] no mochihuatiuh, ye quin ihquac oc ceppa ye no yuh quittatihui, quimahuiçotihui, yn iuh mixtlapachoz tonatiuh. yn motenehua qualoz tonatiuh, yn iuh axcan ypan in xihuitl ticate o topan mochiuh // auh no yhquac. yn o iuh qualoc tonatiuh nimãn ic peuh ỹ nican ciudad mexico miyec tlacatl. oychtaca micq̃ in timacehualtin. yhuã españoles. ỹ quimixilia. huel yuh tlamico ỹ xihuitl de 1611. a^o^s. yn ichtacamicohuac.—

Axcan Domingo. yc .19. mani metztli Junio. de 1611. a^o^s ye teotlac macuilli tzillini ypan tlaco hora, ynic omocallaquico. ciudad Mexico. S.tiago tlatilolco hualmehuiti. yn oncan yc hualmiquanitzino tecpan palacio, mocallaquico, in yehuatzin tlahtohuani Don fray Garcia Guerra arçobispo Mexico. ynic visurrey. mochiuhtzino, yn moch ixquich yc nohuian ypan nueua españa. ye omihto ynin teopixqui Sancto Domingo.

v̲ Martes. yc .24. mani Metztli Março. yn acico, ycedulatzin. yn tohueytlahtocauh Rey Don felipe. tercero. yn quimomaquillico. yehuatzin Excelentissimo Señor Don fray Garcia Guerra arçobispo Mexico. ynic virrey gouernador y capitan general mochiuhtzino ỹ nican ypan nueua españa. yhuan Presidente de la real Audiencia yn ipan moyetzinotica. huel yc mochtin opahpacque ohuelamatque. yn nican tlahtocaaltepehuaque. auh niman hualmohuicazquia yn teoyotica tlahtohuani çan niman oncan hualmehualtizquia. yn itecpanchãtzinco. ynic hualmiquanitzinozquia. huey tecpa Palacio. atle onmantozquia.[4] yn iuh conmonequiltiaya auh yece yn ciudad. tlaca. çã nima amo yuh oquinecq̃. ynic ompa mo-

---

1. For "tamechyolchicahuazque."

2. Such a meaning of *mati* is not common, but the only sense allowed by the general context is that the sun was somehow visible. The verb by origin meant to grasp and still

assemble at the church, here we will raise your spirits."[1] Because of this some people went into the churches. Thereupon [the sun] began to appear again, to show its face, as it passed along and left the moon, which had blocked it, moving away from it, until finally it was fully light again. This befell us right at 3 o'clock in the afternoon, as everyone present saw. In this whole time that darkness had fallen, the whole time the sun could be [perceived],[2] it was clear within the said round space left by the clouds; the clouds only reached that far when it began.[3] [*p. 149*] When it got dark during the eclipse, no more [clouds] at all came over [the sun] or passed by it, and when the whole sun appeared again in its entire roundness it shone brightly. Then the clouds came and spread out over its entire surface, so that everywhere the sky became closed in by the said clouds; the sun didn't appear clearly anywhere before it went down in the west as night came. And the wise men and astrologers said that also because this happened it was a sign that a city, a great altepetl will perish; where it will happen cannot be known, or for what reason it will perish. And a great lord, a royal noble called a prince will die. In what land he will die and who he is cannot be known either, nor where it will happen. That will appear later, at the place where it has happened. But it already appeared in the fact that the surface of the sun was darkened, for that was a sign that it would happen. This then is what happened, so that it is said that the sun was eaten. On the said day of Friday a full account of it was put in order here so that all who are born later and will live here on earth afterward, those who will not ever see the like, will see and find out about it here. Or some of them may indeed see something like this, but it will be sometime a long time from now, many years will pass when again something like this comes to pass and [*p. 150*] happens. At that later time they will again see and behold in the same way how the face of the sun is covered, called the sun being eaten, as befell us now in the present year. // And also when the solar eclipse was over, it began that here in the city of Mexico many people were killed by stealth, we commoners and Spaniards who were stabbed. Right until the end of the year of 1611 people were murdered by stealth. —

Today, Sunday the 19th of the month of June of the year 1611, at half past 5 o'clock in the afternoon, the lord don fray García Guerra, archbishop in Mexico, entered the city of Mexico; he came from Santiago Tlatelolco, from where he moved to the palace and entered it, because he has been made viceroy everywhere in all New Spain. It was already said that he is a Dominican friar.

v Tuesday the 24th of the month of March a cedula of our great ruler the king don Felipe III arrived, granting the most excellent lord don fray García Guerra, archbishop in Mexico, appointment as viceroy, governor, and captain general here in New Spain, and president of the Royal Audiencia which resides there. Each and all of the citizens of the royal altepetl here greatly rejoiced and were content about it, and the priestly ruler was going to come immediately, right away he was going to leave his [archiepiscopal] palace to move to the great governmental palace, [there was to be no delay][4] the way he wanted it; but the members of the [Spanish] cabildo absolutely didn't want him to go there;

---

has implications of feeling.

3. The translation here is particularly speculative.

4. The verb form seems to contain reflexive *ana* in its sense of stretching out.

huicac oc ompa conmotzicalhuique. ynic ompa oc motlatlatolchiallito. atlacohuayan ymacehualpan yn Marques. del valle. vncan vicario. mochiuhtica. ymachtzin. ytoca fray Jeronimo Gerra oc ompa ytlan moyetzticatca. yn oquic tlachichihuallo [*p. 151*] Mocencahua. yn ixquich monequiz. yc namicoz. auh in ye omocencauh mochi yc namicoz. yc niman vmpa hualmehuiti. yn atlacohuayan. ynic on omoteneuh S.tiago. tlatilolco. mohuetziltico. ynic oncan oquimanillito. axcan ypan omoteneuh Domingo. yc .19.tia de Junio. huel yxquichtin. quimanillito. yn tlahtoque audiencia real tlaca oydoresme. yhuan ~~allde~~ de cortesme. yhuan yn ixquichtin. ciudad tlaca. inic ye mochintin castilteca. nimã ya yehuantin. yn Mexica timacehualtin. amo huel mihtoz. motenehuaz. yn ixquich tlacatl vmpa quimonamiquillito. tlatilolco. yn huel oc ompa quimanillito. auh yxquich yn ça otlipan quimonamiquillito. omochiuh huey pahpaquiliznetimaloliztli. yhuan hueylhuichihualiztli, ỹ nican ciudad. yn ipan hualmocallaqui ynic quihualmohuiquillique hualmoyetztitia ypan ce cauallo, ynic maxitico. yn oncan huey puerta motlalliani, tlacuillolo,[1] yn ixpan teopancalli. S. Domingo, yn oncan quinmaca, tlatlapolloni llaues. yn tlahtoque visurreyes. ynic quitlapohua. puerta. ciudad Mexico yn ihquac yancuica yc huallaci, ynic hualcallaq̃. yhuan Juramento. oncan quimanillia

auh yn ihquac ye o no conmanililique Juramento, yhuan in ye oquimotlapolhui omoteneuh puerta. yn tlahtohuani Don fray Garcia Guerra. yc oncan niman quimocaltilique, ytzintla quimocallaquillique cachcalli[2] motenehua palio, yancuic. cenca tlaçotli, ynic oncan quihualmocaltilitiaque, yn queninn iuh namico, oc cequintin visurreyesme, yn huel yancuican hualcallaqui nican ypan ciudad Mexico. auh yc yequene yehuatl in, yn aocmo yequene çan quexquich tlacatl yn amo çan tlapohualli, quimohuiquiliaya. ohtlipan. yc oncã hualmohuicac yn iglesia [*p. 152*] Mayor yc oncan hualmoquixti, yc niman mocallaquico yn tecpan palacio, ynic oncan yxpantzinco quichiuhque yn ixquich tlamantli, yn tetlahtocatlaliliz. nemanilizmachiyotl. ynic tetlahtocatlallilo, ynic oquimocelilique yn audiencia real tlaca. oydoresme. ynic oncan axcan motlatocatillia.

v Axcan viernes. yc .1. mani metztli Julio de 1611. años. ye teotlac macuilli tzillini, yhquac nican ciudad Mexico. S. Franco maxitico, yc mocallaquico. yn Padre fray isidro, yhuan franco faustino, quetzalmaçatzin. ynin donado. teopixque S. Franco. vmpa ohualmohuicaque, yn motenehua yancuic Mexico. çan quinmanillico oc cequintin teopixque, ynic ohualmohuicaque, auh ynin omoteneuh francisco faustino quetzalmaçatzin donado. çan titehuantin nican titlaca Amaquemecan chalco ychã vmpa pilli

v Axcan viernes. yc .26. mani metztli Agosto de 1611. años. ye tlathui yey tztillini. yhquac cenca chicahuac. otlallolin. yn ayc. yuh mochihuani ynic huel omollini tlalli nican ciudad Mexico. yhuan yn huey apan atl yn tepetzinco mani ynic ompa onacitimani tetzcocopa cenca quiquinacatimanca.[3] ynic poçonia. ynic mollininaya yhuan yn oc cequi atl quiyahualotoc ciudad Mexico cenca mochi quiquinacaya ynic poçonia. ynic macocuia. huel yn iuh ypan caquiztia atl ynic tetecuicaya. yuhquin ma cana tepexic hualmotepexihuia yuhquin ma quexquich amo huel mihtoz motenehuaz yc patlahuac huey atoyatl, ynic temamauhti mochiuh ytetecuicaliz atl. auh yn ixquich atlacomolli nohuiã techachan mopia mexico. ynic molliniaya. yuhquin ma ca vmpa yhtic maltiaya. ynic macocuia atl [*p. 153*] Ynic poçonia ynic tzotzopocaya, yc mohuihuitequia. yc hualmomotlaya yn

1. It could have been more a gate than a door, and it might have had writing rather than painting on it.

2. For "cuachcalli" (or "quachcalli").

they detained him, so that he first went to Tacubaya, in the area of the vassals of the Marqués del Valle, to await word. There his nephew, named fray Gerónimo Guerra, holds the post of vicar; he stayed there with him until such time as things should be arranged [*p. 151*] and everything necessary be prepared for his reception. And when everything was prepared to receive him, he came in this direction from Tacubaya and made the said Santiago Tlatelolco his seat, so that they went there today on the said Sunday the 19th of June to pick him up. All the lords of the Royal Audiencia, the civil judges and the court alcaldes, and all the members of the [Spanish] cabildo, and all the Spaniards, and then also all we Mexica commoners went to get him. It can't be said or told how many people went to meet him at Tlatelolco, who went all the way there to get him and how many just went to meet him along the route. There was great rejoicing and celebration of a great feast day here in the city when he entered, as they brought him riding on a horse, when he got to where a great painted door[1] that is usually set up facing the Dominican church, where they give the keys to lords viceroys to open the door of the city of Mexico when they first arrive here, in order to enter, and they take the oaths from them there.

And when they had also taken the oath from the ruler don fray García Guerra and he had opened the said door, they provided him a shelter, they had him enter underneath a cloth covering[2] called a canopy, new and very expensive. They came holding it over him as when other viceroys are received, who come here into the city of Mexico for the very first time. And finally it was a great many people, without number, who accompanied him on the route as he came to the cathedral, [*p. 152*] then came back out and entered the palace, when in his presence they performed all the different signs of assuming the rulership, by which he was installed in the rulership and the judges of the Royal Audiencia received him, so that he is ruler there today.

v Today, Friday the 1st of the month of July of the year 1611, at 5 o'clock in the afternoon, was when there arrived and entered here in the city of Mexico, at [the church of] San Francisco, father fray Isidro and Francisco Faustino Quetzalmaçatzin, a lay brother, who are Franciscans. They came from the so-called New Mexico; the reason they came was to get some other friars. This said Francisco Faustino Quetzalmaçatzin, lay brother, is one of us local people, from Amaquemecan Chalco, a nobleman there.

v Today, Friday the 26th of the month of August of the year 1611, at 3 o'clock in the morning, was when there was a very strong earthquake such as had never happened before, so that the earth here in the city of Mexico actually moved, and the water of the great lake at Tepetzinco, going toward Tetzcoco, made great noises[3] as it boiled and stirred, and the other waters surrounding Mexico City all made large noises as they boiled and flew up. The water slapping made a sound as though something were falling to the ground from a precipice; it cannot be said or expressed how wide the great stream became and how frightful the slapping of the water was. And all the wells in people's homes everywhere stirred as though someone were taking a bath in them, the way the water flew, [*p. 153*] boiled, and splashed, hitting and throwing itself against the cistern walls. And everyone was

3. *Quiquinaca* can refer to a great variety of noises: screaming, buzzing, grunting, growling, muttering, among others.

atlatecochcaltechtli atl. auh yn ixquich tlacatl, cochia yncamapa. yn o yuh quimatque. tlallolini yn cenca chicahuac. mochi tlacatl yc meuhtehuaque yn ĩcochian yn oncan cochia, quiyahuac quiquiztehuaque. yn españoles. yhuan señorati. çan moch iuh quiquiztehuaque. ỹ quenin cochia cequintin çan tlacamisahuia. cequi petlauhtihuitze. yn ithualco hualquizque. cequintin niman otlihpan. momanaco. yuhquin ma ça ticepantlahuanque otochiuhque. ynic titomauhtia. yn tiquitta calli. quemman in mochi ye pachi.[1] yn tlaltitech ye yauh yehica cẽca miyec yn hualtepehuia tetl. yn xamitl calticpac nohuian techachan, tlalli tepehuia. nohuian ytlacauh yn calli yn tepantli moch cuitlatzayan. yn manel yãcuic calli yn quin moch omochiuh omoquetz. mochi oc cenca yehuatl, moch itlacauh tzatzayan, yhuan yn La compañia de Jesus. golesio. teatinos. teopancalli yn icpac yc tetzopqui, tlaco tzayan. auh yn S. Fran[co]. teopancalli, yuh mihto. omapilli ynic tlallac. auh yn S.tiago tlatilolco. teopancalli yancuic achi quezquican yn cuitlatzatzayan. yhuan teocaltepitzitzin occan yn huetz teocaltepantli. ynic ceccan oncan yn S.ta catalina. çacatenco. pachiuh yn capilla. ynic occan vmpa capoltitlan de los Reyes. auh yn calli. cenca miyeccan yn pachiuh yn incal españoles. in ye huecahua huehuey calli yc netlapacholloc, yhuan cequi tepantli miyeccan yn huetzico huel tlaltitech ya. no cequi tepan huetz. yc micohuac cenca achi huel quezquican yn mexico. yc netlapacholoc calli yc micohuac, auh ynic cenchinampa yn culhuacan yn cuitlahuac. oc cenca vmpa yn ciudad xochimilco yn tlatlacauh tlaco yxtlapan yn teopancalli[2] yn huel tlaltitech. ahcico, yhuan yuh machiztico, ỹ nican Me[*p. 154*]Xico, yn ompa motlapachoque. matlactli tlacatl. yn inchachan yn incal ynpan pachiuh yn oncan cochia. yn huel niman micque. yn amo moyolcuitihui, yhuan teocaltepitzitzin. achi quezquican, yn ompa xixitin yn pahpachiuh yca tlallolinaliztli, cenca huel temamauhti. ynic mochiuh yhuan tetlaocolti tlatzatziztlehua yniqu iuh topan ye mochihua, ça huel yayatimani tlalli, aocmo huel titoquetzaya. ça tihuetztihuetzia yn titoquetzaya. huel yuh ypan nemachoc ca yc ye tlami n cemanahuatl, mochi tlacatl. aocac quilnamiquia yn tleyn cecenyaca cecentlacatl ỹchachan quimopiallia. yn teocuitlatl yn tlatquitl. moch callitic mocauhtiquiz. aocac conittac. aocac conmocuitlahui. ynic chollolohuac. ynic necholtiloc quiyahuac. yn ohtlipan, yn ixquichcauh manca tlallolinaliztli, yhuan miyec tlacatl mococo. ynic tlayohuayan chollohuaya. ynic hualquiztiquizque. ynchachan españolesme auh çan tel huel achitonca yn onmanca. tlallolinaliztli ca niman quiz. yece ye omihto huel temamauhti. ynic manca ynic onmochiuh, auh yn otlathuic yn o huel tlanez. yc niman moch nez. yttaloc. yhuã moch machiztic yn ixquich tlamantli oquitlaco. tlallolinaliztli. ynic nohuian nican yhtic ciudad Mexico, yhuan çan ya yhui nemauhtilotoc, ça ticmahmaticate[3] yn iuh omochiuh tlallolinaliz.[4] yey tzilli yohuac. yuhquin ipan titomati, ça yayatimani n tlalli. yuhquĩ ma ye oc ceppa mochihuaz. yn iuh nemachotoc, auh yn o yuh tlathuic yn ipan in omoteneuh cemilhuitl viernes. atle conmotequipachilhui. yn tlahtohuani Don fray Garcia Guerra. arçobispo Mexico. yhuã visurrey mochiuhtzinotica, atle conmitlahui, [*p. 155*] Yn ma tlatlatlauhtilo. yn ma noço tlayahuallolo ma mihto letania. yn ipampa yuh omochiuh cenca temamauhti tlallolinaliztli, yehica ca yuh yntech ca huey tenahuatili huel yntequitzin yn maca ça ychca-

---

1. For "pachihui."

2. Possibly the reference is to the main church of Xochimilco only. Indeed, it is unclear how much of the immediately following refers to Xochimilco specifically, how much to the whole chinampa district.

3. The sense of *mamati* (presumably *mahmati*) in Molina has to do with various kinds

sleeping in their beds. When they realized there was a very strong earthquake, they all got up and ran out of the bedrooms where they were sleeping and hurriedly came outside. The Spanish men and women too all quickly came out just as they had been sleeping. Some were just in shirts, some came out naked into the patios, some then came out into the road. It was as though we had all gotten drunk, we were so afraid when we saw how houses were all collapsing[1] and falling to the ground, for in people's homes everywhere much stone, adobe, and earth came falling in various directions from the tops of the houses. The houses were damaged everywhere; the walls all ripped open even if they were new houses just built; those especially were all damaged and cracked. And at the Theatine college of the Company of Jesus, the stone vaulting above the church ripped in two, and the Franciscan church, as was said, sank into the earth a distance of two inches; and the new church in Santiago Tlatelolco cracked in quite a few places; and the walls of two small churches fell; at the first one, Santa Catalina Çacatenco, the chapel collapsed; the other one was at Capoltitlan de los Reyes. And in very many places houses of Spaniards, old and large houses, collapsed, covering people underneath. And some walls in many places came falling down all the way to the ground; some also fell on people, from which there were fatalities. In quite a few places in Mexico people were buried in houses and died from it. And in the whole chinampa district, in Colhuacan and Cuitlahuac and especially in the city of Xochimilco, there was damage. The churches[2] broke in half and fell right to the ground. And it came to be known here in Mexico [*p. 154*] that ten people were buried there, at their homes, when their houses collapsed on them where they were sleeping, who died right away without confession. And small churches in quite a few places there fell in and collapsed with the shaking of the earth. What happened was very frightening and pitiful; cries arose that such a thing should happen to us; the earth went this way and that and we could not stand, we would quickly fall down when we stood up, and people really thought that the world was ending. No one remembered what money and property each person had in his house, everything was left inside the house, no one looked at it or saw after it while fleeing; everyone fled outside into the road as long as the earthquake lasted, and many people were hurt running out into the night, as the Spaniards came rushing out of their homes. But the earthquake lasted for only a very little while. Right away it stopped, but as was said, it was very frightening when it happened and while it lasted. When dawn came and it got fully light, everything appeared and was seen, and all the different things that the earthquake had damaged everywhere here inside the city of Mexico became known. People were frightened, and we [feared?][3] that as the earthquake[4] happened at 3 o'clock at night and we thought the earth was going this way and that, it may happen again, as people think. And after dawn came on the said day of Friday, nothing worried the ruler don fray García Guerra, who is appointed archbishop in Mexico and viceroy; he did not say [*p. 155*] that there should be prayers or processions or that a litany should be said because such a very frightening earthquake had taken place. For such is the great obligation incumbent upon [priests]. It is really their duty; they are not just

---

of shame and embarrassment, but this form seems somewhat different. It is not clear which parts of this sentence refer to what happened the night before and which parts to the feared recurrence, but there is no doubt that people were worrying that the same thing would happen again.

4. For "tlallolinaliztli."

pixque ca ychcapixque.[1] yn obisposme. yn arçobisposme yn ihquac yuh tley tepan mochihua yn. yn cenca temamauhti, teyçahui yn oquic tzonteconti, moteyacanillia motepachilhuia yn ipan Sancta iglesia. ca yehuantzitzin. achtopa tzatzizque. quiteylhuizque. yc tenemachtizque. yn tleyn. yn catlehuatl huel monequi, yn tlatlatlauhtiliztli yn tlamacehualiztli yn tlayahualoliztli quichihuazque, yn imichcahuan, yn intlapacholhuan, yn altepehuaque, achtopa yehuantin yntech hualpehuaz ỹ tlahtoque yn tlamacehualiztli, ynic yntech quittazque quintocatiquiçazque, yn incuitlapilhuan, yn imatlapalhuan, ynic tlamacehualiztica ynic choquiztica tlaocoyaliztica neçahualiztica quimoyolcehuilizque, yn tt^o^. Dios. yn ipampa, aço totlacocol[2] ypãpa, aço yquallanticatzinco, yn mochihua, yn tley tepan mochihua yn aço cocoliztli yn anoço ytla oc centlamantli, yn çaço quenami yn temamauhti, yn teyçahui yn çaço campa yuh tepan mochihua, yn iuh axcan nican Mexico, o topan mochiuh, auh yn ipã pani. yn iuh nican o topan mochiuh axcan. atle ypã oquimottili, amo quimomauhtilli. yn tlahtohuani Don fr. Garcia Guerra. arçobpo. visurrey. ye motlanahuatilli ynic quaquamiminaloz. yxpantzinco. yn oncan tecpan palacio corral. yehica ca huel ipactzin, yn quaquanmiminaliztli, ynic oncan cenquixohuac netepancaltemaloc, in ye tlamiminalo. yn ipan in cemilhuitl viernes. oncan cenquizque yn tlahtoque [*p. 156*] Yn audiencia real tlaca oncan ytlantzinco cepanpacticate. yn arçobpo visurrey. yn quaquauhtlatlachia. ynic oncan oc ceppa ynpa omochiuh tlallolinaliztli, ye teotlac ypan yey tzillini. ynic oppa omochiuh yc mocuep. yc oquiz yn tlallolinaliztli. auh macihui yn chicahuac o no nicuel mochiuh aocmo cenca yxquich yc chicahuac yn iuh achto yohuac omochiuh, ca ça onquiztiquiz. ça quexquich ynic tlatlaco, yhquac cuitlatlacotzayan, yn iteopancaltzin S Juan bap^ta^, Moyotlan, y motenehua S. Juan de La penitencia, yhuan no yhquac motlapacho. ypan calli actihuetz. ce señora yhuan ypilhuan amo micque ynic ỹpa callitic caltechpa çan tlamach ynpa monacacicmantihuetzico yn calquahuitl ynic quimopalehuili tt^o^. Dios. yhuan oncan ycatzinco tlamahuiçolli. quimochihuili yn itlaçotzin Señor. S. Niculas de tolentino yn ipan señora. yuh mihto, ynin señora yn ihquac oquimah ye tlallolini, yhuã yn oquittac ycal ye ipan huitz. in ye ypã actihuetzi, yn aocmo huel momaquixtia oncan quimotzatzilili ynic quimopalehuiliz. yuh mochiuh quimopalehuili ynic amo mic. çan tlaltitlan yn quiquixtique, ynin iuh mochiuh yc cenca oc hualca yc omahuiçohuac yn S. Nicolas. nican mexico, auh ynic oppa mochihu in tlallolinaliztli teotlac. yc niman tlaocoltzillin nohuian in campanas. yn motenehua tzillin blecarias. yn izquican Monasterios. mexico ynic ye mochi nohuian tehteopan huel nohuian tlaocoltlatzilliniloc, yn ipampa tlallolinaliztli vncã achto peuh yn iglesia mayor. tzillin. campanas. auh yn ipampa yniqu iuh nohuian tlaocoltlatzilliniloc ỹ Mexico. yc cenca tlacox.[3] motequipacho. yn quicac tlahtohuani arçobpo. visurrey. ca noço huel pacticatca [*p. 157*] Yntla. yn tlahtoque, yn quaquauhtlatlachia. cenca quitequipacho, yn tlaocoltlatzilliniliztli quicac nohuiã mantoc, ynic tlaocoyalo netequipacholo. nemauhtillo yhuã tlatlauhtilo yn tt^o^. Dios. ynic techmopalehuiliz. yehica yn ipan in yc oppa mochiuh tlallolinaliztli, oncã caquiztic. yn tleyn caquiztic, mochi tlacatl yuh quicac. yuhquin ce carreda, chachalcatia. ynic motlallo, ynic caquiztic, yn campa hualcaquiztic. cuix tlillitic.[4] cuix noço ylhuicacpa, ca amo huel momati yece huel caquiztic, yn iuhqui ma ytla motlallo, yc no cuel

1. Though the two occurrences of *ichcapixque*, "shepherds," seem to clash with each other somewhat, the intention is clear: bishops are not ordinary shepherds but caretakers for their human flocks, widely responsible for them.

2. Apparently "totlacocol" is for "totlahtlacol" or the like, with the wrong syllable re-

keepers of sheep. Bishops and archbishops are shepherds[1] when something like this happens to people, very frightening and shocking; as long as they are at the head, lead and guide in the holy Church, they are the ones who should first cry out, give instructions, warn people about things, what and what kind of thing is really needed: that their flock, those guided by them, the citizens of the altepetl, should perform prayer, penitence, processions. Penitence should begin first with the rulers, so that their subjects will see it in them and follow them, so that by penitence, tears, sorrowing, fasting they will placate our lord God, because perhaps what is happening to people, disease or something else, or whatever it should be that is frightening and shocking, wherever such things happen to people as have happened to us here in Mexico now, happens because of our [sins],[2] perhaps through his anger, and is fitting. And because the ruler don fray García Guerra, archbishop and viceroy, thought nothing of what has happened to us here now and was not afraid of it, he gave orders that there should be bullfighting in his presence in the palace corral, because he is a great lover of bullfighting, so that everyone assembled and went into the corral, where there was bullfighting all day Friday; there the lords judges of the Royal Audiencia assembled. [*p. 156*] They were enjoying themselves there together with the archbishop and viceroy watching the bulls when an earthquake befell them again, at 3 o'clock in the afternoon, the second time that it happened that the earthquake returned and broke out. And although it was strong again, it wasn't quite as strong as when it first took place at night, it just passed quickly and damaged only a few things. At that time the wall of the church of San Juan Bautista of Moyotlan, called San Juan de la Penitencia, cracked in two, and also at that time a Spanish woman and her children were buried in a house which fell in; they did not die because the beams of the house just fell gently on them inside the house, at the wall, so that the beams lay sideways, by which our lord God helped her. The beloved of our lord God the lord San Nicolás de Tolentino in his name performed a miracle for the Spanish woman. It was said that this woman, when she realized the earth was shaking and saw that her house was coming down on her, was falling in on her and she could no longer be saved, cried out to him to help her. And it came to pass that he helped her, so that she did not die; they pulled her out from on the ground. Because this happened, San Nicolás was worshipped even more here in Mexico. Right after the second time there was an earthquake, in the afternoon, the bells pealed everywhere in mourning; they rang for what are called public prayers at all the monasteries in Mexico. In all the churches absolutely everywhere the bells pealed in mourning because of the earthquake; they began to ring first at the cathedral. And because of this mournful pealing of the bells everywhere in Mexico, the ruler, the archbishop and viceroy became very sad[3] and worried when he heard it, for he was really enjoying himself [*p. 157*] among the lords watching the bulls. He was greatly concerned by the pealing of the bells that he heard spread all around, showing sadness, worry, fear, and prayer to our lord God to aid us, because during this second time that there was an earthquake, there was a sound, and everyone heard what kind of sound it was; it sounded like a cart grating along; it sounded like running. Where the sound came from, whether from inside the earth[4] or from the sky, could not be established, but it was heard clearly, as though something were running, so

---

duplicated. But conceivably it is from *cocoa* and means "our harmful actions."

3. For "tlayocox."
4. For "tlallitic."

yehuatl ypampa yn cenca nemauhtiloc = auh yece in yehuatzin arçobpo visurrey. amo nimã yc mocauhtzino. yn quaquauhtlatlachiaya. macihui n ça tlaocoxticatca, yn quicaqui campanas tzillini amo yc tetlacahualti yn tlamiminallo, çan iuh yohuac, yn tlamiminaloc, yece yuh omihto, ça mocхарактерcotiuh. cuel yn callac tecpan yn icochian, ynic tzonquiz quaquamiminaliztli oncan peuhtica yn, yn ça mocotinemi[1] arçobispo, yn aocmo pactinemi yhuan yhquac oncan[2] in miyec tlacatl españoles. yhuan teopixq̃. ytech quallanque, ynic amo tle yc topan tlahtohua tlatlauhtiliztli, mochihuaz. yn ipampa yuhqui topan omochiuh axcan, ye oc cẽca oquimonequilti yn pahpactinemiz. ynic quaquanminaloz. yn ipan in viernes. yc cenca oquimopinahuilique, oc cenca yehuantzitzin inquisidores. ynic çatepan oquihualmotlacahualtilique. yn aocmo oncan tlamiminaloz. corral, yc oquixitinique mochi yn quauhtlatzatzaqualli oncan quimanca. moch oquiquixtique. [*p. 158*]

v Yn ipan axcan ypehuayan metztli Setiembre de 1611 años yhquac omachiztico. ohualla tlahtolli yn ompa españa. omomiquilli yn licẽciado Diego lanteras. anoço valderas de velasco,[3] oydor del real consejo, de las indias, yehuatl yn visitador. omochiuhtzinoco, nican ypan nueua españa. Mexico. / no ypan in. ytlamian ỹ metztli omoteneuh ỹ nicã mexico. ohuallaque omentin S. Fran^co^ de Paula teopixq̃. ỹ motenehua Minimos.

v Axcan Sabado. yc .10. mani metztli Setiembre de 1611. a^o^s. yhquac pielli omochiuh yn ilhuitzin yc oquiz. señor. S. Niculas de Tolentino. S. Augustin teopixqui, Patron omochiuhtzino. ỹ nican ypan ciudad. Mexico, yn ipampa tlallolinaliztli, omochiuh chicahuac, yn omoteneuh tlacpac. ypan metztli Agosto, mochiuh yn oncã. quimochihuilli ce tlamahuiçolli. S. Niculas. yn ipan ce señora. motlapachoca. ca yehuatl ipampa yn yn iqu intepantlahtocatzin. oquimochihuillique españoles. yhuã tehuantin timacehualti Mexico. oc cenca yehuatzin yn tlahtohuani arçobispo visurrey ySanctotepantlahtocatzin. oquimochihuilli, yn ipampa ça mococotzinotinemi, huell ipan motlahtolti. ynic pieloz. ytlaçoylhuitzin, oc macuililhuitl tacizque. yn ilhuitzin yez. yntzontec.[4] oncan audiencia real, quimocepanhuilique. yn oydoresme ynic Patron mochiuhtzino, yehica amo quiçaznequi, yn tlallolinaliztli, çan momoztlaye, yn tepitzin. yc tlallolini, ynic ompa hualpeuhtica yn omoteneuh cenca chicahuac yc tlallolin ynic axcan Sabado, ye matlacpan tlallolini, çan moztlatica huiptlatica mochiuhtiuh —

v Axcan Juebes. yc .17. mani metztli Nouiembre de 1611. [*p. 159*] Años. huel ypan ylhuitzin Sant. Gregorio. tamadorgo. obispo, Patron. yn nicã ciudad Mexico. yhquac azcapotzalco. quimacato. possion.[5] Juan grande nahuatlahto. yn Don Antonio valeriano telpochtli, vmpa quicahuato. ynic Juez gouernador vmpa mochihuato, compatlato. Don Balthasar m̄n̄. vmpa Juez gouernador catca. nican S. Pablo çoquipan ychan auh ynin omoteneuh Don Antonio valeriano telpochtli fiscal catca. ỹ nican S. Joseph. S. Fran^co^. yn onca yehuac yc mohuicac azcapotzalco, ynin telpochtli, yxhuiuhtzin. yn tlacatl huehue Don Antonio valeriano ychantzinco azcapotzalco. in miyec xihuitl. nican omoJuezgouernadortilico, Mexico tenochtitlan, ypãpa yn inamictzin cihuapilli Doña isabel de aluarado, yn ichpochtzin catca tlacatl Don diego de aluarado. huanitzin tlahtohuani catca tenochtitlan. auh çan tel ychan yn omohuicac azcapotzalco. telpochtli Don Antonio, vmpa cihuapilli, yn inantzin catca. yhuan yn omotocateneuh ycoltzin catca. vmpa chane.

1. For "mococotinemi."
2. Perhaps the meaning is "at that point," merely reinforcing "when."

that everyone was very frightened again because of that. = But the archbishop and viceroy did not therefore stop watching the bulls then; even though he was sad when he heard the bells ringing, he did not therefore halt the bullfighting, but the bullfighting kept on until nightfall. But it was said that he began to get ill as soon as he entered his bedroom in the palace when the bullfighting ended; at that time it began that the archbishop was constantly sick[1] and no longer healthy. And at that time many Spaniards and religious there[2] got angry at him because he did not order prayers said for us because of what just happened to us, and especially he wanted to go about enjoying himself with bullfighting on this Friday, so that they heaped shame on him, especially the inquisitors, so that afterward they prohibited bullfighting in the corral any longer and tore down all the wooden enclosures he had set up there; they removed them all. [*p. 158*]

v Today, at the beginning of the month of September of the year 1611, was when it became known and word came from Spain that licenciado Diego Landeras or Valderas de Velasco,[3] judge of the Royal Council of the Indies, had passed away. He had come here to New Spain and Mexico as inspector general. / Also, at the end of the said month two friars of the order of San Francisco de Paula, called Minimites, came here to Mexico.

v Today, Saturday the 10th of the month of September of the year 1611, was when the feast day of the lord San Nicolás de Tolentino, an Augustinian friar, was observed and celebrated. He has become the patron in the city of Mexico here, because in the strong earthquake that as was mentioned above took place in the month of August, San Nicolás performed a miracle on a Spanish woman who had been buried [under rubble], and it was because of this that the Spaniards, along with us commoners, made him their intercessor. Especially the ruler, the archbishop and viceroy, made him his saintly intercessor, because he was constantly ill. He spoke strongly in favor of holding his precious feast day five days before the day was to come. It was by pronouncement[4] of the Royal Audiencia, done by all the civil judges together, that he was made patron, because the earthquakes do not want to end, every day the earth shakes a little bit. Beginning with the said very strong earthquake until today, Saturday, the earth has shaken ten times; it happens every day or every other day. —

v Today, Thursday the 17th of the month of November of the year 1611, [*p. 159*] right on the feast day of San Gregorio Taumaturgo, bishop, patron here in the city of Mexico, was when Juan Grande, interpreter, took don Antonio Valeriano the younger to Azcapotzalco to give him possession[5] of office, he having been appointed judge-governor there. He replaced don Baltasar Martín, who was judge-governor there and is from San Pablo Çoquipan here. This said don Antonio Valeriano the younger was fiscal here at San Josef at San Francisco, and he left there when he went to Azcapotzalco. This young man is the grandchild of the lord don Antonio Valeriano the elder, from Azcapotzalco, who served as judge-governor for many years here in Mexico Tenochtitlan, because his spouse was the lady doña Isabel de Alvarado, who was the daughter of the lord don Diego de Alvarado Huanitzin, who was a ruler of Tenochtitlan. Thus don Antonio the younger was just going home to Azcapotzalco; his mother was a noblewoman there, and his grandfather whose name was mentioned was from there.

3. See pp. 92–93 at n. 6. Here Ch. uses Velasco, apparently the preferred version.
4. It seems that "yntlatzontec" would be required.
5. For "possession" or the like.

v̲ Axcan Martes. yc 29. mani metztli Nouiembre de 1611. años. yhquac oceppa[1] omocuepque, yn oyahque. yancuic Mexico. yn Padre fray isidro. yn inehuan fran^{co} faustino quetzalmaçatzin donado. amaquemecan ychan. yn quinmanillico oc cequintin S. Fran^{co} teopixque. yn ompa quinmohuiquillia yancuic Mexico. vmpa motemachtilizque. auh çan omacuiltetlMetztico. ỹ nican Mexico tenochtitlan. yn Padre fr. isidro. yn inehuan fran^{co} faustino quetzalmaçatzin.

v̲ Axcan lunes. yc .19. mani metztli de diziembre de 1611. años. yhuac opeuh yn omoman quiyahuitl cehualatl,[2] ynic o[*p. 160*]ceppayauh. yn intech yztac tepetl. yhuan popocatepetl cenca yc moquimiloque, yn ceppayahuitl, yhuan ynic nohuiampa quauhtla, yn intech tetepe, nohuian yntech huetz. yn ceppayahuitl. nahuilhuitl yn cenca cehuac ynic quiyauh ypan Juebes. yn quiçaco cehualatl ynic ceppayauh[3]

¶ iii. tecpatl xihuitl, 1612. años. nican motlallique in al~~ld~~esme Mexico. diego de S. Fran^{co} ychan tequicaltitlan yhuan esteuan ______ ychan S. xp̅o̅ual. xancopincan aztacalco.[4]

v̲ Axcan Sabado. yc 21. mani metztli henero. de 1612. años yhquac notificacion, oquichihuillito. S. Joseph. S. Fran^{co} yn fray Jeronimo de çarate. capellan S. Joseph. yehuatl oncan notificacion quichihuillico, yn señor fran^{co} franco, escriuano audiencia real, yntlanahuatilticatzinco yn señores. oydoresme. yn iuh mochiuh ypampa quiteylhui yn Maria lupez. chocolanamacac.[5] tetzcoco ychã yece nican Mexico tlatilco. omochantico. ye nican moyotlan ponhui. auh ynic quiteylhui fra[6] Jeronimo de çarate, yn Maria lupez. ypampa ynamic yn itoca Juan perez. quipinauhti ypan domingo yn õcã catca yc ychicomeyoc S. Joseph temimiltitech quiquetz. çan petlauhticaca. auh achi cocoxqui. yn oncan ytlanahuatiltica tothatzin. quimecahuitecque. yhquac quicauhque. yn ça yuhqui micqui. yn oçotlahuac. Mecatica, yhuan [*p. 161*] Yca temachti, quihto yn ipan bulpito ca oquipopolo miec tomines. cofradia huentli yhuan yc niman teilpiloyan quihualtehuicalti quitzacuaco. ynic niman quixtlahualtiaya, auh yn icihuauh amo yxpan auh yn ihquac oylhuiloc yn oquimatqui yn iuhqui ypan omochiuh ynamic yc cenca cuallan motequipacho yn mecahuitecoc ynic niman ypampa audiencia real omoteylhuito, no yhuan mocepanteilhuito oc omentin ce Sachristian nemi ytoca Joseph Gomez. ynic ome cihuatzintli ytoca Maria gostança. çan no yuhqui ynpan quichiuh quinpinauhti teyxpan quinquetz. quinpepetlauh yn Joseph Gomez yc teyxpan quiquetz quipepetlauh quiteyttiti quimecahuitec çan quinananquilli yca oncamatl tlahtolli, auh in Maria Gostança ynic teyxpan quiquetz quiteyttiti quipepetlauh ychichihual pani catca çan ipampa ychan canato yn ipan omoteneuh Domingo // quill amo missa quicaquito teopan S. Joseph. auh amo quin iyopa inceltin yuh ynpan quichihu in yn ixquich ica nican yc hualcallac Mexico. ca mochi tlacatl yuh ỹpan quichihuaya. yn Mexica tenochca Moyoteca yehica in tleyn çan tepiton noço huey yc contequipachohuaya quicuallaniaya fr. Jeronimo de çarate ca niman quinpinauhtiaya teyxpan quinquetzaya yhuan oc cequi miec tlamantli in quichihuaya in nicã yc tlatoliniaya. in cequi ca huel tetlatlacoltica in tepinauhtiaya ynic teyxpan tequetzaya.

---

1. Presumably for "oc ceppa."

2. *Cehualatl momana* is in Molina in the Spanish section, under "llouer gran espacio de tiempo," but several other terms are also there, some of which have more connotations than just length. By its roots and the context here *cehualatl* apparently also refers to a cold or freezing rain. See also pp. 240–41 at n. 1.

v Today, Tuesday the 29th of the month of November of the year 1611, was when father fray Isidro, together with Francisco Faustino Quetzalmaçatzin, lay brother from Amaquemecan, they having gone to New Mexico, returned again.[1] They came to get other Franciscan friars to accompany them to New Mexico to preach there. Father fray Isidro together with Francisco Faustino Quetzalmaçatzin spent only five months here in Mexico Tenochtitlan.
v Today, Monday the 19th of the month of December of the year 1611, was when a persistent rain[2] began to set in, and [*p. 160*] on Iztaccihuatl and Popocatepetl it snowed; they were wrapped in a great deal of snow, and snow fell all around in the forests on the mountains. For four days there was a very cold rain; on Thursday the cold rain came to an end [and it snowed?].[3]

¶ 3 Flint Year, 1612. Here were installed the alcaldes in Mexico, Diego de San Francisco from Tequicaltitlan and Esteban ______ from San Cristóbal Xancopincan Aztacalco.[4]

v Today, Saturday the 21st of the month of January of the year 1612, was when they went to San Josef at San Francisco to make a notification to fray Gerónimo de Zárate, chaplain at San Josef; the one who came to notify him there was señor Francisco Franco, notary of the Royal Audiencia. It was done at the order of the lords judges of the Audiencia because of a complaint against him made by María López, chocolate[5] seller, who is from Tetzcoco but came here to Mexico Tlatilco to make her home and now belongs to Moyotlan. She complained of fray[6] Gerónimo de Zárate because he shamed her spouse named Juan Pérez on Sunday a week after [the feast day of] San Josef; he stood him up against a stone pillar, naked and quite ill, where by the order of our father they gave him a lashing. At that time they left him almost dead, having fainted from the lashing. And [*p. 161*] he preached about him, he said in the pulpit that he dissipated much money that had been offered to the cofradía, and then he had people take him to jail and lock him up, so that he would pay it back. This happened when his wife was not present, and when she was told and found out what had happened to her spouse, she got very angry and was worried about his having been given a lashing, so that she went right away to the Royal Audiencia to make a complaint about it. And also two others went jointly to make complaint; one works as a sacristan, named Josef Gómez, and the second is a woman named María Constanza. He did the same thing to them, shamed them in public, standing them up and stripping them. Josef Gómez he publicly stood up, stripped, displayed, and gave a lashing just because he talked back with a few words. And María Constanza he publicly stood up, displayed, stripped; her breasts were exposed. The reason they went to pick her up at her home on the said Sunday was just that // they say she didn't go to hear mass at the church of San Josef. This was not the first time, they were not the only ones to whom he did such things in the time since he entered Mexico here, for he treated all the Mexica Tenochca Moyoteca that way, because when they caused fray Gerónimo de Zárate concern or angered him about something whether little or big, he right away shamed

3. Or on Thursday the cold rain accompanied by snow ended?
4. Space was left for more.
5. The form *chocola-* is probably borrowed back into Nahuatl from Spanish.
6. For "fray."

porbito quihtohuaya ypan Sermon in tleyn tetlatlacol oquitemachili yn aço pinahuiztic yhuan yn manel camo pinahuiztic mochi oncan quihtohuaya yn ipan porbito, quitecaquitiaya yn ipan Sermon. yuhqui ma yehuatl Justicia mayor yhuan yuhquin quisidor mochiuhticatca mochi quimotequitiaya in huehuey Justiciatequitl, yn amoyac oc ce teopixqui yuhqui nican oquichihuaco yn izquĩtin ye quihualpia quihualmocuitlahuia capilla S. Joseph. [*p. 162*] Yhuan tecalnamacaya yn miccacalli yn canin mani tlatlaxillacalpan mochi quitemohuaya yca tlatlania yntla oquilhuito canin mani niman quitequixtiliaya quinamacaya intlanel camo teopan pouhqui. intlanel oncate nemaqueque yn huel tepilhuan ahnoço teyxhuihuan atle ypan quimonpohuaya atle ypan quimittaya huel quincuiliaya yn incal quinhualquixtiaya quinnamaquiliaya yn ipatiuh çan mochi quicuiya fr. Jeronimo de çarate quihtohuaya missas yc niquinchihuiliz in mimicque auh ayac quittaya yhuã ayac quimatiaya in quenin quitechihuiliaya miccamissa. yhuã anotle ytla oncan quinmacaya yn axcahuaque tlatquihuaque. yhuan huel mochi quitemohuaya in testamentos quittaya yniqu itech quimatia in tleyn cecenmimicque oquixexelotiaque auh yntla oquimah mopia testamento ỹtlacamo quititiznequi ỹtlacamo yhciuhca connextiaya yxpan ca yc teylpilloyan tetzacuaya no yc tepinauhtiaya. ynic ça no nepanol[1] onmoztlacahuiaya Mexica yn aquin tleyn quitemachilia. conilhuitimani connextilia ỹ fray Jeronimo de çarate ynic huel quitemoz ynic huel quitechihualtiz pani motlaliz neciz quinextilizque yn çaço tley ytech quittaya testamentos yn miccatlatquitl in manel cenca ye quezqui xihuitl omomiquilli micqui, intlanel ye omoneltilili ytlahtol in tlein ytestamento ytech oquitlalitia yn imiccanenahuatil oc ceppa moch quitemohuaya quiteyxtlahualtiaya. O ca yehuatl in ynic cenca tlatoliniaya omoteneuh Padre fr. Jeronimo de çarate ayac tle ypan quittaya in Mexica yhuã cequi españoles ayac tle ypan quittaya y manel tley yc tepampa quitlatlauhtiaya. yhuan oc cequi miec tlamãtli yn oquichihuaya yn intolliniloca mexica. amo huel mochi nican mihtoz motenehuaz ca cenca miec tlamantli [*p. 163*] Yn tepan quichihuaya amo monequi moch mihtoz. aço qualli ahnoço amo cualli. ma çan icel yc quimomaquiliz cuenta in tt^{o}. Dios. macamo ytalhuillo ma çan motelchihua quiyocolli[2] yehuatl quimati canel teopixqui ytetzinco pouhqui in tt^{o}. dios. ca tel yxpantzinco yxcoyan yc cuenta quimomaquiliz yn ihquac momiquiliz. auh yniqu iuhqui yn ynpan quichihuaya Mexica. ynic quintoliniaya yc cenca quitlahuelilocamatia auh macihui yn itechpa quallania tottatzin mexica. yn iqu iuh quinchihuaya yece çan quihiyohuiaya çan intech quipachohuaya, ayac huel motlapalohuaya in quiteyxpanhuiz quiteilhuiz audiencia real, intlacamo çan yehuatl huel omotlapalo yn omoteneuh Maria Lopez. oquiteilhui ymixpantzinco in tlahtoque oydores. oquichiuh yn iuh mochi omoteneuh ypeticion quicallaqui oncan acuerdo. oncã ytech yn ipeticion quimocaquiltique tlahtoq̃. mochi yn ixquich tlamantli oncan capilla S. Joseph. quichihua ynic tlatollinia moch quimocaquiltique quimomachiltique cenca quimomauhcayttilique. in tlahtoque ynic niman omotlanahuatilique oydores ynic notificacion ochihuililoto fr. Jeronimo de çarate yn axcan ypan omoteneuh Sabado yn oncan capilla San Joseph. ynic aocmo oncan ytequiuh yez capilla callaquiz callihtic motzacuaz conuento aocmo yehuatl

1. For "nepanotl."

2. The phrase *ma motelchihua* is usually an exhortation that a notion or proposal should be rejected in favor of another. We have speculatively translated the puzzling "quiyocolli" as though it were the reflexive *yocoya* (see Molina, "yocoya.nino").

them, stood them up in public, and did many other things here by which he mistreated everyone. In some cases it was for real sins that he would shame people and stand them up in public; he would say in the pulpit during the sermon what sins of people he had found out about. Whether something was shameful or not shameful, he would say it all in the pulpit, he would announce it in the sermon, as though he had been appointed chief justice or inquisitor. He took all the great duties of justice upon himself, as no other friar of all those who came here to be in charge of and take care of the chapel of San Josef did. [*p. 162*] And he would sell people's houses, the houses of the deceased that are in the various tlaxilacalli; he sought it all out and asked about it. If they told him where it was, he would right away take it from people and sell it, even if it did not belong to the church, and even if there were heirs who were truly the children or grandchildren, he would ignore them and consider them as nothing. He would actually take their houses from them, remove them from them and sell them away from them. Fray Gerónimo de Zárate would take all the money they were sold for, saying, "With it I will perform masses for the deceased." But no one saw or found out that he was performing masses for the dead, nor did he give anything to the property owners. He searched out absolutely all of the testaments; he inspected them so that he found out from them what each of the deceased distributed on dying. And if he found out that a testament was in people's custody, if they didn't want to show it to him, if they didn't quickly produce it in his presence, he would lock them up in jail and also shame them for it, so that the Mexica would betray each other;[1] whoever knew something about someone would tell and reveal it to fray Gerónimo de Zárate, so that he could seek it, could have people make it come to the surface and appear and they would reveal it to him. Whatever he saw in testaments in the way of property of the deceased, even though the deceased had passed away quite a few years ago, even though his command had already been carried out, he sought out whatever the testator had ordered in his testament and made people pay it a second time. This then is how the said father fray Gerónimo de Zárate greatly mistreated everyone, he thought nothing of the Mexica, and he thought nothing of some Spaniards, even when they implored him on someone's behalf about something. All of the many other things that he did to mistreat the Mexica cannot be said and told here, for there were a great many things [*p. 163*] that he did to people. It is not necessary to say it all, whether good or bad; let him alone give an accounting to our lord God. Let him not be talked about, forget about that. He did it of his own accord;[2] he is responsible, for he is a friar, he is dedicated to our lord God, and in his presence he will give an accounting to him himself when he dies. Because he did such things to the Mexica and mistreated them, they thought him very evil, but although the Mexica were angry about our father because he treated them like this, they had patience with him, they kept it inside, no one dared to make it public and make complaint to the Royal Audiencia, if it hadn't been for the said María López, who was so bold as to accuse him before the lords judges of the Audiencia. She did all the things aforementioned; she entered a petition when the court was in deliberation, and in her petition she announced to the judges all the different things that he did at the chapel of San Josef to mistreat everyone. The lords heard and found out about all of it, and saw it as a very frightful thing, so that right away the judges ordered that someone go and notify fray Gerónimo de Zárate today on the said Saturday at the chapel of San Josef that his duty would no longer be at the chapel. He was to go inside the monastery, shut

quinmocuitlahuiz in Mexica. yhuã ynic aocmo yuhqui quichihuaz tetolliniliztli tepinauhtiliztli yn temecahuitequiliztli yn iuh ynpan quichihuaya mexica yn necito tlacpac huel yxquich tlamantli quicahualtique ynic aocmo tepinauhtiz ynic aocmo temecahuitequiz ynic aocmo teyxpan tequetzaz. auh yc quipenatique ynic çan tzauhtiaz callihtic conuento yhcuac amo nican catca mexico yn commissario. quauhtemalan mohuicac, yhuan yn prouincial amo no nican mexico moyetzticat[*p. 164*]ca nohuiyan altepetl ypan mohuicac visita quimochihuilito. auh yece in yehuatl omoteneuh fr. Jeronimo de çarate. ca çan quexquichcauh çan quezquilhuitl ynic huel onmocauhca yn. ynic aocmo tle yc quintollini mexica ça mocauhticatca yece amo no yc quicauh in capilla S. Joseph. çan ya yehuatl oncan mocauh. yniqu itequiuh capillero mochiuhticatca —//—

v̲ Axcan lunes yc .30. mani Metztli henero de 1612. años. yhcuac oncan Sancto Domingo teotlac otlayahualoloc ypampatzinco nemecahuitecoc in teoyotica tlahtohuani Don fr. Garcia Guerra arçobispo visurrey. ynic cenca mococotzinoticatca momiquiliznequi, yn quimococolhuia postema ytzcaltzinco motlalli, auh yn omoteneuh yc tlayahualoloc yehuatzin oquimotlayahuallochtilique quimoquixtilique yn christo ymiquiliztzĩ in quimotemohuilitihui quimotoquilitihui mochipa ypan viernes Sancto. y monoltitiuh andasco quimonapalhuitiaque in Sancto Domingo teopixque. yn icatzinco tlatlatlauhtiloc arçobispo visurrey ynic quimopahtiliz quimoquechiliz tt^o^. dios. ynic amo quimotlatlatiliz quimomictiliz. auh yn omoteneuh yc tlayahualoloc ynic hualquixohuac S. Domingo teopan yc niman oncan hualhuilohuac yn iglesia mayor. quimoquixtilico yn inetoquiliz yxiptlatzin x̄p̄o. yc niman quimohuiquilique quimoquixtilito yn la casa professa. anoço San Ignacio. nimann ic quimohuiquilique quimoquixtilito S. Fran^co^. yc niman quimohuiquilique quimoquixtilito visitacion monjas ynic quimocuepilique yc niman huillohuac quimoquixtilito concepcion monjas. ayoticpac, yc niman quimohuiquilique quixohuato S. lurenço monjas. yc niman oc ceppa vmpa quimocallaquillito quimocahuilito yn teopan S. Domingo, auh no yhui yn izquican teopã monasterios yn oncan moyetzticate teopixque frayles [*p. 165*] huel yzquican no ypampatzinco tlatlatlauhtiloc, yn omoteneuhtzino teoyotica tlahtohuani arçobispo, auh çã no yhui yn izquican teopan monasterios monjas tlatlatlauhtiloc huel ce semana yn izquican mixtlapohuiltiticatca Sanctissimo Sacramẽto cecemilhuitl ynic amo momiquiliz. çan quimochicahuiliz in tt^o^. Dios. // auh niman yn ichicomeyoc yn ipan Domingo ynic .5. mani metztli febrero, ye yohua yn oquimotlapolhuilique postema yn omoteneuh motlalli ytzcaltzinco arçobispo. in quimococolhuia temalli yn oncan hualquiz. yevatl ynic momiquiliznequi —

v̲ Axcan Domingo yc .12. mani metztli febrero de 1612 años. yhcuac ye otzonquiz missa huey yn oncan capilla S. Joseph S. Fran^co^. oc achto tetzacualloc amoyac huel hualquiz quiyahuac, auh yn ihcuac ye otzacualloc yc nimã callihticpa yn hualquiz fr. Jeronimo de çarate, omopepetlauh mecatl yn iquechtlan oquitlalli yc oquihualtititztia yn oncan fiscal yc niman altar mayor omotlancuaquetzato yn tottatzin chocatia, quihtotia macamo ximotequipachocan yn anMexica. canel aocmo anquimottitillani yn tetl yn quahuitl, ma nehua nictzacua ynic niman oncan oyah in temimiltitech yn oncan otequetzaya yn otepinauhtiaya huel quinahuatequito yn temimilli oncan ye mohuitequi quilhuia fiscal

himself up there, and no longer take care of the Mexica. No longer was he to perform such mistreatment, shaming, and lashings as he had been inflicting on the Mexica, which appeared above. They stopped him from doing absolutely all the different things, so that he would no longer shame people, give them lashings, or stand them up in public. And they set a fine for him so that he would stay closed up inside the monastery. The commissary was not here in Mexico at that time, having gone to Guatemala, and the provincial head was not here in Mexico either; [*p. 164*] he had gone to the various altepetl all around, carrying out an inspection. But it was only for a little while, a few days, that the said fray Gerónimo de Zárate really stopped mistreating the Mexica in some way. He was stopped for the time being, but he did not therefore leave the chapel of San Josef, he was only prevented from holding the post of chaplain that he had been appointed to. —//—

v Today, Monday the 30th of the month of January of the year 1612, was when there was a procession at Santo Domingo in the afternoon; there was flagellation on account of the spiritual ruler don fray García Guerra, archbishop and viceroy, since he was very sick and on the point of death. An abscess that settled in his right side was hurting him. And for the said procession they took around and brought out the Death of Christ, which they always take down and follow on Good Friday, which lies on a carrying platform. The Dominican friars bore it; they were asked to in the name of the archbishop and viceroy, so that our lord God would heal him and raise him up, so he would not efface him and cause his death. And as to how the said procession went, when they came out of the church of Santo Domingo, they came and passed by the cathedral with the image of the burial of Christ; then they took it and passed by the Casa Profesa, or San Ignacio; then they took it and passed by San Francisco; then they took it and passed by the nunnery of the Visitación, where they turned it around, then went and passed by the nunnery of the Concepción at Ayoticpac with it; then they took it and passed by the nunnery of San Lorenzo; then they once again delivered it to and put it in the church of Santo Domingo. Likewise in all the monastery churches, where the friars are, [*p. 165*] in each one there were also prayers on behalf of the said spiritual ruler, the archbishop, and likewise there were prayers in all the nunnery churches. For a whole week the most Holy Sacrament was open to view every day so that he would not die, but rather our lord God would give him health. // Then on the seventh day [after the procession], on Sunday the 5th of the month of February, at night, they opened the abscess which as mentioned had settled in the archbishop's right side and was hurting him; pus came out of it; for that reason he was at the point of death. —

v Today, Sunday the 12th of the month of February of the year 1612, was when, the high mass at the chapel of San Josef at San Francisco having finished, people were shut in for a while; no one could come outside. And when people were closed in, then fray Gerónimo de Zárate came out from inside the building, stripped, with a rope placed at his neck, by which the fiscal there went pulling him until he knelt at the main altar. Our father went weeping, saying, "Do not worry, Mexica, for you will no longer be shown castigation; let me pay for it." Then he went next to the stone column where he used to stand people up and shame them and put his arms all the way around the column where people were

xinechhuitequi. auh yn fiscal amo tlapalohuaya[1] in quihuitequiz. ynic çan iyoma yehuatl ya mohuitequi tottatzin yc cenca ycahuacaque in Mexica yn quittaq̃. çan ic micahuique[2] quihtoque tleyca yn iuh quimochihuilia yn tottatzin auh çan quitlacahualtique yn tottatzin fr. Jeronimo de çarate ynic amo yuhqui quichihuaz ça caantiaque in callihtic quicallaquique yn ihcuac yn yuhqui quichiuh cenca mochicahua quiteylhuia audiencia real yn Maria Lopez. yece çan concahuaco yn ineteylhuil. amo quitzonquixti, ynic no niman [*p. 166*] Oc ceppa quipehualti omoteneuh fr. Jeronimo de çarate in ye tlatollinia in ye tepinauhtia yn iuh omoteneuh achtopa quichihuaya.

v̲ Axcan miercoles ynic .22. mani Metztli febrero de 1612. a^os. yhcuac omomiquilli in yecmahuizticatlacatzintli teoyotica tlahtohuani Don fray Garcia Guerra arcobispo[3] Mexico yvã visurrey omochiuhtzinoticatca in nican yhuã yn moch ic nohuiyã nueua españa teopixqui S. Domingo. ce tzilini ypan tlaco hora. tlacah yn opeuh ye tzilini ymiccatepoztzin nohuiyan monasterios. auh ynic teoyotica tlahtohuani ynic arçobispo omoyetzticatca Mexico, yexihuitl ypan nauhtetl Metztli ypã cenpohuallonnahui tonatiuh yn axcan ypan yc omomiquillico. auh ynic tlalticpacayotica omotlahtocatilli ynic visurrei omochiuhtzinoticatca. çan chicuetetl Metztli ypan nahuilhuitl yn axcan ypan yc cemilhuitl miercoles omomiquillico, yehuatl yc momiquillico yn omoteneuh postema, yn itzcaltzinco quimotlapohuilique. auh huel mochi tlacatl yuh quihto yn teopixque yhuan españoles. ca çan yehuantin quimomictilique in medigos yn iticitzitzinhuan quimopahtiliaya omentin yn españoles yn ce vmpa quihualmohuiquilli yn españa ytoca Doctor pineda. auh ynic ome amo huel momati yn itoca Doctor.

v̲ Auh ye quin Sabado axcan ynic .25. mani Metztli febrero de 1612. años. yn otococ ynacayotzin yehuatzin teoyotica tlahtohuani Don fray Garcia Guerra arçobispo Mexico yhuan visurrey. ometzticatca. Oc onahuilhuiti yn oonoca ynacayotzin yn oncan Capilla palacio. çaniuh chichiuhtoya yca in teoyotica ytlahtocateopixcanechichihualtzin yn motenehua ornamẽtos. pontificales. yn imitratzin yhuan casulla morada yhuan [*p. 167*] Yn itopiltzin baculo, quimotquilitoya, yhuan in cruz quimoyacaniliaya ynic arçobispo ycxitlantzinco yxpantzinco yhcaya. yhuan yn oc cequi tlamantli ytlahtocamahuizçotzin ynic visurrey. moyetzticatca moch oncan catca ytlantzinco, oncan mochi tlacatl contennamiquia yn imatzin, ynic õcan ytechtzinco mocnopilhuiaya onpohualilhuitl yn tecentlapopolhuiliztli indulgencias. auh yn omoteneuh axcã ypan Sabado. yn oquic ayemo quihualmoquixtiliaya ynacayotzin yn oncan monoltitoya Capilla oncan cecen responso, ypantzinco quimihtalhuito mochintzitzin yn izqui tlamantin nepapan teopixque Mexico onoque, auh yn ihcuac ye otlanque in ye ixquich niman ye netecpano ynic quixohuaz oncan palacio. ye teotlac, auh yn onetecpanoc yc niman peuh in ye quixohua huel yei tzilli ypan tlaco hora, teotlac, auh ynic netecpanoc ynic quixohuac oncan tecpan palacio, huel tlayacac mantiaque in timacehualtĩ mexica, huel yzquicanpa oncã huallaque quihualcencauhque mochintin yn izquicampa Cofradias. quimopialia Mexica, in S. Juan Moyotlan tlaca, yhuan S. Pablo teopan tlaca, yhuã S. sebastian atzacualco tlaca. yhuan S.ta maria cuepopan, yhuã in Sanctiago tlatilolco, huel yzquicampa cecen cruz manca. quihualhuicaque, yhuan cecen estandarte ahnoço vanderra yn izqui ypan Cofradias. mopia huel yzquican hualla, auh yehuãtin tlayacac mantiaque yn omoteneuhque Mexica ynic oncan quixohuac

1. For "amo motlapalohuaya."
2. For "miçahuique."

lashed, and said to the fiscal, "Whip me!" But the fiscal did not dare[1] whip him, so that our father began to whip himself on his own, because of which the Mexica who saw it greatly murmured and were taken aback by it.[2] They said, "Why is our father doing that?" And they restrained our father fray Gerónimo de Zárate from doing it; various of them grabbed him and put him in the interior of the building. When this was done María López was greatly encouraged in her complaint to the Royal Audiencia, but the Audiencia halted her complaint and did not bring it to a conclusion, so that right away [*p. 166*] the said fray Gerónimo de Zárate began again to treat everyone badly and shame people as was mentioned that he had done before.

v Today, Wednesday the 22nd of the month of February of the year 1612, was when the truly reverend lord the spiritual ruler don fray García Guerra, who was archbishop[3] in Mexico and appointed viceroy here and all over New Spain, Dominican friar, passed away. At half past 1 o'clock in the daytime the bells began to toll for him in the monasteries everywhere. Today, on the day he passed away, he had been spiritual ruler and archbishop in Mexico for 3 years, 4 months, and 24 days. And he had ruled in earthly matters, appointed viceroy, for only 8 months and 4 days today on the day of Wednesday when he passed away. He died of the said abscess that they opened on his right side. Absolutely all of the religious and Spaniards said that it was just the doctors, his physicians, who killed him. Two Spaniards were treating him; one he brought here from Spain, named dr. Pineda, and the name of the other doctor cannot be established.

v Not until Saturday, today the 25th of the month of February of the year 1612, was the body of the spiritual ruler don fray García Guerra, late archbishop in Mexico and viceroy, buried. First his body had lain for four days in the palace chapel. He was outfitted in his full normal gear as a priestly ruler, called pontifical ornaments: his miter and purple chasuble, and [*p. 167*] he lay carrying his staff, the crozier; and the cross that used to precede him as archbishop stood at his feet, facing him. And all his other ruler's insignia as viceroy were at his side. Everyone there was kissing his hands, so that thereby they would attain forty days of general pardon, indulgences. And today, on the said Saturday, before they had come to remove his body from where it lay in the chapel, all the different groups of religious who live in Mexico went to say a responsory prayer each for him. And when they had finished, when it was over, everyone lined up to come out of the palace; it was afternoon by then. When they had lined up and began to come out, it was fully half past three o'clock in the afternoon. As to how they were lined up as they came out of the palace, we Mexica commoners went at the very front. Absolutely all the cofradías that the Mexica have for each of the sections came along and had made preparations: the people of San Juan Moyotlan, the people of San Pablo Teopan, the people of San Sebastián Atzaqualco, Santa María Cuepopan, and Santiago Tlatelolco. Every single one each brought a decorated cross and a standard or banner, which are kept by each of the cofradías. They came from absolutely all the sections, and the said Mexica went in a group at the front as people came out of the palace. —

3. For "arçobispo."

tecpan palacio, —

v Auh yc niman yehuantin quimontocatiaque in pipiltzitzinti ycnotlaca in huapahuallo S. Juan de letra in motenehua colegio de los niños, quihuicaq̃. yn incruz teocuitlatl plata tepitzin.

v Auh yc niman yehuantin quimontocatiaque. yn mulatoti inco[*p. 168*]fradia quipia tlayacatitihui // ynic niman yehuantin quimõtocatiaque yn españoles. yn izquicampa Cofradias quipia mexico, çan tel yc cepanmantiaque yn omoteneuhque mulatotih,[1] mochintin cecen quihuicatiaque yn esdantardes yn invamderra, in ye mochi mocenpohua ymaxca españoles cenpohualli. yehuatl tecenpohualca yn iesdantardetzin yn ivamderratzin totlaçonantzin S.ta maria nuestra Señora del rosario, ça tlatocatiuh, yehica ca ya huecahua ca achto motlalli ynon Cofradia S Domingo catqui, ça ce in ye mochi omoteneuh cofradias. çan imamanian in tecpantiaque ynic mantiaque ynic yahtiaque —

v Auh ynic no niman yehuantin quimontocatiaque in motenehua hermanos de convalecientes. yn quimocuitlahuia hospital S.t ipolito, aço çan matlactin yn oncan mantiaq̃. ce yn cruz manca quihuicaque yhuan ytloc mantia ome ciliares, yhuan ce clerigo yncapellan capa quitlalitia, yhuan ytloc mantiaque ome diagonos almaticas quitlalitiaque —

v Auh yc niman yehuantin quimontocatiaque in çã no motenehua hermanos yn ipilhuantzitzin Beato Juan de dios. in çano quimocuitlahuia hospital desmamparados. ahço çã quen matlactlomomentin yn oncan mantiaque. ce yn cruz[2] manca quihuicaque ytloc mantia ome ciliares yhuan ce capa quitlalitia. yehuatl in hermano mayor. ahnoço fundador. sacerdote, yhuan ytloc mantiaque ome diagonos almaticas quitlallitiaque. no sacerdotes, çanno hermanos yn itlatecpampa yn itlaçotzin tt^{o}. Juan de dios. —

v Auh yc niman yehuantzitzin quimonmotoquilitiaque in cẽca mahuiztililoni yxtililoni yn teotlamachilizticatzinco [*p. 169*] Yn motenehua Teopixque La compañia de Jesus. in çan quincuitia yc notzallo teatinos, ca amo yehuantzitzin ynnotzalloca ca oc centlamantin vmpa moyetztica in Roma yhuan Italia in teopixque teatinos. yhuan yc monotza la congregacion de los Clerigos reglares, ynin ypilhuan huel achto ytlatlalilhuan yn Don Pedro carrafa obispo vmpa yn ipan altepetl Teatinense. auh ynin obispo çatepan cardenal omochiuh yequene Sancto Padre mochiuhtzinoco quimotocayotitzino yn ipan yc quimocoronamaquilique Paulo Quarto. o yehuatzin in yn intatzin in huel yehuãtin teopixque motenehua Teatinos yn ayemo hualmohuica nican ypan nueua españa, // ma yc teyollo pachihui ca oc centlamantintzitzin in ye nican moyetzticatca mexico, yn incatzinco titlahtohua, çan huel yxquich ỹnotzallocatzin teopixque la compañia de Jesus. in yehuantzitzin in teopixque aço huel yepohuallonmatlactin. yn oncan momaniltitiaque yn omoteneuh yc tecococ, atle cruz manca quimohuiquilique, çaniuh moquixtique çaniuh mohuicaque yhuan anotle capa quimotlalilitiaq̃. çaniuh mochintzitzin mantiaque yca yn inçodanatzin yhuan inmanteotzin yn iuh mochipa monemiltia — mochintzitzin cecencandelas ỹmactzinco. —

v Auh yc niman yehuantzitzin quimonmotoquilitiaque in cenca mahuiztililoni teopixque in motenehua mercenadios, yn itlaçopilhuantzitzinhuan in tohueycihuatlahtocatecuiyo totlaçomahuiznantzin Sancta maria las mercedes de la redẽption de los cautiuos, ahço huel onpohualtin yn oncan momaniltitiaque omoteneuh yc tetococ, ce yn cruz manca quimohuiquilique ytloc mantia ome ciliares. yhuan ce capa quimotlalilitia[3] yhuan ytloctzinco mantiaque ome diagonos almaticas quitlallitiaq̃. [*p. 170*]

---

1. Another possible interpretation is that the mulattoes went as a group (by themselves).

v And next there followed them the orphaned children who are raised at San Juan de Letrán, which is called the Colegio de los Niños; they took along their small silver cross.

v Then after them followed the mulattoes who have their cofradía, [*p. 168*] going in front [of the Spaniards]. // Then after them followed the Spaniards in all the cofradías they have in Mexico, but they went along in a group with the said mulattoes.[1] They all went carrying a standard or banner each. A total of twenty belong to the Spaniards; the twentieth is the standard and banner of our precious mother Santa María, our lady of the rosary. It came at the end because it has lasted a long time, for that cofradía was first established at Santo Domingo. Each of all the said cofradías was arranged in line in its place [according to seniority] as they went along in groups and proceeded. —
v Then after them followed those called the Brothers of the Convalescents, who take care of the hospital of San Hipólito. Perhaps only ten of them went along in a group carrying a decorated cross; next to it went two processional candlesticks, and a secular priest, their chaplain, wore a cape, and at his side went two deacons wearing their vestments. —
v Then after them followed those likewise called Brothers, the children of the beatified Juan de Dios, who in the same fashion take care of the hospital of Desamparados. Perhaps about twelve of them went along in a group there, carrying a decorated cross,[2] and next to it went two processional candlesticks. The senior brother or founder, a priest, wore a cape, and at his side went two deacons wearing their vestments, also priests and likewise brothers of the order of the beloved of our lord Juan de Dios. —
v Then after them followed those who are very much to be revered and respected for their knowledge of the divinity, [*p. 169*] called the religious of the Company of Jesus, whom they acknowledge to be and are called Theatines, but that is not their [true] appellation, for residing in Rome and Italy is another group of religious, the Theatines, also called the congregation of regular priests. They are the children of and were first founded by don Pedro Caraffa, bishop in the altepetl of Thete. This bishop later became a cardinal, and finally he came to be made pope. At the time they crowned him he took the name of Paul IV. He was the father of the religious who are truly called Theatines, who have not yet come here to New Spain. // May people's minds be put to rest thereby, for it is a different group that is here in Mexico and that we are talking about, whose only real appellation is religious of the Company of Jesus. Perhaps as many as seventy of these religious went along there in a group to the said burial; they did not take any decorated cross, they just came out and went along as they usually are. Nor did they wear capes; they all just went along as usual with their cassocks and long cloaks, as they always go about, each of them with a candle in his hand. —
v Then after them went following the very reverend friars called Mercedarians, the precious children of our great queenly lady, our precious revered mother Santa María de las Mercedes y de la Redención de los Cautivos. Perhaps a full forty of them went along in a group to the said burial, taking with them a decorated cross with two processional candlesticks going beside it; [a priest] went along wearing a cape,[3] and at his side went two deacons wearing their vestments. [*p. 170*]

2. The original could be interpreted as *yncruz*, "their cross," rather than *yn cruz*, "the cross," in this case as in several others.
3. See pp. 204–05, n. 1.

v Auh yc niman yehuantzitzin. quimonmotoquilitiaque, in cenca mahuiztililoni tlaçoteopixque Carmenitas descalsos, in çã no ytlaçopilhuãtzitzinhuan in tohuecihuatlahtocatecuiyo. totlaçomahuiznantzin in moteneuhtzinohua nuestra Señora S.ta maria del carme, amo miequintzitzin ahço çan quen matlactintzitzin yn oncan momaniltitiaque omoteneuh yc tetococ, auh çan cuauhcruz tepitzin nepaniuhqui coztic teocuitlayo. tlapallo, in quimohuiquillique, ytloc mantia ome cuauhciliares, yhuan ce capa quimotlalilitia.[1] yhuan necoc ytloctzinco mantiaq̃. ome diagonos. almaticas quitlalitiaque —

v Auh yc niman yehuantzitzin quimonmotoquilitiaque in cenca mahuiztililoni teopixque hermitaños. yn itlaçopilhuantzitzinhuan totlaçomahuiztatzin S. Augustin. Obispo Hiponia huey yteotlamatilizmatcatzin in Sancta yglesia. ahço huel nauhpohuallonmatlactin yn oncan momaniltitiaque omoteneuh yc tetococ. ce yn cruz manca quimohuiquilique necoc ytloc mantia ome ciliares, yhuan ce capa quimotlalilitia yhuan necoc ytloctzinco mantiaque ome diagonos. almaticas quitlalitiaque —

v Auh yc niman yehuantzitzin quimonmotoquilitiaque in cẽca mahuiztililoni teopixque Menores. yn itlaçopilhuãtzitzinhuan totlaçomahuiztatzin S. Fran^co^ Patriarcha. ahço huel macuilpohuallonmatlactin. yn oncan momaniltitiaque omoteneuh yc tetocac, çan ic mocentlamantiliq̃. çan ic cenyahque çan ic cenmomaniltitiaque. in teopixq̃. descalços, canel çan ic cen ytlaçopilhuantzitzinhuan yn omoteneuhtzino totlaçottatzin S. Fran^co^, no yhuan oncã [*p. 171*] Yntlantzinco momaniltitiaque, yeintin teopixque trinidarios in quimopialia ytech ca ymescapulariotzin yztac ce cruz chichiltic yhuan xoxoctic. in motenehua ytlaçopilhuantzitzinhuã yn ieytilitzin tt^o^. dios. la Sancta Trinidad, ca no yc notzallo de la Redemption de captiuos, auh yn omoteneuhtzinoque teopixque S. Fran^co^. ce yn cruz manca quimohuiquilique necoc ytloc mantia ome ciliares, yhuã ce capa quimotlalilitia yhuan necoc ytloctzinco mantiaque. ome diagonos almaticas quitlalitiaque —

v Auh yc niman yehuantzitzin. in huel yehuantin miccahuaque. quimonmotoquilitiaque. in cenca mahuiztililoni teopixque in moteneuhtzinohua predicadores. yn itlaçopilhuantzitzinhuan totlaçomahuiztatzin, S. Domingo. Patriarcha, ahço huel macuilpohuallonmatlactin, yn oncan momaniltitiaque omoteneuh yc tetococ. ce cruz manca quimohuiquilique necoc ytloc mantia ome ciliares, yhuan ce capa quimotlalilitia yhuan necoc ytloctzinco mantiaque ome diagonos. almaticas quitlalitiaque —

v Auh ynic niman yehuantzitzin quimonmotoquilitiaque in huel tlacpac moyetzticate. in huel teachcauhtzitzinhuan. clerigos. in cabildo tlaca. motenehua Canonigos cathedrales. yn itlaçomahuizpilhuantzitzinhuan totlaçomahuiztatzin Señor S. Pedro. Principe, quihtoznequi tlahtocapiltachcauhtzin yn ipan S.ta yglesia, ynin çan ic mocetilitzinoque çan monepanotzinoque çan mocepanmaniltitiaque. in vela cruz perroquia tlaca clerigos. yhuan S.ta catalina Martyr perroquia tlaca clerigos amo huel mochiuh ynic nononcua mantiazquia, auh mochintintzitzin Sobrepelliz. quimotlalilitiaque ynbonetestzin auh amo huel mopohua in ye mochintzitzin clerigos. oncan [*p. 172*] momaniltitiaque omoteneuh yc tetococ, ca cenca miyequintzitzin, ce yn cruz manca quimohuiquillique necoc ytloc mantia ome ciliares, auh yehuatzin capa quimotlalilitia in cenca mahuiztililoni Señor Doctor Sausedo arcediano, yhuan necoc ytloctzinco mantiaque ome diagonos almaticas tliltic

---

1. The subject of "quimotlaliltia," went wearing, is singular. The only apparent candidate for subject in the immediate vicinity is the cross itself. It was a well established practice to have a priest in a cape surrounded by two deacons on all sorts of ceremonial occasions. We can only presume that Ch. omitted a word for the priest by mistake, or

v Then followed the very reverend precious friars the Discalced Carmelites, who are likewise precious children of our great queenly lady our precious revered mother called our Lady Santa María del Carmen. There were not many of them, perhaps only about ten, who went along to the said burial, and they just took along just a little wooden cross joined together and colored gold. Beside it went two wooden processional candlesticks; [a priest] went wearing[1] a cape, and next to him on both sides went two deacons wearing their vestments. —

v Then followed after them the very reverend friars the Hermits, the precious children of our precious revered father San Agustín, bishop of Hippo, the holy church's great expert on theology. Perhaps a full ninety of them went along in a group to the said burial. They took along a decorated cross; on both sides of it went two processional candlesticks, a priest went wearing a cape, and on both sides next to him went two deacons wearing their vestments. —

v Then after them followed the very reverend Friars Minor, the precious children of our precious revered father San Francisco the patriarch. Perhaps there were a full hundred and ten of them going along in a group to the said burial. The Discalced friars formed a single group with them, they went together and went along as a group, because they are all together precious children of our said precious father San Francisco. And also [*p. 171*] three Trinitarian friars went along among them; they have a white scapular with a red and green cross on it; these said precious children of the three-part nature of our lord God, the Holy Trinity, are also called [by the name of] the Redemption of Captives. And the said Franciscan friars took along a decorated cross; next to it on both sides went two processional candlesticks; [a priest] went wearing a cape, and next to him on both sides went two deacons wearing their vestments. —

v Then after them followed those who were directly bereaved, the very reverend friars called Preachers, the precious children of our precious revered father Santo Domingo the patriarch. There were perhaps a full hundred and ten of them who went along in a group to the said burial. They took along a decorated cross; next to it on both sides went two processional candlesticks, and [a priest] went wearing a cape, and next to him on both sides went two deacons wearing their vestments. —

v Then after them followed the most highly placed, very senior secular priests, the people of the cathedral chapter, called canons of the cathedral, precious revered children of our precious revered father San Pedro the Prince, that is to say, the senior royal noble in the holy Church. With these the secular priests of the Vera Cruz parish and the Santa Catalina Mártir parish were united and joined; it was not possible for them to go as separate groups. They all wore a surplice and bonnet. All the secular priests going along in a group to the said burial cannot be counted, [*p. 172*] for there were very many of them. They took along a decorated cross, and next to it on both sides went two processional candlesticks. The very reverend lord doctor Salcedo, archdeacon, went wearing a cape, and next to him on both sides went two deacons wearing their black vestments, both of them canons with a full ration. And all the canons with a full ration went wearing

possibly taking it for granted. The situation is all the more strange because virtually the same phrase, with exactly the same omission, occurs several more times in following paragraphs. These passages may be testimony to Ch.'s tendency to repeat certain phrases as a refrain almost regardless of their content, as in the resumé of Mexica history earlier.

quimotlalilitiaque ymomextintzitzin Racioneros, auh ynic ye mochtintzitzin Canonigos, Racioneros, mochintin tliltic manto del coro tabetan, in quimotlalilitiaque, yn iuh mochipa ypan quaresmatica quimotlalilitihui yn ipã motenehua La Sena, auh ynic tlamico oncan quixohua palacio capilla. yc ypan macuilli tzilli ypan tlaco hora, ynic quihualmoquixtilique ynacayotzin omoteneuhtzino teoyotica tlahtohuani Don fray Garcia Guerra visurrey. yn oncan monoltitoya cõmanilique achtopa yehuantzitzin yn audiencia real tlaca tlahtoque Oydores. in Andas. yc monoltitoya. quimonapalhuique in tlacpac omoteneuh capilla yc quihualmotemohuillique tlatzintla ynic oncã palacio caltempa quimotequillico ypan quauhtlapechtli motenehua Tumulo yn çan ic tlatlalili ypan quimocehuilizque ynacayotzin miccatzintli, in ye oconmotequilico oncan nimã ic ce responso cuicayo oncan ypantzinco[2] yn inacayotzin quihtoq̃. in capilla tlaca[1] clerigos. yn officiales iglesia mayor, auh yc[3] omoteneuh çaniuh monoltitiuh in andasco yn inacayotzin cencauhtiuh ynic mochi chichiuhtiuh in teoyotica ytlahtocamahuiznechichihualtzin ornamentos pontificales. yevatl ynic centlamantli. amito,[4] niman ye yn alba camisatli, yhuan maquiltitiuh in cassula morada, yhuan cenca tlaçotli yn icpactzinco actiuh Mitra, coztic teocuitlaycpatica yectlamacho. yhuan tlaçoteyo epyolloyo. ymactzinco onotiuh yn ichcapixcatopiltzin baculo, macitica coztic teocuitlayo yn iztac teocuitlatl, auh no yhui yn imatzin haactiuh vandes. yhuan matzatzaztli [*p. 173*] anillos, auh ycxitlantzinco mantiuh yn ibonetetzin. ycpac yetiuh ce yztac borla ynic neztiuh ca maestro omoyetzticatca yn ipan sancta theologia, yhuan yn isomblerotzin huey quiltic çan no ycxitlantzinco mantiuh, auh cayemo huehuentzin omoyetzticatca ca ye quin huel yyolloco oquichtli yuh omihto ye quin ye ompohuallonmatlactli ypã macuilxihuitl oquimopialiaya. auh yn omoteneuh ynic quihualmotemohuilique vmpa capilla palacio, no yehuantin cenpohualloncaxtolli in Doctoresme, yn quihualmololhuilitiaque miccatzintli. in teopixque clerigos Doctores. yhuã frayles maestros oc cenca yehuatzin in cenca mahuiztililoni maestro fr. diego de contreras cathedratico de escriptura. mochintzitzin çan neneliuhtihui yn españoles Doctores ynic moomemaniltitiaque in nepapa yzqui tlamantli yc Doctores. moch quimotlalilitihui yn inquechquentzin in motenehua capirotes. yhuã inBorlas. ymicpac yayatiuh, cecenyacã yntech machioneztiuh yn tlein yc tlamatini tlamachiliznemachtiltica. auh yn omoteneuh miccatzintli yn icquac[5] quihualmoquixtilique tecpan palacio. ca niman hualmotlalli mixtli achi tliltic çan iyoca ypan in ciudad mexico. yc mixtlapacho in tonatiuh. ynic quiquiyahuia. inic yuhquin ma oncan ytech nezqui no yehuatl y nauhtlamantli yn huel peuhcayotl motenehua Elementos no quicoco quitlaocolti yn imiquiliztzin teoyotica tlahtohuani Don fr. Garcia Guerra —

v̲ Auh yn o yuh onmihto yn omoteneuh ce responso, ypan ynacayotzin miccatzintli yn oncan omoteneuh ypan Tumulo. miccatlapechtli in caltempa palacio, yc niman oncan oc yehuantzitzin conmanilique conmonapalhuique yn inacayotzin teoyotica tlahtohuani, in cenca mahuiztililoni [*p. 174*] Canonigos. ynic niman ohtlipan oquimotlatoctilique oquimohuiquilique, tlapohualtepoztli ycal çan ixpan quimoquixtilique ynic tlayahualolotia ynic quimahuiztilique ynacayotzin miccatzintli, auh in yehuantin omoteneuhque Doctoresme. huel yehuantin ytlan omantiaque oquitocatiaque yn omoteneuh miccatzintli, auh ça motlatoquiltitia, ça huel quimotzacuiltitia yn omoteneuhtzin[6] cenca mahuiztililoni Padre

1. Or people of the chapel, perhaps defining the secular priests?
2. For "yxpantzinco."
3. The intention seems to be *ye*, not *yc*.

a black choir cloak of taffeta, like they always wear during Lent at what is called the main meal. When they finished coming out of the palace chapel, it was half past 5 o'clock as they brought out the body of the said spiritual ruler don fray García Guerra, viceroy, from where he was lying. First the lords of the Royal Audiencia, the civil judges, took him in the bier where he was lying and lifted him up in their arms in the above mentioned chapel, and in that fashion they brought him down below, until just outside the palace they laid him on a wooden platform called a catafalque, that had been set up for them to rest the body of the deceased on. When they had laid him there, the [choir members?][1] and the secular priests and officials of the cathedral sang a responsory prayer in the presence of[2] his body. It was already[3] said that his body just lay in the bier, all prepared, all outfitted with his revered equipment as ruler, the pontifical ornaments, which were first the amice,[4] then the alb, a shirt; then he had on the purple chasuble, and on his head a very precious miter, finely embroidered with golden thread and covered with precious stones and pearls, and in his hand lay his shepherd's staff, the crozier, solid silver gilded, and likewise he had gloves on his hands, and rings. [*p. 173*] Below his feet was his bonnet, on top of which was a white tassel showing that he had a master's degree in holy theology, and his large green hat was also at his feet. He was not yet aged, for he was a man just in his full maturity; it was said that he was only fifty-five years old. And when as was mentioned they brought him down from the palace chapel, also thirty-five ecclesiastical holders of the doctorate went gathered around the deceased, secular priests with the doctorate and friars with master's degrees, especially the very reverend master fray Diego de Contreras, professor of scripture. All the Spanish doctors went mixed among one another, so that all the different kinds of doctors went along two by two. They all went wearing neck garments called hoods, and on top of their heads were various tassels, signifying for each person what branch of knowledge he was a scholar in. When[5] they brought the said deceased out of the palace, rather black clouds formed right away, only over the city of Mexico, covering the surface of the sun, and it rained off and on, as though showing thereby that also the four separate things that are the very beginning, called elements, were hurt and moved to pity by the death of the spiritual ruler don fray García Guerra. —

v And when as was mentioned a responsory prayer had been said over the body of the deceased, as was mentioned on the catafalque or platform for the dead, outside the palace, the very reverend canons took and picked up the body of the spiritual ruler. [*p. 174*] Then they directed him along the road and took him to the clock tower; they took him passing right in front of it in their procession in order to honor the body of the deceased. And the said doctors were the very ones who went beside and followed the said deceased; and the said[6] very reverend father master fray Diego de Contreras, Augustinian friar, followed

4. An undervestment around the neck and shoulders.
5. For "ihquac."
6. For "omoteneuhtzino."

Maestro fr. diego de contreras teopixqui S. Augustin yehica ca ye huecauh achto ye maestro ynic nican Mexico —

v Auh yc niman yehuantin quimonmotoquilitiaque mochintin yn ixquichtin cabildo ciudad tlaca, tecpantiaque quintocatia ome vamderra ahnoço esdantarde real ytech icuiliuhtia yn itlahtocatlahuiztzin yn iarmastzin Rey ynin ca tafetan tliltic netloc mantia yyomexti // auh yc niman yehuantin quimontocatiaque yn ixquichtin. Soldadostin yaotiacahuan aço huel chicuepohualtin in ye mochi yn necoccampa motecpanque ynic tlayahualolotia mocuecuentilique ynic tecpancayahque. çan inmac quitetecatiaque yn imarcaboz, yhuan no cecen lanças. inmac quihuicacaya,[1] çan tlalpan quihuillantiaque, amo huel cacocuia, auh yn in omoteneuhque Soldadostin ome yn invamderra yn inquachpan quihuicaque çan tlalpan tlaltitech quihuihuillantiaque amo no huel cacocuia auh no yehuatl yn inyaohuehueuh atambores. chicuacentetl yn oncan quihuicaque quitzotzontiaque, amo cenca caquiztia amo huel nahuatia auh yehica ypampa tlilpalli luto yc quiquimiliuhtia. çan ipan yn quitzotzontiaque, yhuan ome onca quipitztiaque bipano ahnoço blaotas, tliltique cacatzacti amo no cenca quicaquiztilitiaque amo huel quinahuatiltitiaque çan quitlaocolpitztiaque, auh in yehuantin in omoteneuhque Soldadostin [*p. 175*] Yn oncan cenquizque omoteneuh yc tetococ, ca yehuantin y yazque La china in quitequipanozque tohueytlahtocauh rey

v Auh yc niman yehuantzitzin quimonmotoquilitiaque in mochintin Audiencia Real tlaca, tlahtoque Oydoresme, moch luto yn inrobones yn indurga[2] quimotlalilitihui, auh yn omẽtin ymachtzitzinhuan omoteneuhtzino miccatzintli yn arçobispo. ynic ce yehuatzin in Padre fr. Jeronimo Guerra. çanno S. Domingo teopixqui vicario atlacohuayã. ynic ome yehuatl yn capitan de la guardia luto quihuillantiuh, tlanepãtla yhcatihui cẽca otlaocoxtiaq̃. inic quimotepotztoquilitiaq̃. intlaçotlatzin. quinnepantlaquetztiaque yn omoteneuhque oydores, auh yhuan oc no ce tlacatl yn oncan yntlah ycatia tlanepãtla, no luto yn quihuillantia quitquitia yehuatl ce quauhpitzactli hueyac yn icuac tlanepanolli tlacruztlalili oncan ytech pilcatiah çouhtia ce tliltic tepitzin camixatzintli, ytech icuiliuhtia yn itlacamecayotlahuiztzin yn iarmastzin omoteneuhtzino miccatzintli arçobispo visurrey. // Auh yc niman contocatia tlatoquilitiuh ce cauallo tomahuac ỹ nohuiyan ytlacapan çouhtia ynic quimiliuhtia luto huel quihuillantia, yhuã ycximanecuiliuhtia quiztiticque[3] ynic chochollotia omoteneuh cauallo cantiaque yuh mihto huel yehuatl yn iaxcatzin catca yn ipan monemiltiaya omoteneuhtzino teoyotica tlahtohuani arçobispo visurrey. // Auh ynic ontetl cauallo quimontocatia çãno yuh chichiuhtia quimiliuhtia lutotica, no yhuan ycximanecuiliuhtia no quiztiticque no chocholotia, yn iuh yahtia oc cẽtetl omoteneuh cauallo. auh ynin yc ontetl cauallo ypan yatia ce español, tepoztlahuiztica cotatica moyaochichiuhtia motenehua armado, yc yah. quihuicac quitquitia yn vamderra moteneuh Quiyon çan huel tetepitzin ytech icuiliuhtia yn iarmastzin Rey. yehuatl yn castillo yhuan leon. yn itlahtocatlahuiztzin, ynin omoteneuh vanderra tepitzin Quiyon ca yehuatl in quimoyacaniliaya yn ihcuac moquixtiaya yn ix[*p. 176*]quich ica omotlahtocatili ynic visurrey omochiuhtzinoticatca mexico yn oquic mochicahualtitinenca omoteneuhtzino arçobispo. yn

1. For "quihuicaya."

2. It appears that Ch. may not have been familiar with the word *túnica*, "tunic, etc.," so that he may have miscopied "durga" from "duniga" in some earlier text, whether written by himself or another. The form "duniga" in fact occurs elsewhere in the original in a somewhat similar context [pp. 216–17 at n. 2]. In his section on the members of the

everyone and went the very last, because he was the first master [of theology] here in Mexico by a long time. —

v Then after them followed all the members of the [Spanish] cabildo of the city, going in line. Two banners or royal standards went following them, on which were painted the royal insignia, the arms of the king; they were of black taffeta; the two of them went side by side. // Then after them followed all the soldiers, the warriors, perhaps a full hundred and sixty in all. They lined up on both sides of the procession; the lines they went in were not straight; they left their muskets just lying in their arms, and the lances that each one carried[1] in their arms they just dragged on the ground, they could not lift them up. And the said soldiers carried two banners that they just went dragging on the ground; they couldn't lift them up either. And they also took along six war drums, kettle drums, that they went beating; they did not sound loudly or very clearly because they were wrapped in black mourning cloth, and they went along beating them measuredly. And two blacks played fifes or flutes, which they did not play very loudly or clearly either, but went along playing in mourning. The said soldiers [*p. 175*] who assembled for the said burial were the ones who were to go to China [the Philippines] to serve our great ruler the king.

v Then after them followed all the people of the Royal Audiencia, the lords judges; the robes and [tunics][2] that they wore were all of mourning cloth. And the two nephews of the said deceased, the archbishop, of whom the first was father fray Gerónimo Guerra, likewise a Dominican friar, vicar at Tacubaya, and the second was the captain of the guard, who went dragging mourning cloth, went standing in the middle; they went in great sorrow as they followed behind their beloved uncle. The said judges went placing them in their midst. And another person who went standing among them, in the middle, also carried and dragged a sign of mourning, which was a long narrow pole crossed toward one end to make a cross; from it went hanging and was displayed a little black shirt on which were painted the insignia of the said deceased archbishop and viceroy's lineage, his coat of arms. // Then after that followed, coming last, a stout horse on whose sides were everywhere displayed the mourning cloth with which it was wrapped, and it went dragging it. And it went along lame in a forefoot; they had cut a hoof[3] so that the said horse that they went holding went along making leaps. It was said that the horse was the special property of the said spiritual leader, the archbishop and viceroy, when he was alive. // A second horse went following them, likewise outfitted with and wrapped in mourning cloth, which also was lame in a forefoot, whose hoof they also cut, which also went leaping, just like the other said horse. And on this second horse rode a Spaniard, outfitted for war with a metal device, a coat of mail, called a man in armor; as he went he took and carried a banner called an ensign, very small, on which was painted the king's coat of arms, a castle and a lion, his royal device. This said small banner or ensign was the one that preceded him whenever he would come out in public as long [*p. 176*] as he ruled as the viceroy appointed in Mexico, as long as the said archbishop was still in good health,

Royal Audiencia in this funeral procession, Alemán (1911, p. 400), speaks of the wearing of a *loba*, described in the *Diccionario de Autoridades* as a long unfitted garment falling to the feet, in Latin *tunica taladris*.

3. The form is apparently the equivalent of *qu-izti-tecque*. Speaking of this horse Alemán (1911, p. 402) uses the word *despalmado*, with the hoof pared off.

iuh mochintin quinyacana yn oc cequintin tlahtoque visurreyesme yn otlahtocatico nican mexico. yhuan yn oc tlahtocatiquihui in huel yxiptlatzitzinhuan tohueytlahtocatzin Rey yn españa moyetztica

v Auh yc niman yehuantin ça cemi mochintin ontetocatiaque ontlatocatiaque. in teaachhuan yn ibaxehuan omoteneuhtzino miccatzintli arçobispo visurrey omoyetzticatca. huel mochintin tlilpalli luto, quimololotiaque quihuillantiaque. O yhui yn. in quihualquixtique ynacayotzin oncan tecpan palacio. yn omoteneuhtzino miccatzintli teoyotica tlahtohuani Don fr. Garcia Guerra arcobispo[1] visurrey. ynic niman vmpa quimotlacololtilito ynacayotzin, yn calnacazco. ynahuac S. Ilefonso colegio de saminario, ca çan oc conmotlamellahualtilique ynic oncan necololoto ynic niman tlanipa ohtli quimotoctilique ynacayotzin ynin yc quimohuiquillique ca mopapatlatiaque in ixquichtin teopixque nepapanme yhuan tlahtoq̃. ynic quimonapalhuitiaque miccatzintli, ynic niman ypan ohtli S. Domingo. quimoquixtilito quimonamictilito yn ohtli. ynic niman ça tlamellauhca oquihualmocuepillique ca oquihualmotlamellahualtilique. ynic oncan quimoquixtilico yquiyahuac yn iportales Marques del valle. ynic niman oncan oquimocallaquillico miccatzintli iglesia mayor. huel yhcuac onaqui tonatiuh ynic onyohuac in quimaxitilico. auh yn omotenehu in ynic otlipan quihualmohuiquilliq̃. ynic huallayahualolotia ca macuilcan yn otlipan quitlallica quauhtlapechtli. Tumulo. yn ipan quimocecehuilitiaque ynacayotzin miccatzintli arçobispo. yzquican oncã responsos ypantzinco quihtoque [*p. 177*] Yn capilla tlaca[2] clerigos. auh ca amo huel mihtoz. motenehuaz. yhuan amo huel moponhuaz yn ixquich tlacatl catca yn oquimotoquilique[3] miccatzintli. yn españoles. yhuan timacehualtin mexica. amo huel campa tetlan quixohuaya yn otlipan cenca oteten yn tlacatl yhuan yn ça ohtenco otlamahuiçoque otlachixq̃ cenca miec tlacatl yhuan yn calticpac tlapãco cenca no teten yn tlacatl tlachixque, cenca huey tlamahuiztililiztica in quimotoquilique ynacayotzin miccatzintli ca yuhquin ma çã yhcuac viernes Sancto. yc omochiuh yn inetoquiliztzin omoteneuh teoyotica tlahtohuani arçobispo visurrey. auh yn omoteneuh ynacayotzin tococ altar mayor tlamayecamcopa // auh yn o yuh conmotoquilique oncan iglesia mayor, yc niman quixohuac necuepalloc vmpa n tecpan palacio. mocueptzinoque vmpa yn audiencia Real tlaca oydores. yhuan yn oc cequintin Justicias quimocuitlahuia quincahuato yn omentin omoteneuhq̃. ymachtzitzinhuan omoteneuhtzino miccatzintli arçobispo, yhuan yn ibangetzitzinhuan cahualloco, yhuan no tecahuaco y moteneuhque Soldadostin. ynic hualmocuepque ye quihualquechpanotiaque yn imarcaboz. no yhuan ye quihuallacoctiaque yn imalanças.[4] yhuan yn invamderra yn inquachpan

v Auh axcan Juebes yc .8. mani metztli Março. de 1612. años. yhcuac in honrras ymissatzin omochiuh iglesia mayor. in teoyotica tlahtohuani Don fr. Garcia Guerra arçobispo yhuan visurrey moyetzticatca Mexico. // auh çãno ypan in yn omoteneuh ypan cemilhuitl Juebes yn ohualla tlahtolli vmpa españa quitemachiztico ynic omomiquilli yn tohueycihuatlahtocatzin Doña Marcarida de avstria Reyna españa ocatca yn inamictzin tohueytlahtocatzin Don Felipe Tercero Rey españa — [*p. 178*]

v Axcan Juebes yc .15. mani Metztli Março de 1612 años yhcuac yn ohuallathuic ye omomiquilli yohualtica, in cihuapilli Doña Ana de castilla ynamic in Anton[5] de ibarra catca. auh ychpotzin in huehue Don Luis de Velasco. ynic ome visurrey mochihuaco.

1. For "arçobispo."
2. See pp. 206–07 at n. 1.
3. The word could equally well mean "followed."

just as it precedes the other lords viceroys who have come to rule here in Mexico and the other true representatives of our great ruler the king who is in Spain who will come to rule in the future.

v Then finally came following the others, coming last, the pages of the said deceased, the late archbishop and viceroy; every one of them wore black mourning cloth and went dragging it. This then was how they brought the body of the said deceased, the spiritual ruler don fray García Guerra, archbishop[1] and viceroy, out of the palace. Then they took a turn with his body at the corner close to the seminary college of San Ildefonso, for they took him straight until they turned there; there they took his body along the road downward. As they took him all the different ecclesiastics and judges went along taking turns carrying the deceased. Then they brought him to meet the road to Santo Domingo; then they brought him straight back, then they brought him to outside the arcade of the Marqués del Valle, then they brought the deceased inside the cathedral, right at sunset; they brought him in as it got dark. And as they brought him on this said route and came in procession, in five places along the way they had set up a wooden platform, the catafalque, on which they caused the body of the deceased archbishop to rest while the [choir?][2] and secular priests said responsory prayers for him. [*p. 177*] It cannot be said, told, or counted how many people there were who [buried][3] the deceased, Spaniards and we Mexica commoners. It cannot be [said] how, wherever they passed by people on the way, it was full of people; very many people just gazed and looked at things from the roadside, and the housetops, the roofs, were also full of people looking. With very great splendor they buried the body of the deceased; the burial of the said spiritual ruler, the archbishop and viceroy, was performed as though it were Good Friday. And his said body was buried on the right hand side of the main altar. // After they had buried him at the cathedral, everyone came out and returned to the palace. The judges of the Royal Audiencia and the others who administer justice accompanied the two said nephews of the said deceased archbishop there, and his pages were brought there, and also the said soldiers came in accompaniment; as they returned, they shouldered their muskets again, and they again raised their lances[4] and their banners, their cloth flags.

v Today, Thursday the 8th of the month of March of the year 1612, was when the obsequies were held and a mass was performed in the cathedral for the spiritual ruler don fray García Guerra, late archbishop and viceroy in Mexico. // And likewise on the said day of Thursday word came from Spain and it was announced that our great queen doña Margarita de Austria, late queen of Spain, spouse of our great ruler don Felipe III, king of Spain, had passed away. [*p. 178*]

v Today, Thursday the 15th of the month of March of the year 1612, in the night before morning of that day, was when the lady doña Ana de Castilla, who was the spouse of Antón[5] de Ibarra, passed away. She was the daughter of don Luis de Velasco the elder,

4. Probably for "inlanças."

5. The name is given as Diego on pp. 176–77.

nican Mexico nueua españa. auh yhuan ynin omoteneuh Doña Ana de castilla, ca huel ihuan tlacatia huel yuhctzin. ynic ome ytoca Don Luis de Velasco Marques de Salinas. in yehuatl oppa visurrey omochiuh nican Mexico nueua españa. auh çatepan omohuicac yn españa vmpa presidente del consejo de indias omochiuhtzinoto Oquihualmonochilli vmpa yn tohueytlahtocatzin Rey Don Felipe Tercero, auh ynin omoteneuh cihuapilli Doña Ana. S. Domingo. yn tocoto ynacayo yn ompa toctoque ynamic yhuan omoteneuh yttatzin catca huehue Don Luis de Velasco.—

v̲ Axcan Martes yc .20. mani Metztli Março de 1612 años. yn ohuallathuic ye omomiquilli yohualtica in diego cauallero fundador y patron yn oncan Monasterio Sancta ines. monjas. yehuatl ytlatzintil quichiuh yhuan ytlapachol yn omoteneuh monasterio catqui, ynahuac hospital de las bouas. cenca miec yn iaxca ytlatqui quicahuillitia omoteneuh i monasterio —

v̲ Axcan Domingo quaresma ynic .i. mani metztli Abril de 1612. años. yhcuac opeuh in ye quimana tliltique ynic cequintin oquimanque tliltique oncan hospital huitzillan nuestra Señora ye teotlac ypan Sermon quinmachtiaya yn oncan quimanaco Justicia ynic quincallaquique La carcel de Corte quincallaquito yn oncan motenehua calaboços. ypampa yntech tlan quil mach yaoyotl [*p. 179*] quihtohuaya macocuizquia yn ipan Juebes Sancto. quinmictizquia yn intecuiyohuan españoles. —

v̲ Axcan viernes yc .6. mani Metztli Abril de 1612. años. yhcuac nican S. Joseph S. Fran^co^. hualmocallaqui in Padre fr. juã maçura.[1] yehuatzin Capillero mochiuhtzino. quihualmohuiquilli in Padre fr. Sebastian de caribay telpochtli[2] temachtiani mochihuaco S. Joseph. yhcuac quicauh yn itequiuh Padre fr. Jeronimo de çarate ynic Capillero catca yuhquin ceuhtiaq̃. Mexica tenochca yn iuh omoteneuh tlacpac ynic cenca quĩtoliniaya in quinmecahuitequia yhuan quincalnamacaya — capitulo indelmedio ypan in in tequicauh —

v̲ Axcan Martes yc .10. mani Metztli Abril de 1612 años. yhcuac ye teotlac tlaca ypan macuilli tzillini yn oquixohuac oncan tecpan palacio otlayahuallolotia ynic ocallacohua tohueyteopan iglesia mayor. ynic yhonrras yvigiliatzin omochihuilli ynic omomiquilli tohueycihuatlahtocatzin Doña Margarida de Austria Reyna de españa moyetzticatca yn inamictzin ocatca tohueytlahtocatzin Don Felipe Tercero Rey españa yn axcan moyetztica. auh ynic oncan quixohuac tecpan palacio. ca çanno yuh mochiuh yn tlacpac omoteneuh yn iuh mochiuh yn iuh tococ ynacayotzin teoyotica tlahtohuani Don fr. Garcia Guerra arcobispo[3] y virrey yn iuh netecpanoc. çan ye no cuel yuh motecpan yn mochi cofradias. õcatqui mexico. yhuan çan ye nicuel yuh motecpantiaque yn nepapan teopixque monoltitoque Mexico. yn oncan mohuicatza. yhuan yn ciudad cabildo tlaca yhuan oydores. audiencia real tlaca n quinepantlahuitiaque yn tlahtocacorona real quinapalotia ce tlacatl coxin ypan mantia[4] çan ye ynmamanian yn mantiaque. auh yehuatzin yn teoyotica tlahtohuani Don fr. Balthasar Acobarrobias. [*p. 180*] Obispo michhuacan teopixqui S. Augustin, mochichiuhtzino capa quimotlalilitia yhuan Mitra. yhuan yn itlacaychcapixcatopiltzin baculo. quimotquilitia yhuan ome ytloctzinco mantia clerigos capa quitlallitiaq̃. auh ynin Obispo yehuatzin quimihtalhui yhoracio yn ipan omoteneuh yc vigilia mochiuh

1. Name unconfirmed.
2. Or just meaning that he was a young man, or young for a preacher.
3. For "arçobispo."

who came here to Mexico and New Spain appointed as the second viceroy. This said doña Ana de Castilla was a full sibling—he was her younger brother—of the second of the name don Luis de Velasco, Marqués of Salinas, who was made viceroy twice here in Mexico and New Spain and afterward went to Spain, where he was made president of the Council of the Indies; our great ruler the king don Felipe III sent summoning him. The body of this said lady doña Ana was taken to be buried to Santo Domingo, where her spouse and her said late father don Luis de Velasco the elder lie buried.—

v Today, Tuesday the 20th of the month of March of the year 1612, in the night before morning of that day, Diego Caballero, founder and patron of the nunnery of Santa Inés, passed away. He founded the said nunnery, near to the Hospital de las Bubas, and it was under his governance. He bequeathed a very great deal of his property to the said nunnery. —

v Today, a Sunday of Lent, the 1st of the month of April of the year 1612, was when they began to arrest blacks, so that they arrested some blacks at the hospital of Nuestra Señora in Huitzillan in the afternoon. The sermon was being preached to them when the officers of the law came to arrest them and put them in the court jail. They put them in what are called cells because they were accused, according to what they say, that they were declaring war, [*p. 179*] that they were going to rebel on Maundy Thursday and kill their Spanish masters. —

v Today, Friday the 6th of the month of April of the year 1612, was when father fray Juan Mazura[1] entered San Josef here at San Francisco, becoming the chaplain. Father fray Sebastián de Garibay the younger,[2] who had been made preacher at San Josef, brought him when father fray Gerónimo de Zárate relinquished his post as chaplain. Thus the Mexica Tenochca got relief from the way, as was mentioned above, that he had been greatly mistreating them, whipping them, and selling their houses. — It was at an intermediate chapter meeting [of the Franciscan province] that he left office. —

v Today, Tuesday the 10th of the month of April of the year 1612, in the afternoon but still daytime, at 5 o'clock, was when a group came out of the palace and went in procession to enter our great church, the cathedral, to perform the obsequies and vigil for the death of our great queen doña Margarita de Austria, late queen of Spain, who was the spouse of our great ruler don Felipe III, king of Spain, who now rules. They left the palace in the same fashion as was mentioned above with the burial of the body of the spiritual leader don fray García Guerra, archbishop[3] and viceroy. Again all the cofradías there are in Mexico were lined up in the same way, and again all the different religious who dwell in Mexico lined up the same when they came there, and the members of the city cabildo and the judges of the Royal Audiencia. They placed in their midst as they went the royal crown; someone was carrying it on a cushion.[4] They all went along in the same places as before. And the spiritual ruler don fray Baltasar Covarrubias, [*p. 180*] bishop in Michoacan, an Augustinian friar, went along all outfitted, wearing a cape and miter and carrying his staff as a shepherd of people, the crozier, and two secular priests went beside him wearing capes. And this bishop was the one who made the main speech of

4. The way this line is inserted makes it quite clear that the version of the text here is a copy either from an earlier version or from a source.

auh cenca huey yhuan cenca mahuiztic yn cuauhteocalli[1] motlalli oncan yhtic yglesia mayor. mochi tlacatl cenca oquimahuiço yhuã çan ye no yxquich ynic otlayahuallolo axcan yn ixquich moyahuallo yn tlacpac omoteneuh yhcuac tococ ynacayotzin teoyotica tlahtohuani Don Fray Garcia Guerra arçobispo. moyetzticatca. auh niman yn ipan ymoztlayoc miercoles. yn omoteneuhtzino Don Fr. Balthasar Acobarrobias. obispo. yehuatzin quimihtalhui yn Missa. Auh yehuatzin motemachtilli yn Don Alonso de la mota y escobar obpo tlaxcallan anoço ciudad de los Angeles. ynin yc hualmohuicaque omentin omoteneuhque obisposme. ca quimonmonochillique yn tlahtoque oydoresme —

v Axcan Sabado ynic 14. mani metztli Abril de 1612 años. yhcuac yc otzatzihuac yn ihtic ciudad Mexico yn tliltique oquichti aocac espada quitecaz quihualhuicaz. yhuan cuello aocmo quitlalizque no yhui yn tliltique cihua aocmo tliltic manto quitlalizque yhuan mulatati moch quincahualtiq. yhuan pena yc quintlalilique. // auh achtopa yc tzatzihuac nohuiyan yn ihtic ciudad Mexico in yehuantin españoles. yc nahuatilloque, yn aquin quipia chicuacentliltic quinnamacaz yn nahui auh çan oome yn mochi tlacatl quipiaz ytlilticauh. auh yn aquin amo quitlacamatiz Justicia yn iuh tlanahuatia quicuiliz yn omoteneuh nahui ynic aoctle onquiçaz tlatquihua — [*p. 181*]

v Auh ynic omilhuitl axcan ypan Domingo de ramos. ynic 15. mani Metztli Abril yn ipan omoteneuh xihuitl 1612 yhcuac cenca omocomonique yn mochintin españoles yn Mexico onoque cenca omomauhtique miectlamãtli yntechpa oquimotemohuillique yn tliltique yn intlacahuan ça quimimacaztinemia ça ynhuicpa mihmattinemia y manel quintequipanohua. yuh quihtoque mochintin yn españoles. ca otechcentlahtalhuique in techmictizq. totlacahuan yn totlilticahuan ynic cenca quinmauhtiaya ynic niman oquixquetzque yn ipan in omoteneuh cemilhuitl Capitan General quichiuhque yn telpochtli Don fernando altamirano. ynin yxhuiuh yn Don Luis de Velasco Marques de Salinas. yn oppa Visurrey omochiuh nican Mexico. auh yn omoteneuh yxhuiuhtzin yc quitlallique yn tlapiazque nican ypan ciudad Mexico. ynteyacancauh ymachcauh mochiuh yn ixquichtin Soldadostin motlalliq. in yaotlapiazque yn ipampa macocuiznequi in yaoyotl quihtohua tliltique yhuan mulatoti ynpan yn españolesme ynic mochi tlacatl quihtoca ypan yn Juebes Sancto. quichihuazque yn intemictiliz. tliltique —

v Auh yniqueylhuitl axcan Lunes. santo. ynic 16. mani metztli Abril yhcuac yancuican otlayahualloque teotlac ypan ome tzillini yn ompa hualquizque yn teopan yn Sancta maria cuepopan tlaca. ynin prossesion quitlallique yn cofradia yntech pohui yn animasme purgatorio tetlechipahualloyan moyetzticate. auh ynic tlayahualoloc ypan in prossesion oncan quinmoquixtilique yn S. Nicolas de tolentino ynic neci [*p. 182*] Ca yntepalehuicatzin yn omoteneuhque animasme quimõmoquixtilia ytemcopatzinco in tt^{o}. dios. yn ompa omoteneuh purgatorio. ynic omentzitzin oncan quinmoquixtilique yn ipan in tlayahualoliztli yehuatzin yn totlaçottatzin S. Fran^{co}. ynic no yehuatzin ytetzinco neztiuh ca huel no yehuatzin yca yn inelpiayatzin yn icordontzin yn aquique quicelia ynic molpia nican tlalticpac yn ihcuac ye omomiquilique ca yc yehuatl vmpa quimonmoquixtilia quinmopalehuilia yn purgatorio. ytemcopatzinco yn tt^{o}. dios. yn aquin macehualle ycnopille vmpa yauh auh ynic tlayahualloque yn huel ixquich ic oncan ahcico yn S. Francisco. niman la casa professa. niman yglesia mayor. niman yc mocuepque S. Domingo quiçato yc niman S lurenço monjas quiçato. yc niman vmpa yn inteopan ahcito. auh ça ihciuhca ça yxtomac[2] yn ontlayahuallotihuetzque. ca yc niman ynpampa hualquiz yntlahtocatla-

1. The "monument" or catafalque.

prayer when the said vigil was held. A very large and splendid wooden shrine[1] was set up inside the cathedral; everyone greatly marveled at it. The procession went over the same route as told above when the body of the spiritual ruler don fray García Guerra, late archbishop, was buried. Then on the following day, Wednesday, the said don fray Baltasar Covarrubias, bishop, was the one who said the mass. The person who preached was don Alonso de la Mota y Escobar, bishop in Tlaxcala or the city of Los Angeles [Puebla]. These two said bishops came because the lords judges of the Audiencia summoned them. —

v Today, Saturday the 14th of the month of April of the year 1612, was when it was proclaimed in the city of Mexico that black men were no longer to carry swords or wear [Spanish-style] collars, and likewise black women were no longer to wear black veils, and they also prohibited all the mulatto women [from the same thing] and set a fine for them. // But first it was proclaimed everywhere in the city of Mexico and the Spaniards were ordered that whoever has six blacks was to sell four of them, and everyone would have only two blacks each. For whoever would not obey the law it was ordered that the said four be taken from him, so that he would no longer be the owner. [*p. 181*]

v On the second day, today Palm Sunday, the 15th of the month of April in the said year of 1612, was when all the Spaniards who live in Mexico became very agitated and fearful. They investigated many things about their black slaves; they went about in fear of them, they were very watchful about them even though they serve them. All the Spaniards said, "Our black slaves have set and coordinated a time to kill us," which greatly frightened them. Then on the said day they selected and set up don Hernando Altamirano the younger as captain general; he is the grandchild of don Luis de Velasco, Marqués of Salinas, who was made viceroy twice here in Mexico. The reason that those in charge here in the city of Mexico installed his said grandson and made him leader, commander of all the soldiers who were set to stand guard was that the blacks and mulattoes were about to rise and declare war on the Spaniards, so that everyone said that on Maundy Thursday the blacks would do their killing. —

v And on the third day, today Monday of Holy Week on the 16th of the month of April, was when the people of Santa María Cuepopan first came out in procession; at 2 o'clock in the afternoon they came out of the church. The cofradía dedicated to the Souls of Purgatory, where people are purified by fire, organized this procession. And as they went in procession they brought out San Nicolás de Tolentino so that it would be seen [*p. 182*] that he is the helper of the said souls, he redeems them from the said purgatory by order of our lord God. The second one they brought out in the procession was our precious father San Francisco, so that also through him it would be seen that he too, with his belt, his rope, very much receives those who are tied here on earth; when they die, he uses it to help them and redeem from purgatory by order of our lord God those who are deserving to go there. As to how the procession went, they got all the way to San Francisco, then to the Casa Profesa, then to the cathedral; then they turned around and went past Santo Domingo, then they passed by the San Lorenzo nunnery, then they got back to their church. They hastened to go on their procession quickly and [without warning],[2] for right

2. See the use of this root above (pp. 172–73 at n. 4) in a word implying haste, unexpectedness, haphazardness. There too the root is preceded by *iciuhca*, "quickly."

nahuatiltzin yn oydores. motlatzontequillique ynic çan niman acampa ce teopan tlayahualoloz yn ipan in Semana Sancta. auh ynic çã niman ipan in omoteneuh lunes Sancto ye yohua ynic otzatzihuac nohuiyan yhtic ciudad mexico. ynic acan tlayahualoloz. Semana Sancta yehica ypampa ye iuh catca teyollo yn muztla ypan martes Sancto teotlac no omen yancuic tlayahualloliztli prossesion oquiçazquia yn oncan omotlali yancuic cofradias. ynic ce cofradia yehuantin quitlalliq̃. yn españoles. yhuan Mexica Moyoteca oncan yn Monasterio S. Juan de la penitencia monjas. ya yehuantin in in tlayahualozquia ypilhuantzitzin S. Juan // auh ynic ome tlayahualoliztli yancuic oquiçazquia ypan in omoteneuh Martes Sancto. yehuantin yn Mexica tlatilulco S tiago tlaca [*p. 183*] Yn ipilhuantzitzinhuan totlaçomahuiznantzin S. ta maria del rrosario no ihuã motenehua ypilhuãtzitzin el Niño Jesus Perdido cenca miec tetlapopolhuiliztli yndulgencias. oncan quihualmotlalilia in Sancto Padre Paulo Quinto. yn ipan tlayahualoliztli auh ynic huel iuhqui omochihu in ca ytlayhualiztica ytlaytlaniliztica y notlaçoycniuhtzin diego lopez. cuauhtlacuillo[1] yn huel tlatzintille fundador yn ipan ĩ omoteneuh cofradia. yehuantzitzin quimocnopilhuililito ỹ bullas yn totlaçottatzitzinhuan teopixque de la compañia de Jesus yn mohuicaya Roma. auh ca yc ayamo huel mochihu in yqu itlacauh yc çan mocauh yn ipampa yc tzatzihuac in huel yzquilhuitl ypan yc ce Semana Sancta ynic acan tlayahualoloz. yhuan yn manel no ypan xuchipasqua de resurection amo no huel tlayahualoloz. yhuã amonoyac huel mohuitequiz. yn españoles. yhuan yn timacehualtin yn ipan yzquilhuitl omoteneuh Semana Sancta pena motlalli yn aquin duniga[2] yc canazque onpohuallonmatlactli pesos yxtlahualtiloz. yhuan tlatitlanq̃. yn omoteneuhq̃. tlahtoque oydoresme ynic nohuiampa altepetl ipan ynic no amo campa huel tlayahualoloz ypan omoteneuh Semana Sancta çan nohuiyan yaotlapialloz. in teopan ypan Juebes Sãcto ynic quimotzacuilizque tepetlacalco Sanctissimo Sacramento. çan ixquich mochihuaz. atle oc centlamantli yhuan —

v̲ Auh yn axcan ye yc omilhuitl yn ipan Martes Sancto omoteneuh ynic 17. mani Metztli Abril. yhcuac nican caltenco. S. Anton Xolloco ypan huey otli omotlallico miequintin yaotiacahuan Soldadostin españoles yn oyaotlapiaco tlahuiztica no yhui yhuan yn ipan huey otli tepeyacacpa yahticac coyonacazco no miequintin yn oncan motlallito Soldadostin no yhui yn ipan ohtli chapoltepecpa yahticac oncan calyacac[3] temetzcruztitlan[4] no cenca miequintin. yn oncan motlalito [*p. 184*] Soldadostin yhuan ynic nohuiyan yzqui ohtli ypan hualcallaqui ciudad mexico huel yzquican yc yaotlapiallo ça ce ynic nohuiyan in yahualiuhcan yn icaltenyoc[5] yxquich yc ciudad Mexico. yhuan yn ipan huehuey acallotlih nohuiyan ye yaotlapiallo tlachiallo in campa ye quiçaquihui tliltique yn quinmictiquihui españoles. ypampa yuh mihtohuaya vmpa huallazque in ilhuicaatenco in huey atenco acapolco omotlallique cimalonti tliltique yhuan cequintin belacruz huallazque in tliltique cimalõti omocuepque in nican mexico. chollohua yn oquincauhtehuaque yntecuiyohuan

v̲ Auh yn axcan yc yeilhuitl yn ipan Miercoles Sancto cenca yequene mocomonique mo-

---

1. Or it could be taken that he used Quauhtlacuilo as a second surname.

2. See pp. 208–09, n. 2.

3. *Tlayacacac* is sometimes a small inhabited district or settlement, and *calyacac* may have a similar meaning. A similar case on pp. 104–05 at n. 5.

4. The name means literally next to the leaden cross.

afterward came out a royal order of the judges of the Audiencia in which they pronounced that there should not be a procession at any church whatever during Holy Week. Right then on the said Holy Monday, at night, it was proclaimed everywhere in the city of Mexico that there were to be no processions anywhere during Holy Week, because it was people's intention that the next day, on Holy Tuesday afternoon, two more new processions would come out from where new cofradías had been established. The first cofradía was established by the Spaniards and the Mexica of Moyotlan at the nunnery of San Juan de la Penitencia; those who were going to go in procession were the children of San Juan. // And in the second procession on the said Holy Tuesday the Mexica of Santiago Tlatelolco were to come out for the first time, [*p. 183*] the children of our precious revered mother Santa María of the Rosary, also called the children of Niño Jesús Perdido. The Holy Father Paul V granted very many pardons, indulgences, for the occasion of the procession. As to how this could be done, it was through the sending and petitioning of my beloved friend Diego López, a woodcarver,[1] who is the true founder of the said cofradía; [some of] our precious fathers the religious of the Company of Jesus who were going to Rome got the bulls for him. But it was ruined and dropped because of the fact that [the procession] could no longer be held. For it was proclaimed that on absolutely no day during the whole of Holy Week was there to be a procession anywhere. It was not permitted to go in procession even on Easter day, the day of Resurrection, either. Nor could any Spaniards or we commoners scourge themselves on any day of the said Holy Week. A fine was set for whomever they should arrest with a tunic;[2] he would be made to pay 50 pesos. And the said lords judges of the Audiencia sent messages everywhere so that in the altepetl all around there could also not be processions anywhere during the said Holy Week, but everywhere people should stand guard. All that could be done in church on Maundy Thursday was to enclose the most Holy Sacrament in a stone tomb, not a single thing beyond that. —

v̲ Today on the second day [of Holy Week], on the said Holy Tuesday the 17th of the month of April, was when here outside [the church of] San Antón in Xoloco many Spanish warriors, soldiers, came and were stationed on the highway to stand guard with their arms. Likewise many additional soldiers went and were stationed on the highway toward Tepeyacac, going to Coyonacazco, and likewise a great many more soldiers were stationed on the road going toward Chapoltepec, at the [group of houses?][3] at Temetzcruztitlan,[4] [*p. 184*] and all the roads everywhere coming into the city of Mexico they stood guard, absolutely everywhere all around outside the houses[5] in the whole city of Mexico. And everywhere on the great canals they stood guard and looked out for where the blacks would come from who were coming to kill the Spaniards, because it was said that the black renegades who had established themselves at Acapulco would come from the seashore, and that some blacks who had turned renegade and run away from Mexico here, leaving their masters behind, would come here from Veracruz.

v̲ Today, the third day, on Holy Wednesday, when night was coming, the Spaniards came

5. The word has not been found as such. Its components are *calli*, "house"; *tentli*, "edge," and the collective-abstract nominal ending *-yo*. The first two in combination, especially with *-pan*, "in, etc.," often had the meaning at the entrance of a building, outside it, in effect in the street or on the sidewalk if there was one.

mauhtique yn ipan yc hualyohuac yn españoles. cenca tlayohuac mixtica yhuan quiyauh yhuan amo huel momati aquin tzatzitinenca nohuiyan yhtic ciudad Mexico tetzatziliaya amo nel aca telpochtlaveliloc español ynic nohuiyan calnacazco quihtotinenca ca ye oahcico yn tliltique aocmo hueca nemi ma neyaochichihuallo. ynin aquin tzatzitinenca ye quin ipan chiuhcnahui tzilini netetequizpan ynic ça ye catca ynic yequene huel momauhtique españoles. motepetlatzatzacq̃. yn inchachan ynic cenca momauhtique auh in señorati mochintin mochoquiliaya in ye quincahuazque ynnamichuan ypampa yuh mihtohuaya çan yehuantin yn oquichti españoles mictilozque auh in señorati çan cahualozque quinmocihuahuatizque yn tliltique. cenyohual yn amo cochque yxtoçoque nohuiyan tlatlatique[1] yn inchachan omoteneuhque españolesme. çan iuh tlathuilique yn amo cochque. auh yn izquitlamantin teopixque Mexico monoltitoque çan mohuetzquitiaya amo [*p. 185*] Quinmomauhtiliaya yn quimocaquiltiaya yn ipampa yxquich tlamantli mihtohuaya yaotlahtolli yntechpa tliltiq̃. yn cuix quichihuaznequi. auh yn mexica timacehualtin atle ytlan quinmauhtiaya çan tlatlachia yhuan tlatlacaqui çan quinmahuiçohuaya yn españoles. yn iuh mopollohuaya in ĩnemauhtiliztica yniqu iuhqui macamo huel yaotiacahuã ypan nezque —

v̲ Auh yn ipan Juebes Sancto. yn izquican teopan yc mexico, ynic tepetlacalco quimotzacuillique Sanctissimo sacramẽto, ynic hualyohuac çan nohuiyan tzauhcticatca puerta teopan acan tlapoticatca ce yohual ca yuh catca tlahtocatlanahuatilli yc tzatzihuac ya tlathuinahuac yn motlatlapo. in ye ypan viernes Sancto. tlathuico. / auh yn ipan in omoteneuh viernes Sancto. çan occan yn quimotemohuillique cruztitech yn ixiptlatzin tt^o^. Dios. yhuan quimotoquillique ynic ceccan oncan ỹ nican S. Joseph S. Fran^co^. çan callitic yn mochiuh auh ynic occan vmpa n S.tiago tlitilulco[2] quimotoquillique çan no callihtic yn mochiuh yhuan ynic nohuiyan altepetl ipan acan tlayahualoloc çan necomoniloc ynic nohuiyan yaotlapialoc. // auh yn nican Mexico yn izquican ypã ohtli omoteneuh yc yaotlapialloc Sabado Sancto tlamico. ynic callacque ynchachan yn Soldadostin mochiuhca —

v̲ Axcan Miercoles ynic .2. mani Metztli Mayo de 1612. años. yhcuac piloloque cenpohuallonchicuey tlacatl yn tliltique oquichti auh in tliltique cihua chicome tlacatl yn ihuã piloloque in ye mochi yc mocenpohua cenpohuallon[*p. 186*]caxtolli tlacatl in piloloque o ynpan neltico ynic otlatzontequilliloque ynpan yah yn Sentencia yn ipampa yniqu intech tlan ye omoteneuh tlacpac quil macocuizquia quinmictizquia yn intecuiyohuan españoles. yn iuh omoteneuh yuh chihuililoque informacion quil ypan Juebes Sancto yn ihcuac tlayahualolo ynnehuitequian yn españoles quinmictizquia yn iuh quihtoque testigostin ypampa ynic cenca tlamauhtique ypan omoteneuh Semana Sancta ynic amo campa huel tlayahualoloc auh quil yntla huel quinchihuani yntecuiyohuan españoles. yntla huel quinmictiani. quil yc niman. yehuantin tlahtocatizquia quil ce tliltic Rey mochihuazquia yhuan ce mulata morisca[3] quil quimonamictizquia reyna mochihuazquia. ytoca Isabel yn otlahtocatizquia Mexico. auh quil yn ixquich altepetl ynic nohuiyan ypan nueua españa quil ye moch oquimomamacaca yn tliltique yn oncan otlahtocatizquia ynic cequintin Duques. cequintin Marquestin cequintin Condesme quil omochiuhca ynic tinmacehualhuan

1. In the absence of an indication of vowel length, this form could refer to hiding rather than burning things.
2. For "tlatilulco."

to the ultimate of agitation and fright. It was very dark because of clouds, and it rained, and it cannot be found out who went shouting all around the city of Mexico—was it not some mischievous Spanish youth?—shouting to people and going about saying at the corners of houses everywhere that the blacks had arrived, that they were not far away, that everyone should get equipped for fighting. Whoever this was didn't go about shouting until 9 o'clock, the time when everyone goes to bed, so that the Spaniards reached the height of fear; they blocked themselves off in their homes from their great fear. All the Spanish women were weeping, [thinking] that their spouses would leave them, because it was said that only the Spanish men would be killed; the Spanish women would be left and the blacks would take them as wives. All night the said Spaniards did not sleep and kept vigil; everywhere they kept fires going[1] in their houses, and when dawn came they had not slept. And all the different groups of ecclesiastics who live in Mexico were just laughing; they were not [*p. 185*] frightened by what they were hearing about all the different kinds of news of war concerning the blacks, what they supposedly wanted to do. And we Mexica commoners were not at all frightened by it but were just looking and listening, just marveling at how the Spaniards were being destroyed by their fear and didn't appear as such great warriors. —

v On Maundy Thursday, when they enclosed the most Holy Sacrament in a tomb as night came, the doors of the churches everywhere were closed; during the whole night they were open nowhere, for the royal command that had been proclaimed was that they were to be opened close to dawn, as it dawned on Good Friday. / And on the said Good Friday there were only two places where the image of our lord God was taken down from the cross and buried; the first place was here at San Josef at San Francisco; it was done just inside the building. The second place where they buried him was at Santiago Tlatelolco,[2] where it was also done inside. And in the altepetl all around there were no processions anywhere; people were just agitated and stood guard everywhere. // And here in Mexico on Holy Saturday they stopped standing guard on all the roads that were mentioned, so that those who had been made soldiers went to their homes. —

v Today, Wednesday the 2nd of the month of May of the year 1612, was when 28 black men were hanged, and 7 black women were hanged with them; it added up to 35 [*p. 186*] people who were hanged. Verification was made about them so that they were sentenced and a judgment was issued against them because they were accused, as was mentioned above, of reportedly intending to rebel and kill their Spanish masters. According to the investigation made of them they were reportedly going to kill the Spaniards on Maundy Thursday when they were going in procession scourging themselves, as the witnesses said, because of which they caused great general fear during the said Holy Week, so that processions were not permitted anywhere. And reportedly if they had been able to do it to their masters, to kill them, reportedly a black was going to become king and a mulatto woman, a morisca,[3] named Isabel, was reportedly going to marry him and become queen, and they would have been the rulers in Mexico. And reportedly all the different altepetl everywhere in New Spain had been distributed to the blacks, and there they would rule, so that some had reportedly been made dukes, some marqueses, some counts, so that we

3. The exact thrust of this term in this context is not clear. At times Ch. seems to use it as a virtual synonym of mulatto.

otochihuazquia otiquintlacallaquilizquia otiquintlayecoltizquia oc yehuantin ỹ nican titlaca timacehualtin techcamaycuilozquia ynic necizquia ca totecuiyohuan. yhuan yuh mihto. ca çan niman aocac quĩcahuazquia yn oquichtin españoles yn huehuentzitzin yn iyolloco oquichtin yn telpopochtin ça ce ynic ye mochi oquichpipiltzitzinti mochintin quinmictizquia huel quinpopollozquia ynic aocmo yehuãtin tlapilhuatizquia aocmo yehuantin tlacaxinachozquia yhuan quil no quinmictizquia yn señorati in ye yllamatzitzin yn aoctle ynnecoca yhuan in manel quin iyolloco cihua yhuan quil yn manel noço [*p. 187*] Oqu ichpopochtin[1] yntlacamo huel chipahuaque[2] quil yntlacamo huel cualxayaqueque mochintin quinmictizquia. yntla huelitini çan quintlapepenizquia. auh quil ça yehuantin quincahuazquia yn huel chipahuaque[2] señorati yn huel cualxayaqueque in ye yyolloco cihua yhuan yn ichpopochtin ça ce in ye mochintin cihuapipiltotonti yn huel cualxayaqueque çan yehuantin amo quinmictizquia, çan quincahuazquia yehica ypampa quil quinmocihuauhtizquia in tliltique. auh yhuan quil yntla nel quinpilhuatizquia tliltique yn señorati yntla oquichtin yntech quichihuazquia ynpilhuan in ye xeliuhqui ynnacayo[3] yn motenehua mulatos moriscos.tin tlacatizquia, quil niman quinmictizquia amo huel nemizquia amo huel quinhuapahuazquia, auh quil intla ye cihua yntech señorati quinchihuazquia in motenehua ye mulatati muriscastin quil amo quinmictizquia ye nemizquia quinhuapahuazquia ypampa yn ihcuac huehueyazquia ca niman quinmocihuauhtizquia yehuantin in tliltique ynic huel hualmotlilticacuepazquia yn innepilhuatiliz yn intlacamecayo yn intlacaxinacho. auh ne yn ipampa oquichti yn inpilhuan tliltique omoteneuh yn itech quinchihuazquia senorati quil yn ipampa amo quincahuaznequia nemizque ynic amo quinhuapahuaznequia. quil ye yc quimimacacia ypampa yntla huehueyazquia ma quenmanian ytlan ỹpan quichiuhti yn intahuan tliltique in tlamiequiyazquia moriscos. tin ma quilnamicti yn cihuatica yn innanhuan ca españolas. yn intech quiça mahuiztic xinachtli mahuiztic tlacamecayotl yn amo yuh mahuiztic quipia ytechpa yntahuan tliltique. ynic niman aço quinyaotlahtalhuizquia, ahço yc niman quinmictizquia yn intahuan tliltique. quil yehuatl in yc quimimacacia [*p. 188*] Yniqu iuh quihtohuaya quichihuazquia tliltique yntla huelitini yntla huel mochihuani auh quil yn ixquichtin cihuateopixque yn monjastin motzacuiltitoque Monasterios Mexico quil mochintin quinquixtizquia yn ichpopochtin quinmocihuauhtizquia yn tliltique quil oc cenca yehuantin yntech tlahtohuaya yn omentin ychpochhuan tlahtohuani Don Luis de Velasco Marques de Salinas pressidente del consejo de indias. yn españa auh yn omoteneuhque ychpochtzitzinhuan ce ycnocihuatl ytoca Doña Maria dircios. ynin ynamic catca Don Juan altamirano. auh yn oc omentin cihuateopixque monjastin yn oncan moyetzticate monasterio totlaçonantzin Regina ynic ce ytoca Doña Beatriz de la ẽcarnaciõ Abbadessa yn oncan ynic ome ytoca Doña isabel de Jesus. auh quil ça yehuantin yn illamatzitzin vncan mocahuazquia monasterios. yn temachtizquia. auh quil oc yehuantin yn tliltique cihua callaquizquia yn monasterios oncan motzacuazquia ynic oc yehuantin cihuateopixcatizquia monjastin mochihuazquia, auh yhuan yn izquitlamantin teopixque Mexico monoltitoque quil no mochintin quinmictizquia quinpopolozquia, auh quil ça yetlamantin in teopixque quincahuazquia. ynic centlamantin quil yehuantzitzin in teopixque carmenitas descalços. ynic ontlamantin quil yehuantzitzin in teopixque S. Diego moyetzticate descalços. S. Fran^{co}. ypilhuantzitzin. auh yniqu etlamantin quil yehuantzitzin. yn la compañia de Jesus teopixque teatinos. quil ynin yc quin-

1. Or were girls, maidens.
2. The word can also be interpreted as meaning light-skinned.

local people, we commoners, would have become their vassals, we would have paid them tribute and served them, and they would have branded our mouths so it would be seen that they were our masters. It was also said that they were not going to leave any Spanish men at all, whether old men, men in their maturity, or youths; they would kill every last one of all the male children and destroy them absolutely, so that they would no longer have children and reproduce. And reportedly they were also going to kill some of the Spanish women, the old women who were no longer of any use, and even though women were still in the prime of life and reportedly even though [*p. 187*] they were still young,[1] if they weren't really good looking[2] and with comely faces, they were going to kill them all if they had been able; they were going to choose among them. Reportedly they were going to spare only the very good looking[2] Spanish women with very comely faces, the mature women and maidens and all the little girls who were comely of face; they were the only ones that they were not going to kill, that they were going to spare, because reportedly the blacks were going to take them as wives. And also, reportedly, even if the Spanish women had the blacks' male children, if they engendered by them children whose blood[3] was divided, and what are called male mulattoes or moriscos would be born, reportedly they would kill them right away, they would not be permitted to live and be brought up. But reportedly if they should engender females by the Spanish women, called female mulattoes and moriscas, reportedly they would not kill them; they would live and they would bring them up, because when they grew up the blacks would take them as wives so that their procreation, their lineage, their generation would turn black. But about the blacks' male children, as was said, that they would engender by Spanish women, reportedly the reason they didn't want to let them live and to raise them reportedly was that they feared them because when they grew up they might do something sometime to their fathers the blacks, and when the moriscos increased, [they were afraid] lest they remember that their mothers, on the female side, were Spanish women who came from splendid stock, splendid lineage, more splendid than they had on the side of their fathers the blacks, so that perhaps then they would prepare for war against them, perhaps then they would kill their fathers the blacks. Reportedly that was the reason they were afraid of them. [*p. 188*] That is what they said the blacks would have done if they had been able to do it. And reportedly, as to all the nuns who were enclosed in nunneries in Mexico, the blacks were going to bring them all out and take the young ones as wives; reportedly they spoke especially about the two daughters of the ruler don Luis de Velasco, Marqués of Salinas, president of the Council of the Indies in Spain; of the said daughters one is a widow named doña María de Ircio, who was the spouse of don Juan Altamirano, and there are another two who are nuns at the nunnery of our precious mother Regina [Coeli], the first of whom is named doña Beatriz de la Encarnación, abbess there, and the second is named doña Isabel de Jesús. And reportedly only the old women would be left in the nunneries to teach, and reportedly black women would enter the nunneries too and be enclosed there, so that they too would become nuns. And as to all the different groups of ecclesiastics who live in Mexico, reportedly they were going to kill and destroy all of them too. Reportedly they were going to spare only three groups of religious: first, the Discalced Carmelite friars; second, reportedly, the friars of San Diego, who are discalced and the children of San Francisco; third, the Theatine religious of the Company of Jesus; reportedly they

3. Literally flesh.

cahuazquia ypampa ynic quinmachtizquia huel quimixtlamachtizquia yn inpilhuan tliltique yn ica mochi tlamachiliztli yn ixquich quimomachiltia. ynic no oc yehuantin quil teopixcatizquia missa quichihuazquia yn cacatzac cocone yhuan ynic cequintin quil oydoresme mochihuazquia [*p. 189*] Ça ce yn ixquich tlamantli yn intlatecpantlahuiquiliz españoles. quil moch quincuilizquia ynic no yehuantin tliltique ypan yazquia no yc tlamanitizquia auh çan yehuantin ynin omoteneuhque yetlamantin teopixque, yn quil quincuallittaya tliltique ynic quincahuazquia ynic amo quinmictizquia yece macihui yn quincahuazquia yniqu intlan tliltique monemiltizquia yece quil mochintin quinmatequixtilizquia quinmatecuilizquia ynic amo campa huel oc ceme tlapilhuatizquia yntech señorati. ynic quil huel quincenpopoloznequia españoles. O yxquich tlamantli yn yn italhuililoque yn tenehuililoque yn tliltzitzin[1] yhuan oc cequi miectlamãtli yn italhuiloque yn amo huel moch nican motenehuaz tlahtolli ca cenca miec yn intech tlan yn aço nelli quichihuazquia yn anoço amo ca çan iceltzin huel yehuatzin quimomachiltia yn tt^{o}. dios. yntla yuhtica, yehica ypampa ca amo huel mellahuac quimocuititihui yn cequintin yn manel oquitzauhctiaque opiloloque çan oquihtotiaque ma ycatzinco tt^{o}. dios. ticcelican yn miquiztetlatzontequililiztli topan ye mochihua ca amo ticmati yn tleyn in totech tlami ye tictzauhctihui, Auh nican teneuhtica yn intocatzin yn izquintin tlahtoque Oydores. yhuan alcaldes de corte ingouierno ypan moyetzticatca yn huel quimixcahuitzinoticatca tlahtocayotl Mexico yn oquic ayac catca ce tlahtohuani visurrey yn quimochihuilique Justicia. ynpan omoteneuhq̃. tliltique quinmotlatzontequililique ynic piloloque ynic yuhqui ynpan mochiuh. yn iuh mochi tlacatl oquimatqui oquittac. ynic ce tlahtoque yn huel yntiachcauhtzin mochiuhtzinotica oncan audiencia Real yehuatzin

v El licenciado Don Pedro de Otalora Presidente — 1[*p. 190*]
v El licenciado Diego nuñez de Morquecho. — 2
v El Doctor Jhoan quesada de figueroa. — 3
v El licenciado Antonio Rodriguez. — 4
v El licenciado Pedro Suarez de longoria — 5
v El Doctor Don Marcos guerrero. — 6
v El licenciado Aller de Villagomez — 7
v El licendiado Pedro Suarez[2] de molina, — 8
v El licenciado Albar gomez de Abaunça.[3] — 9
v El licenciado ualleçillo fiscal del Rey de lo ciuil — 10

Auh yn alldes de corte

v El Doctor Antonio de morga — ii
v El licenciado Diego Lopez bueno — 12
v El licenciado Don Fran^{co} de Leoz[4] — 13
v El Doctor Valençia fiscal del Rey del crimen — 14

O yzquintin in yn tlahtoque yn quimochihuillique Justicia impan omoteneuhque cenpohualloncaxtolli tliltique ynic piloloque axcan ypan omoteneuh cemilhuitl v oc achtopa quĩtlayahualochtique cauallotì ỹpa quinteyttiq̃ yn otlipã[5] auh yn quinpehualti ye quinpi-

1. The form should be "tlilticatzitzin" or "tlilticatzitzintin."
2. Apparently an original *J* was corrected to *S*.
3. Name unconfirmed.
4. The name is given as Leoz or at times Leos in Monroy Castillo 1987–88, 1: 361;

were going to spare them so that they would teach and instruct the children of the blacks in all knowledge, everything that they know, so that black children too, reportedly, would become religious and perform mass, and so that some reportedly would become judges of the Audiencia. [*p. 189*] All the different things that the Spaniards were responsible for arranging they reportedly were going to take from them so that the blacks also would have access to them, would thereby make the rules of behavior. It was only these three said groups of religious that the blacks reportedly approved of and were going to spare and not kill; but although they were going to spare them so that they would live among the blacks, nevertheless reportedly they were going to remove and take off the testicles of all of them so that one of them somewhere couldn't have children by the Spanish women, so that, reportedly, they wanted to destroy the Spaniards utterly. These then are all the things that were said and told about the blacks;[1] many other additional things were said about them, not all of which tales can be told here, for they were accused of very much that maybe they truly were going to do or maybe not, for only our lord God himself knows whether it is so, because some [of the blacks] did not acknowledge the full truth of it; though they were punished and hanged, they said on dying, "Let us in the name of our lord God accept the death sentence that has been passed upon us, for we do not know what we are accused of that we are being punished for." Here are given the names of all the lords civil and criminal judges of the Audiencia in the time of whose government it was and who ruled all by themselves in Mexico, who as long as there was no lord viceroy administered justice regarding the said blacks and sentenced them to be hanged, as was done to them, as everyone found out and saw. The first of the judges, who had become the most senior in the Royal Audiencia, was:

v licenciado don Pedro de Otalora, president	1 [*p. 190*]
v licenciado Diego Núñez de Morquecho	2
v doctor Juan Quesada de Figueroa	3
v licenciado Antonio Rodríguez	4
v licenciado Pedro Suárez de Longoria	5
v doctor don Marcos Guerrero	6
v licenciado Aller de Villagómez	7
v licenciado Pedro Suárez[2] de Molina	8
v licenciado Alvar Gómez de Abaunza[3]	9
v licenciado Vallecillo, royal prosecutor in civil matters	10
and the court alcaldes,	
v doctor Antonio de Morga	11
v licenciado Diego López Bueno	12
v licenciado don Francisco de Leoz[4]	13
v doctor Valencia, royal prosecutor in criminal matters	14

These then were the judges who administered justice upon the said 35 blacks, so that they were hanged today on the said day. v First they had them go in procession on horses; they displayed them on the roads.[5] And Cristóbal Tranpipitl,[6] a mulatto, began to hang them

---

2: 98, 298.

5. The portion from "oc achtopa" to "yn otlipã," in the English from "First they" to "on the roads," is added in the margin.

6. Name unconfirmed and on the face of it quite unlikely.

pilohua x̄p̄oual tranpipitl[1] mulato matlactli tzillini ypan quarta hora yn tlaca yhcuac yancuican quipalehui yn ipiltzin[2] yniqu inehuan tepilloque oncan tecpan quiyahuac auh chicuetetl in yancuic tepilolcuahuitl inca moquetz tliltique yc chiuhcnauhtetl mochiuh in yeppa ya huecauh yhcac tepilolcuahuitl tlanepantla moquetztiquiz. yehica yn omoteneuh chicuetetl yãcuic tepilolcuahuitl yc quimanque çan quiyahuallochtique [*p. 191*] Auh yehuantin yn achi huey yntlatlacol yntech mihto yeintin in tlanepantla piloloque, auh yn oc cequintin çan quintlayahuallochtique yn itech omoteneuh yancuic tepilolcuahuitl ynic quinpilotiaque mochintin cualtica quimonochilitiaque quimotzatzililitiaque yn intemaquixticatzin tt^o^. Dios. ynic momiquilique mochintin mocencauhtihui moyolcuititihui auh yn tlamico. ynic quinpiloque omoteneuhque tliltique ye ce tzillini huel yei hora in quinpilloque. auh in ye o yuh mochintin quinpilloque çan oc oncan ynpan yohuac cenyohual yn pipilcatimanca. auh no miequintin yn amo piloloque tliltique yhuã mulatoti çan oncan tzauhcticatca yn carcel de corte tlatlatolchixticate

v̲ Auh ye quin iyomilhuiyoc yn ipan Juebes ynic eilhuitl mani n i metztli Mayo. huel ypan ylhuitzin Sancta cruz oquintemohuique in mimicque yn oncan tepilolcuauhtitech auh ynin omoteneuhque mimicque ynic tlatzontequililoque Justiciatica mochintin xexelolozquia ynic ynnacayo miyxtlapanazquia vmpa onmopipilozquia mochi yn ipan yzqui huehuey ohtli ochpantli hualcallaqui Mexico //. auh yn ipampa ĩ yc niman Acuerdo mochiuh yn audiencia real yc mononotzinoque yn tlahtoque no oncan quinmonanamiquilique yn ixquichtin Doctoresme in tepahtiani ynic yncepantlacemihtoltica mochiuh ynic çan quechcotonalloque cenpohuallonchiuhcnahui yn omoteneuhque mimicque auh yn intzonteco oncan tepilolcuauhticpac quinçaçalloque, auh yn intlacnacayo oncan quincallaquique yn contadoria tlatzĩtla ça moch quechcotontia oncan quinquimilloto yn inhuayolque tliltique. auh yn ayac yca mochiuh çan iuhqui auh yc nimã ye teotlac ye ypan chicuacen tzillini yn oncan quimonehualtique vmpa quintocato yn hospital nuestra Señora de [*p. 192*] La misericordia. auh in quinhuicaque yn cuicatiaq̃ clerigos, yhuan in hermanos ypilhuantzitzin Bato[3] Juan de Dios. tehuicaque yhuan cequintzitzin tottatzitzinhuã S. Domingo. yhuan S. Fran^co^. yhuan S. Augustin. yhuan La compañia de Jesus teopixque in motetoquillito. auh niman ya yehuantin in tliltique yhuan achi quezquintin yn españoles. yhuan Mexica cequintin yn timacehualtin tlapallehuique quinnapalloque in mimicque yn atle andas quipia çan petlatica ynic quinhuicaque quintocato // auh yn oc chicuacen omoteneuhque tliltique mimicque quinxexelloque yc cemixtlauh quintlapahtillique ynic mochintin incepanyan xexelolozquia oc cequintin ynic tlatzontequililoque mochintin yn çan otocoque ye omihto, auh ye omoteneuh ça chicuacentlacatl ỹ mimicque quinxexelloque quinpilloto yn ipan omoteneuh yzqui ohtli huehuey hualcallaqui Mexico, auh ynic amo mochintin xexeloloque oc cequĩtin yn omoteneuhque çan tocoque yehica ypampa quihtoque in mochintin tlamatini Doctoresme intla mochintin xexellolozque mimicque auh ynic quinpillotihui ypan yzqui huehuey ohtli yn innacayo. ca oncan mochi pallaniz amo cualli yc mochihuaz yn iyaca yn ipotonca ca cocoliztli mocuepaz auh niman nican hehecatica huallaz yn ihtic ciudad Mexico. topan motecaquiuh ynic techcocolizmacaz. o yehuatl ipampa yn yn intlahtol Doctoresme ynic quinmonanamiquillique tlahtoq̃. oydores yn oncan omoteneuh acuerdo mochiuh ynic çan otocoque oc cequintin mimicque —

v̲ Auh axcan viernes ynic 4. mani Metztli Mayo de 1612 años. ye oquiz yn pascua yhcuac

1. See p. 223, n. 6.
2. Son, surely.

at a quarter past 10 o'clock in the morning; at that time his child[2] helped him for the first time, so that they both together hanged people outside the palace. Eight new gallows had been set up for the blacks; the gallows used as the ninth had been standing there for a long time before; it turned out to stand in the middle because in setting up the said eight new gallows they placed them all around it. [*p. 191*] The three about whom it was said that their crime was greatest were hanged in the middle, and they put the others all around them on the said new gallows. As they went along hanging them they all properly called and cried out to their redeemer our lord God. When they died, all had been prepared and had confessed. Hanging the said blacks came to an end at 1 o'clock; it took three full hours to hang them. After they had all been hanged, they were there until night fell, and they were left hanging all night. Also many blacks and mulattoes who were not hanged were just locked up in the court jail awaiting sentence.

v Not until the second day, on Thursday the 3rd day of the month of May, right on the feast day of Santa Cruz, did they take the dead down from the gallows. According to the official sentence the said dead were all to be cut up and their bodies divided into pieces, which were going to be hung here and there on all the main roads and highways coming into Mexico. // On this matter the Royal Audiencia was then called into session; the judges were summoned for it, and also all the medical doctors assisted them, and it was by their joint pronouncement that 29 of the said dead were only decapitated and their heads stuck on top of the gallows. They put their torsos in the royal accounting office, down below, and the relatives of all the blacks whose heads were cut off went there to shroud them. Nothing was done with any of them, they were just left as they were, and then in the afternoon, at 6 o'clock, they took them away and went to bury them at the hospital of Nuestra Señora de [*p. 192*] la Misericordia. They were accompanied by secular priests who went singing and by the brothers who are the children of the beatified[3] Juan de Dios, and some of our fathers the religious of Santo Domingo, San Francisco, San Agustín, and the Company of Jesus went to the burial. And then the blacks and some few Spaniards and some of us Mexica commoners helped; they carried the dead, who had no biers; they just took them in mats to bury them. // The other said six dead blacks were cut up, with which was made good and with them they made amends for [the sentence] that all of them were going to be cut up together; it was already said how they passed sentence so that all the others were just buried. And with the six dead that as already mentioned they cut up, they hung them in all the said main roads coming into Mexico. The reason that they didn't cut them all up and the said others were just buried is that all the learned doctors said that if all the dead should be cut up and their bodies hung in all the main roads, they would all rot there, it would not be well done, their stench and bad smell would turn into sickness, and then with the wind it would come here inside the city of Mexico and spread among us, making us sick. It was because of these things that the doctors said, then, when they assisted the lords judges of the Audiencia when the said session was held, that the other dead were just buried. —

v Today, Friday the 4th of the month of May of the year 1612, after Easter had been

3. For "Beato."

macoca tlanahuatilli huelitiliztli licēcia audiencia real yn españoles. yn oquitlallique yancuic cofradia oncan omoteneuh S. Juan de la penitencia monjas [*p. 193*] Moyotlan ynic tlayahuallozquia prossion[1] mochihuazquia quiçazquia yn ipilhuantzitzin S. Juan bap^{ta}. tlamaceuhque penitentes inic mohuitequizque. yn ipan ome tzillini teotlac auh ye yuhqui. ye quixohuazquia quiquixtizquia yn ipassiõtzin tt^{o}. dios. auh yece in yehuatl prouisor Don Juan de Salamanca oc polihuia yn ihuelitiliz yn itlanahuatil licencia amo tle quitlanilique ynic çan quihualtzacuilli tlayahualoliztli ynic amo huel mochihuaz. yhuã descomunion quinhuallalili yn españoles. ynic amo huel quiçaz omoteneuh tlayahualloliztli prossion[1] ynic oc nen quitlanilizquia licencia ça ihciuhca prouisor. ça quinhualilhui yn españoles. ca aocmo ymonecyan yn axcan yc quiçaz ytlayhiyohuilitzin yn ipassiontzin ylnamicoca tt^{o}. dios. auh ca ye oquiz in huel ynemacpan cahuitl catca, auh ca ye pahpaquilizcahuitl yn axcã ypan ticate caocmo huel mochihuaz. o yhui yn yn quihualtzauhc prouisor ynic niman ça mixcahuique in tlamaceuhque penitentes quizque yn momecahuitecque ynic yzquican teopan quiquiçato ynic estaciones quichihuato.

v Auh axcan martes ynic 8. mani Metztli Mayo de 1612 años. ye macuilli tzillini teotlac yhcuac otocoque yn intzonteco omoteneuhque tliltique piloloque in yaoyotl quihtohuaya yca çan chicomilhuitique yn oncan cacatca tepilolcuauhticpac ypampa cenca ye iyayaya ynic niman quinquixtique çãno vmpa quihtocato[2] yn omoteneuh hospital de la misericordia

v Axcan Lunes ynic 14. mani metztli Mayo de 1612 años. yhcuac [*p. 194*] Ye no ce tliltic pilolo yn oncan tecpan quiyahuac yncapitan yn achtopa omoteneuhque tliltique piloloque —

v Axcan Sabado ynic 26. mani Metztli Mayo de 1612 años yhcuac nican Mexico quimonpehualtique miequintin tliltique yn ompa quinhuica españa quinmottiliz yn tohueytlahtocatzin Rey yn ipampa yntlatlacol yn omoteneuh ynic macocuizquia yn aço nelli yaoyotl quichihuaznequia nican ypan nueua españa yn oc mocauhque yn amo tehuanme piloloque nican yn iuh ynpan mochiuh oc cequintin tlacpac omoteneuhque tliltique, auh ynin omoteneuhque españa huicoque oncan tetlan yhcuac huicoc yn Anton de loya[3] tliltic çãno ymalguacil catca yn tliltique libres yn tlacallaquia // auh yn ipan in omoteneuh cemilhuitl Sabado no yhcuac omochiuh capitulo. in S. Domingo yehuatzin prouincial mochiuh yn Padre maestro fr. hernando Baçan auh yn iyomilhuiyoc yn ipan Domingo ynic 27. mani metztli Mayo. yhcuac otlayahualoloc yn oncan omoteneuh S. Domingo ycatzinco ypampatzinco yn huey Sancto S. Luis perdra[4] confesor teopixqui S. Domingo. ynic çan oc tlayectenehualtic motenehua Beatificacion ycatzinco yancuica mochiuh yn ompa Roma. in Sancto Padre quinmomacahuilili yhuelitzĩ yn teopixque S. Domingo ynic huel quimolhuichihuililitiazque cecexiuhtica, ynic no nican Mexico. ycatzinco omochiuh yancuican tlayahualoliztli yn ipan in omoteneuh Domingo motlayahualhui yn ixiptlatzin Sancto S Luis. //

v Axcan lunes ynic 28. mani Metztli Mayo de 1612 años yhcuac nican mexico vnmo-

1. For "prossession" or the like.
2. For "quintocato."
3. Name unconfirmed.
4. Stafford Poole has suggested that the person Ch. gives as "S. Luis perdra" was St. Luis Beltrán (1526–1581), known in English as St. Louis Bertrand, a Dominican friar

celebrated, was when an order of permission of the Royal Audiencia had been given to the Spaniards who established the new cofradía at the said nunnery of San Juan de la Penitencia [*p. 193*] in Moyotlan, so that at 2 o'clock in the afternoon the children of San Juan Bautista, the penitents, could come out and go around holding a procession[1] to scourge themselves. Everything was ready, they were going to come out and bring out the Passion of our lord God, but the order of permission of the vicar general don Juan de Salamanca was still lacking, they had not asked him for any, so that he blocked the procession, so that it could not be held, and he excommunicated the Spaniards, so that the said procession[1] could not come out and it would do no good to ask him for permission. The vicar general quickly told the Spaniards that now was no longer a proper time for the suffering and passion in memory of our lord God to be brought out. That had already ended; now we were truly in a time of his grace, in the midst of celebration; it could no longer be done. This then is how the vicar general blocked it, so that then the penitents just came out on their own [as individuals] and scourged themselves, going by each of the churches and making the stations [of the cross].

v Tuesday, the 8th of the month of May of the year 1612, at 5 o'clock in the afternoon, was when the heads of the said blacks who were hanged, who had declared war, were buried. The reason that they were on top of the gallows for only seven days was that they were already smelling very bad, so that then they removed them and buried[2] them likewise at the said hospital of Misericordia.

v Today, Monday the 14th of the month of May of the year 1612, was when [*p. 194*] another black was hanged outside the palace, the captain of the earlier mentioned blacks who were hanged. —

v Today, Saturday the 26th of the month of May of the year 1612, was when they set off from Mexico here with many blacks they were taking to Spain. Our great ruler the king will see them because of their crimes that were mentioned, how they were going to rebel, and if it was true that they were going to make war here in New Spain. Those who were still left, who were not hanged here with the rest as was done with the other blacks mentioned above, these said blacks were taken to Spain. At that time Antón de Loya,[3] a black, was also taken with the rest; he had been the constable of the free blacks who pay tribute. // Also on the said day of Saturday was held the provincial chapter meeting at Santo Domingo; father fray Hernando Bazán, master in theology, became provincial head. And the next day, on Sunday the 27th of the month of May, was when a procession was held at the said [church of] Santo Domingo on account of the great saint San Luis Beltrán,[4] confessor and Dominican friar. Since he has only been blessed for the time being, and what is called beatification was recently performed for him in Rome, the Holy Father granted the Dominican friars his permission for them to go along celebrating his feast day every year, so that also here in Mexico there was a procession for the first time on his behalf; on the said Sunday the image of the saint San Luis went in procession.//

v Today, Monday the 28th of the month of May of the year 1612, was when father fray

---

active in the Caribbean and on the Spanish main, who was ultimately canonized and was named patron saint of New Granada (1690). The form "perdra" is a plausible representation of Beltrán, with the normal substitution *p* for *b*, hypercorrect *r* for *l* and *d* for *t*, and omission of *n*, a ubiquitous phenomenon in Nahuatl writing.

pehualti yn padre fr. [*p. 195*] Antonio de olea el presentado mohuica españa vmpa ychantzĩco ynin ycompañerotzin yn teoyotica tlahtohuani Don fr. Garcia Guerra arçobispo Mexico yhuan visurrey moyetzticatca yn oquimohuiquillitzino tt^{o} . Dios. —
v Axcan Lunes ynic .2. mani Metztli Julio de 1612 años. ypan ylhuitzin visitacion ynic quimotlapalhuito totlaçonantzin S.ta maria yn itlaçopitzin S.ta isabel. yhcuac mochalli ynic yecauh teocalmamallihuac yn oncan yancuic teopan nuestra Señora del colegio de las Niñas. ynin omoteneuh teocalli huel amo huecauh yn omochiuh çan iuhqui yn hualixhuac inic moyancuilli ynic quichiuhque cofrades del Sanctissimo Sacramento. // auh çano ypan in yn omoteneuh lunes yn ohualtlathuic omomiquilli yn fran^{co} de leyba. ynahuatlahtocauh catca visurrey. ynin cenca tlamamauhtiaya nohuiyampa ỹtoca[1] timacehualti ynic cenca tlahueliloc huel teahuani catca yn ipã tleyn tequitl mochihuaya huel tentlahueliloc camachichi catca ayac quixittaya manel gouernadoresme amo tle yc quinmahuiztiliaya yhuan cenca teca omocacayauhtia —

v Axcan Lunes ynic .20. mani Metztli Agosto de 1612 años. yhcuac omomiquilli yn Don Balthasar m̃ĩn chane S. Pablo çoquipan çan atlaca[2] catca amo campa tlahtocayotl ytech quiçaya ynin yehuatl yn gouernador catca azcapotzalco. çan quicahualtique yn igouernacion ynic niman conpatlato Don Antonio Valeriano telpochtli yn iuh omoteneuh tlacpac

v Axcan Miercoles ynic .29. mani Metztli Agosto de 1612 años, yhcuac omomiquilli yn El licenciado Albar gomez de Abaunça oydor catca Mexico. auh ye chicuacen tzillini teotlac yn otocoto ynacayo yn oncan teopan Monasterio de nu[*p. 196*]estra Señora de las mercedes, yn iztac habito teopixque quimotlalilia ynchantzinco[3]

v Axcan Domingo ynic .30. mani Metztli Setiembre de 1612 años ypan ylhuitzin S. Jeronimo. yhcuac omachiztico omomiquilli cuauhtemallan. yn Doctor grauajar. oydor catca yn õpa omoteneuh cuauhtemallan ynin nican Mexico yahca quin icel criyoyo oydor omochiuhtia —

v Axcan Lunes ynic .22. mani Metztli octubre de 1612 a^{o}s. yhcuac nican Mexico ahçico callaquico in El licenciado Don Juan Fernandez de Velasco y horozco al~~lde~~ de corte Mexico vmpa hualla españa ynin yuh omihto criyoyo. nican yahca Mexico ynic oquicuito ytequiuh omochiuh //. auh çãno yhcuac yn hualla yn Don Juan gano Moteuhcçoma,[4] ynic onhuia españa yc expa yllo.[5] // auh çãno ypan in yn omoteneuh lunes. yn ohuallathuic oquichtacamictique yn Miguel Sanchez tecuicitli al~~lde~~ chane S. Pablo ometochtitla oquittato chichinampã huetztoc oquicuallique yn ixayac atlan chaneque[6] oncan yn ichan

1. Despite the plural form, "ỹtoca," the singular must be intended.
2. The form "atlaca" may lack the singular absolutive ending *tl*, or it may be the plural used in a partitive meaning, "one of." The word is probably *ātlahcatl*, a person associated with or inhabitant of the water, which in effect usually means a boatman, sailor, or fisherman. A remote possibility would be *ahtlācatl*, usually meaning an inhuman, monstrous person, but conceivably susceptible of being interpreted as a nobody, a person of very humble origins.

Antonio de Olea, who has been presented [as candidate for archbishop], set out [*p. 195*] to go to Spain where his home is. He was the companion of the spiritual ruler don fray García Guerra, late archbishop in Mexico and viceroy, whom our lord God took. —
v Today, Monday the 2nd of the month of July of the year 1612, on the feast day of Visitación, when our precious mother Santa María went to greet her dear older sister Santa Isabel, was when the new church at Nuestra Señora del Colegio de las Niñas was inaugurated and first dedicated after being finished. It was not very long ago that this said church was built; it is just as though it were branching out and being renovated; the members of the cofradía of the most Holy Sacrament did it. // And also on the said Monday, in the night before morning, Francisco de Leiva passed away; he was the viceroy's interpreter, whose name[1] greatly frightened us commoners everywhere because he was very bad, he used to really scold people about whatever tribute duty was being performed. He really had a bad mouth and spoke bitterly. He respected no one; even though it was a governor he showed no respect. And he greatly cheated people. —
v Today, Monday the 20th of the month of August of the year 1612, was when don Baltasar Martín, from San Pablo Çoquipan, passed away. He was just a [boatman or fisherman],[2] he didn't come from a ruling dynasty anywhere. He was governor of Azcapotzalco, but they made him relinquish his governorship so that then don Antonio Valeriano the younger replaced him, as was said above.
v Today, Wednesday the 29th of the month of August of the year 1612, was when there passed away licenciado Alvar Gómez de Abaunza, who was civil judge of the Audiencia in Mexico, and at 6 o'clock in the afternoon his body was buried at the monastery church of Nuestra [*p. 196*] Señora de las Mercedes; he wore the white habit of the friars in their home establishment.[3]
v Today, Sunday the 30th of the month of September of the year 1612, on the feast day of San Gerónimo, was when it became known that in Guatemala doctor Carvajal, who was a judge in the Audiencia in the said Guatemala, passed away. He had gone from Mexico here, and up to that time he was the only criollo who had been made civil judge in an Audiencia. —
v Today, Monday the 22nd of the month of October of the year 1612, was when licenciado don Juan Fernández de Velasco y Orozco, alcalde de corte in Mexico, got to Mexico here and entered; he came from Spain. It was said that he is a criollo; he had left Mexico here in order to go take the office to which he had been appointed. // Likewise at that time don Juan Cano Moctezuma[4] came back from having gone to Spain; it was the third time that he has come back.[5] // And also on this said Monday, in the night before morning, Miguel Sánchez Teuccitli, alcalde, from San Pablo Ometochtitlan, was secretly killed [murdered]. They found him lying in the chinampas; the fish[6] had chewed at his face. He

---

3. Possibly the passage merely means that the friars wore the white habit; "ynchantzinco" seems to be hanging, not in its usual position.

4. So used in Spanish, as seen on p. 67 at n. 5.

5. Apparently this is the verb *iloti*, to come back from where one has gone, in the preterit without the initial *o*, which Ch. often omits. The standard preterit is *ilot*; the final *t* may have been reduced to an unwritten glottal stop as regularly happened with the verb *mati*, "to know," or it may have been inadvertently omitted.

6. Literally, residents of the water.

yhuino[1] anoço yvinonamacayan Morexon temaztitlan yn quimictique çan quicocohuiteq̃ yca ce gadana çan ihuayolque yn tlẽ yca quimictique cholloque

v̲ Axcan Domingo ynic .28. mani Metztli octubre de 1612 años. huel ypan ymilhuitzin yn Sant. Simon yhuan S. Judas Tadeo, Apostoles. yhcuac nican Mexico tecpã palacio ye ypan chicuacen tzillini teotlac ynic onyohuac yn omocallaquico yn tlahtohuani Don diego fernandez de cordoua [*p. 197*] Marques de guadalcazar comendador S.tiago Visurrey lugartheniente del Rey nuestro Señor gou^{or} y capitan general de la nueua españa, yhuan quihualmohuiquilli yn inamictzin yn cihuapilli ytoca Doña Mariana Riedre[2] Marq̃sa virreyna de la nueua españa. ynin cihuapilli Alemañis ca huel ompa chane yn ciudad Alemañia:[3] vmpa quihualmohuiquilli ycihuapiltzin yhuan ysecretariatzin hualmochiuhtiaca yn tohueycihuatlahtocauh Doña Margarida de Austria Reyna españa omoyetzticatca yn oquimohuiquilli tt^{o}. dios. axcan ce xihuitl ypan ytlaçoylhuitzin S. Fran^{co}, yn momiquilli. // auh yn iteyolcuiticauh yconfesor ohualmochiuhtia Visurrey yn ompa oquihualmohuiquilli españa ce clerigo quitocayotia Doctor Guerrero comendador Calatraba chichiltic cruz yn icomienda quitlalia // yhuan oc ce caualIero ytoca Don fran^{co} de cardona comendador de montesa no chichiltic cruz. çan ixquich nepaniuhqui[4] yn icomienda quitlalia no vmpa hualla yn españa. ynin nican inJuez mochihuaco yn obrajeros.[5] // ynic ey hualla españa yn caualIero[6] ytoca Don Luis de Alçega ybarguen[7] comendador de Alcantara yn icomienda quitlallia quiltic cruz. ynin telpocapiltontli novicio ỹ hualla ayemo monetoltia yca ayemo quichihua profession çan oqu ixquich quihualcuitehua vmpa comienda ynin omoteneuh ynpiltzin ynconeuh yn contador ybarguen catca yhuan Doña catalina de Alçega yn axcan ye ynamic yetica yn Doctor Antonio de Morga al~~lde~~ de corte Mexico. yc ytlacpahuitec yn omoteneuh telpochtli comendador criyoyo

v̲ Axcan viernes ynic 24. mani Metztli Nouiembre de 1612 años. yhcuac oquiz yn inSentencia revista yn audiencia [*p. 198*] real Mexico ynic tlahtoque oydores yhuan virrey oquinmomaquillique yn intlal Mexica tenochca yn ipampa moteylhuique cochtocan y españoles oquicuica ynic ce yehuatl yn Alonso dauilla huehuenton ynic ome yehuatl yn Molison quincahualtique auh yn macoto possesion oc cenca yehuatl yn isabel _______ yhuan ynamic Juan de españa chaneque S.ta maria cuepopan yehuantin huel mochicauhque yn moteilhuique yntlatqui ymixcoyan quipopolloque, auh ça yuhqui yn ontlatoquilitiaque S. Pablo. tlaca yn hernando teuhcxochitzin ynehuan yn Nicolas hernandez tlacayelel /

v̲ Axcan Sabado ynic .8. mani metztli de diziembre de 1612 años. huel ypan ylhuitzin totlaçonantzin Comsepcion yhcuac cenca tlamahuiztililiztica tlayahualoliztica quitocaque coztic teocuitlatl yn teopixque S. Fran^{co}. ypan yn commissario fr. Juan çurida yn ompa totlaçonantzin S ta maria motenehua de la Redonda. cuepopan ynic otlamachiyotique yn

1. Apparently the form "yhuino" is to be read as though it had a hyphen after it, to be completed by "-namacayan," so that Ch. is simply giving two alternatives for spelling the loanword *vino*, probably pronounced with an initial [w] in Nahuatl.

2. For the name see Sánchez 1998, p. 29.

3. Conceivably Ch. means a city in Germany, but since he often equates *ciudad* and *altepetl*, and considers entities such as Japan to be altepetl, it seems more likely that he is calling Germany a city.

was killed at the home and wine tavern[1] of Morrison at Temaztitlan. His throat was cut with a cutlass. It was just [one of?] his relatives who killed him over something, then fled.

v Today, Sunday the 28th of the month of October of the year 1612, right on the feast day of San Simón and San Judas Tadeo the apostles, at 6 o'clock in the afternoon, as night was falling, was when there entered the governmental palace here in Mexico the lord don Diego Fernández de Córdoba, [*p. 197*] Marqués of Guadalcázar, comendador in the order of Santiago, viceroy and deputy of the king our lord, governor and captain general of New Spain, and he brought his spouse, the lady named doña Mariana Riderer,[2] marquise and virreine of New Spain; this lady is German, for she is actually from the city of Germany.[3] She was brought from there as her lady[-in-waiting] and secretary by our great queen doña Margarita de Austria, late queen of Spain, whom our lord God took a year ago now; it was on the precious feast day of San Francisco that she passed away. // And the person who came appointed as the viceroy's confessor, whom he brought from Spain, was a secular priest whom they call doctor Guerrero, comendador in the order of Calatrava; he wears a red cross as his badge. // And another gentleman named don Francisco de Cardona, comendador [of the order of?] Montesa also wears a red cross as his badge, but [doubled?];[4] he too came from Spain, appointed judge of [owners of textile works?].[5] // The third gentleman[6] who came from Spain was called don Luis de Alcega Ibarguen,[7] comendador in the order of Alcántara; he wears a green cross as his badge; he is a youngster, a novice, who came before taking his vows and professing; all he has done so far is get his badge there before leaving. The one we are talking about is the child of the late royal accountant Ibarguen and doña Catalina de Alcega, who has now become the spouse of doctor Antonio de Morga, alcalde of court in Mexico, so that the said youth who is a comendador is his stepson; he is a criollo.

v Today, Friday the 24th of the month of November of the year 1612, was when the sentence after appeal of the Royal Audiencia of Mexico was issued, [*p. 198*] by which the lords judges and the viceroy gave to the Mexica Tenochca their land at Cochtocan about which they had made a complaint, that Spaniards had taken, first the old man Alonso de Avila and second that Morrison. They made them relinquish it, and possession was given to [the Mexica Tenochca], especially Isabel _______ and her spouse Juan de España, citizens of Santa María Cuepopan. They were very energetic in the complaint; it was their own property that they lost, and following them [in pursuing the suit] were the people of San Pablo, Hernando Teucxochitzin together with Nicolás Hernández Tlacaellel. /

v Today, Saturday the 8th of the month of December of the year 1612, right on the feast day of our precious mother of Concepción, was when with very great splendor, in a procession, the Franciscan friars, in the term of the commissary fray Juan de Zorita, buried some gold at [the church of] our precious mother Santa María, called de la Redonda, in Cuepopan, by which they signified that groundbreaking began for building a

4. *Nepaniuhqui* refers to various kinds of folding, doubling, joining.

5. The word *obrajero* was most frequently used in New Spain for the owners or managers of the textile works called *obrajes*, but it could also mean one in charge of public works, contractor.

6. Or knight. All three of those mentioned were knights in military orders.

7. Name unconfirmed.

oncan opeuh yc otlatlallanoc ynic ye mochihua yancuic tlatlapolloyan Porteria yn oncan mochihuaz missa yn oquic mochihuaz yancuic cochiantli yhuan yancuic teopãcalli yntlatquitica yn teopixque ye quimochihuilia — xitiniz yn teopançolli // axcan viernes ynic 28. mani Metztli de diziẽbre de 1612 años ynic nahuilhuitl pascua nauidad yn itlacatillitzin tt^{o} Jesu x̄p̄o. huel ypã ilhuitzin pipiltzitzinti sanctos ynocentes. yhcuac omacoq̃ escabulario yhuã yn capilla in motenehua hermanos conbalecientes ỹ quimocuitlahuia hospital de los Locos. S.t ipolito tlalcozpan .12. monetoltiq̃ profession quichiuhq̃. ymac yn intiachcauh hermano mayor ypan missa yohuatzinco yxpantzinco visurrey yhuã mochi audiencia real tlaca oydores. auh yehuatzin oncan motemachtili ỹ Don fr. diego de cõtreras Electo arçobispo yn la isla S. Domingo ayhtic auh S. Padre ytencopatzinco yn iuh mochiuh —
her^{nos}.[1] de huastepec v̲ Bernardino Aluarez. fundador de los hospitaleros her^{nos}. conualecientes de Mexico. y de otros muchos que estan repartidos por la nueua españa que merecio felicissimo successos de prosperidad para el bien remedio. y salud de muchos

1613.[2] .iiii. calli xihuitl yn ipan in yehuatl [*p. 199*] Gouernador yn Señor Juan Perez de monterrey. ỹ nican Tenochtitlan, auh yn alldesme motlallique S. Juan Moyotlan Diego de S. Fran^{co} chane tequicaltitlan[3] yhuan Augustin Vasquez chane huehuecalco, auh yn alldesme motlallique S. Pablo teopã Juan Ramirez chane çoquipan yhuan Pablo Damian chane ometochtitlan, auh yn alldesme motlallique S. Sebastian atzacualco Don diego luis de Moteuhcçoma chane cuitlahuactõco. yhuan Melchior xuarez. chane tomatla, auh yn alldesme motlallique S.ta maria cuepopan X̄p̄oual pasqual mestiço chane copolco // yhuan Andres de los Angeles chane ____ ynin Andres de los Angeles çan tlaco xihuitl yn alldetic çan õmomiquillico yc niman yehuatl conpatlac yn Pablo corrier[4] chane ____ ynin quitzonquixtico yn omoteneuh xihuitl ynic alldetic
v̲ Axcan Miercoles ohuallathuic ynic omilhuitl mani yancuic Metztli henero No yhuan quin ic omilhuitia yancuic xihuitl de 1613. a^{o}s. yhcuac nican Mexico omixiuh yn cihuapilli Doña Mariana Riedre Marquesa y Virreyna de la nueua españa. yn inamic tlahtohuani Don diego fernandez de cordoua Marques de guadalcaçar Visurrey de la nueua españa, yn ipiltzin otlacat cihuatl ytoca Doña Mariana Manuel auh ynic niman ohualyohuac yn ontzillin horacion ypampa nohuiyan otlatzitzillicac yn huel yzquican teopan monasterios mexico. yhuan nohuiyan cuahuitl oquitlatlahtique yn inquiyahuac yn intlapanco españoles. yhuan candelas sepo tlatlatlac luminarios.
v̲ Axcan martes ynic .15. mani Metztli henero de 1613 años. yhcuac çan ixtomamiquiliztica xoxouhcamiquiliztica[6] momiqui[*p. 200*]lli yn Luy Lopez castiço[5] yn chane ocatca hueycalco yn tictocayotia ychan tonatiuh[7] ynin otlayecoltilloya comendero[8] ocatca. yn

1. This part is in the margin, in Spanish, though in Ch.'s hand. The Spanish here is over-elaborate and not quite in control, reminiscent of the Spanish of some Nahuatl speakers in "Stage 4," in the late eighteenth century. (See Lockhart 1992, pp. 318–23.)

2. The number is accompanied by a precontact-style representation of a house with four dots above.

3. The names in this position throughout the list seem to identify *tlaxilacalli* (constituent subdistricts) within the respective large quarter of Tenochtitlan.

4. Name unconfirmed.

5. As racial mixture proceeded over the decades and centuries, a set of often unrealistic ethnic-racial categories arose to describe different mixtures; a *castizo* was supposed to be

new place where things are opened up, an arcaded entryway [*portería*] where mass will be held until such time as a new dormitory and a new church are built; the friars are doing it with their assets, and the old church will be torn down. // Today, Friday the 28th of the month of December of the year 1612, on the fourth day of the Christmas holiday, the birth of our lord Jesus Christ, right on the feast day of the children, the holy innocents, was when the scapular and hood were given to the said brothers of the convalescents who take care of the Hospital de los Locos at San Hipólito in Tlacozpan; twelve of them took vows and made profession to their most senior member, the eldest brother, at a mass early in the morning in the presence of the viceroy and all the judges of the Royal Audiencia. The person who preached was don fray Diego de Contreras, archbishop elect of the island of Santo Domingo out in the ocean. It was done by order of the Holy Father. —
Brothers[1] of Huaxtepec. v Bernardino Alvarez, founder of the hospitalers, the Hermanos Convalecientes of Mexico, and of many others which are spread throughout New Spain, deserved the happiest results of prosperity for the succor and health of many.

1613,[2] 4 House year. In this year [*p. 199*] señor Juan Pérez de Monterrey was governor here in Tenochtitlan, and as alcaldes Diego de San Francisco, from Tequicaltitlan,[3] and Agustín Vásquez, from Huehuecalco, were installed for San Juan Moyotlan. And for San Pablo Teopan Juan Ramírez, from Çoquipan, and Pablo Damián, from Ometochtitlan, were installed as alcaldes. And for San Sebastián Atzaqualco don Diego Luis de Moteucçoma, from Cuitlahuactonco, and Melchor Juárez, from Tomatla, were installed as alcaldes. And for Santa María Cuepopan Cristóbal Pascual, a mestizo, from Copolco, // and Andrés de los Angeles, from ______, were installed as alcaldes. This Andrés de los Angeles served as alcalde only half a year, for he died, and then Pablo [Corrier],[4] from ______, finished out the said year as alcalde.

v Today, Wednesday before dawn, the 2nd day of the new month, January, also the 2nd day of the new year of 1613, was when the lady doña Mariana Riderer, marquise and vireine of New Spain, spouse of the ruler don Diego Fernández de Córdoba, Marqués of Guadalcázar, viceroy of New Spain, gave birth; her child was born a girl, named doña Mariana Manuela. And then when night was falling and the bells were rung for prayer time, the bells everywhere in absolutely all the churches and monasteries in Mexico pealed, and everywhere the Spaniards burned wood outside their houses and on their roofs, and tallow candles, luminarios, were also burned.

v Today, Tuesday the 15th of the month of January of the year 1613, was when Ruy López, a *castizo*,[5] passed away of an unexpected, premature[6] death; he was a resident of Hueicalco, which we call Ichan Tonatiuh.[7] [*p. 200*] He was served as the encomendero[8]

---

three-fourths Spanish, one-fourth indigenous.

6. See above (pp. 172–73, 214–15), for *ixtomamiquiliztica* used in connection with sudden or unexpected death. *Xoxouhcamiquiliztica* by the context appears to be a synonym; it is used again in connection with *ixtomamiquiliztica* on pp. 250–51. *Xoxouhqui* is something green, including in the sense of unripe, immature.

7. In Book 12 of the Florentine Codex, Moteucçoma talks about taking refuge in *tonatiuh ichan*, possibly a real geographical place, though the phrase means "home of the sun" and referred to a kind of paradise (Lockhart 1993, pp. 88–89).

8. In much Nahuatl usage the *en* of *encomendero* was taken for the subordinator/article *in*, so that it was omitted in the loanword.

azcapotzalco tepanecapan yhuan tenantzinco ça yc yehuatl ytech otlamico ynic niman oquimocuilli ỹ Rey yn omoteneuh altepetl ynin ypiltzin catca yn Juan de Zaucedo Mestiço conquistador. auh yn ical moch itech opouh yn iteyccauh yhermano Miguel Lopez[1] —

v Axcan Martes ynic 22. mani Metztli henero de 1613 años. yhcuac ye tlathui cenca chicahuac oquiyauh ỹ nican Mexico. yhuan ynic nohuiyan cuauhtla o nohuiyan tepeuh[2] yn ceppayahuitl o cepayauh cenca chicahuac in motecac cepayahuitl oc cenca oncan ytech yn chicahuac motecac tepetl yn quitocayotia Tenan ỹ nican tonahuac catqui cuyohuacan çah ce ynic nohuiyan yntech mochi tetepe huel yc moquimilloq̃. yn cepayahuitl yn xochimilco yntech tetepe yhuan oc no cenca vmpa yn chalco Amaquemecan yn intech yztac tepetl yhuan popocatepetl yhuã yn oc cequi tepetl yn intech çaliuhtoque huel ic moquimilloque yn cepayahuitl yhuan yn itech tepetl quitocayotia cilcuaye yn tenanco tepopolla catqui yhuan ytech ỹ quetzaltepetl yn huexotla aculhuacanpa catqui moch iztazque yn tetepe auh ynic omilhuitl ypan miercoles cemilhuitl yn oquiyauh yhuan oceppayauh yn omoteneuh ytech tepetl tenan yhuan cenca ocehuac ỹ nican Mexico // auh çanno yhcuac yn ipan in omoteneuh Metztli henero omachiztico ohualla tlahtolli yn españa ynic hualla acaltepiton naviobiso.[3] yn quenin oncan hualmohuicaya teoyotica tlahtohuani Don Jeronimo de carcamo[4] obsipo de troxillo. pirũ castillampa hualmohuicaya auh çan huey apan [*p. 201*] Onmomiquillico. ynin criyoyo nican tlacat Mexico. nican mohuicac ynic yaca españa.

v Axcan Domingo ynic 27. mani Metztli henero de 1613. años ihcuac oquicuaatequique yn iyacapa yn ipiltzin tlahtohuani Don diego fernandez de cordoua Marques de guadalcazar visurrey de la nueua españa. quitocayotique ynic mocuaatequi ypiltzin ytoca mochiuh Doña Mariana manuel auh yn iPadrino mochiuh ce tottatzin huel sancto ytoca fray Pedro Lazaro teopixqui S. Fran^co^. çan mocnonemiltia yn mahuiztililoni huehue tlacatl motemiccamiquilizpahpalehuillia[5] nohuiyan yn Mexico vmpa mohuica ychan yn aquĩ quimomachiltia cocoxqui españoles yn cenca ye yhiyocahui in ye momiquiliznequi ychan onmocochiltia ynic cenca miec tlatlatlauhtiliztli ỹpan conmihtalhuia yn ixquich ica quiça quincahua ymanimantzin ynic momiquilia tlaca. ynin tottatzin cenca tillahuac ça çan queninami Xerga quimotlatlamanililia[6] yn ihapitotzin quimotlallilitinemi yehuatl in yn tottatzin yconpadre mochiuh visurrey. auh yn cuaatequiloc piltzintli oncan ỹ tecpan palacio capilla real —

v Axcan Sabado ynic .2. mani Metztli febrero de 1613. años. huel ypan ilhuitzin totlaçonantzin Purificacion — yhcuac oncan teopan totlaçonantzin S ta maria nuestra Señora de monserrate tequixquipan omonetoltico oncan profession quichihuaco yn tlacpac omoteneuh Don luis alçega ybarguen cauallero del habito de alcantara ynic Comendador telpocatzin,[7] auh ynic quichihuaco oncan professiõ [*p. 202*] Yehuatl ymactzinco yn Padre Prior

1. It appears that Ruy López de Salcedo was the grandson of the mestizo conqueror Juan de Salcedo. See Gerhard 1972, p. 170. For more on the encomiendas involved see ibid., p. 248, Gibson 1964, p. 414, and Himmerich 1991, p. 235. Ch. uses both the traditional term for younger sibling, *-teiccauh*, and the Spanish for brother, *hermano*, probably because the people involved were Hispanic and Chimalpahin here in all likelihood bases himself ultimately on conversation or writings in Spanish.

2. One must suspect that where we see "tepeuh," "it scattered down," the original intention was something including *tepetl*, "mountains," so that the intended meaning would have been "it snowed in the forests and mountains everywhere."

in Azcapotzalco Tepanecapan and Tenancingo; with him it came to an end, so that the king took [both] the said altepetl. He was the child of Juan de Salcedo, a conqueror who was a mestizo, and his whole house was assigned to his younger brother Miguel López.[1]

v Today, Tuesday the 22nd of the month of January of the year 1613, was when at dawn it rained very heavily here in Mexico. And in the forests all around the snow came down and it snowed.[2] It made a very heavy covering; it covered especially heavily the mountain they call Tenan which is here near to us, in Coyoacan. All the mountains absolutely everywhere were really blanketed in snow; it was on the mountains in Xochimilco, and also very heavily on Iztaccihuatl and Popocatepetl in Chalco Amaquemecan, and it adhered to other mountains, which were entirely blanketed in snow, and on the mountain they call Cilquaye, which is in Tenanco Tepopolla, and on Quetzal mountain in Huejotla, toward the Acolhua region. The mountains were all white. And the second day, Wednesday, it rained all day and snowed on the said mountain Tenan, and it was very cold here in Mexico. // Likewise in this year, in the said month of January, it became known and news arrived from Spain when a small ship, a dispatch ship,[3] came, that the priestly ruler don Gerónimo de Carcamo,[4] bishop of Trujillo, Peru, was coming from there, from Spain, but he passed away on the ocean. [*p. 201*] He was a criollo who was born here in Mexico, and he left from here when he went to Spain.

v Today, Sunday the 27th of the month of January of the year 1613, was when they baptized the first child of the ruler don Diego Fernández de Córdoba, Marqués of Guadalcazar, viceroy of New Spain; when his child was baptized they named her and her name became doña Mariana Manuela, and a very holy father named fray Pedro Lázaro, a Franciscan friar, became her godfather. A venerable ancient person, he lives humbly, he helps people with dying[5] all around Mexico. When he knows Spaniards to be sick, at their last breath and about to die, he goes to their homes; he sleeps there and says many prayers for them until their souls depart and leave them, until the people die. This padre uses any old piece of very rough coarse cloth to fix up his habit that he goes about wearing.[6] This padre became the viceroy's compadre. The child was baptized in the royal chapel of the palace. —

v Today, Saturday the 2nd of the month of February of the year 1613, right on the feast day of our precious mother the Virgin of Purificación, was when at the church of our precious mother Santa María, Our Lady of Monserrat at Tequixquipan, the above mentioned don Luis Alcega Ibarguen took his vows and professed as a knight of the order of Alcántara, as a [junior ?][7] comendador. He professed [*p. 202*] under the direction of the

---

3. Presumably for "navio [de] abiso."
4. Name unconfirmed.
5. There can be little doubt about the general sense of this form, but it is not yet clear why it contains both *micca-* and *miquiliz-*, both "dead person" and "death."
6. It has not been possible to confirm the meanings hazarded here from the relevant Nahuatl vocabulary as seen in reference works.
7. Though the words could indicate status as a novice, they could also mean simply a young comendador.

fray Bernardino de argedas teopixqui S. Benito. yn oncan quimopiallia teopancalli nuestra Señora monserrate, yehica ypampa ynin teopixque Monges yn inteotlatecpannemilitzin yn quinmotlallilitehuac Regla ypan monemitizque ynic quinmonahuatilitehuac yn omoteneuhtzino yntlaçottatzin S. benito. Patriarcha, auh ca çanno yehuatl ocanque oquinmomaquilli ỹ tonantzin Sancta yglesia yn omoteneuh teotlatecpanoctacanemiliztli Regla. yn caualleros comẽdadores yn itech pouhque omoteneuh horden de alcãtara, çanno yehuatl ynnehtol mochihua ynic çan cepãnehtolleque yn omoteneuhque teopixque Monges. San Benito.

v̲ Axcan yc ce Domingo quaresma ynic 24. mani metztli febrero de 1613 años. huel ypan ylhuitzin Sant Matia, yc teotlac ynic nican Mexico onmopehualti ynic ompa mohuica la ciudad de los Angeles cuitlaxcohuapan yn tlahtohuani Señor El licenciado Don Pedro de otalora Presidente yn audiencia real Mexico. ynic ompa mohuica moteochiuhtzinoz ynic teopixqui clerigo mochiuhtzinohua, yhuan yca vmpa yc moteochiuhtzinoz yn EPISTOLA yhuan Euangelio yhuan yn missa yc quimochihuiliz. çan oppa yc quimoteochihuiliz yn ipan in ce cuaresma yn obispo Don Alonso de la mota y escobar yuh quihualmonahuatilia yn Sancto Padre çan eilhuitl mochivaz auh macihui yn iuh catca yn nahuatilli ca ye quin ipan Dominiga yn passion tlamico yn ineteochihualitzin ynic missa quimochihuillico. yn ayc yuhqui oyttoc nican Mexico ce pressidente ahnoço oydor omochiuh clerigo. yn iuh yehuatzin omochiuhtzinoco omoteneuhtzino Don Pedro de otalora yhuan amo yc quimocahuilli yn itequitzin ynic pressidente mochiuhtzinotica [*p. 203*] Audiencia real yuh quimonequiltia yn tohueytlahtocatzĩ moyetztica españa auh yn ixquich ica ayemo tlamia yneteochihualiztzin quaresma yxquichcauh vmpa moyetzticatca cuitlaxcohuapan yhuan vmpa quihualmihtalhuitehuac la compañia de Jesus in yancuic missa ynic niman hualmocueptzino hualmohuicac ỹ nican mexico quimochihuillico yn itlahtocatequitzin ynic pressidente.[1]

v̲ Axcan martes inic .5. mani metztli Março de 1613 años. quaresma yhcuac quimonpehualtique nican ỹ china quinhuicaque españoles cequintin mestiçoti yhuan cequĩtin mulatoti ome tliltic. ey macehualli yn çan tecuitlahuiltiliztica yc hui motenehua forçados.[2] vmpa quinmihualli Justiciatica yn tlahtohani visurrey. tepoçotiaque mochintin cauallo ypan quinhuicaque in ye mochi chiconpohuallonmatlactli yn forçados. ynin yc quinhuicaque cequintin tlatlacolleque cequintin çan vagamundos ynic anoq̃ atle ymofficio quipia. auh yn españoles cequintin huicoque huel momahuiztillitihui ynic huicoq̃ motenehua huel luzidos ynic yahque.[3] cequĩtin namiqueque quincauhtiaq̃. yn innamichuan cequintin quinhuicaque yn incihuahuan. auh yn Soldadostin noncua yahque in çan inyollocacopa hui china amo ynhuan nican mocenpohua[4]

v̲ Axcan miercoles ynic 13 mani metztli Março de 1613 años. Quaresma yhcuac omachiztico nican Mexico vmpa tlahtolli hualla yn acapolco yn quenin ye yc onxiuhtica yc oppa oncan oquiçaco yn Jabon acalli oncan ohualla yn Señor Sebastian vizcayno español ỹ nican Mexico yah onxiuhtica yn omocuepaco. yhuan no oncan ohualla quihualhuica [*p. 204*] Yn teuhctitlantli in Embajador yn ititlan yn quihualtitlani huey tlahtohuani Emperador Jabon, macuilpohualli yn imacehual Jabonti quinhualhuica auh yn quinnahuatlahtalhuitihuitz ce S. Fran^{co} tottatzin descalço

---

1. Compare with the partially identical passage on pp. 248–49.
2. Forced or penal laborers.
3. The words "ynic yahque" could also be taken as referring to how the *lúcidos* went.

father prior fray Bernardino de Arguedas, a monk of St. Benedict, who is in charge of the church of Our Lady of Monserrat, because the holy rules of life of these religious or monks, the rule by which they are to live, that their said precious father St. Benedict the patriarch issued, ordered, and left behind for them was the same one that the knights and comendadores who belonged to the said order of Alcántara took and that our mother the Holy Church gave them, so that they both take the same vows, the said religious or monks of St. Benedict have joint vows with them.

v Today, the first Sunday of Lent, the 24th of the month of February of the year 1613, right on the feast day of San Matías, in the afternoon, was when the lord señor licenciado don Pedro de Otalora, president of the Royal Audiencia of Mexico, set out for the City of the Angels, Puebla; the reason he is going there is to be ordained, for he is becoming a secular priest, and is to be ordained as subdeacon, deacon, and priest who can say mass. The bishop don Alonso de la Mota y Escobar will ordain him twice during one Lent; thus the Holy Father has sent him orders. It is to be done in only three days. But although that was the way the order ran, it wasn't until Sunday at the end of Easter week that his ordainment was finished, so that he performed a mass. Never was the like seen here in Mexico, that a president or civil judge of the Audiencia became a secular priest, as the said don Pedro de Otalora did, and he did not therefore relinquish the office that he had been appointed to of president [*p. 203*] of the Royal Audiencia; so our great ruler who is in Spain wants it to be. Until his ordainment during Lent was finished, he stayed in Puebla; before leaving he said his first mass in the Jesuit church there, and then returned and came back here to Mexico to execute his royal office as president.[1]

v Today, Tuesday the 5th of the month of March of the year 1613, during Lent, was when they caused to depart from here those whom they took to China [the Philippines]: Spaniards, some mestizos, some mulattoes, two blacks, and three commoners, who went by force, called *forzados*;[2] the lord viceroy sent them there by legal sentence. They went in irons; they took them all on horseback. The forzados added up to 150. As to why they took them, some were wrongdoers, some just vagabonds who were arrested because they had no occupation. Some of the Spaniards who were taken went in fine style as they were being taken, called very stylish people. When they went,[3] some of the married men left their spouses behind, and some took their wives along. The soldiers went separately; they are going to China willingly and are not included in the total here.[4]

v Today, Wednesday the 13th of the month of March of the year 1613, during Lent, was when it became known here in Mexico and news came from Acapulco of how in the second year [of its voyage] the Manila galleon landed there for a second time; on it came the Spaniard señor Sebastián Vizcaíno, who left Mexico here two years ago, who has returned and also come bringing there [*p. 204*] the lordly emissary, the ambassador, the messenger who was sent here by the great ruler the emperor in Japan. He brought along a hundred Japanese, [the emperor's] subjects, and a Discalced Franciscan friar came along to interpret for them.

---

4. The following paragraph is crossed out. Other sections have related material but do not duplicate it entirely.

v Auh çãno ypan in yn omoteneuh quaresma de 1613 años. yn opeuhque[1] yn tlacpac omoteneuhque Juan Perez de monterrey Juez gouernador yhuan alldes diego de S. Fran^{co}. yhuan Augustin Vasquez. yhuan Regidores. ynĩ Moyotlan tlaca, yhuan Juan Ramirez. yhuan Pablo Damian alldes S Pablo. yhuan Don diego luis de Moteuhcçoma, yhuan Melchior xuarez ynin alldes. S. Sebastian yhuan xp̄oual pascual yhuan Andres de los Angeles ynĩ alldes. S.ta maria cuepopan ynpan in yn ohualmotlalli oc nahui tomin tlacallaquilli nican tenochtitlan ynic niman opeuhque ye nohuian quitlani ye quinechicohua ye tepan quiça yn ipan in omoteneuh quaresma ca yn achtopa oquimanaya intlacallaquil ỹ namiqueque ce peso yhuan chicome tomin. auh yn axcan ypan in omoteneuh xihuitl ynic ohualmacoc nahui tomin in ye mochi quimana intlacallaquil namiqueque ye ome peso yhuã ey tomin auh ỹ telpochnemi yhuan ichpochnemi ỹ quimana axcã ytlacallaquil ye chiuhcnahui tomin yhuan medio ynic ohualmacoc, ca çan oc chicome tomin yhuã medio ocatca

v Axcan Domingo ynic 24. mani Metztli Março de 1613. años quaresma yhcuac omomiquilli yn Doctor. Don Marcos guerrero. Oydor yhuan allde de corte catca auh qui lunes teotlac teopan S. Augustin yn tocoto ynacayo. oncan mohuicatza motetoquillico tlahtohuani Visurrey yhuan mochintin [*p. 205*] Yn tlahtoque Oydores yn audiencia real tlaca yhuan allde de cortes yhuan mochintin yn ciudad tlaca caualleros. yhuan yn clerigos. yhuan ỹ nepapan teopixque frayles Mexico monoltitoque moch oncan mohuicatza motetoquillico //

v Auh çãno ypan in yn omoteneuh Domingo nepantlah tonatiuh yn tococ ynacayo cihuapilli Doña Martina chane ateponazco ynantzin in yn Nicolas hernandez tlacayeleltzin in momomiquilli[2] Sabado ye yohua chicuey hora. ynic 23. mani metztli Março. auh teopan S. Pablo tococ ynacayotzin // auh yn ipampa yniqu iz nicmachiyotia nehuatl Don domingo de S. Anton Munon Quauhtlehuanitzin yn imiquiliz omoteneuh cihuapilli Doña Martina ca huel nicmati ca ceme oc yehuantin yn inecauhcahuan yn itlaquillohuan[3] yn mihtohua ytzonhuã yztihuã in ye huecauh onemico nican Mexico tenochtitlan yn cẽca otlamamauhtico yn aquin catca huehue tlacayeleltzin cihuacohuatl tlahtocapilli tenochtitlan yn o ỹtlan tlahtoco yn oquinnanamiquico macuiltin huehueyntin tlahtoque tenochtitlan yn itzcohuatl yn huehue Moteuhcçoma ylhuicaminatzin yn Axayaca, yn tiçocic, yn Ahuitzotl, yn izquintin in tlahtoque o yntlan yeco oquinnanamiquico yn ipã yxquich tlamantli oquichihuaco yn omoteneuh huey yaotachcauh Capitan General catca huehue tlacayeleltzin cihuacohuatl ca tel vmpa neztica in tlacpac[4] yn ixquich tlamantli oquichiuhtia yn yn ipan yntlahtocatian yn izquintin omoteneuhque tenochtitlan tlahtoque catca —

v Axcan martes ynic 19. mani Metztli Março de 1613 años. huel ypan ylhuitzin S. Joseph. yhcuac opeuh in ye cehuetzih chicahuac yn ipan ic nohuiyan motenehua nueua españa cenca [*p. 206*] quipolloco yn ixhuacatoctzintli, yhuan yn nopalli celtic mochi quicua yhuan in xochicualli yxochiyo yn ixocoyo mochi quitlaco quitepec[5] çan tel cana in huel quitlaco xochicualli auh macuililhuitl yn cehuetz yn ayc yuh mochihuani çan tel yuhquin tlacuilolchicahuaca cehuetz. —

1. Just what they began is not clear. Such phrases often refer to beginning in office, but these officers were already mentioned above at the beginning of the year. Probably the reference is to their beginning to collect the tax mentioned below, but the sentence breaks off before getting that far.

2. In this form *mo* is inadvertently repeated.

v And likewise during this said Lent of the year of 1613 there began[1] the above mentioned Juan Pérez de Monterrey, judge and governor, and the alcaldes Diego de San Francisco and Agustín Vásquez, along with the regidores—these were Moyotlan people—and Juan Ramírez and Pablo Damián, alcaldes for San Pablo; and don Diego Luis de Moteucçoma and Melchor Juárez, alcaldes for San Sebastián, and Cristóbal Pascual and Andrés de los Angeles, alcaldes for Santa María Cuepopan. During their term an additional four reales of tribute was assessed here in Tenochtitlan. Already then during the said Lent season they began to go around to people and ask for it and collect it. First as their tribute a married couple was paying a peso and 7 reales, and now in the said year it was raised by 4 reales, so that in all a married couple pays as their tribute 2 pesos and 3 reales, and bachelors and spinsters now pay as their tribute $9\frac{1}{2}$ reales, since it was raised, for before it was just $7\frac{1}{2}$ reales.

v Today, Sunday the 24th of the month of March of the year 1613, during Lent, was when dr. don Marcos Guerrero, who had been civil and criminal judge of the Audiencia, passed away. It was not until Monday afternoon that his body was taken to the church of San Agustín and buried; there came to bury him the lord viceroy and all [*p. 205*] the civil and criminal judges of the Royal Audiencia, and all the gentlemen who are on the [Spanish] cabildo, and the secular priests, and all the different friars and members of orders in Mexico were assembled, all came there to the burial. //

v Likewise in this year on the said Sunday at midday there was buried the body of the lady doña Martina, from Ateponazco, the mother of Nicolás Hernández Tlacaelleltzin, who passed away[2] Saturday at 8 o'clock in the evening on the 23rd of the month of March; her body was buried at the church of San Pablo. // The reason why I, don Domingo de San Antón Muñón Quauhtlehuanitzin, record here the death of the said lady doña Martina is that I well know that she is one of the descendants,[3] called the hair and fingernails, of one who lived long ago here in Mexico Tenochtitlan, who was held in great awe, and that was the elder Tlacaellel, the Cihuacoatl, a noble of the royal dynasty of Tenochtitlan, who ruled alongside and aided five great rulers of Tenochtitlan: Itzcoatl, the elder Moteucçoma Ilhuicaminatzin, Axayaca, Tiçocic, and Ahuitzotl. The said great war leader, who was a captain general, the elder Tlacaelleltzin, the Cihuacoatl, stood beside and aided each of the rulers in everything they did, for above[4] appear all the different things he did during the reigns of each of the said late rulers of Tenochtitlan. —

v Today, Tuesday the 19th of the month of March of the year 1613, right on the feast day of San Josef, was when it began to freeze hard everywhere in the said New Spain. [*p. 206*] The freeze greatly destroyed the sprouting stalks of maize, and it ate up all the tender nopal cactus, and it spoiled[5] all the blossoms and buds of the fruit trees, although only here and there did it really ruin the fruit. For five days it froze as never before, although the strong freezing was spotty. —

3. Literally relics and fruits of the tree.
4. Here Ch. apparently refers to another part of his work, apparently considering that some of his accounts referring to precontact history precede the material here within a single framework.
5. The unidentified form "quitepec" seems to reinforce "quitlaco," "spoiled."

v Axcan Sabado in ye ic .23. mani Metztli Março de 1613. años. ye teotlac ihcuac opeuh in çan oc ahuechquiyahuico auh in ye yc omilhuitl ypan Domingo in ye teotlac ye yc cen peuh ỹ momanaco quiyahuitl cehuallatl[1] cenca ytztic yn icecuizyo mochiuh yhuan ceppayauh ỹ nohuiyan cuauhtlah. yxquich ica ynic tlamico Metztli Março. yn quiyauh yn cehuallatl manca yn ayc yuh mochihuani ypan omoteneuh metztli. yhuan cenca chicahuac in yequene momanaco cocoliztli matlaltotonqui[2] yn ipan in omoteneuh Metztli Março. ynic micohuac ynic mochi ypan nohuiyan nueua españa. yn õpa yc hualpeuhtica ytzinecan yn ipan in omoteneuh xihuitl yxquichcauh necocolloc yhuan micohuac ynic yequene axcan chicahuac ye mochihua cocoliztli momiquilia yn timacehualtin yhuã españoles —
v Axcan Lunes Sancto. ynic .i. cemilhuitl mani Metztli Abril de 1613 años teotlac yhcuac yc oppa otlayahualloque yn Sancta Maria cuepopan tlaca yn cofrades yn itech pohui animasme yn ompa quimotlalili ynpalehuiloca in Padre fr. diego Mexia yn ica ymecanelpiayatzin ycordontzin totlaçottatzin S. Fran^{co}. quinmopalehuilia quimonmoquixtilia yn ompa tetlechipahualloyan Purgatorio, ca yuh neztia oncan ynic tlayahualloque [*p. 207*] Quimohuiquillique andasco S. Fran^{co}. quinmoquixtiltiuh yn animasme yn ica omoteneuh ymecanepiayatzin yn icordontzin yn oncan omoteneuh tetlechipahualloyan ytencopatzinco yn tt^{o}. dios. yhuan oc cequi yPassiontzin yn tlayahuallo teotlac yn ompa huallehuaque ynteopan quiçaco concepciõ Monjas. ayoticpac yc niman quiçaco Visitacion monjas. yc niman niman[3] quiçaco S. Fran^{co} teopan. yc niman S. ignacio. la casa professa quiçaco. yc niman oncan yn iglesia mayor quiçaco oncan yc mocuepque yc niman quiçato teopan S. Domĩgo niman S. lurenço quiçato monjas. yc niman vmpa yn inchan ahcito.

v Auh çan no ypan in yn omoteneuh Lunes Sancto no yhcuac teotlac yancuican tlayahualloque yn tlacanechicoltin[4] yn oncan oquitlallique yancuic ỹcofradia yn hospital S. lazaro atenantitech yn itetzinco pohui S. Roche. callaqui tonatiuh yn quizque çan oc quezquintin yglesia mayor ahcico ynic tlayahualloque.

v Auh yn axcan yc omilhuitl martes sancto teotlac yhcuac yequene huel oquizque yn cofrades españoles yn itetzinco ponhui yn ipilhuantzitzinhuan Señor S. Juan bap^{ta}. cenca mahuiztic ynic quizque ynic tlayahualloque oncan quizque yn teopan monasterio monjas motenehua S. Juan la penitencia Moyotlan. auh tlayacac mantiaque in Mexica yn oncan tlaca tequicaltitlan tlaxillacalleque çan oc quezquintin yn oncan tehuan quizque yehica ypampa quimixnamic quintzacuilli in fray Jeronimo de çarate capellan S. Josep. amo quinec yn oncan tehuan quiçazquia Mexica moyoteca yn S. Juan la penitencia. yehica yn oncã quinmoquixtiliz[*p. 208*]quia in yancuicatzitzinti quinmochihuillique Mexica yn imixiptlatzin S. Juan baptistatzin yhuan ymiquillitzin S. Diegotzin. in ye huiptla ypan Domingo de ramos catca yn ihcuac oncan S. Joseph quinmoteochihuilliq̃. yn oquimah fr. Jeronimo de çarate ynin omoteochiuhtzinoque yancuiq̃. Sanctome. yn ca tehuan vmpa motlayahualhuizque Sant Juan la penitencia yn ipan in omoteneuh martes Sancto niman yhcuac yn ipan omoteneuh Domingo de ramos õcan quinmotzacuilili in Mexica S Joseph yn inSanctotzitzinhuan ynic amo vmpa tehuan motlayahualhuizque S. Juã quihto. yn fr.

1. Perhaps also persistent; see pp. 194–95 at n. 2.
2. Typhus; see pp. 92–93 at n. 2.
3. The word "niman" is inadvertently repeated.

v Today, Saturday the 23rd of the month of March of the year 1613, in the afternoon, was when it began to rain, at first just a sprinkle, but on the second day, Sunday in the afternoon, it really began, a freezing rain[1] which became extremely cold, and it snowed everywhere in the woods. There were cold rains until the month of March ended, as had never happened in the said month. And finally, an illness, matlaltotonqui,[2] broke out in the said month of March, causing deaths all over New Spain. It had its beginning [earlier] in the said year, there was sickness and death, until finally now the illness became stronger, and we commoners and Spaniards are dying. —

v Today, Monday of Holy Week, the 1st day of the month of April of the year 1613, in the afternoon, was when for the second time there marched in procession the people of Santa María Cuepopan, the members who belong to the cofradía of the Souls [of Purgatory], that father fray Diego Mejía established there for their help. With his cord girdle, his rope belt, our precious father San Francisco helps them and extracts them from the place where people are purified by fire, purgatory, for so he appeared going along; when they went in procession [*p. 207*] they carried San Francisco on a carrying platform freeing the souls with his said cord girdle, his rope, from the said purgatory by order of our lord God, and other things from his Passion [were in evidence]. The procession was in the afternoon; they started from their church and passed by the nuns of Concepción at Ayoticpac; next they came by the nuns of the Visitación; next[3] they came by the church of San Francisco; next they came by the Casa Profesa of San Ignacio; then they came by the cathedral, where they turned back; next they went by the church of Santo Domingo, next they went by the nuns of San Lorenzo; next they reached their home.

v Likewise on this said Holy Monday, in the afternoon, was when for the first time the people who have come together from various places[4] went in procession; they established their new cofradía at the Hospital of San Lázaro at Atenantitech; it is dedicated to San Roque. The sun was going down as they came out; only a few got as far as the cathedral in their procession.

v Today, the 2nd day [of April and of Holy Week], Holy Tuesday, in the afternoon, was when at last the Spanish cofradía members who are dedicated to and are the children of señor San Juan Bautista were able to come out and went in procession in a very splendid fashion; they came out of the convent church of nuns called San Juan de la Penitencia in Moyotlan. At the front went the Mexica who belong to the tlaxilacalli of Tequicaltitlan; only a few came out there with the others, because fray Gerónimo de Zárate, chaplain at [the chapel of] San Josef, opposed and blocked them. He didn't want the Mexica of Moyotlan to come out with the others at San Juan de la Penitencia, because they were going to bring out [*p. 208*] the new images the Mexica made of San Juan Bautista and the death of San Diego two days before that, on Palm Sunday, when they blessed them at San Josef. When fray Gerónimo de Zárate found out that these new saints had been blessed and that they were to go with the others in procession at San Juan de la Penitencia on the said Holy Tuesday, right then on the said Palm Sunday he locked up the Mexica's saints in San Josef so that they would not go in procession with the others at San Juan. Fray

4. More literally collected people, used by Ch. to refer mainly to indigenous people of other than Nahua ethnicity who migrated to Mexico City on their own. The word also occurs on pp. 242–43 at n. 3 and pp. 246–47 at n. 10.

Jeronimo de çarate amo huel xelihuiz yn altepetl ye quin ic cen yn ipan Juebes Sancto nican S. Joseph motlayahualhuizque yn S. Juan baptista. yhuã ymiquillitzin S. Diegotzin o yehuatl ipampa yn ynic amo huel oncã omotlayahualhuique Sanctome yn monasterio monjas. yn ipan in omoteneuh martes Sancto. yhuã in gou^{or} mexico ynic amo ỹpan mochicauh ytlapacholhuan mexica in miyequintin quinequia oncan tehuan quiçazquia S. Juan inpampa ce oydor anoço al~~lde~~ de corte quixnamic yn omoteneuh gouernador ynic çan mocauh yuh mihto quimotlaquehui yn fr. Jeronimo. ynic ça mixcahui motlayahualhui ce yncrucifixotzin cemanahuatl yn ipan moquetztinotiuh yhuan yn inS. Juan baptistatzin españoles. çan moquetzinotiuh mahcopatlachialtilitiuh yhuã momanepanotzinotiuh[1] yhuan totlaçonantzin —

v̲ Auh no yhuan yn ipan in Omoteneuh Martes Sancto teotlac yhcuac yequene huel no quizque ynic ceppa [*p. 209*] Otlayahualloque yn S.tiago tlatilolco tlaca yn cofrades yn itetzinco pohui ynic mopolihuiltia eilhuitl teotl dios Jesus. piltzintli yn motenehua Niño Jesus Perdido, ynin omoteneuh cofradia. no yhuan yehuatzin ytetinco pohui yn totlaçomahuiznantzin S.ta maria del rrosario ca yuh oquimoneltilili yn Sancto Padre Paulo quinto. yn iuh ytech neztica ome yBullatzin yn quihualmohuiquillique tottatzitzinhuan de La compañia de Jesus teatinos. yntla ytlaniliztica mochiuh oc cenca yehuatl y nocniuhtzin diego lopez cuauhtlacuillo in huel ye tlatzintille quimotlallili ynĩ ome omoteneuh cofradia. fundador mihtohua. auh ynic ome tlacatl ytlaytlaniliztica ytlapalehuiliztica mochiuh yehuatzin yn ompa gouernador Don Melchior de Soto. quinmotlatlauhtilli yn omoteneuhtzinoque tottatzitzinhuan la compañia de Jesus. yni quimocuillito Roma. auh ynic yancuican quizq̃ yn ynic tlayahualloque cenca niman mahuiztic huel cuepontiaque moch yancuic yn andas tlayahuallo yhuan estãdartes cuachpanitl yn iuh mochi tlacatl oquittac ynic mochihu in cenca ypan mochicauhque yn omoteneuhque diego lopez. yhuan gou^{or}. auh ynic tlayahualoloc huel motlayacanilitia yn Jesus piltzintli cruz quimoquechpanilhuitia. auh amo yhuan oncan moquixti amo yhuan oncan motlayahualhui yn totlaçonantzin Rosario yehica quitenhuique yn españoles yn quimopiallia Rosario oncan teopan S. Domingo cofrades. amo quinecque ynic no quinhuelitiltizque tlatilolca auh cenca huey yn quiyahualloque ynic ompa hualquizque ynchan S.tiago tlatilolco. niman quiçaco Sanct ana yc [*p. 210*] niman quiçaco S ta catalina Martyr Perochia. yc niman quiçaco S. Domingo. yc niman ahcico oncan yn iglesia mayor. yc niman quiçato S. ignacio la casa professa. yc niman quiçato S. Fran^{co}. yc niman quiçato Visitacion monjas. yc niman quiçato totlaconantzin[2] concepcion monjas yc niman quiçato Sancta maria cuepopan yc no ceppa ahcito yn inchan S.tiago tlatilolco ynin tlayahualoliztli cenca miec yn tetlapopolhuiliztli indulgencias oncan ytech quicnopilhuia yn aquiq̃. oncan yntlanequiliztica tlayahuallohua yn quimohuiquilia Niño Jesus. —

v̲ Auh yn axcan yqu eilhuitl miercoles Sancto teotlac yhcuac yancuican tlayahualloque yn tlacanechicoltin[3] michhuaq̃. cequi mexica yn oncan yancuic yncofradia oquitlallique hospital real n̄r̄a S^{a}. de la charidad yn oncan tipahtillo timacehualtin[4] ynin ytech pohui ỹ totlaçonantzin omoteneuhtzino ynic ome cofradia õcan ca S. Nicolas de tolentino ytetzinco pohui[5] ynin yc tlayahualloque çan oc quezquintin yhuan huey yn quiyahualloque

1. Possibly joining his hands in prayer.

2. For "totlaçonantzin."

3. See pp. 240–41 at n. 4.

4. This time *timacehualtin* is treated as a true first person plural with an agreeing verb.

Gerónimo de Zárate said, "The altepetl cannot be divided. Not until Maundy Thursday, once and for all, San Juan Bautista and the death of San Diego are to go in procession here at San Josef." It was for this reason, then, that the saints were not able to go in procession at the convent of nuns on the said Holy Tuesday. And the governor in Mexico did not support his Mexica subjects, many of whom wanted to come out with the others at San Juan; because of them a civil judge or a criminal judge of the Audiencia opposed the said governor, so that it was abandoned. It was said that fray Gerónimo paid him off, so that the only thing going in procession was their [Christ on the] cross standing on the world, and the Spaniards' San Juan Bautista went standing looking upward and crossing his arms,[1] along with Our Precious Mother. —

v And also the said Holy Tuesday in the afternoon was when at last also [*p. 209*] the members of the cofradía, people of Santiago Tlatelolco, dedicated to the Child Jesus, the deity and god who was lost for three days, called Niño Jesús Perdido, were able to come out and go in procession once. This said cofradía is also dedicated to our precious revered mother Santa María del Rosario, for thus the Holy Father Paul V confirmed it, as appears in two bulls of his that our fathers of the Company of Jesus, the Theatines, brought back; it was done at the petition especially of my friend Diego López, woodcarver, who was the real beginner, called a founder, who established this said double cofradía. The second person at whose petition and with whose help it was done was the governor there, don Melchor de Soto, who asked our said fathers of the Company of Jesus to go to Rome to get [the bulls]. And when these people first came out in procession, it was very splendid. There were plenty of explosions [of rockets] as they went along, and new carrying platforms and standards, cloth banners, went in procession, as everyone saw. The said Diego López and the governor were very energetic in bringing it about. As to how the procession was, at the very front the Child Jesus went leading the way, shouldering the cross. But our precious mother of the Rosary didn't come out on that occasion, didn't go in procession along with him, because the Spanish cofradía members who have a cofradía of the Rosary at the church of Santo Domingo raised objections to it; they didn't want the Tlatelolca to be given permission too. They went in procession over a very large route; they left from their home base in Santiago Tlatelolco, then they passed by Santa Ana, [*p. 210*] then they passed by the parish of Santa Catalina Mártir, then they passed by Santo Domingo, then they came as far as the cathedral, then they went past the Casa Profesa of San Ignacio, then they went past San Francisco, then they went past the nunnery of the Visitación, then they went past the nunnery of our precious mother[2] of Concepción, then they went past Santa María Cuepopan, until again they got to their home base in Santiago Tlatelolco. Those who went on this procession voluntarily, accompanying the Niño Jesús, earned thereby very many pardons, indulgences. —

v Today, the third day, Holy Wednesday, in the afternoon, was when the miscellaneously assembled people[3] from Michoacan and some Mexica went in procession for the first time; they established their new cofradía at the royal hospital of Nuestra Señora de la Caridad, where we commoners are treated;[4] the cofradía is dedicated to our said precious mother. A second cofradía there is dedicated to[5] San Nicolás de Tolentino; from it only a

---

5. The words "Nicolas de tolentino ytetzinco pohui" were first omitted, then added in the margin. Since the passage makes no sense without these words, we can deduce that Ch. here was quite mechanically making a new copy from something already existing.

ahcico yglesia mayor —

v Auh çano ye no ypan in yn omoteneuh miercoles Sancto. teotlac yhcuac oquizque otlayahualloque yn S.tiago tlatilolco tlaca yn cofrades yn itetzinco pohui ymiquillitzin totlaçottatzin S. Fran^co. no cenca mahuiztic ynic quizq̃. no cenca cuepontiaque oc ceppa oncan ahcico yn iglesia mayor no yxquich quiyahualloque yn ixquich [*p. 211*] Omoteneuh tlacpac in yalhua tlayahualloque yn itetzinco pohui Niño Jesus Perdido. yhuan Rosario y no tlatilolco tlaca
v Auh yn axcan yc nahuilhuitl Juebes Sancto. teotlac ynic otlayahualoloc oncan teopan capilla S. Joseph S Fran^co. ynic mochipa yuh mochihuani cecexiuhtica yn huey tlayahualoliztli auh ya nelli oncan omotlayahualhuique oncan oquinmoquixtillique yn omoteneuhtzinoque tlacpac S. Juan baptista. motlancuaquetzinotiuh yhuan ymiquillitzin S. Diegotzin yn imaxcatzin S. Juan tlaca yn quinmotzacuillica fr. Jeronimo de çarate ca yuh quito yn oncan motlayahualhuizque yn amo vmpa nepa[1] —
v Auh no yhuan yn ipan in omoteneuh Juebes Sancto in Sanctiago, tlatilolco in huey cemaltepetlayahualoliztli yc mochiuh no oncan ahcico yn iglesia mayor yhuan S. Fran^co quiçato ynic mocuepque ca no yxquich quiyahualloque yn ixquich omoteneuh tlacpac yc tlayahualloque yn itetzinco pohui Niño Jesus Perdido yhuan Rosario mopia tlatilolco —
v Auh yn axcan yc macuililhuitl Viernes Sancto ce tzillini ye tlathuitiuh oc huel yohualtica yn oquizque ynic yancuican otlayahualloque yca ynetoquillitzin tt^o. dios. yn Sancta cruz contzinco tlaca. çan yehuatl Dean licencia yhuelitzin quinmomaquilli ypampa pleyto quintlalili quimixnamiquia in hernando de San Martin teuhcxochitzin chane S. Pablo tlachcuititlan amo quinequia ynic noncua tlayahuallozque. çan quinequia ynic oncan mocenchihuaz yntzontecompa S. Pablo. ynic moteylhui yxpan prouisor doctor Don Juan de Salamanca. ynic amo quiçazque noncua. auh in yehuantin Sancta cruz contzinco tlaca ye o[*p. 212*]mihto huel ça oc yohualtica yn tlayahualloque ynic ayac cẽca quimittaz yuhquin çan ichtaca tlayahuallo ynic possesion conanque yca tlayahualloliztli yhuan ynic atle pena quinhuiquilliz ypampa prouisor yn oquic yxpan catqui yneteylhuil hernando de S. m̄n teuhcxochitzin. yn nahui tzillin ye ontlayahualloque ye inchan cate yn S ta cruz contzinco tlaca ynic amo cana ohtlipan monepanozquia yn itlayahualloliz netoquillitzin[2] tt^o dios. quiça S Pablo yn ipã macuilli tzillini ye otlathuic. auh macihui yn pleyto oquĩtlallilica contzinca yn omoteneuh hernando teuhcxochitzin. yn çatepan ca ohuellitiloq̃. ynic huel noncua tlayahuallozque mochipa

v Auh yhuan in ça ye no ypan in viernes Sancto ye tlathui yn oquizque yn otlayahualloque S.tiago tlatilolco tlaca in motenehua Nazarenos. no yglesia mayor ahcico yhuan S. Fran^co quiçato ynic mocuepque
v Auh no yhuan yn ipan in omoteneuh viernes Sancto. yohuatzinco yhcuac yc opah otlayahualloque yn S.tiago. tlatilolco tlaca cofrades yn itetzinco pohui totlaçonantzin ymiquillitzin motenehua nuestra Señora trasito[3] oncan quimohuiquillitiaq̃ andastica mohuetz-

---

1. The passage might be interpreted as meaning that they could go at that point but not back further in time (when they had wanted to). See the entry for April 2nd on pp. 240–43.

few more came along in the procession. They went in procession over a long route, coming as far as the cathedral. —

v Likewise the same said Holy Wednesday in the afternoon was when the cofradía members from Santiago Tlatelolco who are dedicated to the death of our precious father San Francisco came out in procession; they too came out in great splendor, they too went shooting off many rockets, again they came as far as the cathedral; they went in procession over the entire same route [*p. 211*] as told above that the people dedicated to Niño Jesús Perdido and the Rosary, also from Tlatelolco, went over yesterday.

v Today, the fourth day, Maundy Thursday, in the afternoon, there was a procession at the church and chapel of San Josef at San Francisco, the big procession that is always held every year. And truly in that procession went and were brought out the above mentioned kneeling San Juan Bautista and the death of San Diego, belonging to the people of San Juan, that fray Gerónimo de Zárate had blocked [from going out]. He said that they could go in procession [in the immediate area of San Josef?], but not beyond that.[1] —

v And also on the said Maundy Thursday in Santiago Tlatelolco the great general altepetl procession was held; it too came as far as the cathedral and went by San Francisco before turning, for it too went in procession over the entire route mentioned above for those who are dedicated to Niño Jesús Perdido and the Rosary that is kept in Tlatelolco. —

v Today, the fifth day, Good Friday, at 1 o'clock in the morning, while it was still full nighttime, the people of Santa Cruz Contzinco came out and went in procession for the first time with the burial of our lord God. Only the dean [of the cathedral chapter] had given them his permission, for which reason Hernando de San Martín Teucxochitzin, citizen of San Pablo Tlachcuititlan, brought suit against them, opposing them. He didn't want them to go in procession separately, but wanted them to join together with their cabecera, San Pablo, so he brought suit before the vicar general doctor don Juan de Salamanca so that they would not come out separately. But it was already said that the people of Santa Cruz Contzinco [*p. 212*] went in procession while it was still fully night, so that no one would see them very well, as though they were going in procession secretly, whereby they took possession [of the right to hold] processions, and so it would not bring them a fine, because the litigation brought by Hernando de San Martín Teucxochitzin was still pending before the vicar general. At 4 o'clock the people of Santa Cruz Contzinco had already gone in procession and were back home, to avoid meeting somewhere along the way with the procession of the burial of[2] our lord God that came out from San Pablo at 5 o'clock in the morning. But although the said Hernando Teucxochitzin had brought the suit against the Contzinca, afterward they were given perpetual permission to go in procession all by themselves.

v And on the same Good Friday, at dawn, the people of Santiago Tlatelolco called Nazarenes came out in procession; they too came as far as the cathedral and went past San Francisco before returning.

v And also on the said Good Friday, very early in the morning, was when for the second time the cofradía members from Santiago Tlatelolco who are dedicated to the death of our precious mother, called Nuestra Señora del Tránsito,[3] went in procession. They went

2. For "inetoquillitzin."

3. See pp. 74–75 at n. 2.

iltihtiuh ypan chicome tzillini yn oncan ahcico huey teopan yglesia Mayor. ye quiniuhti much oncan tecpantia quihuicatiaque yn izqui tlamantli in huey. in ohui, in mahuiztic yn itlamahuiçollotzin yn imisteriosyotzin tlahtocaychpochtli S.ta Maria ynic yehuatzin Spũ Sancto, miec tlamantli ca yqu expa oyezquia ỹ intla tlayahualoloni ye ce xihuitl[1] [*p. 213*] Yqu itechpatzinco quimopohtilitzinohua, quimonenehuililia yn omoteneuhtzino tlahtocaychpuchtli, yn itechpatzinco quimotlachieltilia, yn huel ytechtzinco pohui yn teotlamatiliztlamahuiçolli ỹ nican motenehua[2] ypan yc tlayahualoloc ynic centlamantli[3] yehuatl yn imachiyoilnamicocatzin yn inezcatlahtollotzin yn ichipahuacanenacayotiliztlacatililocatzin[4] motenehua limpia concepcion yn itech pohui[5] ye in tonatiuh. in Metztli. yn huey citlalli tlathuinahuac hualquiça. in tlatzacuilotl tzauhctiuh, yn iteocaltzin[6] tt^o^. dios. ynic ahuaztli ylhuicac. in çoyatl. yn azetonasquahuitl.[7] yn ahuehuetl, yn tlatzca. yn tezcatl. yn castillan tulpatlachuitztecolxochitl[8] lilio. yn xuchitl Rosa. yn quilmiltepancalli huerto. in huel tzauctica, yn ameyalli fuente in huel tlatzauhctli. yhuan yn oc cequi tlamantli ytetzinco nezcamachiyotlahtoa tlahtocaychpuchtli concepcion. moch oncan quiquixtique yn. auh macihui yn o muchi mahuiznec[9] in ypan tlayahualloliztli. yece camo ynemacpan yn oncan muchi necizquia. yehica ypampa ca çan mixcahuiya yn axcan molnamiqui ymiquiliztlayhiyohuiliztonehuitzin yPassiontzin tt^o^. dios. ca tel yehuantzitzin quimomachiltia yn teopixque yn oquimocelilique yn iuh mochihuaz yn iuh tlayahuallozq̃. omoteneuhque totlaçonantzin ipilhuantzitzin no huey yn quiyahualloque S. Fran^co^. quiçato ynic mocuepq̃. ynchan S.tiago

v Auh yhuan yn axcan ypan in omoteneuh viernes Sancto yn oncan teopan S. Domingo yc oquixohuac ynic otlayahua[*p. 214*]loloc teotlac yn iuh mochipa mochiuhtiuh cecexiuhtica ynic oquimotoquillique yn imiquilizyxiptlatzin tt^o^. dios yn intech ponhui ynic ompa quiça españoles. auh no oncã quiniuhti tlayacac quinmanque quiyacatihtiaque ynic tlayahualoloc in timacehualti yn mixteca tlacanechicolti[10] yn oynnemactic yn oconanque yncapilla catca tliltique yn oquixtilliloque yn cofradia vmpa quipiaya auh ynic niman yehuantin oynnemactic omacoq̃. ynin omoteneuh capilla yn omoteneuhque mixteca ynic oncan oquitlallique yncofradia yn itetzinco pohui totlaçonantzin Rosario. ynic otlayahualoloc axcan yehuatzin oquimohuiquilliq̃. omotlayahualhui yn omoteneuhtzino çan achi tepitzin yn totlaçonantzin Rosario ymaxca macehualti —

v Auh no yhuan yn ipan in omoteneuh viernes Sancto ye teotlac in Santiago tlatilolco yn imiquiliztlayahualoliztococatzin tt^o^. Dios. quin iyopa axcan huel oncan quimaxitillico yn iglesia mayor. ynic otlayahualloque tlatilulca yn ayc oncã huallacini cecexiuhtica cenca mahuiztic ynic tecpantia muchi ypassiontzin tt^o^. Dios. ynin ça huel quitzacuico tlayahualoliztli ynic nicã quizçaco[11] ca achto muchiuh nohuiyan yn izquican nican tenochtitlan yc tlayahualoloc. auh çan no S. Fran^co^ quiçato ynic mocuepque ynchan S.tiago

---

1. The portion in the Nahuatl from "ca yqu expa" to "ce xihuitl" and in the English the part within em dashes was added in the margin.

2. Some of these things are doubtless treated differently in standard church writing.

3. The words "inic centlamantli" are marked over what was apparently "izqui tlamantli," "each of the different things."

4. This word is extraordinarily complex and probably barely grammatical; Carochi complained of the excesses of Nahuatl speakers of his time in creating unwieldy compounds when it came to religious matters. It might be possible grammatically, though hardly logically, to construe Mary as the possessor of the compound.

taking her along reclining on a carrying platform. It was at 7 o'clock that they got as far as the great church here, the cathedral. It was the first time that there were lined up and they went along carrying all the different great, difficult, splendid marvels and mysteries of the queenly maiden Santa María,—it would have been the third time if it had been taken in procession a year ago—[1] [*p. 213*] by which the Holy Spirit equated and compared for the said queenly maiden, by which he made her see, that belong to the marvels of theology and are mentioned here,[2] they went in procession with all the different ones: first,[3] the commemoration of the sign and the announcement of [God's] purely taking on the form of flesh and being born,[4] called the Immaculate Conception, to which belong[5] the sun, the moon, and the great star that comes out close to dawn [Venus], when the gate of our lord God's temple[6] is closing, as a ladder to heaven; the palm tree; the olive tree;[7] the cypress; the mirror; the Spanish flower from a broad-leafed water plant,[8] the lily; the rose; the enclosure for a field of green plants, a garden, entirely enclosed; a spring or fountain, fully enclosed; they brought out all this and other things that speak symbolically of the royal maiden of the Conception. And although everything had a splendid appearance[9] in the procession, nevertheless it was not in the permitted time that it all should appear there, because now people were concentrating on remembering the sufferings in death, the passion, of our lord God; but the religious who accepted it know best about how it is to be done and how the said children of our precious mother are to go in procession. They too went around a long route; they went past San Francisco, from where they returned to their home base of Santiago.

v̲ And also today on the said Good Friday a procession came out from the church of Santo Domingo [*p. 214*] in the afternoon as is always done every year, in which they buried the image of the death of our lord God that belongs to the Spaniards coming out from there. And also for the first time they put us commoners who were Mixtecs, gathered from various places,[10] in the lead, at the front of the procession. They have been granted and took what used to be the chapel of the blacks, from whom the cofradía they had there was taken away, and then the said Mixtecs were granted and given this said chapel, so that they established there their cofradía, dedicated to our precious mother of the Rosary, so that in the procession today the commoners took along in procession our said precious mother of the Rosary, though rather small, that belongs to them. —

v̲ And also on the said Good Friday, in the afternoon, there was a procession for the burial of the death of our lord God from Santiago Tlatelolco; today was the first time that the Tlatelolca brought [the image] all the way to the cathedral in procession, as they had never done each year previously. It was very marvelous how the whole passion of our lord God went lined up. This brought to an end all the processions that have passed by[11] here, for all the different processions here in Tenochtitlan were performed first. They too went

---

5. With which are associated?

6. Meaning the sky?

7. In "azetonasquahuitl," it appears that the *e* may have been meant to be changed to *i*, so that *aceitunas* was intended.

8. The Nahuatl word is literally rush-wide-dark dye-flower.

9. In "mahuiznec" the *c*, taken as preceding *i*, is equivalent to *z*.

10. Here Ch. says "timacehualti," "we commoners," even though the Mixteca are involved. See also pp. 240–41 at n. 4.

11. For "quiçaco."

tlatilulco —

v Auh axcan lunes yc omilhuitl xochipascua [*p. 215*] de Resurreccion ynic .8. mani Metztli Abril de 1613 años yhcuac ohuallathuic otemictiloc yn carcel de corte ey tlacatl yn omictiloque ome españolti ce alcayde ynic ome bastonero. yn iqu ey tlacatl mulato yehuatl in quintlatlaliliaya tepoztli crillos ỹ tlatlacolleque quincallaquia oncar[1] carcel auh yn omoteneuh alcayde ynic quimictique çan quicocotecque niman oncã yc momiquilli auh yn oc omentin çan quĩxixilque ynic quinmictique yohualtica auh in temictique çan timacehualtin ylpiticatca ychtecque yeyntin quinequia yn oncan cholozquia carcel de corte quitlatlapoticauhtiazquia ỹ tlatzacuilotl yntla huel mochihuani auh amo yuh quimonequiltitzino yn tt^o^. Dios. atle nez ỹ llaue ỹ tlatlapolloni otlihcapa ynic quitlapozquia ynic quiçazquia. ynic ça oncan omocauhque oanoque ontzacualloque yequene auh ynin ayc yuhqui ceppa omuchiuh yn iuhqui oquichiuhque yehuantin in ynic oncan in cenca yc otechtlahuelilocamatque yn españoles. auh yn omoteneuhque mimiccatzitzinti ye quin martes ypan tocoque yn innacayo.

v Auh axcan Juebes ynic ii. mani metztli Abril de 1613 años. ye teotlac yhcuac nican Mexico. mocallaquico ynic hualmocueptzino in yehuatzin cenca mahuiztililoni in ye teopixcatlahtohuani omochiuhtzinoto clerigo Don Pedro de otalora Presidẽte audiencia real Mexico. ynic ompa omohuicaya omoteochiuhtzinoto la ciudad de los Angeles cuitlaxcohuapan yn ica epistola yhuan yca Euangelio. yhuan yca yn missa oquimochihuilli çan oppa yca yn oquimoteochihuilli ynic ce quaresma oquiz yn obispo Don Alonso de la mota y escobar. ca yuh hualmotlanahuatilli yn Sancto Padre. ynic çan eilhuitl [*p. 216*] Teochihualoz. auh macihui yn iuh quihualmotlalili yn ytlanahuatiltzin Sancto Padre. yn iuh ycatzinco muchihuaz Señor Don Pedro de otalora. yece ca ye quin ipan Dominiga in Passion[2] tlamico yn ineteochihuallitzin ynic missa quimochihuillico vmpa cuitlaxcohuapan de la compañia de Jesus yn ayc yuhqui oyttoc nican Mexico ce Pressidente ahnoço ce oydor clerigo omuchiuh yn iuh yehuatzin omuchiuhtzinoco axcan Omoteneuhtzino Señor Don Pedro de otalora yhuan amo yc oquimocahuilli yn itequitzin ynic çan ya Pressidente omochiuhtzinoco audiencia real Mexico ca yuh quimonequiltitzinohua yn tohueytlahtocatzin Rey moyetztica españa. auh yn ixquich ica quaresma yn oquic ayemo tlamia yneteochihualiztzin huel yxquichcauh vmpa moyetzticatca yn cuitlaxcohuapan. çan ic ompa quihualmihtalhuitehuac in yancuic missa ynic nimã ohualmohuicac nican Mexico quimochihuillico yn itlahtocatequitzin ynic Pressidente[3]

v Auh axcan Viernes ynic 12. mani Metztli Abril de 1613 años. yhcuac piloloq̃. eintin timacehualtin matlactli tzillini yn tlacah. oquinhualquixtique yn carcel de corte yn omoteneuhque ychteque timacehualtin yn oncan omoteneuh tlacpac carcel de corte temictique yn quinmictique yey tlacatl ome español ce mulato ye omihto yn españolti micque ce alcayde ynic ome Bastonero. auh ynic oncan carcel de corte quinhualquixtique quincuauhtlapechhuique[4] yhuan caualloti yncuitlapiltitech hualilpitia yn incuauhtlapech ynic quinhuillanq̃. ynic oncan quimaxitoco tepilolcuauhtitlan tlanepantla ynepantla yn oc cequi tepilolcuahuitl oncan mani chicuetetl, auh yn o yuh oncan quimaxitico yc niman cecẽyaca [*p. 217*] Cecenme yn inyeccancopamacpal quintehtequillique auh achtopa quimiyxquimilloque ynic quinmacpaltetecque ynic quinmacpaltlazque, auh in ye o yuh quimonma-

---

1. For "oncan."

2. Stafford Poole informs us that at this time Passion Sunday was two weeks before Easter.

by San Francisco before returning to their home base in Santiago Tlatelolco. —
v Today, Monday, the day after Easter, [*p. 215*] on the 8th of the month of April, in the night before morning, there were killings in the court jail; three people were killed: two Spaniards, one a jailer, and the second one a jailer's assistant; the third was a mulatto who used to put shackles on the criminals they put[1] in the jail. They killed the said jailer by cutting his throat; he died of it there immediately. The other two they stabbed. It was night when they killed them. The killers were [of] us commoners, three thieves who were in custody. They wanted to escape from the court jail; they were going to go leaving the door open, if it had been possible, but our lord God did not want it so. The keys to the outside with which they were going to open the door and come out couldn't be found, so they were just left there; finally they were seized and locked up. Nothing like this, like what these fellows did, had ever happened before; because of it the Spaniards thought very badly of us. The bodies of the said dead people were not buried until Tuesday.

v Today, Thursday the 11th of the month of April of the year of 1613, in the afternoon, was when the very reverend don Pedro de Otalora, president of the Royal Audiencia of Mexico, who has now become a priestly ruler and a secular priest, entered Mexico here coming back from having gone to the City of the Angels, Puebla, to be ordained as sub-deacon, deacon, and full priest able to say mass. During the celebration of one Lent the bishop don Alonso de la Mota y Escobar ordained him only twice, for the Holy Father had sent orders that he was to be ordained in only three days. [*p. 216*] But although the Holy Father issued orders that it should be done so with señor don Pedro de Otalora, nevertheless it was not until Passion Sunday[2] that his ordination was finished, so that he performed mass in Puebla at the Company of Jesus. It had never been seen before here in Mexico that a president or judge of the Royal Audiencia became a secular priest as the just mentioned señor don Pedro de Otalora did. And he did not thereby relinquish his office that he was appointed to as president of the Royal Audiencia of Mexico, for so our great ruler the king who is in Spain wishes it. As long as it was Lent, before his ordination was finished, he stayed in Puebla; he left only after having said mass for the first time, and then he came back here to Mexico to perform his governmental duty as president.[3]

v Today, Friday the 12th of the month of April of the year 1613, three of us commoners were hanged. At 10 o'clock in the morning the said thieves, [of] us commoners, were brought out of the court jail, the ones mentioned above who killed people in the said court jail, killing three people, two Spaniards and one mulatto; it was already said that the dead Spaniards were a jailer and second an assistant jailer. As they were brought out of the court jail, a wooden platform[4] was used to carry them, and horses went along with their tails tied to their platform to drag them along and bring them in among the gallows, in the middle of the other eight gallows that are spread out there. When they had brought them there, they cut off the right hand of each of them. [*p. 217*] But first they bound their eyes before they cut off and struck off their hands; when they had cut off their hands, they

3. Compare with the partially identical passage on pp. 236–37.
4. Or separate wooden platforms?

matecque yc niman pilloloque yehuatl ytech yn omoteneuh tlayolloco tlanepantla mani ye huecauh tepilolcuahuitl yn oncan tecpan quiyahuac yhuan xexeloloque yn innacayo yhuan yn intzõteco quincocotonillique, auh oncan ycpac yn omoteneuh tepilolcuahuitl quintlallique yhuan yn inmacpacpal[1] quintetequillique oncan ytlan yhuan tepilolcuauhtitech tepoztica[2] quitetetzotzonque auh yn intzonteco oncan cenpohuallonce tonatiuh yn cacatca tepilolcuauhtitech, auh ye ic omilhuitl mani metztli Mayo Juebes ypan yn quintocaco oncan hospital de la misericordia

v Axcan Juebes ynic .9. mani Metztli Mayo de 1613. años yhcuac çan iciuhca miquiliztica xuxouhcamiquiliztica yxtomamiquiliztica[3] momiquilli yn Secretario Martin de agurto cenca yeyca neyçahuilloc —

v Axcan[4] Sabado ynic .ii. mani Metztli Mayo de 1613 años. yhcuac ohualla yancuica tlahtolli yn españa. yuh machiztico yuh mihto yn tohueytlahtocatzin Rey Don Felipe tercero quihualmotzacuillia yn alla china acalli yn ompa yxquich tlamantli tlatquitl nican Mexico quihualhuicani yn ohualquiçaya oncan huey atenco acapolco. yuh omihto aocmo oncan quiçaquiuh ça nepa ye yc yaz quil vmpa quiçatiuh in motenehua Portugal ynic moch ompa yaz españa in la china tlatquitl quimottiliz yn omoteneuhtzino Rey — ynic çatepan nican Mexico huallaz — [*p. 218*]

v Axcan Domingo ynic .12. mani Metztli Mayo de 1613 años. yhcuac yancuican motenextillitzinoque yn oncan capilla S. Joseph. S. Fran^co^. ynic hualmocallaquique yn Padre fr. Juã Maçurra yehuatzin in Capellan mochiuhtzinoco yn oncan omoteneuh S. Joseph. yhuan ytlantzinco oncan quihuallaq̃. yn telpuchtli padre fr. Sebastian de garibai yntemachticauh muchiuh in Mexica, auh yn fr. Jeronimo de çarate yhcuac quiz yn capillero catca teohuacan yah. auh ynic nican quic in Mexico yn tenochca yuhquin ceuhtiaque yn ipampa yuh omoteneuh tlacpac ynic cenca otlatollinico mexico. ynic nican oyeco tottatzin yn ayac ceppa ce guardian yuh nican otlachihuaco in ye yxquich ica ahcico teopixquę S. Fran^co^ nican ciudad Mexico nueua españa —

v Axcan Viernes ynic 17. mani Metztli Mayo de 1613. años yhcuac Nican Mexico onpeuh ynic yauh españa yn Doña Maria de dircios ycnocihuatl yn inamic catca Don Juã altamirano comendador S.tiago catca auh ynin omoteneuh cihuapilli ynic ompa yah quihualnotz yn ittatzin tlahtohuani Don luis de Velasco marques de Salinas. yhuan Pressidente muchiuhtica in motenehua del consejo de indias yn ompa españa, auh ynic quihualnotz in ychpuch yuh mihto yuh machiztico vmpa quinamictiz yn españa auh ynin omoteneuh cihuapilli ynic ompa yah españa çan quincauhtia yeỹtin yn ipilhuan ynic ce yehuatl yn Don fernando altamirano comendador S.tiago. auh yn oc omentin monjastin oncan cate yntlan [*p. 219*] Yn imahuitzitzinhuan yn oncan monasterio totlaçonantzin Regina Angelorum

v Axcan Viernes ynic .31. mani ytlamian yn Metztli Mayo de 1613. años yhcuac yn omiquico yn Maria ycnocihuatl xocoatolnamacac ynin ynamic yn fran^co^ tlatzonqui Sastre catca nican chaneque ytepotzco yn teopantli yn icaltzin yn notlaçomahuiztatzin S. Antonio Abbad Motenehua tlaxillacalli xulloco. auh yn omoteneuh Maria xucoatolnamacac ynic miquico ca yuh mihto yuh ypan machoc ytechcopa quihtoque ỹ nican tlaca

1. For "inmacpal."
2. Or something else of iron?
3. See the earlier examples of the use of these words (pp. 172–73, 214–15, 232–33);

were hanged on the said gallows that was in the middle and had been there for a long time outside the palace, and their bodies were cut into parts and their heads cut off and placed on top of the said gallows along with their hands[1] that had been cut off, beside them; they hammered them to the gallows with iron [nails].[2] Their heads were on the gallows for 21 days, and on Thursday, the 2nd day of the month of May, they were brought to be buried at the hospital of Misericordia.

v Today, Thursday the 9th of the month of May of 1613, was when the secretary Martín de Agurto quickly died an unexpected and premature death,[3] about which people were greatly shocked. —

v Today,[4] Saturday the 11th of the month of May of the year 1613, was when news came from Spain and it became known and was said that our great ruler the king don Felipe III is closing off the ship to China [the Philippines] that has customarily brought goods of all kinds from there to Mexico here, that docked at Acapulco on the ocean shore. It was said that it will no longer come to dock there, but will go in the other direction and reportedly will go to dock in Portugal, as it is called, so that all the goods from China will go to Spain and the said king will inspect them, so that they will be brought to Mexico here afterward. — [*p. 218*]

v Today, Sunday the 12th of the month of May of the year 1613, was when, at the chapel of San Josef at San Francisco, was first revealed the entry of father fray Juan Mazurra, appointed chaplain at the said San Josef, and along with him was brought the young father fray Sebastián de Garibay, who became the preacher to the Mexica. And at that time fray Gerónimo de Zárate, the former chaplain, left and went to Teohuacan. When he left Mexico here, it was as though the Tenochca were relieved, because of how, as was mentioned above, our father greatly mistreated everyone in Mexico since he came here, as no father guardian had ever done in the whole time since Franciscan friars first reached the city of Mexico here in New Spain. —

v Today, Friday the 17th of the month of May of the year 1613, was when doña María de Ircio, widow, who was the spouse of don Juan Altamirano, late comendador of Santiago, set out from Mexico here to go to Spain. The reason the said noblewoman is going is that her father the ruler don Luis de Velasco, Marqués of Salinas, appointed president in the said Council of the Indies in Spain, summoned her from there. The reason he summoned his daughter, it was said and made public, was to marry her [to someone] in Spain. On going to Spain this said lady left behind three children: the first don Hernando Altamirano, comendador of Santiago, and the other two are nuns who are with [*p. 219*] their aunts at the nunnery of our precious mother Regina Angelorum.

v Today, Friday the 31st, the end of the month of May of the year 1613, was when María, a widow and seller of bitter atole, died. She was the spouse of the late Francisco, a tailor, and they lived here behind the church, the house of my precious revered father San Antonio Abad, [in] the tlaxilacalli of Xoloco, as it is called. The reason that the said María, seller of bitter atole, died, as was said and found out about it, and the local people

---

the meaning quick, premature death is very clear here because of the presence of *iciuhca*, "soon, fast, quick."

4. This paragraph is lightly crossed out in the original.

ypan tlaxillacalli ca çan icuallantzin yçomaltzin ytetzin ycuauhtzin in tt^{o}. Dios quihualmihualli ypan yn omoteneuh cihuatzintli, auh yehica ypampa ytech tlahtohuaya ytech acia yn imahuiçotzin Sancta cruz. ca quimixnamictica amo quinequia ynic oncan quimoquechilizque ohtlipan Yn axcan[1] oncan oquimoquechilique ohnepantla yn icaltepa español hernan m̄n ynin omoteneuhtzino Sancta cruz. ca ymaxcatzin yehuantin yntlaquetzaltzin yn tocniuhtzitzinhuan yn toteyccauhtzitzinhuan Juan morales yhuã yn iyome Bernabe de S. Jeronimo cuechiuhque yhuan incepantlatquitzin oc cequi tlacatl mexica nican chaneque xulloco macihui yn amo muchintin nican ytech pouhticate omoteneuh tlaxillacalli xulloco. Auh ca yuhqui yn yn omochiuh yn axcan ye caxtolli ypan viernes catca in yehuantin omoteneuhque Juan morales yhuan Bernabe de S Jeronimo yhuan yn oc cequi tlacatl yhcuac on[*p. 220*]Can quitequipanohuaya. yn imomuzço yez. yn ipan quimoquechilizque omoteneuhtzino Sancta cruz. quiçallohuaya. auh in yehuatl omoteneuh Maria xucoatolnamacac Justicia canato seral moteylhuito yxpan yn coregidor Don Martin ceron quinteylhuito yn omoteneuhque Juan morales. yhuan Bernabe de S Jeronimo ca noço huel yehuantin yn ipan muchicahua ynic tequipanohua tlaçallohua yn oncan omoteneuh yn caltepa[2] ohnepantla. auh ynin ohtli quimaxcatiaya yn omoteneuh cihuatl Maria xucoatolnamacac ypampa yn moteylhuito. Quito camo vel mochihuaz yn oncã moq̃tzaz cruz ivan quihtohuaya ca ye cualli ỹtla oncã q̃moqueliz q̃[3] cruz ma çan itlatzin nechtlaocollican tomintzin canel naxca n tlalli ypã quitlalia momuztli auh ca amo nelli yn iaxca canel ohtli auh yece amo nelli yn iaxca ca noço otli.[4] auh yn o yuh moteylhuito omoteneuh cihuatl yc niman ce alguacil español quihualtitlan yn coregidor. quimanaco oncan yn tlatequipanohuaya yn omoteneuhque Juan morales yhuan bernabe de S. Jeronimo. amo yhuiyan yn quimanaco ca quinmamaylpica ymomextin auh ça yntepantlahtolliztica yn españoles nican chaneq̃ vezinos[5] ynic quintonque ynic ça matontiaque quinhuicaque Seral vmpa quimilpizquia. auh in yehuatl omoteneuh Maria xucoatolnamacac cenca quintzatzatzillitihuia amo huel mihtoz motenehuaz yn ixquich acualli ayectli tencuicuitlatlahtolli yc quimahuatihuia cenca quinmahuizpollotihuia canel cihuatl, auh amo çan icel ynin cihuatl yhuan ymon yn moteylhuiq̃. auh in yehuantin in omoteneuhque ylpilozquia Seral çan hualmocuepato Seral quiyahuac amo huel quintzacque ytepantlahtolizticatzinco yn Padre fr. Augustin del Spiritu Sancto. ỹ nican quimopiallia teopancalli S. Antonio Abbad. quinmottili oncan yn Seral quiyahuac [*p. 221*] Yn quinhuicaya yniqu ilpillozquia omoteneuhque Juan morales. auh yc niman oncan quinmolhuilli yn coregidor yhuan escriuano Juan Perez de Ribera yhuan nahuatlahtlahto[6] ma xicmomachiltican ca nehuatl nitestigo. ynin cihuatl Maria ca çan oamechmoztlacahuillico ynic oquitoco yn yaxca ytlatqui yn tlalli ypan quimoquechiliznequi Sancta cruz. Yz cate oanoto. ca ohtlipan ohnepantla yn quitlallia yn quiçallohua momuztli yn õcan ypan quimoquechilizque Sancta cruz. ayac aquin in yaxcapan. ma motta. auh in yehuantin omoteneuhque ylpillozquia çan ic huallihualloq̃. quimilhuiq̃. ayatle xicchihuacan ma oc nenemi n pleyto. auh yn o yuh hualnahuatilloque

1. Or recently.

2. One could write "yncaltepa" and translate "their said houses."

3. For "q̃moquechiliz q̃."

4. The portion beginning "Quito camo" and ending "canel ohtli" in the Nahuatl, and in the English beginning "saying" and ending "is the road" is added between the lines and in the margin. Hence the repetition. Once again we have an indication that Ch. was copying from something else.

here in the tlaxilacalli said in this connection, was that our lord God sent down his anger, wrath, and punishment on the said woman. It was because she talked about [disparagingly] and impinged on reverence for the holy Cross, for she opposed and did not want the erection of the one that has now[1] been erected in the road intersection outside the house of the Spaniard Hernán Martín. This said holy Cross was the property of and was raised by our friends and younger brothers Juan Morales and Bernabé de San Gerónimo, who are married to sisters and are skirt makers, and it also belonged jointly to some other Mexica who live here in Xoloco, although not all of them belong to the said tlaxilacalli of Xoloco here. Here is what happened fifteen days ago, on a Friday: at that time the said Juan Morales and Bernabé de San Gerónimo and the others were working on [*p. 220*] what was to be the platform on which the said holy Cross was to be erected; they were putting it together. But the said María, seller of bitter atole, went to get the officers of the law. She went to make a complaint at the municipal building before the corregidor don Martín Cerón; she accused the said Juan Morales and Bernabé de San Gerónimo of being the very ones who were behind working and setting things up there next to the said houses[2] in the road intersection. And the said woman María, seller of bitter atole, claimed this road as her property, which is why she went to make the complaint, saying, "It cannot be done that a cross be erected there." She also said, "Very well, if they erect[3] a cross there, let them concede me just a bit of money, since the land on which they are placing the platform is my property." But it is not in truth her property, for it is the road. But it is not in truth her property, for there is no doubt that it is the road.[4] After the said woman went to make a complaint, the corregidor sent a Spanish constable who came to arrest the said Juan Morales and Bernabé de San Gerónimo, who were working there. They did not take them gently, for they tied the hands of both of them. It was only at the intercession of the Spaniards who live here, the vecinos,[5] that they untied them, and it was with hands untied that they took them to the municipal building, where they were going to keep them in custody. And the said María, seller of bitter atole, went along shouting loudly at them; all the bad and filthy language with which she went scolding at them cannot be said or told. She showed great disrespect for them, for she is a woman. But it was not this woman alone; her son-in-law made the complaint along with her. The said [Juan Morales and Bernabé de San Gerónimo] were going to be detained in the municipal building, but they were brought back outside the building, and they were not able to lock them up because of the intercession of father fray Agustín del Espíritu Santo, who is in charge of the church of San Antonio Abad here. He saw them outside the municipal building [*p. 221*] as the said Juan Morales [and Bernabé de San Gerónimo] were being taken off to be in custody, and then he said to the corregidor and the notary Juan Pérez de Ribera and the interpreter,[6] "May you know that I am a witness that this woman María deceived you when she came saying that the land on which they want to erect the holy Cross is her property. It is in the road, in the intersection that these people here whom they went to arrest are setting up and putting together the platform on which they are to raise the holy Cross. It is not on anyone's property; let it be inspected." And the said people who were going to be detained were sent back; they told them, "Don't do anything yet, let the suit

5. Although meaning only "citizen," the Spanish word *vecino* was ordinarily used for non-indigenous residents only.

6. For "nahuatlahto."

yc niman yhuicpatzinco Visurrey quinmohuiquilli yn Padre fr. Augustin del Spīū Sancto yn omoteneuhque Juã morales yhuan yn oc cequintin ynic yehuatzin Visurrey don diego fernandez de cordoua marques de guada[1] quimitlanililique yhuellitzin licencia quinmomaquilli ynic huel quiquetzazque S.ta cruz. yn oncan ypan omoteneuh ohtli ynic quimixnamiquia omoteneuh cihuatl auh yn o yuh hualmotlanahuatilli yn ohualmofirmatitzino Visurrey. yc niman tlanque yn quiçalloque momuztli quicencauhque. auh in quimolhuichihuillilique ỹ moteochiuhtzino S.ta cruz yancuic nican teopan S. Anton ypan Domingo espīū pascua ynic 26. mani Metztli Mayo, yehuatzin quimoteochihuilli yn cenca mahuiztililoni Padre ye omotocateneuhtzino fr. Augustin del Spīū Sancto. cenca tlamahuiztililiztica tlayahualoliztica yn quimoquechillito oncan omoteneuh ypan omochiuh yancuic momuztli yn ihcuac yn ye mococohua cenca ye tlanahui yn omoteneuh cihuatl xucoatolnamacac. auh yhuan ynic moquetzino ynin omote[*p. 222*]neuhtzino S. ta cruz. no yhuan yhuellitzin ylicenciatzin quimotemaquilli yn provisor Doctor Don Juan de Salamãca. ca quimitlanililique ynic huel moquetzino S.ta cruz. auh yn omoteneuh maria xucoatolnamacac ynic momiquillico amo huecauhtica quitztia yn imõ ytoca catca _______ no momiquilli ca noço quipalehuiaya yn omoteneuh ymonnan ynic moteylhuica

v Auh yn ayemo muchihuaya ỹ yn omoteneuh yn quin tontlami ticpohua yn otoconicuilloque neyxnamiquiliztlahtolli muchiuh yn iuh moteylhuica omoteneuh Maria xucoatolnamacac yn itechcopa Sancta cruz. auh ca yzcatqui oc no centlamantli achtopa omuchiuh çãno nican ypã tlaxillacalli xulloco yhuan mihtohua acatla yn oc centlapal nepa calnacazco ycalnahuac yn español diego Senete. in yehuatl in omoteneuh español yhuan ynamic ytoca Mariana Rodriguez española oquichiuhque neyxnamiquiliztli yn ipehuayan in omoteneuh Metztli Mayo. ynic çã no ytechpa tlahtoque ytech acique yn imahuiçotzin oc ce Sancta cruz. ynic ycatzinco. quimixnamicque yn omoteneuh oncan tlaca tlaxillacalleque yn imaxcatzin omoteneuh Sancta cruz. in cenca ye huecauh yn oncan quimoquechillitiaque yn inttahuan huehuetque catca. auh in yehuantin omoteneuhque español diego Senete yhuan ynamic Mariana Rodriguez. oc cenca yehuatl in yn Señora quimixnamicti. Sancta cruz. amo quinequia ymomextin ynic oncan yncalnahuac yncaltitlan moquetzinoticaz. cruz. auh macihui yn oncan in chaneq̃. ca ye momati ca çan calcohuani tel ye huecauh yn oncã cate ynic chancate çan oc tepitzin ỹ calli yc catca. auh yn axcan ayemo huecauh yn oc cequi miccacalli ynic netech [*p. 223*] Çaliuhtica yncal oquimonnamaquiltitevac yhuan yn fray Jeronimo de çarate yn capillero ocatca S. Joseph S. Fran^co^ ayemo huecauh yn ihcuac ayemo yuh quiça. ynic possesio quinmacaco yn icuac fiscal catca Don Antonio Valleriano yn axcan ye gou^or^ azcaputzalco yn ica calli ynic ça concenmanque ye huecauh yncal, yece amo yhuan quinnamaquilti yhuã amo yhuan ypan possesio yc macoque yn omoteneuh tlalli yn ipan moquetzinoticac Sancta cruz. auh neh yn omoteneuhque español diego Senete yhuan ynamic ye muchi quimaxcatia ỹ tlalli ynic ye quincahualtia omoteneuhque tlaxillacalleque quimilhuique xiquixtican yn amocruz. ca ya taxca yn tlalli ypan moquetzinoticac oticohuillique yn fray Jeronimo de çarate. auh in yehuantin nican tlaxillacalleque amo yuh quimatticatca yntla yhuan oquinnamaquilti tottatzin tlalli çan ic cuallanque yn quicacque tlaxillacalleque ynic oncan ye quinquixtiliznequi yncruztzin ynic ye mixnamiqui, auh yn oc cenca yehuatl ye tlahtohua moteneuh Señora Mariana Rodriguez. in ye quimixnamiqui ye quimahua ye quinmahuizpolohua tlaxillacalleque quexquich

1. For "guadalcaçar."

take its course first." And when they had been dismissed, father fray Agustín del Espíritu Santo took the said Juan de Morales and the others to the viceroy, so that they asked the viceroy don Diego Fernández de Córdoba, Marqués of Guadalcázar,[1] for his permission, and he gave them permission to erect a holy Cross in the said road, which the said woman had opposed. After the orders had been issued and the viceroy had signed, they finished putting together the platform, they got it ready, and they held a feast day for the blessing of the new holy Cross here at the church of San Antonio on the Sunday of the feast of the Holy Spirit, on the 26th of the month of May. The very reverend father whose name was already mentioned, fray Agustín del Espíritu Santo, blessed it. It was with great ceremony and processions that they went to raise it on the said new platform that was built. At this time the said woman seller of bitter atole was sick and very near to death. And when this said holy Cross was erected, [*p. 222*] the vicar general doctor don Juan de Salamanca also gave them his permission, which they had requested, for the holy Cross to be raised. And it was not long after that the said María, seller of bitter atole, passed away; her son-in-law, whose name was ______, also passed away, because he helped his said mother-in-law in the complaint she had made.

v Before this that has been told, that we have just finished recounting and writing about the dispute that happened, how the said María, seller of bitter atole, had made a complaint relating to the holy Cross, here is another thing that happened first, likewise here in the tlaxilacalli of Xoloco and in [a section] called Acatlan, on the other side, at the corner and close to the house of the Spaniard Diego de Senete. The said Spaniard and his spouse named Mariana Rodríguez, a Spanish woman, caused a dispute at the beginning of the said month of May, in which they likewise talked [disparagingly] about and touched on the reverence for another holy Cross, because of which they opposed the people of the said tlaxilacalli there, whose property the said holy Cross was, that their forefathers had erected there a long time ago. The said Spaniard Diego de Senete and his spouse, Mariana Rodríguez, especially this Spanish woman, opposed the holy Cross; neither of them wanted the cross to stand there close to, next to their house. And although they are residents there, it is thought that they just bought their house, although they have been there and made their home there for a long time, but the house was only a little one. Not long ago [fray Gerónimo de Zárate] sold them the house of a deceased person adjacent to their house, [*p. 223*] and it was fray Gerónimo de Zárate, who was chaplain of San Josef at San Francisco, not long ago, before he left, who gave them possession of the house, when don Antonio Valeriano, now governor of Azcapotzalco, was fiscal, so that they amalgamated it with the house they had had for a long time, but he did not sell them, nor did they receive possession of, the said land on which the holy Cross stands. On the other hand the said Spaniard Diego de Senete and his spouse claimed that all the land was their property, so that they ejected the said tlaxilacalli members, telling them, "Remove your cross, for the land it stands on is our property, we bought it from fray Gerónimo de Zárate." But the people of the tlaxilacalli here did not know whether our father had sold them the land along with it, and they were angered when they heard that they wanted to take their cross there away from them and were opposing them. And especially the said Spanish woman Mariana Rodríguez talked about it, opposing, scolding, and showing

yn acualli yectli[1] tencuicuitlatlahtolli quimilhui yn amo huel mihtoz motenehuaz. yhuã huel quineltilizyhtohuaya. yn ca quimoquixtiliz cruz. yn oncan moquetzinoticac. quihto oncan mocaltizque ynic niman omoteilhuito tlacpac yn tlaxillacalleque oquihtoto ca ynhuehuetlatqui yn tlalli ypan moquetzinoticac Sancta cruz. oquicac yn Justicia ynic oquitlalilique pleito diego Senete ynic çan quichtecacuiznequi tlalli ye nemi n pleito, auh yn ipan cemilhuitl y[*p. 224*]n ihcuac omoteneuh ynic mahuaque mixnamicq̃. ypampatzinco Sancta cruz. ca no niman yhcuac peuh in ye mococohua çan oqu itzonteco ynic peuh ye quicocohua yn omoteneuh Señora Mariana Rodriguez. auh yn imuztlayoc yc huallathuic ye omotecac ytlapechco yn mococohua matlaltotonqui yn itech motlalli cenca çã niman chicahuac yhuan niman yglesia mayor quihualmohuiquililique in Sacramẽto. ynic niman quimocelili. auh yniqu eilhuitl yhcuac momiquilli yn Señora auh yuh mihto ypan yuh machoc quihtoque ỹ nican tlaca ypan tlaxillacalli. ca çan ycuallantzin yçomaltzin yn tt^o. Dios. quihualmihualli ypan yn omoteneuh Señora. auh ynic otlamico ynic otzonquiz pleyto. yn Justicia ça oquinmacac in tlalli macehualtin ynic mochipa quipiazque oncan ypã moquetzinoticaz yn Sancta cruz. ayac aquin huel oncan quinquixtiliz. auh yn manel oc nen moteilhuiaya omoteneuh diego Senete. ça nipa hualhuetz. aocmo caquililoc yn ineteilhuil. o yhui yn yn omochiuh ontlamantli tlamahuiçolli nican ypan tlaxillacalli ye omoteneuh xulloco acatla yteopancalnahuactzinco notlaçottatzin S. Antonio Abbad Mexico yn ipehuayan in omoteneuh Metztli Mayo. auh yn ipampa nican onictlalli o-niquicuillo nehuatl Don domingo de S. Anton Muñon Quauhtlehuanitzin ypampa ca huel nixpan yn iyontlamanixti omochiuh huel oniquittac —

v̲ axcan Sabado ynic 22. mani Metztli Junio de 1613 [*p. 225*] Años. yhcuac moman tiyanquiztli yn totlaçonantzin Visitacion yhuan mihtohua nuestra Señora de la biedad huehuetlã yn oncan moyetzticate teopixque S. Domingo. auh ynin yc moman. ynic mochalli omoteneuh tianquintli[2] yehuatl ypã tlahto yn Padre fr. Juan de Bustamante yhcuac oncan tetlan catca —

v̲ Axcan Viernes ynic 28. mani Metztli Junio de 1613. años. yhcuac nican ciudad Mexico otzatzihuac nohuiyan caltzallan ytlanahuatilticatzinco yn tlahtohuani Don diego fernandez de cordoua Marques Visurrey yn ipampa yc aocac macehualli tlamamaz yxcuatica yn iuh muchiuhtihuiz[3] quinmamaltia huehuey cuauhchiquihuitl yhuan yn çaço tley huehuey tlamamalli oquinmamaltiaya frayles yhuan españoles. yn hueca oquihuallehualtiaya quimama quihualcahua nican mexico. ahnoce nican oquihuallanaya in cenca yetic yc quihuica cenca quintollinia ynic oconaxitiaya yn canin altepetl ipan tequiuhtillo macehualtzitzinti concahua, auh yn ipampa aocmo yuhqui mochihuac[4] in Pena yc quinmotlalili yn tlahtohuani yn frayles. yhuan españoles. yuh nahuatilloque yn ipan tecpoyotl tzatzic ça cauallotí yn quintlamamalizque ohtlipan yn tleyn canin quinhuiquilizque yuh hualla yamatzin ycedulatzin yuh hualmotlanahuatilli yn tohueytlahtocatzin Rey Don Felipe Tercero in moyetztica españa —

v̲ Axcan miercoles ynic .4. mani Metztli Setiembre de 1613. años. yhcuac nican tlani[5] centlapal ohmac[6] huel yxpan yn iteopancaltzin notlaçottatzin S. Antonio Abbad xulloco.

1. For "ayectli."
2. For "tianquiztli."
3. For "muchiuhtihuitz."

disrespect for the people of the tlaxilacalli; how much bad,[1] filthy language she used with them cannot be said or told; she said that in all truth she was going to remove the cross standing there, saying that they were going to build a house there. Then the people of the tlaxilacalli above went to make a complaint, saying that the land on which the holy Cross stands is their patrimonial property. The officers of the law heard the complaint, so that they [the tlaxilacalli people] brought suit against Diego de Senete for trying to take the land deceitfully; the suit is now pending. And on the same said day [*p. 224*] when they argued and showed opposition about the holy Cross, the said Spanish woman Mariana Rodríguez began to get sick; at first she just began to have a headache, but the next day in the morning she lay down sick in her bed. She got matlaltotonqui, which soon became very strong, and they brought her the Sacrament from the cathedral, and she received it. On the third day the Spanish woman passed away. And it was said and found out about it, and the local people in the tlaxilacalli said that our lord God sent his anger and wrath down upon the said Spanish woman. When the suit came to an end and was finished, the officers of the law gave the land to the commoners to keep forever; the holy Cross will stand on it and no one will be able to take it away from them. And although the said Diego de Senete tried to make a complaint, it fell to one side; his complaint was not heard. Like this, then, occurred two separate miracles here in the said tlaxilacalli of Acatlan in Xoloco, close to the church of my precious father San Antonio Abad in Mexico, at the beginning of the said month of May. And I, don Domingo de San Antón Muñón Quauhtlehuanitzin, set it down here and wrote it because both things happened right before my eyes, I really saw them. —

v Today, Saturday the 22nd of the month of June of the year 1613, [*p. 225*] was when a market was set up at our precious mother of Visitación, also called Nuestra Señora de la Piedad, in Huehuetlan, where the Dominican friars are. And father fray Juan de Bustamante saw to it that the said market[2] was set up and inaugurated; at that time he was among the people there. —

v Today, Friday the 28th of the month of June of the year 1613, was when it was proclaimed through the streets everywhere in the city of Mexico at the order of the ruler don Diego Fernández de Córdoba, Marqués and viceroy, that commoners are no longer to carry loads using their foreheads, as happens[3] when they load them with large wooden baskets, or when the friars and Spaniards make them bear any kind of heavy load, that they sent them here from far away carrying, that they deliver here in Mexico, or when they came to get something very heavy to take that greatly afflicts them, that they took to whatever altepetl the poor commoners were given the duty of delivering it to. And so that this will no longer be done,[4] the ruler set a fine about it for the friars and Spaniards; they were ordered and the crier proclaimed that only horses are to carry for them on the road whatever they are to take somewhere for them. Thus said the letter that came, the cedula of our great ruler the king don Felipe III who is in Spain; thus he ordered. —

v Today, Wednesday the 4th of the month of September of the year 1613, was when here below,[5] at one side of the road[6] directly facing the church of my precious father San

---

4. Apparently "mochihuac in" is to be understood as "mochihuaz in."

5. Possibly the phrase means in effect below here, though the normal way of saying that something was below something else involved *-tzintlan*.

6. It may be that "ohmac" specifically designates the far side of the road.

O[*p. 226*]Quipehualti tepechtli ynic oncan ye mocaltia yehuatl español ytoca Antonio barreto portugues. ynin omoteneuh tlalli ypan ye mocaltia çan quicouh quicohuilli çãno español ytoca diego Senete ca achto yehuatl in in yaxca catca yn tlalli. auh macihui yn iaxca catca ynin omoteneuh tlalli yece ça atl otentimanca yn oncan cenca achi huecatlah ocatca auh yn o yuh concouh yehuatl omoteneuh Antonio barreto, quin yehuatl oquitlalten ynic oquihuecapano oc cecni oquiçacato yn tlalli oncan oquitetẽmaco ynic oquipollo atl oncan omanca auh in ye o yuh quitlalten çatepa oquicuauhtzotzon miec yn cuamimiltotonti oncan oquicuauhtzotzon ynic chicahuaz tlalli ynic huel ypan ye mocaltia çan oc centetl yn ical oncan oconpehualti ye quichihua ytienda yez. auh ynin omoteneuh yancuic tienda ye muchihua, ca ye quin ic ey tlacatl oncan mocaltia yn oncan in omoteneuh S. Antonio Abbad. yteopancaltzin yxpan yn iuh nezticatqui axcan.[1] ynic ce tlacatl oncan achtopa ye chanchiuhtica. yehuatl ỹ clerigo ytoca licenciado dorosa xuchmilcopa ỹ catqui ycall in tienda quipia, auh ynic ontetl ye huecauh calli oncan mani centetl no tienda muchiuhtica ye yn oztocaltitlan arcotitlan[2] mani ynin calli çan tetlaneuhtillo capellania yc catqui yehuatl yuh quitlalitia yn padre Masares[3] clerigo ca yaxca catca ynin omoteneuh calli ynin ohtenco yn mamani calli auh tlanepantla yn oconquetztihuetz ytienda omoteneuh Antonio barreto. huel amo huecauh yn oconchiuh çan ixquich ica ome metztli yn onmocalti[4] auh yn oc cequi tlalli yn iyanca ypã onmocalti yn ayxtlahuatl[5] muchiuhtoc axcan ach quen ipan muchihuatiuh[6] yn iquin canin quemma yn oc ompa ye tonitztihui aquique yn españoles ypan mocaltitihui auh [*p. 227*] Çan ipampa ỹ nican onicmachiyoti ynic çan oqu excan yn mani calli yxpan omoteneuh yteocaltzin notlaçottatzin S. Antonio. ypampa quittazque quimatizque. yn aquique yn quin nemiquihui yn quin ye tlacatizque Mexica. yhuã yn altepehuaque[7] ca çan oqu iuhcan in yn ihcuac ye nictlallia ye nicmachiyotia yn itlahtollo yn omoteneuh ayxtlahuatl muchiuhtimani axcan yntla çatepan yttoz yn iquin canin quenma ye teopancalli. ye monasterios. ye calli ypan tentoc ye onoc yn axcan ayemo quen neztoc çan atl oncan tentimani nohuiyan ynin tlahtolli nehuatl onicmachiyoti Don domingo de S. Anton Muñon Quauhtlehuanitzin, macihui yn amo nolhuil nomacehual ynic nican nitlatequipanotinemi ychantzinco y notlaçottatzin S. Antonio. ye yxquich ica axcan cenpohualxihuitl yn iuh muchi tlacatl quimati —

v̲ Axcan Juebes ynic .12. mani metztli Setiembre de 1613. años yhcuac nican ciudad Mexico S. Fran^{co}. ahcico callaquico in yancuic comissario ytoca fray chistoual Ramirez. españa hualmohuicac. quihualmohuiquilli yn cenca mahuiztililoni Padre fr. Juan torquemada yn omohuicaya españa çan oncexiuhtito yn ompa nican yc mohuicaca —

v̲ Axcan Viernes ynic 13. mani metztli Setiembre de 1613 años yhcuac nican ciudad Mexico ahcico callaquico ce tottatzin S. Fran^{co}. cuateçontzin vmpa hualla in yancuic Mexico ahnoço huehue Mexico. ynin tottatzin yc hualla çan hualmochtacatitlan quihualhuicac yntlahtol yn ompa motemachtilia oc cequintin teopixque S. Fran^{co}. yc hualmoteil[*p. 228*]huia yxpantzinco tlahtohuani Visurrey yn quenin cenca quintollinia vmpa

1. This clause could be interpreted as "as appears now [from what will be said in a moment]."

2. Literally, next to the arch.

3. Name unconfirmed.

4. The temporal inconsistencies in these annals from parts of passages having been written at a certain time, then added to without thorough revision of what was already

Antonio Abad in Xoloco, [*p. 226*] the Spaniard named Antonio Barreto, who is a Portuguese, began the foundations for the house he is building for himself there. He just bought this said land upon which he is building a house; he bought it from another Spaniard named Diego de Senete, for first the land was his property. But though this said land was his property, it was full of quite deep water. And after the said Antonio Barreto had bought it, he filled it in with earth and raised it. From another place he transported the earth that he filled it in with and got rid of the water that was there. And after he had filled it with earth, he drove in wooden piles, he pounded in many small wooden pillars so the earth will be strengthened, so that he can build himself a house on it. He has begun to build another house there that will be his shop. And this said new shop that is being built makes the third person to build a house facing the said church of San Antonio Abad, as things now appear.[1] The first person who has made a home there is the secular priest named licenciado Tolosa; his house is toward the south and has a shop. Second is a house that has been there for a long time, also made into a shop, at Oztocaltitlan Arcotitlan;[2] this house is rented out to people; it is under a chaplaincy arrangement; that is what was ordered in his testament by father Masares,[3] a secular priest, for this said house was his property. These buildings are spread out at the edge of the road. It is in between that the said Antonio Barreto has quickly built his shop; he took a very short time to build it, in only two months he built the house.[4] The other land, in addition [to what has been built on] is now a lake.[5] Who knows what will happen to it[6] when sometime in the future some Spaniards build on it? [*p. 227*] The reason I have recorded here that there are still only three houses facing the said church of my precious father San Antonio is so that the Mexica and the citizens[7] who live and are born later will see and know that it was still just like this when I set down and recorded the account of the said lake that is there now, if it is later seen at some future time that it is filled with churches, monasteries, and houses that are there where now nothing appears yet and it is full of water all around. This account was recorded by me, don Domingo de San Antón Muñón Quauhtlehuanitzin, who though I am not worthy of it have been serving here at the home of my precious father San Antonio for twenty years now, as everyone knows. —

v Today, Thursday the 12th of the month of September of the year 1613, was when there arrived and entered here in the city of Mexico and at [the church of] San Francisco the new commissary named fray Cristóbal Ramírez; he came from Spain. He was accompanied by the very reverend father fray Juan de Torquemada, who had gone to Spain and spent just a year there since he had left here. —

v Today, Friday the 13th of the month of September of the year 1613, was when there arrived and entered here in the city of Mexico one of our fathers of San Francisco, a lay friar, who came from New Mexico, or Old Mexico. The reason this father of ours came was that he was secretly sent, bringing the statement of the other Franciscan friars who preach there, making a complaint [*p. 228*] before the lord viceroy about how much the

---

written, are particularly apparent in this section.

5. Literally, a watery plain.

6. Or what will be built on it.

7. These "citizens" seem to be distinguished from the Mexica in general. The term *altepehuaque* sometimes means the authorities of an altepetl. Conceivably Ch. is even including the Spaniards.

Gouernador ynic ce ocalcapozhui[1] tottatzin quicxipopoztec yhuan centlapal quimapoztec ynĩ tottatzin cocoloc ytoca fr. Jeronimo de pedraço. yuh machiztico quitlacahualtiayah in teopixque omoteneuh Gou^{or} macayamo cuel ynca mocacayahua macayemo quintollini macehualti canel yancuique in tlaneltoquiliztica ma oc ceppa mocuepti ma motlapololtihti manoçe yaoyotl ynpan quichiuhti yn teopixque yhuan yn españoles. yehuatl in ynic quitlacahualtiaya Gouernador. çan icuallan quittac ynic cenca oquincocolli teopixque

v̲ Axcan Juebes ynic 26. mani Metztli Setiembre de 1613 a^{o}s yhcuac ye yohua ynic hualyohuac maxitico çã mochtacacallaquico ỹ nican ciudad Mexico in cenca mahuiztililoni teoyotica tlahtohuani Doctor Don Juan Perez de la serna arçobispo Mexico ynin clerigo çamora ychantzinco ayac quittac in nican tlaca Mexico ynic hualmocallaqui ychantzinco ayac quimonamiquilli, auh yn huallathuic viernes ye ychantzinco moyetztica çan oc motzauhctzinoticatca ayemo moteyttitzino, auh ynin omoteneuhtzino teoyotica tlahtohuani yn ompa españa ye hualmehuiti ayemo hualtlateochihualtitia yn ica arçobispoyotl. çan niman quihualmihualli yn Rey çan oqu iuhqui hualmacallaquitzino ynic Sacerdote ynic niman omohueyatenquixtico[2] auh yc niman oncan maxitico in la ciudad de los Angeles de la puebla cuitlaxcohuapa. ye yohua çã no mochtacacallaquico yn oncan ynic niman mocehuitzinoco ychan obispo Don [*p. 229*] Alonso de la mota y escobar. quin yehuatl in oncan quimoteochihuilli oncan quimomaquilli yn teoyotica ytlahtocayotzin ynic arçobispo muchiuhtzino. çan callihtic ychan yn omoteneuh obispo ypan ylhuitzin Exaltacion Sancta cruz. ca Sabado ypan motlalli ynic .14. mani metztli omoteneuh Setiembre. yn teochihualloc. auh çan hualmeylhuitiltitiquiz. yn arçobispo yn oncan moyetzticatca la ciudad de los Angeles cuitlaxcohuapa ynic niman oncan hualmehuiti ye hualmonenemitia ynic niman oncan maxitico totlaçonantzin nuestra Señora Sancta Maria de Guadalupe tepeyacac. ynic no ceppa oncan ohualmehuiti ynic omaxitico nican mexico yn ipan axcan omoteneuh cemilhuitl Juebes. ynic çan hualmochtacacallaqui ynic cemilhuitl ypan omoteneuh Viernes mocehuitzino yn ichantzinco çan motzauhctzinoticatca ayemo teyttititzino. —

v̲ Auh ye quin axcan Sabado ynic 28. mani metztli omoteneuh Setiembre in ye yeilhuitiyoc omoteneuh yc hualmocallaqui Mexico yhcuac omotenextillitzinoco omoteyttitzinoco yohuatzinco ypan chiuhcnahui tzillini yn õcan yglesia Mayor yhuan missa quimochihuillico yn omoteneuhtzino yehuatzin teoyotica tlahtohuani Doctor Don Juan Perez de la serna arçobispo. auh ynin ynic ompa ychantzinco hualmoquixti ynic oncan hualmohuicac omoteneuh yglesia mayor çan ic ye oncan mocallaquico yn tecpan quiyahuacpa yn oncã catqui oc ce puerta. auh in yehuantin cabildo tlaca yn Dean yn arcediano. yn chantre yn canonigos yn Racioneros. yn oquimottilique oncan ye õmaxitihtiuh arçobispo. yc niman quihualmonamictiliaya ce palio cuachcalli ynic quimonamiquiliaya. ynic quimocuachcaltilitiazquia ynic on[*p. 230*]mocallaquito Teopan auh in yehuatzin omoteneuhtzino teoyotica tlahtohuani arçobispo. amo quinmocelilili yn omoteneuhque cabildo tlaca yn intenamiquia cuachcalli atle ypan quinmottilili çan iuh ommocallaqui yn teopan. auh yhuan yn manel no vmpa quimoyacanilliaya ynic ye õpa quihualmocallaquiliznequia yn ixcopa teopan yn ompa catqui huey puerta yn huell oncan ycatzinco tlaliloc huey tlacuilolpuerta yn huel tlacencahualli yc tlacuillolli yn huel ycatzinco quichiuh-

1. The meaning may be that the governor merely clubbed the friar with a musket (harquebuse), not that he actually shot him.

governor there mistreats them, that he used a musket on one of our fathers;[1] he shattered his foot [or feet] and broke one of his arms. This father of ours who was hurt is named fray Gerónimo de Pedraza. It became known that the said governor had forbidden the friars to cheat the commoners or mistreat them because they are new in the faith and lest they return to confused beliefs or make war on the friars and the Spaniards. That was why the governor held the friars back; they saw nothing but anger from him, he hated them so much.

v Today, Thursday the 26th of the month of September of the year 1613, at dark as night was coming, was when there arrived and secretly entered in the city of Mexico here the very reverend spiritual ruler doctor don Juan Pérez de la Serna, archbishop of Mexico. He is a secular priest, from Zamora. None of the local people here in Mexico saw him as he entered his home, no one went out to meet him. On Friday morning he was already in his home, but it was still closed; he didn't show himself yet. When this said spiritual ruler left Spain he was not yet consecrated as archbishop. The king just sent him right away, and he was still unconsecrated when he went on board ship, and as a priest he landed on the seashore [of New Spain].[2] Then he reached the City of the Angels, Puebla, at night and likewise entered that place secretly; then he came to the home of the bishop don Alonso de la Mota y Escobar to rest, [*p. 229*] and only then did the latter consecrate him there and gave him his spiritual rulership by which he became archbishop. It was just inside the said bishop's home, on the feast day of the exaltation of the holy Cross, Saturday the 14th of the said month of September, that he was installed and consecrated. And the archbishop left quickly, after only three days of being in Puebla, after which he left and came traveling along in this direction until he reached [the chapel of] our precious mother Nuestra Señora Santa María de Guadalupe at Tepeyacac, from where he again departed to reach Mexico here today on the said day of Thursday, when he came entering secretly, and on the said day of Friday he rested in his home; he was just shut in and didn't show himself yet. —

v It was not until today, Saturday the 28th of the said month of September, three days after he entered Mexico, as was said, that, in the morning at 9 o'clock in the cathedral, the said spiritual ruler doctor don Juan Pérez de la Serna, archbishop, appeared in public and showed himself, and he came to perform mass. But when he came out of his home and came to the said cathedral, he only entered from the direction of the [archiepiscopal] palace exit, where there is another door, and the members of the cathedral chapter, the dean, archdeacon, choirmaster, and the canons who were full prebendaries saw that he was already arriving; then they were coming to meet him with a canopy, a cloth covering, which they were going to hold over him as he entered [*p. 230*] the church; but the said spiritual ruler, the archbishop, did not accept the said cathedral chapter members' sign of greeting, the canopy, he ignored them and went into the church just as he was. And though they were leading him and wanted to bring him in from the front of the church, where the great door is, and right there had been placed in his honor a large painted door,

2. The components of this sentence could be put in somewhat different orders with correspondingly different meanings.

que tlacuilloque yntlanahuatiltica yn omoteneuhque Cabildo tlaca canonigos. yn oncan quitlallique quimanque puerta yxcuac anoço yxco. yn oncan yc quimochialiaya onmocallaquiz teopan arçobispo quimolhuiliaya ynic ye oncan mocallaquiquiuh. auh amo no quimonequilti çã niman amo quimocelili çã niman amo tle ypan quimottilli yn teoyotica tlahtohuani ynic amo oncan yc mocallaqui. // yhuan ỹ nican ciudad Mexico tlaca in tepachohua Regidores españoles. aocmo oquimonamiquillique yn omoteneuhtzino teoyotica tlahtohuani arçobispo. yn iuh ohualmochiuhtihuia yncatzinco yn izquintin arçobisposme achtopa nican Mexico omotlapachilhuico ynic hualmaxitiaya. yancuicã yca palio cuachcaltica oquinmonamiquillique, auh yn axcan caocmo yuh namicozque yn arçobisposme. yn iuh axcan ohualmocallaqui omoteneuhtzino teoyotica tlahtohuani Doctor Don Juan Perez de la Serna, ca yuh axcan ohualmotlanahuatilli caocmo yuh quimonequiltia yn tohueytlahtocatzin Rey Don Felipe Tercero moyetztica españa. aocmo yuh mochihuaz. yn omoteneuhque ciudad tlaca Regidores. aocmo yuh quinnamiquizque cuachcaltica in ihcuac ynic huallacizque yancuicã mexico arçobisposme. ca quinmoquixtililiaya. auh ca ça yehuantin ynneyxcahuilnemac yez. yn tlahtoque yn Visurreyes [*p. 231*] Yn ihcuac huallacizque yancuican Mexico ca yehuantin palio yca cuachcaltica namicozque, auh yn itechpa Sancta yglesia yn Cabildo tlaca, ca ça yehuantin ỹneyxcahuiltequiuh yez. yn paliotica yn cuachcaltica quinmonamiquilizque yn teoyotica tlahtoque arçobisposme. yn ihcuac huallacizque yancuican nican Mexico ỹ nican pouhque quimopializque altepetl tenuchtitlan, auh yece yn axcan ytechpa Sancta yglesia yn Cabildo tlaca yn intenamiquia yn incuachcal. amo oquinmocelilili ynin omoteneuhtzino Doctor Don Juan Perez de la Serna, yhuan yn intlacuilolpuerta ynic çan oc çeccan puerta omocallaqui ynic quimotlapalhuito ytlaçonamictzin Sancta yglesia, yhuan yhtic ye omihto missa quimochihuillito yhuan quinmottilito quinmotlapalhuito yn itlapacholtzitzinhuan Cabildo tlaca canonigos.[1] auh yn o yuh conmuchihuilli missa tepitzin yc niman hualmocueptzino oc ye oncan hualmohuicac yn tecpan palacio. quimottillico quimotlapalhuico yn tlahtohuani Don diego fernandez de cordoua Marques y Visurrey auh yn oconmotlapalhuico yhuan ynamictzin Virreyna, yc niman mocueptzino motlallitzinoto yn ichantzinco arçobispo. ynic niman oncan ocomopehualtilli ytlamanitilitzin ynic ye quimopialia altepetl tenochtitlan cualtica yectica ynic neci cualli ychcapixqui ynic ye quinmopiallia ychcatzitzinhuan Mexico tlaca españoles. yhuan timacehualti yn tixquichtin titlapacholtzitzinhuan ma nechmotlaçopialili yn tt^{o}. dios. miec xihuitl yhuan ma quimochicahuilitzino miecanemiliztica[2] yn iuh timochintin nohuiyampa titlaca tiquellehuia auh yn oc cenca nehuatl noncua yuh catqui oc achi huel nonahuatil nomamal ynic niquelehuia Don [*p. 232*] Domingo de S. Anton Quauhtlehuanitzin chimalpahin[3]

v Auh ynin omoteneuhtzino teoyotica tlahtohuani Don Juan Perez de la Serna arçobispo ynic nican Mexico omaxitico niman oquinmopatilitacico yn Doctor Don Juan de Salamanca prouisor españoles ocatca. auh yehuatl yc quipatlatacico yn itoca licenciado castro. ynin[4] Prouisor españoles omochiuh. auh ynic ome quinmotlalilitacico ytoca licenciado Juan Aguado ynin ayemo quichihua missa yn ihcuac toprouisor omuchiuh timacehualti ynin ymomextin españa quinhualmohuiquilli yn teotica[5] tlahtohuani arçobispo. no yhuan

1. The above account seems quite self-contradictory, but there is relatively little question about what it says.

2. The form seems to contain *miec*, "much," *nemiliztli*, "life," and the instrumental *-tica*, but with the *a* it does not analyze normally.

well prepared with paintings that the painters did precisely in his honor by order of the said chapter members and canons, that they placed and set up there at the portal, or in front of the [main] door, where they waited for the archbishop to go in the church, telling him to come enter that way, nevertheless he didn't want that either, he didn't accept it at all, the spiritual ruler ignored it entirely and didn't go in that way. // And the members of the cabildo of the city of Mexico here, those who govern, the Spanish regidores, did not meet the said spiritual ruler, the archbishop, as had been being done for all the archbishops when they first came here to Mexico to rule, so that when they first arrived they met them with a canopy, a cloth covering. But from now on the archbishops will no longer be met in that fashion, [but] as the said spiritual ruler doctor don Juan Pérez de la Serna just now entered, for now orders have been sent that our great ruler the king don Felipe III who is in Spain no longer wants it to be that way, that it will be done no more; the said cabildo members, the regidores, will no longer greet new archbishops of Mexico with a canopy when they get here, he took [that privilege] away from them. It will be the exclusive right of the rulers the viceroys [*p. 231*] when they first get to Mexico, for they are to be met with a canopy, a cloth covering. And as to the members of the cathedral chapter of the holy church, they will be the only ones who will have the duty of meeting the spiritual rulers, the archbishops, with a canopy, a cloth covering, when they first come here to Mexico and are assigned here to be in charge of the altepetl of Tenochtitlan, despite the fact that now relating to the holy church this said doctor don Juan Pérez de la Serna did not accept the cathedral chapter members' sign of greeting, their canopy, or their painted door, so that he went in by another door to greet his precious spouse the holy church and went inside, as was said, to perform mass and to see and greet his subjects, the cathedral chapter members, the canons.[1] After he had said a low mass, [the archbishop], before coming back, came to the [governmental] palace to see and greet the ruler don Diego Fernández de Córdoba, Marqués and viceroy. After he had greeted him and his spouse the virreine, the archbishop came back and settled in at home, beginning right away his government, by which he is now in charge of the altepetl of Tenochtitlan in a good and proper fashion and appears as a good shepherd, taking care of the people of Mexico as his sheep, Spaniards and us commoners, all of us his subjects. May our lord God deign to guard him for me for many years, may he give him good health and a long life,[2] as we people everywhere wish, and especially to me separately it is an even greater obligation and duty that I, don [*p. 232*] Domingo de San Antón Muñón Quauhtlehuanitzin Chimalpahin, wish it.[3]

v When this said spiritual ruler don Juan Pérez de la Serna, archbishop, arrived here in Mexico, he right away replaced doctor don Juan de Salamanca, who was vicar general for the Spaniards, and the person he replaced him with on arrival was named licenciado Castro,[4] who became vicar general for the Spaniards. And on arrival he installed a second person, named licenciado Juan Aguado, who does not say mass yet, who became at that time the vicar general of us commoners. The spiritual[5] ruler, the archbishop, brought

---

3. The last sentence is a version of a common polite Spanish formula.

4. Here the words "ayemo quichihua missa yn ihcuac ỹ" are marked out in the Nahuatl. They are virtually repeated just below, another indication of copying from an earlier text.

5. For "teoyotica."

yn õpa españa quihualmohuiquilli Masescuela[1] ytoca Don Melchior arindez. nican mexico pouhqui yn.[2] auh çãno ycuac yn mochintin hualmocenhuicaque yn españa in cẽca mahuiztililo teotica[3] tlahtohuani Doctor Juan gutierrez flores ynquisidor menor ytemanahuicatzitzinhuan yn cenquizcacualtlaneltoquiliztli La fee in nican Mexico no yhcuac yn Maxitico yniqu inehuantzin onmotlalitzinoque in yehuatzin ye huecauh nican moyetztica inquisidor mayor Gutierre Bernardo de Quiros.[4] // auh çanno yhcuac yn yancuican ahcico hualla nican Mexico in yancuic coRegidor hualla españa ytoca Don Alonso tello de guzman. yhcuac quicauh yn itequiuh yn Don Martin Ceron coRegidor catca quipatlatacico.

—

v Auh yn axcan Domingo ynic 29. mani metztli Setiembre ynic ye nahuilhuitl omaxitico nican Mexico in yehuatzin omoteneuhtzino teoyotica tlahtohuani don Juan Perez de la Serna arçobispo. yhcuac yn otlayahuallo yn Bulla axcã ypan ylhuitzin S. Miguel archãgel vmpa omanato teopan S. Fran^{co}. niman yehuatzin vmpa yn yomatzinco [*p. 233*] Quimanillito yn omoteneuhtzino teotica[5] tlahtohuani arcobispo.[6] mochi quimotlalilitia yn teotlatquitl yn itlahtocamahuiznechichihualtzin conmotlalilitia yn iMitratzin yhuan Capa quimotlalilitia yc yancuicã quinmottititzino yn muchintin nican altepehuaque auh ytloctzinco mantiaque yn Doctor Saucedo arcediano yhuan Doctor Don Juan de Salamanca chantre capa quitlalitiaque —

v Axcan Domingo ynic .10. mani Metztli Nouiembre de 1613 años. yhcuac oncan huey teopan yglesia mayor Mexico oteochihualloc macoc yn teoyotica ytlahtocayotzin yn cenca mahuiztilliloni Maestro Don fray Diego de contreras. ynic arçobispo muchiuhtzino. ynin teopixqui S. Augustin auh vmpa pouhqui vmpa ytequitzin motlalia vmpa mohuicaz quimopialitiuh yn altepetl ayhtic yn motenehua S. Domingo la ysla, ynin nican motlacatilli nican tepiltzin Mexico criyoyo. auh yehuatzin oquimoteochihuilli yn cenca mahuiztililoni Don Juan Perez de la Serna arçobispo Mexico. quimopalehuillique yn Doctor Saucedo arcediano yhuan Doctor Don Juan de Salamanca chantre Mitra quitlallique yhuan capa de Choro. auh yPadrinotzin muchiuh yn tlahtohuani visurrey Don diego fernandez de cordoua Marques de Guadalcaçar —

v Axcan Domingo ynic 17. mani Metztli Nouiembre de 1613. años. yhcuac yn omachiztic ỹ nican Mexico. in yehuatzin teoyotica tlahtohuani Don Juan Peres de la Serna arçobispo Mexico omentin clerigos S. Pedro ypilhuãtzitzin quinmihualia cecen yn ompa ypan ome alte[*p. 234*]petl ce tetzcoco conmotlalilia ynic ompa teoyotica Sacramentotica[7] quinmocuitlahuitiuh yn ixquichtin vmpa onoque yn ompa chanchihua españoles. aocmo yehuantin frayles teoyotica Sacramentotica quinmocuitlahuizque quĩmoquixtililia yn españoles. auh ça techixcahuizq̃ yn frayles timacehualti techmocuitlahuizque. ce tullocan conmotlalilia clerigo. ynic no vmpa teoyotica Sacramentotica quinmocuitlahuitiuh españoles ca no çenca miequintin yn õpa onoque. ça çe ynic ye nohuian yn izquican ypan huehuey altepetl yn itlapacholpantzinco arçobispo Mexco[8] in motenehua Arçobispado. yn ipan izquican in omoteneuh huehuey altepetl yn campa cenca ye miectin onoque españoles in ye ompa chanonoque nohuiyan vmpa yntlan cecen clerigos quimonmotlaliliznequi ynic

1. For "Maesescuela."
2. Presumably this means he was born in Mexico (Tenochtitlan).
3. For "mahuiztililoni teoyotica."
4. Although this passage seems not to make sense, very likely Quiroz had gone back briefly to Spain to negotiate for his new position after a long time in New Spain.

both of these people from Spain, and also brought from Spain the maestrescuela,[1] named don Melchor Aríndez, who belongs to Mexico here.[2] And at the same time there came all together from Spain: the very reverend spiritual[3] ruler doctor Juan Gutiérrez Flores, lesser inquisitor, [one of the] protectors of the perfect right belief, the faith, here in Mexico; also at that time arrived the main inquisitor, Gutierre Bernardo de Quiroz, who has been here for a long time, so that they were both installed together.[4] // Also at the same time there reached Mexico here and came for the first time the new corregidor who came from Spain, named don Alonso Tello de Guzmán; at that time don Martín Cerón, the former corregidor, relinquished his office; [Tello de Guzmán] replaced him on arrival. —

v Today, Sunday the 29th of the month of September, the fourth day after the said spiritual leader don Juan Pérez de la Serna, archbishop, reached Mexico here, was when a procession, today on the feast day of San Miguel Arcángel went to the church of San Francisco to get a papal bull. The said spiritual[5] ruler, the archbishop,[6] went there in person [*p. 233*] to get it. He went wearing all the holy gear, his splendid attire as a ruler; he went wearing his miter and cape, which is how he showed himself for the first time to all the citizens of the altepetl here. Next to him went doctor Salcedo, the archdeacon, and doctor don Juan de Salamanca, the choirmaster, wearing capes. —

v Today, Sunday the 10th of the month of November of the year 1613, was when at the great church, the cathedral of Mexico, the very reverend master [of theology] don fray Diego de Contreras was consecrated and given the spiritual rulership by which he became archbishop. He is an Augustinian friar, and he is assigned to, his office is established in, he will go to take charge of the altepetl out in the ocean called Santo Domingo de la Isla. He was born here, he is the child of people here in Mexico, a criollo. The very reverend don Juan Pérez de la Serna, archbishop of Mexico, consecrated him; doctor Salcedo, the archdeacon, and doctor don Juan de Salamanca, choirmaster, assisted him. They put on him the miter and the choir cape. The lord viceroy don Diego Fernández de Córdoba, Marqués of Guadalcázar, became his sponsor. —

v Today, Sunday the 17th of the month of November of the year 1613, was when it became known here in Mexico that the spiritual ruler don Juan Pérez de la Serna, archbishop in Mexico, is sending out two secular priests, children of San Pedro, one of them each to two altepetl. [*p. 234*] One he is stationing in Tetzcoco to take care of all the Spaniards who live there and make their homes there in matters of the holy sacraments;[7] no longer are the friars to take care of them in matters of the sacraments, he is taking the Spaniards away from them. The friars will deal exclusively with us commoners and take care of us. One secular priest he is stationing in Toluca, so that he too will take care of the Spaniards there with the holy sacraments, for there are a great many who live there, and everywhere all around in all the large altepetl in the area ruled by the archbishop in Mexico,[8] called the archbishopric, in all the said large altepetl, where a great many Spaniards live and have already established homes there, he wants to station a secular

5. For "teoyotica."
6. For "arçobispo."
7. The words "teoyotica" and "Sacramentotica" are probably synonymous here.
8. For "Mexico."

teoyotica Sacramentotica quinmocuitlahuitihui españoles. ca çan ic pehua yn axcan omachiztic ynic çan oc omentin quinmihualia clerigos ce tetzcoco conmotlalilia yhuan ce tullocan conmotlalilia. auh yn oquimatque yn yn ixquichtin frayles ỹ Fran^cos. yn Dominigos. yn Augustinos. cenca yc omotequipachoque. ynic niman pleyto oquimotlalililique arçobispo. yn oncan audiencia real ymixpantzinco yn Visurrey yhuan oydores omotlalli yn pleyto ye quinemiltia ye quitepotztoca yn iexcampayxti cecenyaca cecemme frayles Procuradores. in ye quinamiqui arçobispo. in ye quimocuitlahuia Pleyto. amo quinequi ynic cecen clerigos ye quinmihualiznequi nohuiyampa ypã arçobispado motlalitihui contraticion yc ye quichihua ỹ frayles. ach quen tzonquiçaz yn inneteylhuil tla oc yehuatzin quimomachiltia yn tt^o. Dios. ca oc ye nemi yn tlahtolli

v Axcan Domingo ynic 24. mani metztli Nouiembre [*p. 235*] de 1613 años. yhcuac oncan teopan S. Augustin omacoc palio yn cenca mahuiztililoni teoyotica tlahtohuani maestro Don fr diego de contreras arçobispo yn ompa ayhtic S. Domingo la ysla. yehuatzin oncan in yacolpan quimotlalililico in palio in cenca mahuiztililoni teoyotica tlahtohuani Don Juã Perez de la Serna arcobispo[1] Mexico. cenca huey tlamahuiztililiztica yn quimotlalilili ca yuh monequi ynin motenehua Palio. ynic tlachiuhtli yuhquin ma çan nelpiloni ypan pohui yn motenehua faxas tepitoton achi onmapilli ynic patlahuac yn moteca quiyahualiuhcaahcitoc yn necoccampa acollipa auh yn itepotzco tlanepantla yn icampa achi hueyac cemiztitl[2] ynic huiac. auh yn ixpan çã ye no yxquich huiac ca tell achiton ynic tepiton, auh ynon yuhqui nelpilloni faxas quicepanpachohua yn acolli yn ica oc cequi faxas yn quiyahuallotoc ytepotzco quechtli, auh ytech quipia ytech tlatlalili ey tepozhuitzmalotl agujas, ahnoço alfileres ca quihtonequi[3] quinezcayotia tlamahuiçolli. auh yn ipipilcaya palio ytech quipia ytech cahca quezquitetl telolotontí temetztli amo huel yztac teocuitlatl yez. auh yhuan ytech quipia ytech cahca cruz chichiltic chicuacen ynitlamellauhyan auh çan ome tlatlapotzco çan itech tlatlamachiuhtli. ynin miec ytech ca quinezcayotia miec teotlamahuiçolli. auh yece yn huel ye tachcauh ynic huey ynic tlateomania[4] cerimonia yn ica arçobispo ytto ynic mahuiztillillo ca yehuatl yca yn palio quitlalia quinemitia auh amo çan ixquich yehuatl ycel yn quihualhuica. ca çan no yhuatl[5] yn Patriarcha yhuan yn motenehua primato auh ca yn ixquich yc huey yn Palio. ca ayac aquin huel quimotocayotiz Patriarcha ahnoço primato. ahnoço Arçobispo ỹtlacamo achtopa quipiaz yn Palio, amo huel ypampa ye quichichihuaz yn iteoyotica yteopixcatlahtocatequiuh[6] in manel çan obispo tlateochihualli amo no huel teotequitiz, yhuã yntla ce tlacatl yc opepenaloc ynic arçobispo omochiuh nican Mexico [*p. 236*] auh yn itech pouhqui nican Sancta yglesia palio maco ỹ nican yancuic arcobispo[7] omotlalli, auh yntla mopatlaz nican mexico arçobispo. yntla oc cecni conicuanicã çan no arçobispoyotl ypan ỹtla ompa ayhtic S. Domingo la ysla, anoço manilla china, ca yuh mihtohua ca quicuitiuh quicelitiuh yn ompa yancuic teopan Sancta yglesia oc ce yancuic palio, auh amo no huel mochihuaz inic ye quicuitaciz ytech quimopohuiliz quitlaliz amo yc huel teoyotica teopixcatlahtocatiz. yn

1. For "arçobispo."
2. Distance between outstretched thumb and forefinger.
3. For "quihtoznequi."
4. Reflexive *teomania* is in Molina's dictionary as "to contemplate, meditate, pray." Perhaps the meaning is that the ceremony induces people to holy thoughts, or simply is impressive, making them think.

priest among them in each place everywhere to take care of the Spaniards with the holy sacraments. It only begins with what was announced today, that for now he is sending only two secular priests, stationing one in Tetzcoco and one in Toluca. When all the friars, the Franciscans, Dominicans, and Augustinians found out about this, they were very worried by it, so that they brought suit against the archbishop in the Royal Audiencia; the suit was brought in the presence of the viceroy and the civil judges; all three groups [of friars] are now involved in it and following it up, each one with its friar as legal representative, opposing the archbishop and taking care of the lawsuit; they do not want that he should try to send out a secular priest who would go to be stationed in each place all around the archbishopric, and the friars contradict it. Who knows how their complaint will end? Only our lord God knows, for the case is still pending.

v Today, Sunday the 24th of the month of November [*p. 235*] of the year 1613, was when in the church of San Agustín the very reverend spiritual ruler the master of theology don fray Diego de Contreras, archbishop out in the ocean, at Santo Domingo de la Isla, was given a pallium. The very reverend spiritual ruler don Juan Pérez de la Serna, archbishop[1] in Mexico, came to place the pallium on his shoulders; he did it with very great ceremony, for so it must be. This item called a pallium is made as follows: it can be looked upon almost as something you tie around you, [consisting of] what they call small sashes, about two inches wide, which spread out so that they reach around the shoulders on both sides; in the back, in the middle, it is rather long, a span[2] long, and in front it is the same length, but a bit smaller. And that thing like a sash to tie around one entirely covers the shoulders with other strips that go around the back of the neck. It has on it, placed on it, three metal needles or pins which mean[3] and signify miracles, and hanging down from it it has and there are on it a few lead pellets, it does not seem to be real silver. It also has and there are on it some red crosses, six in front, and only two behind, embroidered on it; the many that are on it signify many miracles. Although the ceremony by which the archbishop is seen and honored is very preeminent in its greatness and [how it makes people contemplate],[4] because he wears and displays the pallium, it is not just he alone who wears one, but also[5] a patriarch and what is called a primate. So great is the pallium, that no one can be called patriarch, primate, or archbishop if he doesn't have the pallium first; for that reason he cannot carry out his various spiritual duties as priestly ruler.[6] Even though he has been consecrated just as a bishop, he cannot operate in spiritual matters either. And if a person has been chosen and appointed archbishop here in Mexico [*p. 236*] and the holy church here is assigned to him, the new archbishop[7] here is given a pallium when he is installed, but if the archbishop here in Mexico is replaced, if they move him to an archbishopric in another place, out in the ocean at Santo Domingo de la Isla, or Manila in China, it is said that when he gets to the new church he will get and receive another new pallium. Nor can it be done that he should on arrival take, that he should assign to himself, wear, and be able to be a spiritual priest-

5. For "yehuatl."

6. The words should run either "yn iteoyoticateopixcatlahtocatequiuh" or "yn teoyotica yteopixcatlahtocatequiuh."

7. For "arçobispo."

ipalio catca yn quihualtoquilli yntla omomiquilli arçobispo ocatca oncan, auh ca çã huel yancuican quitlaniz oc ce yancuil[1] palio. auh ca macoz auh yntlacamo, amo huel tepachoz am̃o huel tehuillanaz. amo huel ytlatititzaltlapachol[2] mochihuaz yn oc cequi altepetl in yehuatl on huey tzontecoaltepetl muchiuhtica yn oncan ca arçobispo motenehua Metropoli, yhuã amo no huel tenechicoz amo huel tecentlaliz yn teotlaneltililiznenonotzaliztli concilio yc muchihuaz, yhuan amo no huel oncan teteochihuaz yn teopixcayotica. yn ipan Arçobispado yniqu iuh teoyotica tetzonteco oncan Sancta yglesia. ca yn aqui ye omochiuh Arçobispo. ca niman quimitlanililiz yn palio Sancto Padre. huel yehuatl yaz. anoço ytepantlahtocauh yprocurador çan quititlaniz çan ixquich ica chicuacenmetztli quihualhuiquilizq̃ palio auh ynin ca huel yacica ytzonmanca[3] ỹ arcobispoyotl —

v Auh çan acame çan quezquintin yn obisposme oncate y quitlalia yn quinemiltia çan teycneliliztica yn palio yn iuh yehuatl vmpa obispo yn itocayocan luca ypan tlalli Italia, yhuã yehuatl yn obispo Pauia ypan tlalli Lõbardia, auh yn ipan tlalli Alemania yehuatl yn obispo ytocayocan Bãberga, yhuã in yehuatl obispo vmpa ytocayocan Ostiense yntla huel yehuatzin Sancto Padre ymaticatzinco quimoteochihuillia, auh yn francia yehuatl yn obispo ytocayocan Eduense auh amo huel quitlalizq̃ yn yehuãtin in obisposme yn manel yehuãtin Arçobisposme yn palio yntlacamo çan huell oncan ynteteopan yn intlatlapacholpan yhuã amo quezquipa. auh ca çan huel ye yzquipa ypã yazq̃. ynic huel quitlalizque [*p. 237*] Yn iuh quinmotlatlalilia quinmocuaxochtilia yn itech quihualhuica ytech yetihuitz yn iamatehuelitiliztzin yn iamatlacuiloltehuelitiliznemactzin Sancto Padre ynic çan ic cen quihualhuica palio yn ihcuac quinmotitlanililia, auh yn amo huel oncan yc quipanahuizq̃. yn izquilhuipan machiyotic ca yhcuac yn quimochihuilitihui missa yn ica ynteotlatquitlahtocanechichihualtzin motenehua hornamentos Pontifical —

v Axcan Sabado ynic .30. mani Metztli Nouiembre de 1613. años yhcuac ypan ylhuitzin S. Andres Apostol yn oncan teopan S. Fran^co^. yc omotemachtilli yn padre fr. Buenauentura de paredes Guardian nican Mexico. oquinmomachiztilli yn españoles ynic ompa españa ohualla huelitiliztli licencia yn ipampa yn aquique namiqueque[4] quinequi moyollehuazque vezinoz mexico. huel macozque yn habito. yn oncan teopan S. Fran^co^. quicuiquihui ypan çan inchanchan[5] yc quimotlayecoltilizque yn tt^o^. dios. yn iuh tlamani vmpa españa. auh macihui yn centlamantli ỹ yc neci omoteneuh habito. yn axcan yc omotemachtilli Padre Guardian macozque namiqueque yece ca çan no ytetzinco pouhqui çan ye no yhabitotzin yn totlaçottatzin S. Fran^co^ quitocayotia yc quinotza la horden de la Penitencia yhuã ynic ontlamantli quitocayotia la tercera horden de S. Fran^co^ yn ompa castillan quintocayotia tercerones. miec yn inmonasterios vmpa quipia yn aquin quinequi motzacuaz quimotlayecoltiliz tt^o^. dios teopan çan intlanequiliztica yn iuh muchihua motzacua. auh ỹ nican Mexico ynic motlalizque ynic quicuizque ynin omoteneuh tlaquentli yn aquin quinequi ynin quitepotztocaz. yn iuhqui yn teotlamahuiztiliznemiliztli, ca yehuatzin quinmomaquili[*p. 238*]tiaz yn habito yn omoteneuhtzino Padre Guardian yhuan no yehuatzin quinmopachilhuiz. auh yn ihcuac ỹ ca çan oqu icel ye quipia ye quimaquia yn habito yn quitocayotia hermano Alfonso la Tercera horden de S. Fran^co^. ynin hualla españa —

1. For "yancuic."
2. This word has an unusual *ltl* sequence, but Ch. does write it occasionally.
3. The form "ytzonmanca" has not been satisfactorily identified or analyzed, casting doubt on the exact meaning of this clause.

ly ruler with the pallium of the former archbishop there, whom he succeeded, if he has passed away. He has to start all over requesting another new[1] pallium. It will be given to him, but if not, he cannot rule and govern, the other altepetl cannot become his jurisdiction,[2] that is, a great head-altepetl where an archbishop is, called a metropolis. Nor can he gather and assemble people to make a consultation for verifying divine matters, a council. Nor can he ordain priests in the archbishopric as spiritual head in the holy church there. For whoever is appointed archbishop is right away to request the pallium from the holy Father; he himself will go, or he will just send someone to speak for him, his legal representative, and within six months they will bring him back the pallium, and this is the true completion and final touch[3] of the archbishopric. —

v There are just a few bishops who wear and display the pallium by special privilege, like the bishop at the place called Lucca in the land of Italy, and the bishop of Pavia in the land of Lombardy, and in the land of Germany the bishop of the place called Bamberg, and the bishop of the place called Ostia, if the holy Father in person consecrates him by his own hand, and in France the bishop at the place called Autun. But those bishops, and even archbishops, cannot wear the pallium unless they are right where their churches are, in their various jurisdictions, and not just sometimes, but each time they go in it and can wear it, [*p. 237*] it is as the holy Father establishes it for them and sets borders for them in his written authorization, the documentary permission granted by him, that they bring along with and comes with the pallium at the same time it is sent to them, and they cannot exceed the number of days designated for them to go to perform mass with the holy gear that makes their ruler's attire, called pontifical ornaments. —

v Today, Saturday the 30th of the month of November of the year 1613, on the feast day of San Andrés Apóstol, was when at the church of San Francisco father fray Buenaventura de Paredes, father guardian here in Mexico, preached about and announced to the Spaniards that permission had come from Spain that married people,[4] citizens of Mexico, who want to and are so inclined, can be given the habit. They will come to the church of San Francisco to get it, but they will serve our lord God with it just at their various residences,[5] as is the custom in Spain. Although the said habit about which the father guardian just preached and which will be given to married people has a single appearance, the habit of our precious father San Francisco also belongs to what they call the order of Penitence, and secondly to what they call the Tercera Orden de San Francisco, that in Spain they call Tercerones; they have many monasteries there; for whoever wants to be enclosed and serve our lord God in church, if such is his will it is done and he is enclosed. Here in Mexico, as to how those who want to follow such a life of honoring the divine will have arrangements made and wear the said garment, [*p. 238*] the said father guardian will go along giving them the habit and he will also guide them. At present there is still only one person who has and wears the habit, whom they call brother Alfonso of the Tercera Orden de San Francisco; he came from Spain. —

---

4. The Nahuatl is not specific as to the gender of the married people; an entry for the beginning of 1615 (pp. 294–95) makes it clear that they were both men and women.

5. For "inchachan" or "inchahchan."

1614.[1] .v. Tochtli xihuitl yn ipan in xihuitl çan ya oc yehuatl Gouernador yn Juan Perez de monterrey ỹ nican tenochtitlan Auh yn Alldesme motlallique S. Juan Moyotlan çan quitlamellahualti yn diego de S. franco. chane tequicaltitlan. yhuan Balthasar hernandez chane xihuitonco. ynin quininyopa allde omuchiuh // auh yn alldesme motlalliq̃ S Pablo teopan franco Martin chane çoquipan. yhuan Pablo Damian chane ometochtitlan // auh yn alldesme motlallique S. Sebastian atzacualco Melchior xuarez chane tomatla çan quitlamellahualti yn alldeyotl yhuan Sebastian Miguel chane cuitlatlahuactonco.[2] // auh yn alldesme motlalliq̃ Sancta maria cuepopan çan quitlamellahualti yn xp̄oual pascual chane copolco yhuan diego xuarez chane tlocalpan ynin ayac ceme y ytechcopa quiça ỹ nican mexico tlahtocatlacamecayotl —

v Axcan Lunes ynic .13. mani Metztli henero de 1614 años. yhcuac yohuatzinco ỹ omixiuh yn cihuapilli Virreyna Doña Mariana Riedre Marquesa. cihuatl yn quichiuh ytoca Doña brianda yc ome ypilhuantzitzin in ye quinchihua nican ciudad Mexico yn ipilhuantzitzin tlahtohuani Visurrey Don diego fernandez de cordoua Marques de guadalcaçar —

v Axcan Sabado ynic 18. mani metztli henero de 1614 años. yhcuac muchiuh Capitulo. yn xuchmilco. yehuatzin oncan [*p. 239*] quiz muchiuhtzino prouincial yn cenca mahuiztililoni Padre fr. Juan de torquemada, quipatlac oncan quicauh yn itequiuh fr. hernando Duran ynic prouincial catca —

v Axcan Domingo ynic .2. mani Metztli febrero de 1614 años. yhcuac huel ypan ylhuitzin totlaçonantzin de la furipicacion de la candelaria yohualtica ypan ce tzillini ynic ye tlathuitiuh axcan omoteneuh Domingo yn oquitlallique oncan escuellas real ynic oquimacaque yn latintlahtolcopa yn teoamoxtemachtilamapohualiztli yn Padre maestro fr. Gonçalo de hermosillo. teopixqui S. Augustin ynic Cathetradico de escriptura omochiuh yxiptla ypatca muchiuh ỹ yn cenca mahuiztililoni teoyotica tlahtohuani maestro Don fr. diego de contreras arçobispo omochiuhtzino yn ompa ayhtic S. Domingo la ysla, cathetradico moyetzticatca, auh yn omoteneuh Padre maestro fr. Goçalo de hermosillo ynic quicuic huel yaoyotica yn ayc yuhqui oyttoc in ye yxquich ica onca escuella Mexico. auh ynic huel omacoc çan iceltzin quimopallehuilli, yn tlahtohuani Visurrey.[3] ahço huel caxtolilhuitl[4] yn momuztlaye yc nenque tlapohuaya oc cequintin Doctoresme teopixque clerigos. in motlatzohuilique oc cenca. yehuatl ynehuan monamiquia yn fr. ______ Sisneros comendador yn totlaçonantzin nuestra Señora de las mercedes de Redempcion de Captivos. yntepachocauh yn iztac habito quimotlalilia teopixque ynin huel yehuatl macozquia yn omoteneuh la catreda. ypampa muchintin ypan mocuepaya quimopalehuiliaya. yn audiencia real tlaca tlahtoque oydores. ynic yehuatl yez. cualli ynic tlapouh latintlamachiliztica, auh yece ach quenin ça conchiuhque ynic concuillique Sisneros auh yn omoteneuh [*p. 240*] Padre fr. Goçalo de hermosillo, ye omihto ca çan iceltzin quimopalehuilli yn tlahtohuani Visurrey yhuan miequintin clerigos estudiantes. Auh in ye o yuh quiz in ye o yuh motlalli omoteneuh fr. Goçalo de hermosillo cathetradico. in yohualtica niman yhcuac peuh in ye tlatzitzillica vmpa teopan S. Augustin, yhuan yn izquican yc cate Mexico

---

1. The number is preceded by a precontact-style frame with a rabbit inside and five dots above.

2. For "cuitlahuactonco."

1614,[1] 5 Rabbit Year. In this year the governor here in Tenochtitlan was still Juan Pérez de Monterrey. The alcaldes installed for San Juan Moyotlan were Diego de San Francisco, from Tequicaltitlan, who went straight on from before, and Baltasar Hernández, from Xihuitonco, who became alcalde for the first time. // And the alcaldes who were installed for San Pablo Teopan were Francisco Martín from Çoquipan and Pablo Damián from Ometochtitlan. // And the alcaldes who were installed for San Sebastián Atzaqualco were Melchor Juárez, from Tomatla, who kept straight on with the position of alcalde, and Sebastián Miguel, from Cuitlahuactonco.[2] // And the alcaldes who were installed for Santa María Cuepopan were Cristóbal Pascual from Copolco, who went straight on from before, and Diego Juárez from Tlocalpan. None of them comes from the royal line here in Mexico. —

v̲ Today, Monday the 13th of the month of January of the year 1614, early in the morning, was when the lady virreine, doña Mariana Riderer, marquesa, gave birth. It was a girl that she had, named doña Brianda, the second child she has had here in the city of Mexico by the lord viceroy don Diego Fernández de Córdoba, Marqués of Guadalcázar. —

v̲ Today, Saturday the 18th of the month of January of the year 1614, was when a provincial chapter meeting [of the Franciscans] was held at Xochimilco. [*p. 239*] The very reverend father fray Juan de Torquemada turned out to be made provincial head there; he replaced fray Hernando Durán, who at that point relinquished his former post as provincial head. —

v̲ Today, Sunday the 2nd of the month of February of the year 1614, right on the feast day of our precious mother of Purificación de Candelaria, at 1 o'clock at night on the morning of today, the said Sunday, was when at the royal school they installed the father master fray Gonzalo de Hermosillo, Augustinian friar, and gave him the lecturing of the holy book in the Latin language, so that he became holder of the chair of scripture. He took the place of and became the replacement of the very reverend spiritual ruler master don fray Diego de Contreras, who was appointed archbishop out in the ocean at Santo Domingo de la Isla and held the chair previously. And the said father master fray Gonzalo de Hermosillo took [the post] with great strife, the like of which has never been seen ever since there has been a school in Mexico. For [the post] to be able to be given to him, only the lord viceroy helped him.[3] Perhaps for a full fifteen days[4] other doctors, friars and secular priests, were involved in daily lecturing and disputing with each other. The two especially contending with each other were [Hermosillo] and fray [Luis] de Cisneros, comendador of our precious mother Nuestra Señora de las Mercedes de la Redención de Cautivos, superior of the friars who wear the white habit. It was really he who was going to be given the said chair, because all the people of the Royal Audiencia, the lords judges, went over to him and were aiding him so that he would be the one, so well did he lecture in Latin lore. But somehow they managed to take it from Cisneros. The said [*p. 240*] father fray Gonzalo de Hermosillo, as was already said, was helped only by the lord viceroy and many secular priests who were students. And after the said fray Gonzalo de Hermosillo emerged and was installed as the holder of the chair, right then in the night the bells began to peal at the church of San Agustín and at all the places in Mexico where

3. Consider, however, what is said further below.
4. I.e., two weeks, a fortnight.

teopixque S. Augustin yn S. Pablo ỹ S. Sebastian yn Sancta cruz. contzinco, auh teotlac ypan ome tzillini yn oquihualquixtique oncan escuellas ynic oquiteyttitique nohuiyan ohtlipan caltzallan mexico ypã cauallo yn oquipassealoltique ỹnepantla quihuicaque ỹ frayles S. Augustin yhuan miequintin españoles yuhquin çan locoti yc nenque yuh cemilhuitl yn tlatzitzillicac S. Augustin ynic pahpacohuac —

v Axcan yc ome Viernes quaresma ynic 21. mani Metztli Febrero de 1614 años. yhcuac teotlac nahui tzillini ypan tlaco hora, yn oncan teopan S. Augustin, oquiz yãcuic oc ce tlayahualoliztli procession yn momecahuitecque españoles. ypilhuantzitzin ỹ mocentlamachtiani S. Nicolas de tolentino. ynin cofradia yehuantin oquitlallique yn cacahuanamacaque cacavateros[1] españoles. auh yn ipan in tlayahualoliztli procession cenca huey yancuic tetlaocoliliztli Jubileo oncan oncatca mocnopilhui hualla Roma, auh niman cenca miequintin yn españoles yn oncan oquizque yn omohuitecque yn oquinoquique ymezço. auh nahui ynEstandarte tliltic tlayacantiaque ome yztac teocuitlatl plata [*p. 241*] Yn icruzyo[2] tlanepantla mantiaq̃. auh necoc ỹtloc mantiaque quintzatzacuitiaq̃. yn oc ome omoteneuh estandarte çan cuahuitl tecuitlayo[3] yn icruzyo, yc niman contoquillitia ce cruz manca tliltic bordado yztac teocuitlatl plata yn icruzyo, yc niman conmotoquilitia ce crucifixo cenca tlaçotli mahuiztic cenca miec indulgencias ytetzinco mocnopilhuia, yc niman yehuatzin conmotoquilitia ynPadron S. Nicolas de Tolentino motlancuaquetzinotiuh motlactlacopetlahuiltihtiuh. ynic tlachiuhtzintli momecahuitectzinotiuh yhuã ce ymaticatzinco quimotzitzquilitiuh ce crucifixo tepitzin, yc niman conmotoquilitia ce cruz huiyac Cuauhxihxipocho. ahnoço cuauhtzotzocollo[4] ce yztac paño ytech pilcatia, yc niman conmotoquilitia yn lignun cruz. in huel ye ytech momiquilitzino tt^o^. dios. andastica quimonapalhuitiaque yn teopixque yca palio cuachcaltica quimocaltilitiaque, auh tecpan quiyahuac huel palacio yxpan quiçato yn tlayahualloliztli ynic oncan quimottilliq̃ ventana hualmoquetzinoque yn tlahtohuani Visurrey ynehuãtzin yn inamictzin cihuapilli Marquesa. yc niman yglesia mayor quiçato ỹ tlayahualoliztli. niman S. Domingo quiçato, niman S. lurenço monjas quiçato. nimã concepcion monjas quiçato, niman S.ta isabel monjas quiçaco, nimã S. Fran^co^ quiçaco, niman oncan quiçaco yn Colegio de las niñas ynic niman no ceppa ocallaquico yn oncan S. Augustin huey tlayahualloliztli yn omuchiuh axcan —

v Axcan Sabado ynic .i. mani metztli Março de 1614 años yhcuac yancuican nican Mexico omopix pialli omuchiuh [*p. 242*] Yn ilhuitzin mocentlamachtiani Angel cotodio. totepixcatzin ytencopatzinco ytlanahuatilticatzin yn santo padre Paulo quinto. yntlaytlanilizticatzinco quimitlanililique yn españa tlahtoque Reyes Don Felipe tercero. yhuan yn inamictzin omoyetzticatca huey cihuapilli Doña Margarida de Austria. auh ynic nican Mexico yglesia mayor ynic yancuican omochihu in ylhuitl yehuatzin missa quimihtalhui yn cenca mahuiztililoni teoyotica tlahtohuani arcobispo[5] Mexico Don Juan Perez de la serna —

v Axcan Martes ynic .4. mani Metztli Março de 1614 años. yhcuac ye no ceppa ahcico callaquico ỹ nican ihtic ciudad Mexico. in yehuantin Japon[6] tlaca pipiltin tlacauallohuia

---

1. Today *cacahuateros* sell peanuts, but the Nahuatl seems clear that cacao is meant here. Cacao was also very important in the economy of that time.

2. Crossing elements? *Cruz* when possessed does not usually take the suffix *-yo*, so the meaning must be somewhat different here.

3. They could equally well have been covered with silver.

there are Augustinian friars, at San Pablo, San Sebastián, and Santa Cruz Contzinco. And at 2 o'clock in the afternoon they brought him out of the school and showed him in public; they paraded him about on the roads and streets of Mexico on a horse; the Augustinian friars and many Spaniards took him in their midst; they went about like crazy people. The bells rang all day at San Agustín in celebration. —

v Today, the second Friday of Lent, the 21st of the month of February of the year 1614, in the afternoon at half past four o'clock, was when another new procession came out of the church of San Agustín, in which some Spaniards, children of the greatly blessed San Nicolás de Tolentino, scourged themselves. This cofradía was established by the Spanish sellers of cacao.[1] And in this procession a very great new indulgence, the jubilee, was attained; it came from Rome. Very many Spaniards who came out there scourged themselves and spilled their blood. Four black standards went in the lead; two with [crosspieces][2] of silver [*p. 241*] went in the middle, and on both sides next to them went and enclosed them the other two said standards, whose [crosspieces] were just of gilded wood.[3] Following them went a black cross with embroidered ornament, with a silver crosspiece; after that followed a very precious and splendid crucifix; very many indulgences are attained through it. After that followed their patron San Nicolás de Tolentino, made so that he went kneeling and half baring his upper body, scourging himself, and in one hand he went grasping a small crucifix. After that followed a long cross [with bumps or bulges on the wood?],[4] with a white cloth hanging down from it. After that followed a piece of the *lignum crucis*, of the very [cross] on which our lord God died; the friars went carrying it on a platform, sheltering it with a canopy, a cloth covering. The procession went by the governmental palace, right in front of it, so that the lord viceroy together with his spouse the lady marquesa saw it, coming to stand at a window. Next the procession went by the cathedral, then it went by Santo Domingo, then it went by the nunnery of San Lorenzo, then it went by the nunnery of Concepción, then it came by the nunnery of Santa Isabel, then it came by San Francisco, then it came by the Colegio de las Niñas, and then it came into San Agustín again. It was a great procession that was carried out today. —

v Today, Saturday the 1st of the month of March of the year 1614, was when for the first time here in Mexico there was observed and celebrated [*p. 242*] the feast day of the greatly blessed Guardian Angel, our custodian, by order and command of the holy Father Paul V and at the petition of the rulers and monarchs of Spain, don Felipe III and his late spouse the great lady doña Margarita de Austria, who requested it of [the pope]. Since it was the first time the feast day was celebrated here at the cathedral in Mexico, the very reverend spiritual ruler the archbishop[5] in Mexico, don Juan Pérez de la Serna, said mass. —

v Today, Tuesday the 4th of the month of March of the year 1614, was when again there arrived here and entered inside the city of Mexico those Japanese[6] nobles; they came in on

4. See in Molina *quauhtzotzocolli*, *tzotzocolli*, and *xixipachoa*.
5. For "arçobispo."
6. "Jabon?" It seems that in this and other instances of this word below, an attempt was made to change *p* to *b*. Yet it is hard to be certain which was written first. In the following, it has often involved an arbitrary decision whether to write "Jabon" or "Japon."

ynic callaquico ypan matlactlomome tzillini nepantla ca yn tonatiuh, auh quinhualyacantiaque yn inmacehualhuã[1] çan huallacxipanhuitiaque yn quihuallacoctiaque yuhquin cuauhpiaztotonti tliltic cuix ynlanças. tle ynon quinezcayotia. amo nel tlahtocateyacanoni vmpa in Jabon.[2] auh çan iuh hualchichiuhtiaque yn iuh nemi yn iuh vmpa muchichihua ynchan yn iuhqui turga[3] quitlallia ypan mucuitlalpia yhuan yn intzon yncuexcochtlan quilpia. çan oc cenpohualtin in yn axcan nican oahcico: mexico. auh oc otlihpan quihualcauhque in yehuatl teuhctitlantli yn Embaxador yn ititlan yn quihualtitlani vmpa huey tlahtohuani Emperador Japon oqu ihuiyantzin ye yatihuitz. macuilpohualli yn imacehualhuan Jabunti quinhualhuicac auh ce tottatzin descalço teopixqui S. Fran^co^ yn quinnahuatlahtalhuitihuitz. ynin quin ic oppa oncan Acapulco catenquixtico yn imacal Japonti çan muchi[4] [*p. 243*] Tepuztli yn quihualitqui yhuan escriturios. yhuan cequi tilmahtli ỹ nican quinamacazque, no oncan in ohualla yn ihtic omoteneuh Jabon acalli yn Señor Sebastian Vizcayno español vezino Mexico. yn onhuiya otlachiato vmpa Jabun yn queninamican quinhuicaca yn ompa huitza axcan ya yexihuitl oc centlamantin Jabonti yn quinhualhuicaca Don Rodrigo de Viuero yn ompa Gouernadortito. ypan ciudad Manilla china. oc no yhuiyantzin ye yatihuitz mococotihuitz. yn omoteneuh Señor Sebastian Vizcayno quicocoque ynic oncan acapulco quimictique quixillia yn Jabonti. yuh machiztico ỹ nican Mexico ypampa yn ixquich tlamantli vmpa ypial hualmuchiuhtihuia yn tleỹ tetech axihualloni yn tetonaltilloni quihualmahmacac vmpa huey tlahtohuani Emperador. ynic quinhualmotlapalhuia Quinhualmotonaltilia Santo padre Roma moyetztica yhuan tohueytlahtocatzin Rey españa moyetztica, yhuan nican Mexico moyetztica tlahtohuani Visurrey. yn innemactzin yn intonaltzin mochi yehuatl ypialtzin hualmochiuhtihuia huel ymac quihuallali ynic nican caxitiquiuh auh yn amo yehuatl quimacac amo yehuatl ypial hualmochiuhtia yn omoteneuh Embaxador —

v Axcan lunes cuaresma ynic 17. mani Metztli Março de 1614 años. quin ihcuac ypan in nican Mexico ahcico ocallaquico yn omoteneuh Señor Sebastian Vizcayno vezino Mexico. yn onhuiya Japon yn oquicahuato omoteneuhque oc centlamantin achtopa nican Mexico onhuitza Japon tlaca. yexiuhtica yn omocuepaco Señor Sebastian vizcayno. ynic oquinhualhuicac oc ceppa cequintin Jabon tlaca [*p. 244*] Yhuan ce teuhctitlantli ye omoteneuh Embaxador huey tlacatl. yn hualmotitlani —

v Axcan Lunes Sancto ynic 24. mani Metztli Março de 1614 a^os^. ye quin ihcuac yn ỹ nican yhtic ciudad Mexico oancico ocallaquico yn omoteneuh teuhctitlantli Embaxador yn ompa Japon ohualla S. Fran^co^ teopancaltitlan motlallico ce caltica ynin omoteneuh teuhctitlantli Embaxador yn iuh nican Mexico machiztic yuh mihto. yc quihualtitlani yn intlahtocauh Emperador Japon. vmpa yauh yn Roma. quimottiliz yn Sancto Padre Paulo quinto. yhuan quimomaquiliz. yntetlacamachiliz yn itechpa Sancta yglesia ynic chistianosme muchihuaznequi muchtin Japon tlaca mocuaatequizque ynic no teoyotica Sacramentotica ypilhuantzitzinhuan yezque tonantzin Sancta yglesia Romana, muchipa quimotlacamachiltizque teoyotica tlanelnoquiliztica, auh yn ihcuac tla ye oquinmocelili yn cemanahuac teoyotica huey cemichcapixqui Sancto Padre tocentepachocatzin totecemtenecuitlahuicatzin ca no yehuantin ychcatzitzinhuan yezque quinmottiliz quinmiximachiliz.

---

1. The clause could also be construed the opposite way, as meaning that they went leading their vassals.

2. This passage consists more literally of two questions, "What does that signify? Does it not (mean) . . .?" The term *tlatocateyacanoni* appears to be a nonactive instru-

horseback at 12 o'clock noon. Their vassals came ahead of them,[1] just coming on foot, holding high something like little long narrow black poles, maybe their lances; perhaps that signifies royal leadership there in Japan.[2] They came attired just the same way they go about and are attired back at home; they wear something like a tunic,[3] tied in the back, and they tie their hair at the backs of their necks. So far only twenty of them have reached Mexico here; they left behind, still coming along the way, the lordly emissary, the ambassador, the messenger sent here by the great ruler the emperor in Japan, who is still coming at his leisure, bringing a hundred of his Japanese vassals. One of our fathers, a Discalced Franciscan friar, comes interpreting for them. This is the second time that the Japanese have landed one of their ships on the shore at Acapulco; they are transporting here everything [*p. 243*] of[4] iron, and writing desks, and some cloth that they are to sell here. On the said Japanese ship came also señor Sebastián Vizcaíno, a Spaniard, citizen of Mexico, who had gone to Japan to look around, [since] he had taken back the other group of Japanese who had come from there three years ago now, whom don Rodrigo de Vivero, who went to be governor in the city of Manila in China, had brought here. The said señor Sebastián Vizcaíno is also still coming slowly, coming hurt; the Japanese injured him when they beat and stabbed him at Acapulco, as became known here in Mexico, because of all the things coming along that had been made his responsibility in Japan, that the great ruler there, the emperor, gave him to be gifts on arrival, with which from there he greets and makes presents to the holy Father who is in Rome, and the presents assigned to our great ruler the king who is in Spain and to the lord viceroy who is here in Mexico. All that had been made his responsibility, and the said emperor placed it in his hands to get [the things] here; he did not give [the duty] to the said ambassador and it was not made his responsibility. —

v Not until today, Monday, during Lent, the 17th of the month of March of the year 1614, did there reach Mexico here and enter it the said señor Sebastián Vizcaíno, citizen of Mexico, who had gone to Japan to deliver the other said group of Japanese who had come here to Mexico first. After three years señor Sebastián Vizcaíno returned, again bringing some Japanese [*p. 244*] and a lordly emissary, the said ambassador; it is a great personage who has been sent. —

v It was only today, Holy Monday, the 24th of the month of March of the year 1614, that there reached Mexico here and entered it the said lordly emissary, the ambassador, who came from Japan; he was settled in a house next to the church of San Francisco. It became known here in Mexico and was said that the reason their ruler the emperor in Japan sent this said lordly emissary and ambassador here is to go to Rome to see the holy Father, Paul V, and to give him their obedience concerning the holy church, so that all the Japanese want to become Christians; they are to be baptized, so that they will also be children of our mother the holy Roman Church in matters of the holy sacraments and will always obey it in matters of divinity and the faith. And when the great universal spiritual shepherd the holy Father, our universal governor and caretaker, has accepted them, they too will be his sheep. He will see and become acquainted with those who did not belong

mental agentive, "royal means of leading people," but possibly it could mean instead something to lead rulers, that is, some insignia to precede them.

3. See pp. 208–09 at n. 2.

4. Or nothing but.

yn amo yaxcatzitzinhuan yn amo quinmiximachiliaya yn çã campa opoliuhtinenca cuillotla çacatla yxtlahuacan tepetla omaçattitinenca yn axcan mocuepa hui yhuicpatzinco ynic quimiximachilizque yn huel nelli ychcapixqui cemanahuac ymactzinco motlalizque ynic no quinmopializ quinmopachilhuiz quinmocuitlahuitzinoz yn ica ypan mellavac cetiliztlaneltoquiliztli Sancta Fee Catholica ynic aocmo ceppa quimanaz diablo quinmaxcatiz. yn ica [*p. 245*] Tlateotoquiliztli yn tlacatecolonotzaliztli yn iuh axcan nomah ypan cate macihui in ye miectin vmpa oncate christianosme. auh ynin omoteneuh Embaxador ynic nican oahcico Mexico axcan ca çan nican onquiztiquiça çan quezquilhuitl nican motlaliz ynic quimotztilitiquiça tlahtohuani Visurre.[1] auh vmpa españa yhuã ypantzinco quiztiquiçaz yn tohueytlahtocatzin Rey Don Felipe Tercero. quimottiliz yhuan tlamatcayeliztli Paz. quimomaquiliz. ypampa yn intlahtocauh tlahtocati Emperadorti Japom ynic quinextia. ycniuhyotl tlamatcayeliztli cemihcac quihuallalia yn ihuicpatzinco Omoteneuhtzino Rey moyetztica españa. ynic ayc moyaochihuazque çan mochipa motlaçotlazque ynic huel nican Mexico puchtecatiquihui tlanamacaquihui Jabun tlaca. auh intla ye oconmutztilitiquiz Rey. inin Embaxador. ca niman yc nepa yaz Roma. yn iuh omoteneuh yxpantzinco ahciz quimottiliz. yn Sancto Padre ma quimonequiltitzino yn tt^{o}. dios. ma cualli yectli yc mochihua ma tlacenmatican ma ynpan nelti yn cualli yectli yn teocualtiliztli yn teoteyectililiztli gracia yn iuh quinequi, yn iuh quimoyollotia yntla huel nelli yncentlanequiliztica yc hui ma quinmopalehuillitzino ma quinmomaquixtilitzino yn tt^{o}. dios. yniqu ixpãtzinco huel yezque nemizque yollizque muchipa cemihcac Amen —

v̲ Axcan Juebes Sancto ynic 27. mani Metztli Março de 1614 años. yhcuac oc ce yancuic tlayahualloliztli processíon oncan oquiz yn Parrochia de la Vela cruz. [*p. 246*] ynin españoles. yhuan cequintin timacehualtin yn oncan oquitlallique yncofradia animastin yntech pohui. auh no huey yn oquiyahualloque yehuantin in. yglesia mayor. ahcico tlayacac mãtiaque. yn timacehualtin —

v̲ Axcan Lunes ynic .7. mani Metztli Abril de 1614 años yhcuac ỹ vpeuh ỹ nican Mexico. in ye quipopohua in ye quiçoquiquixtia ynic nohuiyan ypan yzqui acallotli. yhcac onoc nican yhtic ciudad Mexico ytencopatzinco tlahtohuani Visurrey ynic nohuiyampa altepehuaque ohuallaque oquichihuaco oquiyectico acallotli —

v̲ Axcan miercoles ynic .9. mani Metztli Abril de 1614 años yhcuac ỹ oncan teopan S. Fran^{co}. mocuaatequique cenpohualli tlacatl yn Japonti yehuatzin yn Padre commissario. quinmocuaatequilli, auh yn teoyotica tettahuan yn Padrinos[2] mochiuhtzinoque çanno yehuantzitzin yn huehuetque tottatzitzinhuan frayles Fran^{cos}. auh in yehuatl teuhctitlantli Embaxador amo quinec ỹ nican mocuaatequiz. yuh mihto ye quin ompa yn españa mocuaatequiz. —

v̲ Axcan Sabado ynic .19. mani metztli Abril de 1614 años. yhcuac nican Mexico ome Capitulo quichiuhque yn S. Augustin teopixque. ynic ce capitulo oncan quichiuhque yn inteopan S. Augustin yehuatl oncan quitlallique prouincial mochiuh yn Padre maestro fr. francisco muñuz. ynin nican pouhqui[3] tlapachoz ypan prouincia Mexico. yn ipan yxquich ytlatititzal muchiuhtoc, auh ynic ome capitulo mochiuh oncan yn teopan colegio S. Pablo. no õcan oc ce prouincial quitlallique ompa pouhqui vmpa [*p. 247*] Ytlapachol mochihua yn ipan yc ome prouincia quipia michhuacan ca vmpa huallaque ynin teopixque S. Pablo. oquichihuaco capitulo ytencopatzinco tlahtohuani Visurrey don diego fernandez

1. For "Visurrey."
2. Perhaps this should be construed as "ynteoyoticatettahuan ynPadrinos," "their

to him and whom he did not know, who had just wandered lost somewhere in the thickets, the deserts, the plains, the mountains, and lived bestially, who now are converted and go toward him to become acquainted with the really true universal shepherd and place themselves in his hands so that he will guard, govern, and take care of them too with and in the true unified belief, the holy Catholic faith, so that the devil will never seize them again and make them his through [*p. 245*] idolatry and the worship of devils, in which they now still are, although there are already many Christians there. And this said ambassador who reached Mexico here is just quickly passing through here now, he will stay here only a few days to see the lord viceroy[1] quickly. And also he will quickly pass by our great ruler the king don Felipe III to see him and to offer him peace, because their ruler who serves as emperor in Japan to show friendship has established eternal peace toward the said king who is in Spain, so that they will never make war on each other but will always love each other, so that the Japanese can come here to Mexico to act as merchants and sell things. And once this ambassador has seen the king in passing, he is to go on beyond that to Rome; as was said, he is to reach the presence of the holy Father and see him. May it be our lord God's desire that it go well; may they be diligent, may the good and pure, divine goodness and purity, grace, be realized upon them, as they want and are inspired, if it goes with their whole true desire; may our lord God help them and redeem them so that they can be and live in his presence forever and ever. Amen. —

v Today, Maundy Thursday, the 27th of the month of March of the year 1614, was when another new procession came out from the parish of Vera Cruz. [*p. 246*] The Spaniards and some of us commoners have established a cofradía there dedicated to the souls [of purgatory]. They also went around a long route, reaching the cathedral. We commoners went in the lead. —

v Today, Monday the 7th of the month of April of the year 1614, was when by order of the lord viceroy they began here in Mexico to clean and remove mud from all the canals that are here everywhere inside the city of Mexico, for which the people of the altepetl all around came to do it, to clean the canals. —

v Today, Wednesday the 9th of the month of April of the year 1614, was when at the church of San Francisco twenty Japanese were baptized; the father commissary baptized them, and it was likewise the eldest among our fathers the Franciscan friars who became the spiritual fathers, the sponsors.[2] But the lordly emissary, the ambassador, did not want to be baptized here; it was said that he will be baptized later in Spain. —

v Today, Saturday the 19th of the month of April of the year 1614, was when here in Mexico the Augustinian friars held two chapter meetings. The first meeting they held at their church of San Agustín; there they installed someone who was made provincial head, father master fray Francisco Muñoz, who belongs here;[3] he is to govern in the province of Mexico and in its whole jurisdiction. The second chapter meeting was held at the church of the Colegio de San Pablo, and there they installed another provincial head who belongs there and [*p. 247*] whose jurisdiction is in a second province that Michoacan has, for from there came these friars to hold the chapter meeting at San Pablo by order of the

---

spiritual fathers, their sponsors."

3. Is assigned here in Mexico? Is assigned in the province of Mexico?

de cordoua Marques. yhuan audiencia real tlaca tlahtoque oydores. ypampa cenca mochallaniaya in teopixq̃. yn ompa tlaca ypan omoteneuh prouincia michhuacan auh ynic oncan quichiuhque S. Pablo. capitulo. huel yxpantzinco tlahtohuani Visurrey yn motlalli prouincial oncan omilhuitl mohuicatza ynic amo ytlah yc monepanoltolinizque teopixque quin iyopa yuh nican omochihu in —

v̲ Axcan Domingo ynic .20. mani Metztli Abril de 1614 a^{o}s. yhcuac teotlac ye no cenpohuallomome Japon tlaca omocuaatequique yn oncan teopan S. Fran^{co}. yehuatzin oncan oquinmocuaatequillico in teoyotica tlahtohuani arçobispo. Mexico Don Juan Perez de la serna —

v̲ Axcan Viernes ynic 25. mani Metztli Abril de 1614 a^{o}s. yhcuac teotlac huel ypan ylhuitzin S. Marcos Euangelista. yn teoyotica tlahtohuani arçobispo Don Juan Perez de la serna oncan yglesia mayor, oquinmomaquilli teoyotica techicahualiztli confirmacion quicuique yn omoteneuhque tlacpac yn yancuique nican X̄ptianosme omochihuaco Japon tlaca. in yehuantin in epohualli yhuan ey tlacatl yn confirmacion quicuiq̃. ce ynpillo yn confirmacion quicuic auh yehuatl quimopalehuilli yn llicenciado Vallezillo fiscal del Rey de lo ciuil teoyotica tettatzin padrino muchiuh —

v̲ Axcan Martes ynic 29. mani Metztli Abril de 1614. años. [*p. 248*] Yhcuac huel ypan ylhuitzin yn mocentlamachtiani S. Pedro Martyr, ohualla tlahtolli españa, yn ipampa yehuatzin Rey quihualmopatilia ỹ nican ytlachixcatzin fiscal del rey ocatca el licenciado vallezillo. auh oc yehuatl ytlachixcatzin fiscal del rey de lo ciuil quihualmochihuilia yn gardos[1] de valencia al~~lde~~ de corte ocatca Auh yn omoteneuh el licenciado vallezillo yn al~~lde~~ de corte quihualmochihuilli ỹ nicã Mexico / auh çãno yhcuac yn omachiztico yn quenin españa yehuatzin Rey ce yhuayolcatzin oquimixquechilli vmpa Principe de esquirachi ynic yehuatl Visurrey oquihualmochihuilli oncan huallamellahua Pirũ. ynic oncan tlahtocatiz quimopatiliz yn oncan tlahtocati Don Juan de Mendoça y luna Marques de Montesclaros. mohuicaz mocuepaz yn ichan españa. ynin achto nican Mexico tlahtocatitiquiz. Visurreytitiquiz ynic ompa nican mohuicac Pirũ. vmpa conmicuanilli yn Rey // auh çano yhcuac yn omachiztico ynic ohualla tlahtolli españa. yn quenin yehuatzin Rey quihualmihuallia ce comendador clerigo Dean muchiuhtihuitz oncan quihualmotlalilia yn Pirũ. ynic oncan quinpachoz clerigos. ynin omoteneuh comendador ca canonigo reglar ytetzinco pouhqui yteopixcatzin ypiltzin yn huey Patriarcha S Antonio Abbad notlaçottatzin. yhuã yuh machiztico ynin omoteneuh comendador ynic ontlamantli ytequiuh vmpa Perũ muchihuaz. quil yhuellitzin ylicenciatzin quihuica oquimomaquilli yn comendador mayor general Don frey fran^{co} de la pressa y mota moyetztica castroxeriz españa, ynic ompa Perũ yteocaltzin S. Antonio quiquetzaz quichihuaz hospital ynic oncan pahtilozque cocoxque yn intech ca tlecocoliztli motenehua [*p. 249*] Ytletzin San Anton.[2] yhuan quinmacaz yn iTautzin yn icruztzin yn icomiendatzin xoxoctic S. Antonio yn aquique ompa españoles ynpilhuan quinequizque conanazque ytetzinco mopohuazque ynic teopixcatizque ynic no ypilhuantzitzinhuã yezque S. Antonio. yn quimocuitlahuizque yn ihospitaltzĩ vmpa moquetzaz mochihuaz. yn iuh tlamanitia mochintĩ comendadores yn ompa yc nohuian moyetzticate francia, Italia. españa. yn izquican yc quimopielilia yteocaltzin yn ihospitaltzin yntlaçottatzin S. Antonio Abbad. canel ylhuicacpa tlamahuiçol-

1. Name unconfirmed.

lord viceroy don Diego Fernández de Córdoba, Marqués, and the people of the Royal Audiencia, the lords judges, because the friars there in the said province of Michoacan had argued greatly. And when they held the meeting at San Pablo, it was right in the presence of the lord viceroy that the provincial head was installed; he came for two days so that the friars wouldn't mistreat one another about something; it was the first time such a thing has been done here. —

v Today, Sunday the 20th of the month of April of the year 1614, another 22 Japanese were baptized at the church of San Francisco. The spiritual ruler the archbishop in Mexico, don Juan Pérez de la Serna, came to baptize them. —

v Today, Friday the 25th of the month of April of the year 1614, in the afternoon, right on the feast day of San Marcos Evangelista, at the cathedral, the spiritual ruler the archbishop don Juan Pérez de la Serna gave holy confirmation to and it was received by the above mentioned Japanese who became new Christians here; 63 people received confirmation. One of their nobles received confirmation, and he was aided by licenciado Vallecillo, the royal prosecutor for civil matters, who became the spiritual father, the sponsor. —

v Today, Tuesday the 29th of the month of April of the year 1614, [*p. 248*] right on the feast day of the greatly blessed San Pedro Mártir, was when news came from Spain that the king is sending orders replacing his lookout here, the royal prosecutor, who was licenciado Vallecillo, and for now is making [Galdós][1] de Valencia, who was an alcalde of the court, his lookout, the royal prosecutor in civil matters. He made the said licenciado Vallecillo alcalde of court here in Mexico. / At the same time it became known how in Spain the king has appointed and made a relative of his, the prince of Esquilache, viceroy. He is coming straight to Peru to rule there and replace don Juan de Mendoza y Luna, Marqués of Montesclaros, who is ruling there and will go and return home to Spain; he first served briefly as ruler and viceroy here in Mexico until he went from here to Peru, to where the king transferred him. // At the same time it became known and news came from Spain how the king is sending here a comendador, a secular priest, who is coming with an appointment as dean and is stationed in Peru to rule the secular priests there. This said comendador is a canon who at the same time belongs to an order; he is dedicated to and is the priest and child of the great patriarch San Antonio Abad, my precious father. And as became known, this said comendador will have two separate duties in Peru: reportedly he carries the authorization and permission given to him by the high general comendador, don frey Francisco de la Presa y Mota who is in Castrojerez in Spain, to erect a church of San Antonio in Peru and to build a hospital where the sick who suffer from the fire-disease called Saint Anthony's fire[2] will be treated. [*p. 249*] And he is to give San Antonio's Tau, his cross, his green badge to those children of Spaniards there who want to take it and dedicate themselves to him so that they will become priests and also be children of San Antonio, taking care of his hospital that will be erected and built there, as is done by all the comendadores who are all around France, Italy, and Spain, wherever they are in charge of the churches and hospitals of their precious father San Antonio

2. A family of skin inflammations.

tica yc quinhualmotlalili yhuelitilizticatzinco yn tt^{o}. dios. ynic oncan otzintique opeuhque yehuantzitzin in omoteneuhque tlaçopipiltin[1] teopixque clerigos comendadores ynic monetoltia quimocuitlahuitzinohua hospitales. —

v auh no yhcuac ỹ. quihualmonahuatili ỹ Rey ỹ Doctor Antonio de morga. al~~lde~~ de corte nican Mexico ynic Presidẽte mochiuhtzino vmpa Piru. mohuicac[2]

v Auh yn oquic ytechpa yn nitlahtohua ma ça noço achitzin nican noconiciuhcanextitihuetzi ma çan noconiciuhcayttotihuetzi yn iuh peuhtica yn iuh tzintitica ynin yancuic yn itzintica ypeuhca ynic hualpeuh yancuic teopixcatlatecpantli horden ynic notzallo tocayotillo S. Anton yhuã yn imachiyo Tau ahnoço cruz xoxoctic yn quinemiltia quitlalia quihualhuica ytech ỹnechichihualtzin yntlaquentzin ymhabitotzin in yehuantzitzin teopixque nehtolleque yn ipan in teopixcanemiliztlatecpantli // ynin vmpa tzintic vmpa peuh cecni yn ipan ce altepetl yn itech pohui yn itlatititzalpan yn itlahuillanalpan yn huey altepetl Arçobispado Viena ytocayocan Mota // Auh ca yuhqui yn yn omochiuh yn ihcuac Sancto Padre muchiuhtzinotica Vrbano Segundo yn õpa Roma yn ipan yxiuhtzin tt^{o}. Dios. de 1095. años. in [*p. 250*] Ye ontzonxihuitl ypan matlacpohualxihuitl ypan nauhpohualloncaxtolli xihuitl motlacatillitzino nelli dios ytlaçomahuizpiltzin. auh in yehuatzin S. Antonio Abbad yn ihcuac yn ye o yuh nepa centzonxihuitl ypan caxtolpohualxihuitl ypan onpohuallonchicome xihuitl momiquillitzino yn ompa ytocayocan Thebas Egipto. yn tepetla texcalla cuauhtla çacatla yxtlahuacan yn oncan motlamacehuilli Sancto. ca ye yxquichcauhtica yn yn ihcuac ypan omoteneuh xihuitl yn quihualmonextilitzino quihualmottititzino yhuan quihualmonahuatilli ylhuicacpa S. Antonio. ynic tleyn quichihuaz quipehualtiz ipãpatzinco ce huey tlaçopilli cauallero yn ompa ypan huey altepetl Prouincia yn itocayocan Viena huel ynezyan yc machiyoticatca yn iteycnoyttaliz. ytoca Don Gaston ynic quintlaliz teopixq̃. comẽdadores. ytetzinco povizq̃.[3]

v Auh ynin yc peuh yancuic teopixcatlatecpantli horden yn itetzinco pohui S. Antonio ca hospitalleque oncan pahtililo in tlecocoliztli ahnoço ytletzin mihtohua S. Antonio. yntech ca. ynin ye omoteneuh yehuãtin quitzintique quipehualtique omentin tlaçopipiltin caualleros vmpa chaneque yn Viena Francia ynic ce yc omotocateneuh ytoca Don Gaston yhuan ypiltzin ytoca Don Girondo. Auh ye quinmomaquilli yn tonãtzin Sancta yglesia yn iteooctacanemilizmachiyotzin yn ireglatzin S. Augustin yn iteopixcatenemitiayatzin in teoyotica nehtolli, auh quihualhuica quitllallia yehuatl ymhabitotzin ypan pohui yn çan ixquich yc machiyotinemi ce cruz ahnoço ce Tau xoxoctic, ynin miec Abbadias yhuan Prioratos oncatqui [*p. 251*] Yn Francia yhuan Italia yn ompa yn huel motlacamati mocuiltonohua yhuan yn españa oncatqui nepapan hospitales yn oncan pahtilillo cocoxque yn icocoliztzin S. Anton ca yehuatzin quimopialia yntatzin mochiuhtzinohua S. Antonio Abbad. yn omoteneuhque canonigos reglares clerigos comendadores, auh ynin omoteneuh yancuic teopixcatlatecpantli yn ihordetzin S. Antonio, yn oncan yc hualtzintic yn oncan yc hualpeuh yn ipan omoteneuh xihuitl. 1095. yn ihcuac ypan in yc quihualmonextilitzino quihualmottititzino yca yn icruztzin yn icomiendatzin quihualmonahuatilli yn S. Antonio. yn omoteneuh ytetlaçotlacatzin yn itetlayecolticatzin Don Gaston ynic

1. The words "in omoteneuhque tlaçopipiltin" do not seem integrated into the grammar of the sentence. Also, despite the use of "omoteneuhque," "said," these people have not been mentioned before. Perhaps the phrase was added inadvertently, a partial anticipation of what comes below.

Abad, for by a miracle from heaven he established them with the authority of our lord God, so that priests who were secular priests and comendadores, vowing to take care of the hospitals, were founded and begun [by?] the said high nobles.[1] —

v And also at this time the king sent orders to doctor Antonio de Morga, alcalde of court here in Mexico, so that he went to Peru with an appointment as president of the Royal Audiencia.[2]

v As long as I am talking about this, let me very quickly reveal a bit of how this new priestly order began and was founded and quickly tell of its beginning and foundation, this new order named and called after San Antón, whose sign is the Tau or the green cross that the priests who have taken vows in this order of priestly living display, wear, and attach to their outfits, their garments, their habits. // It was founded and began in a particular altepetl called Mota that belongs to the jurisdiction and dependent area of the great altepetl and archbishopric of Vienne. // It was like this that it happened, when Urban II was holy Father in Rome in the year of our lord God of 1095, [*p. 250*] 1095 years after the precious revered child of the true God was born. At that time it had been 747 years since San Antonio Abad had passed away at thc place called Thebes in Egypt, where among mountains, crags, forests, grassy deserts and plains the saint did penance. It had been that long when in the said year from heaven San Antonio appeared to, showed himself to, and gave orders to a great high noble, a gentleman named don Gastón, of the great altepetl and province called Vienne, his very place of appearance marked by his mercy, about what he was to do and undertake on his behalf, to establish priests who were comendadores and would be dedicated to him.[3]

v With him began the new priestly order dedicated to San Antonio; they have hospitals where those who suffer from the fire-sickness, or what is called Saint Anthony's fire, are treated. It was already said that it was founded and begun by two high noblemen, gentlemen, who lived in Vienne, France, the first of whom was named don Gastón, and his child named don Girondo. And our mother the holy church gave them the example of divine living, the rule, of San Agustín, his means of making people live a priestly life, as their spiritual vow. And the habit they wear is equivalent except that it is distinguished by a green cross or Tau. There are many of these abbeys and priories [*p. 251*] in France and Italy, where they are very prosperous and rich, and there are also various hospitals in Spain where those sick with Saint Anthony's disease are treated. The said canons who are at the same time regular, secular priests, and comendadores have San Antonio Abad as their father. This said new priestly order, the order of San Antonio, which was founded and began in the said year of 1095, in which San Antonio appeared to, showed himself to with his cross as his badge, and gave orders to the said don Gastón, who loved and served

---

2. This is true in a sense, but Morga actually became president in Quito.

3. This last part from *res* in the word "comẽdadores" is between the lines though not an afterthought, another indication that parts of the text we know are copied mechanically from something already written.

quintlalli omoteneuhque comendadores clerigos. yhuan ynic quichiuh quiquetz ce hospital tzontecomatl mochiuhtica. yn oncan huel peuhqui ca axcan ye centzonxihuitl ypan chicuacẽpohualxihuitl hue[1] yxquich oahcic axcan yn ipan ticate xihuitl de 1614 años —

v̲ Axcan Juebes ynic 15. mani Metztli Mayo de 1614 años yhcuac tlamico yn ỹ nican Mexico ynic mopopouh moçoquiquixti yn izqui acallohtli omoteneuh tlacpac cenca yc motollinique yn macehualtin cequintin oncan opeuhque yn omococoque Mexica yhuan cequintin altepehuaque ce yc momiquilli nican chane S Pablo tlachcuititlan ynic nemonhuac çoquiquixtiloc ce metztli ypan chicueylhuitl —

v̲ Axcan Juebes ynic 29. mani Metztli Mayo de 1614 años. [*p. 252*] Yhcuac ypan in omotlallico[2] yn itlaçoylhuitzin santissimo sacramento çan ic onquiz in yn ilhuitl çan iquezquilhuiyoc ynic niman nican ompeuh yahqui yn ompa yc yauh españa. yn omoteneuh teuhctitlantli Embaxador. chane Japon ynin yc yah çan quinxellotehuac yn imacehualhuan yxquich quinhuicac no yxquich nican quincauhtiquiz yn Japonti. ynic nican tiyamiquizque tlanamacazque puchteca, auh yn omoteneuh Embaxador ynic nican onpeuh ynic yah españa. Nican cantiquiz Mexico quihuicac ce español. amo huel momati yn itoca inhermano yn Doctor Martinez ySecretario muchiuhtiuh ytencopatzinco nican visurrey ypampa quimati yn intlahtol Japonti ca ompa ỹtlan onemito yn ihcuac Soldado catca —

v̲ Axcan Lunes ynic 4. mani Metztli Agosto de 1614 años yhcuac huel ypan ylhuitzin S. Domingo yn ohuallathuic omomiquilli yn Doña Augustina de guzman cihuapilli cuyohuacan yn inamic Don Constantino chacalli michhuacan tlahtohuani Auh yn omoteneuh Doña Augustina de guzman micqui ca chillapan tlacatito ynin cuyohuacan ehuac yn inantzin vmpa quihuallitlan yn Don Augustin ixcuinan tlahtohuani chillapan ynic oncan tlacatito. Omoteneuh axcan omomiquilli Doña Augustina de guzman. auh ynic oc ceppa ycuitlahuic ohuallaca oncan cuyohuacan ca çan centlamanpa iyachton[3] yPrimo hermano y conitlanca ynic hualla oncan cuyohuacan yn quihualmonamictica achtopa ytoca Don felipe [*p. 253*] de guzman ynin çatepan ogouernadortito yn oncan cuyohuacan ypiltzin in yn Don Juan de guzman tlahtoque tlahtocatepilhuan catca yn oncan cuyohuacan auh ayac ce yconetzin quicauhtiuh ynic onmomiquillico yn omoteneuh cihuapilli Doña Augustina de guzman çan mixpopolotiuh —

v̲ Axcan Juebes ynic 14. mani Metztli Agosto de 1614 años yhcuac nican Mexico machiztico hualla tlahtolli huaxacac ynic ompa omomiquilli teoyotica tlahtohuani Don Juan de Seruantes Obispo huaxacac ynic ompa teoyotica tlahtocatito. çan macuilxihuitl ypan etetl metztli ypan caxtolli tonatiuh ynic niman omomiquillico ynin nican tlacat nican tepiltzin Mexico conquistadores yntechpa quiz. yhuan yehuatl in yn tlacpac mieccan omoteneuh yn itoca ca achtopa etlamantli ytequiuh mochiuh ỹ nican Mexico. yn ayemo yuh obispo mochiuhtzinohuaya ynic centlamantli nican yglesia mayor arcediano catca, ynic ontlamantli ytequitzin muchiuh yGouernador quihualmochihuillica nican Mexico yn teoyotica tlahtohuani Don Alonso Fernandez de Bonilla arçobispo Mexico yn oc yxquich ica vmpa monemiltiaya yn yn oquic Visita quimochihuiliaya yn ompa ypan tlahtocaaltepetl Piru. ynic ompa ypan momiquilli ytequitzin amo huel hualmohuicac ỹ mexico. yniqu etlamãntli ytequitzin muchiuh Don Juan de ceruantes Cathetradico catca yn ica escriptura quiponhuaya ỹ nican de La Viversidad escuella Mexico — Ynic niman çatepan

1. For "huel."

2. The role of this word in the sentence is not clear. Perhaps it refers to the fact that

him, to establish the said comendadores and secular priests, and he built and erected a hospital which became the headquarters, where it really began. It is now a full[1] 520 years ago up to the present year of 1614. —

v Today, Thursday the 15th of the month of May of the year 1614, was when they finished cleaning and clearing mud from all the canals here in Mexico, as mentioned above. The commoners were greatly afflicted by it; some Mexica began to get sick, as well as some people from other altepetl. One person died of it who was a resident here in San Pablo, in Tlachcuititlan. They were engaged in clearing mud for a month and 8 days. —

v Thursday the 29th of the month of May of the year 1614, [*p. 252*] when the precious feast day of the most Holy Sacrament had passed, a few days afterward, [it was established that ?][2] the said lordly emissary, the ambassador from Japan, set out and left for Spain. In going he divided his vassals; he took a certain number of Japanese, and he left an equal number here as merchants to trade and sell things. As the said ambassador left Mexico here to go to Spain he took along a Spaniard, whose name cannot be established, a brother of doctor Martínez, who by order of the viceroy here went appointed as his secretary because he knows the language of the Japanese, for he went to live among them when he was a soldier. —

v Today, Monday the 4th of the month of August of the year 1614, right on the feast day of Santo Domingo, overnight, doña Agustina de Guzmán, a noblewoman of Coyoacan, spouse of don Constantino Chacalin, a ruler from Michoacan, passed away. The said deceased doña Agustina de Guzmán was born in Chilapan although she had affiliations in Coyoacan. Don Agustín Itzcuinnan, ruler in Chilapan, asked for her mother [in marriage], so that the said doña Agustina de Guzmán who just died was born there. The reason she came back again to Coyoacan was that her older brother[3] once removed, her first cousin, had asked for her [in marriage], so that she came to Coyoacan, where she married first the person named don Felipe [*p. 253*] de Guzmán, who later became governor in Coyoacan and was the child of don Juan de Guzmán; they were rulers and members of the royal dynasty in Coyoacan. The said noblewoman doña Agustina de Guzmán left no children behind; [her line] was extinguished. —

v Today, Thursday the 14th of the month of August of the year 1614, was when it became known here in Mexico and news came from Oaxaca that there had died there the spiritual ruler don Juan de Cervantes, bishop in Oaxaca, who had been spiritual ruler there only 5 years, 3 months, and 15 days before he died. He was born here, the child of people here in Mexico; he descended from conquerors. His name has been mentioned in many places above, for he held three separate offices here in Mexico before he became bishop. First, he was archdeacon in the cathedral here; the second office he held was that the spiritual ruler don Alonso Fernández de Bonilla, archbishop in Mexico, made him his governor here in Mexico for as long as he was occupied in the royal altepetl of Peru making an inspection, but he died there during his assignment and was not able to come to Mexico; the third office don Juan de Cervantes held was the chair of scripture in which he lectured here at the university and school in Mexico, until later he became bishop in

---

the ambassador had stayed in Mexico for a while.

3. The word *-achton* usually means great-grandfather. Older brother or cousin of a female is normally *-ach* (reverential *-achtzin*).

Obispo mochiuhtzino huaxacac ynic ompa omomiquillito. ynic ohualla axcan ytenyotzin — [*p. 254*]

v Axcan Viernes ynic 15. mani Metztli Agosto de 1614 años. yhcuac huel ypan ytlaçoylhuitzin totlaçonantzin Sancta Maria nuestra Señora Assumpcion teotlac ypan macuilli tzilli yn omomiquilli Don Antonio cortes totoquihuaztli telpochtli Gouernador catca tlacopa. çan nahuilhuitl yn omococo amo huel oneztia yn tley cocoliztli yc omomiquilli yn aço matlaltotonqui amo huel momati çã yn iuh omihto ca çan miec netequipacholli oquimopialiaya yehuatl ynic omomiquilli quiteylhuiyaya yn imacehualhuan tepaneca tlacopaneca.

v Axcan Sabado ynic 16. mani Metztli Agosto de 1614. años. yhcuac yancuican omopix yn ilhuitzin mocẽtlamachtiani S. Roque. yn ompa quimopielia hospital S. Lazaro. atenantitech ytencopatzinco muchiuh yn arçobispo Mexico. ytlaytlaniliztica mochiuh ỹ clerigo Augustin de leon Patron yn oncan omoteneuh hospital S. Lazaro. // auh çãno yhcuac ỹ yn ipan omoteneuh cemilhuitl Sabado yn otococ ynacayotzin yn omoteneuh tlacpac Don Antonio cortes totoquihuaztli telpochtli tlacopan Gouernador catca auh çan omentin çihuatzitzinti tepitzitzin yn ipilhuantzitzinhuan oquincauhtia, ynin tlahtohuani huel oc yehuantin yntechpa oquiçaco yn izquintin otlahtocatico tlahtoque tlacopa ynic ompa hualtzintitica oncan tlahtocayotl —

v Axcan miercoles ynic 20. mani Metztli Agosto de 1614. años. yhcuac omomiquilli yn el licenciado Aller [*p. 255*] de Villagomez. Oydor catca nican audiencia real yn inacayo teopan S. Augustin tocoto oncan motetoquillico Visurrey yhuã mochintin tlahtoque oydores audiencia real tlaca —

v Axcan Sabado ynic 23. mani Metztli Agosto de 1614 a^{o}s. yhcuac nican Mexico tlacpac[1] yn tlahtohuani Visurrey quimomaquilli yn tlacopan gouernacion Don diego cortes huanitzin ynic ompa Gouernador muchiuh ynin huel yteyccauh yn tlacpac omoteneuh miccatzintli Don Antonio cortes totoquihuaztli Gou^{or}. catca tlacopa ynin o yuh momiquilli çan ichicueylhuiyoc yn conan yteyccauhtzin Gouernacion —

v Axcan Sabado ynic. 6. mani Metztli Septiembre de 1614 años yhcuac teotlac ypan chicuacen tzillini yn momiquilli cenca mahuiztililoni yxtililoni Padre Doctor P^{o}. de Morales de la Compañia de Jesus teopixqui omoyetzticatca yhuan quimotocayotiliaya el Pontifice chiquito. yehica ypampa Ca huey tetlaocoliliztli Jubileos.[2] quimotenemactiliaya ypampatzinco yca ytocatzin yn Sancto Padre. ỹ nican Mexico yn çaço campa moyetzticatca ỹteopanchantzinco oncan quimotenemactiliaya Jubileo yn ihcuac aquique yntech monequi oquimitlanililiaya yn aquin sancto ytetzinco quiponhua ahnoço altar animas ytech quipohua yn inpalehuilloca Porgaturio tlayhiyohuiticate mochi ytechpa yn oquimotemaquiliaya yn Jubileo. ca yuh ocatca ynahuatiltzin yuh quimohuelitizmaquili yn Sancto Padre ______ yn ihcuac vmpa mohuicaya Roma. ynic procura[*p. 256*]dor de indias mochiuhtzinoto yhcuac vmpa quihualmomaquilli yn bulla yn brebes oquimopieliaya ynic huell omohuelitiliaya nican ypan nueua españa. yhuan huel iuhqui yn itetopillo ytenetlaquechillo omochiuhtzinoticatca oquimotzitziquilliticatca tlamachilizmiyahuayotica ỹ nican altepetl Mexico. yhuan ynic nohuiyan nueua españa. ynteyacancatzin ymachcauhtzin ytetzinco oytzticatca yn mochintin nican oncate tlamatinime yn Doctoresme, ynic cenca oquimotemachililiaya oquimitlanililiaya yn itlamachiliztenonotzaliztzin yteyx-

1. The word "tlacpac," "above," does not fit in the sentence as it exists; perhaps the word "omoteneuh," "mentioned," was inadvertently omitted. It was probably going to

Oaxaca, where he died after going there, of which word came today. — [*p. 254*]

v Today, Friday the 15th of the month of August of the year 1614, right on the precious feast day of our precious mother Santa María, Nuestra Señora de la Asunción, in the afternoon at 5 o'clock, was when there passed away don Antonio Cortés Totoquihuaztli the younger, who was governor in Tacuba. He was sick for only four days; it was not clear of what illness he died, maybe matlaltotonqui, it couldn't be established, but it was said that he had many worries, and that was what he died of; his vassals the Tepaneca of Tacuba had been making complaints about him.

v Today, Saturday the 16th of the month of August of the year 1614, was when for the first time the feast day of the greatly blessed San Roque was observed; it was observed at the hospital of San Lázaro at Atenantitech. It was done by order of the archbishop in Mexico at the request of the secular priest Agustín de León, patron of the said hospital of San Lázaro. // It was at the same time, on the said Saturday, that the body of the above mentioned don Antonio Cortés Totoquihuaztli the younger, late governor in Tacuba, was buried. He left behind only two small girls as his children. This ruler still descended in the direct line from all the rulers who have ruled in Tacuba since the rulership was founded there. —

v Today, Wednesday the 20th of the month of August of the year 1614, was when there passed away licenciado Aller [*p. 255*] de Villagómez, who was a civil judge in the Royal Audiencia here. His body was taken to be buried in the church of San Agustín; the viceroy and all the lords judges of the Royal Audiencia came to the burial. —

v Today, Saturday the 23rd of the month of August of the year 1614, was when here in Mexico the above [mentioned?][1] lord viceroy gave don Diego Cortés Huanitzin the governorship of Tacuba, so that he became governor there. He is the full younger sibling of the above mentioned deceased don Antonio Cortés Totoquihuaztli, late governor in Tacuba. His younger sibling took the governorship only eight days after he had passed away. —

v Today, Saturday the 6th of the month of September of the year 1614, in the afternoon at 6 o'clock, was when there passed away the very reverend and estimable father doctor Pedro de Morales, who was a religious of the Company of Jesus, and they called him the little pope because he used to bestow great indulgences, the jubilee,[2] on people here in Mexico on behalf of and in name of the holy Father. Whatever church it was in, he would issue a jubilee there. When anyone would request of him something needed, to dedicate to some saint or at the altar of the souls of purgatory to dedicate to the aid of those who are suffering in purgatory, he would grant a jubilee for them all, for he had that faculty and the holy Father ______ had authorized him when he went to Rome appointed legal representative [*p. 256*] of the Indies. There he gave him a bull and apostolic briefs that he kept by which he was fully authorized here in New Spain. And he became like the staff and support that people would grasp as to the pinnacle of wisdom here in the altepetl of Mexico and all over New Spain, the leader and most preeminent of all the scholars and doctors who are here, to whom they would look, so that they would have great confidence in him and would ask him for his advice on matters of knowledge, his guidance, his

refer to don Antonio Cortés, with whom this phrase is used just below.

2. Special plenary indulgence for a year.

tlatilitzin ytenanamiquiliztlahtoltzin quimotemaquiliaya ynic tleyn huel mochihuaz. moyectiliz yn ihquac tleỹ yn itlah huehuey netequipacholli yn aço neyxnamiquiliztli acame o ynpan motlaliaya ca cenca oquinmopalehuiliaya yhuan nohuiyampa omotlananamiquiliaya yn ipan Sancto officio ynQuisisio. yhuã yn tlahtoq̃ arçobispos. obispos. oydores. no quenmanian oquinmonanamiquiliaya ytlamachiliztlahtolticatzinco ynehuantzin y Padre Pº. hordigosa çãno vmpa teopixqui de la compañia de Jesus. yn axcan moyetztica. yn ihcuac cenca monequi omotlananamiquillique. auh ynin omoteneuhtzino miccatzintli Padre Pº. de morales ynic hualmohuicac españa ca oydor hualmochiuhtzinotia vmpa mohuicazquia ỹ nueuo granada Piru, auh nican mexico yn quimoyollotillico ttº. Dios. ynic nican mocallaqui nican quimocuilli ỹ habito de la compañia de Jesus. ynic oncan axcan oquimopolhuico ttº. dios. oquimohuiquilli yn ichantzinco ylhuicac canel oquimotlayecoltilli ma quimotimalhui

v Auh ye quin axcan yc omilhuitl ypan Domingo ynic .7. mani [*p. 257*] Metztli Septiembre teotlac ypan macuilli tzillini yn oquimotoquillique ynacayotzin yn oncan teopan de la compania de Jesus colegio yn omoteneuhtzino Padre Doctor Pedro de morales. cenca quimomahuiztililique moch oncan mocenquixtique quimololhuillique ỹ tlaçoteopixq̃. tottatzitzinhuan prouincial[1] de la compañia de Jesus. yhuan yglesia mayor capilla officiales cantores. y cuicato yc quimotoquilliq̃. yhuan oncan motetoquillico ce ynQuisidor yhuan ce oydor yhuan miequintin pipiltin españoles auh yn ipampa yc nican nictlallia nicmachiyotia yn imiquilitzin ynin omoteneuhtzino huey teopixqui omoyetzticatca yniqu iuhqui yxiptlatzin omochiuhtzinoticatca nican Sancto Padre ynic huel omohuelitiltiaya yniqu icatzinco ypampatzinco miec Jubileos oquimotemaquillitia yn iuh otiquittaque auh monequi no quimatizque oncan in quittazque ytocatenehuallocatzin yn aquique çatepan ye nemiquihui yn amo quimottilique yn amo quimiximachilique ynin yc huey teopixqui ocatca ypampa yuh ninomati caocac yuhqui nican Mexico oc ce teopixqui yttoz yn oc ompa ye tonitztihui ypan cahuitl —

v Axcan Lunes ynic 8. mani Metztli Septiembre de 1614 años teotlac huel ypan ylhuitzin ytlacatilitzin totlaçonantzin Sancta maria de la natiuidad yn momiquilli Alonso Rodriguez delgado fundador yn oquichiuh hospital del Sp̄ū Sancto yn acallotenco[2] ynahuac San Ignacio la casa proffesa. ynin yhospital oncan quincauhtia yn hermanos de huaxtepec motenehua conbalecientes in quimocuitlahuia hospitales auh yn omoteneuh miccatzintli Alonso Rodriguez ye [*p. 258*] quin martes teotlac ynic omilhuitl otococ ynacayo ypan macuilli tzillini yn oncan yteopan hospital yglesia mayor officiales cantores yn cuicaco yn quitocaco yhuan oncan mohuicatza motetoquillico in teoyotica tlahtohuani Don Juan Perez de la serna arçobispo Mexico //

v Axcan Juebes ynic 18. mani Metztli Septiembre de 1614 años yhcuac teotlac yc otzatzihuac nohuiya yn ihtic ciudad Mexico Pena yc motlalli mochi tlacatl cuahuitl quitlatiz yn españoles ỹchachan yn intlapanco anoço ỹcaltenpa ypampatzinco motemachizti ynic yancuican ohualla españa yn iyectenehualiztlahtollotzin huey Sancta tenantzin la madre Theresa de Jesus. ynic motenehua Beatificacion çan oc ycatzinco Oquimochihuilli yn Roma Sancto Padre Paulo quinto auh ynic Pena motlalli yn aquin atle cuahuitl quitlatiz ychan matlactli Peso quixtlahuaz. auh ynic nimã yc onyohuac çan huel yc ontzillin yn horacion anoço Auemaria, yc niman achtopa vmpa peuh yn teopan monasterio

1. This word is written above the line, but it seems to refer to the Jesuits. The religious referred to are probably all Jesuits.

helpful words which he would bestow on people, about what could be done to fix it when some great concerns or struggles had come upon some of them; he greatly aided them, and he helped people everywhere, including at the holy Office of the Inquisition, and sometimes he would help the lords archbishops, bishops, and judges of the Audiencia with his words of wisdom, along with father Pedro Ortigosa, also a religious of the Company of Jesus, who is alive now; when it was very necessary, they helped. And when this said deceased father Pedro de Morales came from Spain he came appointed as an Audiencia judge and was going to go to New Granada in Peru, but here in Mexico our lord God inspired him to enter the Company of Jesus here and take its habit until our lord God just now effaced him and took him to his home in heaven, for he served him; may he exalt him.

v It was only later, today the second day, on Sunday the 7th of the [*p. 257*] month of September at 5 o'clock in the afternoon, that they buried the body of the said father doctor Pedro de Morales at the church and college of the Company of Jesus. They greatly honored him; all the precious religious, our fathers, assembled and gathered around him, and the provincial head[1] of the Company of Jesus, and the professional singers of the cathedral choir came there to sing at his burial, and an inquisitor and a judge of the Royal Audiencia, along with many noble Spaniards, came to the burial. The reason that I set down and record here the death of this said late great religious is that he became like the representative of the holy Father here because he was fully authorized to go along issuing many jubilees in his name and on his behalf, as we saw. And also those who will live later, who didn't see and know how great a religious he was, need to know of him and see his name mentioned, because I think that in future times another religious like him will not be seen again here in Mexico. —

v Today, Monday the 8th of the month of September of the year 1614, in the afternoon, right on the feast day of the birth of our precious mother Santa María de la Natividad, there passed away Alonso Rodríguez Delgado, the founder who built the hospital of Espíritu Santo on the bank of the canal[2] close to the Casa Profesa of San Ignacio. At this hospital he left behind the Brothers of Huaxtepec, called Convalecientes, who take care of hospitals. And the body of the said deceased Alonso Rodríguez [*p. 258*] was buried later, on Tuesday in the afternoon at 5 o'clock, on the second day, at the hospital church. The professional singers of the cathedral came to sing and bury him, and the spiritual ruler don Juan Pérez de la Serna, archbishop in Mexico, came to the burial. //

v Today, Thursday the 18th of the month of September of the year 1614, in the afternoon, was when a proclamation was made everywhere in the city of Mexico, setting a fine, that all Spaniards were to burn wood at their homes on their roofs or on the streets outside their houses because, it was announced, there had newly come from Spain the statement, called beatification, blessing the great saint mother Teresa de Jesús, which the holy Father in Rome, Paul V, provisionally made in her name. The fine that was set was that whoever didn't burn wood at home would pay 10 pesos. And then when it got dark, right when they were ringing for prayers or the Ave María, pealing the bells began first at

2. Possibly a place name, Acalotenco.

nuestra Señora del carme in ye tlatzitzillica in ye tlapitzallo vandera tlapanco motehtecac yhuã miec cuahuitl tlatlac yn tlapanco yhuã covetes quitlatlazque auh yniqu ipampa vmpa peuh yc tlatzitzillicac carme ca yehica ypampa ynin omoteneuhtzino Sancta ca huel ynantzin yehuatzin oc ceppa quinmoyancuilili yn teopixcatlatecpancanahuatilli regla achto ynic quimochicahuacapielia vmpa moyetzticate carme teopixque [*p. 259*] Carmelitas descalços.[1] ca huel ytlatlaliltzitzinhuan ynic ompa huel y tzintia achto motlallique ynin frayles descarços carmelitas yn ipan altepetl Manzera españa ytlahuillanalpan in huey altepetl Salamanca, yehuatzin oncan tzontecomatl muchiuh yn cenca mahuiztililoni Padre Maestro fr. Antonio de Heredia ypan yxiuhtzin tt^{o}. Dios. de 1564. auh in yehuatzin Sancta Theresa de Jesus. yn quinmotlalili quinmocaltili ymõjastzitzinhuan descalças in S. Josef. oncan yn ipan altepetl Auila: auh amo yhuan yntech nican nitlahtohua yn oc cequintin teopixque carmelitas yn calçados çapatoseque ca ynon ca yeppa cenca ye miec xihuitl oncate ayemo hualhui ỹ nican Mexico. auh niquihtohua yn o yuh peuh tlatzitzillica nican carme no niman yc peuh in ye tlatzitzillicac yglesia mayor. yhuã ça ce ynic nohuiyan mochi teopan monasterios yn oncã moyetzticate teopixque frayles. yhuan monjas. tlatzitzillicac yhuan cenca huel nohuiyan tlatlac ỹ cuahuitl ciudad. mexico yn inchan yn intlatlapanco yn incaltenpa españoles. ça ce ynic nohuiyan ohtlipan tlatlac yuhquin tlaztalotl moquetz mexico. auh yn monasterios teopixcan mochi sepo candelas yn teopantlapanticpac tlatlatlac yn iuh mochi tlacatl oquittac —

v̲ Axcan Domingo ynic .5. mani Metztli octubre de 1614 años. yhcuac yn opeuh yn ompa totlaçonantzin Sancta Maria del carme, yn ilhuitzin ye quimochihuililia in omoteneuhtzino tenantzin La madre Sancta [*p. 260*] Theresa de Jesus Virgen carmelita descalça[2] ynin ye omito ayemo ycenyo çan oc Beatificacion ynic quimolhuichihuililia yniqu icatzinco moteylhuicohuanochilia ypilhuantzitzinhuan teopixque carme, yn axcan ypan omoteneuh Domingo. yc opeuh ylhuitl clerigos cabilto tlaca yn oquimochihuililito missa Sancta Theresa. yhuan yehuatl otemachtito yn Doctor Muñoz canonigo. // Auh yn ipan lunes yc omilhuitl yehuantzitzin yn teopixque Dominigos oquimochihuililito missa Sancta yhuã ce temachti // Auh yn ipan Martes ynic eylhuitl yehuãtzitzin yn teopixque Fran^{cos}. quimochihuililito missa Sancta. yhuan no ce temachti // Auh yn ipan miercoles ynic nahuilhuitl yehuantzitzin yn teopixque Augustinos. quimochihuililito missa Sancta yehuatzin motemachtilito in teoyotica tlahtohuani Don fr. Diego de contreras arçobispo S. Domingo la ysla ayhtic, // Auh yn ipan Juebes ynic macuililhuitl yehuantzitzin yn teopixque mercenadios quimolhuichihuililito Sancta no ce temachti // Auh yn ipan Viernes. ynic chicuacemilhuitl yehuantzitzin yn teopixque yn itehuicaltzitzinhuan Jesus ỹ tocayotillo de los Padres de la compañia de Jesus yehuatzin motemachtilli yn inProuincial // Auh yn ipan Sabado ynic chicomilhuitl yehuantzitzin yn teopixque Fran^{cos} descalços. yn quimolhuichihuililito Sancta no ce temachti // Auh yn ipan Domingo yn ichicueylhuiyoc yehuatzin in teoyotica tlahtohuani Don Juan Perez de la Serna Arçobispo Mexico yn quimochihuililito ymissatzin Sancta Theresa de Jesus. yhuã motemachtilli [*p. 261*] Ça motlatzacuilli yehuatzin yniqu ilhuitl quimochihuili.

v̲ Axcan Sabado ynic .11. mani metztli octubre de 1614 años. yhcuac nican ciudad Mexico Teopan San Augustin omaxitico in Teoyotica tlahtohuani Don fray Juan çapata y Sandoual Obispo teopixq̃ S. Augustin ompa ytequitzin motlalia quimopieliz. yn altepetl

---

1. In this word *l* was marked over *r*.

the nunnery church of Nuestra Señora del Carmen. Wind instruments began to be played, and banners were displayed on roofs, and much wood was burned on roofs, and they shot off rockets. The reason that the bellringing began at Carmen is that the said saint was really the mother of and renewed for them the priestly constitutional ordinance, the rule, that was first strictly observed by the Carmelite friars there [in Spain], [*p. 259*] the Discalced[1] Carmelites, for they were truly founded by her, so that these Discalced Carmelite friars were really founded and first established in the altepetl of Mancera, Spain, in the jurisdiction of the great altepetl of Salamanca; the person who became the head was the very reverend father master fray Antonio de Heredia, in the year of our lord God 1564. And Santa Teresa de Jesús established and housed her discalced nuns at San Josef in the altepetl of Avila. I do not speak here in addition of the other Carmelite friars, the shod, who wear shoes, for they have already existed for very many years; they have not yet come here to Mexico. And I say that after the ringing had begun here at Carmen, ringing began also at the cathedral, and there was ringing everywhere at all the monastery churches where there are friars and nuns, and absolutely everywhere in the city of Mexico wood was burned at the homes of the Spaniards, on their roofs and outside their houses, and there were fires absolutely everywhere on the roads; it became as bright in Mexico as the coming of dawn's light. And in all the monasteries, where there are friars, tallow candles were burned on the roofs of the churches, as everyone saw. —
v Today, Sunday the 5th of the month of October of the year 1614, at our precious mother Santa María del Carmen, was when the celebration of the feast day of the said holy mother [*p. 260*] Santa Teresa de Jesús the virgin, a Discalced Carmelite,[2] began; as was said, her [sainthood] is not yet complete, it is for now only her beatification that is being celebrated, so that in her name her children the Carmelite friars invite people to the feast. Today on the said Sunday the feast day began with the secular priests who are members of the cathedral chapter, who went to say mass for Santa Teresa, and doctor Muñoz, a canon, preached. // On Monday, the second day, the Dominican friars went to say mass for the saint, and one of them preached. // On Tuesday, the third day, the Franciscan friars went to say mass for the saint, and one of them preached too. // On Wednesday, the fourth day, the Augustinian friars went to say mass for the saint; the spiritual ruler don fray Diego de Contreras, archbishop in Santo Domingo de la Isla, out in the ocean, preached. // On Thursday, the fifth day, the Mercedarian friars went to celebrate the feast of the saint, and one of them preached too. // On Friday, the sixth day, it was the religious who are in the following of Jesus, who are called the fathers of the Company of Jesus; their provincial head preached. // On Saturday, the seventh day, it was the Discalced Franciscan friars who went to celebrate the feast of the saint, and one of them preached too. // On Sunday, the eighth day, the spiritual ruler don Juan Pérez de la Serna, archbishop in Mexico, went to say a mass for Santa Teresa de Jesús, and he preached; [*p. 261*] he closed the celebration of the feast.

v Today, Saturday the 11th of the month of October of the year 1614, was when the spiritual ruler don fray Juan de Zapata y Sandoval, bishop, Augustinian friar, reached the church of San Agustín here in the city of Mexico. It is established as his assignment that

2. Or a Discalced Carmelite virgin.

ciudad chiapa. ynin nican. mexico chane nican tepiltzin motenehua criollo españa hualmohuicac nican mohuicac huecauh ompa omoyetzticatca yn españa ynic ompa oquimomaquilli Rey in Teoyotica ytlahtocayotzin. auh ynic hualmohuicac ye quin oncan yn ciudad de los Angeles. cuetlaxcohuapan y hualmoteochiuhtzinotiquiz in Teoyotica ytlahtocayotzin ymactzinco quihualmocuilitiquiz. yn oncan Obispo Don Alonso de la muta y escobar huel ipan ylhuitzin S. Miguel.

v̲ Axcan martes ynic 14. mani metztli octubre de 1614 años. yhcuac nican Mexico. onpeuhque cequintin Jabun tlaca oyahque in inchan Japon onauhxiuhtico ỹ nican mexico onemico. cequintin oc nican omocauhtiaque motlaecoltia. tiamiqui quinamaca nican yn intlatqui ompa quihualcuique Japon

v̲ Axcan Jueues ynic 23. mani metztli octubre de 1614. años. yhcuac nican Mexico onmopehualtihque omẽtin Teopixque S. Fran^{co} descalços mohuica Japon ompa motemachtilizque

v̲ Axcan Lunes ynic .20.[1] mani metztli octubre de 1614. años. ihcuac nican yhtic huey altepetl ciudad Mexico ocallaquico yn Don Gaspar de albeal cauallero. [*p. 262*] quitlalia yComiendatzin yn Santiago. ompa mohuica ompa motlalia ytequitzin ompa motepachilhuiz Gouernador mochiuhtzinohua ompa motenehua de la nueua Viscaya en guatiana de la nueua España, çan onmoquixtihtiquiça nican Mexico españa ohualmohuicac. quin yehuatl ocõpehualtico yn Gouernacion. ompa guatiana.

v̲ Axcan miercoles ynic 29. mani Metztli octubre de 1614 años. ihcuac omomiquilli yn cihuapilli Doña Ana de Mendoça ycnocihuatl ynamic catca Doctor rriego Pressidente catca yn audiencia real mexico. yehuantin tlatzintileque fundadores quimochihuillique yn cihuateopixcacalli Monasterio monjas San lurenço yn oncan cate omentin ymichpotzitzinhuan oncan yn otocoto ynacayo omoteneuh cihuapilli Doña Ana de Mendoça no yehuatzin quimotoquilito yn tlahtohuani Don diego fernandez de cordoua Visurrey yhuan mochintin yn audiencia real tlaca.

v̲ Axcan Jueues ynic .30. mani ytlamian yn Metztli octubre de 1614 años ihcuac teotlac ye chicuacen tzillini omomiquilli yn licenciado Antonio Rodriquez. oydor catca nican Mexico audiencia real auh ye quin imoztlayoc ipan viernes teotlac in motocac ynacayo S. Fran^{co}, oncan no motetoquillico tlahtohuani Visurrey Don diego fernandez de cordoua. yhuan mochintin yn audiencia real tlaca oydores all~~de~~s de cortes, yhuan i yehuatzin yn Arçobispo Don Juan Perez de la serna.

v̲ Axcan Sabado ynic .15. mani Metztli Nouiembre de 1614 años. yhcuac yancuican ipan navioviso[2] [*p. 263*] Omotlatitlani yn españa y nothatzin Padre fray Augustin del espiritu Sancto Patron quimopachilhuia y huel yxcoyantzinco yaxcatzin ynic quimopielia yn iteopancaltzin notlaçomahuizthatzin yn hueytzintli S. Antonio Abad ỹ nican ciudad Mexico. ynehuantzin motlatitlania yn Señor Doctor Antonio Roque. ynic ompa tetech conmocahuilia españa çan oc tlatlaniliztli conmochihuilia campa e in moetzticate teopixq̃. Sanct antonio ma cuix hualmomachiztilican ahço vel hualmohuicazq̃. yehuantin in comendadores onmotetlacuilhuililia ynic ma ynhuelitzintica yn Sancto Padre Paulo Quinto. yhuan yehuatzin Rey españa Don Felipe. Tercero. ynic ma quinmomacahuilican ma hualmohuicacan ỹ nican ipan ciudad Mexico nueua España. ma motlalitzinoqui ma quimopieliqui yn omoteneuhtzino S. Antonio Abad yn iteopancaltzin y huel yehuan-

1. The date is out of order. The days of the week, however, work out right with the 20th and 23rd.

he is to be in charge of the altepetl and city of Chiapas. He is from Mexico here, a child of people here, what is called a criollo. He came back from Spain; he left here and was in Spain for a long time, so that the king gave him his spiritual rulership there, but it wasn't until he came back that he was consecrated as spiritual ruler in passing through the City of the Angels, Puebla, on the way here; he received it from the hands of the bishop there, don Alonso de la Mota y Escobar, right on the feast day of San Miguel.

v Today, Tuesday the 14th of the month of October of the year 1614, was when some Japanese set out from Mexico here going home to Japan; they lived here in Mexico for four years. Some still remained here; they earn a living trading and selling here the goods they brought with them from Japan.

v Today, Thursday the 23rd of the month of October of the year 1614, was when two Discalced Franciscan friars set out from Mexico here; they are going to Japan, where they will preach.

v Today, Monday the 20th[1] of the month of October of the year 1614, was when there entered the great altepetl and city of Mexico here don Gaspar de Alvear, a gentleman [*p. 262*] who wears the insignia of Santiago. He is going to, his assignment is established at, he will rule people in and has been appointed governor in what is called New Biscay, in Guadiana in New Spain. He is just quickly passing through Mexico here; he came from Spain. He is the first one who has come to begin the governorship at Guadiana.

v Today, Monday the 29th of the month of October of the year 1614, was when there passed away the noblewoman doña Ana de Mendoza, widow, who was the spouse of doctor Riego, late president of the Royal Audiencia of Mexico. They were the founders of and built the nunnery of San Lorenzo, where two of their daughters are. It was there that the body of the said lady doña Ana de Mendoza was taken to be buried. Also the lord viceroy don Diego Fernández de Córdoba and all the members of the Royal Audiencia went to bury her.

v Today, Thursday the 30th, at the end of the month of October of the year 1614, at six o'clock in the afternoon, was when there passed away licenciado Antonio Rodríguez, who was a civil judge in the Royal Audiencia here in Mexico. It was later, the next day, on Friday afternoon, that his body was buried at San Francisco. Also the lord viceroy don Diego Fernández de Córdoba and all the members of the Royal Audiencia, the civil judges and alcaldes of court, and the archbishop, don Juan Pérez de la Serna, came to the burial.

v Today, Saturday the 15th of the month of November of the year 1614, was when for the first time [*p. 263*] my father, father fray Agustín del Espíritu Santo, the patron, who governs and as his very own property has charge of the church of my precious revered father the great San Antonio Abad here in the city of Mexico, sent a message to Spain in the dispatch ship,[2] and he and señor doctor Antonio Roque are sending a message together, in which they entrust people in Spain to make inquiries where there are religious of San Antonio and to have it announced to them that perhaps the comendadores to whom they write can come here by authorization of the holy Father Paul V and the king of Spain don Felipe III, hoping that they would allow them to come here to the city of Mexico in New Spain; let them come establish themselves and take charge of the said church of San Antonio Abad, those precious revered religious, who are called monks who live by

2. Once again "navioviso" or "naviobiso" appears for *navío de aviso*, suggesting that the form is normal for Ch. See also pp. 234–35 at n. 3.

tzitzin tlaçomahuizteopixque moteneuhtzinohua ycel yyoca nencatzitzinti Mongestin y huel ypilhuantzitzinhuan y huel ytlacahuillohuan yn nican tlalticpac quinmocahuilitia yn ihcuac momiquilitzino omoteneuhtzino notlaçomahuizthatzin S. Antonio Abad, y ye yxquich ica[1]
auh yehuatl ipan mohuica yc teoyotica monemiliznehtoltihtzinohua yn teoyotica yoctacatlatecpantzin yn motenehua yn ireglatzin in Totlaçomahuizthatzin hueytzintli S. Basilio Magno Doctor yteotlanextzin in Sancta yglesia. yhuan Arçobispo moyetzticatca yn ompa ipan huey ciudad de Cesarea. de Capadocia. en Grecia, ypan tlalli Assia, yn tonatiuh yquiçayampa. Auh ca çãno [*p. 264*] San Antonio Teopixqui moyetzticatca yn omoteneuhtzino hueytzintli San Basilio Magno. yece in çatepan oc ceppa ye no yehuatzin motlayancuililico. motlapahpatillico yn itechpa yn oc tleỹ ytlacahuia teopixcanemiliztli. yn ipan teopixcayotl S. Antonio Auh yn ipampa ye no yehuatzin omoteneuhtzino San Basilio Magno. ynic yenohuatzin[2] omotlayancuilili yn omotlapahpatilli ynic oquinmomaquillico oc cẽtlamantli yn omoteneuh teoyotica yoctacateopixcatlatecpantenemitiayatzin yn iReglatzin ynic oquinmomaquillico y huel quinmocemaxcatilli cemihcac. yn itlaçoteopixcateyccauhtzitzinhuan yn omoteneuhtzinoque ycel yyoca nencatzitzinti Mongestin, yehuatl ipan mohuica yn axcan ynic teoyotica monemiliznehtoltitzinohua in tlaçoteopixque S. Antonio. yc ipampa on oquimocentocayotitzinoco Teopixque Basilios. ynic axcan yc monotzinohua, yece ca yqu imomextintzitzin ynthatzitzinhuan mochiuhtzinoticate in S. Antonio Abad, yhuan S. Basilio Magno, yn ipan in ce ynteopixcanemilitzin tlaçoteopixque Mongestin y ye moteneuhtzinohua Basilios. yn ompa yn ayemo no huecauh yn ayemo. miec xihuitl omotlalitzinoco España. ompa ohualmohuicaque yn italia. yhuan francia. oc cenca ompa yn miequintin onmoyetzticate yn tonatiuh yquiçayampa motenehua en Grecia yhuan yn ipan ome tlalli motenehua Armenias in hueycan yhuan ipan Tepiton Armenia ihuan Moscouia yhuan Ethiopia yn itlahtocatlapacholpan huey tlahtohuani yn tocayotillo Preste Juan. huel cenca tlamaceuhque yhuan motlatequipanilhuiani yn inma[*p. 265*]Ticatzinco Tequitini. auh in tlein ceceyaca quimixnextilia conmotlalilia yn ompa intlacentlaliayantzinco motenehua Comunidad, yniqu incepanyantzinco yntetzinco monequi. O yhui n in y motlamaniltilia yn intlatecpanpantzinco tlaçoteopixque, ma yuh mochi tlacatl quimati ca yuh quinmottilizque intla quimonequiltitzinoz. ytla itlanequiliztzin. tt°. Dios. ca hualmohuicazq̃. tiquihtotilizq̃.[3] ỹ nican S. Anton Mexico nueua españa, auh ytlacamo ytlanequilizticatzinco mochihuaz tt° Dios. ca amo huel hualmohuicazque.
v Auh çano ypan in yn omoteneuh cemilhuitl Sabado. ihcuac nican Mexico Omoquixti in licenciado Don Pedro de Otalora Presidente ỹ nican Mexico audiencia real, yn oquimottilito. yn oquimoyahualhuito nohuiyampa in techyahualotoc huey atl. ompa hualmopehualtito yn xuchimilco oquimottilito atl, yn quenin mani yc niman ompa moquixtito yn Tulyahualco, niman moquixtito cuitlatetelco, niman yc ompa moquixtito yn ayotzinco, niman moquixtito chalco atenco, niman moquixtito chimalhuacan atẽco, niman moquixtito yn ipan huey alte[266]Petl Tetzcuco, yhuiyantzin yn mohuicatia ynic nohuiyampa quimootztilitia atl ynic niman ça yc ompa mocauhtzinoto ỹ citlaltepec, yn quimot-

1. The sentence is apparently left incomplete.
2. For "no yehuatzin."
3. The verb *i(h)totia* is to dance. It is normally reflexive. When it has a nonreflexive object instead, it means to cause someone else to dance. "We will dance to or for it or

themselves and alone, who are the true children and relics that my said precious revered father San Antonio Abad left here on earth when he died until such time as____[1]

They go in, they take their vows for a spiritual life with, the spiritual exemplary arrangement called the rule of our precious revered father the great San Basilio Magno, a doctor, the divine light of the holy Church, who was archbishop in the great city of Caesarea in Cappadocia, in Greece, in Asia Minor, in the East. [*p. 264*] The said great San Basilio Magno was likewise a religious of San Antonio, but afterward he again renewed and corrected what was still wrong with priestly life in the priesthood of San Antonio. And because the said San Basilio Magno when he[2] renewed and corrected things and gave them another separate said exemplary arrangement for living a spiritual, priestly life, his rule, which he gave to and entirely made the eternal property of his precious younger siblings as priests, who as mentioned live by themselves and alone, monks, in which the precious religious of San Antonio now are guided by and take their vows for a spiritual life, for that reason they came to call them all by the same name of Basilian religious, as they are now called, but the two of them have different fathers, San Antonio Abad and San Basilio Magno, within a single priestly life of the precious religious, monks. The said Basilians, not long ago, not many years ago came to establish themselves in Spain; they came from Italy and France, and especially there are many in the east, in what is called Greece, and in two lands called the Armenias, the big and the small Armenia, and in Moscovia, and in Ethiopia, in the royal jurisdiction of the great ruler called Prester John. They are great penitents and workers, [*p. 265*] working with their hands, and what each one acquires he places in their joint gathering place, called the community, so that they can use it jointly. Like this, then, the precious religious govern themselves in their rule. Let everyone know that they will see them if our lord God wishes it; if it is his will, they will come here. [We will dance to it ?][3] here at San Antón in Mexico, in New Spain. But if it is not done by the will of our lord God, they will not be able to come.

v On the same said day of Saturday was when licenciado don Pedro de Otalora, president of the Royal Audiencia here in Mexico, left Mexico to go to inspect and to go all around the great lake that surrounds us. He began in Xochimilco, inspecting the level of the water; then he passed through Tolyahualco; then he passed through Cuitlatetelco; then he passed through Ayotzinco; then he passed through Chalco Atenco; then he passed through Chimalhuacan Atenco; then he passed through the great altepetl [*p. 266*] of Tetzcoco. He went slowly because he went inspecting the waters in each place everywhere, until finally he stopped at Citlaltepec to inspect the water excavation [drainage] being done there. The

---

him," in Ch.'s style, would be "tictihtotilizq̃." A sense "we will celebrate it" would be very appropriate here, but the form here does not say that unless we assume that a mistake was made. A causative from *i(h)toa* might give the right sense, but that would normally be *i(h)toltia*, hence "tictihtoltilizq̃."

tilito, yn ompa mochihua atataquiliztli, yn macehualtzitzinti ompa quitatacaya ce tepetl yn quicuitlacoyoniaya,[1] yn amo huel mochihua mohuitia ynic ompa quiçaz atl,[2] omoteneuh ỹ nican techyahualotoc yn capachoznequi ciudad Mexico, yc mocauh ayocmo omochiuh yn motatacaz. yuh omihto ypampa ca cenca miequintin ỹ macehualtzitzin hueca tlaca huel yxquich cincuenta mil yn oncan omomiquillico atatacoyan, y nohuiyampa tlaca, cẽca omotolinique, yhuan yuh omihto ca ce millon, yn oncan ye popolihui ytlatquitzin Rey. Auh yn ohualmocueptzino yn omocallaquico nican Mexico. yn omoteneuhtzino Señor licenciado Don Pedro de Otalora. ye ipan Metztli de diziembre. in ça ye ipan ye itlamian yn omoteneuh xihuitl de 1614. años huel ipan yc cemilhuitl ypehuayan. ynic ce ymissatzin yn iaquillantotzin[3] totlaçomahuiznantzin yn mochiuhtiuh yn chiuhcnahui y ye ytlacatilizhuallalizpantzinco tt^{o}. Dios. yn iuh mochipa cecexiuhtica mochiuhtiuh oquimoneltililito yn Presidente ytequitzin. [*p. 267*]

vi.[4] Acatl xihuitl 1615. años. yn ipan yn ipehuayan in omoteneuh yancuic xihuitl yhuan metztli henero. yhcuac cenca chicahuac. omomanaco çahuatl motenehua saranpio, yntech motlalli yn inpilhuan españoles, yhuan timacehualtin topilhuan

v̲ Yhuan yn ipan yn ipehuayan in omoteneuh yãcuic xihuitl yhuan metztli henero yhcuac opohualloque ye cuel yxquich chicuacenpohualli yn oncate yn españoles. yhuan españolas. teoyotica nenque yn oquicuique yn itlaquentzin yn iauitotzin totlaçothatzin S. Fran^{co}, yn quiyahuac tlaca yn omopouhque yn iexcantlatecpampantzinco. y ye motenehua la tercera orden de s. Fran^{co}. yn çan inchachan quipia quimonemiliztia yn toquichtin yhuan cihua[5] yn iexcantlatecpantzin Señor S. Fran^{co}. yn omotlalique nican ipan huey altepetl ciudad Mexico Tenuchtitlan.

v̲ Axcan domingo ynic cemilhuitl mani metztli de febrero de 1615. años. yhcuac cenca chicahuac ocehuetzico yn ayc yuh mochihuani nican Mexico. oc cenca ompa yn izquican chalco. mochi cecualloc. y nochiznopalli yn oquitocaca [*p. 268*] ytencopa Jues español topille[6] yn quimocuitlahuiaya. ye otlatzicoca ye omozcaltiaya huel tlaltitech oquihuicac ynic oquipollo cetl[7] huel ce semana yn chicahuac ocehuetz.

v̲ Axcan lunes ynic .2. mani Metztli de febrero de 1615. años. yhcuac nican ciudad Mexico. onmopehualti in teoyotica tlahtohuani Don fray Juan çapata y sandoual obispo. ompa mohuica yn ipan ciudad chiapa ompa quimopieliz yn altepetl. çan ey metztli ipan tlaco nican mexico metzticatca. ynic niman omohuicac.

v̲ Axcan sabado ynic .7. mani metztli de febrero de 1615. años. ihcuac nican mexico onpeuhque matlactin Japon tlaca. ompa hui yn inchã Japon nican Mexico opochtecatico.

v̲ Axcan sabado ynic 14. mani Metztli de febrero de 1615. años. yhcuac oceppayauh yn intech nohuiayan tetepe. yn iztac tepetl ytech yhuan ytech popocatepetl, yhuan ytech tepetl ytoca cilcuaye, yn ayotzinco nepa catqui chalco, yhuan ytech quetzaltepetl, yn tetzcucopa catqui, yhuan cenca chicahuac oyehecac, omilhuitl yn ohuetz ceppayahuitl. yn

1. Or through it?
2. Or a channel cannot be made for the water to come out.
3. Usually a Christmas or New Year's present, often from a superior to subordinates.
4. Space was left in front for a pictorial year sign not actually filled in.
5. In this case *toquichtin*, "we men," a way of referring to groups of men that Ch.

poor commoners were excavating a mountain there, making a hole in the side of it,[1] where the said waters that as said surround us and are about to flood the city of Mexico cannot find a channel to come out.[2] It was halted, and the excavation was done no more, because, it was said, a great many poor commoners from far away, a full 50,000, died at the place of excavation; people from all around were greatly afflicted. And it was said that a million [pesos] of the king's assets were spent there. When the said señor licenciado don Pedro de Otalora returned to and entered Mexico here, it was already in the month of December, at the end of the said year of 1614; it was right on the first day, beginning, and first mass of the *aguinaldo*[3] of our precious revered mother, of which nine go along being performed at the time of the birth and coming of our lord God, as is always done every year, that the president finished carrying out his assignment. [*p. 267*]

6[4] Reed Year, 1615. At the beginning of the said new year and of the month of January was when a very severe pox broke out, called measles; the children of the Spaniards and the children of us commoners caught it.

v Also at the beginning of the said new year and of the month of January was when there were counted the Spanish men and women who live in legitimate marriage who have taken the attire and habit of our precious father San Francisco, the people outside [the monastery], who joined the third order [of San Francisco], called the Tercera Orden de San Francisco, the men and women[5] who just observe at home and give themselves to the life of the third order of lord San Francisco established here in the great altepetl and city of Mexico Tenochtitlan. There were already a full hundred and twenty of them.

v Today, Sunday the first day of the month of February of the year 1615, was when there was a very severe freeze such as had never happened here in Mexico. Especially all over Chalco all the cochineal cactus froze that had been planted [*p. 268*] at the order of a Spanish judge, [a constable].[6] The [cactus] that they were cultivating had already taken root and started to grow, but the ice[7] destroyed it and knocked it all the way down to the ground. For a whole week it froze severely.

v Today, Monday the 2nd of the month of February of the year 1615, was when the spiritual ruler don fray Juan de Zapata y Sandoval, bishop, set out from the city of Mexico here to go to the city of Chiapas, where he will be in charge of the altepetl. He was here in Mexico for only three and a half months before he left.

v Today, Saturday the 7th of the month of February of the year 1615, was when ten Japanese set out from Mexico here to go home to Japan; they came here to Mexico to act as merchants.

v Today, Saturday the 14th of February of the year 1615, was when it snowed on the mountains everywhere, on Iztaccihuatl and on Popocatepetl, and on the mountain called Cilquaye in Ayotzinco on the far side of Chalco, and on Quetzaltepetl, which is toward Tetzcoco. And there was a very strong wind. For two days the snow fell. On Sunday, after

---

often reserves for indigenous men, refers to Spanish men instead. Often, too, *cihua*, "women," refers primarily to indigenous people, but not here.

6. The word *topile* is often glossed as constable, but it can apply to a large range of middle-level officials, all those who hold a staff as a sign of some special assignment.

7. Or cold.

ipan Domingo. ohuallathuic ye[*p. 269*]quene nohuiyan ynic cenchalco oceppayauh yn intech tetepe. ça tel quexquich yn onhuetz ayocmo cenca chicahuac, yece çan ye yhui cenca chicahuac yn oyehecac. ye ome tzillini ipan tlaco hora yn omocehuico hehecatl huel itztic yn omochiuh omilhuitl.

v Axcan martes ynic .3. mani Metztli Março de 1615 años. yhcuac nican Mexico onpeuhque onpohualtin yn Portuguestin ytencopatzinco visurrey ompa hui yaotlapiazque y huey atenco Acapolco, ypampa omachiztico nican Mexico oncan ohuallaque yn tlahueliloque ỹ motenehua landenses,[1] yhuan pichilinquez, ychtecque huey apan nemi,

v Axcan yc ce viernes yn ipan quaresma ynic 6. mani Metztli Março de 1615. años ihcuac omotlalli opeuh. otzintic yn estaciones sant ipolito yn oncan motenehua Monte caluario. yehuatzin oquimotlalili yn señor Don gabriel guerrero tlatzintille fundador omochiuhtzino yca ytlatquitzin yn oquimochihuilli. auh ypan omotlahtolti ypan huel omochicauhtzino yn Padre fray Alonso de Molina lego quateçontzin S. Fran[co] teopixqui yntepantlahtocatzin in animas no yehuatzin in tlatzintile fundador omochiuhtzino. ynic mochi tlacatl oncan onmoteochihua yn ipan chicome viernes quaresma [*p. 270*] ynic amo çan quexquich oncan õmocnopilhuia tecentlapopolhuiliztli yndulugencias.

v Axcan sabado ynic .7. mani metztli Março de 1615. años huel ipan ilhuitzin san[to], thomas de Aquino ihcuac nican Mexico quimonehualtilique matlacpohualli ipan chiuhcnahui tlacatl in forçados. yn españoles. temac ohuetzque bagamondos. yhuan cequintin tlahtlacolleque temictiliztica cequintin tliltique. cequintin mulados. cequintin mestiçostin. yhuan macuiltin timacehualtin indios. in huicoque la china justiçiatica mochintin tepoçotiaque yhuã mailpitiaque. // Yhuan in ipan in omoteneuh metztli Março cenca momiquillique in pipiltzitzinti yn ica çahuatl saranpio. mochintin intech motlalli yn inpilhuan españoles. yhuã tliltique.

v Axcan miercoles ynic .ii. mani metztli Março de 1615. años. yhcuac nican mexico quimaxitico Eyntin españoles. de la guardia yehuantin quinpixtihuia in forçados la china quinhuica Justiciatica in tlacpac omoteneuhque corte quimontzaq̃. auh iuh machiztico yuh mihto yn nican Mexico. Epohuallonmatlactli in quinchololtito tepetitech tlecoque in forçados. auh ce tlacatl tepixtihuia de la guardia quimictitehuaque. yhuan ce tehuicac in tepixtihuia. Auh inic niman yn ipan viernes. ynic 13. mani metztli Março. nican mexico onpeuhque oyahque onpohuallonmatlactli soldadostin tiacahuan ce tlacatl Capitan mochiuhtia Comission qui[*p. 271*]huicac. ynic nohuiyan quintemozque. yn ocholloto forçados. yn iuh yatia itlanahuatiltzin tlacatl visurrey intla oquimittaque cholloque intlacamo çan ihuiyan hualmotemacazque. intla mocuecuetzozque niman ompa tepuztlahuitoltica pistoletetica quinmiminazque quinmictizque. yhuan caxtolpohualli macehualtin tlaminani quinhuicaque quimantiquizque ohtlipan in quinpalehuizque Joldadostin in quinmiminazque quinmictizque in forçados choloque. ca iuh motlanahuatilli in visurrey.

v Axcan viernes. ynic .20. mani metztli Março de 1615 años. ihcuac ipan in oquihuallicuanique in intlayahualoliz. in inprossesion in cofrades. yn itetzinco pohui yn ipilhuantzitzin tlacemicnopilhuiani San Roque. yn ompa quiçani atenantitech hospital s. lazaro. acalcalco.[2] yn españoles. yhuan timacehualtin yn oquiçaya lunes sancto. // Auh

1. This form doubtless derives from Flandes, Flanders, with a Latinate ending. Nahuatl would be prone to omit [f] before [l].

midnight and before dawn, [*p. 269*] it finally snowed everywhere all over Chalco on the mountains, though only a certain amount fell; it was no longer very strong, but there was a very vigorous, strong wind. At half past 2 o'clock the wind abated. It was very cold for two days.

v Today, Tuesday the 3rd of the month of March of the year 1615, was when 40 Portuguese set out from Mexico here by order of the viceroy; they are going to stand guard at the seashore at Acapulco, because it became known here in Mexico that the wicked people called the Flemish[1] and pirates, thieves who go on the sea, had come there.

v Today, the first Friday of Lent, the 6th of the month of March of the year 1615, was when [the practice] of setting up the stations [of the cross] began and was founded at San Hipólito, at the place called Monte Calvario. It was set up by señor don Gabriel Guerrero, who became the founder; it was with his own assets that he did it, and father fray Alonso de Molina, a lay brother, a Franciscan friar, the intercessor for the souls of the dead, also spoke in favor of it and really urged it; he too became a founder, so that everyone goes there to pray on the seven Fridays of Lent, [*p. 270*] so that a great many general pardons, indulgences, are earned there.

v Today, Saturday the 7th of the month of March of the year 1615, right on the feast day of Santo Tomás de Aquino, was when they set out from Mexico here taking 209 people condemned to forced labor: Spaniards, vagabonds who had been apprehended, some people guilty of murder, some blacks, some mulattoes, some mestizos, and five of us commoners, Indians, who were taken to China [the Philippines] by order of the law. All of them went in shackles and with their hands tied. // And in the said month of March many children died from a pox, measles; all the children of Spaniards and blacks caught it.

v Today, Wednesday the 11th of the month of March of the year 1615, was when they brought here to Mexico three Spanish guards who had been going along guarding those condemned to forced labor [*forzados*] in the Philippines; they took the above mentioned [guards] by order of the law and locked them in the court [jail]. It became known and was said here in Mexico that they let 70 of those condemned to forced labor get away and climb the mountains, and they left dead one guard who went along guarding them, and one who was guarding they took along. And then on Friday the 13th of the month of March, 50 soldiers, warriors, set out from and left Mexico here. One person went appointed as captain; he carried a commission [*p. 271*] to seek everywhere the condemned to labor who had run away. According to the order of the lord viceroy, if they saw those who fled, if they didn't give themselves up peacefully, if they made a motion, right away they were to shoot and kill them with a metal crossbow, that is, with a pistol. And they took along 300 commoners who were archers; they took them along on the road to help the soldiers, to shoot and kill the condemned to labor who had fled. That is what the viceroy ordered.

v Today, Friday the 20th of the month of March of the year 1615, was when the cofradía members who are dedicated to and the children of the all-deserving San Roque moved their procession. The Spaniards and we commoners used to come out from the hospital of San Lázaro at Atenantitech, at Acalcalco,[2] on the Monday of Holy Week. // But they came out

2. In another instance (pp. 54–55, entry for the end of December, 1595), referring to this same site, the word is given as "acalcaltitlan." We take it for a varying place name, but the meaning might be at or next to the boat house(s).

çan ye ipan in teotlac nahui tzillini oquizque axcan ipan cemilhuitl viernes.
v̲ Axcan martes ynic .24. mani Metztli Març̧o de 1615. años. ihcuac nahuintin forçados. oncan temac huetzico in culhuacan yehuantin in tlacpac omoteneuhque yn ohtlipan chol-loto in quinhuicaya la china. auh ic hualmocuepaya. çan ichtaca yohualtica ỹ nican Mexico callaquizquia oncan quimittac in culhuacan teniente, ynic niman oc nẽ callactihuetzca teopan. oncan quinquixtizquia [*p. 272*] yn omoteneuh teniente. ynic oncan quihualmotlaque tepuztlahuitoltica. pistoletetica, ic yehuatl niman momiquilli in teniente. ynin temictihque ye omoteneuh yehuantin yn españoles Eyntin. yhuã ce tliltic ahnoço mulato. auh ça omentin y huel quimanque teomeca[1] in tliltic ynehuan yn español huel ayaxcan in quimanque ompa chaneque çan timacehualtin in teahcique. huel quinhuihuitecque ynic quimanque niman ompa quinmictilique. auh ça mimicque in quimaxitico nican mexico teotlac. innahuixtin yn ipan in omoteneuh cemilhuitl martes. oquinxexeloque yhuan in intzonteco oncan tecpan quiyahuac. tepilolcuauhticpac oquinçaçaloque. yhuan yn inmayeccamcopamacpal quintehtequilique oncan itlan yn intzonteco quiçaçalloque.

v̲ axcan sabado ynic .4. mani metztli Abril de 1615. años. ihcuac yohuatzinco yn opeuh ye tlatzillini yglesia mayor. ynic oquimotlalili descomunio Prouisor ytocatzin castro yn inpan alldes de cortes. impampa omentin quintlatzontequilique Justiciatica pilolozquia omentin españoles. ce corona quipia ce teopan quiquixtique auh Eilhuitl in inpampa descomunio intech catca omoteneuhque alldes de cortes, cemilhuitl in tlatzillin ipan omoteneuh Sabado, yhuan ipan domingo. yhuan ipan lunes. ye yohua mocahuaco. yn o iuh ontzillin Oracion Cenca ic ne[*p. 273*]içahuilloc, yc netetzanhuilloc. in nican ipan ciudad. Mexico. // Auh no ihcuac yn. ocehuico yn cocoliztli çahuatl motenehua saranpio.

v̲ Jueues ynic 21. mani Metztli Mayo de 1615 años ihcuac yohuatzinco chiuhcnahui tzillini nican ciudad Mexico. ommopehualti in cenca mahuiztililoni teoyotica tlahtohuani Maestro Don fr. Diego de contreras. Arçobispo. teopixqui S. Augustin nican mexico motlacatilli nican ypiltzin y huei altepetl ompa mohuica ompa motlallia itequitzin yn atl itic S^{to}. Domingo la ysla ompa quimopieliz in Sta. yglesia. yn iuhqui hualmotlachicahuililia S^{to}. Padre de Roma. yhuan yn iuh oquimocnelili yn iuh oquihualmonahuatilli tohueytlahtocatzin Don felipeh tercero Rey españa.
v̲ Martes. ynic .19.[2] mani Metztli Mayo. de 1615. años. ynic hualyohuac ihcuac omomiquilli yn çihuapilli Doña isabel de Muteuhcçuma cihuateupixqui Monja omoetzticatca omopohuiltiaya itlatecpanpantzinco in totlaçomahuiznantzin in itlaçomahuizchipahuacanenacayotiliztzin Sancta Maria nuestra señora de la consepçion yn oncan Monasterio ayoticpac. ipan tlaxillacalli cihuatlan yuh yehuantin quitocayotiaya i ye huecauh tlaca catca Mexica huehuetque. ynin omoteneuhtzino cihuateupixqui, ca mes[*p. 274*]tiça ỹtech quiz huel ymichputzin yn Gozallo gano español Conquistador. ynehuan ynamic Doña isabel tecuichpotzin de Muteuhcçuma tepeticpac cihuapilli. yhuan mihtohuaya Tecaman çihuapilli. ynin omoteneuh tlahtocacihuapilli infanta Doña isabel tecuichputzin de Muteuhcçuma, huel ichputzin in huey tlahtohuani catca Muteuhcçumatzin xocoyotl. ynic

1. In his writing Ch. often uses a rare form consisting of *te-*, a number, and *-ca*. It usually has an ordinal sense, which would here be "the second of them," but that meaning does not seem appropriate.

today, on a Friday, at 4 o'clock in the afternoon.

v Today, Tuesday the 24th of the month of March of the year 1615, was when four of those condemned to forced labor were apprehended in Colhuacan; they were of the group mentioned above who fled along the way while they were taking them to the Philippines. The reason they were coming back was that they were going to enter Mexico here secretly, at night. The deputy magistrate in Colhuacan saw them, whereupon they quickly tried to enter the church; the said deputy was going to remove them from there [*p. 272*] when they shot back at him with a metal crossbow, a pistol, of which the deputy died right away. These killers, as was already said, were three Spaniards and a black or mulatto. They were able to take only two of them; it was with great difficulty that people living there were able to take [the other two],[1] the black and a Spaniard. It was just some of us commoners who caught them; they gave them a real beating when they took them; then and there they killed them. All four of them were dead when they brought them here to Mexico in the afternoon of the said day of Tuesday. They cut them into parts and stuck their heads on the gallows outside the palace, and they cut off their right hands and stuck them next to their heads.

v Today, Saturday the 4th of the month of April of the year 1615, early in the morning, was when the bells began to peal at the cathedral because the vicar general named Castro had placed the alcaldes of court under excommunication on account of two Spaniards whom they had sentenced by legal process and who were going to be hanged, one who has the tonsure and one whom they removed from a church. Because of them the alcaldes of court were excommunicated for three days; the bells pealed the whole day on the said Saturday and on Sunday, and on Monday at dark it was halted, after the bells rang for prayers. People here in the city of Mexico were greatly taken aback [*p. 273*] and shocked by it. // At the same time the sickness of pox called measles abated.

v Thursday, the 21st of the month of May of the year 1615, in the morning at 9 o'clock, was when there set out from the city of Mexico here the very reverend spiritual ruler master don fray Diego de Contreras, archbishop, Augustinian friar, who was born here in Mexico and is the child of the great altepetl here; he is going and his assignment is established out in the ocean, at Santo Domingo de la Isla, where he will be in charge of the holy church, [his office] having been confirmed by the holy Father in Rome and granted him by order of our great ruler don Felipe III, the king of Spain.

v Tuesday the 19th[2] of May of the year 1615, as night was coming, was when there passed away the noblewoman doña Isabel de Moteucçoma, who was a female religious, a nun, belonging to the order of the precious revered pure conception of our precious revered mother, Santa María, Nuestra Señora de la Concepción, in the nunnery at Ayoticpac in the tlaxilacalli of Cihuatlan, as the people of long ago, the ancient Mexica, used to call it. This said female religious was a mestiza; [*p. 274*] she descended from and was the true daughter of Gonzalo Cano, a Spanish conqueror, together with his spouse doña Isabel Teucichpochtzin de Moteucçoma. She was a lady from Tepeticpac, and it is said from Tecaman. This said royal noblewoman or infanta doña Isabel Teucichpochtzin de Moteucçoma was the true daughter of the former great ruler Moteucçomatzin the younger,

2. The date is out of order, although the days of this entry and the previous one are compatible.

teomeca yn iuhqui yntoca ỹ nican Mexico Tenuchtitlan tlahtoque catca auh ypampa ynic nican motenehua huey tlahtohuani catca Moteuhcçumatzin xocoyotl. Ca huel ixhuiuhtzin yn omoteneuh cihuateupixqui Doña isabel de Muteuhcçuma yn axcan omomiquilli ipan cemilhuitl omoteneuh. ca yuh mihtohua huel no yehuantzitzin ceme in tlapehualtileque tlatzintileque y huel achtopa ic motlalitzinoque cihuateupixque Monjastin yn oncan omoteneuh cihuateupixcacalli monasterio consepçion ayoticpac cihuatlan, in quimopehualtillique omoteneuh cihuateupixcayotl ynehuantzin yn iuhctzin. y huel ynehuantzin mehualtiaya itoca Doña Catalina de S. Miguel de Muteuhcçuma oncan moquixtihque in motenehuaya in colegio mestiçati yn oncan axcan ye motenehua colegio de las niñas, y huel ynahuac ytloc monasterio. S. Fran^co^ yni mochtintzitzin oncan moquixtihque [*p. 275*] Ca çan oc señorati,[1] auh ynin omoteneuhque çihuateupixque monjastin in ihcuac motlalique yn inhuan omentzitzin mestiçati ye omoteneuh yxhuiuhtzitzinhuã in tlacatl catca Muteuhcçumatzin Xocoyotl. ca ihcuac ipantzinco nican Mexico Motlahtocatilia y yehuatzin tlacatl Excelentissimo señor huehue Don luis de velaso, ynic ome Visurrey y mochiuhtzinoco Mexico, auh no yehuatzin ipantzinco in teuyotica tlahtohuani su señoria Don fr. Juan de çumarraga. i huel achto çan oc obispo moetzicatca nican Mexico teupixqui S. Fran^co^.[2] auh no yehuatl ipan in tlacatl Don Diego de S. Fran^co^. Tehuetzquititzin Gouernador nican Mexico Tenuchtitlan chane catca S. Pablo. Teupan xuchititlan, auh yn oncan monasterio mochiuh consepcio ca ichan catca yn Andres de Tapia cõquistador, auh yn omoteneuhtzino Doña isabel ca ye quin imoztlayoc ipan miercoles. teotlac macuilli tzilli ynic .20. mani metzli Mayo. yn otococ ynacayotzin. oncan monasterio. cõsepcio. ymixpantzinco yn ihuayolque. y ye españoles. omocuepque. quintocayotia andradas. [*p. 276*]

v̲ Jueues ynic 28. mani metztli Mayo de 1615. años. ye itlamian ynin metztli yn ohuaquico yn atl nican ixpan mani iteupancaltzin totlaçothatzin S. Antonio Abbad // auh çã no ihcuac yn ipan in omoteneuh cemilhuitl Jueues ipan ilhuitzin tt^o^. dios Assencion ynetlecahuilitzin[3] ihcuac ic oppa motlacuilhui yn españa. fr. augustin del esp̅ı̅u̅ sancto, ynnehuantzin doctor antonio Roque ipan flotas i ya cartas çan ye oc tlatlaniliztli conmochihuilia in inpampa in campa e moyetzticate yn ahço huel hualmohuicazque yn S. Antonio teopixque comendadores huallazq̃ nican mexico.

v̲ lunes ynic .i. cemilhuitl mani metztli Junio de 1615. años. yhcuac oquipehualtico. i ye quicuauhtzotzona huey aohtli in xuchimilcopa huitz. yn ixquich ic patlahuac ic catqui nican quiça y huel ixpan iteupan ithualtzin totlaçothatzin S. Antonio abbad. nican xolloco. ynic omocuauhtzotzon yehuatl[4] oquichiuh itencopa Alexo m̅ı̅n̅ Juez Repartidor nican mexico. ynic omotlapacho ynic omotetzop. omoteneuh ahotli. fuente[5] ynic hualcallacohua teopan omotlaxtlahui ynic oquichihuaco.

v̲ Auh çanno itlamian yn omoteneuh metztli Mayo. yn oquipehualtihque españoles. ytech ye tlataca chapultepetl.[6] ytencopatzinco tlahtohuani visurrey Don diego fernandez de

1. Another possibility might be: All the [mestizas] came out of there, [*p. 275*] for [it was to be] just for Spanish women from then on.

2. Velasco and Zumárraga did not actually coincide in New Spain, if that is Ch.'s meaning.

3. This word is in the wrong place, but apparently was meant here.

4. The word "yehuatl," which repeats or anticipates the subject of "oquichiuh," "did it,"

the second of two rulers here in Mexico Tenochtitlan who had that name, and that is why here the great former ruler is called Moteucçoma the younger. The said female religious doña Isabel de Moteucçoma who died now on the said day is truly his grandchild. It is said that she together with her younger full sibling named doña Catalina de San Miguel de Moteucçoma were truly among the beginners and founders when female religious, nuns, were established for the very first time at the said house for female religious, nunnery, of Concepción at Ayoticpac in Cihuatlan; they initiated the said nunnery. They came from what was called the Colegio de Mestizas, which now is called the Colegio de las Niñas, very close to the monastery of San Francisco. All the others who came from there [*p. 275*] were just Spanish women.[1] And these said female religious, nuns, established themselves then along with the two mestizas, who as was said were grandchildren of the lord Moteucçoma the younger. That was in the time when the most excellent lord the elder don Luis de Velasco ruled here in Mexico, the second viceroy appointed in Mexico, and also in the time of the spiritual ruler, his lordship don fray Juan de Zumárraga, the very first bishop here in Mexico—he wasn't archbishop yet—, a Franciscan friar,[2] and also in the time of the lord don Diego de San Francisco Tehuetzquititzin, governor here in Mexico Tenochtitlan, from San Pablo Teopan, in Xochititlan. And where the nunnery of Concepción was built was the home of Andrés de Tapia, a conqueror. It was later, the next day, Wednesday afternoon, the 20th of May, at 5 o'clock, that the body of the said doña Isabel was buried at the nunnery of Concepción, in the presence of her relatives, who have become Spaniards and are called the Andradas. [*p. 276*]

v Thursday, the 28th of the month of May of the year 1615, at the end of this month, the water that is spread out here in front of the church of our precious father San Antonio Abad dried up. // And likewise on the said day of Thursday, on the feast day of the rising up[3] of our lord God, Ascensión, was when fray Agustín de Espíritu Santo together with doctor Antonio Roque wrote to Spain again; the letters went in the fleet. They are making another similar request that wherever there are religious of San Antonio, comendadores, perhaps they will be able to come, to come here to Mexico.

v Monday, the 1st day of the month of June of the year 1615, was when they began to drive piles in the great canal coming from Xochimilco, which in its full width passes by here right in front of the square of the church of our precious father San Antonio Abad here in Xoloco; when the piles were driven, [someone][4] arranged by order of Alejo Martín, distributor [of draft labor] here in Mexico, that the said canal was covered and vaulted over with stone, [making] a bridge,[5] where people enter the church; he was paid for coming to do it.

v Likewise in the said month of May, at the end of it, the Spaniards began to dig on Chapoltepetl[6] by order of the lord viceroy don Diego Fernández de Córdoba, Marqués de

---

here "arranged," has no crossreferent. Possibly, despite the grammatical oddity, Alejo Martín himself is meant and is also the person at the end of the paragraph who was paid.

5. In the Nahuatl of Stage 2, *f* and *p* were equivalent, both being pronounced [p], so that by hypercorrection *fuente* could mean *puente*.

6. That is, the hill or mountain at Chapoltepec, though in fact the settlement derives its name from the hill.

cordoua Marques de Guadarcaçar. quitemohuaya ytech teocuitlatl yn tepetzintli. aquique yn quimoztlacahuilique visurrey ca ytech toctitica miec coztic teocuitlatl. yehuatl in quitemohuaya. auh in ça tepan atle nez çan quicauhque in tlatlatacaya mochi quintlazque quintepeuhque yn ixquich ahuehuetl oncan onoyah quinxexeloque quitlatlapanque hualla nican palaçio oncan tlatlac cozina, huel [*p. 277*] ic tlaixpoliuh in chapultepec, oncan quitepeuh sebada yn capitan de la guardia Don P^o^. serrano. huel yehuatl yn tlanahuatiaya ynic tlaixpoliuh ca huel mahuizcã catca yn chapultepec.

v Miercoles ynic .10. mani Metztli de Junio de 1615. años. ihcuac. oquinmachiztito citaçion oquinchihuillito. yn amaquemecan chalco tlaca. ynic yca çan merced. ye quinmomaquiliznequi visurrey iztac tepetl in teopixq̃ itehuicaltzitzinhuan Jesus. yn moteneuhtzinohua tothatzitzinhuan de la compañia de Jesus. yhuan tocayotillo. Teatinos. yhuan ome cidios de estancia moch in cuahuitl quimaniliznequia teopixque ychcame oncan nemizquia yn imaxcahuan. auh ahuel mochiuh ca ye moteilhuico yn amaqumeq̃. yhuan tlalmanalca macehualtin yc macomanq̃. mochintin in teupixq̃. dominigos. yhuan Fran^cos^. yn ompa quimopielia altepetl yhuan ompa vezinos españoles. yc formacion quichiuhque in macehualtin yn quenin huell imaxca tepetl yc moteilhuico ixpantzinco visurrey. yc pleito mochiuh. testigos mochiuhque yn frayles. yhuan españoles yn intechpa macehualtin chalca, ynic çan quicauhque motzinquixtitzinoque in teupixque la compañia de Jesus. auh çãno ic quicauhque inPleito macehualtin amo quitzonquixtihque oncan mocauh yn proseso. amacalco palaçio.

v Auh çãno ipehuayan in yn omoteneuh metztli Junio de 1615. años. ihcuac. ompa cuyohuacan ynahuac San jacinto [*p. 278*] cecni huerta. omotlalitzinoto. in tlaçoteupixque yn itlaçopilhuantzitzin totlaçomahuiznantzin nuestra Señora del carme in motlacxipanhuilia ahnoço mocxipetlahuiltihtinemi moteneuhtzinohua descalços. yn oncan motlalitzinoto. yhuerta catca in cuyohuacan tlahtohuani catca Don Juan de guzman itzllolinqui, ye ipilhuan ixhuihuan yn oquinnamaquiltico huerta yn omoteneuhtzinoque teupixque yn oncan incolegiotzin quimochihuilique yc motlatocamaquilique San Angel Martyr. yn oncã quimomachtitzinohua latin telpopuchtin teupixque.[1]

v Lunes ynic .15. mani metztli Junio de 1615. años. ihcuac nican Mexico. onpeuh yn Doctor Antonio de Morga. ynic ompa mohuicac Perũ ompa Presidente mochiuhtzinoto. yn audiencia real, ompa quihualmicuanilli yn Rey[2]

v Domingo inic .21. mani metztli Junio de 1615. años. ihcuac ilhuitzin mochiuh sacramento. in san Fran^co^. ihcuac no mochalli omoman yn omotlapallicuillo yancuic rrejas tepoztli, yn oncan callihtic capilla mayor, españa hualla cenca mahuiztic ynic oquitlapallicuilloque xoxoctic. yhuan cequi coztic. cequi yca coztic teocuitlatl, ynic omicuillo icpac motlalli yn itocatzin Jesus. auh quin iyocan teupan. yuhqui rrejas tepoztli, omotlalli, yn ayemocan oc cecni teupan yuhqui motlalia.

v Domingo inic .5. mani metztli Julio de 1615. años. ihucuac [*p. 279*] ye yohua ye ipan horaçion tzillini yn omomiquilli Doctor Don Juan de Salamanca chantre omoetzticatca ỹ nican Sancta yglesia Mexico. ynin ye huehue tlacatl omoetzticatca huel nican motlacatilli nican chane Mexico. Tenuchtitlan, motenehua criollo, yhuan huecauh o no moProuisor-

1. The meaning could be all ecclesiastics, only religious, only friars, or perhaps only members of their order.

Guadalcázar; they were searching for gold on the hill. Someone falsely told the viceroy that much gold lies buried on it, and that was what they were looking for, but afterward nothing could be found, and they halted the excavation. They knocked down all the cypresses that were there and left them scattered around; they cut them up and split them and they were brought here to the palace, where they were burned in the kitchen; [*p. 277*] with that things were left very bare at Chapoltepec. The captain of the guard don Pedro Serrano scattered barley [seed] there. It was he himself who gave the orders by which things were left bare; Chapoltepec used to be a very marvelous place.

v Wednesday, the 10th of the month of June of the year 1615, was when they went to inform and formally notify the people of Amaquemecan Chalco that just by a grant the viceroy wants to give Iztaccihuatl, with two estancia sites, to the religious who are followers of Jesus, called our fathers of the Company of Jesus, also given the name of Theatines; the religious wanted to take all the forest, and sheep belonging to them would live there. But it could not be done, for the commoners of Amaquemecan and Tlalmanalco made a complaint about it; all the Dominican and Franciscan friars who are in charge of altepetl there, and the Spanish residents there, were upset by it, so that the commoners provided formal proof of how the mountain is really their property. They made complaint about it before the viceroy and a suit was brought about it; the friars and the Spaniards became witnesses for the Chalca commoners, so that the religious of the Company of Jesus abandoned [their plans] and withdrew. Because of that the commoners likewise dropped their suit and did not finish it; the papers of the suit were left in the palace archive.

v Likewise at the beginning of the said month of June of the year 1615 was when the precious friars who are precious children of our precious revered mother Nuestra Señora del Carmen, who go on foot, or rather go about with bare feet, called Discalced, went to establish themselves in Coyoacan near San Jacinto, [*p. 278*] in an orchard. They established themselves in an orchard that used to belong to the late ruler in Coyoacan don Juan de Guzmán Itztlolinqui; his children and grandchildren sold the orchard to the said friars. They built their colegio there, giving it the name of San Angel Mártir, where they teach Latin to young ecclesiastics.[1]

v Monday, the 15th of the month of June of the year 1615, was when doctor Antonio de Morga set out from Mexico here to go to Peru, where he has been made president of the Royal Audiencia; the king transferred him there.[2]

v Sunday, the 21st of the month of June of the year 1615, was when the feast day of the Sacrament was celebrated at San Francisco, and also when the new painted iron grill inside, in the main chapel, was set up and inaugurated; it came from Spain, very splendidly painted, green and some of it yellow, and some with gold, where the name of Jesus is written on top of it. This is the first place where such iron grillwork has been put in a church (here); such a thing has not yet been put in any other church.

v Sunday, the 5th of the month of July of the year 1615, when [*p. 279*] it was already dark and bells were ringing for prayer, was when there passed away doctor don Juan de Salamanca, who was choirmaster here in the holy church in Mexico. He was already an old man, born right here, a person native to Mexico Tenochtitlan, called a criollo, and he

2. See pp. 280–81 at n. 2.

tilitia. ỹ nican mexico. yn intechcopa españoles. auh ye quin teotlac lunes yn otococ ynacayotzin oncan yglesia mayor. oncan motetoquillico in teoyotica tlahtohuani Don Juan Perez de la Serna arçobispo. mexico, yhuan mochintin yn cabilto tlaca oncan otetocaco, yhuan omentin oydores yn oncan oquimotoquillico.

v Miercoles ynic .9. mani metztli Septiembre de 1615. años ipan matlactlonce tzillini tlahca, yn opeuh ye tlatzitzilica ompa teupan S. Augustin, yhuan colegio. S. Pablo. yhuan Sancta Cruz. contzinco, yhuan S. Sebastian, yhuan Totlaçonantzin nuestra Señora de las mercedes. yhuan la casa profesa, yc omotemachizti, in quenin çan nican ce macehualli Mexicacihuatl yconeuh quin cexiuhtia piltzintli ipan tlaco xihuitl quipia yn ohuetzca poçoco yn aolhuaztonco. in piltzintli oquichtontli, auh oncan tlamahuiçoltica oquimopalehuilli oquimozcalili in S. Nicolas de Tolentino, ça yuh moztla ilhuitzin auh yn omoteneuh piltzintli ca huel micca ca oMe hora ihuan tlaco hora in mictoca. ynic ni niman[1] oquimozcalili omoteneuhtzino Sancto, auh y ye yohua ynic hualyohuac, yc nohuiyan otlatzitzi[*p. 280*]licac yn izquican Teupan ynic cenMexico, yn iglesia mayor, yhuan monasterios. oc cenca ompa S. Augustin, yhuan nohuiyan cuahuitl quitlahtlatique yn intlapanco españoles. yhuan cequi yncaltempa quitlahtlatihque, yhuan in cequi monasterios. cohuetes oquitlatlazque, yhuan no yuhqui miequintin macehualtin Mexica, yuh quichiuhque quitlahtlatihque in intlapanco cuahuitl ynic cenca pahpacohuac ycatzinco S. Nicolas. nican Mexico. oncan peuhtica y, ynic ye mochipa hueylhuichihualiztli ye mochiuhtiuh ipan ilhuitzin S. Nicolas de Tolentino nican mexico in cecexiuhtica —

v Auh çan ye no ipan in yn omoteneuh cemilhuitl Miercoles. yhuan yn ipan omoteneuh ynic ohualyohuac. ihcuac omomiquilli yn Juan grande español. nahuatlahtohuaya itlantzinco tlahtohuani visurrey. cenca ohuehuetitia yhuan miec xihuitl onahuatlahto yn intloctzinco oc cequintzitzin teteuhctin tlahtoque visurreyesme yn izquintin ye hualmohuica nican ipan nueua españa, hualmotlahtocatilia, auh huel cualli tlacatl ocatca yn omoteneuh Juan grande, amo imca omocacayahuaya macehualtzitzinti in Pleito quihualchihua imixpantzinco visurreyesme, yn iuhqui oc ce tlacatl catca yn achtopa omic nahuatlahto yn itoca catca fran^co^ de leyba ynic tlahueliloc catca cẽca quintoliniaya macehualtzitzinti, auh [*p. 281*] Auh yn omoteneu[h Juan gr]ande[2] in nican Mexico Tenuchtitlan Gouer[nador catca] yehuatl iyaxca catca quimomaquilitia [in tlahto]huani Visurrey Don luis de velasco Marques [de sali]nas. ca macuilxihuitl yn itech ocatca gouernacio. auh in tlacpac omotocateneuh mestiço. yn itoca Don Juan Perez de monterrey ca çan ixiptla. çan quipalehuia çan itlaquehual mochiuhtica ynic huel yehuatl Gouernador mochiuhtica moteneuh nican Mexico Tenuchtitlan auh in salario yuh mihtohua imomextin oquimoxelhuiaya. yn omoteneuh Juan Grande.

v Martes ynic .6. mani Metztli octubre de 1615. años. ye yohua ihcuac ohualla tlahtolli correo. quihualhuicac ompa yn acapulco. inic quenin oncan macuilli acal[. . .]que[3] nemi huey apan yn quintocayotia inglesestin inglatera tlaca tlahueliloque chicotlaneltocanime motenehua Eregesme. yuh omihto ca quichiaco oncan in la china acalli ye huitz. oncan quinamoyazque in ixquich tlatquitl quihualhuica yc cenca onemauhtiloc ỹ nican ciudad Mexico. ynic çan niman ymoztlayoc ipan miercoles matlactlõce tzillini tlahca. yn on-

1. The "ni" of "niman" was inadvertently repeated.

2. These portions are presently missing in the Paris original. We have supplied them from the corresponding transcriptions of Zimmermann (Chimalpahin 1963–65), though it is not clear that the originals were more complete even at the time when Zimmermann

also served for a long time here in Mexico as vicar general for the Spaniards. Later, Monday in the afternoon, his body was buried in the cathedral; the spiritual ruler don Juan Pérez de la Serna, archbishop in Mexico, came to the burial, and all the members of the cathedral chapter came to the burial, and two judges of the Audiencia came to bury him.
v Wednesday, the 9th of the month of September of the year 1615, at 11 o'clock in the morning, bells began to ring at the church of San Agustín, and at the colegio of San Pablo, at Santa Cruz Contzinco, at San Sebastián, at our precious mother Nuestra Señora de las Mercedes, and at the Casa Profesa, announcing that the child of a Mexica commoner woman here, an infant just a year and a half old, a little boy, had fallen into a small well, and by a miracle San Nicolás de Tolentino helped and revived him on the eve of his feast day. The said child had really died, for he lay dead for two and a half hours until[1] the said saint revived him. And when it was dark, as night was coming, the bells pealed everywhere [*p. 280*] in all the churches all over Mexico, at the cathedral and the monasteries, especially at San Agustín, and the Spaniards everywhere burned wood on their roofs, and some burned it in the street outside their houses, and in some monasteries they shot off rockets, and many Mexica commoners did the same, burning wood on their roofs, in great celebration in the name of San Nicolás here in Mexico. From this time it began that a great celebration is always held every year on the feast day of San Nicolás de Tolentino here in Mexico. —

v On the same said day of Wednesday in the said [month], as night came, was when there passed away Juan Grande, a Spaniard, who interpreted for the lord viceroy; he died very old, and for many years he interpreted for other lords viceroys, all those who have come here to New Spain and ruled. The said Juan Grande was a very good person; he did not cheat poor commoners who come to bring suit before the viceroys, like another person who interpreted, who died earlier, whose name was Francisco de Leiva; he was evil and greatly mistreated the poor commoners. [*p. 281*] The said Juan Grande[2] was governor here in Mexico Tenochtitlan; [the office] belonged to him, given to him by the lord viceroy don Luis de Velasco, Marqués de Salinas, and for five years he held the governorship. The mestizo whose name was mentioned above, named don Juan Pérez de Monterrey, is just his representative and helps him, is just hired by him, so that he himself is the appointed governor here in Mexico Tenochtitlan, and it is said that the two of them, [Pérez de Monterrey] and the said Juan Grande, share the salary.

v Tuesday, the 6th of the month of October of the year 1615, when it was already dark, was when news came, brought by courier from Acapulco, how five ships [of pirates?][3] are going about on the ocean there; they call them Englishmen, people from England, wicked people, wrong believers called heretics. It was said that they came there to wait for the coming of the ship from China [the Philippines], and there they will rob it of all the goods it is bringing. There was great fear here in the city of Mexico about it, so that right

saw them. But probability dictates that Zimmermann's additions are substantially correct.

3. Or pirates in five ships? There is a gap in the original. A word with the "que" plural would not normally refer to the ships themselves. The original words may have been "macuilli acalco tenamoyaque," literally "robbers in five ships," or the like.

peuhque Tiyacahuan Joldadostin ahçonpohuallonmatlactin çan mochintin palacio nemi[1] yn oyahque tlapiazque huey atenco Acapulco, yhuan ompa quichiazque yn omoteneuh la china acalli ynic aciquiuh //. Auh yniqueilhuitl yn ipan Jueues. oc ceppa cenpohuallonnahui Tiyacahuan Joldadostin nican Mexico. onpeuhq̃. yn om[*p. 282*]pa hui omoteneuh acapu[lco a]hçizque[2] y yaotlapiazque.

v̲ Viernes. ynic .9. mani [metztli oc]tubre de 1615. ihcuac omotlalitzino yancuic Prouisor yehuatzin in Doctor P°. leon y plaça. auh in castro Prouisor catca ohuetz.[3] çã̃n onxihuitl yn otequipano visita chihuililoc mochintin yn oncan oficialti españoles. yn audiencia arçobispal. ynic cenca teca mocacayahua[4] ytencopatzinco yn arcobispo Don Juan de la serna.

v̲ Sabado ynic .10. mani metztli octubre in ipan omoteneuh xihuitl no cuel cenpohuallonchiuhcnahui tlacatl in tiyacahuan soldadostin o no yahque yn ompa omoteneuh acapulco,

v̲ Miercoles. ynic .14. mani Metztli octubre de 1615. años. ihcuac nohuian teupan ynic cenciu[dad][5] Mexico. otlatlatlauhtilloc otlayahualoloc. yn inpa[mpa] omoteneuhque tlacpac toyaohuan in teohuatentli quitocatinemi yn techyahuallotinemi,[6]

---

1. Possibly the meaning is rather that they were all of those stationed there.

2. See p. 304, n. 2.

3. "Was removed" is virtually the only sense the context permits, though it is an unfamiliar meaning. Presumably it indicates "fell" in the sense that a government falls.

away the next day, Wednesday, at 11 o'clock in the morning, soldiers, warriors, set out, perhaps 50 of them, who are all stationed at the palace,[1] who went to stand guard at the ocean shore at Acapulco and await there the arrival of the said ship from China. // On the third day, Thursday, again soldiers, warriors, 24 of them, set out from Mexico here [*p. 282*] to reach the said Acapulco[2] and stand guard.

v Friday, the 9th of the month of October of 1615, was when there was installed a new vicar general, doctor Pedro León y Plaza, and Castro, the previous vicar general, [was removed][3] after serving for only two years; by order of the archbishop don Juan de la Serna a review was made of all the Spanish officers of the Archiepiscopal Audiencia, [according to which] he was taking great advantage of people.[4]

v Saturday, the 10th of the month of October in the said year, again 29 soldiers, warriors, left for the said Acapulco.

v Wednesday, the 14th of the month of October of 1615, was when in all the churches all over the city[5] of Mexico there were prayers and processions on account of our above mentioned enemies who are going along the seashore and surround us.[6]

---

4. Or simply was cheating them.

5. See p. 304, n. 2.

6. The last entry stops well short of the bottom of the page, something hardly seen in the rest of the work, indicating an at least temporary halt of the writing.

Glossary

Certain special terms which appear only a single time and are defined in a footnote at that point are not included in this listing.

AUDIENCIA, ROYAL AUDIENCIA. High court of New Spain.

ALCALDE. First-instance judge (full title *alcalde ordinario*), also a member of a local municipal council or cabildo.

ALCALDE DE CORTE. Criminal judge belonging to the high court of the Audiencia and viceroy in the viceregal palace.

ALCALDE MAYOR. Chief magistrate of a large and usually indigenous district; always a Spaniard. Often virtually synonymous with corregidor.

ALTEPETL. Nahuatl word for any potentially independent sociopolitical entity; in central Mexican conditions, usually city-state sized, originating in precontact times and continuing after the conquest. See Introduction, pp. 6–8, 18.

ATOLE. A maize gruel.

BEATA. Literally a blessed woman; a woman wearing a religious habit and often maintaining some connection with a religious order, but usually living at home and not an official member of the order.

CABILDO. A municipal council in the Spanish style.

CATANA. An Asian-style cutlass.

CHINA. In the Mexican Spanish of the time, often reflected in Nahuatl, the Philippines; alternatively, the whole Far East.

CHINAMPA. Strip of land built up in the midst of water, extremely productive.

CHIRIMÍA. A loud single-reed wind instrument.

CIHUACOATL. In preconquest Mexico Tenochtitlan, a very high official second only to the principal ruler.

COFRADÍA. Sodality, lay brotherhood for religious purposes.

COMENDADOR. Rank in a military order or in some other orders.

COMMONER. Translation of the ambiguous *macehualli*, sometimes meaning an indigenous person of lower rank, but here, and especially in the plural, more often indigenous person in general. See Introduction, p. 17.

CONGREGACIÓN. The act of assembling indigenous people in a more compact settlement, or the resulting settlement.

CORREGIDOR. Chief magistrate of a large district; always a Spaniard. Often virtually synonymous with alcalde mayor.

CRIOLLO. An ethnic term apparently quite new to Chimalpahin, defined by him as someone born "here," in most cases right in the capital. All the examples he gives are of ethnic Spaniards.

DEFINIDORES. In the Franciscan order, members of a council set up to resolve serious problems presenting themselves.

DON. Spanish title primarily for high nobility or holders of some high offices, also used for preeminent indigenous men.

DOÑA. The approximate feminine equivalent of don.

ENCOMIENDA. Governmental grant, usually to a Spaniard, of tribute and/or labor rights from an indigenous entity, usually an altepetl.

ESTANCIA. (1) a private land grant, originally intended for livestock, usually but not invariably held by a Spaniard; in effect comes to mean Spanish rural property. (2) An outlying constituent unit of an altepetl, located at some remove from the entity's core.

FISCAL. Name of various offices. Here often the chief steward of a church; applied primarily to indigenous people. When associated with the Royal Audiencia, chief royal prosecutor.

FORZADO. A person condemned to forced labor, usually in a remote site.

GOVERNOR. Often the same as a judge-governor, highest official of an altepetl. Other times a Spaniard holding any of various types of governorships, secular or ecclesiastic.

GUARDIAN, FATHER GUARDIAN. The prior of a Franciscan establishment.

JUBILEE. Special plenary indulgence for a year.

JUDGE-GOVERNOR. An indigenous person holding the highest office in an altepetl as reorganized under the Spaniards, successor of the preconquest *tlatoani*, ruler.

HOLY FATHER. The pope.

LICENCIADO. Licentiate, title of one holding a degree, most often in law, beyond the bachelorate.

MAESTRESCUELA. A cathedral dignitary nominally charged with teaching divinity.

MATLALTOTONQUI. An epidemic fever, apparently typhus.

MANTILLA. Spanish headgear for women, a light scarf over head and shoulders.

MESTIZO, MESTIZA. Person of mixed Spanish and indigenous descent; by the strict interpretation, often violated, half Spanish and half indigenous.

MEXICO. Here, the combined entities of the Spanish Mexico City and the indigenous Mexico Tenochtitlan, or the area holding them.

MONASTERY. Since the Spaniards universally used this term (*monasterio*) for a friary of one of the mendicant orders, we follow them in that usage.

MONUMENT. A term used for an elaborate wooden catafalque set up in churches in front of the main altar at Easter time and for important funerals, often in the form of a church itself.

MORILLO. A round wooden beam used for rafters, pilings, etc.

MORISCO, MORISCA. Literally a person of Moorish descent, apparently used in Chimalpahin in virtually the same meaning as mulatto.

PALLIUM. An important insignia of the archbishopric.

PULQUE. The primary indigenous alcoholic drink, made from the juice of the maguey plant.

REAL. A coin and a monetary value, one-eighth of a peso.

REGIDOR. One of several councilmen in a Spanish-style municipal council or cabildo.

REGIDOR MAYOR. Chief regidor, ranking above the others.

RELIGIOUS (noun). Member of a clerical order, as opposed to the secular clergy.

REPARTIMIENTO (labor). A system of draft rotary labor instituted by the Spaniards on the basis of the indigenous *coatequitl*, "turn work," and still often called that by the Nahuas.

SEÑOR. Lord, also a courtesy title for men of prominence or holding certain offices.

SEÑORA. Approximate feminine equivalent of señor; sometimes used specifically as a second-class title with certain women lacking the doña.

SUJETO. Spanish term for a constituent entity of a larger indigenous polity.

TENIENTE. Deputy, lieutenant, here a Spanish magistrate subordinate to an alcalde mayor or corregidor.

THEATINES. An unofficial, technically incorrect, but widespread term used for the Jesuits.

TLAXILACALLI. One of the constituent parts or subdistricts of an altepetl. See Introduction, pp. 6, 18.

Bibliography

Alemán, Mateo. 1911. "Sucesos de d. fray García Guerra . . . (1613)," *Revue Hispanique* 68: 378–457.

Anderson, Arthur. J. O., Frances Berdan, and James Lockhart, eds. and trans. 1976. *Beyond the Codices*. Berkeley and Los Angeles: University of California Press.

Andrews, J. Richard. 1975. *Introduction to Classical Nahuatl*. Austin: University of Texas Press.

Boban, Eugène. 1891. *Documents pour servir à l'histoire du Mexique. Catalogue raisonné de la collection du M. E. Eugène Goupil.* Ancienne Collection J. M. A. Aubin. 2 vols. Paris: Ernest Leroux.

Boyer, Richard. 1980. "La ciudad de México en 1628: la visión de Juan Gómez de Trasmonte." *Historia Mexicana*, 29: 447–71.

Brewer, Forest, and Jean G. Brewer. 1971. *Vocabulario mexicano de Tetelcingo, Morelos*. 2d ed. México: Instituto Lingüistico de Verano.

Carochi, Horacio. 2001. *Grammar of the Mexican Language, with an Explanation of its Adverbs (1645)*. Ed. and trans. by James Lockhart. UCLA Latin American Center Nahuatl Studies Series, 7. Stanford, Calif: Stanford University Press and UCLA Latin American Center Publications.

Chimalpahin Quauhtlehuanitzin, don Domingo de San Antón Muñón. 1889. *Annales de Domingo Francisco de San Antón Muñón Chimalpahin Quauhtlehuanitzin. Sixième et septième relations (1258–1612)*. Ed. and trans. by Rémi Siméon. Paris: Maisonneuve et Ch. LeClerc, Éditeurs.

_____. 1944. *Diferentes historias originales de los reynos de Culhuacan y México, y de otras provincias. El Autor de ellas dicho Don Domingo Chimalpahin. Das Manuscrit Mexicain No. 74 der Bibliothèque Nationale de Paris, 5. Relación*. Ed. and trans. by Ernst Mengin. Hamburg: Cram, De Gruyter.

_____. 1949, 1950, 1952. *Diferentes historias originales de los reynos de Culhuacan, y México, y de otras provincias. El autor de ellas dicho Don Domingo Chimalpahin. Manuscrit Mexicain No. 74. Liber in lingua mexicana manuscriptus ut est conservatus in Bibliotheca Nationis Gallicae Parisiense sub numero LXXIV*. Ed. by Ernst Mengin. 3 vols. Corpus Codicum Americanorum Medii Aevi, vol. 3. Copenhagen: Einar Munksgaard.

_____. 1958. *Das memorial breve acerca de la fundación de la ciudad de Culhuacan*. Ed. and trans. by Walter Lehmann and Gerdt Kutscher. Stuttgart: W. Kohlhammer Verlag.

_____. 1960. *Das Geschichtswerk des Domingo de Muñón Chimalpahin Quauhtlehuanitzin*. Ed. and trans. by Günter Zimmermann. Hamburg: Museum für Völkerkunde und Vorgeschichte.

_____. 1963–65. *Die Relationen Chimalpahin's zur Geschichte Mexico's*. Ed. by Günter Zimmermann. 2 vols. Hamburg: Cram, De Gruyter.

_____. 1997. *Codex Chimalpahin: Society and Politics in Mexico Tenochtitlan, Tlatelolco, Texcoco, Culhuacan, and Other Nahua Altepetl in Central Mexico*. 2 vols. Ed. and trans. by Arthur J. O. Anderson and Susan Schroeder. Norman: University of Oklahoma Press.

_____. (given here as Chimalpáhin, Domingo). 1998. *Las ocho relaciones y el memorial de Colhuacan.* 2 vols. Ed. and trans. by Rafael Tena. México: Cien de México.

_____ (given here as Chimalpáhin, Domingo). 2001. *Diario.* Ed. and trans. by Rafael Tena. México: Cien de México.

_____. 2001A. *Diferentes Historias Originales.* 2 vols. Ed. and trans. by Elke Ruhnau. Markt Schwaben, Germany: Verlag Anton Saurwein.

Códice Osuna. Pintura del governador, alcaldes y regidores de México (1565). 1973. Ed. by Vicenta Cortés Alonso. Madrid: Ministerio de Educación.

Cook, Noble David. 1998. *Born to Die: Disease and New World Conquest, 1492–1650.* Cambridge: Cambridge University Press.

Cruz, Martín de la. 1996. *Libellus de medicinalibus indorum herbis.* Trans. by Juan Badiano. 2 vols. México: Fondo de Cultura Económica.

Diccionario de Autoridades. 1984. Facsimile edition. 3 vols. Biblioteca Románica Hispánica: Diccionarios, 3. Madrid: Gredos.

Durán, fray Diego. 1994. *The History of the Indies of New Spain.* Trans. by Doris Heyden. Norman: University of Oklahoma Press.

Gerhard, Peter. 1972. *A Guide to the Historical Geography of New Spain.* Cambridge: Cambridge University Press.

Gibson, Charles. 1964. *The Aztecs Under Spanish Rule.* Stanford, Calif.: Stanford University Press.

Gómez de Cervantes, Gonzalo. 1994. *La orden económica y social de Nueva España al finalizar el siglo XVI.* Ed. by Alberto María Carreño. Biblioteca Histórica de Obras Inéditas, series 1, 19. México: Antigua Librería Robredo.

Guijo, Gregorio Martín de. 1952–1953. *Diario, 1648–1664.* 2 vols. México: Porrúa.

Hernández, Francisco. 2000. *The Mexican Treasury: The Writings of Dr. Francisco Hernández.* Trans. and ed. by Rafael Chabrón, Cynthia L. Chamberlin, and Simon Varey. Stanford, Calif.: Stanford University Press.

Himmerich y Valencia, Robert. 1991. *The Encomenderos of New Spain, 1521–1555.* Austin: University of Texas Press.

Karttunen, Frances. 1983. *An Analytical Dictionary of Nahuatl.* Austin: University of Texas Press. Reprinted in 1992 by University of Oklahoma Press, Norman.

Karttunen, Frances, and James Lockhart, eds. and trans. 1987. *The Art of Nahuatl Speech: The Bancroft Dialogues.* UCLA Latin American Center Nahuatl Studies Series, 2. Los Angeles: UCLA Latin American Center Publications.

Launey, Michel. 1979. *Introduction à la langue et à la littérature aztèques.* Vol. 1: *Grammaire.* Paris: L'Harmattan.

Lockhart, James. 1992. *The Nahuas After the Conquest.* Stanford, Calif.: Stanford University Press.

_____. 1995. "A Double Tradition: Editing Book Twelve of the Florentine Codex." In: *Critical Issues in Editing Exploration Texts,* ed. by Germaine Warkentin, pp. 125–148. Toronto: University of Toronto Press.

_____. 2001. *Nahuatl as Written: Lessons in Older Written Nahuatl, with Copious Examples and Texts.* UCLA Latin American Center Nahuatl Studies Series, 6. Stanford, Calif: Stanford University Press and UCLA Latin American Center Publications.

Lockhart, James, ed. and trans. 1993. *We People Here: Nahuatl Accounts of the Conquest of Mexico.* Repertorium Columbianum, 1. Berkeley: University of California Press and UCLA Center for Medieval and Renaissance Studies.

Martínez, Henrico. 1948. *Reportorio de los tiempos e Historia natural de Nueva España.* México: Secretaría de Educación Pública.

Mendieta, fray Gerónimo de. 1980. *Historia eclesiástica indiana.* México: Porrúa.

Molina, fray Alonso de. 1970. *Vocabulario en lengua castellana y mexicana y mexicana y castellana* (1571). México: Porrúa.

Monroy Castillo, María Isabel. 1987–88. *Guía de las actas de cabildo de la ciudad de México: Años 1601–1610 y 1611–1620.* 2 vols. México: Departamento del Distrito Federal.

Muriel, Josefina. 1990, 1991. *Hospitales de la Nueva España.* 2 vols. México: Universidad Nacional Autónoma de México and Cruz Roja Mexicana.

Namala, Doris. 2002. "Chimalpahin in His Time: An Analysis of the Writings of a Nahua Annalist of Seventeenth-Century Mexico Concerning his own Lifetime." Doctoral dissertation, UCLA.

Pizzigoni, Caterina. 2002. "Between Resistance and Assimilation: Rural Nahua Women in the Valley of Toluca in the Early Eighteenth Century." Doctoral dissertation, King's College, University of London.

Reyes García, Luis. 1971. "Un nuevo manuscrito de Chimalpahin," *Anales del Instituto Nacional de Antropología e Historia*, 2: 333–48.

_____, ed. and trans. 2001. *Anales de Juan Bautista.* México: Centro de Investigaciones y Estudios Superiores en Antropología Social and Biblioteca Lorenzo Boturini, Insigne y Nacional Basílica de Guadalupe.

Sahagún, fray Bernardino de. 1979. *Códice florentino.* El Manuscrito 218–220 de la colección Palatina de la Biblioteca Medicea Laurenziana. Facsimile edition. Florence: Giunti Barbera and the Archivo General de la Nación.

_____. *Florentine Codex: General History of the Things of New Spain.* 1950–1982. Trans. by Arthur J. O. Anderson and Charles E. Dibble. 13 parts. Salt Lake City and Santa Fe: University of Utah Press and School of American Research. [Note: Part 1 is an introduction and index volume, so that each of the twelve books represents a part one number higher than the volume number; Book 10 is Part 11 or vol. 11. Yet nearly all readers are aware only of the book numbers, so that in our references we say for example Sahagún 1950–1982, Book 10, p. 151, not Sahagún 1950–1982, 11: 151.]

Sánchez, Magdalena S. 1998. *The Empress, the Queen, and the Nun: Women and Power in the Court of Philip III of Spain.* Baltimore: Johns Hopkins University Press.

Sarabia Viejo, María Justina. 1978. *Don Luis de Velasco, virrey de Nueva España.* Seville: Escuela de Estudios Hispano-Americanos.

Schäfer, Ernesto, ed. 1934. *Las rúbricas del Consejo Real y Supremo de las Indias desde la fundación del Consejo en 1524 hasta la terminación del reinado de los Austrias.* Seville: Imprenta Alemana.

Schroeder, Susan. 1991. *Chimalpahin & the Kingdoms of Chalco.* Tucson: University of Arizona Press.

Sousa, Lisa, Stafford Poole, C.M., and James Lockhart, eds. and trans. 1998. *The Story of Guadalupe: Luis Laso de la Vega's* Huei tlamahuiçoltica *of 1649*. UCLA Latin American Center Nahuatl Studies Series, 5. Stanford, Calif.: Stanford University Press and UCLA Latin American Center Publications.

Torquemada, fray Juan de. 1975. *Monarquía indiana.* 3 vols. México: Porrúa.

Index

Index entries are listed under the categories of *Individuals*, *Locales and Associated Ethnic Groups*, and *Subjects*. In the many cases where the item is on facing pages in both Nahuatl and English, only the recto page, with the form in the English translation, is given; the Nahuatl equivalent will be found on the facing verso. Non-English words other than proper names are given in italics even if mainly in roman in the body of the book.

Individuals

Locales and Associated Ethnic Groups

Subjects